ID0906997

The Sociogenesis of Language and Human Conduct

The Sociogenesis of Language and Human Conduct

Edited by

Bruce Bain

University of Alberta
Edmonton, Alberta, Canada

Plenum Press • *New York and London*

831559

Library of Congress Cataloging in Publication Data

Main entry under title:

The Sociogenesis of language and human conduct.

Includes bibliographical references and index.
1. Language and languages — Addresses, essays, lectures. 2. Linguistics — Addresses, essays, lectures. I. Bain, Bruce, date-
P106.S584 1983   401′.9   83-4036
ISBN 0-306-41041-9

© 1983 Plenum Press, New York
A Division of Plenum Publishing Corporation
233 Spring Street, New York, N.Y. 10013

Printed in the United States of America

**In memory of
Alexander Luria**

Contributors

René Appel • Institute for General Linguistics, University of Amsterdam, Amsterdam, Holland

Bruce Bain • Department of Educational Psychology, University of Alberta, Edmonton, Alberta, Canada

John W. Berry • Department of Psychology, Queen's University, Kingston, Ontario, Canada

Elizabeth A. Brandt • Department of Anthropology, Arizona State University, Tempe, Arizona

Courtney B. Cazden • Graduate School of Education, Harvard University, Cambridge, Massachusetts

Michael Cole • Laboratory of Comparative Cognition, University of California, San Diego, La Jolla, California

Diane de Terra • School of Oriental and African Studies, University of London, and Consultant, Development Anthropology, Washington, D.C.

Norbert Dittmar • Department of Linguistics, Free University of Berlin, Berlin, Federal Republic of Germany

Elizabeth C. Fisk • Department of Higher and Adult Education, Arizona State University, Tempe, Arizona

Tamotsu Fujinaga • Departments of Education and Psychology, Ochanomizu University, Tokyo, Japan

Hans Furth • Center for the Study of Youth Development, Catholic University, Washington, D.C.

Howard Giles • Department of Psychology, University of Bristol, Bristol, England

Patricia Marks Greenfield • Department of Psychology, University of California at Los Angeles, Los Angeles, California

Adrienne Harris • Psychology Department, Newark College of Arts and Sciences, Rutgers—The State University of New Jersey, Newark, New Jersey

Miles Hewstone • Maison des Sciences de l'Homme, Paris, France

Dell Hymes • Graduate School of Education, University of Pennsylvania, Philadelphia, Pennsylvania

Ivan Illich • CIDOC, Cuernavaca, Morelos, Mexico

Vera John-Steiner • Departments of Linguistics and Educational Foundations, The University of New Mexico, Albuquerque, New Mexico

Catharina Jonsson • Lund, Sweden

Steinar Kvale • Institute of Psychology, University of Aarhus, Aarhus, Denmark

Vandra Lea Masemann • Inter Cultural Associates, Toronto, Ontario, Canada

John A. Meacham • Department of Psychology, State University of New York at Buffalo, Buffalo, New York

Ashley Montagu • Department of Anthropology, Princeton University, Princeton, New Jersey

Mihai Nadin • Liberal Arts, Rhode Island School of Design, and Center for Semiotic Research, Brown University, Providence, Rhode Island

Morris A. Okun • Department of Higher and Adult Education, Arizona State University, Tempe, Arizona

Harry Osser • Faculty of Education, Queen's University, Kingston, Ontario, Canada

Ian Parker • Department of Economics, Scarborough College, University of Toronto, West Hill, Ontario, Canada

Shelley Phillips • Unit for Child Studies, School of Education, University of New South Wales, Kensington, New South Wales, Australia

Jan Prucha • Institute for Educational Research, Czechoslovak Academy of Sciences, Prague, Czechoslovakia

Catrin Roberts • Department of Education, University of Manchester, Manchester, England

Guilem Rodrigues da Silva • Lund, Sweden

Francine Ruskin • New York, New York

Josef Schubert • Department of Psychology, University of Regina, Regina, Saskatchewan, Canada

Tatiana Slama-Cazacu • Laboratory of Psycholinguistics, University of Bucharest, Bucharest, Rumania

Philip M. Smith • Department of Psychology, University of British Columbia, Vancouver, British Columbia, Canada

Howard F. Stein • Department of Family Medicine, University of Oklahoma Health Sciences Center, Oklahoma City, Oklahoma

Paul Tatter • All Indian Pueblo Council Teacher Education Program, Department of Elementary Education, The University of New Mexico, Albuquerque, New Mexico

Renzo Titone • Department of Psychology, University of Rome, Rome, Italy

Hervé Varenne • Department of Family and Community Education, Teachers College, Columbia University, New York, New York

James V. Wertsch • Department of Linguistics, Northwestern University, Evanston, Illinois

Glyn Williams • Department of Social Theory and Institution, University of North Wales, Bangor, Great Britain

Roy Williams • Communication Department, University of South Africa, Pretoria, South Africa

Foreword

Michael Cole

To the unwary reader, even the table of contents of this book will appear incongruous. What notion, let alone set of principles, could bring coherence to the following concepts: playing peekaboo with small children, aging, human alienation, conversations with Uzbeki peasants, toolmaking, sexism, the world of the deaf, the ecology of hunting groups? After s/he has had a chance to scan the entire set, the reader can see that this book seems to center on language. But it clearly is not a book *about* linguistics. It is about a notion that combines two other notions that we usually find located in very different kinds of books, *language* and *human nature*. There is no widely accepted term for this combined notion. It does not fit into those ways of thinking of the world that have gotten us where we are. Walker Percy, philosopher-novelist, succinctly nails the source of our problem:

> The importance of a study of language, as opposed to a scientific study of a space-time event like a solar eclipse or rat behavior is that as soon as one scratches the surface of the familiar and comes face to face with the nature of language, one also finds himself face to face with the nature of man. (1975, p. 10)

Once we reinvent this insight, its implications begin to work into our lives; our central problem becomes to figure out how to deal with the dilemmas it implies.

The essays in this volume all explore a strategy for dealing with the intertwining of language and human nature, a strategy which the editor describes to us in his introduction. He calls this strategy a "sociogenetic" approach to the origins of language and human conduct.

Sociogenetic is not precisely a buzzword in the English language, nor will it be a precise word when all of the reading is done. After the current fashion, we might call it a "fuzzy concept" and feel satisfied. Professor Bain calls it a collage and provides an exceedingly useful catalogue of the elements that enter into it, names and concepts most readers will have encountered. These elements will be an invaluable resource in guiding the reading of this book. But I prefer the term *montage*.

This choice is more than the whim of an overzealous social scientist. Professor

Bain has dedicated his book to Alexander Luria, the Soviet psychologist who, as my teacher, helped to arrange my interest in sociogenesis. It was Luria who intrigued me with the possibility that his ideas and Sergei Eisenstein's ideas were somehow part of a larger discussion about the reconstruction of the humane sciences in the twentieth century. And it was Eisenstein who explained that montage is more than a collage; it is a unifying principle arising from the nature and juxtaposition of elements that constitute it:

> Each montage piece exists no longer as something unrelated, but as a given *particular representation* of the general theme that in equal measure penetrates *all* the shot-pieces. The juxtaposition of these partial details in a given montage construction calls to life and forces into the light that *general* quality in which each detail has participated and which binds together all the details into a *whole,* namely, into that generalized *image,* wherein the creator, followed by the spectator, experiences the theme. (1975, p. 11)

Eisenstein was talking about film shots of course, but he believed that process to be entirely general. So did Luria. So do I, for it does for me just what a concept should do: it organizes my activities, it makes coherence where I experienced chaos, it connects previously experienced ideas and events in ways that give me a feeling I understand better the phenomena that I seek to study.

Of course, as Eisenstein knew full well, effective juxtaposition of elements is not an automatic process; it occurs only when the "partial details" are shared by creator and recipient. It requires a lot of shared knowledge to make the process go. It also requires what we call "artful" arrangements of the elements.

In the essays which follow there are many partial details of the concept of sociogenesis. Professor Bain has named what he considers to be shared aspects of the details that are relevant to experiencing the unifying principle. By providing us with a name highlighting details that appear relevant and artfully arranging them for us to interact with, Professor Bain invites us to form a useful concept. In so doing, he is following Eisenstein again.

> These mechanics in the formation of an image interest us because the mechanics of its formation in life turn out to be the prototype of the method of creating images in art. (1975, p. 14)

And in science too, Luria would have added approvingly.

References

Eisenstein, S. *The film sense* (J. Leyda, Trans.). New York: Harcourt Brace Jovanovich, 1975.
Percy, W. *The message in the bottle.* New York: Farrar, Straus and Giroux, 1975.

Acknowledgments

It is a pleasure to be able to use this opportunity to thank so many for their help in making this book a reality. To the late Alexander Luria, I should like to dedicate this book as a whole. We are all indebted to Professor Luria for his early championing of the sociogenetic approach. To the current standardbearer, Michael Cole, I am indebted for his foreword to this book, written despite the pressure of his other commitments. Actual work on the book begain in 1978 while I was on sabbatical leave at the University of Hawaii in the Department of English as a Second Language. The generous use of the university's facilities and the guiding hand of Richard Day are remembered with gratitude. Harvey Zingle, Ted Aoki, Max van Manen, Harry Garfinkle, Wilfred Schmidt, Garry Prideaux, Ana Maria Fantino, Robert Haymond, Emma Collins, Josephine Milne-Home, Jim Davies, and especially Agnes Yu and the late Ludwig Bertalanffy, all of the University of Alberta, are hereby given my warmest thanks. My graduate and undergraduate students at Alberta and Hawaii who reacted to the chapter drafts and helped me guide the contributors are likewise appreciated. Several friends and colleagues also helped with general editorial work. Foremost among these are Jan Prucha, Hartmut Haberland, Tove Stutnabb-Kangas, David Ho, Walburga von Raffler-Engel, Bi Jiwan, Lars Ekstrand, Mel Watkins, and Ferruccio Rossi-Landi. My respect and deep regard for the contributors comes from their dedication to scholarship and from their good humor in dealing with my dictatorial directives. Catharina Jonsson translated da Silva's poems from Portuguese to English and recaptured their beautiful resonance. The last acknowledgment must go to Leonard Pace, Naomi Segal, and Anne Koenig, because their faith and guidance helped bring this volume to fruition.

BRUCE BAIN

Contents

Introduction

Bruce Bain

The time is ripe for a multidisciplinary book of readings addressed to various aspects of the theme that the genesis—the origins and development—of language and human conduct are to be found in the practical or social relations between people. With this sociogenetic theme as their heuristic guide, I have brought together anthropologists, educators, linguists, psychologists, semiologists, sociologists, and a political economist in an attempt to raise the level of theoretical analysis of the problem of individual, language, and society.

Traditionally, this problem was couched in terms of individual experience and social structure. In recent years there has been a belated recognition of the privileged position of language in that matrix. Further, although individual, language, and society are conceptually distinct and, in themselves, legitimate objects of inquiry, instrumentally and phenomenally they are irreducible.

Apart from the issue of the formal relationship of psychology, linguistics, and sociology, contemporary students of the problem are now in a quandary. As is often the case in science or any human endeavor, a plateau has been reached. The popular theoretical positions of the past decades which had achieved that status for good reason now seem to have leveled off epistemologically. Social scientists know or think they know where they ought now to be going with their analyses, but the popular theories do not seem to be viable roadmaps to the new horizons. The contemporary "conceptual scent" is beckoning toward sociofunctional approaches to the problem. Insofar as it is possible to capture the essence of this zeitgeist in a sentence, it could be said that social scientists are coming to appreciate as never before that *language is an evolutionary confluence of biological, psychological, and sociohistorical determinants.* The popular positions tended to be *pars pro toto;* they tended to take one or two streams of determinants for the whole. This tendency can be clearly seen in the linguistic works of Chomsky, the psychological works of Piaget, and the sociological works of Bernstein.

Chomsky's transformational grammar vividly revealed that grammaticality cannot be equated with making sense (which unfortunately gave rise to a line of research that tried to cut up meaning to fit the procrustean bed of ideal syntax) and that the acquisition of syntactical rules cannot be reduced to passive imitation (which fortunately sounded the death knell to the concept of tabula rasa). But by tying his theory to formal logic and notions of innateness, Chomsky missed the psychological and sociohistorical influences in language. Chomsky seemed to have inviolate syntax using people rather than people using contextual syntax as well as other semiological means. Moreover, a theory must ultimately be useful in practice. Following an initial flurry of interest, language teachers soon reverted to more useful contextual or communicative competency models of pedagogy.

Piaget's genetic epistemology captured the evolutionary, constructive nature of individual cognitive processes and, along with Hans Furth's work, convincingly demonstrated to psychologists what other professionals had long known—that language is but one semiotic means among many, albeit a mighty important one. Piaget nonetheless skirted sociohistorical influences and rested on his axioms of rationalism and biological imperatives. In practice this theory implied that there was little parents or others could do to socialize, to educate and miseducate, their children. In the final analysis Piaget insisted that mind was impervious to the vicissitudes of intention and social experience, a rather unlikely premise.

Bernstein's sociology of language comes closest to the contemporary zeitgeist. His theory was not burdened with esoteric neo-Kantianisms as were Chomsky's and Piaget's, and his image of (wo)man was recognizably human. Unlike other sociological theorists, Bernstein built language into his theory not as an option but as an integral component. He insisted on the genetic mutuality of individual, language, and society. Nonetheless, Bernstein's sociology seems unsatisfactory to contemporary students. Theory and practice seem unrelated in his thesis. Although he fully recognized that individual linguistic and cognitive processes were originally real relations among people, Bernstein consistently concluded that the social barriers between classes are due to the fact that some cannot articulate as well as others. In practice, Bernstein (and especially some of his less cautious followers) seemed to advocate middle-class speech training as the palliative of social and psychological ills. The psychosocial problems of the disenfranchised, which originate in sociopolitical and politicoeconomic relations between people, were somehow imagined to be treatable through a kind of speech therapy for the masses.

No attempt is being made here to provide a substantive criticism of the works of Chomsky, Piaget, or Bernstein. Their place in history is assured and by now well known. Nor do I wish to leave the impression that theirs were the only significant works in the past decades. Obviously there were others. The point is that they are representative of establishment Linguistics, Psychology, and Sociology. They were accepted by that time-honored intellectual tradition which has taken great delight in the elaboration of dichotomies. Mind–body, real–ideal, maturation–learning, individual–society, theory–practice are but some of the dubious dichotomies that are chiseled throughout the works of this tradition. Findings of various degrees of legitimacy on one side of a dichotomized category were typically used as conceptual pilings on which to build bridges to the severed half. Although motivated by the valid desire to join conceptually what common sense suggested was united empirically, the traditional training in "divide and solve" social science often resulted in premature claims of universal findings. The status of many of these claims is reminiscent of the now famous quip that by indiscriminately using an overwrought metaphysic, behaviorists found more and more about less and less until they found out everything about nothing.

It also became apparent that dialogues across the divides were mutual embarrassments. Psychologists' discussions of social institutions seemed to sociologists to have an air of *joyeux naiveté;* linguists' discussions of mind seemed to psychologists to have arrived deus ex machina; while anthropologists' and sociologists' discussions of linguistic phenomena seemed to linguists to be much ado about very little linguistic. That period in the history of social science is coming to an end. Social science has now, I believe, reached a level of theoretical sophistication where a genuine integrative approach is possible, at least vis-à-vis the problem of language.

Alongside the establishment tradition there have been a number of researchers who rather independently came to the conclusion that a new, conceptually synthetic definition of the problem is necessary, one which, in Halliday's phrase, sees language as "social semiotic." In this regard the names which come readily to mind are Barthes, Bruner, Fishman, Freire, Gumperz, Halliday, Hjelmslev, Labov, Leontiev, Merleau-Ponty, Perelman, Reigel, Rommetveit, Schaff, and Werner. Their concern is not just with what people do with language—as a specific kind of praxis—but also with what people do to themselves and to each other through social semiotics—as in the general praxes of social relations, economics, and history. A part of the concern is still the traditional search for the laws that pertain to language, but with the recognition that it is neither thing nor mind; that it is simultaneously immanent and transcendent; that it cannot be grasped directly, only exercised. This reader is an attempt to accelerate the process of adopting an integrative approach to the study of language by focusing on a general position which has already played a significant role in this process, namely, sociogenesis.

Before commenting on the sociogenetic position, it is necessary to say something about the term *conduct* found in the title of the reader. *Behavior* would be an acceptable general synonym. The term *conduct,* however, is more specifically intended to connote not only the "what" of an act of behavior, but also the "why," the motive, the ideology that prompts the act. Questions of why are of course fraught with epistemological and theoretical dangers. But to ignore these human considerations leads to the reified, excessively rationalistic constructs that have for too long characterized the problem of language.

The term *sociogenesis* by itself could mean almost anything or nothing at all. It connotes more a loosely structured set of attitudes than a specific theoretical framework. It also suggests a particular stance toward the problem of language and human conduct based on those attitudes. I do not think of it as the sociogenetic school of thought founded by *patresfamilias* such as Bertalanffy (anthropogenesis); Marx and Engels (historical materialism); Saussure (semiotics); Humboldt and Sapir (cultural anthropology); and Mead, Dewey, Peirce, and Bruner (pragmatics) and propagated now by a dedicated band of disciples. The theoretical inheritance of those thinkers is acknowledged without being carved in stone. Petrified schools focus attention on the past rather than on the present and future; they encourage exegesis rather than innovative research and constant testing of assumptions. I would therefore ask you the readers to consider the sociogenetic stance not as a school of thought but as a constantly evolving collage of attitudes: a general image of humanness, one which is not the property of a single discipline, one which is not confined by geographical, ideological, or political boundaries.

Sociogenetic attitudes are few in number: that of Bertalanffy, that the human organism is the only member of the animal kingdom that makes and is made by the social signs that constitute its existence; that of Cassirer, that the sign system par excellence is language; that of Saussure, that language is a social fact; that of Humboldt, that language is not *ergon* but *energia,* and thus should be studied genetically and not as a constant product; that of Marx and Engels, that language is thought made real and is subject to the dynamics of social history; that of Mead, Dewey, Peirce, and Bruner, that the earliest and most fundamental function of speech is pragmatic—to direct, control, and alter human activities—and thus is inseparable from social relations; that of Sapir, that consciousness is largely verbal in nature; in sum, that the problem of the individual, language, and society is defined in terms of instrumental linguistics, or the study of language for the purpose of understanding something else: the social system, personality, alienation, values, consciousness, cognition, and so forth.

These attitudes are represented in the chapters in this reader with varying emphasis depending on the particular topic of each contributor. Similarly represented are the seminal ideas of an early advocate of a sociogenetic stance, Lev Vygotsky. Vygotsky's recognition that *behind all high mental processes stand real relations among people* is the leitmotiv of sociogenetic thought.

However, there is no slavish adherence to doctrine or discipline by the contributors. Each in his/her own way insists on testing the limits of ideas—mercifully without the feeling of contempt for other lines of thought which so often accompanies enterprises of this nature—and on integrating what seems relevant in neighbor disciplines. This reader is thus multidisciplinary in two ways. First, the professional training of the contributors spans the traditional disciplines of the social sciences. Second, while the legitimacy of discipline-specific theories and methods is recognized, the contributors ignore territorial taboos in search of a more holistic way of posing the problem. There is also a liberal sprinkling of psychologists among the contributors, although not ones which are readily recognizable in conventional psychology. I felt it was necessary to so encourage psychologists because, unlike representatives of other disciplines who have long been advocating unified approaches to specific problems, psychologists—with noteworthy exceptions—have been slow in getting out of the laboratory and into the real world. It is hoped that the impetus of this reader will be a vehicle whereby psychologists in general will engage other social scientists in productive dialogues.

A few comments about the structure of this reader are necessary. It was of course contradictory to the spirit of the book to impose a format on each chapter/contributor. On the one hand, I was anxious for the readings to appeal to general readers and to students and professors in a wide range of departments. At the same time, I had to deny admission to a number of substantive contributions of a more traditional nature in favor of contributions that were sociogenetic in stance. On the other hand, I accepted a few contributions that in themselves were more traditionally conceived, but either answered a specific concern or, in conjunction with others, fleshed out a relevant idea or method. Terminology was inevitably a problem. To get around this problem of writing for a broader audience than some contributors were used to, they were instructed to err on the side of description where a term might otherwise have sufficed. The result was longer sentences in some cases, but I believe the necessary clarity has been achieved in the main. Another terminological—and ideological—problem was sexist language. "His/her," "s/he," "(wo)man" lack the elegance and euphony that is part of historical English. "Man makes himself" is a more beautiful, solid feeling phrase than is "(Wo)man makes him/herself." But until a poet or person of letters creates a new symphony of sounds and concepts that are gender free, I felt that these historical compromises should be used.

Because of their multidisciplinary nature, the chapters did not lend themselves to conventional groupings. By design the chapters have ties to more than one topic or discipline. Making a virtue out of necessity, I tried to sequence the chapters so that the evolutionary flow of an argument, concept, assumption, or method followed from one chapter to the next. It turned out rather better than expected in that the progression from considerations of phylogenesis to ontogenesis to theory to practice is the order in which students prefer to read about these topics. The parts of this reader parallel that progression. Because the sociogenetic attitudes and central issues recur throughout the reader, the number of chapters in each part is arbitrary. The part dividers simply serve as aids in organizing the reader's thoughts or course materials and lectures. They could easily be ignored, and the text could be read from beginning to end. Finally, in a volume of this nature it was necessary to have some means of linking the recurring and contrasting points made in each chapter. Toward that end, in choice spots, cross-reference reminders have been inserted. These take the form "cf. Jones, this volume." This innovation allows the reader to flip to Jones's chapter to see how the point in question was used or abused by Jones.

Part I consists of one chapter. In addition to those mentioned above, this unusual procedure is valid for two reasons—the necessarily speculative nature of the topic and the scholarship of the contributor. The topic is the evolutionary origins and development of (wo)man. It is scholarly in that it is based on substantive research and a finely honed sense of what must have been. Part II contains ten chapters. These chapters focus on the genesis of language, self, and consciousness. The influence of Vygotsky and Mead is felt strongly in these chapters as the contributors try to come to grips with the panorama of individual mind as shaped and determined by social relations. Theoretical and research issues are treated with an overriding concern for the inseparability of individual dynamics, social semiotics, and social relations. Part III contains fourteen chapters. These deal with major theoretical issues in the sociology, the psychology, and the political economics of language; the semiological nature of ideas and informatics; psychoanalytic anthropology; and methodology. These are massive issues in which the whole is more than the sum of the parts. These chapters may well be a significant backdrop to inquiry in the next decade. Part IV contains six chapters and deals with issues of praxis. The concern here is how the "ideological sense" of signs is tied to social history and to social institutions. A refreshing concern for humanized change, which is also ideological, characterizes this reader. This concern is particularly evident in Part IV.

I expect that the parts and the sequencing of chapters reflect my personal idiosyncracies and may be less useful in the future as the problems of and with this sociogenetic stance become evident. Perhaps this future direction will emerge from the poetry of Guilem Rodrigues da Silva, which graces the epilogue.

Homo Loquens, Homo Faber, Animal Economicum: An Anthropologist's Conception of the Dawn of Human Conduct

I

Toolmaking, Hunting, and the Origin of Language

Ashley Montagu

To the inarticulateness of nature (wo)man has added a new dimension—speech. S/He is the only creature who talks, in the sense of using a shared set of abstract rules for creating and communicating ideas about the world. Hence, it has more than once been suggested that, instead of being called by that oafishly arrogant, prematurely self-bestowed name *Homo sapiens,* s/he would be more accurately described as *Homo loquens.*

In this chapter, which is in two parts, I shall be concerned first with a brief inquiry into some of the factors that may have contributed to the origin and development of speech and second with a discussion of the importance of the study of prehistoric tools as a means of learning something about the behavior of early humans. The intelligibility of speech is nothing but the unintelligibility of behavior made artificially clear.

Let me begin, then, by saying that there exists a widespread belief among those of us who should know better that the tools of the early Oldowans were of the simplest kind, typically represented by the unifacial and bifacial choppers that one sees almost exclusively illustrated in books—mine, I regret to say, among them—on prehistoric (wo)man. Indeed, for a long time I believed that this was the only type of tool that had been found at the oldest Olduvai levels. Illustrations should present assemblages of the tools found, *not* figures of a single allegedly "typical" implement. Otherwise, it is easy to fall victim to the imprinting of the "typical pebble tool" solecism. It is easy enough to point to the mistakes of others; what is more difficult is for us to digest the unpalatable truth that such mistakes are equaled only by those we ourselves commit. In that spirit may I then, as uncaptiously as possible, note that

Revised from *Origins and Evolution of Language and Speech* edited by Stevan R. Harnad, Horst D. Steklis, and Jane Lancaster, *Annals of the New York Academy of Sciences,* 1976, *280,* 266–274. Copyright 1976 by the New York Academy of Sciences. Reprinted by permission.

Ashley Montagu ● Department of Anthropology, Princeton University, Princeton, New Jersey 08544.

in the proceedings of a recently published conference on the origin and evolution of language and speech we find one of the contributors stating that "the first tools, which are associated with the australopithecines and *Homo habilis,* are either unshaped stones or stones that have a flake or two taken off them" (Lieberman, 1975a). Curiously, in his references the author lists Mary Leakey's superb description of the tools and other artifacts found in Beds I and II at Olduvai (Leakey, 1971). That work showed that the early Oldowans used quite a variety of skillfully made tools, not only of stone but also some of bone. There was evidence also of several other interesting artifacts.

The tools from Bed I (site DK 1A) are typically Oldowan. They are made from two kinds of lava, as well as from chert and tuff, and consist of five types of choppers, polyhedrons, discoids, light duty scrapers, burins, and other varieties of heavy duty tools. In addition, artificially flaked and abraded bone tools were recovered. It was at this level also that the remains were found of a loosely piled circle of stones suggestive of an artificial structure. No primate fossil remains have been found at this level, but the tools suggest use in cutting, pounding, scraping, and the butchering of small animals.

Whoever made these tools must have been able not only to select the appropriate materials—bone, various kinds of stone, and possibly wood—but also to shape them for a particular purpose and to teach the techniques of making them to others.

It is suggested that the kind of cognitive processes involved in the making and the transmission of the art of making the Oldowan-type tools mentioned implies the existence of some form of speech, however rudimentary. We know that it is possible to think without speech; deaf-mutes do it. It is not, however, possible to speak without thinking. A creature that learns to make tools to a complex preexisting pattern, calculated to serve a series of complex future purposes, among them the making of other tools, must have the kind of abstracting mind that would be of high selective value in facilitating the development of the ability to communicate such skills by the necessary verbal acts.

It is further suggested that it was toolmaking in interactive relationship with small-game hunting that supplied the other necessary factor that constituted the sufficient conditions which led to speech.

It has on several occasions been suggested that big-game hunting was probably a principal condition in the origination of speech. I am suggesting here that speech originated earlier than that.

At a stage probably somewhat earlier than the Oldowan, small-game hunting led to the development of tools for the more efficient butchering of the kill. We know that small-game hunting in itself would not lead to speech, since chimpanzees and some baboons engage in that activity (Teleki, 1975). Furthermore, small-game hunting is usually pursued in silence. Food-gathering and the securing of skins, tendons, bones, and possibly other useful parts of the bodies of animals seem to have been among the main reasons for the gradual invention and development of a variety of tools designed to secure those ends.

It hardly need be said that speech did not spring full-blown from the heads of early humans, but that it must have been at first quite rudimentary and practical, restricted to simple names for things and words for processes, relating principally to toolmaking and usage, as well as to the hunt.

At Olduvai, site FLK North, there were five fossil-bearing levels, four of these being living floors and the fifth a butchering site where the skeleton of an elephant was found embedded in clay associated with tools and flakes. All levels contained large quantities of microfauna, including reptiles, rodents, insectivores, small birds, and so on. Mary Leakey has said that the repeated discovery of the skeletal remains of large animals embedded in clay—antelope *(Paramularius altidens),* goats *(Pelorovis oldowayensis),* a *Deinotherium,* and an elephant—associated with numbers of stone tools leads us to believe that these animals may have been deliberately driven into swamps by early hominids. Depressed fractures above the orbits on the antelope skulls suggest that these animals were killed by means of an accurately placed blow (Leakey, 1971, p. 61).

If elephants (*Elephas* and *Deinotherium*) were in fact driven into swamps and either killed or allowed to die there, then we can see how the beginnings of big-game hunting may have come about. In Bed II at site SHK and Bed IVa the remains of two herds of antelope similarly embedded in clay have been found. The suggestion is that they were driven into the swamps by early Oldowans.

In addition, other evidence of the mental development of the early Oldowans is the curiously grooved and pecked phonolite cobble found at level I in Upper Bed I at FLK North. This stone, which has been artificially shaped and seems unlikely to have served as a tool for any practical purpose, bears a striking resemblance to the head of a baboon. A similar quartzite cobble, which appears to have been naturally produced, has been described by Dart (1959) from Makapansgat. As Mary Leakey said, "The occurrence of such stones at hominid sites in such remote periods is of considerable interest" (Leakey, 1971, p. 269).

Also at level I in Upper Bed I FLK North, symmetrical stone balls first make their appearance. Such spheroids are relatively rare at this level, but become markedly more numerous in Middle and Upper Bed II, where they never constitute less than 20% of the tools and where they range in size more extensively than in earlier assemblages (Leakey, 1971, p. 266). Mary Leakey thinks they may have served as the essential parts of bolas. The different sizes of the stones suggest that, if they were used as bolas, animals of different sizes were the targets. Bolas are missiles that can bring animals down by entangling their legs both on the ground and in the air. Richard Leakey has shown that a pair of such spheroids, each attached to a cord about a yard long, entangles more effectively around upright posts than a group of three (Leakey, 1971, p. 266). Such spheroids have been found in association with *Homo erectus* and Neanderthal (wo)man, facts which tend to strengthen the belief that these stones may well have been used as parts of an ingenious hunting implement.

The probability that such a sophisticated hunting implement was made and used by the early Oldowans, taken together with the other evidence of their economic activities, renders it very difficult to believe that they had not customarily employed some form of speech (cf. Prucha, this volume).

Everyone agrees that the development of big-game hunting (and we follow Teleki, 1975, here in accepting any animal weighing 10 kg or more as big game) was closely related to the elaboration of speech. It seems to me however that the evidence indicates that speech originated prior to the development of big-game hunting and that rather than speech being the result of such hunting, the latter was one of the effects of speech; that speech in fact made big-game hunting possible or at least contributed to making it possible.

Much more is involved in big- than in small-game hunting at many complex levels. Most important would have been the planning and attention to logistics, strategy, and roles. Crude as all this preparation may have been, it would undoubtedly have been most economically achieved by verbal means, just as communication during the hunt would have been.

The influence of toolmaking on the development of intelligence must have been considerable. The intimate relation between the skillful hand and the intelligent mind has often been the subject of comment. It is not surprising that the hand should have formed the subject of one of the earliest and greatest contributors to our understanding of the nervous system, Charles Bell, in his Bridgewater treatise of 1833. Nor did the relationship between hand, brain, and the erect posture escape the acute mind of Frederick Engels, in 1896, in his *Dialectics of Nature*. In his *Creative Evolution,* published in 1902, Bergson discussed at considerable length the relationship between the invention of tools and the development of intelligence, and another philosopher with anthropological interest, Lucien Lévy-Bruhl (1910, p. 76) observed that "the progress of the mind is due to the co-operation between the mind and the hand." The idea is implicit throughout Frederic Wood Jones's (1920) notable book on the hand and in many references to the subject since. It is to be noted that the area of the brain devoted to the hand is remarkably large. In this connection it has more than once been observed that the size of the cerebral and cerebellar areas devoted to any function is related not so much to the size of the structure of the part of the body involved as to the skill in using it (Gerard, 1959). It is also not without significance that the areas of the cerebral cortex for hand, tongue, and speech situated within the left hemisphere, as well as the area for hand gestures during speech, are all closely associated with the areas for logical analytical operations on perceptual material and temporal sequential ordering. In this connection, David Katz, in his path-breaking monograph of 1925, suggested that the hand be regarded as the organ of touch.

Toolmaking greatly contributed to skill in the use of the hands and to mental development in a feedback interactive relationship that led to a continuing reinforcement in the skills of both, that is, mental and manual skills.

(Wo)Man's ideas, his/her words, are conceptual tools, mental analogs of material tools. (Wo)Man has to learn how to "handle" these conceptual tools, just as s/he does other implements. Prehension, meaning "to grasp," "to lay hold of," is a function both of the hand and of the mind. In their book *Biogenetic Structuralism* Laughlin and d'Aquili (1974) defined prehension as "the inputting of data through any of the sensory receptors into the brain plus the simultaneous association of those data with other data and associations of data stored in memory within the brain." Mind and hand work interoperatively together. Thought constitutes (wo)man's principal adaptive response to the challenges of the environment. Laughlin and d'Aquili took a similar view when they wrote of "prehension being cognitively extended, enabling protohominids to predict the utility of a hand-held tool beyond the period of immediate use" (p. 93), beyond immediately prehended relationships to more expansive ones in time and space. In short, with the domination of inert matter and the ability to mold it to one's needs for some future purpose must have gone the ability to conjure with the "not-here" and the "not-now." Language is molded on matter and on humans' action on matter, resulting in an instrument free from matter, a device to triumph over mechanism.

Bergson (1902) postulated that "intelligence in its initial form may be considered to be the ability to produce artificial objects, particularly tools, and to continue making them by a variety of methods." And he went on to suggest that if we would ignore pride and allow ourselves to be guided by history and prehistory, we would call ourselves not *Homo sapiens* but *Homo faber*. The toolmaking kind of intelligence Bergson called "creative intelligence" (the "practical intelligence" of later writers), believing that the evidence of prehistory and history shows that creative intelligence preceded rational intelligence.

By creative or practical intelligence is meant, unlike conceptual or logical intelligence, not the application of abstractions to facts, but the purposeful use of movements and actions for dealing with the shape of objects and with external events (Viaud, 1969).

The Bergsonian distinction between creative or practical intelligence and rational intelligence has a certain validity, as Piaget's (1952) and other studies of children have shown, and it is not unreasonable to suppose that the earliest toolmaking, well antedating the toolmaking of the early Oldowans, was the product of the practical intelligence (cf. Schubert, this volume).

It seems probable that success in small-game hunting, assisted by the making of a variety of implements useful in securing quarry and by the manufacture of other tools useful in butchering, sharing, and utilizing various parts of the remains, would have served to improve the general conditions of life and contributed to social development. The growing mastery of the environment would have produced a novel form of interactivity among the members of the group, in which speech facilitated the communication of practical ideas relating to the manufacture of tools to serve various purposes in response to the challenges presented by the variety of animal food. In this way, in a quite complex feedback interrelationship, small-game hunting, toolmaking, and speech would have reciprocally served to provoke each other to further advances. In this manner speech itself would develop as a special kind of tool designed to operate on humans themselves (Viaud, 1960, p. 20; cf. John-Steiner & Tatter, this volume).

It has been observed by more than one writer on the subject that any description of the processes involved in language or speech could also be employed to describe the processes of toolmaking, that there exists, in short, a grammar of toolmaking in much the same sense as there exists a grammar of language and of speech.

Speech is designed to communicate meaning to others, to put oneself "in touch" with others. This is accomplished by the use of certain formal rules relating to the modification, transformation, and positioning of certain stylized, chopped-up segments of sound. The techniques of producing these sounds must be learned according to a particular pattern and transmitted by those who are familiar with it to those who are not. Briefly summarized, these are exactly the kinds of processes that occur in toolmaking. At a more detailed level of analysis the parallel between language and toolmaking becomes even more striking, but although several writers on the subject have seen this (Holloway, 1969; Lieberman, 1975a,b), none, so far as I know, seems to have made a detailed study of toolmaking as a clue to the cognitive processes of early humans and the origin and evolution of language and speech. What is needed is a scientific study of tools, a science, as it may be called, of *hoplonology* (Gr. *Oplon,* a tool, implement). The hope is that by giving such a science-to-be a name, it may be conjured into existence. Such a scientific study of tools could go a long way toward the reconstruction of something of the character and evolution of the behavioral characteristics of early humans. As Sollas (1924) put it many years ago, "The works of man's hands are his embodied thought." Recently Cahen, Keeley, and Van Noten (1979) have discussed the evidence provided by tools from a single paleolithic site for the behavior of their makers.

But to return to the grammar of toolmaking. Every technical skill is an intellectual achievement. In toolmaking it is the hand and mind in a continuous feedback of learned muscular acts, involving touch, pressure, and temperature senses, that is responsible for the hand's activities (Schiff & Foulke, 1982). For the making of each tool, it is clear that a quite specific sequence of acts is required, each one of which must follow the other in a strictly ordered manner. It is suggested that a certain isomorphism exists between the grammar of toolmaking and the grammar of speech.

The grammatical precision of toolmaking at a level as old as Bed I at Olduvai strongly suggests that speech was already well established among the makers of those tools, so that for the origins of language and speech we shall have to look to earlier horizons and perhaps to even earlier forms of humans. It seems to me, however, that in broad outline the conditions to which I have referred were probably responsible for the origination of language and speech based possibly on a repertory of vocalizations long practiced by the human's immediate ancestors.

When one studies in detail the manufacture of stone tools, one soon discovers that a very clear and purposive idea lies behind every motion that has been employed to create them (Semenov, 1964). I can best illustrate this point with the aid of some Acheulean tools from the Lower and Middle Gravels of Swanscombe, in Kent, England. From the study of these implements it is possible to determine not only how they were held, and hence what they were most likely used for, but also to discern what went on in the minds of the individuals who made them. And this is what we find:

First, that each tool was probably made to fit the hand of the individual who intended to use it. This means that although many tools could have been used by everyone, there were others that were specially made for the use of a particular individual. The smaller hand axes may have been made for the use of females, and the really small ones, about three inches in length, beautifully finished, may well have been made for children—which does not exclude their possible use by adults. The really large hand axes, about ten inches or more in length, were probably manufactured for exclusive use by males, for they are very heavy and must have required the employment of both hands when in use.

Second, to accommodate every part of the palmar surface of the hand, a specific area was shaped on the stone (Figure 1). Thus, for the palm, the original rough surface was left untouched in order to afford a firmer grip. Immediately above this area a large flake was removed, leaving a concave surface (E) for the reception of the thenar eminence. Extending from this concavity an area was prepared, also by flaking, for the reception of the thumb. On the reverse side, portions of the stone were prepared in such a way that the tip of each finger would find a firm resting place. In the example illustrated here, the ingenious prehistoric manufacturer has prepared the areas for the reception of the tip and ball of the index and especially the middle finger in the form of double-indented triangular fossae (D, A, and a). This, so far as anyone knows, is unique among Acheulean implements, but quite clearly what the inventor—for such s/he may well have been—had in mind was the establishment of as firm a grip as possible on the implement. Toward that end s/he made certain that his/her fingers would never slip to the slightest degree. The result is an implement that can be held so firmly in the hand that under the greatest application of pushing, pressing, or pulling forces, it remains steady and immovable.

Third, the position in which this tool was held in the hand indicates that it was indeed used as a hand ax, but mainly for digging up thickly rooted plants and tubers of various sorts.

Fourth, it is clear that each flake has been removed in order to produce the cutting edges and point of the tool with the minimum number of strokes; for if one examines this tool carefully, one may readily perceive that no more flakes have been removed than were minimally necessary to produce the desired result.

Turning to another hand ax from Swanscombe (Figure 2), this time from the Lower Gravels, and hence early Acheulean, one can immediately see that the maker had much the same end in view as the maker of the middle Acheulean hand ax, except that the earlier Acheulean tool is rather more crudely made. All the elements of the middle Acheulean implement are present, but they are far less economically and skillfully executed. The thenar concavity is evident and so are the prepared areas for the tips of the fingers and the thumb. If my interpretation of these areas is correct, then this particular tool was probably made and used by a left-handed individual, for the artificially prepared surfaces fit far better in the left hand than they do in the right, with more of the tool remaining with which to work.

Finally, I wish to draw attention to the middle Acheulean tool, also from Swanscombe, which was clearly devised for the cutting of animal skins (Figure 3). Among the remarkable things about this tool is the fact that it almost exactly resembles the modern furrier's knife—except that the Acheulean tool is far more versatile. The Acheulean knife is serrulated, and in one place notched, along its lower edge and also along the anterior half of its upper edge, which, like a modern cutting knife, curves downward to meet the lower edge in a point. The upper cutting edge is designed to be rotated downward so that it becomes a lower cutting edge, used for purposes requiring greater precision and the cutting of small areas of skin. It is a very remarkable instrument indeed. Its surfaces are prepared in such a way as to

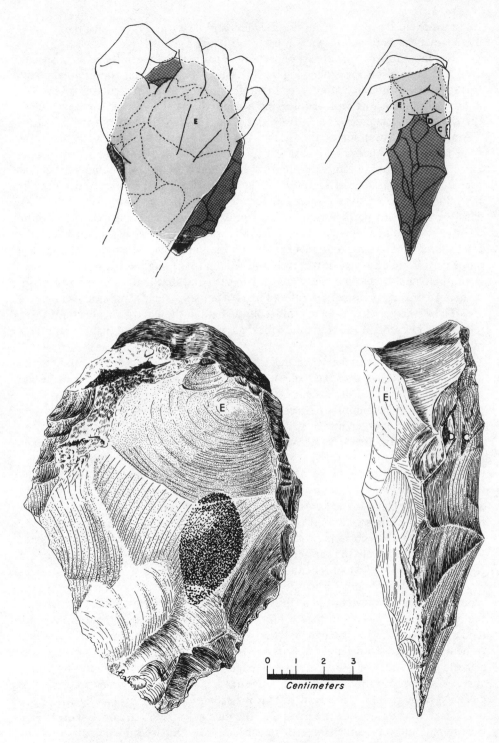

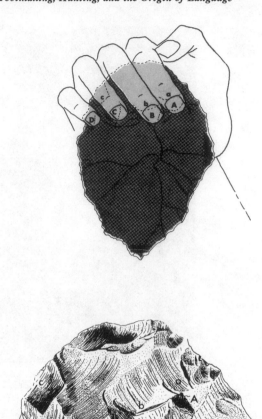

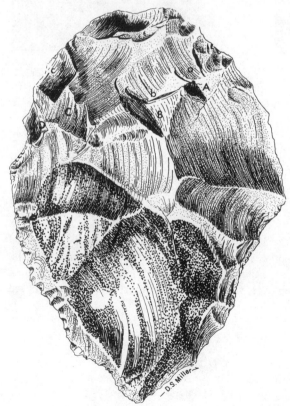

Figure 1. Acheulean hand ax from the Middle Gravels of Swanscombe, Kent, England. E, Thenar fossa; D, Flaked depression for little finger; C, depression for tip of ring finger; c, depression for ball of ring finger; B, depression for tip of middle finger; b, depression for ball of middle finger; A, depression for tip of index finger; a, depression for ball of index finger. To the side of the latter on the untreated rough surface of the flint there is a rest position for the thumb.

Figure 2. Acheulean hand ax from the Lower Gravels of Swanscombe, Kent, England. Left: Palmar surface showing thenar fossa. Right: finger surface. The flaked areas for the reception of index finger and thumb are, unfortunately, in shadow. The tip of the tool was broken away not long after it was made.

render the instrument stable in the hand whatever the cutting edge to which one has rotated it. The individual making such a tool must have been characterized by a very high grade of intelligence, and I think there can be little doubt that he was capable of speech of a quite complex order.

The tools I have described were made by humans who lived considerably after the earliest hominids. I have discussed these tools first because they happen to be the only ones available to me and second because they serve as simple illustrations of the kind of inferences that can be drawn concerning the behavior of early humans at every level, from the congealed behavior, as it were, by which they were represented in their tools.

Acknowledgments

I owe many thanks to the late Paul Fejos, Director, and the Wenner-Gren Foundation for Anthropological Research for a grant which made possible the dig at Swanscombe from which the tools described in this paper were recovered by the writer. I also wish to thank Don Miller for the great pains he took in making the drawing of the tools figured here.

Figure 3. Acheulean furrier's knife from the Middle Gravels of Swanscombe, Kent, England. The stone knife is shown together with a modern furrier's knife (the cutting blade has not been inserted in the beaked area of the latter). The lower back portion of the stone knife was broken away some time after its manufacture. The earlier 20th century furrier's knife even more closely resembled the Acheulean tool than the latest version shown here.

References

Bell, C. *The hand: Its mechanism and vital endowments as evincing design*. London: Pickering, 1833.

Bergson, H. *Creative evolution*. London: Macmillan, 1902.

Cahen, D., Keeley, L. H., & Van Noten, F. L. Stone tools, toolkits, and human behavior. *Current Anthropology*, 1979, *20*, 661–683.

Dart, R. A. How human were the South African man-apes? *South African Panorama*, November 1959, pp. 18–211.

Engels, F. *Dialectics of nature*. New York: International Publishers, 1896.

Gerard, R. Brains and behavior. In J. N. Spuhler (Ed.), *The evolution of man's capacity for culture*. Detroit: Wayne State University Press, 1959, pp. 14–20.

Holloway, R. Culture: A human domain. *Current Anthropology*, 1969, *10*, 395–412.

Katz, D. Der Aufbau der Tastwelt. *Zeitschrift für Psychologie*, 1925, Erganzungsband II.

Laughlin, C. D., Jr., & d'Aquili, E. G. *Biogenetic structuralism*. New York: Columbia University Press, 1974.

Leakey, M. D. *Olduvai Gorge: Excavations in Beds I and II 1960–1963*. New York: Cambridge University Press, 1971.

Lévy-Bruhl, L. *Les fonctions mentales dans les sociétés infrieures*. Paris: Presses Universitaires de France, 1910.

Lieberman, P. The evolution of speech and language. In J. F. Kavanaugh & J. E. Cutting (Eds.), *The role of speech in language*. Cambridge, Mass.: MIT Press, 1975, p. 102. (a)

Lieberman, P. *On the origins of language*. New York: Macmillan, 1975. (b)

Piaget, J. *The origins of intelligence in children*. New York: International Universities Press, 1952.

Schiff, W., & Foulke, E. (Eds.). *Tactual perception: A sourcebook*. New York: Cambridge University Press, 1982.

Semenov, S. A. *Prehistoric technology*. New York: Barnes & Noble, 1964.

Sollas, W. J. *Ancient hunters: 67* (3rd ed.). New York: Macmillan, 1924.

Teleki, G. Primate subsistence patterns: Collector-predators and gatherer-hunters. *Journal of Human Evolution,* 1975, *4,* 125–184.

Viaud, G. *Intelligence: Its evolution and forms: 20*. New York: Harper & Bros., 1960.

Wood Jones, F. *The principles of anatomy as seen in the hand* (2nd ed.). London: Balliere, Tindall & Cox, 1920.

II

The Reconstitution of Humanity: Genesis of Language, Self, and Consciousness

2

The Role of Semiosis in L. S. Vygotsky's Theory of Human Cognition

James V. Wertsch

One of the twentieth century's most imaginative accounts of how human mental activity derives from social activity was outlined by the Soviet psychologist Lev Semenovich Vygotsky (1896–1934). Although nearly half a century has passed since his death, Vygotsky's ideas continue to motivate a great deal of interesting research in psychology and semiotics in the USSR and are beginning to be more widely utilized in the West. In this chapter I will outline three central themes in Vygotsky's account of social and psychological functioning. I will examine these themes one by one, but I will also demonstrate how they are interrelated in a single theoretical framework. The three themes to be examined are: (1) the use of developmental, or genetic, analysis; (2) the claim that individuals' psychological processes emerge out of social processes; and (3) the claim that the mediational means used in individuals' psychological processes result from the mastery and internalization of social sign systems, especially language.

Vygotsky developed a theoretical approach built around these three themes in order to deal with what he viewed as the "crisis in psychology." Although he was addressing issues that had arisen in the early twentieth century, his comments about this crisis have a great deal of relevance for contemporary psychology and for social science in general. His concern was that no overarching theoretical framework existed that could provide an integrated explanation of psychological phenomena. Not only had research findings and hypotheses failed to be interrelated, they often seemed to be contradictory. Borrowing from Brentano, Vygotsky (1956) wrote that "there exist many psychologies, but there does not exist a unified psychology" (p. 57). He went on to point out that the implications of such a state of affairs are quite serious.

James V. Wertsch ● Department of Linguistics, Northwestern University, Evanston, Illinois 60201.

> The absence of a single scientific system that would embrace and combine all
> of our contemporary knowledge in psychology results in a situation in which
> every new factual discovery ... that is more than a simple accumulation of
> details *is forced* to create its own special theory and explanatory system. In
> order to understand facts and relationships investigators are forced to create
> their own psychology—one of many psychologies. (1956, pp. 57–58)

Vygotsky's response to this crisis was to propose a scheme for reformulating
psychology on Marxist foundations. In this reformulation he focused on the relationship between the individual and the social world in which the individual develops.
However, he never lost sight of the fact that the human individual is also a biological
organism. As we will see, he developed a theoretical framework that attempts to
interrelate these issues rather than consider them in isolation. His sociohistorical
approach to the study of mind is the result of this effort. It was in the context of this
general approach that he developed the three themes that I will outline here.

The First Theme: Genetic Analysis

A fundamental assumption in Vygotsky's approach is that human behavior can
be understood only by considering its position in genetic transition. He argued that
we must develop an approach that focuses on process rather than product, on movement and transformation rather than static structure.

> We need to concentrate not on the *product* of development but on the very *pro-
> cess* by which higher forms are established. ... To encompass in research the
> process of a given thing's development in all its phases and changes—from birth
> to death—fundamentally means to discover its nature, its essence, for "it is only
> in movement that a body shows what it is." Thus, the historical [i.e., in the
> broadest sense of "history"] study of behavior is not an auxiliary aspect of the-
> oretical study, but rather forms its very base. (1978, pp. 64–65)

Vygotsky is widely known for his studies of ontogenesis, but this is only one of
several types of development that he investigated. Overall, he utilized a variety of
what I will term *genetic domains*. These included phylogenesis, sociocultural history,
ontogenesis, and microgenesis.

Vygotsky relied heavily on phylogenetic comparisons in outlining his account of
how tools and signs come to mediate activity. For example, he often drew on Köhler's
studies of primitive problem-solving activity in apes to examine the origins of intelligence in humans. His assumption was that this type of activity is similar to the
primitive problem-solving activity seen in early phases of human ontogenesis. He saw
the need for phylogenetic comparison as arising from the fact that we usually cannot
isolate this primitive problem-solving activity in human ontogenesis because social
activity begins to affect the child's development at a very early age. Thus phylogenetic comparison is needed to conduct a "developmental analysis that returns to the
source and reconstructs all the points in the development of a given structure" (1978,
p. 65; cf. Montagu, this volume).

In light of recent investigations on chimp language, it is interesting to note that
in a manuscript written in 1930 Vygotsky (1960) argued that a phylogenetic analysis

of sign-mediated intelligence would remain incomplete until researchers had considered apes' ability to learn non-oral language. He noted that all existing attempts to teach apes language had rested on the assumption that their vocal apparatus was capable of carrying out the complex muscle movements required, and he argued that the issue of how language might transform the practical intelligence of apes would remain open until researchers tried to teach apes a language that does not rely on oral speech. He suggested sign language as a good place to begin this research.

The second genetic domain that Vygotsky examined was social history. Although it was only one of several types of development in his analysis, it played such a central role that in the USSR his theory is referred to as the "sociohistorical" or "cultural-historical" approach (cf. Smirnov, 1975; see also Luria, 1971). In this connection, Vygotsky was especially interested in the evolution of sign systems that mediate human activity. For example, he examined mnemonic devices introduced over the course of various cultures' history, and he analyzed the history of word meanings. Also, this concern led to a series of empirical studies that he and Luria carried out in Soviet Central Asia in the early 1930s. While these would be considered to be cross-cultural studies in today's parlance, it would be more accurate to label Vygotsky's and Luria's concerns as "cross-historical" since for them the studies served to make comparisons of the mental functioning of people from societies at different sociohistorical levels (cf. Illich; Parker, this volume).

The third genetic domain for Vygotsky was ontogenesis. Although he developed much of his theoretical framework on the basis of cross-historical comparisons, he carried out most of his empirical research on ontogenetic transition. This was both because he was heavily involved in the practical problems of education and rehabilitation and because ontogenesis was one of the most accessible domains for empirical research. Since my examination of Vygotsky's other two themes will rely primarily on ontogenetic comparison, I will not go into it in detail here.

The final genetic domain explored by Vygotsky was microgenesis (cf. Wertsch & Stone, 1978). The two types of microgenetic transition that he examined were (1) the evolution of a single psychological act as it unfolds, usually over the course of milliseconds, and (2) the development of an individual or social activity as it is repeated and transformed during a single training session. In connection with this second type of microgenesis, Vygotsky argued that psychological studies conducted in experimental laboratories often fail to utilize what may be the most interesting data they generate because they involve training a subject "to criterion" before beginning the observations.

> Uniformity was sought, so that it was never possible to grasp the process in flight; instead, researchers routinely discarded the critical time when a reaction appears and when its functional links are established and adjusted. Such practices lead us to characterize the responses as "fossilized." They reflect the fact that these psychologists were not interested in complex reactions as a process of development. (1978, p. 68)

Vygotsky utilized each of these four genetic domains at one time or another in his writings. He viewed various types of genetic analysis as capable of contributing different parts to the overall picture he was trying to construct. For example, although ontogenesis is more accessible in the sense that it can be directly observed in its entirety, the fact that several forces of development are simultaneously in operation makes it advisable to supplement the study of the human life span with other types of genetic analysis. Social history can be important in this respect because it allows the investigator to study social evolution independently of biological evolution. As Tulviste (1978) has pointed out:

> In contrast to ontogenesis, the natural maturation of the brain does not play a role in the course of historical development (Vygotsky, 1960; Luria, 1971). The natural cause of the historical development of cognitive processes is the historical development of society. (p. 83)

Thus while the rest of this paper will focus primarily on ontogenesis, it should be kept in mind that this is only one of several genetic domains investigated by Vygotsky.

When examining any of these genetic domains, Vygotsky's basic line of reasoning focused on how separate lines of development come into contact, transform one another, and thereby reorganize the process of development. In this chapter I will outline two of the most important of these reorganizations. The first reorganization results from the introduction of social forces into a form of development that had formerly been primarily biological in nature. I will term this the *social reorganization of development*. The second reorganization involves the further transformation that results in the emergence of individual consciousness, especially in the form of higher mental functions (e.g., voluntary memory, voluntary attention, thinking). I will term this the *psychological reorganization of development*.

Vygotsky emphasized that such reorganizations involve a change in the very nature of development. By this he meant that at certain points in development we must recognize that the principles which had been capable of explaining changes are no longer sufficient. Rather, the explanatory framework must be revised to incorporate a new type of developmental force. This line of reasoning had previously been proposed in connection with certain phylogenetic and sociohistorical transitions, but as we will see, one of Vygotsky's accomplishments was to demonstrate how it applies to ontogenesis.

The social reorganization of development results from the impact of social processes on development that had previously been explainable in terms of biological processes. In making this argument Vygotsky was clearly influenced by claims made by Marx (1906) and especially Engels (1940) about phylogenesis and social history. Like them, Vygotsky argued that with the appearance of social life in history we can no longer explain the development of humans solely on the basis of principles of Darwinian evolution. There is a switch in the very nature of development (i.e., in the explanatory principles that are applicable). In Vygotsky's words,

> one form of development is not simply a direct continuation of the other. Rather, *the type of development itself has changed* from biological to socio historical. (1956, p. 146)

Vygotsky (1956, 1960, 1972) extended this line of reasoning by applying it to ontogenesis. Perhaps the most forceful statement of his argument can be found in his critique of child development theories which were based on the assumption that a single set of principles can explain all ontogenetic change. For example, Vygotsky criticized Blonskii (1921) for trying to account for all ontogenetic change on the basis of physiological principles, and he criticized other investigators for basing their entire analysis on other dimensions such as sexual maturation.

> These schemes do not take into account the reorganizations of the process of development itself, by virtue of which the importance and significance of any characteristic is constantly changing from age to age. This excludes the possibility of using a single criterion to divide all of childhood up into separate epochs. Child development is a very complex process in which none of its stages can be fully defined solely on the basis of one characteristic. (1972, p. 115)

Vygotsky argued that the most frequent problem in this regard was that investigators fail to recognize that biological principles cannot serve as the sole basis for explaining psychological phenomena. While he never disputed the importance of biological principles in explaining psychological phenomena, he argued that as a result of the social reorganization of development, the burden of explanation shifts from biological to social factors as they operate within a given biological environment. This does not mean that biological factors no longer play a role, but it does mean that they are subordinated to and transformed by social factors. For example, he contrasted embryological and psychological development on this basis:

> The embryological development of the child . . . in no way can be considered on the same level as the postnatal development of the child as a social being. Embryological development is a quite special type of development subordinated to different patterns than is the development of the child's personality which begins at birth. Embryological development is studied by an independent science—embryology which cannot be considered as one of the chapters of psychology. . . . Psychology does not study heredity or prenatal development as such, but only the role and influence of heredity and prenatal development of the child in the process of social development. (1972, p. 123)

Thus for Vygotsky the explanation of the ontogenesis of human consciousness was clearly not based solely on biological principles. I would again emphasize, however, that this does not constitute a rejection of the notion that biological forces play an important role in development. Rather, it means that biological principles must be considered from the perspective of how they operate in a broader explanatory system (cf. Fujinaga; Furth, this volume).

Before turning to the psychological reorganization of development I should point out that Vygotsky's account of the biological or "natural" line of development in ontogenesis is one of the weakest parts of his theoretical approach. From his writings it is sometimes not clear whether he was dealing with neurophysiological maturation or with a type of sensorimotor intelligence. In outlining his ideas on this topic, he simply incorporated findings from others (e.g., Köhler, 1921; Yerkes, 1916) and produced a very sketchy outline of the practical intelligence of apes and young children. This weakness is particularly apparent today given the mass of recent research on early intellectual development in humans (e.g., Bruner, 1968, 1973; Piaget, 1963, 1971). However, the fact that very little was known about the natural line of development at the time Vygotsky was writing and that he therefore treated it in an oversimplified way does not reduce the merit of his general argument about the relationship between biological and social factors in ontogenesis. The reorganization that he envisioned in this connection awaits serious study.

The Second Theme: The Social Origins of Individuals' Psychological Processes

Vygotsky made explicit claims about a developmental reorganization in ontogenesis only in connection with the relationship between biological and social principles. I would argue, however, that the same line of reasoning applies to the relationship between social processes and individual human consciousness. That is, I would argue that Vygotsky's theoretical framework assumes that the set of principles that are capable of explaining social interaction must be revised with the emergence of higher mental functions in individual humans.

Although this second reorganization obviously could be considered under the first theme in Vygotsky's approach (genetic analysis), I will consider it separately since it was the focus of so much of his theoretical and empirical research. His primary emphasis was on how individual human consciousness, personality *(lichnost'),* and higher mental functions derive from the social environment. His line of reasoning on this issue was heavily influenced by Marx's claims about the emergence of human consciousness. Like Marx, Vygotsky (1979) argued that "the social dimension of consciousness is primary in time and fact. The individual dimension of consciousness is derivative and secondary, based on the social" (p. 30).

This position led Vygotsky to criticize traditional psychological research in a way that is strikingly similar to the position then being developed independently by Mead (1934). In a 1931 paper entitled "The Genesis of Higher Mental Functions" Vygotsky wrote:

> To paraphrase a well-known position of Marx's, we could say that humans' psychological nature represents the aggregate of internalized social relations that have become functions for the individual and the form of his/her structure. . . .
> Formerly, psychologists tried to derive social behavior from individual behavior. They investigated individual responses observed in the laboratory and then studied them in the collective. . . . Posing the problem in such a way is, of course, quite legitimate; but genetically speaking, it deals with the second level in behavioral development. The first problem is to show how the individual response emerges from the forms of collective life. (1981a, pp. 164–165)

This passage reveals that Vygotsky's claim about the social origins of higher mental functions has clear implications for how it is possible to investigate the psychological make-up of the individual. As his student Luria (1982) has pointed out, it means that we must begin by stepping *outside* the study of the individual.

> [Vygotsky's] basic position sounds paradoxical. It is as follows: *In order to explain the highly complex forms of human consciousness one must go beyond the human organism. One must seek the origins of conscious activity and "categorical" behavior not in the recesses of the human brain or in the depths of the spirit, but in the external conditions of life. Above all, this means that one must*

> *seek these origins in the external processes of social life, in the social and his-*
> *torical forms of human existence.* (1982, p. 25)

Marxist research on this issue is usually concerned with social history. Again, Vygotsky's contribution was to explicate the implications of this claim for ontogenesis. It was in this connection that he proposed the following "general law of cultural development."

> Any function in the child's cultural development appears twice, or on two planes. First it appears on the social plane, and then on the psychological plane. First it appears between people as an interpsychological category, and then within the child as an intrapsychological category. This is equally true with regard to voluntary attention, logical memory, the formation of concepts, and the development of volition. (1981a, p. 163)

For Vygotsky it is the emergence of this intrapsychological functioning that produces the psychological reorganization of ontogenesis. The very nature of development changes once again, and a new set of principles concerned with the child's psychological processes must be incorporated into the explanatory system. As is the case with the social reorganization of ontogenesis, the incorporation of these new principles changes the overall explanatory system. Thus social interaction cannot be viewed as continuing to occur as it had earlier, the only change being that it now involves genuine psychological beings. Rather, the emergence of consciousness in the child changes the nature of social interaction as well (cf. John-Steiner & Tatter; Cazden, this volume).

An essential aspect of Vygotsky's account of the psychological reorganization is that he saw the processes and mediational means of individual psychological functioning as resulting from the mastery and internalization of social processes. This feature contrasts with the social reorganization where there is no such claim. The bulk of Vygotsky's empirical research on ontogenesis was concerned with how individuals' mental processes emerge out of social interaction. He argued that the genetic relationship between social and psychological processes produces the result that the latter have a social or quasi-social nature.

> All higher mental functions are internalized social relationships. . . . Their composition, genetic structure, and means of action—in a word, their whole nature—is social. Even when we turn to mental processes, their nature remains quasi-social. In their own private sphere, human beings retain the functions of social interaction. (1981a, p. 164)

The Third Theme: Semiotic Mediation of Social and Individual Functioning

Up to this point in my explication of Vygotsky's approach I have avoided introducing any of his specific claims about the role of sign systems in development. I have done this in an attempt to provide an independent account of his first two themes. As we will see in the rest of this chapter, however, the nature of these first two themes cannot be fully appreciated independently of Vygotsky's semiotic analysis. In fact, without this semiotic analysis Vygotsky's theory seems to offer few original insights. For example, his genetic analysis would seem to be a simple extension of points made by Marx (1906) and Engels (1940). When we turn to his interpretation of the social origins of intrapsychological processes, we once again find a large debt to Marxist theory, and figures such as the French psychiatrist Janet (1928, 1929) were espousing similar ideas at the time (and indeed had a direct influence on Vygotsky).

In order to understand the role of semiotic analysis in Vygotsky's work it is useful to point out a fact about his intellectual biography. Prior to his career in academic psychology, Vygotsky was interested in problems of poetics, literary criticism, and philology. While he tended to be concerned with the nature of the psychological response created by text, he insisted that the study of aesthetic responses must be grounded in the analysis of the objective semiotic properties of texts. Vygotsky's interest in semiotic analysis continued throughout his career. For example, as noted by Ivanov (1976), he participated in an ongoing series of seminars on semiotics with the linguist Marr and the cinematographer and semiotician Eisenstein during the early 1930s. In addition, the influence of scholars of language such as Potebnya (1913) and Yakubinskii (1923) is apparent in Vygotsky's writings. And finally, Ivanov (1976) and Bibler (1975) have argued that the semiotician Bakhtin (1973) and his colleagues (e.g., Voloshinov, 1973) influenced Vygotsky's later writings.

Ivanov (1977) has outlined the central tenet of Vygotsky's notion of the semiotic mediation of human activity as follows:

> As the outstanding Soviet psychologist L. S. Vygotsky observed in the 1930's signs are a means of controlling human behavior. Man cannot govern his own behavior directly and creates signs in order to control it indirectly. The history of a culture can be described to a great extent as the transmission in time of sign systems serving to control behavior. Semiotic systems for the programmed control of human behavior are elaborated due to the internalization of external signs, a process that can partly be compared to the emergence of internal speech. Investigation of children's speech makes it possible to ascertain that speech arises initially only as a means of communication and a way for adults to control the infant's behavior. (1977, pp. 29–30)

As this passage reveals, the main semiotic issue for Vygotsky was how sign systems, especially speech, control human activity. What specifically is meant by "control" here? In order to answer this question I must return to the developmental reorganizations I outlined earlier. (Perhaps more accurately I should emphasize that these reorganizations can be fully understood only when we understand semiotic mediation or control.)

Vygotsky's account of the social reorganization of development was based primarily on his observations of how the child's integration into verbally mediated social interaction creates the conditions for the transformation of the practical intelligence of the natural line of development.

> The most significant moment in the course of intellectual development, which gives birth to the purely human forms of practical and abstract intelligence, occurs when speech and practical activity, two previously completely independent lines of development, converge. Although children's use of tools during the

preverbal period is comparable to that of apes, as soon as speech and the use of signs are incorporated into any action, the action becomes transformed and organized along entirely new lines. The specifically human use of tools is thus realized, going beyond the more limited use of tools possible among the higher animals. (1978, p. 24)[1]

Vygotsky argued that this line of reasoning applied to all uniquely human higher mental functions. For example, in the case of perception he wrote:

The role of language in perception is striking because of the opposing tendencies in the nature of visual perception and language. The independent elements in a visual field are simultaneously perceived; in this sense, *visual perception is integral*. Speech, on the other hand, requires sequential processing. Each element is separately labeled and then connected in a sentence structure, *making speech essentially analytical*.

Our research has shown that even at very early stages of development, language and perception are linked. In the solution of non-verbal tasks, even if a problem is solved without a sound being uttered language plays a role in the outcome.... A special feature of human perception—which arises at a very young age—is the *perception of real objects*. This is something for which there is no analogy in animal perception. By this term I mean that I do not see the world simply in color and shape but also as a world with sense and meaning. I do not merely see something round and black with two hands; I see a clock and I can distinguish one hand from the other.... These observations suggest that all human perception consists of categorized rather than isolated perceptions. (1978, p. 33)

These passages reveal the main points in Vygotsky's argument about how natural processes are transformed when they come into contact with semiotically mediated processes. We can see that his claim was not that speech somehow creates psychological processes and categories; rather, speech was viewed as transforming and reorganizing preexisting natural processes. Also, his comment about the sequentiality of speech reflects the fact that he viewed speech, rather than some form of nonlinguistic social interaction, as the central mechanism for transforming the products of the natural line of development.

Vygotsky's use of the term *categorized perception* in the preceding passage and Luria's mention of *categorical behavior* in an earlier passage indicate one of the basic properties of language that the members of this school of Soviet psychology saw as causing the social reorganization of development. This is the fact that the use of language involves generalization and the categorization of experience. Vygotsky's argument on this issue begins with the axiom that categorization in the form of generalized word meaning is inextricably tied to human social interaction. Borrowing from Sapir (1921) he wrote:

In order to transmit some experience or content of consciousness to another person, there is no other path than to ascribe the content to a known class, to a known group of phenomena, and as we know this necessarily involves *general-*

---

[1] Vygotsky's statement here that speech and activity meet after having been "two previously completely independent lines of development" once again reflects the oversimplified notion he had of early social and sensorimotor intelligence.

ization. Thus it turns out that *social interaction necessarily presupposes generalization and the development of word meaning,* i.e., generalization becomes
possible with the development of social interaction. Thus higher, uniquely
human forms of psychological social interaction are possible only because
human thinking reflects reality in a generalized way. (1956, p. 51)

Vygotsky was quite explicit about how he viewed the implications of this line of
reasoning for ontogenesis. According to him,

The levels of generalization in a child correspond strictly to the levels in the
development of social interaction. Any new level in the child's generalization
signifies a new level in the possibility for social interaction. (1956, p. 432)

Vygotsky's comments here about levels of generalization and levels in the development of social interaction reflect an important aspect of his semiotic analysis. In
developing his genetic argument he did not assume that generalized word meaning
suddenly appears on the scene. In fact he was quite critical of Stern's (1928) analysis
in which a child is thought to "discover" the symbolic function of the word between
the ages of 18 and 24 months. Instead he argued that a detailed analysis of children's
speech reveals that the development of categorical word meaning is not complete
until early adolescence. For him, genetic analysis must document its origins and
development rather than assume its presence.

Vygotsky began such a genetic analysis by arguing that during early phases of
ontogenesis the child's understanding of words is specifically *not* based on their categorical meaning. Rather, he argued that

our initial words have indicatory meaning for the child. In this, it seems to me
that we have identified the *original function of speech,* which has not been
appreciated by other researchers. The original function of speech is not that the
word has meaning for the child; it is not that a corresponding new connection
is created with the help of the word. Rather, the *word is initially an indicator.*
The word as an indicator is the primary function in the development of speech,
from which all others may be derived. (1981b, p. 219)

Vygotsky's notion of an "indicator" here is very similar to Peirce's (1931–1935)
notion of an "indexical sign." As Silverstein (in press) has pointed out, the indexical
function of the sign during early phases of ontogenesis is precisely the mechanism
that makes it possible for communication to affect the primitive practical activity of
the natural line of development and thus to begin the social reorganization of development (cf. Williams; Nadin, this volume).

Of course, if the child is to become part of the semiotically mediated social
world, s/he soon must advance beyond understanding and using words as indexes.
This development requires at least primitive forms of categorization. Vygotsky's
explanation of how this advancement occurs is again based on the semiotic mechanisms that make it possible for the child to participate in progressively higher levels
of social interaction with experienced members of a culture. Specifically, he utilized
the distinction between meaning *(znachenie)* and object reference *(predmetnaya otne-
sennost').* Borrowing from Husserl, he outlined this distinction as follows:

It is necessary to distinguish . . . the meaning of a word or expression from its
referent, i.e., the objects designated by the word or expression. There may be
one meaning and different objects or conversely, different meanings and one

object. Whether we say "the victor at Jena" or "the loser at Waterloo," we refer to the same person (Napoleon). The meaning of the two expressions, however, is different. (1956, p. 191)

Vygotsky argued that this distinction "provides the key to the correct analysis of the development of early stages in children's thinking" (1956, p. 192). Its importance lies in the fact that it allowed Vygotsky to deal with the function of referring, or picking out particular objects, independently of the function of classifying or categorizing these objects in terms of some generalized meaning. Furthermore, it allowed him to deal with early forms of categorization based on concrete perceptual features independently of categorization based on decontextualized semantic relationships (cf. Greenfield, this volume). His account of the indicatory function of the word is the beginning of this analysis. In this case, referring is largely independent of any linguistic categorical system. He extended this analysis (and hence his critique of Stern) by arguing that children go through a sequence of stages culminating in an abstract (i.e., decontextualized) form of categorization. The preliminary stages in this development in one way or another involve restrictions imposed by the concrete context.[2]

For Vygotsky the essential point in this argument is that word meaning continues to develop long after the point when new words (i.e., phonetic forms) first appear in children's speech (cf. Dittmar, this volume). He argued that although it is tempting to attribute a complete understanding of word meaning to children when they begin to use word forms, the appearance of new words marks only the beginning rather than the end point in the development of meaning. In Vygotsky's opinion this is a crucial fact that investigators of language development often fail to understand.

> The outward similarity between the thinking of the 3-year-old and the adult, the practical coincidence in the child's and adult's word meaning that makes verbal social interaction possible, the mutual understanding of adult and child, the functional equivalence of the complex and concepts—all these things have led investigators to the false conclusion that the 3-year-old's thinking is already present. True, they assumed that this thinking is undeveloped, but they nonetheless assume that it has the full set of forms found in adult intellectual activity. Consequently, it is assumed that during the transitional period there is no fundamental change, no essential new step in the mastery of concepts. The origins of this mistake are very easy to understand. At a very early age the child acquires many words whose meanings for him/her coincide with those of adults. Because of the possibility of understanding, the impression has been created that *the end point of development in word meaning coincides with the beginning point,* that a ready-made concept is given from the very beginning, and consequently that there is no room for development. Those investigators (e.g., Ach) who equate the concept with the initial meaning of the word thereby inevitably arrive at false conclusions based on an illusion. (1956, pp. 179–180)

In developing a proposal that would overcome this problem, Vygotsky (1956) outlined a series of ontogenetic stages in concept development. He documented these

---

[2]This line of reasoning is based on Vygotsky's assumption that abstract, decontextualized mental functioning represents an advanced level of psychological development that emerges with the evolution of the social institution of formal schooling. The specific claims involved in this assumption are explored more fully by Luria (1976).

stages through the use of a block sorting and classification task (cf. Schubert, this volume). Based on his observations of the sorting strategy used by subjects, he concluded that the stable, decontextualized categorization and generalization which adults are capable of using does not emerge until early adolescence. Before then children may appear to have a great deal of overlap with adults in their identification of the objects to which a word may be used to refer, but Vygotsky demonstrated that this overlap does not imply that they are using the same meanings and cognitive processes as those used by adults. In particular, he found that whereas adults are capable of sorting on the basis of stable categories and of reasoning abstractly (i.e., independently of the concrete set of referents) about these categories and their interrelationships, children are often tied to the concrete context provided by the blocks. On the basis of this result he argued that

> we could say that the child's word coincides with the adult's word in their object reference, i.e., they point to or indicate one and the same set of objects, they relate to one and the same set of phenomena. But they do not coincide in meaning.
>
> Again, this *agreement on the object reference of a word and lack of agreement on the meaning,* which we have disclosed as a major characteristic of childhood thinking in complexes, is not the exception but the rule in the development of language. We said earlier in summing up the most important result in our investigation that in connection with a word's meaning a child thinks of the same things as the adult, i.e., the same objects. However, the child thinks about the same content differently, with different means, with the help of different intellectual operations. (1956, p. 196)

Thus we see why Vygotsky saw the distinction between meaning and reference as a key element in the social reorganization of ontogenesis. The fact that primitive, context-bound communication is possible on the basis of agreement on reference provides an "entry point" for the adult to come into contact with the child's natural line of development. However, the fact that the adult understands and uses words in terms of a culturally constituted sign system (i.e., language) means that the social interaction is structured such that the child is encouraged to master a system of decontextualized, categorical word meanings. Vygotsky outlined this form of the adult's influence in the following terms:

> We have seen that the speech of those adults surrounding the child, with its constant, determinant word meanings, determines the paths of the development of children's generalizations, the circle of complexes. The child does not select the meaning for a word. It is given to him/her in the process of verbal social interaction with adults. The child does not construct his/her own complexes freely. He/she finds them already constructed in the process of understanding others' speech. He/she does not freely select various concrete elements and include them in one or another complex. He/she receives a group of concrete objects in an already prepared form of generalization provided by a word. . . .
> In general, a child does not create his/her own speech; he/she masters the existing speech of surrounding adults. (1956, pp. 180–181)

It may strike some readers that what I have said so far about the emergence of generalization applies more readily to the psychological reorganization of ontogenesis than to the social reorganization. In fact, the close connection that Vygotsky saw between social and individual functioning means that in his approach there is no sharp cut-off point between interpsychological and intrapsychological processes or between the social and psychological reorganization of ontogenesis. The advanced phases of the social are neccessarily the early phases of the individual. When we come to the final phases of the development of word meaning, however, we find a transition that is clearly a part of the psychological reorganization of ontogenesis.

The final stage in concept development is the emergence of "scientific concepts." According to Vygotsky the child develops scientific concepts in response to the requirements of formal instruction. In school there is an emphasis on learning concepts or word meanings by relating them to other word meanings rather than through direct experience with referents. Whereas earlier forms of conceptual development had relied primarily on word–object relations the scientific concept involves

> both a relationship to an object and a relationship to another concept, i.e., the initial elements of a system of concepts. (1956, p. 249)

The development of systems of hierarchically interrelated concepts is the hallmark of this stage of development. Such systems are necessarily based on decontextualized meanings rather than concrete reference. Thus the developmental path Vygotsky outlined begins with word–object relations and culminates in meaning–meaning relationships. The relationships among meanings inherent in scientific concepts make possible abstract propositional reasoning such as that studied by Luria (1976) and Tulviste (1975, 1977). The development of this form of reasoning is clearly concerned with the psychological reorganization of ontogenesis. It involves a form of individual psychological functioning that derives from, and changes, the social functioning that had preceded it. This development reflects the conscious realization and voluntary control that Vygotsky viewed as so central for the forms of intrapsychological functioning valued in Western technological societies.

> Thus *the generalization of genuine mental processes that leads to their mastery lies at the foundation of conscious realization.* Above all else instruction plays a decisive role in this process. Scientific concepts with their unique relationship to objects, with their mediation through other concepts, with their internal hierarchical system of interrelationships among themselves are the area in which the conscious realization of concepts, i.e., their generalization and mastery, emerges first and foremost. (1956, p. 247)

Thus we see how the development of word meaning involves increasingly stable and decontextualized categorical behavior. As I have argued elsewhere (Wertsch, in preparation), this is only one aspect of the larger picture proposed by Vygotsky for how semiotic mechanisms function to transfer the locus of control for human action from the natural line of development to the plane of interpsychological (between persons) functioning and finally to the intrapsychological (within individuals) plane of functioning.

In his analysis of all of these issues Vygotsky's line of reasoning involves the three themes that I have outlined in this chapter. It begins with the assumption that "we need to concentrate not on the *product* of development but on the *process* by which higher forms are established" (1978, p. 64). That is, it begins with the assumption that genetic analysis is the appropriate method. Included in Vygotsky's understanding of genetic analysis is the idea that *"the type of development iself has changed"* (1956, p. 146). In particular, his line of reasoning means that we must be prepared to study the social and the psychological reorganizations of development. Vygotsky's major focus was on the latter, especially as it occurs in ontogenesis. Thus the bulk of his writings was concerned with the "general law of cultural development" that "any function in children's cultural development appears . . . [first] on the social plane and then on the psychological plane" (1981a). He viewed the genetic relationship between these two planes such that intrapsychological functioning reflects interpsychological functioning in several important respects. His analysis of the semiotic mechanisms provided the foundation for the investigation of the concrete link between social and individual functioning. In this chapter, I outlined Vygotsky's account of one of the semiotic issues he examined, word meaning.

The ultimate goal of this chapter, however, is not to present Vygotsky's account of categorical word meaning. Rather, it is to outline a general theoretical approach that I see as quite relevant to the problems encountered in contemporary studies of the relationship between society and the human individual. As I noted, certain of Vygotsky's claims are naive and oversimplified in light of recent empirical research. However, the scope and theoretical integration inherent in his approach provide some very timely suggestions for how we might reformulate social science questions today.

References

Bakhtin, M. M. *Problems of Dostoevsky's poetics.* Ann Arbor: Ardis, 1973.
Bibler, V. S. *Thinking as creation: An introduction to the logic of mental dialogue.* Moscow: Political Literature Press, 1975. (in Russian)
Blonskii, P. P. *Essays in scientific psychology.* Moscow: State Publishing House, 1921. (in Russian)
Bruner, J. S. *Processes of cognitive growth: Infancy.* Worcester, Mass.: Clark University Press, 1968.
Bruner, J. S. Organization of early skilled action. *Child Development,* 1973, *44,* 1–11.
Engels, F. *Dialectics of nature.* New York: International Publishers, 1940.
Ivanov, V. V. *Essays on the history of semiotics in the USSR.* Moscow: Nauka Press, 1976. (in Russian)
Ivanov, V. V. The role of semiotics in the cybernetic study of man and collective. In D. P. Lucid (Ed.), *Soviet semiotics: An anthology.* Baltimore: Johns Hopkins Press, 1977.
Janet, P. *L'évolution de la mémoire et de la notion du temps.* Compte-rendu intégral des conférences d'après les notes sténographiques. Paris: A. Chahine, 1928.
Janet, P. *L'évolution psychologique de la personnalité.* Compte-rendu intégral des conférence d'après les notes sténographiques. Paris: A. Chahine, 1929.
Köhler, W. *Intelligenzprüfungen an Menschenaffen.* Berlin: Springer, 1921.
Luria, A. R. Towards the problem of the historical nature of psychological processes. *International Journal of Psychology,* 1971, *6*(4), 259–272.
Luria, A. R. *Cognitive development: Its cultural and social foundations.* Cambridge, Mass.: Harvard University Press, 1976.
Luria, A. R. *Language and cognition.* New York: Wiley-Interscience, 1982.
Marx, K. *Capital.* Chicago: Kerr, 1906.
Mead, G. H. *Mind, self, and society.* Chicago: University of Chicago Press, 1934.
Peirce, C. S. *Collected papers.* Cambridge, Mass.: Harvard University Press, 1931–1935.
Piaget, J. *The origins of intelligence in the child.* New York: Norton, 1963.
Piaget, J. *The construction of reality in the child.* New York: Ballantine, 1971.
Potebnya, A. A. *Thought and language.* Khar'kov, 1913. (in Russian)

Sapir, E. *Language*. New York: Harcourt, Brace and World, 1921.

Silverstein, M. The functional stratification of language and ontogenesis. In J. V. Wertsch (Ed.), *Culture, communication and cognition: Vygotskian perspectives*. New York: Cambridge University Press, in press.

Smirnov, A. A. *The development and present status of psychology in the USSR*. Moscow: Pedagogika Press, 1975. (in Russian)

Stern, C. *Die Kindersprache*. Leipzig: Barth, 1928.

Tulviste, P. *The socio-historical development of cognitive processes (based on materials of foreign experimental psychological research)*. Candidate's dissertation abstract, Moscow, 1975. (in Russian)

Tulviste, P. The interpretation of parallels between the ontogenetic and historical development of thinking. *Papers on sign systems* (Vol. 8). Tartu: Tartu University Press, 1977. (in Russian)

Tulviste, P. On the theoretical problems of the historical development of thinking. In L. I. Antsyferova (Ed.), *The principle of development in psychology*. Moscow: Nauka Press, 1978. (in Russian)

Voloshinov, V. N. *Marxism and the philosophy of language*. New York: Seminar Press, 1973.

Vygotsky, L. S. *Selected psychological research*. Moscow: Academy of Pedagogical Sciences Press, 1956. (in Russian)

Vygotsky, L. S. *The development of higher mental functions*. Moscow: Academy of Pedagogical Sciences Press, 1960. (in Russian)

Vygotsky, L. S. The problem of stage periodization in child development. *Problems of Psychology, 1972, 2*, 114–123. (in Russian)

Vygotsky, L. S. *Mind in society: The development of higher psychological processes* (M. Cole, V. John-Steiner, S. Scribner, & E. Souberman, Eds.). Cambridge, Mass.: Harvard University Press, 1978.

Vygotsky, L. S. Consciousness as a problem in the psychology of behavior. *Soviet Psychology, 1979, 17*(4), 3–35.

Vygotsky, L. S. The genesis of higher mental functions. In J. V. Wertsch (Ed.), *The concept of activity in Soviet psychology*. Armonk, N.Y.: M. E. Sharpe, 1981. (a)

Vygotsky, L. S. The development of higher forms of attention in childhood. In J. V. Wertsch (Ed.), *The concept of activity in Soviet psychology*. Armonk, N.Y.: M. E. Sharpe, 1981. (b)

Wertsch, J. V. *Cognitive developmental theory: A Vygotskian approach*. Cambridge, Mass.: Harvard University Press, in preparation.

Wertsch, J. V., & Stone, C. A. Microgenesis as a tool for developmental analysis. *The quarterly newsletter of the Laboratory of Comparative Human Cognition*. University of California, San Diego, September 1978, *1*(1), 8–10.

Yakubinskii, L. P. *On dialogic speech*. Petrograd: Works of the Phonetics Institute of the Practical Study of Languages, 1923. (in Russian)

Yerkes, R. M. The mental life of monkeys and apes. *Behavioral Monographs*, 1916, *3*(1).

3

Peekaboo as an Instructional Model: Discourse Development at Home and at School

Courtney B. Cazden

I have spent my professional life going back and forth between the language worlds of the child at home and the child at school. For several years, I participated actively in research on early language acquisition. Recently, my work has returned to elementary school classrooms, where I started out. Questions about language in education were on my mind when I went back to graduate school at Harvard in 1961, and my primary professional commitment is to understand the complexities of how language is used, and could be used, in schools. This paper is an exploration of relationships between the two research enterprises that are focused separately on the language of home and of school, to see if a comparison between them yields new insights about either one.

The past five years have seen a marked increase in descriptions of classroom talk that are informed by theory and methodology from the ethnography of speaking and sociolinguistics. I will start with examples of this work, look back at mother–child interaction studies for comparison, and then, from the perspective of Vygotsky's zone of proximal development, return to speculations about what language in the classroom could be.

Discourse in the Classroom

Recent ethnographic studies of language in the classroom—sometimes called microethnographies because the unit is a classroom rather than a culture—follow a methodology described by Frake:

Courtney B. Cazden ● Graduate School of Education, Harvard University, Cambridge, Massachusetts 02138. This is a revised version of a paper that was written while the author was a Fellow at the Center for Advanced Study in the Behavioral Sciences with support from the National Endowment for the Humanities and the Spencer Foundation, and appeared in the *Papers and Reports on Child Language Development No. 17,* Stanford University, Department of Linguistics, 1979, pp. 1–29.

A description of a culture derives from an ethnographer's observations of the stream of activities performed by the people he is studying. As a first step toward producing an ethnographic statement, the investigator must segment and classify the events of this behavior stream so that he can say, for example of two successive events, that they are repetitions of the "same" activity. . . . Information about what is the "same" and what is "different" can only come from the interpretation of events made by the people being studied. (1972, p. 110)

Because of the importance of language to the goals of schools, one very useful aim of this kind of educational research would be a typology of the kinds of talking that occur in classrooms, and then a typology of classrooms according to the types and frequencies of talking that occur. Such a cross-classroom comparison—a subset of cross-cultural ethnographies of communication—would surely be more informative than the usual classification of classrooms on global terms like "structured" and "open." We are a long way from such a typology, but a start has been made in segmenting the complex stream of behaviors and analyzing the structure of some of the segments. (See Erickson & Shultz, 1977, for a methodological discussion.)

In thinking about the kinds of talk that occur in classrooms, it seems useful to preserve Hymes's distinction between a speech situation and a speech event, at least as ends of a continuum (Bauman & Sherzer, 1975; Hymes, 1972). A speech *situation* contains speech, but it is organized in terms of some nonverbal activity. Watching a football game would be one example. There is talk among the spectators; there will be regularities in that talk as the spectators assemble and find their seats and the game begins. But the situation is not constituted in terms of rules for speaking. A speech *event,* by contrast, is "directly governed by rules or norms for the use of speech" (Hymes, 1972, p. 56). Among classroom contexts, a ticktacktoe game is a speech situation, and teacher-led lessons are one kind of speech event.

Complementing analyses of situations and events are analyses—more sociolinguistic than ethnographic—of particular speech *acts,* such as requests for clarification. The relationship between these two levels of analysis presents important problems. One cannot describe the structure of an event without deciding what each slot in the event structure can be filled with—decisions about "same" and "different" at another level. Just as to say that "S → NP + VP" assumes decisions about what counts as an NP and a VP, so to say that "Instructional sequence [in a lesson] → Initiation + Reply + Evaluation" (Mehan, 1979, p. 75) assumes decisions about membership in those categories. Conversely, though perhaps less obviously, decisions about speech act assignment may depend on where in a speech event structure an utterance appears. (Mishler, 1979, discussed this problem in an analysis of children's bargaining sequences.) Even more fundamental and pervasive are questions about the level of interpretation of intentions that controls sequencing (Labov & Fanshel, 1977; cf. Dittmar, this volume). I do not want to enter these controversies here and only use the terms *situation, event,* and *act* as labels for types of recent classroom research.

Speech Situation: The Ticktacktoe Game

Shultz (1979) described one speech situation, a ticktacktoe game, in a kindergarten–first grade class in a Boston suburb. Activities in this classroom alternated between those in which the whole group was assembled on the rug for some joint

Table I. Behaviors in Three Phases of a Ticktacktoe Game[a]

	Setup (161 seconds)	Serious play (184 seconds)	Windup (33 seconds)
	C_1 asks C_2 to play until beginning of game	From 1st move of game to teacher's statement that no one will win	From T's statement until C_2 sent off to take test
Teacher's position while seated: (1) upright, (2) leaning forward slightly, (3) leaning far forward	All 3	Always leaning in (2 or 3); never straight up	All 3
Successful interruptions by outsiders/attempts	7/7	0/2	3/3
Topics permitted	C_1's comment to T: *I saw Kevin's father today,* responded to even though not game-related	C_2's comment to T: *I'm gonna tell my Mommy again,* also unrelated to game, ignored	

[a]Based on Shultz (1979).

endeavor—called *circles*—and those in which the children were dispersed around the room performing a variety of tasks—called *small group periods.* One of the tokens of the small group situation was called *workperiod,* and one of its tokens (of which many may occur simultaneously and sequentially as children move from one activity to another) was a ticktacktoe game. This speech situation is structured around the game—here played by the teacher and three children, one of whom, C_2, is a kinder-gartner who is being taught how to play. What Shultz discovered is that the three phases of the game situation—setup, serious play, and windup—are organized in ways that have consequences for the talk that does and does not occur. These phases are marked by changes in the teacher's posture, by the frequency and success of attempted interruptions of the game by children who are not players, and by what topics can "get the floor," as shown in Table I. The teacher's posture, always leaning in during serious play, may be a significant "contextualization cue" (Gumperz, 1976) for the children, telling them nonverbally "that she was very deeply engrossed in what she was doing and was therefore not available to be interrupted" (Shultz, 1979). Note particularly that a child's comment about a nongame topic—actually a nonschool topic—is responded to by the teacher during the setup phase, but a similar comment in the serious play phase is ignored. The fact that the kindergarten child, C_2, attempted such a conversation at that time is seen by observers and the teacher as evidence that s/he is not yet a competent member of this classroom community.

Speech Event: The Lesson

Some segments of classroom life are organized for and by talk alone. By far the most common focus for classroom interaction research is the *lesson.* Focus on lessons may have been initially influenced by their greater audibility to human observers or overhead microphones; during lessons teachers and children talk up, and they talk (pretty much) one at a time. Without wireless microphones, other speech situations like the ticktacktoe game are as hard to overhear as talk at restaurant tables. But attention to lessons may also be justified by their status as the focal instance, the enactment of the central tendency, of the larger category of classroom talk, especially in the density of known-answer test questions and teacher evaluations of student replies. The most detailed and formalized analysis of classroom lessons is Mehan's (1979) book-length description of nine lessons in a multiethnic, inner-city Primary classroom in San Diego.[1]

The lesson, like the ticktacktoe game, has three phases: *opening,* the *instructional core,* and *closing.* During the opening and closing phases, the teacher issues directives, such as "Alberto, turn around so you can see the blackboard," and informatives, such as "The people who haven't had a turn and would like to may do it tomorrow." In the instructional core, three-part sequences of teacher initiation, student reply, and teacher evaluation are organized into what Mehan called topically related sets. Table II illustrates one set from the "Namecards" lesson, conducted on the fourth day of the first week of school in September.

According to Mehan, the beginning of each topically related set is signaled by a combination of kinesic, verbal, and paralinguistic behavior. The teacher physically orients toward the instructional materials to be used, in this case a namecard held up in front of the class. There is a closed set of markers that appear nowhere else in the lessons, including *um, now, let's see,* and *last of all.* The cadence of the teacher's voice quickens as the set beings. Each set contains a basic sequence; sometimes there are conditional sequences as well. In the Namecards lesson, the basic sequence is the identification of one student's name on a namecard. With some cards, more frequently near the beginning of the lesson, the student who read the card is asked to identify the actual student or explain how s/he knew the answer. The teacher then confirms the reading of the name with its owner. The set closes in ways complementary to the opening: the teacher lowers the material and marks the end with a finite set of markers like "That's right," often with the correct reply repeated, and the cadence slows with these words (paraphrased from Mehan, 1979, pp. 65–70).

A further aspect of the lesson structure is how each teacher initiation functions to allocate turns at speaking. Mehan identified three turn-allocation procedures that accounted for 80% of the 480 initiations in all nine lessons:

- *Invitations to bid:* "Who knows . . .?" or "Who could tell us?" as in Table II, 4:9 and 4:10.

---

[1] I was the classroom teacher in these lessons, but my personal involvement is not relevant to this discussion. I have discussed my experience as teacher in Cazden (1976, 1979, 1982); I have reported analyses of the language of children in that classroom in Cazden (1975), Cazden, Cox, Dickinson, Steinberg, and Stone (1979), and Carrasco, Vera, and Cazden (1981). Later in this paper I will comment briefly on some of my own utterances as teacher. Until now, I have left such comments to others, but if child-language-researcher parents can analyze their interactions with their own children, why not a teacher too?

Table II. A Representative Example of a Topically Related Set[a]

	Initiation		Reply		Evaluation
4:9					
T:	Who knows whose namecard this is? (holds up namecard)	P: C:	Mine. (raises hand)	T:	Ah, if you see, if it's your namecard don't give the secret away if you, if . . .
4:10					
T:	Let's see, I'll just take some of the people who are here. Um, if it's your namecard, don't give away the secret. Whose namecard, who could tell us whose namecard this is? (holds card up)	C:	(raises hand)		
4:11					
T:	Carolyn.	C:	Patricia.		
4:12					
T:	Can you point to Patricia?	C:	(points to Patricia)	T:	That's right.
4:13					
T:	Is this your namecard?	P:	(nods yes)		

[a]From *Learning Lessons* by H. Mehan, Cambridge, Massachusetts: Harvard University Press, 1979, p. 69. Copyright 1979 by Harvard University Press. Reprinted by permission.

- *Individual nominations:* A particular respondent is named or identified by gaze and pronoun as in Table II, 4:11, 4:12, and 4:13.
- *Invitation to reply:* Later in the Namecards lesson, "And last of all, anybody, whose name is this?" to which anyone may answer, alone or in chorus.

Various types of formal statements of rules for speaking have been attempted. Mehan formalized the lesson structure into a set of rewrite rules (1979, p. 75) and formalized the possible combinations of normal forms and sanctioned violations of the turn-allocation procedures in a set of flow charts (pp. 104–105). The purpose of such formal statements was explained by Hymes:

> When prose descriptions of events have been so restated, there has been a considerable gain in understanding of structure; or, one might say, a considerable clarification of what one understood to be the structure has been demanded. The form of the events is disengaged, as it were, from the verbal foliage obligatory in prose sentences, and can be more readily *seen.* In order to compare events within a society, and across societies, some concise and standard formats are needed. Comparison cannot depend upon memorization or shuffling of prose paragraphs vastly different in verbal style. And *it is through some form of formal statement that one can commit oneself to a precise claim as to what it is a member of society knows in knowing how to participate in a speech act.* (1972, p. 66, emphasis added)

Hymes's last sentence gets to the heart of one purpose of this set of microethnographic studies. Just as a description of language (a grammar) asserts hypotheses about what the speaker of a language must learn, so a description of a lesson asserts hypotheses about what children must learn in order to participate fully in classroom talk and to be judged as interactionally, as well as academically, competent students.

Also analogous to analyses of language learning is the concept of interference between what could be called first and second discourse development, interference between what children have learned about appropriate ways of talking at home and the interactional demands of school. A model for such analyses has been Philips's (1972) research on the Warm Springs Reservation.

A recent analysis of interference is Michaels and Cook-Gumperz's (1979) study of the narratives of personal experience offered by white and black first-grade children during sharing time, a common speech event in kindergarten and primary classrooms. All the children used a special and highly marked intonation contour and formulaic beginnings such as "Yesterday" (even when the topic in fact happened last night or last year). All the narratives differed from usual intraconversational narratives in several ways: the teacher holds the floor for the speaker; the narrator does not have to tie the story to previous discourse topics; and the teacher actively collaborates by interjecting questions, comments, and reactions. The interference is produced by a mismatch between the narrative style of some of the children, often the black children, and the model implicit in the teacher's collaborative efforts. Her collaboration fits and sometimes even enhances what Michaels and Cook-Gumperz called a "topic-centered" style, but not a differently structured "topic-chaining" style.

Table III gives examples of each style, retaining the division into lines but not the transcriptions of prosodic and paralinguistic features of the original. Whereas Jenny receives a confirming "Oh great," Deena is cut off with criticism for what the teacher refers to as her "filibusters." Although we regret the teacher's insensitivity and her egocentric notion of what's "really very important," we may still recognize, I believe, that Jenny's narrative—with its greater detail about a single event—is more interesting to listen to or to read.

As important as differences in the children's styles are differences in the teacher's help. With children who used a topic-centered style, the teacher was highly successful at "tuning in" and helping them produce more focused and lexically explicit discourse through her questions and comments (Michaels, 1981). With many of the black children, on the other hand, the teacher's questions were often mistimed—stopping the child in midclause—and thematically inappropriate—interrupting the child's train of thought rather than collaborating with it. Such a mismatch between the teacher and the child's prosodic signaling system and narrative schemata made it harder for the teacher, despite the best educational intentions, to help precisely those children who needed help most.

These studies of discourse interference assume that such interference will affect the children's success in school. Interestingly, in this particular case Deena was one of the best readers in the class. Michaels and Cook-Gumperz commented:

> Furthermore, while Deena's reading, math, and spelling skills have all shown
> marked improvement over the course of the school year, her sharing discourse

Table III. Two Styles of Sharing Time Narratives[a]

Topic-centered		Topic-chaining	
Jenny:	Yesterday	Deena:	I went to the beach Sunday
	my mom		and to McDonald's
	and my whole family		and to the park
	went with me to a party		and I got this for my birthday
	and it was a thanksgiving party		My mother bought it for me
	where and we		and I had two dollars for
St.T:	} mm		my birthday
Jenny:	} my mom		and I put it in here
	we had to get dress up as		and I went to where my friend
	Pilgrims		names GiGi
	and my mom made me this hat for a		I went over to my grandmother's
	Pilgrim		house with her
St.T:	Oh great.		and she was on my back
			and I and we was walking around
			by my house
			and she was heavy
			She⟨ was in the sixth or seventh
			{ grade
		T:	(OK I'm going to stop you.
			I want you to talk about things
			that are really really
			very important.

[a]From *A Study of Sharing Time with First Grade Students: Discourse Narratives in the Classroom.* by S. Michaels and J. Cook-Gumperz, Berkeley, California: Berkeley Linguistics Society, 1979. Copyright 1979 by the Berkeley Linguistics Society. Reprinted by permission.

style has remained unchanged. And so, while sharing can be seen as an oral preparation for literacy, this has, as yet, had no influence on her progress in reading. However, Deena's topic-chaining oral discourse style may, in time, greatly interfere with her ability to produce literate sounding descriptive prose. (1979, p. 12)

Speech Act: Requests for Clarification

Some research on classroom language has selected a particular speech act as the focus of analysis. A set of utterances is selected from a set of protocols as tokens of an utterance type defined by its function and the tokens are then analyzed for formal variants and for the frequency and pattern of their distribution. A large study of children's functional language in nursery, kindergarten, and the primary grades in a Washington, D.C., private school conducted at the Center for Applied Linguistics included an analysis of requests for clarification (Christian & Tripp, 1978). Here are two kindergarten examples, one asked of the teacher, the second of another child:

T: All my other students have always called it the Ed and Edna game.
Ashley: *The what?*
T: The Ed and Edna game. (p. 14)

Joyce: You get to put the chapstick on.
Mary: *On what?*
Joyce: On her lips. (p. 16)

Requests for clarification were selected both because of their presumed importance in education and because of the existing sociolinguistic research of Garvey (1977) and others to draw on.

A corpus of videotapes was selected such that each of 40 children, 8 at each grade level (nursery through third grade), could be followed for two hours, divided evenly between large group and small group activities. All instances of requests for clarification on these tapes were then analyzed. The researchers were interested in whether the use of these requests differentiated between those children whom the teacher had identified as more and less competent language users and in the distribution of these requests by addressee and group size. Briefly, the use of these requests did not differentiate the children according to the teacher's ratings, but there was a strong effect of addressee and situation. The percentage addressed to teachers dropped from 69% in the nursery to only 6% in third grade; and only 11% of all the requests were asked in large group settings. The researchers related this situational difference in frequency to the kind of lesson structure described by Mehan:

> Most large group situations, especially in classrooms, involve certain rules about turns of speaking to maintain order. In order to issue a request for clarification, it is often the case that one of these rules that maintain order would need to be violated so that the request can be appropriately timed. For example, it would be virtually impossible to observe a rule about raising your hand to be given a turn and then to make one of these requests. This relationship between requesting clarification and situation in terms of group size then follows naturally from features of the behaviors associated with each. (1979)

Thus an analysis that starts with speech acts leads to questions about the structure of the speech event in which they occur in order to explain patterns of use.

Discourse at Home

What do we know about speech situations and speech events in the child's preschool life that are similar to those at school—similar in the sense that there is a context, a sequential structure, that creates slots of certain shapes in which the child comes to speak. In a general sense, all conversation fits this description, but the closest similarity between classroom and home seems to be the language games with infants that Bruner has analyzed: social exchange games such as peekaboo (Ratner & Bruner, 1978) and picture-book reading (Ninio & Bruner, 1978). A closer look at those games relates them, and by extension more of early mother–child conversation as it is described in the research literature, to Vygotsky's concept of the "zone of proximal development," and suggests what may be essential qualities of the most powerful learning environments. Now to take the steps in that argument one at a time.

Happily, we all know how to play peekaboo. Ratner and Bruner's description reminds us how this familiar activity exemplifies four special features of these early games: a restricted format, clear and repetitive structure, positions for appropriate vocalizations, and reversible role relationships (1978, p. 391). Here is a representative peekaboo game between Richard and his mother.

> In the beginning [6–11 months] agency was almost always handled by the mother. She always did the hiding, about half the time covering herself. By 1;2, the pattern was transformed: nine out of ten times, it was the CHILD who did the hiding, and inevitably he hid himself. In reappearance, again the mother initiated most of the time in the early months, invariably appearing with a smile and *hello.!*
>
> As he moved from the role of spectator in the first phase to that of actor in the second, his vocalizations changed. . . . while in the earlier period his vocalizations were excited babbles, the later period was marked by lexemic-like PCF [phonetically consistent form] sounds, principally directed to the partner in the game, including (at 1;3.21), *peeboo, da, hi da, dere, ahh.*
>
> By 1;3 and after, Richard and his mother played peekaboo rarely. But object hiding continued. The last appearances of peekaboo surfaced six months later (1;9.14), after Richard had acquired a fair amount of language. But interestingly enough, this time it was a solo, between Richard and objects HE had hidden and then caused to reappear. . . . He could also [now] manage interchangeable roles. The following month, for example, HE asked *Where Mummy* when she hid and said *hello* when she reappeared—roles hitherto controlled by his mother only. (Ratner & Bruner, 1978, pp. 398, 400)

If peekaboo is considered a speech situation, structured around the physical activities of hiding and finding, picture-book reading is an equally ritualized speech event where talk is the primary purpose—not just phatic communication and greetings as in peekaboo, but labeling for which the book provides clear and present referents for the talk. In the family described by Ninio and Bruner (presumably the same "Richard" as in the peekaboo game), picture-book reading early in the child's second year has a four-part event structure (paraphrased from Ninio & Bruner, 1978, p. 6):

- An attentive vocative, such as *Look*
- A query, such as *What's that?*
- A label, such as *It's an X*
- A feedback utterance, such as *Yes, that's an X* (if the child has provided the label)

As with peekaboo, as Richard's development proceeds, he takes over more and more of the script.

The similarity between the basic picture-book reading structure and Mehan's analysis of classroom lessons is striking. With the mother's attentional vocative replacing the teacher's turn-allocation procedures, the remaining parts of the book-reading fit exactly the initiation–reply–evaluation sequence of the lessons. Moreover, the initiations in both events are questions to which the adult asker knows the answer. In studies of the antecedents of school success, many researchers have found a high correlation between being read to and succeeding in school and have remarked on the special linguistic features of written text and of the conversation interpolated into the text-reading scene (e.g., Chomsky, 1972; Snow, 1977b). The structural similarities suggest that picture-book reading may, in addition to its substantive contribution, provide preparation for participation in the discourse of classroom lessons several years later.

There can even be an analogue to interference in this early learning. As Ninio and Bruner point out, picture-book reading has a different structure if the mother reads a nursery rhyme and leaves a slot for the child to fill in at the end of each line. A graduate student at Harvard, Sharon Haselkorn, reported interference between the patterns of mother and researcher that she encountered with book reading at this early age. Sharon was used to playing the "What's that?" game, but one of her young subjects had learned the fill-in-the-blank game, and they had a very hard time getting their speech event together (personal communication, 1978).

But there are important differences between these home and school events as well as similarities. Very different from the classroom is the change in these home language games as the child develops. While the mother can and does enact the entire script herself in the beginning, the child gradually assumes a more and more active role. Variations in the games over time are critical: the adult so structures the game that the child can be a successful participant from the beginning; then as the child's competence grows, the game changes so that there is always something new to be learned and tried out, including taking over what had been the mother's role. When variations are no longer interesting, the game is abandoned and replaced. In Bruner's words, "the only way in which the child can be kept communicating in a format is by altering or varying it—he or his mother taking the lead" (1978, p. 254).

Bruner's term *scaffold* has become a common caption for the adult's role in these games, but it is a good name only if one remembers that this is a very special kind of scaffold that self-destructs gradually as the need lessens and is then replaced by a new structure for a more elaborate construction. Another metaphor for the same relationship is what musicians know as *music-minus-one* or *add-a-part* records: chamber music records, each with a missing part to be supplied by the novice, in a graduated series of difficulty. Neither scaffolds nor add-a-part records are as dynamic and interactional as the language games, but if these limitations are kept in mind, they may be helpful metaphors.[2]

The language games described by Bruner and his associates are only one set of examples—admittedly in concentrated, exaggerated, ritualized form—of a more widespread occurrence of forms of adult support in talk with young children. In selecting these forms for special attention here, I am not talking about their possible assistance to the child's acquisition of syntax (see Ervin-Tripp, 1977, on that topic). My concern rather is with the child's acquisition of particular conversational patterns and discourse forms, which I assume to be more dependent on particular forms of help than is syntax.

First, there is Snow's (1977) description of the development of conversation between mothers and their 3- to 18-month-old babies. She described how hard the mothers worked to maintain a conversation despite the inadequacies of their conversational partners. At first they accepted burps, yawns, and coughs as well as laughs and coos—but not arm waving or head movements—as the baby's turn. They filled

---

[2]In an interesting book, *Metaphors We Live By*, Lakoff and Johnson (1980) present many examples of how "we tend to structure the less concrete and inherently vaguer concepts (like those for the emotions) in terms of more concrete concepts, which are more clearly delineated in our experience" (p. 112). In keeping with the directionality they point out, I am using the concepts of scaffold and (later) ratchet from the more concrete domains of construction and tool use to conceptualize the vaguer domain of interaction.

in for the babies by asking and answering their own questions and by phrasing questions so that a minimal response could be treated as a reply. Then by seven months the babies became considerably more active partners, and the mothers no longer accepted all the baby's vocalizations, only vocalic or consonantal babbles. As the mother raises the ante, the child's development proceeds.

From later adult–child talk, there are reports of possible antecedents of one discourse form, the narrative of personal experience that Michaels and Cook-Gumperz heard during first-grade sharing time. The most complete description is Scollon and Scollon's (1981) account of the antecedents of their daughter Rachel's ability to tell the kind of narrative that they, like Michaels and Cook-Gumperz, believe to be related to later acquisition of literacy in school. A few days before her third birthday, Rachel silently "wrote" a story in circular scribbles, and then "read" it to her parents. Here is the story, with division into lines to indicate pauses, dots (·) to indicate breaths, and double slashes (//) to indicate an intonation contour of high rise and then fall, which serves to close an information unit and yet communicates an intention to continue reading.

> There was a b-
> girl
> she
> went out to get snow//
> ·
> she
> she made a hole//
> ·
> she
> ·
> she went back
> she cried//
> she went back in tel m-
> ·
> her
> her Mom to get
> tel—old her Mom, to
> give her apple//
> so she gived her apple///
> ·
> she got
> ·
> she went out again
> got sn-
> some more snow?//
> (pp. 66–67)

While most discussions of preparations for literacy focus on what young children learn from being read to and being around adults and older children who read and write frequently and happily, the Scollons acknowledged such influences and went on to suggest how Rachel received preparation for two characteristics of what they called "essayist literacy" through adult–child interaction as well.

One characteristic is the provision of new information in each utterance. The Scollons believed that this provision is taught by the young child's caregiver in "vertical constructions," in which the adult asks the child for additional new information in each utterance. The result has what Bruner metaphorically called a "ratchet-like" quality (personal communication, 1980), with the adult helping to "hold" each previous utterance in focal attention while asking the child to say still more. In the Scollons' words:

> The child says something, the mother asks about it and the child says something further. The first can be seen as a topic statement, the mother's comment as a request for a comment and the child's answer as giving that comment.
>
> As the child develops she begins to take over both roles. That is, Brenda [the subject of R. Scollon's previous study, 1976] soon began to say both the topic and the comment. As soon as these became prosodically linked as a single utterance the whole process shifted up a level. The whole topic–comment pair was taken as a given and the interlocutor sought another comment. An example of one of these more elaborate pairs is as follows:

> | Brenda: | Tape recorder |
> | | Use it |
> | | Use it |
> | Int.: | Use it for what? |
> | Brenda: | Talk |
> | | corder talk |
> | | Brenda talk |

> Two things are important for this discussion. One is that this development is based on interaction with other speakers. The other is that it involves the progressive incorporation within a single tone group of greater amounts of new information. (1981, p. 92)

R. Scollon first described vertical constructions in his study of Brenda (1976). At that time he believed that they provide assistance in the child's development of syntax. Because of intervening evidence from other researchers that children develop syntax in the absence of this particular form of interaction, the Scollons have revised this view. In 1981, Scollon and Scollon wrote: "The vertical construction is a discourse process as is the information structuring of essayist literacy. We now see the former as an important means of teaching the latter" (p. 93).

Whereas such vertical constructions are excellent examples of interactional scaffolds, assistance to Rachel's development of the other characteristic of literacy came through the provision of adult models. This characteristic is what the Scollons called the *fictionalization of the self,* the ability to distance oneself from participation in an event and describe it to someone else. They believed that caregivers who are literate themselves coach young children in such narrative accounting by speaking for them before they can speak for themselves, either telling a child a story about herself after it has happened ("Once upon a time there was a little girl named Rachel . . .") or giving a running account of an activity as it is taking place ("See look, we throw it up and we catch it. . . ."). With these kinds of help, Rachel constructed—with self-corrections from "Mom" to "her Mom" and from "tell" to "told"—a narrative in the third person about an incident in her own life a few days before. (Not surprisingly, problems remain. The referents for the same sex pronouns in "*she* gived *her* apple" are ambiguous, but this is a specific problem in anaphora that persists well into the elementary school years.)

Brenda was talking about an object, the tape recorder, present at the moment of speaking, and special problems confront the child who, like Rachel, is struggling to encode a narrative of a past event. Sachs (1977) analyzed the first attempts to talk about absent objects and persons by her own daughter, Naomi. In the period she studied, starting at 17 months, conversation about the "there and then" was not always successful. Sachs reported that one helpful strategy was a conversational routine, for example about the absent parent:

> These conversations were initially very primitive as conversations go, but over time the child progressed from a small set of learned responses [*Daddy at the lab?*] to using appropriate, variable speech content. As other types of displaced reference appeared in the parent-child discourse, they also tended to make their first appearance in conversational routines. (p. 58)

Stoel-Gammon and Cabral (1977) described the development of the same "reportative function" in Brazilian children 20 to 24 months old. They found that attempts to tell narratives of past experience usually occurred first in a dialogue in which the adult asked questions that acted as prompts. For example, when a 20-month-old child reported "Fell ground," the adult prompted more information by asking how and where it happened and "Who pushed you down?" These early reports were most successful when the adult had been with the child at the event and later asked the child to relate what had happened to some third person. The questions of a companion thus not only elicit progressively more information from the child; they also indicate to the child what aspects of the past event are significant and notable, focusing the child's mental image on those aspects that should be replayed in the present account.

It is important to recognize that all the above examples of help for discourse learning at home are from families with highly educated parents. Unfortunately, at least in part for understandable reasons of access, demographic characteristics of the children whose language development has been studied in the past 20 years are much more limited than characteristics of the children in current research on language in the classroom. Consider the research reports in *Talking to Children* (Snow & Ferguson, 1977). The range of non-English language included in the book is admirable. But within the English-speaking world of the United States and Australia, all of the identified subjects are white, middle-class, and college educated. Children and their families from other groups are still nearly invisible in our child language research. (Adam and Sarah were exceptions in the 1973 study by Brown; Adam was black, the child of a minister; Sarah's father was a clerk in a store and neither of her parents had gone beyond high school.)

Two recent theses by students of Lois Bloom, Miller (1981) in working-class South Baltimore and Schieffelin (1979a,b) in Papua New Guinea, provide vivid linguistic and ethnographic descriptions of children learning to talk in non-middle-class and even nonwestern homes. We find in these reports both similarities to and differences from our more familiar accounts. For similarities, Schieffelin reported that in Papua New Guinea, Kaluli children play peekaboo (1979a, p. 87). And all three of Miller's mothers made requests for names, sometimes while looking at books, with one of these forms:

> *Say X* and what-question, alone or in combination;
> *That X* (or *There X, Look X,* etc) and what-question, alone or in combination.

For one child and her mother, Amy and Marlene, there were enough data to show how development proceeded:

> Over the first six samples [when Amy was 18–22 months], the form of Marlene's requests for names changed from predominantly *Say X* to predominantly what-questions. During this time Amy consistently achieved a high level of correct naming even though her mother offered fewer and fewer names for imitation. By the sixth sample Amy not only responded correctly, with minimal help, to her mother's what-questions, but addressed what-questions to her mother. (paraphrased from Miller, 1981, pp. 89–92)

As Miller pointed out, her description of Amy starts about where Ninio and Bruner's Richard stopped. After the children can answer wh-questions without help, they reverse the roles and ask the questions themselves.

As a difference, both Miller and Schieffelin reported far more direct instruction in how to speak than had been reported before, where direct instruction can be defined as an imperative of a verb of speaking plus an utterance to be repeated: *say, tell,* or *ask* X, or as in Kaluli, X *elema.* In both South Baltimore and New Guinea, direct instruction is used to teach interpersonal uses of speech in triadic encounters in which adults give children lines to say.

Amy	*Mother*
	Oh, what did she [Kris] do?
my baby	
	Tell her [Kris], say 'keep off.'
keep off	
keep off	
	Say 'you hurt it'.
you hurt it	

(Miller, 1981, p. 75)

In New Guinea, parents use direct instruction to teach young children the basic cultural modality of assertion. Here is an extended elema sequence with Meli, one of Schieffelin's three subjects (1979a, pp. 126–127, intonation notation deleted):

> Meli (24.3), Mother and Father at home. Cousin Mama (3¼ years) is outside; she had taken Meli's gourd.

> *Note:* All speech from Mother and Father to Meli is further directed to Mama.

[Parents]	[Meli]
[1]Mother–Meli: Mama! elema.	
	[2]Mama!
[3]Yes, Mama! elema.	
[4]to Meli (softly): While sitting *here,* call out. Mama will hit you (if you go out). While sitting here call out.	
	[5]Mama!
[6]Bring the gourd! elema.	
	[7]bring the gourd!

[8]Quickly!

[9]bring!

[10]Quickly!

[11]quickly!

[12]Bring!

[13]bring!

[14]Father–Meli: Is it yours to take?! elema.

[15]is it yours to take?!

[16]Mother–Meli: Aren't you ashamed of yourself?! elema.

[17]aren't you ashamed of yourself?!

[18]Be ashamed! elema.

(no response)

[19]Mama! elema.
(Meli sees marble on floor, picking it up)

[20](look at) this!

[21]Marble, I took the marble. elema.
(Meli is busy examining the marble and loses interest in what her mother is saying)

Miller and Schieffelin's work suggests what we will find as our sample of families expands: not that the same kinds of interactional scaffolds, mature models, and direct instruction will be provided in all subcultural groups, but rather that functional equivalents of those described here will occur for those discourse patterns considered important in the child's family and culture. Direct instruction provides especially strong evidence for that importance. Where something is being explicitly taught, something believed to be important is there to be learned.

Vygotsky's Zone of Proximal Development

Vygotsky discussed his concept of the zone of proximal, or potential, development, in both *Thought and Language* (1972) and *Mind in Society* (1978):

> It is the distance between the actual developmental level as determined by independent problem solving and the level of potential development as determined through problem solving under adult guidance or in collaboration with peers. (1978, p. 86)

Soviet psychologists apply the concept both to diagnosis and to instruction. In diagnosis, measurement of the width of the zone—that is, of how much children can do with help that they can not do alone—is used to differentiate learning-disabled children from the mentally retarded; in instruction, it is basic to a philosophy of education that learning must lead development:

> What the child can do in co-operation today he can do alone tomorrow. Therefore the only good kind of instruction is that which marches ahead of development and leads it; it must be aimed not so much at the ripe as at the ripening function. (1972, p. 104)

To make the concept of the zone of proximal development more concrete, consider an actual test developed and used at the Institute of Defectology of the National Academy of Pedagogical Sciences in Moscow by psychologists working in the Vygotsky tradition.[3] The test begins as a version of a pattern-matching test item commonly included in tests of intelligence. The subject is given pieces of a geometric puzzle to assemble and a picture of how the completed puzzle should look. The picture gives only the external outline of the finished puzzle and is smaller in scale than the pieces themselves. If the subject can complete the puzzle, s/he goes on to the next item. If not, the subject is offered, one by one, a series of "graduated aids." First, the picture is changed to the same scale as the pieces. Then, if further help is needed, the subject is given a second picture, again in the right scale, but now with the internal divisions of the puzzle shown. Finally, if still more help is needed, s/he can assemble the puzzle pieces right on top of the picture. When that puzzle is completed, the subject is given another puzzle, for which the same series of graduated aids is available. The second puzzle is harder in that it has more, and more difficult, pieces, but at least one part of the new puzzle can be completed by combining pieces just as they were combined in the previous puzzle. Thus there is the possibility of transfer of some of the actual construction, as well as a chance to complete subsequent puzzles with fewer of the graduated aids. There is a critical difference between this puzzle and the kind of testing and learning environments it exemplifies on the one hand, and our usual testing situation on the other: instead of presenting children with a standardized task and noting whether they succeed or fail, the adult presents the task, offering simplifying aids in a principled way until the child succeeds, and then omits the aids as they are no longer needed.

This puzzle is a completely nonverbal item, but the concept of a zone within which a child can accomplish with help what s/he can later accomplish alone applies to aspects of language learning as well. Vygotsky's own language application is to the child's internalization of interpersonal speech as an internal self-regulatory function, or in Wertsch's (1979) terms, adult–child interaction as one of the antecedents of the child's independent metacognition (cf. Furth; Fujinaga, this volume). (According to Wertsch, personal communication, 1979, the correct translation of Vygotsky's monograph, *Myshlenie i Rech* is *Thought and Speech*.) But the concept can also apply to the child's acquisition of patterns of conversation and discourse. If we substitute "speaking" for "problem-solving" in Vygotsky's definition, then the zone of proximal development for speaking is the distance between the actual developmental level as determined by independent speaking and the level of potential development as determined through speaking under adult guidance or in collaboration with peers. "Speaking under adult guidance" is just what the children were doing in all the above examples of discourse development in the home.

In stopping an analysis of the zone of proximal development at this point, I am

---

[3]These tests were observed in Moscow, in December 1978, while I was there with a group of psychologists as part of agreements between the Academies of Science of our two countries. I am most grateful to V. I. Lubovsky and T. V. Rozanova of the Institute of Defectology of the Academy of Pedagogical Science for their time and hospitality. See Brown & French (n.d.) for Ann Brown's comments on this same visit.

knowingly being vague about exactly what kind of help has what kind of conse-quences for what kind of learning and am avoiding distinctions that I don't yet under-stand enough to clarify. Let me note them here, as a place holder for analyses that need to be done. As Brown and French (n.d.) pointed out in their more extended discussion of the application of the concept to testing, the provision of graduated aids depends on an analysis of the task and the dimensions along which it can be simpli-fied. Wertsch (1979) presented an analysis of the directives with which mothers talk young children through a puzzle-matching task. In particular, it is important to understand the effect of presenting to the child a mature version of the task first, and then simplifications. See the related discussions by Pascual-Leone, Goodman, Ammon, and Subelman (1978) on "graded learning loops" that are sequences from hard to easy within segments, and then easy to hard across segments, exactly like the Vygotsky puzzles. (I am grateful to Paul Ammon for calling my attention to this work.)

How do these distinctions apply not to problem-solving but to speaking, to aspects of discourse development with which we are concerned here? We need more analyses of assistance to children's learning of discourse—of the kinds of scaffolds, models, and direct instruction that children are provided—not only to understand more fully what happens at home, but to find ways to extend that learning more effectively at school.

Back in the Classroom

What kind of assistance to discourse development through "speaking under adult guidance" do children get in school? It is my impression from both personal experience as a teacher and from the research literature that children get help in answering teacher questions; more rarely, they get help in participating in the dis-course structure typical of classroom lessons; and there is even less evidence of assis-tance to other discourse forms. More about each of these impressions will follow.

Help with Particular Questions

It is important to distinguish between help that somehow gets a child to produce the right answer and help from which the child might learn how to answer similar questions in the future. Only the latter is of educational interest. All teachers some-times have to get the answer said somehow in order to keep the lesson going for the sake of social order, what Mehan empathetically calls "getting through" (1979, pp. 111–114); but one cannot defend the value of such sequences to the individual child. If, for example, when a child cannot read the word *bus* on a word card, the teacher prompts the answer with the question "What do you ride to school on?" the child may correctly now say "bus." But that is not a prompt that the child could give to himself/herself the next time, because the prompt depends on the very knowledge of the word that it is supposed to cue. We are looking for assistance that at least has the possibility of helping children learn how to answer, even if we lack evidence that it in fact does.

Here are two examples from reading lessons with first-grade children analyzed by Mehan (1979, pp. 44, 58–59). From one theoretical perspective, these are excellent examples of "negotiated interactions" or "interactional accomplishments": the children get the teacher to give them the clues they need to find the answer. (I am grateful to Peg Griffin for this observation.) But, speaking for the teacher, I want to suggest another noncontradictory perspective: that the teacher was providing implicit information about how to answer such questions—information that is applicable, and ideally eventually transferred, beyond the particular instance.

Examples of Question Sequences

(1)	T.	OK, what's the name of this story? (points to title of story)
	Ss.	(no response)
	T.	Who remembers, what's the name, what's the story about?
	Ss.	(no response)
	T.	Is it about taking a bath?
	Ss.	No.
	T.	Is it about the sunshine?
	Ss.	No.
	T.	Edward, what's it about?
	Edward.	The map.
	T.	The map. That's right. This says 'the map.'
(2)	T.	What else, what else, Edward, what do you think we could put there that starts with an M?
	Edward.	(no answer)
	T.	Somebody in your family, Edward.
	. . .	
	Audrey.	I know. I know.
	T.	What?
	Audrey.	Man.
	T.	Man, good for you, Audrey.

In the first example, the implicit message is about the meaning of the question "What's the story about?" The form of simplification here is from the initial wh-question to yes/no alternatives, a sequence common in adult talk to children. The specific alternatives are deliberately absurd members of the category of things that could answer that question. In Churchill's (1978) analysis of disconfirming answers to yes/no ("specific proposal") questions, his "generalized invitation maxim" says in part: "If you are asked a specific proposal question and . . . your answer is the disconfirming one, either give the disconfirming answer and then give the correct answer or give the correct answer only" (p. 48). Presumably the teacher would have welcomed a one-turn answer that followed this maxim:

> Is it about taking a bath?
> No, it's about the map.

But that did not happen. Whether for developmental or situational reasons, the children answered only "no"; and a separate teacher turn was necessary to elicit the correct answer. In the second example, the general wh-question about "What else . . . starts with M?" is followed by a hint that when you want to think of a word, a useful heuristic is to narrow the field to a small set you can run through in your mind.

Blank (1973) gave a detailed analysis of how teachers can respond to children's wrong answers. Wertsch believes (1979), as I do, that teachers do more of such meta-cognitive teaching while working with individual children at their seats than in group lessons. Such tutorial dialogues can be recorded easily with wireless microphones, but detailed analysis might still be difficult unless a videocamera captured the work that was the referent for the talk. And, of course, we would still lack evidence that such teaching actually helps.

Help with Participation in Lessons

There are various reasons why help with particular questions may not be enough, why children may need help with known-answer questions in general and the lesson structure in which they are embedded. They may be newcomers to school; they may need to get used to the particular lessons enacted in particular classrooms; they may come from a cultural background that does not include the kind of practice in labeling that some children get in picture-book-reading events. Here is one example of successful learning in each case.

One description of how nursery school teachers in England inducted 3-year-old children into the rules of classroom discourse sounds strikingly like Snow's conversation between mothers and babies reported above. Willes (1981) began her observations with the youngest children because she assumed that "the rules of classroom discourse, like those of any other game, have to be learnt by those to whom they are new," and that it would be some time before the talk between teacher and these very young children began "to resemble classroom discourse and to be analysable as such" according to the Sinclair and Coulthard (1975) scheme. She was in for a surprise.

> Once the children had 'settled' teachers consistently spoke *as if* children knew how to behave and respond as pupils. If they did not get an expected and acceptable response, they would interpret a look, a gesture, or silence *as if* it were at least an attempted response, and evaluate it. If the response were noise, they would impose on it a prompt, or even an answer. (1981; emphasis in the original)

With such help, Willes found that the kind of sociolinguistic competence required of a pupil is learned very rapidly, sometimes in the course of a single session.

Mehan (1979) also observed growth over time in lesson participation. Since the children he observed were in primary grades and had all been in school before, this development was presumably due to growing familiarity with the patterns of their particular teacher. Without any discernible help, as the year went on, the children became more effective in responding appropriately (in timing and form) as well as correctly (in content) to the teacher's questions. They were less frequently negatively sanctioned for saying the wrong thing at the wrong time, and they became more and more successful in initiating sequences of interactions themselves. Less than 10% of their attempted initiations became incorporated into lesson topics in the fall, but this percentage increased to nearly 50 by the winter. That is, the children became interactionally more competent in tacitly understanding the structure of the lessons and functioning within that structure for their purposes as well as the teacher's. Since none of the participants, not even the teacher, knew this discourse structure explicitly, the children had to learn it as they learn syntax, without explicit tuition. As with syntax, they learned more than anyone could have explicitly taught. Unfortunately, we do not yet have a principled distinction between aspects of discourse that children can learn as they learn syntax, out of awareness, and aspects that benefit from more explicit help.

Cultural differences seem to matter more. Despite considerable research attention to cultural differences in patterns of interaction between home and school, there are few descriptions of what can be called "second discourse teaching." More attention has been given by researchers to how the teacher can adapt to children's preferred ways of interacting than to how teachers can help children adapt to the school, even though Philips (1972) presented both alternatives in the concluding section of her influential paper (cf. Greenfield, this volume). One important exception is Heath's (1982) work with teachers in a black community in the southeastern United States that she calls Trackton. When the teachers complained that children did not participate in lessons, Heath helped them understand what she had learned from five years of ethnographic field work in the Trackton community. For example, the children were not used to known-answer questions about the labels and attributes of objects and events; as one third grade boy complained, "Ain't nobody can talk about things being about theirselves." She then worked with the teachers to try out changes in their classrooms.

These changes consisted of the following sequence:

- Start with familiar content and familiar kinds of talk about that content.
- Go on to new kinds of talk, still about the familiar content, and provide peer models, available for rehearing on audiocassettes.
- Provide opportunities for the Trackton children to practice the new kinds of talk, first out of the public arena and also on tape, and then in actual lessons.
- Finally, talk with the children about talk itself.

Because Heath's work is such an imaginative and rare example of assistance to children's discourse development in school, I quote at some length:

> For some portions of the curriculum, teachers adapted some teaching materials and techniques in accordance with what they had learned about questions in Trackton. For example, in early units on social studies, which taught about "our community," teachers began to use photographs of sections of different local communities, public buildings of the town, and scenes from the nearby countryside. Teachers then asked not for the identification of specific objects or attributes of the objects in these photographs, but questions such as:
>
> > What's happening here?
> > Have you even been here?
> > Tell me what you did when you were there.
> > What's this like? (pointing to a scene, or item in a scene)
>
> Responses of children were far different than those given in usual social studies lessons. Trackton children talked, actively and aggressively became involved in the lesson, and offered useful information about their past experiences. For specific lessons, responses of children were taped; after class, teachers then added to the tapes specific questions and statements identifying objects, attributes, etc.

Answers to these questions were provided by children adept at responding to these types of questions. Class members then used these tapes in learning centers. Trackton students were particularly drawn to these, presumably because they could hear themselves in responses similar in type to those used in their own community. In addition, they benefitted from hearing the kinds of questions and answers teachers used when talking about things. On the tapes, they heard appropriate classroom discourse strategies. Learning these strategies from tapes was less threatening then acquiring them in actual classroom activities where the facility of other students with recall questions enabled them to dominate teacher-student interactions. Gradually, teachers asked specific Trackton students to work with them in preparing recall questions and answers to add to the tapes. Trackton students then began to hear *themselves* in successful classroom responses to questions such as "What is that?" "What kind of community helper works there?"

In addition to using the tapes, teachers openly discussed different types of questions with students, and the class talked about the kinds of answers called for by certain questions. For example, *who, when,* and *what* questions could often be answered orally by single words; other kinds of questions were often answered with many words which made up sentences and paragraphs when put into writing. (Heath, 1982, pp. 124–125)

Help with Other Discourse Forms

Ideally, one would hope to find classroom opportunities for children to practice a growing range of discourse functions (explaining, narrating, etc.) first in situations in which a scaffold or model of some appropriate kind is available, and then gradually with less and less help. Such opportunities should be especially important for practice in the various kinds of extended monologues that children are expected to write in assigned themes. Imagine, for example, the kind of help Heath's teachers gave for question answering also available for the children telling narratives in the Berkeley classroom observed by Michaels and Cook-Gumperz.

In the San Diego classroom described by Mehan, we created one special speech situation that we called an instructional chain (IC) (Cazden, Cox, Dickinson, Steinberg, & Stone, 1979). Briefly, in each IC the teacher taught a lesson to one child who then taught the same lesson to one or more peers. Leola, a black third grader, was asked to learn and then teach a language arts task. Here are the first three items on her worksheet in completed form.

1. new   Y ø ł o d u   2. t y ɛ o l ʂ d   3. m ø ꞑ e
2. no
3. off   Y o u   t o l d   m e

Figure 1 gives a skeletal version, minus repetitions, corrections, etc., of the teacher's directions as she talked Leola through the first two items on the task, and the full transcript of Leola's subsequent directions first back to the teacher as a rehearsal, and then in actual instruction of her peers. Note in passing that the teacher's questions served to talk Leola through the task until she could do it herself. That such aid can indeed be graduated is shown by a comparison of the teacher's instructions

---

Teacher's Instructions to Leola

Item 1			Item 2	
Teacher	Leola		Teacher	Leola
OK, now number one here says *new*.			OK, now number 2 here says– *No*. What's the opposite of	No.
What's the opposite of *new*?	Old		*no?*	Yes.
			OK, how do you spell *yes*?	Y–E–S
Old. How would you spell *old*?	O–L–D		All right, now what are you	(L. crosses
OK, in the letters that are on this paper, cross out the letters you just used for spelling *old*.	(L. does it)		doing–	out the letters Y–E–S) Told
Good. What word is left?	Y–O–U			
What does that spell?	You			
OK, and down here you'll write *you*.				

Leola's Versions of the Instructions

In rehearsal to the teacher:

L: Spell these letters, and then put out that letter, and then have another letter left.

L: (later after T goes over the instructions again)
To do the opposite of this. You got to write old. I'm gonna tell 'em: you gotta write old, cross old out and you have another letter left.

In actual instruction of her peers:

(1) [Goes to get pencils, then returns to work desk and sits down.] It is hard.... You gotta write— what's the opposite of "new" is "old."

So you got—so you gotta cross O, L and D, and you have a letter left, and you—you put the letter left in these words.

(2) You cross it—you see, you got to do the opposite of "n-no" i—"no" is "yes" on number two. "No"—"no" is "yes," so you gotta write Y–E–S. And you have a "told" left, so

(3) you write T–O–L–D. See d-do the op—the op—the opposite of ah—uh—"off" is "on," so you gotta cross, on number three, you gotta cross "on" off. O–N. And you—it is "me" left, M–E.

Figure 1

---

for the first and second items. The first three parts were repeated, but then a much vaguer and incomplete question, "Now what are you going to-," was sufficient, and Leola took off on her own.

The important aspect of this IC for thinking about discourse development at school is the development of articulateness and precision in Leola's instructions from her first rehearsal to the teacher, "Spell these letters, and then put out that letter, and then have another letter left," to the most elaborated version in item 3. Here it is without the hesitations and self-repairs: "The opposite of *off* is *on,* so on number 3, you gotta cross *on* off. O–N. And it is *me* left, M–E." This is a good example of what Wertsch & Stone (1978), following the Soviet psychologists, called "microgenesis"—that is, development within an observable time period—and it is a kind of development that Leola seemed to need. In the nine lessons analyzed by Mehan, some three hours of talk in all, she spoke four times, and only twice more than one word. This is not to say that she was in any way nonverbal, but it is to suggest that she could benefit from challenges to talk about academic topics, not just in response to questions. Another competency stimulated by taking on the role of tutor for their peers was the crisp pronunciation of English consonants by a strong black dialect speaker and a Spanish-dominant bilingual child who were both asked to present sentences or words to their tutees in other language arts tasks. (See Carrasco, Vera, & Cazden, 1981, and Cazden *et al.,* 1979, for a further discussion of the ICs.)

Another example of a microgenetic sequence came from McNamee's studies of help to children's story retelling within a Vygotskian perspective. In her first observational study of one kindergarten teacher, McNamee (1979) had analyzed the series of questions by which that teacher talked a child through a story until the child could retell it alone. Then, in a more controlled experiment, she read a story to 12 kindergarten children and asked each child to retell it three times. At each retelling, the adult helped with a series of questions designed in a Vygotskian sequence, providing minimum help at first and then more and more specific help as needed:

(1) repeat back the last sentence that the child said;
(2) ask: "What happened next?" or "So what happened?" or "What happened in the beginning/end?";
(3) ask a wh-question that probes for the next piece of information;
(4) supply the next piece of information needed in the narrative in the form of a tag question. (McNamee, 1980, p. 96)

McNamee found that the children needed help with fewer story events in the second retelling, and that in the third retelling, the number of events on which the children needed help stayed the same, but the kind of help needed shifted from more specific to the more general. When a second story was presented in order to see whether the children had internalized the story retelling skills, the children reverted approximately to the second retelling stage: needing less help than with the first retelling, but more specific help than with the third.

Earlier I pointed out the obvious difference between helping a child somehow get a particular answer and helping a child gain some conceptual understanding from which answers to similar questions can be generated alone at a future time. We can think about this distinction more generally as different relationships between performance and competence.

Child discourse under adult guidance that is more advanced than what the child can speak alone can be called "performance without competence." Gleason and Weintraub (1976) first pointed out the existence of such performance in early social routines like *bye-bye, thank you,* and *trick-or-treat.* I am generalizing their description to other kinds of adult-assisted talk. In the school examples, the teacher assumes—with Vygotsky—that the assisted performance is not just performance *without* competence, but performance *before* competence—that the assisted performance does indeed contribute to subsequent development. A task for researchers is to find out if and how that happens.

Conclusions

I started with a quotation from Frake because of the importance of the "class-room as culture" metaphor in current classroom language research. Like any meta-phor, this one highlights some features and leaves others in shadow. To assume that a classroom is like a culture highlights the process of inducting new members, and so most current studies take place in the primary grades. With this metaphor, change is expected only in those who are becoming members, not in the culture itself (cf. Nadin, this volume).

Remember that one of the special characteristics of both the early language games in the home and the Vygotsky puzzles is that the games and puzzles them-selves get more complicated as development proceeds. A major contrast between dis-course development at home and at school, at least as described in our current research, is that we have no record of such change in the school. We have no reports yet of how school language games themselves become more complex as the school years go on.

Yet classrooms are, or should be, very special cultures—a community of people who are themselves changing, and whose change the environment is specifically designed to support. That's why another metaphor, peekaboo as an instructional model, is so important for both teachers and researchers to keep in mind.

References

Bauman, R., & Sherzer, J. The ethnography of speaking. *Annual Review of Anthropology*, 1975, *4*, 95–119.

Blank, M. *Teaching learning in the preschool: A dialogue approach*. Columbus, Ohio: Charles E. Mer-rill, 1973.

Brown, A. L., & French, L. A. *The zone of potential development: Implications for intelligence testing in the year 2000*. Urbana, Ill.: University of Illinois, Center for the Study of Reading, n.d.

Bruner, J. S. The role of dialogue in language acquisition. In A. Sinclair, R. J. Jarvella, & W. J. M. Levalt (Eds.), *The child's conception of language*. New York: Springer-Verlag, 1978.

Carrasco, R. L., Vera, A., & Cazden, C. B. Aspects of bilingual students' communicative competence in the classroom: A case study. In R. Duran (Ed.), *Latino language and communicative behavior. Advances in discourse processes* (Vol. 6). Norwood, N.J.: Ablex, 1981, pp. 237–269.

Cazden, C. B. Hypercorrection in test responses. *Theory into Practice*, 1975, *14*, 343–346.

Cazden, C. B. How knowledge about language helps the classroom teacher—or does it: A personal account. *The Urban Review*, 1976, *9*, 74–90.

Cazden, C. B. Foreword. In H. Mehan, *Learning lessons*. Cambridge, Mass.: Harvard University Press, 1979, pp. vii–xii.

Cazden, C. B. Four comments. In P. Gilmore & A. Glatthorn (Eds.), *Ethnography and education: Children out of school*. Washington, D.C.: Center for Applied Linguistics, 1982, pp. 209–226.

Cazden, C. B., Cox, M., Dickinson, D., Steinberg, Z., & Stone, C. "You all gonna hafta listen": Peer teaching in a primary classroom. In W. A. Collins (Ed.), *Children's language and communication*. Hillsboro, N.J.: Lawrence Erlbaum, 1979.

Chomsky, C. Stages in language development and reading exposure. *Harvard Educational Review*, 1972, *42*, 1–33.

Christian, D., & Tripp, R. Teacher's perceptions and children's language use. In P. Griffin & R. Shuy,

Final report to Carnegie Corporation of New York: *Children's functional language and education in the early years*. Arlington, Va.: Center for Applied Linguistics, 1978.

Churchill, L. *Questioning strategies in sociolinguistics*. Rowley, Mass.: Newbury House, 1978.

Erickson, F., & Schultz, J. When is a context? Some issues and methods in the analysis of social competence. *Quarterly Newsletter of the Institute for Comparative Human Development*, 1977, *1*(2), 5–10.

Ervin-Tripp, S. M. From conversation to syntax. In *Papers and reports of child language development* (Vol. 13). Stanford, Calif.: Stanford University, Department of Linguistics, 1977, pp. 11–21.

Frake, C. O. "Struck by speech": The Yakan concept of litigation. In J. J. Gumperz & D. Hymes (Eds.), *Directions in sociolinguistics*. New York: Holt, Rinehart & Winston, 1972, pp. 106–129.

Garvey, C. The contingent query: A dependent act in conversation. In M. Lewis & L. Rosenblum (Eds.), *Interactions, conversation, and the development of language*. New York: Wiley, 1977, pp. 63–93.

Gleason, J. B., & Weintraub, S. The acquisition of routines in child language. *Language in Society*, 1976, *5*, 129–136.

Gumperz, J. J. Language, communication, and public negotiation. In P. R. Sanday (Ed.), *Anthropology and the public interest*. New York: Academic Press, 1976.

Heath, S. B. Questioning at home and at school. In G. Spindler (Ed.), *The ethnography of schooling: Educational anthropology in action*. New York: Holt, Rinehart, & Winston, 1982, pp. 102–131.

Hymes, D. Models of the interaction of language and social life. In J. J. Gumperz & D. Hymes (Eds.), *Directions in sociolinguistics: The ethnography of communication*. New York: Holt, Rinehart & Winston, 1972, pp. 35–71.

Labov, W., & Fanshel, D. *Therapeutic discourse: Psychotherapy as conversation*. New York: Academic Press, 1977.

Lakoff, G., & Johnson, M. *Metaphors we live by*. Chicago: University of Chicago Press, 1980.

McNamee, G. D. The social interaction origin of narrative skills. *The Quarterly Newsletter of the Laboratory of Comparative Human Cognition*, October 1979.

McNamee, G. D. *The social origin of narrative skills*. Unpublished doctoral dissertation, Northwestern University, 1980.

Mehan, H. *Learning lessons*. Cambridge, Mass.: Harvard University Press, 1979.

Michaels, S. "Sharing time": Children's narrative styles and differential access to literacy. *Language in Society*, 1981, *10*, 423–442.

Michaels, S., & Cook-Gumperz, J. *A study of sharing time with first grade students: Discourse narratives in the classroom*. Berkeley, Calif.: Berkeley Linguistics Society, 1979.

Miller, P. J. *Amy, Wendy and Beth: Learning language in South Baltimore*. Austin: University of Texas Press, 1981.

Mishler, E. G. "Wou' you trade cookies with the popcorn?": The talk of trades among six year olds. In O. K. Garnica & M. L. King (Eds.), *Language, children and society: The effect of social factors on children learning to communicate*. Elmsford, N.Y.: Pergamon Press, 1979.

Ninio, A., & Bruner, J. The achievement and antecedents of labeling. *Journal of Child Language*, 1978, *5*, 1–15.

Pascual-Leone, J., Goodman, D., Ammon, P., & Subelman, I. Piagetian theory and neo-Piagetian analysis as psychological guides in education. In J. M. Gallagher & J. A. Easley (Eds.), *Knowledge and development*. New York: Plenum Press, 1978.

Philips, S. U. Participant structures and communicative competence: Warm Springs children in community and classroom. In C. B. Cazden, V. P. John, & D. Hymes (Eds.), *Functions of language in the classroom*. New York: Teachers College Press, 1972, pp. 370–394.

Ratner, N., & Bruner, J. Games, social exchange and the acquisition of language. *Journal of Child Language*, 1978, *5*, 391–401.

Sachs, J. Talking about the there and then. *Papers and reports of child language development* (Vol. 13). Stanford, Calif.: Stanford University, Department of Linguistics, 1977, pp. 56–63.

Schieffelin, B. B. *How Kaluli children learn what to say, what to do, and how to feel: An ethnographic study of the development of communicative competence*. Unpublished doctoral dissertation, Columbia University, 1979. (a)

Schieffelin, B. B. Getting it together: An ethnographic approach to the study of the development of communicative competence. In E. Ochs & B. B. Schieffelin (Eds.), *Developmental pragmatics.* New York: Academic Press, 1979, pp. 73–108. (b)

Scollon, R. *Conversations with a one year old: A case study of the developmental foundation of syntax.* Honolulu: University Press of Hawaii, 1976.

Scollon, R., & Scollon, S. B. K. Narrative, literacy and face in interethnic communication. *Advances in discourse processes* (Vol. 7). Norwood, N.J.: Ablex, 1981.

Shultz, J. It's not whether you win or lose, it's how you play the game: A microethnographic analysis of game-playing in a kindergarten/first grade classroom. In O. K. Garnica & M. L. King (Eds.), *Language, children and society: The effect of social factors on children learning to communicate.* Elmsford, N.Y.: Pergamon Press, 1979.

Sinclair, J. M., & Coulthard, R. M. *Toward an analysis of discourse.* New York: Oxford University Press, 1975.

Snow C. E. The development of conversation between mothers and babies. *Journal of Child Language,* 1977, *4,* 1–22. (a)

Snow, C. E. Mothers' speech research: From input to interaction. In C. E. Snow & C. A. Ferguson (Eds.), *Talking to children: Language input and acquisition.* New York: Cambridge University Press, 1977, pp. 31–49. (b)

Snow, C. E., & Ferguson, C. A. (Eds.). *Talking to children.* Cambridge: Cambridge University Press, 1977.

Stoel-Gammon, C., & Cabral, L. S. Learning how to tell it like it is: The development of the reportative function in children's speech. *Papers and Reports of Child Language Development* (Vol. 13). Stanford, Calif.: Stanford University, Department of Linguistics, 1977, pp. 64–71.

Vygotsky, L. S. *Thought and language.* Cambridge, Mass.: MIT Press, 1972.

Vygotsky, L. S. *Mind in society: The development of higher psychological processes.* Cambridge, Mass.: Harvard University Press, 1978.

Wertsch, J. V. From social interaction to higher psychological processes: A clarification and application of Vygotsky's theory. *Human Development,* 1979, *22,* 1–22.

Wertsch, J. V., & Stone, C. A. Microgenesis as a tool for developmental analysis. *Quarterly Newsletter of the Laboratory of Comparative Human Cognition* (Center for Human Information Processing, University of California, San Diego), 1978, *1*(1).

Willes, M. J. Early lessons learned too well. In C. Adelman (Ed.), *Uttering, muttering: Collecting, using and reporting talk for social and educational research.* London: Grant McIntyre, 1981.

4

The Implications of Luria's Theories for Cross-cultural Research on Language and Intelligence

Josef Schubert

The work of A. R. Luria (1960, 1961b, 1963a) on the development of the *second signal system* combines a biological approach to the study of human behavior with an analysis of the social conditions determining its development. The biological approach is represented by Luria's research about the stages of development of verbal regulation of behavior. It is complemented by the principle that the content of the second signal system as well as the modes of verbal regulation of behavior are developed through social interaction.

This paper will summarize Luria's theories on the development of the second signal system and will discuss their general implications. This discussion will be followed by a report on the standardization of some of his experiments and the application of his methods in a cross-cultural setting. It will be argued that an adequate analysis of language development must be based on the study of the interaction between social determinants and developmental stages and that the study of verbal regulation of behavior can shed light on the relationship between language development, intelligence, and social-economic conditions.

The Second Signal System and Verbal Regulation of Behavior

The term *second signal system* was introduced by Pavlov (1951, cited in Luria, 1961b). It became known to Western psychologists mainly through Luria's reports of his studies on verbal regulation of behavior (Luria, 1957, 1958, 1959a,b, 1960,

Josef Schubert ● Department of Psychology, University of Regina, Regina, Saskatchewan S4S 0A2, Canada.

1961a,b, 1963a,b). However, the impact of these studies on American psychology was minimal. Contemporary texts of psychology and even advanced theoretical books hardly mention Luria's work or discuss its implications. The reason for this lack of communication is not merely linguistic, because by now an impressive body of Soviet psychological literature is available in English. It is partly a consequence of Luria's theoretical approach, which is far removed from American behaviorism. It also reflects the difficulties Western investigators have had in replicating his results (Wozniak, 1972). A brief review of Luria's work in the area is therefore indicated.

The Function of the Second Signal System

The theory is based on Pavlov's conception of the development of higher nervous activity and on Vygotsky's (1962) work on the development of language and thought in children. Luria (1961b) defined psychology as the study of the "formation of mental processes" (p. 16). This formation involves the establishment of conditional "links" between stimuli. These links constitute the *first signal system*. The speed of its formation and its stability are a function of external conditions as well as of properties of the nervous system.

In contrast to animals, whose learning is confined to the development of the first signal system, humans develop the *second signal system*. A connection of the first signal system is a link between two concrete stimuli (e.g., when a specific sound becomes the signal for the appearance of meat). The sign represents only itself, in all its concrete aspects. A word, in contrast, represents a class of stimuli. Thus the word *cup* abstracts certain features of a particular object and generalizes to many objects which differ in their concrete stimulus aspects.

Language has several functions. The first is that of communication; it enables humans to assimilate the experience of many generations. Language is also a major instrument of thinking. By naming an object children organize their experience; by mastering complex grammatical expressions they learn new methods of analysis and synthesis. Finally, language is the basis of conscious and voluntary behavior.

Learning based on the second signal system differs fundamentally from learning based on the first signal system in the following respects: (1) There is no need for incessant reinforcement. (2) Links are maintained even when reinforcement is absent for a long time. (3) The system established is more mobile; it is easy to change the meaning of a signal. (4) The signaling property may easily take an abstract form. An animal orients itself only to concrete signals and has great difficulties in learning that involves abstractions.

Luria (1961b) and Liublinskaya (1957, 1961) reported many investigations that demonstrate the influence of verbal articulation on the learning of preschool children. In these experiments, children were taught to talk about their experiences—for instance, to name sounds and smells or to describe their activities. These experiments show transfer of training, the establishment of learning sets (Harlow, 1959), or central processes comprising strategies for processing information (Hunt, 1961). Luria concluded that all higher mental activity is based on verbal processes. Language development is a necessary condition for normal mental development; verbal training enriches perceptual discrimination and develops intelligence.

The Development of Verbal Regulation of Behavior

Words do not merely communicate knowledge; they also can be commands. The regulation of behavior by means of speech is social in origin. It starts when a mother diverts the child's attention and initiates specific actions through a verbal request. At a later age the children use speech in order to regulate their own actions, to divert them toward conscious goals, and to eliminate irrelevant responses. Finally, the child will inhibit overt speech, and the regulation of behavior will be a function of internal speech, that is, thought. Thus, verbal regulation of behavior is a necessary condition for conscious voluntary activity.

Luria designed a series of experiments for the investigation of the stages of verbal regulation of behavior. In these experiments the child is requested to squeeze a rubber bulb or to press a button in response to a signal, for example, light or a verbal command. The task then becomes more complicated through: (1) the introduction of additional stimuli which must be discriminated, (2) the introduction of different modes of response (weak and strong, left and right hand, etc.), (3) the introduction of verbal response ("Say 'go' and squeeze"), (4) changes in the rhythm of stimulus presentation (speed of presentation and changes in the probability of stimulus sequences), and (5) the differentiation of physically identical stimuli according to abstract principles.

Only few statistical data were reported by Luria; age placements were general and probably tentative. The main stages of verbal regulation of behavior, described by Luria, are as follows:

1. Age 1–2 Years. Behavior is not yet regulated by speech. The word is still a part of the total concrete situation. It may initiate behavior, but only if the verbal instruction does not interfere with the current activity of the child.

2. Age 2–3 Years. At this age, verbal instruction may interrupt current activity and initiate a new activity. A system of speech association is developed and behavior begins to assume an active voluntary character. However, there is no true verbal regulation of behavior in the sense that future activity is planned. At this stage children are able to learn a rule if constant verbal reinforcement is given.

At the beginning of this stage, regulation of behavior is achieved either through separation of action into its components or by exteroceptive feedback. They are unable to learn a combined verbal-motor response. Either they press or say "go." Their own verbal response does not help to regulate their behavior, but confuses them.

During the first and second stages learning is furthered by verbal reinforcement given by the adult.

3. Age 3–4½ Years. Words may now begin to regulate subsequent action. The child is capable of following a simple conditional instruction and can wait for the appearance of a signal. The important development at this age is that the child's own verbal reaction helps him/her to execute the motor response. S/He will make fewer mistakes during the combined motor-verbal response. Ordinarily the length of his/her response will be determined by the length of the stimulus. However, if s/he says "go" while s/he presses, the motor reaction becomes independent of the length of the stimulus. Saying "one, two" helps the child to press twice.

Some experiments indicate that regulation of behavior at this stage is mainly determined by the impulsive aspect of the words and not by their significative aspect. Thus the child is able to learn a discrimination between two stimuli, but the combined response (say "yes" and "no" and press for the positive light) will result in an increase of mistakes. Saying the word "no" is an impulse to act. Similarly, saying the word "twice" constitutes an impulse to squeeze once because "twice" is a monosyllabic word.

4. Age 4–5 Years.

The regulatory function is steadily transfered from the impulse side of speech to the analytic system of elective significative connections which are produced by speech. Moreover, and this is most interesting, it simultaneously shifts *from the external to the internal speech of the child.* (Luria, 1961b, p. 92)

The child easily grasps complicated instructions (e.g., alternation of signals). During spontaneous play the child accompanies his/her activity with verbal comments, which finally become internalized. The combined verbal and motor response helps the child to eliminate mistakes.

5. Age 6–7 Years.
Silent speech is predominant. Internalized speech constitutes an essential component of thought and volitional action.

The verbal analysis of the situation begins to play an important role in the establishment of new connections; the child orients himself to the given signals with the help of the rule he has verbally formulated for himself. (Luria, 1961b, p. 96)

The development of verbal regulation of behavior is thus characterized by (1) an increased dominance of the significative aspect of words and (2) an increased autonomy, a shift from regulation by external stimuli to internalized verbal control.

Theoretical Implications

The introduction of the concept of the second signal system makes Luria's psychology a truly developmental theory. American learning theory has until recently been nondevelopmental. The laws which describe the learning of rats are said to be the same as the laws which describe the laws of human learning (cf. Seligman, 1972). Differences between human learning and animal learning are not in the form of the law, but in the values to be given to various constants. We thus hope to account for all forms of human learning, including verbal behavior, by one simple set of basic laws.

Luria's (1961b) position is diametrically different:

The formation of systems of mental process in which speech plays an integral part ... *considerably modifies the basic laws of the formation of temporary links.* (p. 42)

Historically, in the life of every individual, the second signal system has its origins in classical conditioning.

That these laws are fundamental is beyond doubt. It is noteworthy, however, that none of them applies in full force when we come to analyzing the process of the formation of new links in human beings. (p. 43)

No amount of conditioning can generate the organizing activity which is evident in the second signal system. With its emergence the laws of conditioning are superseded. "The complex and indirect nature of temporary links in man means a considerable modification in all their laws of evolution" (p. 44). The practical implication of this view is that human learning must be studied by observing humans. The theoretical implication is that laws of human psychology cannot be derived from laws of animal psychology. A developmental approach is evident not only in the assumption of species-specific differences in learning but also in the assumption of biologically determined developmental stages.

Learning is described as an *interaction* between environmental conditions and biological characteristics. The term interaction is used here in its narrow technical sense; it does not merely state that both heredity and environment are necessary for learning—which is a self-evident platitude—but that the impact of a specific environmental condition is a function of the organism's developmental state and, at the same time, that the environment which is needed and effective at a specific moment is also a function of the organism's developmental status (cf. Fujinaga, this volume).

This developmental principle is well illustrated by the following interchange which occurred during the Second Conference on the Central Nervous System and Behavior. Luria (1960) had discussed the stages of verbal regulation of behavior and described the inability of a 2-year-old child to wait for the appearance of the light before squeezing the rubber bulb.

> Leese: Professor Luria, in experiments of this type, have you tried to modify the motivation of these children by a system of reward and punishment?
> Luria: I have tried but failed, because, when I say, 'You will get a candy for this,' the child becomes so interested in the candy that he fails in his work. (p. 378)

Besides suggesting a wholesome similarity between Russian and American children, the point is clear: the effect of the stimulus in such a learning situation differs at various age levels. This does not imply that the 2-year-old is impervious to social influence. Luria described in detail didactic methods which enabled him to teach the child the appropriate response (1960, pp. 363–367; 1961b, pp. 59–68). The child who is supposed to learn a specific activity needs different teaching methods at different ages.

It must be stressed that the differences in learning between preschool children of different ages do not merely reflect differential amounts of previous experience. The behavioral differences observed in the child are not supposed to reflect differences in conditioning experience but in biological readiness to learn.

Luria stated that the development of the second signal system is a specifically human achievement. He agreed, however, that this is not an essential part of his theory (personal communication, August 9, 1966). There is evidence of second signal learning in animals. This is a minor point, the major issue being that second signal system learning differs fundamentally from first signal learning and that it forms the basis of human learning and cultural development.

A problem is created by the apparent identification of the second signal system with human speech. However, Luria agreed (personal communication) that in principle any stimulus may become a second signal stimulus, representing a concept and not a concrete event. The case of Helen Keller illustrates how a tactual stimulus—a line traced on the child's hand—can acquire the significance of a word. The second signal system is a system of language, the symbols of which are not necessarily sounds. Furth (1966) has presented evidence for nonverbal thinking in deaf children. His data do not contradict Luria's theories: they demonstrate that visual stimuli such as geometrical patterns may acquire a second signal system significance (cf. Furth, this volume). However, in general one may assume that for most humans the second signal system is practically identical with their vocabulary. Therefore, Luria's illustrations of the second signal system refer to words, and he talks about *verbal* regulation of behavior (VRB).

Because the second signal system is not identical with human speech, Luria had little to say about the development of syntax. He did not address himself to the questions raised by Chomsky (1967) and Lenneberg (1967). And, indeed, speech development does not appear to be identical with the development of the second signal system. The evidence for the independence of speech and learning ability is summarized by Smith and Wilson (1979). The difference between speech fluency and intellectual development can be demonstrated by VRB experiments with oligophrenics, that is, children whose intellectual retardation is biologically determined. I observed, for example, a 7-year-old girl with myelomeningocele who chatted freely. She asked about the experimenter's name, occupation, place of residence, and family. At the same time she was unable to carry out the simple instruction "Wait until the light goes on and then squeeze the rubber bulb." I have also observed severely retarded adolescents with IQs in the 50–60 range who talked quite fluently in several languages.

We find, therefore, that the second signal system differs from speech in two important aspects: (1) Second signal system development may proceed without verbal language; (2) The development of syntactic speech proceeds in relative independence from the development of verbal regulation of behavior. There is, however, no complete independence, because the development of syntactic speech appears to depend on a minimum level of second signal system development, and adequate regulation of behavior depends on language articulation. Without the ability to form sentences there is no verbal regulation or conscious thought. The assumed relationship between thought and word is well expressed by Vygotsky (1962):

> We found no specific interdependence between the genetic roots of thought and of word. . . . Thought and word are not connected by a primary bond. (p. 119)

The relationship between word and thought is not a "prerequisite for but rather a product of, the historical development of human consciousness" (p. 119). Nevertheless, Vygotsky rejected an analysis which

> sought to explain the properties of verbal thought by breaking it up into its component elements, thought and word, neither of which, taken separately, possesses the property of the whole. (p. 120)

The biological basis of syntactic speech differs from the biological basis of the second signal system, but the two cannot be separated in adult thinking: "A word devoid of thought is a dead thing, and a thought unembodied in words remains a shadow" (p. 153).

Luria's Cross-cultural Research

We have seen that Luria's description of the second signal system implies two evolutionary-development premises. The first is that human learning is species-specific. The second is that the development of the second signal system follows biologically determined stages, which must be considered in the study of intellectual development. However, and this idea distinguished Luria's approach from crass nativism, the learning process cannot be understood or even defined without specification of the developmentally relevant environmental event. For the human species this means social interaction. Both the content of the second signal system and the strategies employed in conscious planning are developed through social experience and reflect the socioeconomic conditions of the society in which the learning occurs. "A child's mental activities are conditioned from the very beginning by his social relationship with adults" (Luria, 1961b, p. 16).

The relevant event in a learning situation is not merely a physical stimulus or environmental contingencies but the event in its social context. It follows that it is futile to investigate either semantics—the relationship between words and their references—or pragmatics—the relationship between words and the way they are used—without reference to the society which constitutes the relevant background (cf. Cazden, this volume).

Language develops in a context of doing, of one person doing something to or for another person, or of doing things together. Human intelligence is therefore closely related to another form of species-specific behavior: humans work together and produce within a framework of social organization. It is not merely that humans use tools; animals have been observed to do this also. Nor is it merely cooperation in food gathering: animals hunt together. Human species-specific activity is the cooperative use of tools in the production and acquisition of food and other goods. Such organized economic activity is not conceivable without the development of the second signal system, which is necessary both for the transmission of experience through generations and for long-term planning.

Speech enables humans to form an infinite number of new sentences, to develop new concepts, to elaborate constantly on the meaning of words, and to form an infinite number of strategies for the planning of new activities. Speech opens the road to intellectual diversity. Neither the organization of society nor the organization of mental processes is immutable. They evolve through mutual regulation. "The structure of mental activity . . . change[s] in the course of historical development" (Luria, 1976, p. 8). The socioeconomic structure of society will determine the content and the strategy that are important and that form a part of the intelligence of adults. "Important manifestations of human consciousness have been directly shaped by the basic practices of human activity and the actual forms of culture" (p. 3).

To paraphrase Erikson (1950), every society needs to develop in its members certain modes of thinking in order to maintain itself and needs to transmit those modes of thinking to the next generation. Conversely, the development of the second signal system in a society determines the way it looks at its environment.

These considerations lead to the contemplation of cross-cultural research. Luria's (1976) basic question is

> whether changes in sociohistorical structures . . . result only in broadened experience, acquisition of new habits and knowledge, literacy, and so forth, or whether they result in radical organization of mental processes . . . and the formation of new mental systems. Proof of the latter would be of fundamental significance for psychology as a science of social history. (p. 19)

In order to test this theory Luria conducted field studies in Uzbekistan and Kirgizia in 1931–1932. The material was published only in 1974 and was translated into English in 1976 under the title *Cognitive Development: Its Cultural and Social Foundations*. In this study Luria investigated the relationship between intelligence—here called cognitive function—and changes in socioeconomic conditions (cf. Illich; Parker, this volume). This work preceded Luria's investigations of VRB and did not mention the term *second signal system*. The hypothesis of the close relationship between thinking and language is, however, fully developed: "Words . . . carry not only meaning but also the fundamental units of consciousness reflecting the external world" (p. 9).

The subjects of this inquiry were adults who differed widely in previous exposure to Russian culture and education and who lived under conditions of rapid cultural change. Some of Luria's subjects were older women living according to traditional life-styles "in remote villages, who were illiterate and not involved in any modern social activities" (p. 15). Others were kolkhoz workers who were actively involved in running the farm and women students admitted to a teacher's training after two or three years of study.

Luria's research method was essentially clinical and bears similarity to Piaget's technique. He presented his adult subjects with a specific task and then engaged in a detailed inquiry in order to elucidate the processes of reasoning which led to the first answer given. His tasks were not taken from conventional tests. "It would have been foolish to give them problems they would have regarded as pointless" (p. 17).

The scope of the inquiry was extended. The problems were in the area of perception, abstraction, inference, problem solving, imagination, and self-awareness. The problems presented to the subjects could be solved either on a "concrete, graphic-functional level or on an abstract, verbal, and logical one" (p. 18). Luria predicted that with increased acculturation to modern Soviet society there would be a shift from a practical, immediate, functional mental approach to abstract, reflective, and logical thinking.

> We assumed [that] . . . the perception of oneself results from the clear perception of others and the processes of self-perception are shaped through social activity, which presupposes collaboration with others and an analysis of their behavioral patterns. Thus the final aim of our investigation was the study of how self-consciousness is shaped in the course of human social activity. (p. 19)

Luria reported differences in the predicted direction in all the areas investigated. His final conclusion was that "sociohistorical shifts not only introduce new content into the mental world of human beings; they also create new . . . structures of cognitive functioning. They advance human consciousness to new levels" (p. 163). We shall return to the discussion of these findings after presenting some results of cross-cultural research in VRB with Canadian Indian children.

The VRB Apparatus

The Standardization of the VRB Procedure

The VRB apparatus was designed by the author for the standardized administration of experiments in verbal regulation of behavior. It follows Luria's original procedures but specifies exactly both the order of stimulus presentation and scoring criteria. A detailed description of the procedure is given in Schubert (1969, 1970) and Schubert and Cropley (1972). A manual of administration is available from Schubert (1973). In addition to the problems described by Luria, more complicated tasks were introduced, which were specifically designed to investigate the subject's ability to use internal instructions in the solution of new problems.

The apparatus displays lights in various colors and positions. Each light may be "positive" or "negative." Stimuli are presented at irregular intervals at a predetermined rhythm. The subject is asked to give a *motor response* (squeezing a rubber bulb or pulling a string) or a *verbal response* (say "Yes," "No," "Twice") or a *combined verbal/motor response*. A correct response elicits a reward light; an incorrect response is indicated by the sound of a buzzer. Problems may be presented at three levels of difficulty: the first two levels reported by Luria and the third level designed by Schubert.

I. Training. At the first level the experimenter gives continuous instructions during the presentation of the stimuli.

II. Statement of the Rule. At this level the rule is told to the child. The child must give a delayed response.

III. Discovery of Rule. The subject is not told the rule. He must discover it himself in the light of positive and negative indications given by the apparatus and then must act appropriately upon it.

The procedure has been administered to about 800 children in the United Kingdom and Canada. Split-half reliabilities for various samples range from .88 to .92. Test–retest reliability for Canadian school children ($n = 166$) is .80. VRB scores are significantly related to IQ and age ($p < .001$). Normative sampling of the general population was not attempted, since we did not intend to develop another intelligence test but to offer a standardized investigation procedure.

We were able to confirm Luria's findings on the development of verbal regulation of behavior of preschool children: (1) Normal children learn to carry out delayed instructions between the age of 3 and 4 years. An inability to do so after the age of 5 years is a sign of oligophrenia. (2) Up to the age of 5 years the combined verbal/motor response is more difficult than a motor response alone. The disinhibition of a motor response when the child says "no" to a negative stimulus disappears at about age 6 years. Children of 8 years or more who cannot carry out a combined verbal/motor response are severely retarded (IQ below 50). (3) Up to about age 7 years most children cannot say "twice" and give two motor responses at the same time. (4) The ability to give a correct combined verbal/motor response excludes biologically determined mental retardation. If a child succeeds on these problems and has an IQ below 50, the latter does not validly reflect his/her biological capacity. This phenomenon has been demonstrated especially for cerebral palsied children, as reported by Burland (1969) and Schubert and Burland (1973). Thus, for example, VRB scores predicted the educational achievement of severely handicapped cerebral palsied children.

The VRB apparatus was originally designed as part of a research project investigating the intellectual development of physically handicapped children. We were looking for a procedure which would discriminate between children whose low IQ reflects limited biological capacity and children whose retardation is the result of experiential deprivation. Luria's approach appeared promising for several reasons. First of all, it makes a clear distinction between the biological concept *intelligence-capacity* and the psychological concept of *intelligence-ability*. The first refers to the characteristics which make the development of intelligent behavior possible. The second refers to the "strategies for processing of information that have been differentiated and have achieved the mobility which permits them to be available in a variety of situations" (Hunt, 1961, p. 354). Oligophrenia is reflected in a disturbance of the regulatory function of the second signal system, while experiential deprivation is reflected in the paucity of the content of the second signal system.

Thus experiments in verbal regulation of behavior are directly related to a theory of intelligence. In this respect Luria's approach is similar to that of Piaget. It is a test of operational intelligence (Furth, 1973) and can be contrasted with the psychometric approach. A statement about a subject's intelligence which is based on an IQ score merely states the degree of success on the test in relation to an age norm. The successful solution of a VRB problem identifies a stage of intellectual development which the subject has reached. The validity of the IQ score depends on the validity of the test standardization. The validity of a statement based on VRB experiments depends on the validity of the theoretical framework.

Another advantage of the procedure is that VRB tasks appear to depend on very little culture-specific information. A subject who is able to comprehend any language at all and to utilize the second signal system while processing information should be able to solve all the problems appropriate to his/her developmental level. While the content and complexity of the second signal system may be reduced because of experiential deprivation, the basic stages of verbal regulation of behavior should be achieved by all children of normal intellectual capacity.

Finally, an important aspect of the VRB procedure is that the subject is observed in a learning situation and conclusions are not based only on initial achievement. In this connection Luria (1961b) stated:

> Would it not be more proper ... to reject the static principle of assessing a child's independent performance of a given task in favor of that of comparing the success of his independent performance with that achieved with *adult help?* (p. 41)

Because of these considerations the VRB procedure appears to be a suitable technique for cross-cultural research.

VRB Research with Canadian Indian Children

Some data about Canadian Indian children were reported in Schubert and Cropley (1972) and Steinberg (1974/1975). They were collected in two locations. The Northern Group (*N*) lived on a reservation which had not been accessible by road until shortly before testing. The children spoke Cree at home and many of the adult women of the community did not speak English at all. Until recently the majority of the population lived by fishing and trapping. All the children of this group had been at school for at least five years. They communicated fluently in English. The other reservation was located near a white urban center in central Saskatchewan (Group *C*). The population speaks English and most of the children could not speak Cree. The majority of this population lived on welfare.

Both reservations were approached through the Saskatchewan Indian Federation and their approval was obtained before the educational authorities were approached. I visited the *N* reservation during the summer vacation and spent some time there camping with one of my sons, who made friends with the local children. I was invited to the homes of several families and was well known to the children before the testing started. There was no problem of verbal communication with the children who were tested.

The mean IQ of the *N* group was 20 points below that of the *C* group. The mean verbal IQ of the 11-year-old children was 64, the mean verbal IQ of the 12- to 14-year-old children was 72. However, these low IQ scores did not reflect reduced biological capacity. The children passed all those VRB problems which differentiate between oligophrenia and environmentally determined retardation. Schubert and Cropley (1972) concluded:

> Despite their low scores on the conventional intelligence test, the Indian children with IQs below 70 had a significantly higher verbal regulation of behavior score than white children in the same IQ range. (p. 300)

Striking differences between the remote Northern Indians (*N*) and the centrally located Indians (*C*) were found in their ability to verbalize the rules which they discovered themselves. The *N* group did almost as well as the *C* group on the motor level but were unable to state the rule which guided their behavior. It also appeared that those children who were able to formulate the correct rule about the problems which they had solved proceeded easily to more complex problems. Those children who solved the problem on the motor level only, showed perseveration when confronted with a new, similar, more complicated problem.

> The major difference between the northern Indian child and the urban child looks to lie in the fact that the former does not habitually and spontaneously analyze his experience in verbal terms and does not formulate internalized rules that might guide him in new learning situations. (Schubert & Cropley, 1972, p. 300)

Two years later Steinberg (1974/1975) collected data for the entire school population of the *C* reservation. The age range of the 70 children was 6 to 16 years. Forty-five children had been tested previously (Schubert & Cropley, 1972). Psychometric intelligence was assessed through the Wechsler Intelligence Scale for Children (WISC). Operative intelligence (Furth, 1973) was measured by the VRB pro-

Table I. *VRB and Piagetian Cognitive*
Tasks: Mean Scores and Standard
Deviations for 70 Canadian Indian
School Children[a]

Age range	n	VRB		Cognitive	
		M	SD	M	SD
6:3–8:6[b]	25	9.4	4.7	4.0	1.5
8:7–10:10	15	13.9	1.6	6.1	1.0
10:11–12:6	14	15.0	2.0	6.9	1.3
12:7–16:2	16	14.9	3.2	5.8	1.3

[a]Adapted from Steinberg (1974/1975).
[b]6:3 means 6 years, 3 months.

cedure and a series of specifically designed Piagetian problems on cognitive and moral development.

The mean performance IQ of the four age groups fluctuated about 100, and the mean verbal IQ of the younger children fluctuated about 90. However, the oldest group (grades 5–9, age 12–16) showed a significant decrease of verbal IQ ($\overline{X} = 80.7$).

Steinberg defined three VRB stages for her population. Stage I (VRB score 1–6) was called *external rule following*. This means that the child is able to remember simple instructions and carry them out; the verbal response will not interfere with the motor response. Stage II (VRB score 7–11) was labeled *internalized rule using*. At this stage the child can discover the rule by trial and error. VRB score 12–15 represents the transitional Stage IIa. Here an attempt at verbalizing the rule is made but the child cannot give correct systematic explanations. Stage III (VRB score 16–20) is called *verbalization of rule*. It indicates that the child is able to give a correct verbal explanation of the rule.

Piagetian tasks were also scored on three levels: preoperational (score 1–4), concrete operations (score 5–8), and formal logic (score 9–11).

Table I summarizes the data for VRB scores and Piagetian cognitive tasks. For both measures there was a significant increase in mean score between group 1 (age 6–8) and the three older groups ($p < .001$) but no significant increase after age 8 years. The level of VRB scores of the younger children was comparable to that of white children of similar age. The fact that all subjects of the older group reached the *internalized rule using* stage indicates that they were of biologically normal intelligence. The fact that they did not progress beyond the transitional Stage IIa shows retardation in the articulation of the second signal system. This retardation is also reflected in the Piagetian measures, where the subjects did not progress beyond the stage of concrete operations.

Separate factor analyses of the youngest and the three older groups as well as factor analysis for the combined total sample yielded a *cognitive* factor with the highest loadings for the VRB problems and Piagetian cognitive measures. This factor accounted for 40% of the variance in the younger sample but only for 13% of the variance of the older sample. In contrast, the *verbal comprehension* factor, with the highest loadings on the verbal subtests of the WISC, accounted for 16% of the variance in the younger group and for 55% of the variance of the older group. These results, as well as the reduction of verbal IQ in the oldest group, show an increase with age of educational influence on the general performance of the children.

The third study[1] investigated whether the training procedures described by Luria (1961b) and Liublinskaya (1957, 1961) would result in increased articulation of the second signal system and whether this increase would be reflected in the children's IQ score. We designed an intensive program based on the experiments cited by these authors (Schubert & Bergman, 1974). The program was administered to the first and second grades of the *N* reservation and in several integrated white–Indian schools in central Saskatchewan.

The teaching material consisted of large posters with pictures relevant to a common theme. Examples are fish of northern Saskatchewan, large animals of northern Saskatchewan, fishing lures, winter footwear, and handtools. A similar series of posters with different animals, plants, and tools was prepared for use in the central Saskatchewan region.

The teachers were carefully trained in the administration of the program. They used the material daily for about 20 minutes. The children were engaged in various verbal games. For example, in games of identification the children were asked, and later encouraged to formulate, questions such as "Which bird has a *long straight beak* and *webbed feet* and *black and white feathers* and a *white head?*" Or the children were asked to give a detailed verbal analysis of everyday activities as, for example, "set a beaver trap; build a fire; build a log cabin; make moccasins; bead a necklace; start an outboard motor." Another game involved the use of local prepositions: "Take a ball *out* of the box, walk *around* the desk and put it *under* the table." A lotto game was designed to teach the children that an item can be classified in several manners, according to shape or according to color; according to use or according to origin.

The children liked these activities, and after a year an increase in spontaneous use of English among them was observed. Unfortunately, the analysis of the results met with difficulties, because of a number of technical-administrative problems beyond our control. We were therefore unable to ascertain whether the significant increase in IQ which was observed after a year was related to our program or not. At present all that can be said is that such a teaching program can be easily carried out, catches the interest of the children, and appears to have some effect on their verbal habits.

The three studies confirm Schubert and Cropley's (1972) conclusion that these children "have not developed the kinds of information-processing strategies which are necessary to function adequately in a Western educational system" (p. 301). Nevertheless, these were bright children, well adapted to a hunting society, as can be easily ascertained by observing them outside of school. It is therefore misleading to talk about "experiential deprivation" in these communities. The children we observed were not deprived of the experience necessary for intellectual development

[1]The financial support of Canada Council Grant is gratefully acknowledged.

within the framework of their culture. I have seen a 4-year-old boy being taken on a sledge by his father to the traplines, where he stayed for several days. I assume that he learned by observation and imitation rather than by verbal analysis of similarities and differences between various traps. No doubt the holistic approach to the totality of experience which characterizes Indian thinking makes sense in this environment. But, of course, it does not foster that analytical thinking which leads to a high Similarities score. This point is well illustrated by the following incident, which occurred during one of the training sessions. The teacher discussed the picture of animals in the *N* reservation. The exercise was: the bear has a large paw; the fox has a small paw. The children thought that this statement was very funny. It turned out that in Cree "bear paw" is different from "fox paw." Therefore a bear with a large paw is a bear with an overgrown bear paw, and the fox with a small paw is a fox with a small fox paw. This difference in perception illustrates the influence of the cultural background on thought. The analytical approach states: This is a paw and it can be considered abstractly, independently from the total animal. Such fragmentation is strange to a hunting society which looks at the totality of events. A global approach may be more suitable for a hunting society. If you see a paw in a bush it is not very useful to think "This is a paw." You should be thinking "This is a bear." If, however, you are expected to manage a sawmill and to be able to order spare parts from the manufacturer, then attention to details is of paramount importance. It is doubtful whether the abilities required in a highly technological society will develop without a higher level of articulation of the second signal system.

Comment: The Implications of Cross-cultural Research for the Study of Intelligence

We have shown that the conceptualization of the second signal system is relevant for a definition of *intelligent behavior, intellectual ability,* and *intellectual capacity* (cf. Montagu, this volume). Luria successfully identified some critical tasks the completion of which depends on the child's maturational stage. Although at present we have data about the development of verbal regulation of behavior in three cultural groups only, it appears to be a reasonable hypothesis that these developmental stages can be demonstrated in any human society. We are therefore suggesting that the capacity to develop the second signal system and to regulate behavior is the biological substratum that is common to the "intelligence" of mankind—irrespective of cultural background.

However, because the second signal system is an open system, it permits the development of an infinite, nonpredictable variety of intellectual abilities or strategies for the processing of information. The cross-cultural research described by Luria, as well as our own research, shows that these differences in intellectual abilities can be meaningfully analyzed in terms of the *content* of the second signal system as well as in terms of articulation of *problem-solving strategies.* It further suggests that these features can only be understood with reference to the socioeconomic conditions of the societies in which they were developed.

Although Luria's cross-cultural data and our own were collected 40 years apart, in two samples differing widely in cultural background and age, the results show clear differences between the groups investigated and Western European populations. The two central Asian groups as well as the Canadian Indians relied mainly on a global, functional approach to problem solving but had not developed the abstract-analytical approach which characterizes Western thinking. These differences are not simply an artifact of the testing situation but reflect real differences in the way people adapt to their respective environments. Every society develops the "intelligence" which is needed for its functioning. Comprehensive research on intelligence must therefore be cross-cultural.

Wober (1967) distinguished two approaches to cross-cultural research. The *centri-cultural* approach is an attempt to measure how well "they" do "our" tricks. The true *cross-cultural* approach attempts to measure how "they" do "their" tricks. I think that there is a third approach which aims to find out how we all come to do our tricks (cf. Berry, this volume). If it is true that intelligence is shaped by culture, then only a comparison of cultures can open our eyes to the structure of intelligence. Research that is restricted to the investigator's own society is an attempt by Münchhausen to pull himself out of the bog by his own hair. It will turn out to be a futile attempt to refute Gödel's theorem.

Our results were obtained by white investigators. Would Indian investigators have obtained similar results? Perhaps not. Their entire approach might have been different. The issue is not that VRB problems could have been administered in the Cree language but that Cree investigators would have asked different questions. Ideally we need an Indian psychologist doing research on the intelligence of white children. However, our attempts to ask our questions in other cultures can also shed light on the development of white children. The very fact that our questions, originally designed for our populations, occasionally turn out to be inadequate will open up a new vista of looking at ourselves. I suggest therefore that the value of cross-cultural research is that it enables us to view our own behavior in a new light. Indeed, the research described above highlights an aspect of intelligence which has hitherto been woefully neglected in psychological research.

Intelligence is not merely a matter of concept formation; it is also a matter of planning. Knowledge transmitted to the child remains arid unless it is integrated into the planning of activity. The extent of a person's temporal horizon is an important aspect of intelligent behavior. Hearnshaw (1956) suggested that the ability to organize temporal sequences is perhaps the most distinguishing feat of human behavior.

> Temporal integration essentially involves the formation, from temporally disparate units, of configurations in which the present moment and immediate stimuli lose the dominance they possess at the perceptual level. The capacity to form and to scan such temporal configurations frees the organism from control by the present situation, and is the foundation of most of man's characteristic attributes. (p. 17)

Contemporary research neglects temporal integration.[2] There are hardly any tasks in conventional intelligence tests which measure the complexity of temporary

[2]Temporal integration is related to Luria's (1966) concept of *successive synthesis,* namely, the "synthesis of separate elements into successive series" (p. 74, footnote 1). Successive synthesis is not the "mere successive (and often rote) recall of stimuli, requiring little or no transformation, reorganization or manipulation of sensory input," as has been claimed by Vernon, Ryba, and Lang (1978, p. 2). It is an active organizing process which may occur at different levels of complexity.

gestalten. Some VRB problems require the integration of temporal sequences. It might be worthwhile to develop tests of hidden movements, rhythm analysis, or time perspective. I suggest therefore that intelligence is not merely a function of the problem-solving tricks available but is also related to motivational factors and is a function of the long-term goals which a person is able to articulate. Could it be that some goals are more "intelligent" than others? *"It might be fruitful to define stages of intelligence not only on the basis of complexity of behavior, but on the basis of complexity of the goals which have been articulated"* (Schubert, 1973, p. 18).

These considerations suggest that societies will differ in the level of intelligence which they foster. This is Luria's position (1976):

> Before the revolution, the people of Uzbekistan lived in a backward economy . . . When the socialist revolution eliminated dominance and submission as class relations, . . . people for the first time . . . experienced responsibility for their own future. (p. 13)

According to this view societies can be graded as to the stage of socioeconomic organization which they have achieved, the final stage presumably being an industrial, classless society. The progress of intelligence goes hand in hand with social progress. It may be noted that this position evoked considerable criticism at the time of its original presentation:

> Critics pointed out that [Luria's] data could be read as an insult to the people with whom he had been working (Razmyslov, 1934). . . . It was definitely not acceptable to say anything that could be interpreted as negative about these people. (Cole, 1976, p. xiv)

This thorny issue is very much alive today. It is often argued that although different societies may foster different abilities, it is improper to talk about more or less "advanced" societies. Any value statement of this sort is centri-cultural and implies a chauvinistic missionary spirit. Not only does each society stand on its own merits, but the very forms of intelligence which are fostered by European-American civilization are ultimately detrimental to the development of humankind. There is no doubt about Luria's attitude in this matter. The ideal society he envisaged is one that needs people who are capable of abstract thinking and who are ready to take responsibility for the planning of their life. Any attempt to foster such development is progressive; any attempt to delay it in the name of traditional values is essentially reactionary and antisocial.

It has often been suggested that research on intelligence and testing is invidious and antisocial, because it tends to rationalize discrimination. From this point of view, testing is seen as a tool to maintain the class structure; cross-cultural research, especially where it leads to suggestions of change in the abilities of an "underdeveloped" society, is said to be a tool of Western imperialism. These arguments neglect to consider that political equality without equality of competence is illusory. Differences in ability are not abolished by ignoring them. Success, leadership, and meaningful participation in the political, economic, and cultural life of contemporary industrial society demand a reasonable development of those abilities which are measured by conventional intelligence tests. Abolishing university entrance examinations by itself does not guarantee equality of educational opportunity. The idea that Western philosophical thought is the crowning achievement of humankind and that its benefits must be conferred on our poor Indian brothers, whether they like it or not, represents cultural imperialism. The other side of the coin is the withholding of information that may help minorities to become integrated within the technological society, should they wish to do so. Ignoring the task of carrying out relevant research can be as bad as imposing it. *The paternalistic revolutionary who tries to convince the Indian that the mastery of Western skills enslaves him/her to Western devils is no less pernicious than the capitalist who develops his/her intelligence in order to procure a more efficient labor force.*

The question of experiential deprivation and remedies to overcome it becomes acute when the full integration of minorities is attempted. Whether full integration is desirable is a political question to which our research does not address itself. It appears to me—notwithstanding Luria's social vision—that the extent and speed of change should be controlled by Indians themselves. Our research addresses itself to the fashioning of tools which help it.

> Early development of the second signal system should be fostered, if Indians desire to develop those kinds of abilities in their children. . . . However, whether Indians wish to adopt such a model of intelligence involves a set of values about the goals of life, a set of values which the Indian communities may not wish to adopt. (Schubert and Cropley, 1972, p. 301)

This is the area in which the practical implications of cross-cultural research in verbal regulation of behavior become relevant. We have shown that the development of the intellectual abilities required in a society built on a Western European model depends on the articulation of the second signal system. From this point of view, a child who grows up in an environment that does not encourage verbal reflection and articulation is deprived even if his/her emotional experience is rich and varied. To counteract this deprivation it is necessary to develop educational programs which will systematically encourage children to analyze their environments, their activities, their perceptions in verbal terms. It goes without saying that such a program must reflect the daily life situation of the children to whom it is offered. A program of Indian education for Indian school children should be developed by Indian teachers at home among Indian traditions. Otherwise the result will be assimilation, not integration of cultures.

Our results suggest an additional important implication: It is not enough to foster knowledge and problem-solving tricks. It is unfortunate if remedial educational programs concentrate on the accumulation of memorized knowledge—including problem-solving skills—but neglect planning. If, as I have suggested, the major index of intellectual development is the ability to plan behavior and to take responsibility for it, then the educational system should encourage children to ask new questions and to look for new goals. At present we lack even the diagnostic tools to measure the scope of a person's temporal world and the sophistication of his/her goal system. We tend to substitute teaching machines for education.

Holzkamp (1970) suggested that modern society is in danger of being subjected to a regime that will duplicate the essential features of the psychological laboratory: control over the subjects' motivation, limited access to information, and restriction of behavioral alternatives. Such strictures ensure the applicability of the behavioristic "laws of learning" but impede intellectual development. Our analysis suggests that the development of intelligence is highly dependent on the power structure maintained within a society: who is allowed to plan and who is encouraged to plan. Intellectual progress in a society depends in the final analysis on the ability of its members to ask new questions and to conceive new plans. It is quite possible that a true change in general intelligence (ability) will not occur without a change in social structure.

Every form of teaching is a form of brainwashing, of structuring the way in which the environment is perceived. There are, however, two fundamentally different approaches to teaching (cf. Greenfield, this volume). The first brings the organism under increased stimulus control and decreases autonomy. This learning has been investigated in the American psychological laboratory. The organism is exposed to rigid schedules of reinforcement and his/her freedom of action is restrained. Such a regime may bring about a stable and predictable conditional response. The other kind of learning leads to the development of internal regulation of behavior and the ability to formulate new questions and new answers. As far as we know, humans are the only species predisposed to develop such a system. For this reason human behavior is essentially unpredictable and undetermined. The possibility of regulation of behavior gives humanity a freedom which is more than the "recognition of necessity," the freedom of true creativity. The development of this kind of freedom is the noblest purpose of education, and the investigation of the conditions leading to it is the ultimate task of the study of intellectual development.

Acknowledgment

The author is indebted to C. R. Jillings, University of Regina, for his helpful comments after reviewing the manuscript of this chapter.

References

Burland, R. The development of verbal regulation of behavior in cerebrally palsied (multiply handicapped) children. *Journal of Mental Subnormality,* 1969, *15,* 85–89.

Chomsky, N. Appendix: The formal nature of language. In E. H. Lenneberg, *Biological foundations of language.* New York: John Wiley & Sons, 1967.

Cole, M. Foreword. In A. R. Luria, *Cognitive development: Its cultural and social foundations.* Cambridge, Mass.: Harvard University Press, 1976.

Erikson, E. H. *Childhood and society.* New York: Norton, 1950.

Furth, H. G. *Thinking without language.* New York: Free Press, 1966.

Furth, H. G. Piaget, IQ and the nature-nurture controversy. *Human Development,* 1973, *16,* 61–73.

Harlow, H. F. Learning set and error factor theory. In S. Koch (Ed.), *Psychology: A study of a science* (Vol. 2). New York: McGraw-Hill, 1959.

Hearnshaw, L. S. Temporal integration and behavior. *Bulletin of the British Psychological Society,* 1956, *30,* 1–20.

Holzkamp, K. Zum Problem der Relevanz psychologischer Forschung für die Praxis. *Psychologische Rundschau,* 1970, *21,* 1–22.

Hunt, J. McV. *Intelligence and experience.* New York: Ronald Press, 1961.

Lenneberg, E. H. *Biological foundations of language.* New York: John Wiley & Sons, 1967.

Liublinskaya, A. A. The development of children's speech and thought. In B. Simon (Ed.), *Psychology in the Soviet Union*. London: Routledge and Kegan Paul, 1957.

[Liublinskaya, A. A.] Ljublinskaja, A. A. *Die psychische Entwicklung des Kindes*. Berlin: Volk und Wissen Volkseigener Verlag, 1961.

Luria, A. R. The role of language in the formation of temporary connections. In B. Simon (Ed.), *Psychology in the Soviet Union*. London: Routledge and Kegan Paul, 1957.

Luria, A. R. Brain disorders and language analysis. *Language and Speech*, 1958, *1*, 14–34.

Luria, A. R. The directive function of speech in development and dissolution. *Word*, 1959, *15*, 341–352; 453–464. (a)

Luria, A. R. Experimental study of the higher nervous activity of the child. *Journal of Mental Deficiency Research*, 1959, *3*, 1–22. (b)

Luria, A. R. Verbal regulation of behavior. In M. A. B. Brazier (Ed.), *The central nervous system and behavior*. New York: Josiah Macy, Jr. Foundation, National Science Fund, 1960.

Luria, A. R. The genesis of voluntary movements. In N. O'Connor (Ed.), *Recent Soviet psychology*. London: Pergamon Press, 1961. (a)

Luria, A. R. *The role of speech in the regulation of normal and abnormal behavior*. London: Pergamon Press, 1961. (b)

Luria, A. R. (Ed.). *The mentally retarded child*. Oxford: Pergamon Press, 1963. (a)

Luria, A. R. Psychological studies of mental deficiency in the Soviet Union. In N. R. Ellis (Ed.), *Handbook of mental deficiency*. New York: McGraw-Hill, 1963. (b)

Luria, A. R. *Higher cortical functions in man*. New York: Basic Books, 1966.

Luria, A. R. *Cognitive development: Its cultural and social foundations*. Cambridge, Mass.: Harvard University Press, 1976.

Schubert, J. The VRB apparatus: An experimental procedure for the investigation of the development of verbal regulation of behavior. *Journal of Genetic Psychology*, 1969, *114*, 237–252.

Schubert, J. The VRB apparatus: A cross-validation. *Psychological Reports*, 1970, *27*, 571–574.

Schubert, J. *The VRB apparatus* (manual). Mimeographed edition. Regina, Saskatchewan: University of Saskatchewan, 1973. (Available from author on request.)

Schubert, J., & Bergman, A. *Learning concepts from everyday experiences: Revised manual*. Mimeographed edition. Regina, Saskatchewan: University of Regina, Department of Psychology, 1974. (Available from author on request.)

Schubert, J., & Burland, R. The performance of cerebrally palsied children on the VRB test. *British Journal of Social and Clinical Psychology*, 1973, *12*, 96–97.

Schubert, J., & Cropley, A. J. Verbal regulation of behavior and IQ in Canadian Indian and White children. *Developmental Psychology*, 1972, *7*, 295–301.

Seligman, M. *Biological boundaries of learning*. New York: Appleton-Century-Crofts, 1972.

Smith, N., & Wilson, D. *Modern linguistics: The results of Chomsky's revolution*. Brighton, Sussex: Harvester Press, 1979.

Steinberg, R. H. *Psychometric and operative intelligence in an Indian school population*. Doctoral thesis. University of Saskatchewan, Regina Campus, 1974. Ottawa: National Library of Canada, 1975 (Microfiche).

Vernon, P. E., Ryba, K. A., & Lang, R. J. Simultaneous and successive processing: An attempt at replication. *Canadian Journal of Behavioral Science*, 1978, *10*, 1–15.

Vygotsky, L. D. *Thought and language*. Cambridge, Mass.: MIT Press, 1962.

Wober, M. Distinguishing centri-cultural from cross-cultural research. *International Journal of Psychology*, 1967, *2*, 233–250.

Wozniak, R. H. Verbal regulation of motor behavior: Soviet research and non-Soviet replications. *Human Development*, 1972, *15*, 13–57.

5

An Interactionist Model of Language Development

Vera John-Steiner and Paul Tatter

Few domains within the social and behavioral sciences can match the study of language development in theoretical richness, in breadth and inventiveness of research approaches, and in the liveliness of debates among its students. However, these characteristics of a flourishing interdisciplinary field have arisen only recently.

Early in this century, studies of language development were primarily descriptive; they documented the rapid increase in vocabulary and grammatical complexity of young children's utterances (McCarthy, 1954). The behaviorists only marginally considered the development of children's language, inasmuch as they preferred the use of nonverbal subjects for their studies of learning. Investigations that did include "verbal behavior" relied for their analyses on the concepts of stimulus generalization, response classes, and reinforcement (Salzinger, 1967). The central and reciprocal roles of language and social interaction in human learning and thought were articulated by philosophers concerned with processes, such as Peirce, Mead, Dewey, Whitehead, and Wittgenstein. But their important work in this area was largely ignored by researchers in the middle of this century.

The scope and direction of the study of language changed dramatically after the publication of Chomsky's *Syntactic Structures* in 1957. His rationalist theory appealed to diverse groups of researchers, including linguists, cognitive psychologists, and students of development, who had rejected the assumptions of behaviorism. On the basis of Chomsky's bold hypothesis, that children have an a priori knowledge of

An earlier version of this chapter was presented at the meeting of the New York Academy of Sciences, January 1979.

Vera John-Steiner ● Departments of Linguistics and Educational Foundations, The University of New Mexico, Albuquerque, New Mexico 87131.   *Paul Tatter* ● All Indian Pueblo Council Teacher Education Program, Department of Elementary Education, The University of New Mexico, Albuquerque, New Mexico 87131.

the rules of grammar and generate specific hypotheses about their native languages in the course of maturation, the analysis of language development began anew.

In the decade that followed, researchers working longitudinally with small numbers of subjects focused on the emergent grammars of child language. McNeill (1970) summarized the assumptions that governed this approach as follows:

> Every language utilizes the same basic syntactic categories, arranged in the same way—such categories as sentences, noun phrases, verb phrases. Every language utilizes the same basic grammatical categories among these categories—such relations as subject and predicate of a sentence, verb and object of a verb phrase and modification within a noun phrase. Every language can recursively include sentences within sentences. And every language distinguishes between deep and surface structure, and so is transformational. (p. 1088)

The role of transformations in the development of langauge was stressed by McNeill in his analysis: "The interaction between children's innate capacities and their linguistic experience occurs at this point, in the acquisition of transformations—and it is here that parental speech must make a contribution." Nevertheless, language development was seen by most of the nativist theoreticians in the 1960s as primarily preprogrammed. The astonishingly rapid mastery by children of a highly complex linguistic system contributed to the acceptance by many researchers of the notion of an innate language acquisition device.

The search for a universal child grammar was implicit in the increasing number of longitudinal studies where children's utterances were recorded in naturalistic settings such as their homes. This approach, akin to Piaget's successful clinical method of developmental inquiry, was first elaborated by Brown and his co-workers (Brown & Fraser, 1964). Ten years after the Harvard study of Adam, Eve, and Sarah was initiated, there were 24 well-documented cases available to Brown from his own and other research. Different groups of developmental psycholinguists described similar stages of early language development. For example, a period of single word utterances by children was inevitably followed by the production of two-word utterances as they reached 18 to 24 months of age. The observation that children proceed in such small steps in developing language was accounted for by the argument that the language acquisition device had a fairly fixed and short programming span during the early stages of maturation.

The construction of a universal theory required researchers not only to replicate each other's work within a certain speech community but also to go outside of it. Slobin's (1967) *A Field Manual for Cross-cultural Study of the Acquisition of Communicative Competence* was aimed at this endeavor and was widely used, first by students of Slobin, Ervin-Tripp, and Gumperz at Berkeley, and later by an increasing number of linguists and psychologists within and outside of the United States. The data thus collected revealed some commonalities across languages, particularly during the stage of two-word utterances. But under closer analysis, a strictly syntactic interpretation of these early expressions became insufficient. For instance, Bloom (1970) found that the same noun–noun combinations expressed at least five different relations: conjunction ("block dolly"), attribution ("party hat"), genitive ("daddy hat"), subject–locative ("sweater chair"), and subject–object ("mommy book").

The many examples in Bloom's work convincingly demonstrate that beginning speakers convey a variety of semantic intentions beyond their ability to use linguistic devices which differentiate them. In their interpretations of these utterances, caretakers rely on the nonverbal context in which the child's language is produced. That context is the ongoing exchange between young children and their elders—a social structuring of the processes of language development.

In the late 1960s, some researchers, particularly those psycholinguists who worked in field situations, realized the significance of the social and ecological sources of the child's developing language. Kernan (1969), whose study of Samoan child language was one of the cross-cultural studies initiated at Berkeley, was critical of an abstract syntactic theory of development. He stressed that there were many structured and recurrent events in the life of a young child which constituted a critical framework for early dialogues. The semantic notions of "Agent + Action" could best be understood in the context of these events. This relationship of language to its social and behavioral context was particularly striking to those who examined child language in cultural environments other than their own.

Nevertheless, it was difficult for many psycholinguists to abandon the Chomskian paradigm of a preprogrammed language acquisition device and the notion of an innate and universal grammar at the basis of the complex processes of language development. The first changes in approach to the study of child language were seen as representing minor modifications of this paradigm. Bloom interpreted her results in this way. But an increasing interest in the cognitive precursors of language development and the work of speech act theorists such as Austin, Grice, and Searle accelerated the proliferation of new ways to examine child language.

The first definitive statement of the paradigmatic shift which emerged during the early 1970s was the closely reasoned argument in Brown's book, *A First Language* (1973). In this detailed study, Brown identified eight semantic relations (action–agent, action–object, etc.) which accounted for the meanings of children's two-word utterances. These semantic relations were subsequently used by researchers in analyzing maternal input language (Snow & Ferguson, 1977). The nativists had regarded input language as lacking in distinctiveness and as marred by disfluencies and disruptions, while the behaviorists had regarded it as a form of reinforcement or shaping. But the careful study of "motherese" (Newport, 1976) led to a recognition of finely tuned interactions between children and their caretakers. In summarizing her findings on maternal input, Toni Cross (1977) stressed this relationship:

> In general, it appears that at the discourse level of description, mothers' speech is more finely tuned to the child's linguistic, psycholinguistic and communicative abilities than to age. It has been argued that the discourse adjustments found to be most sensitive to child level in this study are precisely those that provide the child with ideal opportunities to learn the structure of his language. . . . If children acquire the form of language through the process of comprehension, then the mothers of rapidly developing children seem to make it easy for them to do so. (p. 172)

Such insights, gained from the new focus on the language children hear, became manifest in a widespread reexamination of the sources of language development.

The studies of input language, together with an increasing concern for cognitive, semantic, functional, and pragmatic aspects of language, have created the ground-work for a new *interactionist model*. In a relatively short time, the view of child language as an abstract system has given way to an approach that places speech within the context of communication and social life. Bruner (1978b) expressed this change when he wrote:

> If the semantic and the functional primacists are to be taken seriously, language emerges as a procedural acquisition to deal with events that the child already understands conceptually and to achieve communicative objectives that the child, at least partially, can already realize by other means. (p. 247)

A social interpretation of language and meaning forms the core of the work of Michael Halliday:

> Language arises in the life of the individual through an ongoing exchange of meanings with significant others. A child creates, first his child tongue, then his mother tongue, in interaction with that little coterie of people who constitute his meaning group. In this sense, language is a product of the social process. (1978, p. 1)

A child is born into this process. Infants communicate through cries, gestures, and intonation, and their caretakers respond by a multiplicity of means, constructing and sustaining a crucial dialogue.

Halliday documented the growth of these exchanges in *Learning How to Mean* (1975). There are some parallels between his work on the prelinguistic phases of communication and Bates's (1976) research on the pragmatics of child language. But Halliday's approach is primarily sociolinguistic, while Bates structures her inquiry with the help of Piaget's stages of cognitive development. It seems to us that these differences represent a common trend in contemporary language studies: namely, a separation between a primarily social, external approach on the one hand and a primarily cognitive, internal focus on the other. It is our belief that an inter-actionist theory of language development must integrate these two perspectives.

A unification of these approaches cannot be achieved, however, without a care-ful attempt at making explicit some of the philosophical and psychological assump-tions which govern contemporary analyses of language and its development. There is a danger that much of the recent work which is so promising will remain frag-mented without such an effort at the tentative theoretical integration of what may be the desired features of a new paradigm. Although the Chomskian rationalist view of language and mind is now a minority position among researchers, it did point out the critical importance of making clear the philosophical—ontological and episte-mological—notions which govern the examination of the development of language.

The emerging interactionist model of language development is not the work of any single theorist or researcher; it is the joint product of recent thinkers as well as of individuals who worked during the first half of this century. In the writings of the American pragmatists, in the European Marxist approach to language and thought represented by Vygotsky and Luria, and in the broad and integrative thinking of Bruner and Halliday we find the scaffolding for a new interactionist paradigm. In examining their work we try to clarify and to integrate their contributory conceptions as constituent parts of this perspective. The numbered assumptions which follow are the tentative results of this effort, strands in the coalescence toward what Toulmin (1978) saw in Vygotsky's work: "the novel unification of Nature and Culture" (p. 57).

Social and Functional Sources of Language

1. The development of human cognitive and linguistic processes is effectually and causally linked with complex social and cultural practices. The higher mental processes, such as verbal thought, cannot develop apart from the appropriate forms of social life. From birth, the social forms of child–caretaker interactions, the tools used by humans in society to manipulate the environment, the culturally institution-alized patterns of social relations, and language, operating together as a socio-semiotic system, are used by the child in cooperation with adults to organize behavior, perception, memory, and complex mental processes. For children, the development of language is a development of social existence into individuated persons and into culture.

An extensive, historical resource for the emerging perspective on the semiotic process can be found in the work of the American pragmatists. Because this tradition has been largely neglected by contemporaries, its contributions, drawn in summary form from the writings of Charles S. Peirce, John Dewey, and George Herbert Mead, are incorporated into the following discussion.[1]

To the pragmatists, the semiotic process is intrinsically social. It originates, develops, operates, and has meaning only within and for a social process of human interaction and communication. Some aspect of it is embedded in every human institution and social interaction. It is continuous with physical and biological processes without being identical or reducible to them, growing out of organic activities as the emergence of new modes of activity in connection with wider cultural processes. It participates in genuine transformations (Dewey, 1938; Mead, 1938; Peirce, 1932; cf. Wertsch, this volume).

As a process it is dynamic and developmental. It plays a key and multifaceted role in human development and has, in its operation, its own developmental characteristics, including the emergence of new forms. "Symbols grow," said Peirce (1932, p. 169). The relationships among signs are more than merely formal because they have a developmental time dimension (Dewey, 1938; Peirce, 1931; cf. Nadin, this volume).

Furthermore, the semiotic process is purposive, having a directed flow. It functions to choreograph and to harmonize the mutual adjustments necessary for the carrying out of human social activities. It has its sign function only within the intentional context of social cooperation and direction, in which past and future phases of activity are brought to bear upon the present. In this context, the semiotic process creates meanings and sign functions insofar as it provides the conditions through which anything is taken as a sign. It is thus a wider process than that commonly

[1]Citations of principal sources are provided. However, the text attempts to summarize positions for which there is evidence of general agreement among the pragmatists.

understood by the term language and encompasses all means or media of communication, including tools, monuments, formalized arts, and institutionalized or conventionalized patterns of behavior (Dewey, 1929; Mead, 1934). The conception of language as part of an interactive, biosociosemiotic system is fundamental in the work of the pragmatists and informs our formulation of the explanatory context of language.

2. We assume that an explanatory account cannot state the character of language development in itself apart from its relations, but rather must state an organized system of interactive relations as a whole in terms of which the development of language may be explained. These interactive relations are of an organismic-environmental complex; the dynamic, dialectical, and developmental relations of an ecosystem as a natural, functioning whole. Within this sociosemiotic ecosystem, interaction refers to a dialectical unity of biological and cultural aspects of development, to the dynamic relations among people, other material objects and social patterns, and to developmental consequences or transformations in the semiotic process which issue in language. The full development of symbolic language is possible only for humans who are essentially intact biological organisms within essentially intact social environments.

From their unifying conception of context, the pragmatists analyze the semiotic process in such a way as to distinguish related classes of signs. Signs are classified according as the relation of the sign to its object consists, first, in the sign's having some character in itself, an icon, which acts as a sign insofar as it is like its object and used as a sign of it; second, in some existential relation to its object, an index, which refers by virtue of being really affected by that object; or third, in its relation to an interpretant, a symbol, which refers by virtue of a law or a series of symbols in a universe of discourse (Peirce, 1932).

These classes of signs are inextricably related in the language process, and it is through this relation that language possesses its operational force: the connection with things which symbols by themselves lack and the function of mediating social activities. A sign is significant only insofar as it stands, directly or eventually through a series of symbols, in this triadic relation—insofar as there is someone for whom it is a sign of something in relation to some interpretant. The characteristic of relations among symbols as interpretants, which provides the possibility of an eventual but not immediate realization of the triadic relation or a possible postponement of the operational force in behavior of the triadic relation, allows for the representation of events removed in origin, participants, objects, time, or space from the present occurrence. It is in this manner that symbols contribute to the development of thought (Dewey, 1938; Peirce, 1934).

The process through which these relations develop and through which signs become meaningful to individuals is a social process, beginning at birth, in which the reciprocating roles in shared interaction of infant and caretaker use the pauses between reciprocations to indicate a coming phase of the cooperative or conjoint activity. The signs involved in this turn taking or role alternation become significant symbols or language for the child when they implicitly educe in the child who is making them a tendency into responses that are functionally the same as those which the signs explicitly call out in the other participants. These attitudes, or beginnings of the acts of others, in the child are integrated by the child into its experience as past or future phases of the ongoing, conjoint activity, and thus enable the participants alternately to readjust their subsequent behavior to each other so as to carry out their parts of the whole activity. In the purposive context of cooperative social activity, the same meaning or tendency into response may mediate a whole series of different but appropriate contributions (Mead, 1934, 1964).

It was the tendency of the pragmatists to explain the relations among signs, to account for and to explain language in terms of its function in a context of social interaction, and to assume the social field as a necessity. In the work of Mead, attention began to be directed toward the operation and effects of this social field in the development of significance and meaning. Mead attempted to explain the operation of the symbolic process in its functional context on the basis of its biological and social conditions. But this biosocial account of language function did not provide a complete ontogenetic account of its genesis and development in the growth of a human individual. It did, however, place it explicitly within a sociosemiotic system.

The concern with meaning, which is central to the pragmatists' view of the semiotic process as an aspect of functional relations among biologically grounded activities, social interaction, culturally organized behavior, and language, has reappeared in the last decade through the work of Halliday, Bruner, Bernstein, and Labov. This concern has both returned the study of language development to a larger sociosemiotic field and made possible an account of the developmental relationships between a child's preverbal interactions, protolanguage, and subsequent adult language. From the perspective of expression, there are dramatic discontinuities among these phases of development. However, from a social perspective there appear continuities in function. For Halliday, the operation of language in social life provides a framework which is essential in understanding the development of language in children. And the study of language functions for children provides insights for understanding language as a semiotic system.

Halliday (1978) interpreted social reality, or culture, in semiotic terms, as "an edifice of meanings—a semiotic construct" (p. 2). "From a sociolinguistic viewpoint, the semantic system can be defined as a functional or function-oriented meaning potential; a network of options for the encoding of some extralinguistic semiotic system" (p. 79). This higher-level semiotic may be viewed as a conceptual or cognitive, logical, ideological, aesthetic, or social system (cf. Stein, this volume).

Language is seen as a system of meaning potential, a semantic system, which is a realization, encoding, or projection of a higher-level semiotic, a behavioral system or social semiotic. The lexicogrammatical system operates as a realization of the semantic system. These three systems are related in a system of multiple coding, as one system coded or actualized in another. Their interface is a relation of realization. Thus the examination of any part of the semantic system must involve its relation to other parts of the same system and its relation of realizing an aspect of the social system and of being realized in the lexicogrammatical one (cf. Williams, this volume).

This perspective was used by Halliday to show how the development of language by the child is organized around a set of social functions, and why the linguistic system has to be explained in functional terms.

> A child learning his mother tongue is learning how to mean; he is building up a meaning potential in respect of a limited number of social functions. These functions constitute the semiotic environment of a very small child, and may be thought of as universals of human culture. (1978, p. 121)

The functions are seen as "language-engendering" and form the context of development of the child's protolanguage.

With regard to how a child makes the transition from its protolanguage into the adult semiotic system, Halliday suggested a role for the fact that adults interpret the child's utterances in terms of functions recognized by the adults as plausible ways of using language. He also suggested that the child internalizes a distinction between pragmatic uses of language, as a means of doing, requiring a response, and "mathetic" uses, as a means of knowing, not requiring a response. The introduction of a syntax which allows the simultaneous expression of these modes of meaning makes possible a semiotic reflexivity in verbal interaction. Through this process the social functions of the child's protolanguage become reinterpreted as metafunctional components in the organization of the semantic system. Halliday's account of this transition resists a thorough attempt to explain the role of the cognitive processes involved.

The theoretical separation of nature and culture is likely to be perpetuated if these processes are not accounted for. Progress in understanding the development of language requires the effort to overcome this dichotomy between the internal and the external, between the cognitive and the social. The promise of an interactionist perspective resides in the unification of these domains. It is to the processes of unification that this discussion now turns.

The Dynamic Sources of Language Development

3. The prolonged dependence of young children on their caretakers is a basic condition of human life. The adult–child interactions during this period of dependency form the primary social sources for the development of linguistic and cognitive processes. The subsequent mastery of language, extending the meaning and scope of these early reciprocal exchanges, enables growing children to internalize the cultural knowledge of their communities and to reflect on their experiences. There is both receptivity to others and self-initiated exploration in the behavioral repertoire of very young children. The tension between these two highly adaptive tendencies contributes to the processes of individuation and enculturation in the course of children's semiotic development.

The dependency needs of newborns constitute a crucial biological universal which shapes the profoundly social nature of human learning (cf. Fujinaga, this volume). The first year of life provides "both an unparalleled opportunity for mental and emotional development and a period of vulnerability to profound distortion by neglect," wrote the child psychiatrist Leon Eisenberg (1972, p. 127). The central role of this dependence is specific to our species, as the attachment of the young in other mammalian species is frequently discouraged or abruptly terminated by the mother (Rosenblatt, 1965).

A comparison to other species highlights the relatively indeterminate nature of the human newborn's behavior and the consequent socially mediated means–ends relationships needed for the infant's survival. This characteristic may be considered a clear and specific biological adaptation necessary to cultural organisms. Through dependency and behavioral adaptability, it provides the contextual conditions for the correlative processes of individuation and enculturation, both of which are essential to the development of language. From the moment of birth this adaptation places the infant into social relations with already individuated and enculturated adults and through them into a sociocultural system of meaning. Thus the requirements of care allow the infant's individuality to develop with cultural sources and also provide the communicative formats necessary for the development of language.

The first formats of communication are established in the context of the reciprocity of eye-to-eye contact, smiling, and vocalizing exchanges, which provide caretakers with signs of mutual recognition and a sense of pleasure in the midst of this arduous period of dependency. Bruner (1978a) has linked the precursors of language to the caretaker's effective interpretation of the infant's gestures and vocalizations, to the joint attention to objects and novel occurrences, and to the many games of appearance and disappearance that they engage in during the later period of infancy. He described this fluid course of development as follows:

> Much of that learning [of pragmatics] is based upon the mother interpreting the child's intent, the child sometimes conforming with the interpretation, sometimes not, but learning, *en route,* what interpretations his efforts evoke and how these may be modified. (p. 28)

Caretakers act as though infants begin life as persons with intentions, "competent to participate in social exchanges" (Shotter, 1978, p. 56). As caretakers weave their own behavior into the rhythmic alternations of the infants' activities, the reciprocity of a dialogue format becomes the primary form of social exchange. The adults bring to these exchanges both their knowledge of what is meaningful in ordinary human discourse and their specific familiarity with the young child in their care. They rely on these sources in interpreting the infant's actions as means, as communicating to the adult an intent or purpose which can be realized with the adult's cooperation. Thus, the beginnings of the infant's activity—the incipient acts—are interpreted by the caretaker as gestural signs appropriate to culturally patterned interactions.

When the adult responds to imputed gesture with gesture, the infant's subsequent response is an adjustment to the gestural phase of the conjoint activity; the exchange becomes *a conversation of gestures.* Opportunities for such exchanges are provided by the early "games of the person" and "games with objects" (Trevarthen & Hubley, 1978), "transfer of objects" (Clark, 1978), "the threatening head" (Newson, 1978), and "peekaboo" (Bruner & Sherwood, 1976). Their mutual adjustments to the beginnings of each other's actions create what Bruner (1978a) called a "transactional situation: their joint behavior determining its own future course" (p. 26). Slowly the child assumes an increasingly larger share of the "alternating sequence of communication gestures" (Newson, 1978, p. 41). The result is a gestural elaboration of the period of inhibition in activity—the mediated suspension of the directed flow of a course of action—which Mead (1938) referred to as the manipulatory phase of the act.

In a similar analysis Vygotsky (1978) described the development of pointing:

> Initially, this gesture is nothing more than an unsuccessful attempt to grasp something, a movement aimed at a certain object which designates forthcoming activity. The child attempts to grasp an object placed beyond his reach; his hands, stretched toward that object, remain poised in the air. His fingers make grasping movements. . . . When the mother comes to the child's aid and realizes his movement indicates something, the situation changes fundamentally. Pointing becomes a gesture for others. The child's unsuccessful attempt engenders a reaction not from the object he seeks but *from another person.* (p. 56)

In these early stages, the development of both child–adult interactions and child–object interactions is of significance. As children become more skillful in handling objects through playful explorations and manipulatory formats are developed, the child's anticipation of a coming phase of manipulation is used to control the ongoing activity. The anticipated future activity has a hypothetical character, which is called to the child's attention by the redirective interventions of the caretaker. The child is afforded the opportunity to focus increasingly on alternatives in action, in relation to both objects and other people. Thus, two lines of development—object-oriented and person-oriented activities—are woven together. The cognitive consequences of dealing with alternatives form the basis of an early dialectic in the child's behavior.

When the possibilities for future activity are implicated in the conversation of gestures, the alternative available to the child is an interpretive action of the adult. The consequence is that child and caretaker become engaged in a process of creating intentions in each other through their mutual adjustments to competing alternatives in behavior. The creation of an intention, or tendency into action, in another is characteristic of human communication. However, for communication to become referential, it is necessary that the child's incipient act create for the child an intention which has the same consequence as the intention created for the adult by the same act. *For the development of language, communicative interaction must be reflexive as well as reciprocal.*

The role of the adult in conjoint activity is both interpretive and contradictory. Because this process is dialectical, the period of inhibition in the child's activity is more than a mere blocking or frustration of action attempting to run its course. Rather, it becomes the entertaining of alternative courses of action which are temporarily in conflict. In the context of the systems of meaning provided by communicative formats, the alternative to action in inhibition is a sign of the coming phase of conjoint action. The implication of the adult's gesture is developed in the child's own activity. As a result, the role of the adult is taken during the exchange. The subsequent incipient act of the child has the same implication for the child's future activity as for the adult's. The shifting of roles in discourse, which Bruner (1978a) described as the essential prerequisite for deixis, is controlled by the negotiated resolution of the contradictions between the incipient acts of child and caretaker.

It is immaterial that in early infancy the child is unaware of the incipient act or gesture as a sign. It is sufficient that attention is brought to it and that it is the focus of adjustment. The formats described by Bruner are habituations of activity patterns with such a focus. In Mead's words:

> Awareness or consciousness is not necessary to the presence of meaning in the process of social experience. A gesture on the part of one organism in any given social act calls out a response on the part of another organism which is directly related to the action of the first organism and its outcome; and a gesture is a symbol of the result of the given social act of one organism (the organism making it) in so far as it is responded to by another organism (thereby also involved in that act) as indicating that result. The mechanism of meaning is thus present in the social act before the emergence of consciousness or awareness of meaning occurs.... Language simply lifts out of the social process a situation which is logically or implicity there already. (1934, pp. 77–79)

While Mead saw the sources of reflexivity in the dialectics of mutual action, Vygotsky identified social interaction and cognitive generalizations necessary for word meaning as the dual roots of such development. Our account of the development of language incorporates both of these perspectives.

As seen by Mead, the development of the symbolic function, including the growth of language, is grounded in reciprocal reflexivity: when children find themselves responding to their incipient acts in the attitude of another and others do the same, then the gestures are functioning as symbols to the children in the control of their activity. The symbolic function requires that the child develop a concept of the relationship between a distinct self and another, because taking the attitude or role of another into the meaning of one's own communicative behavior involves a reference to the self. Consequently, the process of becoming a culturally individuated person is an essential aspect of the development of language. The self develops as a complex sign representing both *I* as agent-doer and *me* as agent-representative,[2] as giver and receiver, as willful and cooperative. The linking of self, other, and object which this development makes possible, in conjunction with the linking of meaning to speech, leads to the transformation of referential communication into language.

There are many parallels between Mead's analysis of sign functions and Vygotsky's description of the development of language. They both stress the transformation from interpersonal or social sources of development to intrapersonal processes. According to Vygotsky:

> *An operation that initially represents an external activity is reconstructed and begins to occur internally....* Every function in the child's cultural development appears twice: first, on the social level, and later, on the individual level; first *between* people *(interpsychological),* and then *inside* the child *(intrapsychological).* This applies equally to voluntary attention, to logical memory, and to the formation of concepts. All the higher functions originate as actual relations between human individuals. (1978, pp. 56–57)

Although Vygotsky highlighted the social sources of psychological processes, he also stressed that the reconstruction of interpersonal into intrapersonal functions is

---

[2]The term *agent-representative* calls attention to the social-behavioral use of *agent* rather than the solely performative use of *agent* in the linguistic literature. "What turns out to be crucial in this connection of person with agent is the representative character of relationships designated as personal" (Rucker, 1980, p. 107).

not simply a linear transition. The reconstruction occurs as part of an ongoing dialectic, in which the unification of diverse lines of development results in a transformation of the original processes. "At a certain moment at about the age of two the curves of development of thought and speech, till then separate, meet and join to initiate a new form of behavior" (Vygotsky, 1962, p. 43). At the point where two different processes are linked together, the communicative and cognitive possibilities of language are deepened (Bronckart & Ventouras-Spycher, 1979). An earlier example is the linkage of sound to gesture in infancy; while the former serves primarily expressive functions, gestures acquire important sign functions as described above. But gestures require that communicative exchanges take place in face-to-face situations, while vocalizations are not spatially restrictive.

The full use of language brings about the decontextualization of communicative exchanges; the generalizations necessary in the construction of word meanings allow the child to overcome the limitations of gesture. The trajectory that leads from protolanguage to the fully developed use of language requires that the conceptual and communicative achievements of the young child be linked to linguistic input. "In an effort to adapt to the world of linguistic communication, the child cognitively reorganizes these conceptual and communicative inputs into a grammar, with the aid of a purely linguistic input" (Dore, 1978, p. 88).

The importance of linguistic input was neglected in earlier theories. But recent research (Nelson, 1978; Snow & Ferguson, 1977) has established that the role of adult language input is critical in bringing about the expansion and transformation of communicatively and cognitively limited exchanges. It is in joint effort with adult speakers that young children actively forge the integration of these diverse lines of development. Although all speakers contribute to this integration, "children whose linguistic input comes primarily from adults (as opposed to peers and older children) are at an advantage in language learning" (Bates, Bretherton, Beeghly-Smith, & McNew, 1982, p. 48).

The adaptation of caretakers' speech to the psycholinguistic needs of young children is not the result of a consciously developed language teaching strategy. Rather, it results from the adults' attempts to maximize communicative effectiveness with linguistically immature children. "What adults are chiefly trying to do, when they use BT [baby talk] with children is to communicate, to understand and be understood, to keep two minds focussed on the same topic" (Brown, 1977, p. 12). These early conversations exhibit a functional continuity with the conversations of gestures prevalent during the prelinguistic phases of development. Adults who are effective in tailoring their language to the communicative requirements of their young interlocutors are continuing an approach first used with infants. For example, toward the end of their first year, infants whose varied patterns of crying have been responded to differentially by caretakers cry less and vocalize more than do infants not so sensitively attended (Ainsworth & Bell, 1974). Similarly, children engaged in well-modulated verbal exchanges with adults reveal accelerated development in their speech.

When children begin speaking in holophrases—combining these with actions, gestures, and the use of nonverbal context to signal their intentions—caretakers change their mode of addressing them. They speak to them in a higher pitch, use more whispering, and lengthen the duration of verbs as part of the prosodic style of their baby talk (Garnica, 1977). Processes of *simplification* (at the phonological, grammatical, and syntactic level), *clarification* (such as lengthening of word segments, repetition of words and phrases), as well as *expressive* and *identifying* processes (the use of diminutive suffixes, softening of consonants, and sharpening of vowels), are among the baby-talk features Ferguson (1977) identified in a variety of languages throughout the world.

It has been found that both the quantity of adult input as well as some specific discourse features of "motherese" contribute to the rate and breadth of children's language development. In research with rapidly developing speakers Cross (1977) reported that maternal discourse adjustments were highly correlated with children's receptiveness scores, a measure of the "child's ability to process and decode sentences" (p. 157). Mothers whose children acquired language rapidly paid close attention to possible misunderstandings in their exchanges. While their children were still verbally immature, these mothers used repetition and expansion of their children's utterances, a strategy which Newport, Gleitman, and Gleitman (1977) found to be "positively correlated with every measure of child sophistication" (p. 129). The children's concerns frequently governed exchanges at this stage: Cross (1977) found that 55% of the mothers' utterances were semantically linked to the children's topics of conversation. In the presence of more linguistically developed children, these mothers produced semantically novel utterances.

Maternal input studies show less evidence for direct effects of syntactic modeling in baby talk. Although Newport and her colleagues (1977) reported significant correlation between questions used by mothers (e.g., "Are you getting hungry?") and the use of such forms by children in later sessions, they found no such correlations for the use of complex sentences or other indexes of grammatical development. In a carefully designed intervention study, Nelson (1977) did obtain more positive results for the modeling of complex questions and verb forms.

Some critics of sociogenetic theories of language have claimed that the paucity of specific effects of maternal input on children's syntactic development undermines the explanatory power of such theories. After reviewing the literature, Bates and her co-workers (1982) concluded that a cognitive-causal theory had greater empirical support than theories that stressed the social sources of language development. However, their analysis is limited by a narrow interpretation of social sources, the causal effects of which they equate with varying rates of development. Vygotsky (1962) raised a similar issue in his criticism of Stern's personalistic theory of language development:

> Stern does say quite emphatically, it is true, that social environment is the main factor in speech development, but in reality he limits its role to merely accelerating or slowing down the development, which obeys its own immanent laws. (p. 31)

The fundamental weakness of such a limited perspective is that it considers cognitive and social processes to be separate or parallel phenomena with respect to language. Thus the mode of explanation used looks for statistically measurable influences of one on the other, a position which assumes that the processes are not integrated in the course of development. The difficulty which researchers have had in finding linear influences may provide evidence for the insufficiency of parallelistic accounts, but it does not diminish the credibility of an interactionist model. The strength of an interactionist perspective is that it focuses on the unification and transformation of cognitive and social processes, which requires that the development of language be examined in the context of an organized system of interactive relations (see assumption 2). The relations of particular significance to the development of language are those formed by the unification of cultural, communicative, cognitive, and linguistic processes. The joining of these lines of development arises from the dependence relation as an active process, in which both child and caretaker participate in the scaffolding of knowledge necessary for the child's movement from dependence toward competence and independence.

4. *A requisite for the adequate account of language development is a unification in analysis of social, cultural processes and conditions with cognitive, psychological processes and conditions. The unification of these diverse lines of development in children is not simply additive. It entails the transformation of these processes and of both overt and covert language. In an interactionist model, it is assumed that the ontogenetic development of language evolves from the interwoven unification of nature and culture.*

Language Transformations and Writing

As children master the complex forms of adult language—following the initial interweaving of the communicative, cognitive, and linguistic lines of development— an important cognitive transformation takes place as "thought becomes verbal and speech rational" (Vygotsky, 1962, p. 44). During the course of further development, speech for the self is progressively differentiated from speech for others. In the late twenties, Piaget described "egocentric speech" while observing children at play. Vygotsky subsequently delineated the role of this form of speech in the critical transition from interpsychological to intrapsychological functioning, from overt language to the inner use of language in thought (1962).

The interest in private speech (a term which is less ambiguous than egocentric speech) has grown in the last decade. American researchers have extended the work of Vygotsky's Soviet students Luria, Levina, and Gal'perin. They have examined the regulatory role of private speech during motor activities as well as during problem solving and exploratory play. Private speech does not have a unitary function: it serves both cognitive and affective purposes. As observed by psychologists, its functional categories include children's word play and repetitions, remarks to nonhuman subjects, descriptions of one's own activities, self-guiding comments, and expressions of relief and pleasure, such as "I did it" (Zivin, 1979).

During the early phases of reliance on private speech, children do not differentiate between the overt and covert forms of this language function. Some researchers assume that inner speech is substantially the same in form and function as external speech. The internalization of speech for the self was described by Vygotsky as a series of stages in a transformation leading to the "ingrowth" stage when "the external operation turns inward and undergoes a profound change in the process" (1962, p. 47). One of the characteristics of this internal process is its condensed and predicative nature. Vygotsky's description of private speech as predicative has been related by Wertsch (1979) to Chafe's distinction between given and new information. Wertsch and Stone (1980) further analyzed the developmental progression leading from overt expression to internal representation. They suggested that the crucial link between external and internal activities resides in semiotic processes: "When a child comes to understand and master the significance (i.e., meaning or sense) of a sign form, there is often no need to invoke an additional process of moving underground" (p. 37). Their description of the role of sign functions in internalization is similar to the one proposed in this account, which views semiotic activities as central to intellectual development.

5. *The internalization of the culturally prevalent semiotic system links human cognitive and linguistic development to its interpersonal sources. The consequences of this internalization process are enculturation on the one hand and access to the means of individuation on the other. These dual developments give rise to the symbolic functions required for higher mental processes. From the correlative process of externalization emerge novel meanings and the sharing of these personal achievements with others in one's collectivity.*

In the following discussion of internalization and externalization, we will focus on language and literacy, on the back and forth movements between internal representation and external codes. The research on writing conducted by Elsasser and John-Steiner (1977) is based on the description of language codes provided by Vygotsky:

> There are other important functional distinctions in speech. One of them is the distinction between dialogue and monologue. Written and inner speech represent the monologue; oral speech, in most cases, the dialogue. Dialogue always presupposes in the partners sufficient knowledge of the subject to permit abbreviated speech. . . . It also presupposes that each person can see his partners, their facial expressions and gestures, and hear the tone of their voices. . . . In written speech, lacking situational and expressive supports, communication must be achieved only through words and their combinations; this requires the speech activity to take complicated forms—hence the use of first drafts. The evolution from the draft to the final copy reflects our mental processes. (1962, pp. 142–144)

In general, individuals do not keep a copy of their first drafts. Thus it is difficult to document the mental processes involved in extending the semantic shorthand of inner speech into effective writing. But in the notebooks and journals of writers, one occasionally encounters samples of inner-speech writing. These condensed notes exemplify the usually covert processes which precede the externalization of novel meanings. Such a writing for the self is found in Virginia Woolf's *A Writer's Diary* (1953). When she was working on her biography of Roger Fry, she wrote a telegraphic outline of her next chapter:

> Suppose I make a break after H.'s death (madness). A separate paragraph quoting what R. himself said. Then a break. Then begin definitely with the first meeting. That is the first impression: a man of the world, not professor or Bohemian. . . .
> The first 1910 show. . . .
> Give the pre-war atmosphere. Ott. Duncan. France. Letter to Bridges about beauty and sensuality. His exactingness. Logic. (pp. 292–293)

The meaning of this entry is accessible only through the finished biography, in which these telegraphic thoughts are expanded, connected, and crafted into a clearly formulated text (John-Steiner, 1983).

For many writers, inner-speech writing has the function of planning, of moving rapidly ahead while exploring the connections among a complex of thoughts which may be lost without the permanence of written form (Smith, 1977). In utilizing this function of inner speech, the writer, turned inward toward thought, is not attempting to communicate with others, but to discover.

The movements from thought to text require transformations which are frequently unrealized in the work of inexperienced writers. They are not able to transform their semantically condensed inner thoughts into a communicatively effective external code. They frequently construct their writing in the open-ended fashion of conversation, assuming that their potential readers share their experience or point of view. In a recent study, Collins and Williamson (1981) used a Vygotskian perspective to focus on two features of students' writings: the prevalence of semantic abbreviations and the role of the audience. Writers whose compositions were part of a national assessment study differed with respect to these features. Those judged as strong writers decreased the use of condensed, inner-speech forms in their work from 4th to 8th grade. The weak writers produced a higher percentage of semantic abbreviations in all grades, and did not show a decrease in this respect even at the 12th grade level. A sensitivity to audience requirements was revealed in the work of strong writers, whose compositions minimized the use of semantic abbreviations when their intended reader was an editor, while showing more of these forms when addressing a parent. These differentiations were absent in the compositions of students characterized as weak writers.

In our own studies of writing (Elsasser & John-Steiner, 1977), we have found that it is difficult for inexperienced adult writers to shift their perspective from an immediate audience, which shares the writers' experience and frame of reference, to an unfamiliar and abstract audience. It is even more difficult for such writers to unfold their compact inner speech into the detailed, sequenced, and expanded writing which effectively communicates with readers.

These findings deepen the realization of one of the themes in this account of the development of language, namely, that the full use of the symbolic function, and specifically of the varied codes of human language, cannot be achieved without the internalization of a concept of the self in relation to others. Lacking such a conceptual understanding of one's audience and of the dynamic and developmental relations which govern one's interactions, language remains an external medium of communication instead of becoming a controlled system of reflexive, cognitive, and communicative means.

Conclusion

We have stated the case for the emergence of a new paradigm of language development, a paradigm that is the logical outcome of recent studies of maternal input language and of the delineation of previously neglected cognitive, semantic, functional, and pragmatic aspects of language. Bruner has played a central role in both shaping and documenting this contemporary view which followed the "*productively* wrong and enormously fruitful" nativist model (1978b, p. 245). There have been a variety of characterizations of this model. Bruner wrote of a transactional model while Bates referred to it as the social bases of language approach.

The choice of *interactionist* as a label for this paradigm is governed by the historical status of the interactive stance in the social sciences. Nevertheless, it is clear to us that this term presents some difficulties because it confounds two different levels of analysis. At one level, an interactionist model refers to the role of interactions in the development of language. It is in this way that Berko-Gleason and Weintraub (1978) used the term when they wrote:

> The acquisition of communicative competence can be seen *as a product of the child's active participation in interaction with the environment,* rather than as the unfolding of preprogrammed behavior. In this case, the environment is totally provided by other human beings, who are themselves tuned to the linguistic needs of the child and whose speech is characterized by special features that mesh with those needs. (p. 214, emphasis added)

In a broader philosophical and psychological context, *interactionist* refers to the unification of nature and culture in the course of ontogenetic development, as conceptualized in the theories of Mead and Vygotsky. This unified sense of interaction provides the basis for a powerful model of language development. While the implications of this emerging model have been used in research to substantially explore the early phases of language development, the later phases, such as the mastery of writing, have yet to be examined in depth.

References

Ainsworth, M. D., & Bell, S. M. Mother-infant interaction and the development of competence. In K. Connolly & J. S. Bruner (Eds.), *The growth of competence.* New York: Academic Press, 1974.

Bates, E. *Language and context: The acquisition of pragmatics.* New York: Academic Press, 1976.

Bates, E., Bretherton, I., Beeghly-Smith, M., & McNew, S. Social bases of language development. In H. W. Reese & L. P. Lipsitt (Eds.), *Advances in child development and behavior* (Vol. 16). New York: Academic Press, 1982.

Berko-Gleason, J., & Weintraub, S. Input language and the acquisition of communicative competence. In K. E. Nelson (Ed.), *Children's language* (Vol. 1). New York: Gardner Press, 1978.

Bloom, L. *Language development: Form and function in emerging grammars.* Cambridge, Mass.: MIT Press, 1970.

Bronckart, J., & Ventouras-Spycher, M. The Piagetian concept of representation and the Soviet-inspired view of self-regulation. In G. Zivin (Ed.), *The development of self-regulation through private speech.* New York: Wiley, 1979.

Brown, R. *A first language: The early stages.* Cambridge, Mass.: Harvard University Press, 1973.

Brown, R. Introduction. In C. E. Snow & C. A. Ferguson (Eds.), *Talking to children.* London: Cambridge University Press, 1977.

Brown, R., & Fraser, C. The acquisition of syntax. In U. Bellugi & R. Brown (Eds.), The acquisition of language. *Monographs of the Society for Research in Child Development, 1964, 29* (Serial 92), 43–79.

Bruner, J. S. From communication to language: A psychological perspective. In I. Marková (Ed.), *The social context of language.* New York: Wiley, 1978, pp. 17–48. (a)

Bruner, J. S. The role of dialogue in language acquisition. In A. Sinclair, R. J. Jarvella, & W. J. M. Levelt (Eds.), *The child's conception of language*. New York: Springer-Verlag, 1978, pp. 241–256. (b)

Bruner, J. S., & Sherwood, V. Early rule structure: The case of peekaboo. In J. S. Bruner, A. Jolly, & K. Sylva (Eds.), *Play: Its role in development and evolution*. New York: Basic Books, 1976.

Chomsky, N. *Syntactic structures*. The Hague: Mouton, 1957.

Clark, R. A. The transition from action to gesture. In A. Lock (Ed.), *Action, gesture and symbol: The emergence of language*. London: Academic Press, 1978, pp. 231–257.

Collins, J. L., & Williamson, M. Spoken language and semantic abbreviation in writing. *Research in the Teaching of English*, 1981, *15* (23).

Cross, T. G. Mother's speech: The role of child listener variables. In C. E. Snow & C. A. Ferguson (Eds.), *Talking to children*. London: Cambridge University Press, 1977, pp. 151–188.

Dewey, J. *Experience and nature* (2nd ed.). LaSalle, Ill.: Open Court, 1929.

Dewey, J. *Logic: The theory of inquiry*. New York: Holt, Rinehart, 1938.

Dore, J. Conditions for the acquisition of speech acts. In I. Markova (Ed.), *The social context of language*. New York: Wiley, 1978, pp. 87–111.

Eisenberg, L. The 'human' nature of human nature. *Science*, 1972, *176*, 123–128.

Elsasser, N., & John-Steiner, V. An interactionist approach to advancing literacy. *Harvard Educational Review*, 1977, *47*, 355–369.

Ferguson, C. A. Baby talk as a simplified register. In C. E. Snow & C. A. Ferguson (Eds.), *Talking to children*. London: Cambridge University Press, 1977.

Garnica, O. K. Some prosodic and paralinguistic features of speech to young children. In C. E. Snow & C. A. Ferguson (Eds.), *Talking to children*. London: Cambridge University Press, 1977.

Halliday, M. A. K. *Learning how to mean: Explorations in the development of language*. New York: Elsevier, 1975.

Halliday, M. A. K. *Language as social semiotic: The social interpretation of language and meaning*. London: Edward Arnold, 1978.

John-Steiner, V. *Notebooks of the mind*. Albuquerque, N.M.: University of New Mexico Press, 1983.

Kernan, K. T. *The acquisition of language by Samoan children*. Unpublished doctoral dissertation, University of California, Berkeley, 1969.

McCarthy, D. Language development in children. In L. Carmichael (Ed.), *Manual of child psychology* (2nd ed.). New York: Wiley, 1954.

McNeill, D. The development of language. In P. H. Mussen (Ed.), *Carmichael's manual of child psychology* (3rd ed.). New York: Wiley, 1970.

Mead, G. H. *Mind, self, and society* (C. W. Morris, Ed.). Chicago: University of Chicago Press, 1934.

Mead, G. H. *The philosophy of the act* (C. W. Morris, Ed.). Chicago: University of Chicago Press, 1938.

Mead, G. H. *Selected writings* (A. J. Reck, Ed.). Indianapolis: Bobbs-Merrill, 1964.

Nelson, K. E. Facilitating children's syntax acquisition. *Developmental Psychology*, 1977, *13*, 101–107.

Nelson, K. E. (Ed.). *Children's language* (Vol. 1). New York: Gardner Press, 1978.

Newport, E. Motherese: The speech of mothers to young children. In N. Castellan, D. Pisoni, & G. Potts (Eds.), *Cognitive theory* (Vol. 2). Hillsdale, N.J.: Lawrence Erlbaum, 1976.

Newport E., Gleitman, L., & Gleitman, H. Mother I'd rather do it myself: Some effects and non-effects of motherese. In C. E. Snow & C. A. Ferguson (Eds.), *Talking to children: Language input and acquisition*. London: Cambridge University Press, 1977, pp. 109–149.

Newson, J. Dialogue and development. In A. Lock (Ed.), *Action, gesture and symbol: The emergence of language*. London: Academic Press, 1978, pp. 31–42.

Peirce, C. S. Principles of philosophy. In C. Hartshorne & P. Weiss (Eds.), *Collected papers of C. S. Peirce* (Vol. 1). Cambridge, Mass.: Harvard University Press, 1931.

Peirce, C. S. Elements of logic. In C. Hartshorne & P. Weiss (Eds.), *Collected papers of C. S. Peirce* (Vol. 2). Cambridge, Mass.: Harvard University Press, 1932.

Peirce, C. S. Pragmatism and pragmaticism. In C. Hartshorne & P. Weiss (Eds.), *Collected papers of C. S. Peirce* (Vol. 5). Cambridge, Mass.: Harvard University Press, 1934.

Rosenblatt, J. S. The basis of synchrony in the behavioral interaction between the mother and her offspring in the laboratory rat. In B. M. Foss (Ed.), *Determinants of infant behavior* (Vol. 1). New York: Wiley, 1965, pp. 3–45.

Rucker, D. Selves into persons: Another legacy from John Dewey. *Rice University Studies, 1980, 66,* 103–118.

Salzinger, K. The problem of response class in verbal behavior. In K. Salzinger & S. Salzinger (Eds.), *Verbal behavior and some neurophysiological implications.* New York: Academic Press, 1967.

Shotter, J. The cultural context of communication studies: Theoretical and methodological issues. In A. Lock (Ed.), *Action, gesture and symbol: The emergence of language.* London: Academic Press, 1978, pp. 43–78.

Slobin, D. I. (Ed.). *A field manual for cross-cultural study of the acquisition of communicative competence.* Unpublished manuscript, University of California, Berkeley, 1967.

Smith, F. The uses of language. *Language Arts, 1977, 54,* 638–644.

Snow, C. E., & Ferguson, C. A. (Eds.). *Talking to children: Language input and acquisition.* London: Cambridge University Press, 1977.

Toulmin, S. The Mozart of psychology. *New York Review of Books, 1978, 25*(14), 51–57.

Trevarthen, C., & Hubley, P. Secondary intersubjectivity: Confidence, confiding and acts of meaning in the first year. In A. Lock (Ed.), *Action, gesture and symbol: The emergence of language.* London: Academic Press, 1978, pp. 183–229.

Vygotsky, L. S. *Thought and language* (E. Hanfmann & G. Vakar, Eds.). Cambridge, Mass.: MIT Press, 1962.

Vygotsky, L. S. *Mind in society: The development of higher psychological processes* (M. Cole, V. John-Steiner, S. Scribner, & E. Souberman, Eds.). Cambridge, Mass.: Harvard University Press, 1978.

Wertsch, J. V. The regulation of human action and the given-new organization of private speech. In G. Zivin (Ed.), *The development of self-regulation through private speech.* New York: Wiley, 1979, pp. 79–98.

Wertsch, J. V., & Stone, C. A. The concept of internalization in Vygotsky's account of the genesis of higher mental functions. Paper presented at the conference *Culture, communication, and cognition: Vygotskian perspectives,* Center for Psychosocial Studies, Chicago, October 1980.

Woolf, V. *A writer's diary* (L. Woolf, Ed.). New York: Harcourt Brace Jovanovich, 1953.

Zivin, G. (Ed.). *The development of self-regulation through private speech.* New York: Wiley, 1979.

6

Language and Alienation

Adrienne Harris

Introduction

The claim I will examine here is that the capacity to participate in the speech community, constituted first as the family, then as the school, and finally as the larger culture, is the outcome of a social process. *Language learning is the by-product of entering and altering the ensemble of social relations.* If we are to treat the development of language activity—and in particular language knowledge—as the product of the social and historical context, we must swim upstream against the dominant views of contemporary psychology and contemporary psycholinguistics (cf. Dittmar, this volume).

In this chapter I will outline both some aspects and some problems of the sociogenetic approach to language development, considering both phylogenetic and ontogenetic transformations. The perspective I speak from is that of dialectical psychology, with lines of influence from Hegel and from Marx, and within psychology from Baldwin (1897), Piaget (1963), Vygotsky (1962), and Mead (1934). Dialectics as a method and as a theoretical approach has a long history in the social sciences (Horkheimer, 1972; Wozniak, 1973; cf. Okun, Fisk, & Brandt, this volume). What is entailed in this approach for psychology and for the psychology of language development can be briefly summarized.

Dialectics

Dialectical psychology's key feature is reflectivity (Riegel, 1975, 1976). It is a dual and somewhat contradictory approach to studying social phenomena. This approach requires an assumption that the domain of the "psychological" is both real

Adrienne Harris ● Psychology Department, Newark College of Arts and Sciences, Rutgers—The State University of New Jersey, Newark, New Jersey 07102.

and illusory. It assumes real subjective experience, historically and socially determined and susceptible to analysis, reflection, and interpretation. The approach to
language and thinking developed most fruitfully by Vygotsky (1962), by Luria
(1961, 1967), and by the British linguist Halliday (1975) typifies dialectical theory.
The origins of the individual's power over language (in planning, in representation,
and in communication) lie in social dialogue and in the historically mediated and
class-specific understanding of what speech activity constitutes and intends.

Additionally, dialectical psychology entails a critique of psychology as ideology
(Buss, 1975). It is thus not merely an approach to understanding social and psychological phenomena but also an approach to systems of scientific understanding and
their production. Dialectics in this way is self-reflective. There are two actions in this
critical work. First, we can analyze the degree to which psychological theory and
practice function as apparatuses of the dominant ideology, presenting special interests as universal, transhistorical and objective (Mannheim, 1936). Second, we see
that in modern mass culture, psychological knowledge is itself a feature of the massive "disinformation" which enters, constructs, and potentially distorts consciousness.
In a doubling mirroring function, psychology as a scientific discipline mystifies the
degree to which individual consciousness is a social construction and at the same time
becomes part of the internalized self-knowledge by which we interpret ourselves and
others.

This contradictory duality is exquisitely captured in psychology's analysis of
speech activity and language development. Linguistic signs are social signifiers. They
are ambiguous, equivocal in meaning, representing subjective experience *in* socially
derived symbols. Volosinov (1973) continues:

> Ideology may not be divorced from the material reality of sign. . . . The sign
> may not be divorced from the concrete forms of social intercourse. . . . Com-
> munication and the forms of communication may not be divorced from the
> material base. (p. 21)

Speech activity, then, utilizes material that is always social and ideological.

A dialectical analysis of the development of speech and language knowledge
must thus consider how individuals extract meaning and competence from social discourse. Simultaneously, we understand that the internalizing of the word gives power
to the user and at the same time constitutes a mechanism whereby the state and the
dominant culture maintain certain kinds of controls over the individual (cf. Phillips;
Kvale, this volume). Speech is the agency both for socialization and for resistance.
We may illuminate this point by considering the paradox embedded in Luria's model
for verbal regulation (Luria, 1961).

The capacity to plan, to inhibit, and to program one's own actions, that is, to
control oneself, comes with the internalization of the processes of social exchange
whereby the parent exerts power over a child's action. It is an internalized power
relation. However, the capacity to plan cannot be extracted from the content and
dynamic of the controls. One's relationship to words and to their control function and
one's belief in the instructive and planning capabilities of words are factors that
affect self-regulation. Instructions for behavior are often coded for gender, for class,
for ethnicity. The force of state control, cultural control, or, more immediately, family control is masked in the misnaming of social control as self-regulation.

Sociogenesis

In outlining a sociogenetic theory of language acquisition we must first locate the study of child language in the framework of contemporary psycholinguistics, examining the theoretical soil in which any new model must be planted. There is a strong tropism in psychology toward focus on the individual, on monads, atomized traits, and abstracted skills. Currently, developmental psychology and developmental psycholinguistics betray an additional tropism toward the biologic and the rational. This conceptually inconsistent situation bears elucidation.

Current studies of the development of communicative competence are strongly influenced by models from ethology (Stern, 1977), by a rather biologically flavored form of systems theory (Brazelton, 1974; Lewis & Rosenblum, 1974), and by a marked tendency to present reciprocal interactions of mother and child as organic, innately rooted, and unmodulated by learning (Brazelton, 1974). In this respect, psychology functions to transform the social into the biological. Interaction is treated as a form of natural mutual conditioning. This approach entails an odd mixture of mechanical and organic modeling. The infant in the social dyad of mother and child is characterized as the controller, a participant in feedback systems and reciprocal regulation. Infant mind, in particular where language knowledge is considered, is seen as rational, technological (infant as information processor), goal oriented, and hierarchical. Considering both the waves of theoretical writing in linguistics and the influences from ethology, it is apparent that there is a strong tendency in psychology toward what can be called the "rationalization of infancy."

The post-Chomskian developments in child language study have never fully recovered from the thoroughgoing commitment Chomsky's theory makes to rationalism, to innate ideas, and to the characterization of language knowledge as hierarchical structures (Chomsky, 1965, 1968, 1975). The very first models of child language were pursuant to Chomsky's own earliest project: to design a grammar which could decode sentences without recourse to meaning or context (Chomsky, 1957). In what was a logical extension of his views on the cognitive apparatus necessary for grammatical knowledge, early child language studies viewed such knowledge as essentially unlearned (McNeill, 1970). Much ground has been covered since then. Semantic structures increasingly play a central role. The psychological reality of and even the formal necessity for deep structure are seriously queried (McCawley, 1968). More recently the impact of context on speech activity (cf. Cazden, this volume) and an interest in dialogue (Harris, 1975; Schaeffer, 1979), in motherese (Snow & Ferguson, 1977), and in the properties of discourse have served to socialize child language study.

Another key development has been the adoption of pragmatics as a new source for model building (Bates, 1976; Dore, 1977). Regardless of the linguistic paradigm, the strategy is still to take structural models as the format or description of knowledge internalized by the child. Interpretation is used primarily as a disambiguating device (both intuitively by the parent and more formally by the observing linguist) to clarify infant intention. Sentence meaning and language knowledge are still seen as individual property.

Developmental psycholinguists, using speech act theory or some variant of pragmatics, focus on the dual level in language activity. Intentions to express something are conceptually distinct from realization rules and procedures for expression. Searle's (1969) influential essay on speech act theory raises important questions regarding the application of this perspective to mother–child dialogues. There are two conceptual distinctions to bear in mind. First, we can distinguish between the intention to mean and the effect of the utterance on the listener. This distinction may be crucial in considering infant utterances to mother. Second, we can distinguish between the intention to mean and the realization of an expression. As we will see later, it is into these gaps between intention and realization that certain promising psychoanalytic work has been directed. It is also important to note that Searle is describing idealized communication in which comprehension and interpretation are achieved intersubjectively in a situation in which all participants in discourse share meaning systems, interpretive strategies, and conditions of input and output. These conditions clearly do not fully hold in dialogues between parent and language-learning child. Intention to mean and realization rules may have a somewhat imperfect fit in all real life speakers. Certainly this is likely to be profoundly so in the case of the young child. To think otherwise is to opt for innate language rules and grammar as a feature of infant mind.

What is missing from the application of pragmatics to child language learning is an understanding of the situation which would render it fully social and interactive. We would also miss the view of the child, articulated in psychoanalytic theory, in which early thought and early interpersonal attributions are conceived of as more unconscious, inchoate, and undifferentiated. The connection between intention and realization is both a process of elaboration (in the sense that Vygotsky has outlined the mutual interdependence of thinking and speaking) and a process of distortion and alienation. What is required is an analysis of the mother–child dyad in terms of power dynamics. Meaning and the ascription of intention or decoding are built up over dialogue. They are negotiated and understood intersubjectively in a relationship in which the adult (usually mother) holds particular and complex forms of power.

Bridging the Gaps

There is a connection between pragmatic theories of language and object relations theory which may illuminate our understanding of the development of dialogue between parent and child. Pragmatic theory, as Peirce (1955) initially and Habermas (1976) more recently noted, depends on a triadic system of meaning in which intention of the speaker, interpretation of the listener, and realized speech act are involved. To engage in discourse (leaving aside the thorny problems of obfuscation and deception) entails at least some rough equivalence of meaning systems among participants and some rough (if not fully conscious) acceptance of the validity claims raised by each utterance. In human interactional terms, this system of communicated understandings capitalizes on primary modes of interaction and perception: projection, introjection, and the implicated mechanism of identification. In psychotherapy, the transference phenomenon (the tendency to hear and understand the therapist as some residue or stand-in for an early parental imago) is but a special case of the language user's tendency to make attributions and identification in speech dialogue.

Interpretation is thus hinged to mutual recognition and identification (cf. Stein, this volume). In mother–child dialogue we see differing developmental levels and differing processes of attachment and attribution which may all affect the negotiation of meaning. Above all we note the differing levels of social and linguistic power.

The full application of speech act models and pragmatics to child language study will require an abandonment of the systems theory approach which describes a sort of pseudomutuality and thereby disguises the real social actors in the communicative matrix within families. The child's meaning for the mother, which may well have gender specific and class specific implications; the mother's theory of how and why her child will speak and what will or should be talked about; and the family's pattern of communication must all be considered. Paradoxically (and ironically) the mother operates as one of the agents of distortion in her child's socialization into the symbol-using community. Mother's organization of the child's communications into particular meanings, that is, her control over the conversational negotiations, is one aspect of the restructuring of desire into need (in the Lacanian sense) and the introduction of the child into the social semiotic (in Halliday's sense).

Phylogenesis

In reflecting on a social and materialist model for language development, we may look to research and theory in language evolution. Research on individual transformation and on phylogenetic change in the domain of language has been subject to much cross-fertilization and mutual influence. Vygotsky's work on the evolution of word meaning is perhaps the contemporary benchmark.

One important line of evidence comes from the orchestration of information from anthropology, fossil remains, and developmental neurophysiology. Speculations tie symbolic behavior to material transformation in brain function, in hand usage, in tool development, and in social structuring necessary or compatible with systematic changes in food-gathering techniques. Although this analysis is primarily ingenious speculation and manifests a somewhat mechanical materialism, it may offer important insights for understanding speech activity in early development.

The question of how language abilities interweave with and are dependent on social praxis, labor, and evolutionary pressures is a difficult one. Can we combine evolutionary theory, an understanding of adaptation and natural selection, with a dialectical understanding of the reciprocal impact of individual, social, and biological functioning? One strategy has been to tie language to action and labor, that is, to speculate on the processes which might have to underlie the capacity to work and thence to speak. Some features of memory, some capacity to anticipate, and a level of mental representation would seem the necessary prerequisites for the capacity to imagine the structuring of an activity over time in order to produce some object, that is, to work. To the degree that labor is social, some degree of communication must arise to sustain and coordinate collective work (cf. Montagu, this volume). Recently, Parker and Gibson (1979) generated an extensive discussion of the cognitive underpinnings for language skill in which certain labor (in particular agricultural and food gathering) was considered crucial. Memory and some topographic representation (essential for planting, storing, and extracting food) are implicated. In addition, play and playful symbolizing are proposed as essential for the transmission of technique and work skill between generations.

In addition to social and historical features attendant on language development, there is an extensive literature on biological correlates for language (Lenneberg, 1967, 1975). Morphological changes in the peripheral musculature, changes in the construction of the vocal chords and jaw, and increase in areas of the cortex committed to language-related motor processes have all been documented (Lenneberg, 1967). Language skills are also implicated in ways not yet well understood with the evolution of a time sharing system and some pacing mechanisms. Speech and various metabolic processes must smoothly utilize the same system—breathing.

These mechanical and physiological conditions are assumed to be important and effective in both central nervous system functioning and motor coordination involved in high speed production of articulated speech. Lieberman (1975) has analyzed fossil remains of prehominids to suggest the evolutionary point at which complexity of the peripheral structure would permit the set of distinctive sounds which make up human phonological systems.

All this work, whether speculative reconstruction or empirical analysis, describes the mechanical preconditions for the human capacity to reproduce language on the sound stream and to use such a system in communication or in representation.

An additional piece of the evolutionary puzzle is lateralization. Kinsbourne (1978) has speculated on a connection among attentional processes, handedness, and lateralization. In his argument, lateralization is viewed as a genetically controlled trait observable prenatally and at birth. Infants systematically demonstrate a preference for right orientation. Lateralization thus preconditions infants to orient asymmetrically. For right handers, that orientation is to the right in accompaniment with right hand dominance in gross and fine motor skills. The right hand then becomes the primary instrument whereby the child selects, points to, and alters objects. Attentional mechanisms also direct the child to objects in the right visual field. The hand is thus the body part most intricately bound with tool use and communication. Referring, a linguistic activity as well as an action, thus occurs through the use of the right hand which points, gestures, selects, and draws attention.

Cradled by the prior conditions of functional cortical asymmetry, there is hypothesized both a structural and functional overlay of hand and voice usage. Language activities thus arise in support of, as an extension of, and in concert with tool use and thus with social functions. This view is close to the perspective on speech developed by Grace de Laguna (1963) and by the anthropologist Gordon Hewes (1973a,b), as well as that developed by Vygotsky (cf. Wertsch, this volume).

Ontogenesis

Developmental data are supportive here in that early preverbal communication seems to be built around an intricate and ingenious combination of sounds, gestures, and actions which carry increasingly complex meaning. This view of language development (one taken by Halliday and the pragmatist language philosophers) assumes a tight developmental progression from action to sound to symbol (and supportive grammatical structure).

Werner and Kaplan (1963) and, more recently, Sigel and Cocking (1979) have developed an analysis of the development of symbol capacity through which we could argue the primacy of language over work. In their discussions of the concept of "distancing" they alert us to one of the most extraordinary aspects of symbolic behavior, that is, its impact on our experience of the external world.

The ability to use a sound that exists in abstract relationship to the object signified and to use that sound consciously in reference to some aspect of the external world is not only an exteriorization of subjectivity but simultaneously a transformation of that subjectivity and a transformation of the phenomenally experienced world. The speaker changes his relationship to nature when he can name it. Symbolizing, which reaches its most highly evolved form in human speech, is an aspect of the separation of man from nature and a potential avenue for our interaction with and transformation of nature. In that act, man is also transformed. Symbol making puts man in a relationship to the external world such that transforming it through work is imaginable.

At this stage in our understanding we can identify the conditions within the individual implicated in speech and language. We can speculate on the social and material conditions in which coordinated production and communication would have a decided evolutionary advantage and we can see a process whereby individuals in interaction transform each other and, in acting on nature, transform it and themselves. We see also that the development of the capacity to work and to speak, although arising socially, has individual implications. Speech and symbolizing require a social situation for development (in both the phylogenetic and the ontogenetic sense). At the same time this capacity, internalized in the individual, becomes available for private play, for fantasy and creativity.

The functional connection between action and language is compatible with theories of individual development, in particular Piaget's. Piaget's work has been a source of influence on the comparative work that Parker and Gibson report and has itself been influenced by evolutionary theory. The child's representative capacities are built on sensorimotor schemes. In Piaget's theory (and in Chomskian psycholinguistics) language knowledge is modulated in an intricate process of assimilation and accommodation to an external language system. The social agent (i.e., mother) is considered an objective and detached interpretive guide.

Alienation

There is, however, a shadowed side to language. Symbolizing raises a multiplicity of meanings. "A symbol is a double meaning linguistic expression that requires an interpretation" (Ricoeur, 1970). Speech is often equivocal. Language and work may be mutually supportive but words and work can also be systems of social control. Language can mystify and distort as well as represent. *Language is at the service of relations of production and reproduction which also distort and alienate.*

It is interesting that developmental psycholinguistics has been influenced more by the rationalizing tendencies in linguistic theory than by ego development and the onset of symbolizing capacities. Psychoanalytic theory assumes a radical asynchrony. A vulnerable infant with underdeveloped and often undifferentiated motor capacities and with immature systems for sensory integration manifests nonetheless an acutely developed capacity to imagine and fantasize. The asynchrony becomes the precondition for terror, for the defensive fantasies required to ward off loss, for the splitting which protects against annihilating rage and the terror of being devoured (Klein, 1975; Klein & Riviere, 1964). A paradox explored most fully by Lacan (1968, 1978) is that the defensive action, insofar as it utilizes symbolizing functions and ultimately language, both represents and distorts (cf. Stein, this volume). Ego structuring, the development of personality which takes a crucial turn when the child enters—and is transformed by—the language community, is understood as a fundamental loss of subjectivity.

Conclusion

A sociogenetic account of language development will need to focus on the dialectical nonidentity between intention and subjectivity and on the socially constrained and socially constructed rules of discourse and language. Sensitivity to the development of consciousness and to the unformed, inchoate, undifferentiated nature of the child's earliest apperceptions will be an effective antidote to the excessive rationalizing characterizing child language studies.

One implication of this approach is the reconsideration of classic Marxist notions of alienation. Meszaros (1970) developed a distinction, which he found in Marxist and pre-Marxist thought, between primary and secondary alienation, the latter being the particular loss of products and labor power under certain conditions of production. These forms of alienation are, in theory, distinct from primary alienation, a construct roughly akin to Werner and Kaplan's notion of distancing, the capacity of the symbol to alter the symbol user's relationship to objects, to nature, and to himself/herself. This distinction collapses in the discovery that the symbol system which enables a changed relation to objects and to nature is not itself neutral and is decidedly not the product of free labor or free social relations.

The new member of any language community internalizes a preexisting social semiotic, a system of linguistic relations which expresses social relations, domination, and hierarchy. Indeed, although the initial language instructor is usually a woman, the language system also is an expression of patriarchy. The emancipating action of learning to speak is simultaneously imprisoning. The new social actor enters a system of words and work in which power and possibility have been constrained by conditions of class, race, gender, and (often) family pathology.

It is interesting to consider that in the concept of distancing we record the alienation of speaker from object and in the internalization of language and discourse competence we record the alienation from self and subjectivity.

In sketching a sociogenetic and dialectical approach to language evolution and language development, I have been exploring in part the difficulty in reconciling a materialist account of the process of language acquisition with a theoretical and scientific climate that is often at odds and sometimes frankly contradictory to this approach. A sociogenetic theory of language activity will tie speech and language to relations of production and of reproduction and to the process of social labor. Additionally, in focusing on the child's entrance into the speaking community we must, I believe, be particularly alert to the ideological claims which social science makes concerning this process. In this regard, I have tried to suggest that a closer reading of psychoanalytic literature, in particular the work on object relations and early ego development, may prove fruitful.

References

Baldwin, J. M. *Mental development in the child and in the race: Methods and processes.* New York: Macmillan, 1897.

Bates, E. *Language and context: The acquisition of pragmatics.* New York: Academic Press, 1976.

Brazelton, T. B. The origins of reciprocity: Early mother-infant interaction. In M. Lewis & L. Rosenblum (Eds.), *The effect of the infant on its caregiver: The origins of behavior* (Vol. 1). New York: Wiley, 1974.

Buss, A. The emerging field of the sociology of psychological knowledge. *American Psychologist,* 1975, *30,* 988–1002.

Chomsky, N. *Syntactic structures.* The Hague: Mouton, 1957.

Chomsky, N. *Aspects of a theory of syntax.* Cambridge, Mass.: MIT Press, 1965.

Chomsky, N. *Language and mind.* New York: Harcourt Brace, 1968.

Chomsky, N. *Reflections on language.* New York: Pantheon, 1975.

de Laguna, G. *Speech: Its function and development.* Bloomington, Ind.: Indiana University Press, 1963.

Dore, J. *The development of speech acts.* The Hague: Mouton, 1977.

Habermas, J. *Communication and the evolution of society.* Boston: Beacon Press, 1976.

Halliday, M. A. K. *Learning how to mean: Explorations in the development of language.* London: Arnold, 1975.

Harris, A. E. Social dialectics and language: Mother and child construct the discourse. *Human Development,* 1975, *18,* 80–96.

Hewes, G. Primate communication and the gestural origin of language. *Current Anthropology,* 1973, *14,* 5–24. (a)

Hewes, G. An explicit formulation of the relationship between tool using, tool making and the emergence of language. *Visible Language,* 1973, *7*(2), 101–127. (b)

Horkheimer, M. *Critical theory* (M. O'Connell *et al.,* trans.). New York: Herder & Herder, 1972.

Kinsbourne, M. (Ed.). *Asymmetrical functions of the brain.* Cambridge: Cambridge University Press, 1978.

Klein, M. *Envy and gratitude and other works.* New York: Delta, 1975.

Klein, M., & Riviere, J. *Love, hate and reparation.* New York: Norton, 1964.

Lacan, J. *The language of the self* (A. Wilden, trans.). Baltimore: Johns Hopkins Press, 1968.

Lacan, J. *The four fundamental concepts of psychoanalysis.* New York: Norton, 1978.

Lenneberg, E. *Biological foundations of language.* New York: Wiley, 1967.

Lenneberg, E., & Lenneberg, F. *Foundations of language development* (Vols. 1 & 2). New York: Academic Press, 1975.

Lewis, M., & Rosenblum, L. *The effect of the infant on its caregiver: The origins of behavior* (Vol. 1). New York: Wiley, 1974.

Lewis, M., & Rosenblum, L. *Interaction, conversation and the development of language.* New York: Wiley, 1977.

Lieberman, P. *On the origin of language.* New York: Macmillan, 1975.

Luria, A. R. *The role of speech in the regulation of normal and abnormal behavior*. New York: Liveright, 1961.

Luria, A. R. The regulative function of speech in its development and dissolution. In K. Salzinger & S. Salzinger (Eds.), *Research in verbal behavior and some neurological implications*. New York: Academic Press, 1967.

Mannheim, K. *Ideology and utopia*. London: Routledge and Kegan Paul, 1936.

McCawley, R. The role of semantics in a grammar. In E. Bach & R. Harms (Eds.), *Universals in linguistic theory*. New York: Holt, Rinehart & Winston, 1968.

McNeill, D. *The acquisition of language*. New York: Harper & Row, 1970.

Mead, G. H. *Mind, self and society*. Chicago: University of Chicago Press, 1934.

Meszaros, I. *Marx's theory of alienation*. London: Merlin Press, 1970.

Parker, S., & Gibson, K. A developmental model for the evolution of language and intelligence in early hominids. *Behavioral and Brain Sciences*, 1979, *2*, 367–408.

Peirce, C. S. *Philosophical writings of Peirce* (J. Buchler, Ed.). New York: Dover, 1955.

Piaget, J. *The origins of intelligence in children*. New York: Norton, 1963.

Ricoeur, P. *An essay on interpretation*. New Haven, Conn.: Yale University Press, 1970.

Riegel, K. F. (Ed.). The development of dialectical operations. *Human Development*, 1975, no. 18.

Riegel, K. F. The dialectics of human development. *American Psychologist*, 1976, *31*(10), 689–700.

Schaeffer, H. R. Acquiring the concept of the dialogue. In M. Bornstein & W. Kessen (Eds.), *Psychological development from infancy: Image to intention*. Hillsdale, N.J.: Erlbaum, 1979.

Searle, J. *Speech acts: An essay in the philosophy of language*. Cambridge: Cambridge University Press, 1969.

Sigel, I. E., & Cocking, R. Cognition and communication: A dialectical paradigm for development. In M. Lewis & L. Rosenblum (Eds.), *Communication and language: The origins of behavior* (Vol. 5). New York: Wiley, 1979.

Snow, C., & Ferguson, C. *Talking to children: Language input and acquisition*. Cambridge: Cambridge University Press, 1977.

Stern, D. *The first relationship*. New York: Academic Press, 1977.

Volosinov, V. N. *Marxism and the philosophy of language*. New York: Seminar Press, 1973.

Vygotsky, L. S. *Thought and language*. Cambridge, Mass.: MIT Press, 1962.

Werner, H., & Kaplan, B. *Symbol formation: An organismic developmental approach to language and the expression of thought*. New York: Wiley, 1963.

Wozniak, R. Structuralism, dialectical materialism and cognitive developmental theory. In K. Riegel (Ed.), *Issues in developmental and historical structuralism*. Basel: S. Karger, 1973.

7

Ontogenesis, Use, and Representation of Cultural Categories: A Psychological Perspective

Patricia Marks Greenfield

In 1966, I was asked to write a review of the volume emanating from the 1963 Merida Conference on transcultural studies in cognition (Greenfield, 1967). The report of that conference (Romney & D'Andrade, 1964) identified an important gap between the fields of anthropology and psychology in their approach to the transcultural study of cognition: anthropological study focuses on relatively static cognitive *products* while psychological research concentrates more on dynamic cognitive *processes*. Romney and D'Andrade, in their "Summary of Participants' Discussion," pointed out diverging assumptions on the part of the two fields: on the one hand the "assumption by anthropologists that 'cognition' is equivalent to the code held by a group of individuals" and on the other hand "the psychologists' assumption . . . that 'cognition' is equivalent to mental capacities or intellective processes" (p. 239). Indeed, after reviewing the conference as a whole, Romney and D'Andrade said that "it began to appear as though many of the issues could be reduced to one: whether the transcultural study of cognition is primarily a study of codes or of intellective processes" (p. 234).

   In this chapter, I will try to close this gap, to link cognitive processes with cultural codes. Indeed, a similar mandate was put forth by Roger Brown (1964) in his concluding statement of the 1963 Merida Conference; he said there that eventually someone is going to have to nail together the mind as template—a categorical grid imposed on reality—and the mind as transformer—an active cognitive processor.

   Within cognitive anthropology, the years since the conference have witnessed

An earlier version of this chapter was presented at the Conference on Anthropology, Psychology and Cognitive Structures, University of California, Riverside, May 1979.

Patricia Marks Greenfield ● Department of Psychology, University of California at Los Angeles, Los Angeles, California 90024.

progress in this task of integrating cognitive processes—the mind as transformer—with cultural codes—the mind as a categorical template. For example, Kronenfeld (1979) has applied George Miller's (1956) magical number 7 ± 2 in conjunction with Bruner, Goodnow, and Austin's (1956) concept-attainment strategies to the analysis of decision making processes in various societies. In this work the concern is not with culturally standardized *products* but rather with culturally standardized *processes*. A paper by Berlin, Boster, and O'Neill (1979) integrates process with code in another way, by demonstrating how processes of visual perception affect a cultural system for classifying birds.

I will continue this integrated approach to the study of cognitive process and cultural product by considering several methodological and substantive approaches to understanding the dynamic processes involved in the ontogenesis, representation, and use of culturally standardized cognitive structures. A major question to which I will return at the end is the extent to which individual cognitive processes are determined by the nature of a culture's relatively standardized category systems, both linguistic and nonlinguistic.

The Ontogenesis of Cultural Codes: An Example from the Domain of Kinship

My concern here is with the developmental acquisition of specific kinds of cognitive processing constraints stemming from the acquisition of kin terms.

This particular study, which I carried out in collaboration with Carla Childs (Greenfield & Childs, 1978), examines the development of sibling terms in Zinacantan, a Maya Indian community in Chiapas, Mexico. It also presents a new methodological procedure for studying kinship knowledge. The method is a comprehension task in which the subject is given a series of kinship terms and must name a person or people to whom each term applies. This method has an advantage for developmental research in that it maximizes the display of competence concerning kinship terminology at each point in development. This is the case because comprehension generally develops before production. The child need only name particular people in his or her family to answer each question. This skill is generally acquired before the production of kinship terms. In other words, the kinship terms are given and the child replies, displaying his or her understanding of the term by naming a person to whom it applies. To give an example from English, a question might be "Who is your sister?" This question presents the kinship term "sister." The reply might be "Alice," the name of a person in the family. Kronenfeld and Gladwin (n.d.) listed eight broad questions which formal analysis of kinship systems has sought to answer. Our method involves the inverse of one of their questions, the calculation of kin terminology from the user's point of view. Instead of calculating which *kin term* applies to a given person, our procedure involves calculating which *person* is referred to by a given term. For example, the kind of calculation which Kronenfeld and Gladwin referred to would be involved in the question "What is Alice to you?" to which the answer would be "sister." Here the name of the person is given and the subject must calculate the relationship to that person. In contrast, our procedure gives the kin term and the child responds with the name of a person to whom it applies.

Our data were collected in the Zinacanteco hamlet of Nabencauk under the aegis of the Harvard Chiapas Project. Our sample consisted of 66 subjects varying along three dimensions: age, sex, and schooling; however, sex and schooling did not turn out to affect the results, so I will not say anything more about those variables. For present purposes, therefore, this was a developmental study involving the comparison of three age groups: 4- to 5-year-olds, 8- to 10-year-olds, and 13- to 18-year-olds. (Sample sizes were 13, 33, and 19 respectively.)

Before asking our subjects any questions, we obtained family trees from their mothers. These trees gave the names of all household members and showed the kinship relationships between them. We used these family trees to compose a set of questions for each subject relating to his or her nuclear family, the basic residential unit in Zinacantan. The questions that will be discussed all involved Zinacanteco sibling terms. They were of two types: egocentric and other-centered. The term *egocentric* is used here somewhat differently from the way it is used in componential analyses of kinship; *ego* refers specifically to the subject who is being questioned, not to the general reference point for the terminological system, which we call *reference point,* as will be clear later. Egocentric questions concerned the relationship of an individual participant to his or her siblings. Figure 1 presents an example. For this family tree we had composed three egocentric questions for Chepil: "What's the name of your older sister?" (Shunka); "What's the name of your younger brother?" (Petul); "What's the name of your younger sister?" (Maruch). Other-centered questions concerned a given sibling's relation to his or her siblings. Here are examples: "As for your older sister, Shunka, what's the name of her younger sister?" (Maruch); "As for your younger brother, Petul, what is the name of his older sister?" (Shunka). We asked all questions in a singular form even when a correct answer included more than one person. However, after each response we asked the subject, "Does the person have any more in this category?" For example, Shunka has two younger brothers, Chepil and Petul. If we asked "As for your older sister, Shunka, what's the name of her younger brother?" and the subject answered "Petul," we would then ask "Does she have any more younger brothers?" We would repeat this question until the subject told us that there were no more.

Our main theoretical purpose was to test out the value of componential analyses, cultural values, and Piagetian theory in accounting for the ontogenetic development of the Zinacanteco system of sibling terminology. However, in reconsidering this research for the present chapter, I realized that our results also point to the value of

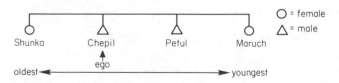

Figure 1. Sample Zinacanteco family tree showing sibling relationships.

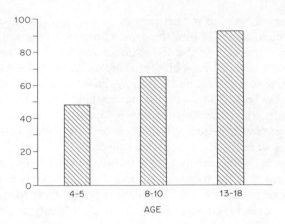

Figure 2. Percentage of questions answered correctly at different ages.

extensionist semantics for their explanation. Under such an analysis, knowledge begins with focal examples of relationships and extends outward to similar instances. In the area of kinship, this sort of analysis was first proposed by Lounsbury (1964) and further developed by Kronenfeld (1973) for kinship systems as they exist in mature adults.

Here are the results. From a developmental point of view, the most basic, although not particularly unusual, results are shown in Figure 2. This figure shows that the ability to apply sibling terms correctly is acquired gradually. It is clear that an increasing number of questions was correctly answered at each age level. The 13- through 18-year-olds approached perfect knowledge, correctly answering 94% of the questions. This information by itself does not favor any particular developmental model, but it does show that the sibling system does not arise full-blown at some point in time. Some model of progressive acquisition is required.

What does it mean to say that a componential analysis can account for development? Basically, the claim is that the conceptual components posited for the analysis guide the learning process. This claim can be tested through the patterning of errors.

	SIBLING			
	OLDER		YOUNGER	
	THAN REFERENCE POINT			
	FEMALE	MALE	FEMALE	MALE
FEMALE	VISH (girl's or boy's older sister)	SHIBNEL (girl's older brother)	MUK (girl's younger sibling)	
REFERENCE POINT				
MALE		BANKIL (boy's older brother)	ISHLEL (boy's younger sister)	IZ'IN (boy's younger brother)

Figure 3. Three-dimensional componential analysis of Zinacanteco sibling terms.

In this regard there are three different componential analyses, each with its particular developmental implications. I will start with two traditional analyses of Zinacanteco sibling terms of reference, both developed by Collier (1969). The first, shown in Figure 3, is based on three dimensions: sex of reference point (which would be sex of ego in componential analysis terminology), sex of sibling, and age of sibling relative to reference point. That is to say, a Zinacanteco speaker would use a different word to describe a sibling depending on whether the *speaker* is male or female and whether the *sibling* is male or female, younger or older. The distinction in two of the semantic components of the dimensions are, however, incompletely realized, as the figure shows. Sex of reference point is not distinguished in the term for older sister, *vish,* which is the same for both male and female reference points. Sex of sibling is not distinguished in naming a female's younger sibling. The basic term *muk* applies to younger siblings, both boys and girls. It can, however, be modified to specify sex by the addition of the Tzotzil word for boy or girl. If these three semantic components, or dimensions, guide the acquisition process, then one would expect the child's comp :hension of the terms at different stages to reflect the gradual acquisition of the three semantic components. The second way in which semantic components should be reflected in the acquisition process is that componentially more complex terms would be learned before componentially simpler ones. For example, *bankil* (boy's older brother) and *shibnel* (girl's older brother) are componentially more complex than *vish* (older sister) because the latter does not involve the component of sex of reference point, whereas the former two terms do.

Let us now turn to Collier's second componential analysis (Figure 4). This analysis is based on reciprocity and relative age. The relative age dimension is the same as in the three-dimensional analysis that we saw before, but the two sex dimensions have been replaced by a single reciprocity component. The idea of reciprocity is embodied in the example. Shibnel and *ishlel* are a reciprocal pair of terms because if you are my *shibnel,* I am your *ishlel.* This model substitutes one relational component, reciprocity, for two categorical components, sex of reference point and sex of sibling. Since all sibling terms now have the same number of components, this model reduces them to the same componential complexity. Hence our prediction from this model is that all terms would develop at the same rate and that error patterns would reflect the components of relative age and reciprocity.

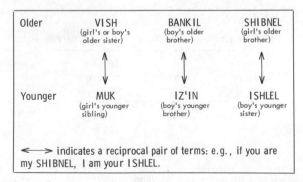

Figure 4. Two-dimensional componential analysis of Zinacanteco sibling terms.

The third type of componential analysis comes from Haviland and Clark (1974). Their analysis combines the two already presented and also adds a relational feature: that siblings have common parents. For the present purposes, it is not necessary to go into the details of Haviland and Clark's model. Suffice it to note that the predictions based on relative complexity would be the same as for the first model.

Evaluation of the models with respect to actual findings produced some interesting contrasts. (In order to hold category size constant, this data analysis is based on questions for which there is only one correct answer, i.e., one family member falling into a particular category. The effects of category size will be considered separately in the memory analysis to be reported later.) Our first finding regarding the patterning of errors is that, overall, no term is more difficult than another. This result goes against the complexity predictions of the first componential analysis of Collier and against that of Haviland and Clark. The result is in accord with the complexity predictions from Collier's second model. At this point then, Collier's first model and Haviland and Clark's model are eliminated, and we shall proceed with further consideration only of Collier's second model.

Let us further analyze Collier's second model. The developmental implications of this model are that children would use the older/younger dimension and the reciprocal relation between pairs of terms in order to learn the system. Let us proceed now to look at errors of commission in order to see whether the components hypothesized by this model mediate the learning process. Errors of commission are of particular interest because they can be used to see whether the participants of various ages have analyzed sibling terms into various components. A pattern in errors of commission reveals the existence of a concept, as opposed to knowledge of specific examples. (Nevertheless, keep in mind the fact that only 11% of all errors were errors of commission; the majority of errors by far were errors of omission.) Table I groups errors of commission according to which semantic component is maintained. Let us consider specifically those semantic components presumed by Collier's second model, the model which our results thus far indicate is the most promising for developmental explanation. To understand what maintaining common parentage, maintaining right sex, and so on, mean in this table, consider this example: If the experimenter asks a boy "What is your older brother's name?" and the boy responds with the name of his younger brother, his wrong answer is not totally wrong; it maintains the sex—

Table I. Errors of Commission at Different Ages[a]

	Maintain common parentage	Maintain right sex	Maintain relative age	Stay within reciprocal pair	Number of questions
Age 4–5	75%	46%	38%	23%	20
Age 8–10	94%	80%	16%	30%	55
Age 13–18	100%	79%	21%	14%	14
					89

[a]The percentages do not add up to 100 because each one represents a binary split of the complete data for a particular age group. The small number of errors that referred to people outside the sibling group were not included on the age, sex, and reciprocity analyses, because we sometimes did not know who these people were.

male—of the correct answer and stays in the same reciprocal pair—older brother and younger brother. If he responds by naming his older sister, he maintains relative age of the correct answer, but not sex or the reciprocal pair. The only semantic component consistently maintained by the youngest children was common parentage. That is, they infrequently named people outside their sibling group in answer to sibling questions. But this component is not even part of Collier's second model. One could say, however, that this model was just taking the sibling system in isolation and that if it had been considered as part of a larger componential analysis, then common parentage would certainly have been included.

Let us, nonetheless, proceed to more telling facts. It can be seen that the middle and oldest age groups maintained the attribute of sex as well as common parentage. Neither relative age nor reciprocal pairs were maintained by any age group. But the maintenance of reciprocal pairs in errors of commission would be required at some point in development by the model now under consideration. There is additional evidence in our data that reciprocity is not used in learning the sibling system; this evidence is fully presented in an article by Greenfield and Childs (1978). The important point is that the analysis of errors of commission does not show the semantic addition of components required by any of the three models. Children seem to be acquiring comprehension of the sibling system of terminology by learning how to label individual relationships between particular people rather than by use of conceptual components. These individual relationships can be thought of as focal instances. Here is one piece of evidence that focal instances are critical in the developmental acquisition of kinships terms.

Let us first consider a point that was mentioned before: the fact that 75% of all errors maintained common parentage. This result means (1) that most errors did not extend beyond the nuclear family and (2) that most errors stayed within the correct generation. This first characteristic agrees with the Kronenfeld (1973) analysis of Fanti kin terms, which showed that nuclear family terms are extended outward to apply to relatives outside the nuclear family. This result seems to indicate that children do not start their acquisition of kin terms by discriminating nuclear family from others. In a way, others are nonexistent. What the children do is simply learn to identify members of the nuclear family. Common parentage is a core common to all sibling terms and this core seems to be learned first.

What is the significance of the second characteristic, that errors do not cross generations? It does not imply that children are learning the component of generation. The children named people in their own generation, yet limited themselves to that generation within the nuclear family. If generation were acquired as a generalized component, this component could be maintained while naming cousins outside the nuclear family; but this type of error was made very rarely.

Another point that emerges from Table I relates to a cultural emphasis in Zinacantan. In that culture, relative age is a salient social characteristic. Comparing age with sex, one could say that within families in general, not just the Zinacantecos, relative age would have more behavioral significance for sibling relationships and roles than does sex. Yet it can be seen from the table that the attribute of sex is preserved before the attribute of relative age. This result seems to indicate that cultural and behavioral salience is not a factor in developmental acquisition. On the other hand, our finding is in accord with Piaget's view that absolute attributes are learned before relational ones. Sex is a categorical attribute. Age is a relative or relational attribute. On the other hand, common parentage, the first components to be acquired as a component, is also relational, and this result contradicts Piaget. Thus, the results are mixed with respect to Piaget's idea that absolute attributes should be acquired before relational ones. What is suggested, however, is that the core concept of sibling is acquired before the various sibling relationships are differentiated.

There is also some additional evidence showing how the developmental acquisition of sibling terms moves outward from focal instances. The particular focal instances are those predicted by Piagetian analysis (1928): that the child will be able to apply terms first in response to egocentric questions. These are questions concerning the relationship of the subject to his siblings, for example, "What is the name of your older sister?" Only later should the child be able to answer questions concerning relations between two siblings apart from self, for example, a question to Chepil in the family shown in Figure 1: "As for Maruch, what is the name of her older sister?" The final stage, according to Piaget, involves the child's ability to see himself or herself from the point of view of another person. The child must reverse perspectives. The following question–answer pair, again addressed to Chepil in Figure 1, requires a reversal of perspective: "As for Maruch, who is her younger brother?" (me). Figure 5 shows this developmental progression from being able to answer questions where the subject is the reference point to being able to answer questions with other reference points; it also shows the still greater difficulty of other-centered questions about relations to ego. These are basically questions where the answer is me. What this graph shows is that, among the youngest children, we have a situation where the child can name, for example, her older brother but cannot answer a question about

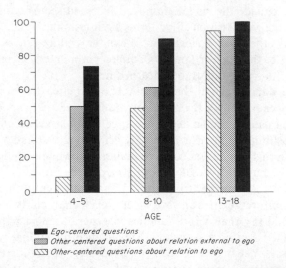

Figure 5. Percentage of questions concerning different types of example answered correctly at different ages.

her older brother's older brother. Nor can she name herself as her older brother's younger sister. For the 4- and 5-year-olds we see a neat progression: they answer most of the egocentric questions; a lower percentage of other-centered questions, involving a relationship totally external to ego; and, finally, very few questions which involve taking another person's perspective on self. Figure 5 shows that this ordering of difficulty of the questions is maintained for children in the middle age range, although their performance with each type is better than that of the youngest children. It is only with the 13- to 18-year-olds, however, who can answer virtually any type of question, that the gap between question types closes. The evidence indicates that knowledge moves outward from one particular focal relationship, the relationship of other people to oneself. The important theoretical point is that no characteristic of sibling terms *per se* predicts error patterns as well as the nature of the example on which the child is being questioned. In concrete terms, this means that whether a child is being questioned about a *vish* or *shibnel* does not affect the difficulty of the question while the sibling system is in the process of development. What does matter, though, is whether you are asking the child about *his/her shibnel* or someone else's.

It is interesting to consider why Haviland and Clark (1974) would find their componential analysis explanatory in the case of English kin terms, whereas we did not in the case of Zinacantan kin terms. The answer lies not in the difference between the two languages or between the two cultures but rather in the task itself. Haviland and Clark were asking for definitions, whereas we were asking for the application of kin terms. *Development in the application of kin terms is intrinsically different from definitional development.* Indeed, a closer look at their results indicates that there is no conflict with our data. Haviland and Clark, as well as Danziger (1957), found an early stage in the definition of kin terms before semantic components appeared. At this point, the child could name examples of terms but could not define them. In essence, our task required naming rather than definition, and our results suggest that children learn kin terms as labels for specific relations before the labels themselves are organized into the conceptual components necessary to formulate definitions. Development in the application of kin terms differs in another respect from development of kin term definitions. Whereas Piaget (1928) found that very young children define brother as "boy," using an absolute attribute, errors of commission in our task show that, when applying sibling terms within their own family, children do *not* think that a brother can be any boy whatsoever. A brother must be a sibling. Nelson (1973) has found that a new word is first used to refer to something in a particular *functional* relationship to the child but that generalization to new instances will occur on the basis of perceptual attributes. If we consider definition a form of generalization, Nelson's conceptualization would account for the findings of Piaget (1928) and Haviland and Clark (1974) that the earliest *definitions* of kin terms refer to perceptual attributes like sex (for example, defining brother as a boy). However, earliest *application* of the term involves referents that are of functional importance to the child, that is, siblings (cf. Cazden, this volume).

This difference between the ability to *define* and the ability to *use* a term shows that we must be careful in taking conscious conceptualization as an index of behavioral categorization. (This difference should have been taken into account by Colby, 1979, when he proposed that written material be used to study behavioral roles in a culture. Certainly there will be a relationship between more conscious knowledge of roles, as it appears in verbal texts, and the less conscious way in which roles are actualized in behavior. But this relationship needs explicit study. Here the emerging area of metacognition, e.g., Flavell & Wellman, 1977, in developmental psychology is of relevance. This is the area of investigation in which conscious knowledge *about* cognitive process and *about* behavior is studied in itself apart from the development of the cognition or behavior themselves.) In general, it has been found that knowledge of behavior or cognition lags behind the behavior or cognition itself. Thus one is likely to underestimate the complexity of a category system by relying exclusively on verbal descriptions of it.

Using Sibling Terms: The Role of Memory Development

It is productive to use our sibling data to illustrate how the development of kin term usage is affected by the development of the cognitive process of memory. Here I will be considering the interaction of a cognitive processing constraint with the cultural system itself. Because larger families require the child to remember more individual relations, we were able to utilize the variability of Zinacanteco family size as a natural experiment and to study the role of memory factors in our kinship task. To demonstrate the influence of this factor, we compared responses to questions for which there is but a single correct answer (the body of data discussed up to this point) with responses to questions for which a correct answer involves naming more than one person. If memory is a factor and if sibling terms can be used to access items in memory, then the more members there are in the category being recalled, the greater the probability will be of recalling at least one member. The slopes of the lines in Figure 6 show that this is the case for every age group except the oldest, for whom there is a ceiling effect. At the same time, comparison of the graph for the

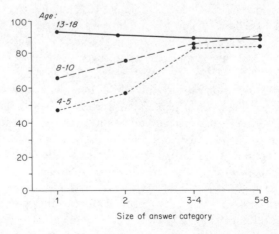

Figure 6. Percentage of questions eliciting at least one correct answer as a function of category size for children of different ages.

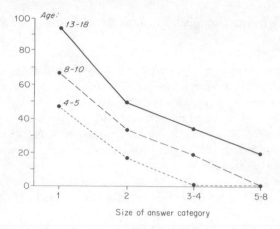

Figure 7. Percentage of questions completely answered by children of different ages as a function of category size.

different age groups shows the progressive development of memory with age. More specifically, the youngest children are as likely to produce at least one correct answer as the older children for kin categories containing three or more members in the household but not for the smaller categories, those containing one or two members. For those categories, the probability of producing at least one correct answer increases with age. The difference in the lines' slopes indicates that the constraining effects of memory decline with age.

These results can also be looked at another way: they demonstrate the influence of the terminological system on memory. That is to say, the probability of recalling one correct answer would increase with size of the category only if the category referred to by a particular sibling term were an organizing factor in memory. Category would not help or hinder performance if a particular sibling's name could not be retrieved in terms of the particular relationship being asked about. This result also shows that sibling terminology is an organizing factor in children's memory.

Another memory skill that is called for when there is more than one sibling in an answer category is the ability to make a list. This skill requires not only retrieval of data but *ordered* retrieval, so that one can remember which items have already been retrieved and which have not. The larger the answer category, the longer the list and the more difficult it should be to retrieve the complete list. Figure 7 shows that this is indeed the case. The downward sloping lines from left to right show that the probability that a question will be completely answered declines as the size of the required list gets larger. The different heights of the three graph lines show that, in general, the ability to construct lists of any given size becomes progressively greater as age increases. The only deviation from this pattern is due to a floor factor for the youngest children such that they are not able to generate any complete list for categories containing three or more members. This type of analysis illustrates a method for studying the developmental interaction of a cognitive constraint, memory, with a culturally prescribed cognitive system, sibling terminology.

Representing Cultural Categories: The Role of Cognitive Development and Task Structure

There is yet another sort of cognitive analysis of culturally standardized categories. We can consider the representation of examplars of culturally prescribed categories, analyzing how this representation is constrained by cognitive development on the side of the organism and by task structure on the side of the environment. Recent concern with the internal structure of categories (e.g., Berlin & Kay, 1969; Berlin *et al.*, 1979; Rosch, 1973) has considered intension—the category's definition—only indirectly through the study of extension—its exemplars. In the study I will now describe, Childs and I (Greenfield & Childs, 1977) approached the internal structure of categories through the direct study of intension in a nonverbal representational task.

The categories in question are two patterns woven in Zinacantan. We examined the difference between concrete exemplars of the two categories and their representation by native Zinacantecos. To examine the constraining factors in the representation of these patterns, it was necessary to introduce a new method for investigating visual representation of a cultural object.

Note the categories themselves. Figure 8 shows two exemplars of each of the two categories. The top pair is the pattern used for the male pancho called a *pok' k'u*ul*. The bottom one shows two examples of the pattern used for the female shawl called a *pok' mocebal*. Each variant of a given pattern has certain features in common. The male pattern is essentially the repeated pattern of a red stripe followed by a broader white stripe. The female pattern, in contrast, also involves red and white alternation, but the red stripe is actually a complex unit consisting of three red stripes separated by two white stripes. The task, shown in Figure 9, involved placing sticks in a frame in order to form striped patterns. For the part of the experiment concerned with the woven patterns, the subject placed sticks in a frame in order to make first a *pok' k'u*ul* then a *pok' mocebal*. Both articles of clothing were continuously present during the task, and the relevant one was always pointed out to the subject.

Two Pok' K'u*uls

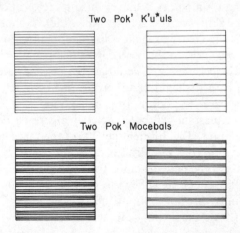

Two Pok' Mocebals

Figure 8. Categories of Zinacanteco woven patterns. Black lines represent red stripes; white spaces represent white stripes.

Figure 9. Experimental setup for pattern representation task.

An interesting phenomenon concerned how cognitive development constrains the representation of these two categories of woven pattern. As in the kinship study, we had 4- and 5-year-olds, 8- to 10-year-olds, and 13- to 18-year-olds. Most of the youngest children had not reached the stage where they could represent both patterns as a simple alternation. None could differentiate the two patterns. Most of the 8- to 10-year-olds could represent the patterns in one way or another. Nevertheless only one child in this age group differentiated between the patterns. The modal strategy, used by six children, was to represent both patterns as a regular alternation of red and white. Thus the female pattern containing three differentiated parts or elements became identical with the two-part male pattern. It is clear that the general failure to differentiate the two patterns stemmed from failure to differentiate the elements within the more complex pattern. The tendency of this age group to simplify the more complex patterns was also manifest in pattern continuation tasks in which the experimenters started a novel pattern and the task of the child was to continue it. The same progressive differentiation of parts in representing complex patterns has been found in the development of patterning tasks in a variety of cultures. Hence, our results show evidence of highly generalized constraints on cognitive development.

More interesting, though, are the constraints imposed by the differing behavioral roles in relation to the two patterns. The two behavioral roles with which we were concerned were (1) weaving the patterns, using them, and viewing them and

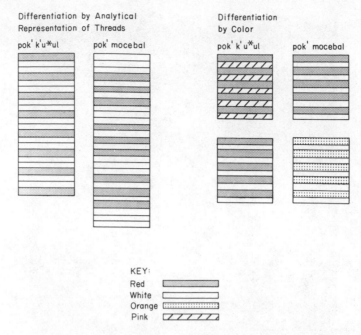

Figure 10. Zinacanteco ways of representing two woven patterns.

(2) simply using the patterns and looking at them. Figure 10 shows two strategies for representing the patterns. The crucial feature of the representational strategy on the left is maintaining the configuration of stripes in the two patterns, including the thin white stripes in the female pattern. This type of representation was more than twice as frequent among weavers, represented by the girls in our oldest groups, as opposed to nonweavers, represented by the oldest boys. This comparison refers to subjects who had never attended school. This type of analytic representation is what one would expect from people who are involved in the actual construction of patterns, as weavers must be.

This strategy becomes more interesting, however, when we compare it with a strategy used by the nonweaving boys of a similar age, shown on the right side of Figure 10. Essentially about a third of the oldest boys used color to differentiate the male and female patterns. Zinacanteco boys are clothes conscious too, but this type of representation shows that they consider a different aspect of the pattern significant. When the male garment is seen from a distance, the thin stripes seem to disappear and the pattern looks like a solid pink or light red color; therefore, the *pok' k'u*ul* gives the impression of being more red or more pink than the *pok' mocebal* even though the threads in the two garments are exactly the same color. None of the girls (weavers) used color to differentiate the two woven patterns.

The girls' attention to the structural detail of the pattern contrasts with the boys' representation of a difference in superficial appearance, a difference nonetheless important in making the distinction between male and female Zinacanteco clothing.

The role requirements of Zinacanteco women in relation to clothing are different. Girls need to know and use the detailed analytical aspects of the patterns more than boys do, and so they are more apt to choose those aspects when representing them. Thus we found that behavioral role, specifically the task in which a pattern category is embedded, affects the salience of different attributes of that pattern.

Which attributes will be highlighted on the verbal level is also a function of a particular task environment. Frake (1962) pointed out a relevant example a long time ago. At a party where two aunts are present, most people would refer to one as "my mother's sister" and the other as "my father's sister." If only one aunt were present in the same setting, however, it is more than likely that one would use the simple term *aunt*. The former terms make the feature side-of-family salient, whereas the term *aunt* does not.

We have found very similar phenomena in the developmental study of communication (Greenfield & Dent, 1980). In this study the task was to explain to another person how to combine some simple objects (beads in a cup or a series of cups) in a situation where the second person cannot see what the first is doing but has the same materials. We found that attributes are coded verbally when they are necessary to make discriminations relevant to the task, but not otherwise. For example, when a 6-year-old or a 10-year-old child explained how to seriate a sequence of cups of different sizes and different colors, the word *cup* was rarely used. Instead, the cups were identified by their color. In this situation, the word *cup* does not distinguish among alternatives required to carry out the task. On the other hand, color words do. Olson (1970) has integrated this notion into a general theory of semantics. He posited "that words designate, signal or specify an intended referent relative to the set of alternatives from which it must be differentiated" (p. 264). Olson cited Brown's (1958) idea that objects are usually named at the level of generality which allows them to be differentiated from other objects of contrasting function. Thus, the fact that we use the term *ball* more often than *baseball* or *sphere* reflects the nature of potential alternative referents: not usually golfballs or cubes but rather bats, rackets, kites, or skateboards. Thus the very choice of a label reflects the set of alternatives potentially in a given context. In putting forth this idea of relative salience, I am not trying to denigrate absolute bases for salience in the perceptual system; I only want to point out that these absolute factors can be modified through task structures which selectively render particular distinctions functional for a particular task. This could be an important concept in further elucidating the relation between perceptual categories and linguistic encoding.

Our study of pattern representation indicates that the task relevance of categories affects the salience of their features and that this differential salience can be manifest in nonverbal representation, as other studies have shown for verbal representation.

Cognitive Effects of Superordinate Category Labels

We now turn from the cognitive causes to the cognitive effects of a culturally standard category system. My topic now is the cognitive implications of superordi-

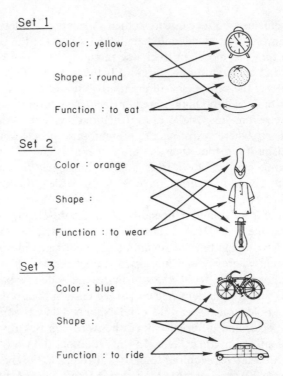

Figure 11. Diagram of stimuli in grouping experiment.

nate labels in a hierarchically organized terminological system. Here I shall be drawing on a study which was carried out in Senegal and involved a grouping task (Greenfield, Reich, & Olver, 1966). This study was done with Wolof children from three different milieus in Senegal. One group had neither schooling nor urban influence; the setting was a traditional Wolof village. The second milieu was the same traditional rural milieu plus schooling. The third milieu was school plus urban influence. These children attended public school in Dakar, the country's capital. The children in each milieu represented three grade levels or age groups: first, third, and sixth grade and for the unschooled groups, the age equivalents 6 and 7, 8 and 9, and 11 to 13. The materials for the grouping experiment consisted of three sets of three pictures each. In each set it was possible to form a pair on the basis of color, form, or function of the objects pictured, as Figure 11 shows. Children were asked to show the experimenter two pictures out of each set of three that were most alike. They were then asked the reason for their choice. After they had gone through this procedure once, the three displays were exhibited a second time with the instructions to show the experimenter two other pictures that were alike in a threesome. Again the question "why?" was asked. At the end the children were asked to identify the pictures. Pretests had been conducted in order to ensure that the objects pictured would be equally familiar in urban and rural environments. Figure 11 shows the different ways the pictures could be grouped. Thus, in Set 1, the clock and the banana could be grouped together by color; the orange and the clock could be grouped together as round; the banana and the orange could be grouped together because both are to eat or both are fruit. Although the school children were learning French in school, the results to be reported were based on testing in Wolof, the children's first language.

There has been much controversy about the place of superordinate words in conceptual thought. In this experiment, superordinate words are words like *color* or *shape,* as opposed to specific color words like *blue* or specific shape words, *round* or *square.* The Wolof language, in contrast to French or English, has neither the word *color* nor the word *shape.* We found in our grouping task that lack of the word *color* did not hinder color groupings from being formed. In fact, unschooled Wolof children used color more than any other attribute to make the groupings. Are there, then, any cognitive implications of the absence of superordinate words? First, we found that use of superordinate words increases with age among the children who attend school. This sort of finding is in itself nothing new. The same trend has been observed before in the development of children's vocabularies (Brown, 1958). *It becomes interesting only when one realizes that such development takes place among the unschooled Wolofs only to the extent that French words are assimilated to their Wolof language because these words do not exist in Wolof.*

But these facts still do not answer the question of whether this terminological development or its absence has extralinguistic cognitive consequences. Let us now consider Figure 12. If this hierarchical organization corresponds to the type of structure generated by the subject in order to deal with the task, then his or her use of the superordinate words *color* or *shape* should indicate that the person is at the top of the hierarchy and has access to the entire hierarchy. We would predict, then, that he or she would be able to supply more than one kind of attribute if pressed. For the person is plainly contrasting, say, color with shape or with use. By the same reasoning his or her use of shape names or color names alone (for example "round" or "yellow") would mean that he or she was operating one level lower in the hierarchy. The person would then be cut off from the top of the hierarchy and its connections with other branches and would be less likely to operate in branches other than the one in which he or she was already located. A concept is defined as much by what it excludes as by what it includes, that is, by its contrast class. The concept of color, therefore, comes into being with the appearance of an opposing idea, and this opposing concept cannot exist on the level of specific color names. *Round* contrasts only with other shapes; *yellow* only with other colors. If this reasoning is correct then we would expect that if a child ever used an abstract word like *color* or *shape* he or she would vary his or choice of grouping attributes when asked to make a first and second

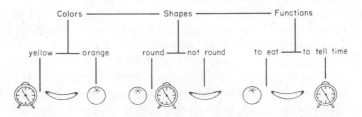

Figure 12. Possible hierarchical organization of first set of pictures.

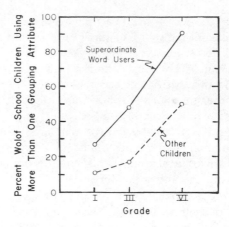

Figure 13. Percentage of Wolof school children using more than one grouping attribute.

choice of pairs for each of three sets of pictures. If he or she used only concrete words like yellow, then we would expect the person to form nothing but color grouping in all six tasks. The results presented in Figure 13 indicate that there is an important association between the use of superordinate words like *color* or *shape* and the use of a variety of attribute types for grouping. The results are presented separately for each grade level, so that it is clear that this relationship holds when all other factors such as knowledge of French and school grade are held constant. Thus if a Wolof child used a superordinate word, his or her chances of grouping by a variety of attributes are twice as great as those of a child who utilizes no superordinate vocabulary in this task. Recall that when a Wolof child uses the word *color,* it is a French word that he or she is introducing into a Wolof linguistic context. In 1958, Roger Brown hypothesized that superordinate class words are basically a luxury for people who do not have to deal with concrete phenomena. Our findings show, however, that superordinate words can be used to integrate different domains of words and objects into hierarchical structures. Our results show an association between the hierarchical depth of a taxonomic structure and flexibility in category use (cf. Bain, 1980).

Open and Closed Category Systems

Finally, let us consider the learning and developmental consequences of an aspect of culturally standardized category systems that has not been considered by cognitive or other branches of anthropology. That is the question of an open versus closed category system. The concern here is once more with categories of woven patterns, and I will use this domain to illustrate what I mean by an open or closed system. The Zinacantecos have a closed system in the sense that there are discrete, finite, and, as it happens, very few categories of patterns in the culture; furthermore, this pattern set is not meant to be added to. In contrast, many other peoples, including other Maya groups for whom weaving is important, place a premium on pattern innovation. In these cultures, the domain of pattern categories is an open system with a constantly increasing or changing inventory of patterns.

In one study, Childs and Greenfield (1980) investigated how Zinacantecos learn to weave. Our findings concerning this learning process may well be a consequence of the closed quality of the system of woven patterns. In the instructional process, we found an emphasis on modeling and observation, which yielded basically errorless learning. That is to say, instructional intervention was done selectively in such a way that whenever the learner reached a part of the process where she was having difficulty, the teacher intervened by either helping or totally taking over, in the latter case providing a model for observation. This type of selective intervention not only provided a model for the girl, but also prevented her from making errors. This kind of instruction is in sharp contrast with methods of teaching and learning which depend more on trial and error. Our hypothesis (Greenfield & Lave, 1982) is that trial-and-error learning becomes functional when it is used in connection with an open system of product categories, such as patterns in weaving (cf. Schubert, this volume). The essence of trial and error is that the learner learns by experimenting. In the process of experimenting, the learner makes mistakes, but also may make discoveries, for example, may invent a new pattern. At the present time, I have reports from two cultures in which weaving is important and in which pattern innovation is not only permitted, but also very much valued. One of these cultures, studied by Lisa Aronson (personal communication, 1978), is the Ibo town of Akwete in eastern Nigeria. The other is, like the Zinacantecos, a Maya group, but one located in the highlands of Guatemala and studied by James and Maria Loucky (personal communication, 1978). Both sets of investigators report that girls learn to weave through a process of trial and error. Initially little miniature looms are set up, and the young girls are given odd leftover scraps of material or grass to weave with. Later when they start weaving real items on a real loom, they are basically left alone. That is to say, there is no teacher hovering over the learner, waiting to intervene at the slightest sign of an error. The only people around are siblings, who give advice but generally do not know how to weave themselves. Hence, the evidence thus far indicates a correlation between instructional method and whether the category system relating to a cultural product is an open or closed one. *Errorless learning based on observation and selective intervention by a teacher seems to go with a closed system or product categories, while trial-and-error learning based on experimentation seems to go with open systems of product categories in which innovation is valued.*

Conclusions

In conclusion, I would like to pull together the diverse threads of this chapter. First, I have tried to present models for the developmental acquisition of culturally standardized category systems by focusing on two such systems, kinship and weaving patterns, and two aspects of the system, one linguistic and one nonlinguistic. Kinship was investigated on the linguistic level, whereas patterns were investigated in terms of their visual representation. The first finding emerging from the study of kinship was that extensional semantics—adding the Piagetian notion of decentering to identify focal instances—presents a good model of the development of sibling-term comprehension in Zinacantan. The second finding from the kinship study had to do with the influence of memory development on the application of sibling terminology. In the domain of pattern representation, another cognitive developmental factor—differentiation—played a role. That study also demonstrated the influence of a social factor—the task for which a category will be used—on the internal structure of a category. The next topic was an investigation of the cognitive consequences of a formal aspect of a category system, degree of depth in a hierarchically organized structure. Here I found that the presence of a superordinate level not only integrated what would otherwise be separate taxonomic structures, but also facilitated the flexible use of alternative modes of categorization. Finally, I looked at the relationship between culturally standardized category systems and methods of socialization, looking specifically at the relationship between the openness of category systems and methods by which the system is taught. Here my tentative conclusion was that closed category systems are associated with errorless methods of learning and teaching and are more dependent on observation and modeling, whereas open systems are taught with trial-and-error methods, leading to innovation as well as error.

For each of these topics I have tried to describe empirical techniques which could be applied by cognitive anthropologists to substantially broaden their inquiry into the effects of environmental and cognitive processing constraints on culturally standardized cognitive structures. My hope is that these methods and concepts will prove useful in the future, furthering not only research, but also productive interchange between anthropology and psychology (cf. Okun & Fisk, this volume).

In terms of the relationship between the individual, language, and society, it is clear that the mere existence of a culturally standardized category system, whether represented verbally or nonverbally, does not determine the use to which it is put by an individual. Factors of cognitive development influence its use at different points in time, as was clear with both our kinship task, a verbal one, and our pattern representation task, essentially nonverbal. These cognitive developmental constraints appear to have a stronger influence than the culturally specific form of the category system itself. Thus, in our kinship study, egocentrism influenced the pattern of development more than did the structure of Zinacanteco sibling terminology. Potentially universal factors of cognitive development emerge more readily than do culture-specific ones. For example, the growth of memory, an apparently universal phenomenon, played a role in the kinship task, but the culturally important discrimination of relative age did not seem to.

The flexibility of culturally standard categories to individual needs was also revealed. The study of weaving patterns showed that the same categories will be represented in quite different ways within a given culture depending on roles relative to those categories. Thus, although it could be claimed that the Zinacantecos have a single system of pattern categories, weavers represent them quite differently, on the average, than do nonweavers. Here, differentiated social roles within a society moderate the influence of uniform cultural products. The other direction of influence, from static category system to dynamic psychological process, was shown in the work on hierarchical category depth. There the presence of superordinate terms, available in some languages but not others, affected the flexibility of categorization processes.

Finally, I identified differences between societies in terms of whether a category system is open or closed. One might conclude that closed category systems stamp their impression on the members of a culture more than open ones do. For in the latter, cultural products are not merely taught to individuals, they are also created by them. Thus, the dynamic cognitive processes of the developing individual moderate and modulate the influence of static cultural products, while at the same time being influenced by them (cf. Nadin, this volume).

References

Bain, B., Being in the world bilingually. In M. Simpson (Ed.), *Clinical psycholinguistics.* New York: Irvington, 1980.

Berlin, B., & Kay, P. *Basic color terms: Their university and evolution.* Berkeley, Calif.: University of California Press, 1969.

Berlin, B., Boster, J. S., & O'Neill, J. P. *The perceptual bases of ethnobiological classification: Evidence from Aguaruna Jivaro ornithology.* Paper presented at the Conference on Anthropology, Psychology and Cognitive Structures, University of California, Riverside, May 1979.

Brown, R. *Words and things.* Glencoe, Ill.: Free Press, 1958.

Brown, R. Discussion of the conference. In A. K. Romney & R. G. D'Andrade (Eds.), Transcultural studies in cognition. *American Anthropologist,* 1964, *66,* 243–253. (special publication)

Bruner, J. S., Goodnow, J. J., & Austin, G. A. *A study of thinking.* New York: Wiley, 1956.

Childs, C. P., & Greenfield, P. M. Informal modes of learning and teaching: The case of Zinacanteco weaving. In N. Warren (Ed.), *Studies in cross-cultural psychology* (Vol. 2). London: Academic Press, 1980.

Colby, B. N. *Computer-assisted text ethnography and the building of knowledge structures.* Paper presented at the Conference on Anthropology, Psychology and Cognitive Structures, University of California, Riverside, May 1979.

Collier, J. F. *Changing kinship terminology in a Tzotzil Maya community.* Unpublished manuscript, 1969.

Danziger, K. The child's understanding of kinship terms: A study in the development of relational concepts. *Journal of Genetic Psychology,* 1957, *91,* 213–232.

Flavell, J. H., & Wellman, H. M. Metamemory. In R. Kail & J. Hagen (Eds.), *Perspectives on the development of memory and cognition.* Hillsdale, N.J.: Erlbaum, 1977.

Frake, C. O. The ethnographic study of cognitive systems. In T. Gladwin & W. C. Sturtevant (Eds.), *Anthropology and human behavior.* Washington, D.C.: Anthropological Society of Washington, 1962.

Greenfield, P. M. Mind active, mind static (Review of *Transcultural studies in cognition,* edited by A. K. Romney and R. G. D'Andrade). *Contemporary Psychology,* 1967, *12,* 105.

Greenfield, P. M., & Childs, C. P. Weaving, color terms, and pattern representation: Cultural influences and cognitive development among the Zinacantecos of Southern Mexico. *Interamerican Journal of Psychology,* 1977, *11,* 23–48.

Greenfield, P. M., & Childs, C. P. Understanding sibling concepts: A developmental study of kin terms in Zinacantan. In P. Dasen (Ed.), *Piagetian psychology: Cross-cultural contributions.* New York: Gardner Press, 1978.

Greenfield, P. M., & Dent, C. H. A developmental study of the communication of meaning: The role of uncertainty and information. In K. Nelson (Ed.), *Children's language* (Vol. 2). New York: Gardner Press, 1980.

Greenfield, P., & Lave, J. Cognitive aspects of informal education. In D. Wagner & H. W. Stevenson (Eds.), *Cultural perspectives on child development.* San Francisco: Freeman, 1982.

Greenfield, P. M., Reich, L. C., & Olver, R. R. On culture and equivalence-II. In J. S. Bruner, R. R. Olver, & P. M. Greenfield (Eds.), *Studies in cognitive growth.* New York: Wiley, 1966.

Haviland, S. E., & Clark, E. V. "This man's father is my father's son": A study of the acquisition of English kin terms. *Journal of Child Language,* 1974, *1,* 23–48.

Kronenfeld, D. B. Fanti kinship: The structure of terminology and behavior. *American Anthropologist,* 1973, *75,* 1577–1595.

Kronenfeld, D. B. *Information processing and cognitive structures*. Paper presented at the Conference on Anthropology, Psychology, and Cognitive Structures, University of California, Riverside, May 1979.

Kronenfeld, D. B., & Gladwin, H. *Introduction*. Unpublished paper, no date.

Lounsbury, F. G. A formal account of Crow- and Omaha-type kinship terminologies. In W. H. Goodenough (Ed.), *Explorations in cultural anthropology*. New York: McGraw-Hill, 1964.

Miller, G. A. The magical number seven, plus or minus two: Some limits in our capacity for processing information. *Psychological Review,* 1956, *63,* 81–97.

Nelson, K. Structure and strategy in learning to talk. *Monographs of the Society for Research in Child Development,* 1973, *38*(1–2, Serial No. 149).

Olson, D. R. Language and thought: Aspects of a cognitive theory of semantics. *Psychological Review,* 1970, *77,* 257–273.

Piaget, J. *Judgment and reasoning in the child*. New York: Harcourt, Brace, 1928.

Romney, A. K., & D'Andrade, R. G. Transcultural studies in cognition. *American Anthropologist,* 1964, *66* (Special publication).

Rosch, E. H. On the internal structure of perceptual and semantic categories. In T. E. Moore (Ed.), *Cognitive development and the acquisition of language*. New York: Academic Press, 1973.

Self-concept and Sexism in Language

Shelley Phillips

Introduction

In the not-so-distant past, it was fashionable to suggest that language development was essentially a product of innate dispositions. Later research challenges that approach (Snow & Ferguson, 1977) and emphasizes, as Vygotsky had done earlier, the overriding influence of the social-historical context. As Vygotsky (1962, 1966) saw it, a communication situation is a social situation and the language of communication should be studied in the social context. This is not to say that laboratory studies do not have their place, but that they are merely one aspect of reality. There are other realities given by other perspectives and other methodologies. One of these is interactional analysis, which takes into account all the relevant situational factors. On such a basis, language can be described as a set of social conventions which reflect socioeconomic relations. This emphasis is most relevant to the self-concept and sexism in language.

One of the most significant aspects of social relationships in Western societies has been the distinctiveness of role division between the sexes. Our language abounds in terms, concepts, and labels that signify what is appropriate for female or male behavior. A popular explanation of these distinctions rests on the peculiarities of economic relations in Western societies, which are typically competitive: capital, profit, the battle for markets, and consumerism are their basic economic characteristics, and their management depends on the hierarchical organization of roles and the division of labor. Childbearing, along with its significance for the inheritance of property and the provision of future factory workers, is seen as fundamental to the division of male and female roles as we know them. Men busied themselves with power and competition in the market place, but they also needed housekeepers, emotional support, the provision of a base, and sexual partners; through traditionalized social and

Shelley Phillips ● Unit for Child Studies, School of Education, University of New South Wales, Kensington 2033, New South Wales, Australia.

economic pressures, women have been taught to supply these needs and have come to occupy these distinctive roles as men have theirs. The language of sex roles and sex stereotypes reflects these socially structured relations.

More recently, this interpretation has not been seen as sufficient, for while there have been noncompetitive societies which lack our sex-role divisions (Leacock, 1977), there are also noncompetitive ones which have subordinated women as much as Western society has. Adrienne Rich (1977) saw the sex-role division and the subordination of women as having ancient and precapitalist origins in the male's envy, awe, and dread of the female capacity to create life. She saw this envy as having led to the disavowal of other aspects of female creativity. These fears are well illustrated in the language of ancient mythology and folklore (Slater, 1970). The emergence of patriarchy, as Rich saw it, was a retaliation; she believed that historical research demonstrates that men, denied the ability to nurture life within their bodies, have sought immortality in power and possessions.

The reality may possibly embrace both of these theories and others as well. In any case, it is clear that there are sex-role divisions within our society, and that typically the arrangement has been a predominance of males in government and decision-making committees in all aspects of society. There is also clearly a language to suit this hierarchy.

Language Mirrors Socioeconomic Relations

An outstanding example of language as a set of conventions reflecting socioeconomic relations can be seen in the use of the prescriptive *he* in Western literature. Female readers are required to be a "generic man" and an "invisible woman" (Bate, 1975). Here, language mirrors the power structure of the hundreds of societies in which males have presided over the powerful policy-making. Yet, consider the effect of the prescriptive *he* on the female reader. Some researchers have suggested that its unrelenting use in the past entailed a diminished self-concept for female readers (Bate, 1975). Lakoff (1973) argued that this problem is trivial, but such research has been criticized for failing to distinguish between evaluation and description in language (Bem & Bem, 1974; Geiwitz, 1978; Miller & Swift, 1976). Prescriptive *he* is seen as evaluative, with all the characteristics of an effective propaganda technique, and as a subtle and powerful source for shaping attitudes. As far as psychology is concerned, the age-old usage is a new problem, and to many researchers, determining the full extent of the psychological effect of prescriptive *he* presents a major challenge for the social psychology of language (Mackay, 1980).

Language is seen as reflecting socioeconomic relations in many other ways (cf. Parker, de Terra, this volume). Feminist research argues convincingly that historical records, literature, and psychology are generally male-oriented because men have predominated throughout Western history in selection and assessment committees. They have attended to and treated as significant only what men say (D. E. Smith, 1978). Recent discoveries of exceedingly talented but previously unknown female writers and artists by feminist historians offer support for these claims. This research also suggests that female contributions to language and culture have been significant but disregarded as invalid, unreal, trivial, or stupid. In this evaluative way, woman's perceptions, experience, and judgment have been excluded from the processes by which language is created.

These outcomes have been possible because the knowledge and language created by men has been seen as a universal reality, independent of the knower. The assumption that language and knowledge can be sex-free permits the exclusion of the interpretations of women (Hextall, 1976).

Communication between the Sexes

The possibility that males' and females' interpretation of knowledge and, therefore, their use of language are different has been recognized in the past. That women's interpretations should be regarded as being as valid as those of men has only recently begun to emerge as a serious topic for research (Haas, 1979). Wood (1966), analyzing the speech of a small sample of college students in response to a photograph of a man's face, found males referred more to concrete features, while women were more interpretive. Barron (1971), studying the speech of pupils and teachers, found that females used more participative and purposive cases and focused on how people felt and behaved, whereas men used more instrumental and objective cases and attended to objects and actions related to objects. Alvy (1973) and Strodtbeck and Mann (1956) similarly found that emotional sensitivity and support of other speakers is more characteristic of females of all ages.

Many other studies underline this relationship between linguistic form and social function. Leet-Pellegrini (1980), for example, found that even when both men and women are seen as experts in a particular area, which puts them in a position of power in relation to their peers, male experts pursue a style of interacting based on power, while female experts pursue a style based on solidarity and support. On the other hand, expert males interacting with other males do not maintain a dominant stance throughout discussions as they do with females. Whereas the name of the man's game appears to be "Have I won?", the name of the women's game is "Have I been sufficiently helpful?" (Leet-Pellegrini, 1980).

This distinction in language usage appears in many other ways. Primary school boys have been reported to use more words relating to possessions (Garvey & Dickstein, 1972), whereas female's speech is found to be nonassertive (Lakoff, 1975) and tentative with more use of "perhaps" and "I suppose" (Hartman, 1976; Swacker, 1975). Men rarely follow topics initiated by women in mixed sex conversations (Bernard, 1972), and men and women issue requests differently, with women stating them and men demanding them (Lakoff, 1975).

As a result of the accumulation of this kind of evidence, Jong (1977), along with many others, suspects that men and women are not really speaking the same language. At best, there is frustratingly poor communication between the sexes.

The Language of Psychology and Psychiatry

Another important area in which knowledge and language are being examined and found to reflect the dominance of the male in the socioeconomic sphere is that of psychology and psychiatry. Psychology and psychiatry emerge increasingly from the research as essentially status quo preserving subjects, dedicated to the elevation of male values and power. When women do not conform to the concepts and norms of male behavior, the psychological conclusion is that there is something wrong with them. Women have also been used projectively by men. For example, knowledge and language emanating from the male perspective resulted in the Freudian concept of penis envy, now much discredited by anthropological and feminist research. Although equally undermined by anthropological research, the male-oriented term *oedipal conflict* survives. In conceiving of it, Freud extrapolated the term, derived from his observation of male jealousy, to the behavior of the female. He rationalized its interpretation since it did not quite fit and came to the masterly conclusion that, since women were not men, they lacked the clear-cut oedipal resolution open to men. This lack, he claimed, results in a developmental failure in the female as a consequence of which women have "less sense of justice than men" (1925/1961, p. 257).

That point of view also appears in the contemporary theory of Laurence Kohlberg (1969, 1971). The theory has been increasingly discredited for many reasons (Trainer, 1976), but one of the most telling is that pointed out by Gilligan (1979), who highlights the fact that on the basis of an originally *all male* sample, Kohlberg developed a six-stage theory of moral development. The ultimate sixth stage is a legalistic one, in which rights and noninterference predominate in judgments of justice, and is seen to be more typically attained by "mature" males. Women, on the whole, tend to make lower, third-stage judgments, which are concerned with relationships and pleasing others. Thus, in Freud's footsteps, Kohlberg's criteria relegate women to a lesser sense of morality than men and, in doing so, judge them on male terms.

The method and the findings also highlight the distinctive moral language by which females are socialized and condemned. Concepts such as "unselfishness" and "responsibility" are instilled by constant association and reinforcement through approval. Morality for the female becomes "taking care of others" (Gilligan, 1979), whereas in men, for whom the socialization process stresses competition (McClelland, 1961), it becomes "legality." Thus, the one linguistic term tends to have different meanings for the sexes throughout socialization. What is more, while women have been socialized to take care of men, men, in their psychological theories of development, have either taken for granted or devalued that care. Thus, the language of women as well as what it represents has lesser currency than that of men. In Kohlberg's terms, it is generally reflected in the more "immature" third stage of development.

The devaluation of women and their relegation to dependency can also be seen in the theory and language of Eric Erikson (1968). For Erikson, the linguistic concept of *identity* is forged by the male in adolescence, involving "autonomy, initiative and industry." Just how male-laden these concepts are is clear when, conversely, he describes the female as holding her identity in "abeyance" until she finds a man to rescue her from her emptiness and loneliness by filling "the inner space."

The psychological concepts of competition and achievement are among many other possible illustrations of how psychological language means different things for each sex. Whereas for men the problem involves motives to approach success and to avoid failure (McClelland, 1961), for women it involves another dimension: fear of success (Horner, 1971). This occurs because for most women the anticipation of success in competitive achievement, especially against men, produces anticipation of certain consequences such as threat of social rejection and loss of femininity.

The Language of Fairy Tales and School Texts

The Judeo-Christian doctrine which has been an essential aspect of Western society is also steeped in the male perspective with a language to match. *Paradise lost* are emotion-laden words expressing man's distrust of woman and his superiority. Within those words lies the tale of Adam, who was a man alone, in God's grace and the first on earth. As the word implies, *woman* was constructed from him. She led him into *temptation* and paradise was lost.

Variations on this theme are an essential part of the language of socialization for very young children. For example, in the preschool years, the child is introduced to the language of fairy tales. Much of it is symbolic of culturally accepted sex roles and stereotyping. A common theme concerns the male's struggle with the father, elder brothers, or the environment during adolescence, as illustrated in the story of "Jack and the Beanstalk" and Jack's successful killing of the giant. In contrast, on the edge of puberty, the girl's first bleeding is followed by a period of passivity, symbolized by the deep sleep of Snow White and the Sleeping Beauty. Each is rescued by a male and marriage. In his famous Freudian analysis of fairy tales, Bettelheim (1976) argues that, since identity for women in our society is bound up with intimacy, this theme in fairy tales helps in the early socialization of female children into that role.

This pervasive doctrinal language is further repeated, with variations, in the language of the basic school texts to which every child in Western society is subject. There are some females in elementary readers, but typically 70–80% are male and only 20% are female (Lorimer & Long, 1979–1980). Of the men, 90% are presented in a large variety of activities, but women are presented in a significantly narrower range (Linn, 1976).

What is more, these sex differences are bound to characterizations which are value-laden. Girl children may appear in the school texts and readers in active, outside-the-home roles for 36% of the time, but women appear in such roles much less often. Given the fact that the ratio of the sexes in the population is approximately 50–50, this emphasis suggests that activities in which women participate are not important enough to be written about in school readers (Lorimer & Long, 1979–1980). The suggestion is borne out in the research. Asked to rate a variety of home activities, such as cooking, cleaning, and caring for children, and outside activities, such as mending a fence, using a sledge hammer, and being a policeman, children of 6 to 10 years chose the latter, to a highly significant degree, as more important (Phillips, 1979). Above all, significantly more little girls wanted to be little boys than vice versa, which suggested that they had already learned to see males as being in an enviable position; their comments indicated that this was because they saw boys as having access to the most attractive activities.

Generally, three times as much character-trait language is applied to men (big, strong, active, competitive), all of which emphasizes dominance, while for women there are fewer character-trait descriptions, and those few imply subdominance (pretty, accepting, admiring, a good companion) (Lorimer & Long, 1979–1980). If women do assume leadership, it is during the absence of men; in this role, they are not always considered as capable as men are and are sometimes described as disagreeable. The narrow range of traits for women in the language of school texts suggest they are more stereotyped than males. Yet many have led and still lead remarkably varied lives to which many private but few public histories attest. The little that has been written about women in history more often than not places them in nurturant and supportive background roles, just as school readers do; their fame derives from, or is noticed because of, the fact that they are the wives or mistresses of famous men.

In the face of the continually inferior social position in which women are placed and the barrage of language which attests to this inferiority, what are the predictions and findings about the female self-concept?

Language and the Self-concept

Sullivan (1953), Mead (1934), and Cooley (1902) saw children as immersed in a continual stream of interpersonal situations in which they are recipients of a never-ending flow of "reflected appraisals" which develop their self-concepts. If the child assimilates positive and constructive appraisals, then the child's feelings are more inclined to be positive and approving. However, if the appraisals have been mostly derogatory and rejecting, then the self-concept is apt to be disparaging and hostile.

The self-concept is not only directly conditioned by the language applied to it, it is also indirectly influenced by language mediated by cognitive development. The cognitive structural limitations of young, pre-operational-thinking children narrow their field of awareness and constrict their ability to weigh appraisals reflected in the spoken word. They cannot yet hold multiple points of view and understand the impact of the values, the goals, and the judgmental competence of those who verbally appraise them. Their abilities to differentiate and abstract are severely limited. Hence they are, as Piaget suggests, under adult constraint, and they take into themselves the linguistically expressed view that others have of them (cf. John-Steiner & Tatter, this volume).

We are all aware of the cultural variations in the self-concept. Some cultures encourage cooperativeness, others aggrandizement or arrogance, and others humility.

We are also aware of the influence of varying socioeconomic and environmental factors on the self-concept within cultures. A recent study (Fahey & Phillips, 1981) suggested that disadvantaged children have a poor view of self components which relate to possessions, skills, and schoolwork. In these areas, the value put on self is an outcome of socioeconomic structure. Of course for some the socioeconomic status may change and, as a result, the self-concept changes under the influence of a new set of environmental values. The verbal appraisals of others may also enhance the self-concept as one acquires socioeconomic power, increases in maturity, or learns to express or develop one's potential and talents.

Thus, for some, the hierarchical relationships and their linguistic labels, which have considerable effect on the self-concept, may change. However, in one major area the child is presented with a single dimensional order of human relationships (Lorimer & Long, 1979–1980) and an inescapable linguistic category. *The child learns that class, age, and socioeconomic status may change, but sex and the language labels that go with it do not.* Thus one would expect that females, since they are generally in a socially inferior position, should have poor self-concepts. Much research, mostly done by males, suggests that this is so (I. D. Smith, 1975). In the light of the previous discussion of the male-oriented bias in psychology, one wonders whether the methodology embraced but one aspect of reality or whether there was poor communication. Perhaps recognition of an inferior social position was confused with "feelings" of inferiority; the two are quite different.

To illustrate the problem, the research interpretations of Lakoff (1979) and Fishman (1980) are of interest. Both based their research on the proposition that linguistic behavior, like other aspects of behavior, is predominantly a product of learning. They also both argued that style of speech and choice of words reflect the self-image and that through socialization the male/female power hierarchy is internalized and reproduced in differing linguistic styles. However, Lakoff (1979) argued that, on this basis, the language of women is more insecure, dependent, submissive, and emotional than that of men. Fishman (1980) proposed a different analysis on the basis of examining the interactional situation, which produces differences in male/female language.

For example, women tend to ask more questions than men. Whereas Lakoff saw this as an expression of an insecure personality, Fishman (1978) noted that in interaction with men women succeed only 36% of the time in getting their topics to become actual conversations. However, when one looks at the topics which women successfully introduce with a question, their success rate jumps to 72%. It is suggested, therefore, that in interaction with men the greater use of questions is an attempt to solve a conversational problem. Men often do not do the necessary work to keep the conversation going. Thus, women ask questions so often because of the conversational power of questions, not because of personality weakness. Fishman argues that women's conversational troubles, in this and many other ways, reflect not inferior social training, as Lakoff claims, but their inferior social position. Socially structured power relations are reproduced and actively maintained in linguistic interactions. The question of the self-concept of women needs further research, research which assesses self-esteem within the female as well as the male perspective.

The Self-concept and Stereotyped Language

Linked with this problem is another. In the use of sex-stereotyped labels, language again appears to play an important part in maintaining and reflecting socially structured power relations (cf. Harris, this volume). Some of these stereotypes were found in the earlier discussion on school readers. In general, our stereotyped language of sex roles suggests that women are better at verbal tasks, think more globally, are more empathic, are more apt to allow intuition and emotion to influence their judgment, and are less aggressive (Gilligan, 1979). Males are stereotyped as being aggressive, competitive, and analytical. Are these stereotypes but one spectrum of reality or all of it?

Of special interest in this context is the recent research on androgyny. Bem (1975), Bem and Lenney (1976), Bem, Martyna, and Watson (1976), and Jones, Chernovetz, and Hansson (1978) believe that persons who indicate high levels of masculine and feminine language in their self-descriptions are adaptive, flexible, and unusually skillful in social situations. Ickes and Barnes (1978) found that whereas the usual role-stereotyped dyads are highly incompatible and display dysfunctional interpersonal behavior, those containing at least one androgynous person are much more successful (Jose, Crosby, & Wong-McCarthy, 1980). This finding suggests that genuine communication between the sexes can be increased by reducing stereotyping.

The research also suggests that severe conditioning of the unidimensional male or female aspects of personality through linguistic and physical reinforcement can be related to pathology which is the outcome of the severe repression of some facets of the personality. Psychopathy and passive-aggressive personality disorders tend to account for significantly more male than female cases (Dacey, 1979) and have been related to the discouraging of emotion and the encouraging of competition in males. Conversely, socialization pressures to take on the female stereotype appear to be related to the fact that significantly more females than males suffer from anxiety disorders, depression, and obsessive compulsive reactions. Even when one casts culturally induced pathology aside, the fact remains that sexual stereotypes may offer both sexes but a segment of all the personality possibilities open to them. Perhaps instead of aiming to educate men and women toward a rounded capacity for both empathic and legalistic attitudes, we have circulated the myth that these are opposites which cannot grow together and so deprive our children of optimum cognitive and personal growth. Much more research is needed on the effects on personality and self where socially structured power relations are reproduced and actively maintained in linguistic interaction and reinforcement. One such attempt is the research outlined in the following chapter.

References

Alvy, K. T. The development of listener adapted communications in grade-school children from different social-class backgrounds. *Genetic Psychology Monographs*, 1973, *87*, 33–104.

Barron, N. Sex-typed language: The production of grammatical cases. *Acta Psychologica*, 1971, *14*, 24–72.

Bate, B. A. Generic man, invisible woman: Language, thought and social change. *Michigan Papers in Women's Studies*, 1975, *2*, 1–13.

Bem, S. L. Sex role adaptibility: One consequence of psychological androgyny. *Journal of Personality and Social Psychology*, 1975, *31*, 634–643.

Bem, S. L., & Bem, D. Does sex-biased job advertising "aid and abet" sex discrimination? *Journal of Applied Social Psychology*, 1974, *24*, 142–149.

Bem, S. L., & Lenney, E. Sex typing and the avoidance of cross sex behavior. *Journal of Personality and Social Psychology*, 1976, *33*, 48–54.

Bem, S. L., Martyna, W., & Watson, C. Sex typing and androgyny: Further explorations of the expressive domain. *Journal of Personality and Social Psychology*, 1976, *34*, 1016–1023.

Bernard, J. *The sex game*. Englewood Cliffs, N.J.: Prentice Hall, 1972.

Bettelheim, B. *The uses of enchantment*. New York: Knopf, 1976.

Cooley, C. *Human nature and the social order*. New York: Scribner, 1902.

Dacey, J. S. *Adolescence today*. Pacific Palisades, Calif.: Goodyear, 1979.

Erikson, E. *Identity: Youth and crisis*. New York: Norton, 1968.

Fahey, M., & Phillips, S. The self concept of disadvantaged children: An exploratory study in middle childhood. *Journal of Psychology*, 1981, *109*, 223–232.

Fishman, P. M. Interaction: The work women do. *Social Problems*, 1978, *25*, 397–406.

Fishman, P. M. Conversational insecurity. In H. Giles, W. P. Robinson, & P. M. Smith (Eds.), *Language: Social psychological perspectives*. New York: Pergamon Press, 1980.

Freud, S. Some physical consequences of the anatomical distinction between the sexes. In J. Strachey (Ed.), *The standard edition of the complete psychological works of Sigmund Freud* (Vol. 19). London: Hogarth Press, 1961. (Originally published, 1925.)

Garvey, C., & Dickstein, E. Levels of analysis and social class differences in language. *Language and Speech*, 1972, *15*, 375–384.

Geiwitz, J. Another plea for *E. A.P.A. Monitor*, August 1978, pp. 3–10.

Gilligan, C. Woman's place in man's life cycle. *Harvard Educational Review*, 1979, *49*(4), 431–445.

Haas, A. Male and female spoken language differences, stereotypes and evidence. *Psychological Bulletin*, 1979, *86*(3), 616–626.

Hartman, M. A. A descriptive study of the language of men and women born in Maine, around 1900 as it reflects the Lakoff hypothesis in "Language and women's place." In B. L. Dubois & I. Couch (Eds.), *The sociology of the languages of American women*. San Antonio, Tex.: Trinity University Press, 1976.

Hextall, I. Marking work. In G. Whitty & M. Young (Eds.), *Exploration in the politics of school knowledge*. Driffield: Nafferton Books, 1976.

Horner, M. Toward an understanding of achievement-related conflicts in women. *Journal of Social Issues*, 1972, *28*(2), 157–174.

Ickes, W., & Barnes, R. D. Boys and girls together—and alienated: On enacting stereotyped sex roles in mixed-sex dyads. *Journal of Personality and Social Psychology*, 1978, *36*, 669–683.

Jones, W. H., Chernovetz, M. E. O., & Hansson, R. O. The enigma of androgyny: Differential implications for males and females? *Journal of Consulting and Clinical Psychology*, 1978, *46*, 298–313.

Jong, E. *How to save your own life*. New York: Holt, Rinehart & Winston, 1977.

Jose, P. E., Crosby, F., & Wong-McCarthy, W. S. Androgyny, dyadic compatibility and conversational behavior. In H. Giles, N. P. Robinson, & P. M. Smith (Eds.), *Language: Social psychological perspectives*. New York: Pergamon Press, 1980.

Kohlberg, L., & Kramer, R. Continuities and discontinuities in childhood and adult moral development. *Human Development*, 1969, *12*, 93–120.

Kohlberg, L. From is to ought: How to commit the naturalistic fallacy and get away with it in the study of moral development. In T. Mischel (Ed.), *Cognitive development and epistemology*. New York: Academic Press, 1971.

Lakoff, R. T. Language and women's place. *Language and Society*, 1973, *2*, 45–80.

Lakoff, R. T. Women's language. In D. Butturff & E. L. Epstein (Eds.), *Women's language and style*. Akron, Ohio: University of Akron, 1979.

Lakoff, R. T. *Language and women's place*. New York: Harper Colophon Books, 1975.

Leacock, E. The changing family and living—Strauss or whatever happened to fathers. *Social Research,* 1977, *44,* 2.

Leet-Pellegrini, H. M. Conversational dominance as a function of gender and expertise. In H. Giles, P. Robinson, & P. M. Smith (Eds.), *Language: Social psychological perspectives.* New York: Pergamon Press, 1980

Linn, J. *Language patterns.* Toronto: Holt, Rinehart & Winston, 1976.

Lorimer, R., & Long, M. Sex-role stereotyping in elementary readers. *Interchange,* 1979–1980, *10*(2), 25–45.

Mackay, D. G. Language, thought and social attitudes. In H. Giles, P. Robinson, & P. M. Smith (Eds.), *Language: Social psychological perspectives.* New York: Pergamon Press, 1980.

McClelland, D. *The achieving society.* New York: Van Nostrand, 1961.

Mead, G. *Mind, self and society.* Chicago: University of Chicago Press, 1934.

Miller, C., & Swift, K. *Words and women: New language in new times.* Garden City, N.J.: Doubleday, 1976.

Phillips, S. *Sex bias in children's choice of roles and tasks.* Unpublished research report, School of Education, University of New South Wales, 1979.

Rich, A. *Of woman born: Motherhood as experience and institution.* New York: Bantam Books, 1977.

Slater, P. *The pursuit of loneliness.* Boston: Beacon Press, 1970.

Smith, D. E. A peculiar eclipsing: Women's exclusion from man's culture. *Women's Studies International Quarterly,* 1978, *1,* 281–295.

Smith, I. D. Sex differences in the self concept of primary school children. *Australian Psychologist,* 1975, *10*(1), 59–63.

Snow, C. E., & Ferguson, C. A. (Eds.). *Talking to children: Language input and acquisition.* Cambridge: Cambridge University Press, 1977.

Strodtbeck, F. L., & Mann, R. D. Sex role differentiation in jury deliberations. *Sociometry,* 1956, *19,* 3–11.

Sullivan, H. S. *The interpersonal theory of psychiatry.* New York: Norton, 1953.

Swacker, M. The role of the speaker as a sociolinguistic variable. In B. Thorne & N. Henley (Eds.), *Language and sex: Differences and dominance.* Rowley, Mass.: Newbury House, 1975.

Trainer, F. E. A critical analysis of Kohlberg's contributions to the study of moral thought. *Journal for the Theory of Social Behavior,* 1976, *1*(1), 19.

Vygotsky, L. S. *Thought and language.* New York: Wiley, 1962.

Vygotsky, L. S. Development of higher mental functions. In *Psychological research in the U.S.S.R.* Moscow: Progress Publishers, 1966.

Wood, M. The influence of sex and knowledge of communication effectiveness on spontaneous speech. *Word,* 1966, *22,* 112–137.

Sexism and Self-concept in the Language of Children: A Middle Childhood Survey

Shelley Phillips

This study attempts to examine whether children are affected by the presentation of the single dimensional order of human sexual relationships through stereotypic linguistic labels. The method involved looking at primary school children's attitudes toward their own and the opposite sex in a large Australian city with a diverse socioeconomic and cultural background. The research findings suggest that, as early as the age of 10 years, female characteristics are seen as undesirable by 50% or more of male children and that this phenomenon cannot be dismissed as unimportant or a mere function of developmental age as is typically done in traditional psychological theories.

Method

Subjects

The participants in the main study were 2,279 fifth- and sixth-grade pupils, from a random sample of government, independent, and alternative primary schools.

The government-controlled state schools in the sample (36) are coeducational and non-fee-paying and embrace predominantly working-class children, although many include a considerable percentage of children with middle-class and professional backgrounds, depending on the area in which the school is situated, as indicated later. The four independent schools in the sample were old, well-established, traditionally oriented, expensive, fee-paying, single-sex schools, representing predom-

Shelley Phillips ● Unit for Child Studies, School of Education, University of New South Wales, Kensington 2033, New South Wales, Australia.

inantly upper-middle-class children from the high status areas 1 and 2 (Congalton, 1969). The alternative school in the sample is also independent of government control and expensive, but it is coeducational and prides itself on a progressive, antiauthoritarian stance on education. Its pupils are from well-to-do, intellectual backgrounds and the higher socioeconomic status areas 1 to 3 (Congalton, 1969). The distribution of schools in the random sample was representative of that in the total school population. Numbers of children from each school ranged from 33 to 67.

The schools were distributed randomly throughout all socioeconomic strata of inner- and outer-metropolitan Sydney according to Congalton's 7-point scale (1969) and included children of 57 different nationalities. The subsamples of various ages were: 9 years, $n = 19$; 10 years, $n = 732$; 11 years, $n = 1,078$; 12 years, $n = 439$; 13 years, $n = 14$. Six children gave no age. The grade subsample was: fifth grade, $n = 967$, and sixth grade, $n = 1,277$. One child was in the fourth grade and 34 had no grade recorded. There were 1,119 girls and 1,158 boys. The sex of two children was not recorded.

During the pilot studies a random sample of 500 children from status areas 1, 3, 4, and 5 were interviewed.

Independent Variables

Socioeconomic Status. The socioeconomic status of the suburb in which the children attended school was derived from Congalton's 7-point scale (1969) and checked against Congalton's ongoing research. The ranking was derived from population estimates of the desirability of a suburb in relation to middle-class values (professional status, education, wealth, and what Hirsch, 1977, describes as "positional good") and ranges from a ranking of 1 for the highest status suburbs to 7 for the lowest status suburbs.

Educational Area. The educational area was defined by an analysis of census figures by Davis and Spearritt (1974). It ranges from 1 to 6 as follows:

	Percentages of Adults in the Area Who Have Completed
Area	*School to University Entrance Requirements*
1	50–80
2	40–50
3	30–40
4	20–30
5	10–20
6	9–10

The Development of the Items

The first stage of the study consisted of free discussion with 500 children in schools from status areas 1, 3, 4, and 5 about playmates and the collection of statements made most frequently by them about the opposite sex. There were many stereotyped descriptions by both sexes; insignificantly few of these were derogatory descriptions of boys by girls but there was a high percentage of derogatory descriptions of girls by boys. A selection of the most common statements was made as follows:

1. Boys make better leaders than girls.
2. It is silly for men to be nurses.
3. You can trust boys more than you can girls.
4. Girls are weak and silly.
5. Boys are better at maths and science than girls.
6. Father should be head of the house.
7. Girls should learn only things that are useful around the house.
8. Boys are cleverer than girls.
9. Girls wouldn't make good engineers.

In order to estimate whether the single direction of each statement might bias the results with a larger sample, the opposite sex was substituted in each case and the items were also reversed. For example, in the case of the original item 1, described here as 1a: "Boys make better leaders than girls," the following variations were included:

1b. Girls make better leaders than boys.
1c. Boys do not make better leaders than girls.
1d. Girls do not make better leaders than boys.

The variations for each of these items (36) were included with 36 additional items which were being tested for another aspect of the research and given to the 500 pilot subjects. Analysis indicated that the children answered all questions consistently. If they agreed with version 1a, they disagreed with 1b and 1c and agreed with 1d, and vice versa. Less than 2% of the children changed the direction of their answers. This trend applied to all nine items, and with this degree of reliability, the stereotyped statements given by the children themselves were deemed the most suitable for the main study. They had the advantage of being derived from the children's language and their own methods of evaluating, judging, and defining. Extrapolation of adult language and attitudes to those of children has resulted previously in unreliable questionnaires for them.

There was also an attempt in the pilot studies to question the children fully on each of the statements to establish that the intent and meaning fully agreed with the statement. Observations of behavior between the sexes also indicated a high correlation between denigratory statements and avoidance and uncomplimentary behavior, such as orders to girls to get out of boys' games and aggressive teasing ("We don't want any fat tarts here").

Procedures

The nine items were then given to the main sample of 2,279 children as part of a 54-item paper-and-pencil questionnaire which included a number of other attitudes (Phillips, 1979a,b). It included prior instructions and practice examples in answering procedures and the statement "The paper before you has questions about what you think and what your interests are." It was administered by a trained psychologist. Pearson's correlation coefficient, χ^2, and the paired sample t test (Nie, Hull, Jenkins, Steinbrenner, & Dent, 1975) were used in the analysis.

Results

Cluster Analysis

In a cluster analysis of the 54 items on the total questionnaire, the nine items under discussion formed cluster I with a correlation of .633. That correlation and the ensuing factor analysis suggested that the items had something strongly in common (Phillips, 1979a).

Reliability and Validity

After a six-month interval, 530 children from grades five and six were given the questionnaire a second time. The test–retest correlation (paired sample) for the nine items was .94. The time interval was unavoidable, and this interval and maturational and learning effects could contribute to error variance. Nevertheless, the test–retest coefficient suggests that the attitudes sampled have a strong reliability overtone.

Responses

Sex Differences in Acceptance of Stereotyped Language. Table I gives the percentages of the total population and the percentages of boys and girls agreeing with each of the nine items. The group of items (3, 4, 5, and 8) which relate to traditional stereotypes about male superiority combined with denigratory attitudes toward females shows the most marked differences. Only a small percentage of girls agree with these statements in contrast to a large percentage of boys. Items 1 and 7, which are more indirectly derogatory, show a slight increase in female agreement. Most

Table I. Percentage of Total Population and Each Sex Agreeing with Nine Items

Item	Total population	Girls	Boys	χ^{2a}	p
1. Boys make better leaders than girls.	46.2	14.0	77.2	926.18677	.0000
2. It is silly for men to be nurses.	44.5	40.2	48.6	19.10428	.0040
3. You can trust boys more than you can trust girls.	30.1	8.8	50.4	477.55037	.0000
4. Girls are weak and silly.	25.1	2.0	47.5	635.67187	.0000
5. Boys are better at maths and science than girls.	30.6	8.8	51.7	509.70164	.0000
6. Father should be head of the house.	69	63.5	74.2	31.91892	.0000
7. Girls should learn only things that are useful around the house.	29.7	16.1	42.9	199.78861	.0000
8. Boys are cleverer than girls.	30.3	5.1	54.6	668.78816	.0000
9. Girls wouldn't make good engineers.	47.6	34.6	60.2	151.74657	.0000

[a] χ^2 is for boy–girl population only.

Table II. A Comparison of Boys within Status Areas 3 and 7 Agreeing with Each of the Nine Items

Item	Status area	Percentage agreeing	Mean	SD	SE	t
1. Boys make better leaders than girls.	3	64.3	1.36	.48	.04	3.68[a]
	7	87.8	1.22	.33	.05	
2. It is silly for men to be nurses.	3	38.1	1.62	.49	.04	1.82
	7	46.9	1.45	.58	.08	
3. You can trust boys more than you can girls.	3	34.9	1.63	.50	.045	4.11[a]
	7	69.4	1.30	.47	.067	
4. Girls are weak and silly.	3	31.0	1.69	.46	.04	3.17[b]
	7	57.1	1.43	.50	.07	
5. Boys are better at maths and science than girls.	3	34.1	1.66	.48	.04	5.14[a]
	7	73.5	1.27	.45	.06	
6. Father should be head of the house.	3	57.1	1.43	.50	.04	3.90[a]
	7	81.6	1.14	.41	.06	
7. Girls should learn only things that are useful around the house.	3	21.4	1.79	.41	.04	6.31[a]
	7	69.4	1.31	.47	.07	
8. Boys are cleverer than girls.	3	27.8	1.72	.45	.04	4.42[a]
	7	63.3	1.37	.49	.07	
9. Girls wouldn't make good engineers.	3	44.4	1.56	50	.04	.78
	7	51.0	1.49	.51	.07	

[a] $p < .001$ (two-tailed test).
[b] $p < .01$ (two-tailed test).

agreement between the sexes, but with a tendency for females to agree less, occurs in support of the expectation that males fulfill stereotyped masculine job roles (item 2) and that females cannot fill these satisfactorily (item 9). Above all, note how firmly the concept of male dominance in the social hierarchy is accepted by both sexes in item 6, although again with less females in agreement.

Effects of Socioeconomic Status on Acceptance of Stereotyped Language. It is necessary to ask whether these differences are not simply an artifact of socioeconomic differences as suggested by some other studies (McCandless, 1967). In the present study, the results of the possible influence of the socioeconomic status of parents on the preparedness of children to agree with stereotyped statements were confused by the fact that all children in status 1 and in most in status 2 suburbs (Congalton, 1969) were attending single-sex private schools. Such schools appear to have some effect which increases acceptance of prejudiced statements in boys and will be discussed later. Thus, status area 3 best represented boys who were from a middle-class background but not in a single-sex school. Boys from these suburbs were significantly less inclined to agree with the traditional stereotypes about females and males than boys in all other status areas. Table II compares status areas 3 and 7— the latter representing strongly working-class areas with a high proportion of immigrants.

Nevertheless, it should be noted that the percentages of middle-class boys agree-

Table III. A Comparison of Boys within Education Areas 1 and 6 Agreeing with Each of the Nine Items

Item	Status area	Percentage agreeing	Mean	SD	SE	t
1. Boys make better leaders than girls.	1	68.5	1.3	.48	.04	2.57[a]
	6	81.3	1.19	.39	.02	
2. It is silly for men to be nurses.	1	39.2	1.59	.51	.04	2.24
	6	50.6	1.48	.51	.03	
3. You can trust boys more than you can girls.	1	42.0	1.58	.50	.04	2.79[a]
	6	55.0	1.45	.50	.03	
4. Girls are weak and silly.	1	38.5	1.62	.49	.04	2.80[a]
	6	51.9	1.48	.50	.03	
5. Boys are better at maths and science than girls.	1	42.7	1.56	.51	.04	2.46[a]
	6	56.3	1.44	.50	.05	
6. Father should be head of the house.	1	66.4	1.34	.47	.04	2.04[a]
	6	76.7	1.23	.43	.02	
7. Girls should learn only things that are useful around the house.	1	26.6	1.72	.47	.04	4.90[b]
	6	49.9	1.49	.51	.03	
8. Boys are cleverer than girls.	1	35.0	1.66	.48	.04	5.87[b]
	6	61.6	1.37	.50	.03	
9. Girls wouldn't make good engineers.	1	51.0	1.49	.50	.04	2.44[a]
	6	62.9	1.37	.48	.02	

[a]$p < .01$ (two-tailed test).
[b]$p < .001$ (two-tailed test).

ing with these statements, although lower than in other suburbs, are still very high on items relating to male superiority combined with denigratory attitudes to females (items 1, 3, and 4). Their tolerance is only somewhat improved in their attitudes to the domestic stereotyping of females (item 7) and the stereotyping of female intelligence (item 8).

Effects of Parental Education on Stereotyped Language. Table III compares area 1, where the majority of parents have completed six years of secondary school, with area 6, where only 10% of parents have attained this level. Comments for socioeconomic differences apply equally. Education reduces preparedness to agree with stereotyped and denigratory descriptions of females; nevertheless, stereotyped language is still embraced by a large percentage of males from favored educational backgrounds.

Age and Grade Effects. There was a nonsignificant but general decline (1–2%) in the tendency to agree with the nine items as age increased. For both sexes on item 2, and for boys on items 4, 5, 6, and 9, the decline was greater, but still insignificant at 10%. In many cases the tendency to agree went up again with 12 year olds. This increase could be a matter of intelligence, since a child who is 12 and still in fifth year class is generally less intelligent than average.

The Impact of the Single-Sex School on Stereotyped Language

Boys. Table IV compares the percentage of boys in the expensive, high-status, single-sex, independent schools with boys in coeducational, non-fee-paying, government schools from all status areas.

It should be noted that, with the exception of item 7 on the expectations of domesticity, boys from independent, single-sex schools are even more prepared to agree with negative and stereotyped statements about females than are the already highly prejudiced boys from coeducational, government-controlled state schools. Indeed, boys from these single-sex schools are as conformist and denigratory of females as are boys from strongly working-class areas and boys from immigrant cultures where sex roles are markedly traditional. Thus, the single-sex school for boys appears to introduce factors that negate the usually more tolerating influence of middle-class family environments and higher education. It may be that there are forces at work in these schools that negate the nonsexist atmosphere and training in some homes. The fact that boys in the alternative school agreed with none of these stereotyped statements suggests that positive alternatives are available; this suggestion will be discussed later.

Girls. Whereas there appears to be a significant increase in negativism in language relating to females in single-sex schools for boys, the reverse is true for girls.

Table IV. A Comparison of Boys within State Coed and Independent Single-Sex Schools Agreeing with Nine Items

Item	School type	Percentage agreeing	Mean	SD	SE	t
1. Boys make better leaders than girls.	Coed	76.9	1.22	.43	.01	2.57[a]
	Single-sex	91.2	1.09	.29	.05	
2. It is silly for men to be nurses.	Coed	48.6	1.51	.51	.02	.40
	Single-sex	52.9	1.48	.51	.09	
3. You can trust boys more than you can girls.	Coed	49.9	1.49	.51	.02	2.92[a]
	Single-sex	73.5	1.26	.45	.08	
4. Girls are weak and silly.	Coed	47.1	1.53	.51	.02	2.05[b]
	Single-sex	64.7	1.35	.49	.08	
5. Boys are better at maths and science than girls.	Coed	51.3	1.47	.52	.02	2.23[b]
	Single-sex	91.2	1.29	.46	.08	
6. Father should be head of the house.	Coed	73.8	1.26	.44	.01	3.26[a]
	Single-sex	91.2	1.09	.29	.05	
7. Girls should learn only things that are useful around the house.	Coed	43.2	1.56	.51	.02	−.66
	Single-sex	38.2	1.62	.49	.09	
8. Boys are cleverer than girls.	Coed	54.5	1.44	.52	.02	.36
	Single-sex	58.8	1.41	.50	.09	
9. Girls wouldn't make good engineers.	Coed	59.8	1.40	.50	.02	2.69[a]
	Single-sex	74.4	1.21	.41	.07	

[a] $p < .01$ (two-tailed test).
[b] $p < .05$ (two-tailed test).

Girls in independent, single-sex schools are significantly less inclined to agree with prejudiced items 3 and 4 ($p > .05$), which relate to blatant denigration of females, and item 7, which stereotypes their domestic role (6% agreed), than are girls in coeducational schools (9% agreed). However, when it came to accepting descriptions of themselves as not competent in what have been seen traditionally as exclusively male job roles—math and science (item 5) and engineering (item 9)—significantly ($p < .01$) more girls from single-sex schools (28% and 44%) were prepared to agree than were girls from coeducational state schools (7.9% and 34.2%).

This result suggests that in some respects single-sex schools for girls, while generating greater self-respect and less rigidity in the expectation of pure domesticity, are discouraging girls from competing in traditionally male-dominated professions. An inspection of the academic syllabus in the schools in the sample further supports this hypothesis.

In contrast to their acceptance of stereotyped statements about their own professional roles, the single-sex, independent school girls' stereotyping of the male professional role (item 2) is significantly less ($p < .01$) (27.8% agreed) than that of coeducational state school girls (40.9% agreed). This finding suggests, as does other research (McCandless, 1967), that when compared to those of lower socioeconomic status, Sydney's upper middle classes have a less stereotyped demand of masculinity for their males. Girls from the alternative school, unlike state and single-sex independent schools, agreed with none of the stereotyped statements.

Discussion

The Single-Sex School: Language and Self-concept

It seems reasonable to assume that the language of these children reflects their social conventions at this age, since the observations of behavior between the sexes and careful checking of the intention of their language in the pilot studies and the retests suggest that they are highly related. Certainly the single-sex school appears as a confounding variable not sufficiently accounted for in previous research on sexual stereotyping in language. The findings here also suggest that coeducation is not necessarily the best alternative for all. While coeducation may reduce sexist language in boys, it appears to encourage in girls a willingness to accept language reflecting a poor view of femininity. These findings put the educator in a dilemma in which there are no immediate answers.

The research suggests that single-sex schools have advantages for girls in a male-dominated society. Girls in single-sex schools are less willing to accept denigratory statements about their sex than are girls in the coeducational schools. They presumably have better self-concepts when they are not in contact with boys in the school situation. On the other hand, if the aim is to reduce sexism in boys, the research suggests that the single-sex school is not a good proposition. It appears to have more effect in inducing male chauvinistic language and attitudes than does the family. The issue is of particular concern because it is boys from these schools who typically become Australia's top lawyers, doctors, and bureaucrats and enter positions which dominate the lives of females as well as males and perpetuate the divisive language of the single dimensional hierarchy in boardrooms, psychiatric consulting rooms, and economic and cultural settings. The position appears to be similar to that in many other Western democracies.

For the sake of the boys, should we sacrifice girls to coeducation? Since the problem of single-sex schools is one of degree (sexism in boys is high even in coeducational schools), the answer is not easy. The research suggests that there may be another alternative. It is to be noted that not one child of either sex in the alternative school agreed with any of the nine statements. This school is one in which parents and school work closely together, and both are dedicated to the elimination of authoritarianism in all forms, including sexual stereotyping. The language of school texts and every activity is carefully monitored to this end, as are cooperative living and learning in all areas. Further research on similar schools and their effects, with careful control of extraneous variables, is needed.

Reducing Stereotyped Language

Measures to reduce sexist language in school texts have been taken by the Education Department of New South Wales, which controls the government coeducational schools in the Sydney sample. For example, they have tried to remove language which stereotypes sex roles from their textbooks. Unfortunately, because there was no prior study, we cannot tell whether this action has improved attitudes. Have girls of this age always been persuaded by the absurdity of such prejudiced statements about their sex, or were school children of this age even more prejudiced against females several decades ago, before the improved texts were introduced? In either case, 50–70% of boys remain uninfluenced or unconvinced. It would seem that these programs controlling textbook language are not sufficient and the total situation needs evaluation, including teacher, peer, and parental language and behavior. The results could also suggest that the elimination of stereotyped language in respect of roles has more effect on girls than it does on boys. This suggestion also needs investigation.

Explanations in Existing Psychological Language

In seeking some of the factors which might encourage primary school boys to use less stereotyped language about females, one might begin by asking whether there is underlying behavior which is crucial to the occurrence of the stereotyped language used. An explanation is to be found in one well-known interpretational concept in the language of psychology. This is the concept of "latency." The concept was first offered by the Victorian male psychiatrist Sigmund Freud (1856–1934) and has since gained considerable currency in lay and professional circles, although the latter do not always recognize its originator, in spite of the fact that anthropological research threw doubt on the generality of the application of many of Freud's concepts across cultures decades ago.

As indicated earlier, from his clinical observations of his patients, Freud applied what he saw as the male oedipal crisis to both sexes. The essence of the argument is that through fear of threat and loss of support the male child represses oedipal incestuous wishes for the mother and aggressive feelings against the parent of the same sex. Through these inhibitions and sublimations, the sexual interest of the male child subsides. The process for the female is a mirror reflection of that of the male and thus, for both sexes, through anxiety, the love for the parent becomes desexualized; the process extends in such a way that the child also temporarily gives up interest in others of the opposite sex. Freud labeled this the *latency* period and the concept is presumed to apply to all children in primary school years. Freud hypothesized that the latency of sexual interest between children of 6 and 11 years is why, at that age, boys play mostly with boys and girls play more often than not with girls. The theory is now part of cultural folklore and language, and there is a generally held belief that a disinterest and hostility between the sexes in primary school is natural.

Alternative Realities in Language

Could the latency concept be yet another example of language in psychology describing but one reality or the reality of the male perspective? Has this perspective been falsely rationalized to include females in an explanation which does not apply to their experiences and development? Is this oversight the product of a methodology which fails to take account of the social and economic dimensions which are different for the sexes in our society? Certainly, the results in the present research suggest a divisive socialization process internalized through stereotyped language. The results also suggest that middle childhood is not a time of carefree indifference between the sexes, as the latency concept and popular belief would have it. Rather, the findings here suggest that there is a one-sided rejection and that we are witness to a crucial stage in the developmental and socialization process, necessitating the assertion of masculinity and the denigration of femininity. A language of hostile stereotypes reflects and internalizes this process.

The limitation of personal development and freedom implied in the dichotomy of sex roles in our language has already been discussed. To develop and maintain the exclusively masculine traits of competitiveness and aggressiveness, to conceal softness and emotionality, not to cry in the face of hurt, and never to show fear are the basic elements of the educational diet and language conditioning process for most males in our society. It appears to be an unrealistically harsh education and most males recall the anxiety associated with the fear of being labeled a "sissy" or behaving "like a girl." Thus, the male child, anxious about hiding his fears and softness, tends to reduce that anxiety by projecting his denigration of the feminine aspects of himself onto members of the opposite sex, who are indeed feminine, and thus female children become the target for his denigratory language. This prejudiced language reflects not only his inner anxiety but social conditions. In Western society such language is encouraged and institutionalized as "normal" during the crucial socialization period of middle childhood. Not until the male child is more confident of his ability to play the masculine role does his fear and derision of females diminish. With some, this may occur in adolescence, and with others, never. Psychoanalytic language reflected these social conventions and preserved and reinforced them with concepts that suggested they were inevitable.

Toward a Comprehensive Language

The problem is that psychological research has not utilized the interactional/situational model often enough. This means that the power structure and the unidimensional nature of society can be overlooked in studying linguistic conventions. In such cases, certain aspects of human behavior may be encapsulated in psychological language which describes those aspects as "in the nature of things" (and the latency concept is but one example) when, in fact, the behavior in question is a product of particular social influences (cf. Meacham, this volume). Distortion of reality is particularly apparent where female development and behavior are regularly subsumed under linguistic labels which better describe male processes. The point is not that everyone should have the same views about language and social structure, but that the experiences, perceptions, and interpretations of females should be acknowledged as legitimate and part of reality. Without this comprehension, psychology and the psychology of language are but half a science and half of reality.

References

Congalton, A. A. *Status and prestige in Australia.* Sydney: Cheshire, 1969.

Davis, J. R., & Spearritt, P. *Sydney at the census, 1971: A social atlas.* Canberra: Urban Research Unit, A.N.U., 1974.

Hirsch, F. *Social limits to growth.* London: Routledge and Kegan Paul, 1977.

McCandless, B. R. *Children, behaviour and development.* New York: Holt, Rinehart & Winston, 1967.

Nie, N., Hull, C., Jenkins, J., Steinbrenner, K., & Bent, D. *Statistical package for the social sciences* (2nd ed.). New York: McGraw-Hill, 1975.

Phillips, S. Authoritarianism: Factor structure of a middle childhood scale. *Child Study Journal,* 1979, *9,* 1. (a)

Phillips, S. *Young Australians: The attitudes of our children.* Sydney: Harper & Row, 1979. (b)

9

Aging, Work, and Youth: New Words for a New Age of Old Age

John A. Meacham

We are currently in a period of transition from an understanding and experience of late adulthood and old age that was valid for thousands of years to a new age of old age. In the United States, for example, the number of people over the age of 60 will increase by 16 million in the next 30 years, an increase of 50% over the current 32 million. These older people will be better educated, healthier, and better organized politically. They will expect a higher level of educational and recreational opportunities, health benefits, and other social services than what is now provided. There will likely be profound changes in how older people perceive themselves and how society in general regards older people.

There are a number of symptoms of this transition to a new age of old age. One of these is the great variety of conceptual models employed both by social scientists and by the general public for organizing and interpreting information about aging. Kalish (1979), for example, has described several such models, including the pathology model, in which sickness is the principal characteristic of aging, and the minimal change model, in which the continuity of late adulthood with earlier periods is emphasized. Most gerontologists subscribe to the normal person model, in which older people are seen to be as diverse as people of other ages and their individual characteristics are understandable in terms of unique and complex life experiences. Kalish warns against two models that unfortunately involve ageist stereotyping: the incompetence model, in which the needs of older people are overemphasized in order to obtain funding for social services programs, and the geriactivist model, in which active social and political participation is prescribed as a behavioral norm for all older people. Kalish advocates a variation on the normal person model, the personal growth model, in which the later years can be for some people a period of fewer work

---

John A. Meacham ● Department of Psychology, State University of New York at Buffalo, Buffalo, New York 14226.

and family constraints, increased leisure time, and motivation to concentrate on what is deemed truly important, whether this be politics, painting, or reminiscing.

A second symptom of the transition in understanding is the open discussion of what to call people who are living in late adulthood and old age and who are the object of study by social scientists. Although there is widespread agreement on designation of younger people as infants, children, adolescents, and adults, there is no agreement on a noun for referring to older people. Schmerl (1975) has reviewed several alternatives in current use, including senior citizen, which some regard as patronizing and as connoting dependency, and aged, which often connotes being quite old and in very poor health. Other terms—older adult, elderly, older person—are derived from implicit comparisons with younger people, rather than being based on the characteristics of late adulthood and old age. Schmerl suggests adoption of the term elder, which connotes not only advanced age but also status, gentility, and the improvements that come with age. Other gerontologists distinguish between the young-old, ranging between 60 and 75 years of age, and the old-old, who are more likely to be in poor health. It is not the purpose of this chapter to advocate any particular terminology. (The problem may be more acute in English than in some other languages.) Rather, it will be argued that the words that are employed during this transition will have a critical relationship to whether the incompetence model, the personal growth model, or any other model is widely applied to the understanding of aging. More generally, discussion of the relationship between words, conceptual models, and the place of older people in society will serve to illustrate the need for social scientists to abandon input-output models in favor of metaphors such as interpenetration, transaction, or dialectics (Meacham, 1981).

Identity and the Social Context

The experiences of older people are based primarily on their relations with the social context. These relations include acting on the social context as well as responding to the social context. Consider as a social event that someone has called attention to the graying hair of a middle-aged person. How does this person act on or otherwise understand this event? The understanding will be influenced by the structure of the person's identity: if feeling young is an important aspect of identity, this person may be threatened by gray hair; if feeling mature is important, this person may welcome the gray hair. In summary, from this constructivist perspective, events in the social context have no inherent meaning, but acquire meaning by being understood within a structure of knowledge. Of course, the identity of an older person may be influenced by the social context. Frequent mention of graying hair by one's friends may, along with other events, be instrumental in bringing about a change in identity from youthful to mature. The relations of acting on the social context (assimilating) and responding to the social context (accommodating) exist simultaneously and may be considered two aspects of the process of adaptation. Whitbourne and Weinstock (1979) have detailed this general model for social and personality development and refer to these relations that link identity and experiences as deductive and inductive differentiation. Of course, these relations hold not only for older people but for people of all ages.

Ideally, the relations of acting upon and responding to the social context should be in approximate balance. Kuypers and Bengtson (1973) argue, however, that the identities of many older people are unduly influenced by events in their social environment. This influence is possible because their identities are diffuse and weak due to the loss of familiar roles through retirement, widowhood, and the deaths of friends; the lack of clearly defined age-appropriate behavioral norms; and the lack of appropriate reference groups that might provide social support. An older person in such a condition of identity diffusion then becomes too easily influenced by and dependent on information available within the social context. Unfortunately, this information is often incorrect in many respects and in general supports a stereotyped view of aging as a period of increasing incompetence and dependency (McTavish, 1971). Nevertheless, this stereotype of aging becomes the basis for construction of a new negative identity during aging. This identity in turn provides the framework for understanding events in the social context, and so a vicious circle is initiated. The circle becomes a self-fulfilling prophecy, both for older people and for society in general. Kuypers and Bengtson refer to this process as one of social breakdown, in which the apparent symptoms of old age within individuals derive from structural, social changes such as retirement and from negative stereotypes of aging prevalent within the social context.

Kuypers and Bengtson (1973) suggest several procedures for intervening in the social breakdown process. For example, one can aid in the efforts of older people to cope with poor environmental conditions (health care, housing, etc.). Second, feelings of competence and control can be increased by encouraging older people—for example, clients or patients—to be involved in decision making, policy formation, and administration of social services programs.

The Stereotype and Reality of Aging

A third intervention in the social breakdown process is to correct the stereotype of older people as incompetent, useless, obsolete, dependent, and so on. This negative stereotype derives in part from neglect of three important principles in the understanding of adult development and aging. The first principle is that older people are a heterogeneous group, and so the stereotype of aging is unfair—as are all stereotypes—in its failure to recognize and to give credit to the wide range of differences in interests, values, and abilities among older people. One would rarely consider grouping people between the ages of 5 and 35 and then describing this group with a common set of adjectives. Yet our general unfamiliarity with the reality of aging encourages us to do this with people from 55 to 85—also a range of 30 years. Much social science research includes samples from each decade from 20 to 50, but the last, undifferentiated group is merely "65-plus." There is considerable continuity between the interests, values, and abilities of early adulthood and those of later adulthood; the wide range of differences among children and young adults also exists among older people.

A second principle whose neglect supports the negative stereotype of aging involves health. The principle is that many apparent changes with age reflect instead poor health. The association of aging and poor health is not a necessary one; only a small proportion of older people are in poor health at any point in time. Just as it is possible to consider the social and psychological changes of infancy and childhood apart from the incidence of accidents and disease, so it is possible to consider the changes of late adulthood and old age as these occur for healthy people. The importance of good health for psychological functioning was demonstrated in an investigation of older men living in the community and apparently free of symptoms of poor health (Botwinick & Birren, 1963). The men were divided into two groups on the basis of a rigorous medical examination. The examination revealed for some of the men incipient arteriosclerosis, a thickening of the lining of the arteries so that the ability of the lungs and heart to provide oxygen to the brain is diminished. Although the differences in health were minor, the healthy group performed better than the unhealthy group, and better than a group of younger people, on a variety of cognitive and personality measures. Unfortunately, much social science research compares young, healthy people—college students, for example—with older people in poor health—institutionalized elderly or clinic outpatients—and so age and health are not separated as possible explanations for any observed age differences. Similarly, the common stereotype of aging fails to distinguish necessary or typical changes with age from the effects of poor health *per se*.

A third principle is that many apparent changes with age reflect instead differences between generations. People's interests, personalities, and abilities derive from their unique experiences. These experiences change in a regular way from one generation to the next. Successive generations have had greater opportunities for education, good health care, travel and leisure activities, and jobs that require little physical effort and have few health hazards. Successive generations also have unique intersections of life stages with specific historical events. For example, the generation born in 1910 began to raise families and establish careers during the Depression; the generation of 1930 began these tasks during the affluence of the 1950s. Certainly, the different social and economic conditions influenced the expectations and achievements of these two generations and contributed to the development of interests and values that have been carried forward into late adulthood and old age. The common stereotype of aging, therefore, fails to recognize that many of the characteristics of the people who are old today reflect lack of education, poor health care, restricted career opportunities, and the like during the lives of these people. The people who will be old in the future will have different characteristics, reflecting the experiences of their own time in history.

What can be said, then, about the reality of aging? Setting aside the first principle of heterogeneity for the sake of brevity, and keeping in mind the principles of health and generational differences, a few broad conclusions emerge. A major feature of the negative stereotype of aging is that the ability to remember diminishes. This is not so for healthy people, at least when one considers people's ability to retain information over extended periods of time. Hulicka and Weiss (1965) compared the ability of older and younger people to retain associations between various geometric shapes and names over periods of 20 minutes and one week. First, however, they had each group learn the associations to the same criterion, namely, one error-free pass through the list of shapes and names. This procedure ensured that both age groups had acquired the information before the test for retention. The number of items retained and subsequently recalled was found to be the same for the older and younger people.

It is likely that apparent problems of remembering in older people reflect instead a problem of acquiring or learning the material in the first place. For example, not knowing a person's name may reveal not that the name was not remembered, but rather that the name was not heard distinctly or attended to when the person was first introduced. Learning in older people follows precisely the same principles as learning in younger people: learning is facilitated if the material to be learned is presented at a proper pace, if the new information is made meaningful and familiar so that the learner can build on previous knowledge, and if the learner is properly motivated. Unfortunately, many of the specific techniques employed by our educational institutions, as well as procedures employed by educators and social scientists for assessing learning abilities, have been designed with younger people in mind and do not mesh well with the interests, needs, and motivations of older people from earlier generations. The learning and problem-solving performance of older people can be substantially improved by changing materials originally designed for children or for laboratory research to make the materials more relevant for older people (Arenberg, 1968; Hulicka, 1967). Learning can also be improved by attending carefully to the level of motivation or arousal of older learners. Many older people, perhaps as a reaction to the stereotype that older people are poor learners, become over-aroused and anxious in learning situations and their learning performance suffers. Eisdorfer, Nowlin, and Wilkie (1970) have provided evidence that anxiety hinders learning by comparing the performance of older people who had received a calming drug with a group that had received a placebo. The calm drug group made fewer errors on the learning task than the placebo group, whose arousal level increased.

Intelligence is not considered by most psychologists to be a general ability, but rather a combination of several more specific abilities. When these specific abilities are assessed for people between the ages of 20 and 80, some abilities are found to increase, some to decline, and some to remain unchanged (Nesselroade, Schaie, & Baltes, 1972). For example, one of these more specific abilities is crystallized intelligence, which involves the understanding of language and mathematical skills. As people get older, performance on measures of crystallized intelligence increases. A second ability has been termed visuo-motor flexibility and involves making repeated changes in what one is doing while working rapidly without making errors. Older people do not perform as well on measures of visuo-motor flexibility as do younger people (nor in general on tests that call for very rapid responding). The decline in this ability begins not in late adulthood, however, but in early adulthood. In short, it is not the case that there is a general decline in cognitive or intellectual functioning during aging. Whether a decline for a specific ability is significant depends on the circumstances of each older person. For example, the decline would likely be important if the ability were required for work and the job could not be restructured to compensate for the change in ability.

Although the common stereotype of aging implies that there is considerable personality change, research evidence supports the conclusion that there is continuity of personality throughout life. The one exception to the picture of continuity is a subtle change in feelings of mastery from active to passive and an increased orientation toward the inner, psychological world rather than the outer world (Neugarten, 1973). There are, however, differences in personality from one generation to the next. Schaie and Parham (1976) have gathered personality data for people born between 1890 and 1940, that is, people who were approximately 75 to 25 years of age. They found that people born around 1900 were more outgoing, excitable, and relaxed and had greater humanitarian concern. People born in the 1920s and 1930s were more conscientious, harder to fool, more conservative (not critical or free thinking), and more group oriented (dependency, community involvement). These generational differences in personality likely reflect early socialization experiences within the family and the impact of major social and economic events, such as the Depression, on individual development.

In summary, the stereotype of aging implies that there are major discontinuities in interests, abilities, and personality between early and late adulthood. In reality, the continuities, at least for people who remain in good health, are far more impressive. Even when evidence exists for psychological changes with aging, one must be cautious in concluding that younger and older people are markedly different. For example, it has been found that reaction times (for example, the time required to respond to a buzzer by pushing a button) of older people are slower than those of younger people. Botwinick and Thompson (1968), however, have observed that when the younger group is divided into athletes and nonathletes, the reaction times of the latter are similar to those of older people.

Work, Identity, and Youth

Correcting the negative, incorrect stereotype of aging through research and education is an intervention in the social breakdown process aimed at decreasing the negative impact of the social context on the identities of older people. A fourth intervention, in addition to improving environmental conditions, increasing feelings of control, and correcting stereotypes, is to eliminate the condition of susceptibility—identity diffusion—that permits the process of social breakdown to begin. Kuypers and Bengtson (1973) suggest that a major factor in becoming susceptible to the social breakdown process is the loss, primarily through retirement, of the role of a productive worker within a society that equates personal worth with economic utility. A variety of anecdotal and survey data demonstrate the significance of working in the lives of people of all ages. What one does as work is a major dimension of identity and of relations with other people so that we describe and introduce ourselves by referring to our work: "I'm a teacher," "I'm a steelworker," etc. Work is a major source of self-esteem, for it provides opportunities to achieve mastery over problems and to produce something of value to others within an organization and within society. Work also provides a primary means of initiating and maintaining friendships.

The consequences of denying work are illustrated by the story of Mr. Winter (Margolis & Kroes, 1974), who was forced to retire as a business executive at age 65. Mr. Winter became isolated from people, and less than a year later was hospitalized with a diagnosis of senile psychosis. A year later, the young person whom Mr. Winter had trained suddenly died. Since only Mr. Winter understood this particular job, he was asked to return from retirement and was soon working at full steam. Unfortunately, after he had trained a new young person, Mr. Winter was retired for a second time and within six months was again hospitalized. Various surveys document the importance of work in the lives of older people. Typical of these is a study by Powers and Goudy (1971), who asked older workers whether they would be willing to accept an annuity providing a comfortable living for the rest of their lives, on the condition that they no longer worked for pay or profit. Prior to retirement workers were more willing to quit work and accept the annuity than after retirement, when half would prefer to refuse the annuity and continue working.

In view of the significance of work for identity, and the likelihood that the work role will be lost through retirement, the fourth intervention in the social breakdown process is to liberate older people from their dependence on the economic role as the single, dominating basis for identity and self-esteem. Instead, people should be encouraged to develop other bases, including expressive, creative, introspective, and interpersonal activities that can be engaged in throughout the life span (Kuypers & Bengtson, 1973). Having an identity that is multidimensional, reflecting interests and strengths in a variety of domains, can provide a good defense against becoming susceptible to the social breakdown process.

There seem to be no obstacles to the development of a differentiated identity at any time in adulthood. Nevertheless, the period of youth stands out as a critical time in which the work role is established as the foundation of identity and other possible dimensions are deemphasized. For Erikson (1963), the sense of ego identity reflects the confidence that there is agreement with others regarding one's role—primarily an occupational identity or career—within society. The developmental tasks of youth include preparing for, gaining entry into, and making a commitment to the world of work. It is unfortunate that for many accomplishing these tasks precludes the establishment of a differentiated identity, based on a wide range of interests, including the arts and humanities, and activities, such as family life and service to others, that can serve to maintain feelings of competence and friendships throughout the life span and especially during retirement when the work role is lost. This differentiation is certainly the best possible preparation during youth for aging.

Language, Stereotypes, and Identity

In the preceding sections, the relations between society's negative stereotype of older people, on the one hand, and the identity, self-esteem, and psychological development of older people, on the other, have been outlined. A symptom of the change in these relations for newer generations is the continuing discussion of how to refer to older people—as senior citizens, the elderly, elders, the aged, and so on. This discussion reflects the important role that language plays for society in facilitating the construction of stereotypes and for individuals in constructing personal identities or self-concepts (cf. Phillips, this volume). The role of language during this transition in understanding of aging parallels the role that language has played as various minorities and women have struggled to construct identities and to achieve equality within the framework of society. Numerous ethnic and racial groups have protested not only against obvious derogatory terms, but also against terms that do not reflect the identity that the minority group holds for itself. A recent example is the preference of Afro-Americans to be referred to as Blacks rather than Negroes; similarly, many females prefer to be referred to as women rather than girls. For many women, an important issue has been to eliminate generic use of words such as he, his, him, and man, since these are likely to be confused with or imply merely the specific male meaning. Moulton, Robinson, and Elias (1978) have provided evidence that even when such words are used in a gender-neutral sense, people more often think of the male referent than when an explicitly neutral word is used, thus validating the claim that the words are discriminatory. Just as language can be racist and sexist, so can it be ageist.

The claim that a word can have such a powerful influence may be doubted by some. The reasonableness of the claim depends on a rejection of input–output models in favor of metaphors such as interpenetration (Meacham, 1981), transaction (Meacham, 1977), or dialectics (Riegel & Meacham, 1978). Input–output models suggest that human development—the output—may be understood and even predicted by describing the proportional amounts of various independent inputs. Large increments in input are expected to be related directly to large increments in output. From this perspective, it would appear unlikely that a single word—for example, *senior*—could strongly influence a process such as that of social breakdown. Nevertheless, although the input–output model may be a reasonable description of many processes—for example, increasing the number of workers to produce more units of a particular product—it may not hold for some important developmental processes. As an alternative, it is necessary to move beyond a consideration of merely the nature and the proportion of the inputs and to focus instead on processes. For example, a common process in chemistry is catalysis, in which a minute amount of a particular input may change the final product dramatically (even though the input itself remains unchanged during the course of the reaction). We need to remain open to the possibility that, in human development as well, apparently minor inputs can lead to major differences in outcome (see Riegel & Meacham, 1978, for further discussion and examples). In particular, a single word—for example, *elder*—may serve as a catalyst in determining whether the relations between the social context and the identities of older people are ones of social breakdown or of positive growth and development.

In summary, words such as senior, aged, elder, and the like, with their associated meanings, provide the initial framework on which society constructs its stereotype of older people and on which older people reconstruct their identities following retirement and associated role losses. Thus human development—in particular, the interests and abilities of older people—must be understood not as the emergence of characteristics that somehow are inherent within individuals, but as a product of the relations that bind individuals to the social context. Recognition of these relations, and of the role that language plays in these relations, is just beginning. In order to understand the historical development of these relations and to grasp how new words might reflect the restructuring of these relations in a new age of old age, it will be necessary to consider closely whose interests are served by these words and by the relations which they imply. Whose interests are served by language that is consistent with the incompetence model rather than the personal growth model (cf. Kvale, this volume) of aging, thus supporting the exclusion of older people from opportunities for working, the failure of employers to provide continuing training so that skills do not become obsolete, as well as the denial of adequate health care, housing, and income during retirement? Dowd (1981) suggests that ageism is an ideology, supporting the exploitation of older people by those who continue to benefit from the system. The language of ageism supports labeling, finding defects in, and blaming the victims (Ryan, 1976; cf. Appel, this volume), thus diverting attention from the profound influence that social relations and the structure of society have on the course of human development. Ironically, perpetuation of the ideology depends on the continued, successful socialization within youths of a unidimensional, production-oriented identity, simultaneously preparing them to be victims during their own aging.

References

Arenberg, D. Concept problem solving in young and old adults. *Journal of Gerontology*, 1968, *23*, 279–282.

Botwinick, J., & Birren, J. E. Cognitive processes: Mental abilities and psychomotor responses in healthy aged men. In J. E. Birren, R. N. Butler, W. W. Greenhouse, L. Sokoloff, & M. R. Yarrow (Eds.), *Human aging: A biological and behavioral study*. Washington, D.C.: U.S. Government Printing Office, 1963.

Botwinick, J., & Thompson, L. W. Age differences in reaction time: An artifact? *The Gerontologist*, 1968, *8*, 25–28.

Dowd, J. J. Age and inequality: A critique of the age stratification model. *Human Development*, 1981, *24*, 157–171.

Eisdorfer, C., Nowlin, J., & Wilkie, F. Improvement in learning in the aged by modification of autonomic nervous system activity. *Science*, 1970, *170*, 1327–1329.

Erikson, E. H. *Childhood and society*. New York: Norton, 1963.

Hulicka, I. M. Age differences in retention as a function of interference. *Journal of Gerontology*, 1967, *22*, 180–184.

Hulicka, I. M., & Weiss, R. L. Age differences in retention as a function of learning. *Journal of Consulting Psychology*, 1965, *2*, 125–129.

Kalish, R. A. The new ageism and the failure models: A polemic. *The Gerontologist*, 1979, *19*, 398–402.

Kuypers, J. A., & Bengtson, V. L. Social breakdown and competence: A model of normal aging. *Human Development*, 1973, *16*, 181–201.

Margolis, B. L., & Kroes, W. H. Work and the health of man. In J. O'Toole (Ed.), *Work and the quality of life*. Cambridge, Mass.: MIT Press, 1974.

McTavish, D. G. Perceptions of old people: A review of research methodologies and findings. *The Gerontologist*, 1971, *11*, 90–101.

Meacham, J. A. A transactional model of remembering. In N. Datan & H. W. Reese (Eds.), *Life-span developmental psychology: Dialectical perspectives on experimental research*. New York: Academic Press, 1977.

Meacham, J. A. Political values, conceptual models, and research. In R. M. Lerner & N. A. Busch-Rossnagel (Eds.), *Individuals as producers of their development: A life-span perspective*. New York: Academic Press, 1981.

Moulton, J., Robinson, G. M., & Elias, C. Sex bias in language use: "Neutral" pronouns that aren't. *American Psychologist*, 1978, *33*, 1032–1036.

Nesselroade, J. R., Schaie, K. W., & Baltes, P. B. Ontogenetic and generational components of structural and quantitative change in adult cognitive behavior. *Journal of Gerontology*, 1972, *27*, 222–228.

Neugarten, B. L. Personality change in later life: A developmental perspective. In C. Eisdorfer & M. P. Lawton (Eds.), *The psychology of adult development and aging*. Washington, D.C.: American Psychological Association, 1973.

Powers, E., & Goudy, W. J. Examination of the meaning of work to older workers. *International Journal of Aging and Human Development*, 1971, *2*, 38–45.

Riegel, K. F., & Meacham, J. A. Dialectics, transaction, and Piaget's theory. In L. A. Pervin & M. Lewis (Eds.), *Perspectives in interactional psychology*. New York: Plenum Press, 1978.

Ryan, W. *Blaming the victim*. New York: Random House, 1976.

Schaie, K. W., & Parham, I. A. Stability of adult personality traits: Fact or fable? *Journal of Personality and Social Psychology*, 1976, *34*, 146–157.

Schmerl, E. F. In the name of the elder—An essay. *The Gerontologist*, 1975, *15*, 386.

Whitbourne, S. K., & Weinstock, C. S. *Adult development: The differentiation of experience*. New York: Holt, Rinehart and Winston, 1979.

10

Beyond Societal Language: The Development of the Deaf Person

Hans Furth

Thinking without Language

The social sciences cannot lay claim to astonishing discoveries in the sense in which natural sciences constantly enlarge society's knowledge with new physical and biological understanding. Even so-called revolutionary insights, such as those of Marx or Freud, do not quite have the stamp of utter newness. Not only is it possible to point to the forerunners, albeit in the writings of philosophers or poets, but, what is even more remarkable, once accepted in the culture, the new insights become a part of common knowledge, understandable to any educated person.

Within this perspective, the research efforts which I started in 1959 and first published seven years later (Furth, 1966) yielded rather astonishing results in the form of a definite answer to an important psychological question. The question concerned the language–thinking relation, particularly, to what extent and in what manner logical thinking is dependent on language. No better scientific strategy can be devised than to eliminate the presumed causal variable and observe what happens to the effect. Profoundly deaf children provided the unique opportunity to study individuals not steeped in a natural language as is the case for all hearing children. A system of conventional manual symbols, such as the American Sign Language (ASL), is certainly included in the meaning of a natural language. However, at the time of my research manual communication at a young age was neither taught nor encouraged and deaf children of deaf parents (who might be presumed to be familiar with ASL) were excluded from my samples. I went to some length to discover areas of intellectual functioning in which deaf children would show a systematic deficit. The answer was loud and clear—there were none. No direct and systematic influence

Hans Furth ● Center for the Study of Youth Development, Catholic University, Washington, D.C. 20064.

of language on logical thinking could be demonstrated. At first blush such a statement seems preposterous, considering how closely language and knowledge are related in the form of the written or the spoken word.

For a number of years after 1966 I continued research in the hope of finding a causal link between linguistic and logical knowledge. Of course, I studied the research of others and collected in two review articles (Furth, 1964, 1971) more than one hundred pertinent studies. Everything confirmed the original answer. Knowing or not knowing a societal language does not make a decisive difference in the developmental acquisition of an individual's reasoning capacity. (I take it for granted that the individual lives in a society and that a society cannot be conceived without a natural language.)

Whether or not this finding strikes you as important or new depends to a great extent on your own assumptions and interests. In any case it provides conclusive support for a theory of knowledge development, such as Piaget's, which is based on personal interactions and deals a decisive blow to any theory of knowledge which has recourse to language. However, you may circumvent my argument by pointing out that deaf children, although they may not know a particular societal language, such as German, English, or ASL, have an implicit, "inner" language. If you now ask yourself what you mean by "inner language," you may discover that the analysis of this concept covers much more than knowing and speaking a societal language. The meaning of "inner language" goes beyond linguistic and intellectual competence and encompasses emotions, values, indeed the entire psychology of the person.

The purpose of this chapter is to underscore the proposition that personal relations are the matrix out of which the child develops as a thinking and communicating person. The developmental achievement of a certain stage of relating and thinking is the foundation that makes possible the function of language and speech. In the final analysis the most astonishing discovery of my research seems to me not so much that young deaf children develop logical reasoning without the direct aid of natural language but that they can develop into socially related and relating persons (Furth, 1973). I would therefore like to explore in some detail why "thinking without language" and "communication without language" mutually imply each other, so that the possibility of one guarantees the possibility of the other. Although asking what comes first may appear to be a chicken and egg question, I would put communication first for the obvious reason that small infants certainly communicate but do not yet know a language.

Personal Relations and Object Formation

Insofar as deafness frequently remains unrecognized for at least the first year, deaf children—in marked contrast for instance to blind children (who become linguistically competent)—are freed from the pressures of guilt and anxiety on the part of their parents and can experience a normal personal-social development. Between the ages of 1 and 3 a major revolution in the infant's world occurs, which both Freud and Piaget connect with the notion that objects are permanent. For Freud this refers to the relation between the child and the human object of emotional attachment, for Piaget to the relation between the child and the object of theoretical knowing. In both cases this is a new relation which is founded on a separation from a more primitive state where the self and the other were undifferentiated.

Freudians talk of an early "symbiotic" relation; Piaget refers to "sensorimotor" interactions. At this stage infants have the experience of relating to (or interacting with) others. But neither self nor others are experienced as entities separate from the relating in the sense in which older children can separate the action from the self (the agent) and the other toward whom the action is directed. This idea can be put conversely: neither the self as agent nor the other as object are known as entities apart from the present action. However, once these entities begin to be experienced as separate from present action (e.g., people or things do not cease to exist when they are out of sight, the child knows theoretically that they—as well as the self—are "permanent objects"), it stands to reason that the early undifferentiated relationship takes on a new character. The 3-year-old child knows "I am a self who relates to my parents and other people"; similarly, "I know that an ordered world of things and people exists among whom I am a person who knows this." Notwithstanding that it will take 15 or more years before these concepts are adequately understood, 3-year-old children have already made the qualitative jump into a theoretical world. This new capacity is properly named by the term *thinking* (in terms of theoretical knowledge) or *personal relating* (in terms of responsible emotional attachment).

In its full development, the transition from the first (undifferentiated) to the second (differentiated) stage leads to mature personal relating and rational thinking. In its beginning the transition is obviously not dependent on linguistic communication since the progress toward that achievement takes place before language acquisition. But one could still conceivably hypothesize that language competence is the critical difference for full entry into the second stage. One could, except that countless numbers of deaf children, well beyond the age of 2 or 3, provide palpable evidence to the contrary. But empirical evidence alone is never enough to persuade a person who does not have a rational framework into which the "facts" can fit.

Which of the two theories is a more difficult framework—the Freudian notion of the construction of object attachment or the Piagetian notion of the construction of the theoretical object? Clearly, it is Piaget's that is difficult to grasp. For the prevailing correspondence theory of knowledge (namely, that knowledge is an internalization of a given, outside reality) is contradictory to the notion of the construction of the object (that knowledge constructs a reality and poses it as outside the self). Moreover, this theory makes use of a societal language as the principal instrument by means of which knowledge is "transmitted." Analogously to this correspondence theory of knowledge, the further socialization of the child is also assumed to be mediated principally through language.

The relational-constructivist theory, which I espouse in free interpretation of Piaget and Freud, has no need of an external instrument, such as society's language, to develop the socially related and thinking individual. For in this interpretation interpersonal relating and reasonable ordering of experiences are part of human life in accordance with what Piaget calls "expanding equilibration." This concept is the key to an autonomous (from within) development ("expanding") and to an adaptive, coordinated balancing ("equilibration") of personal and knowing relations (Furth, 1981, Chapter 15).

The capacity to form representative symbols is a natural consequence of object formation: Children can make present (represent) absent events which they know (theoretically) as objects; e.g., a little boy can think of driving in a car and represent this thinking in symbolic play or in internal imagination. Because of this general symbolic capacity, communication takes on a symbolic character. The most common symbolic system of communication is of course society's language, and hearing children, having developed that symbolic capacity, readily assimilate language and make it their own. However, spontaneously constructed gestural and mental representations (as action images) are the primary symbol forms for all people, hearing or deaf. Deaf children apparently use these spontaneous symbols in the service of communication and thinking. In other words, they construct on their own a symbolic gestural language—clear evidence that societal language, far from being the source of thinking or communication, always presupposes object (or objective) thinking which is intrinsically communicative.

Deaf infants, like all infants, are born into a world of personal relating, and their development as persons is the history of these interrelations (cf. Fujinaga, this volume). The relating of you and me is the basic human act. It includes for the infant what will eventually come to be differentiated as specific psychological acts, such as feelings, actions, communication, knowing (including perceiving), and remembering. The long slow track of separating the as yet unseparated subject–action–object (self–action–other) matrix begins during infancy. The developmental course continues in an uninterrupted and open-ended direction toward "objective" knowing. It covers the years from the object concept of the 2-year-old child to the first stable but incomplete mental frameworks at around age 7 (Piaget's "concrete operations") and the psychologically and logically mature frameworks of the socialized adolescent and adult ("formal operations").

The development in knowing necessarily changes the nature of personal relations and communication. First, personal interrelations and feelings take on the quality of increasingly personal and responsible actions: they are founded on the differentiated ("objective") knowledge of the other and are not merely the undifferentiated ("subjective") reactions of a stimulated organism (Macmurray, 1961). Second, as mentioned previously, objective knowledge implies the capacity to make present (to make real) absent events. This is representation and its results are symbols. Symbolic behavior can be external, such as gestures or play, or internal, such as mental images or imagination. Third, by means of symbols, communication can take place in separation from present feelings and actions. This separation is also called *displacement*. In other words, while previously communication could not but engage the total person in interpersonal relations, symbolic communication can take the form of an impersonal transmission of information. This is particularly true of society's language, which is a communication system imposed from outside on a mind as yet unformed.

Communication as Co-construction of Knowledge

It is perhaps unnecessary to stress the risk of an inappropriate use of language if hearing children live in a "good enough" home atmosphere. It is, however, a clear and present danger in the situation of deaf children and their hearing parents. There is no need to mention the irrational feelings of guilt and regret that almost invariably threaten to deform an adequate healthy interrelation; no need to insist that nothing but total acceptance of their deaf child is an absolute precondition for the parents to play a constructive role in their child's personality development; no need to recall the unrealistic propaganda of certain programs with their alluring promises and veiled threats. Of course, parents should be taught the decisive place of communication in personal development. But this importance of communication should not be interpreted in a misleading sense as if the hearing parents had to succeed in teaching a language under pain of crippling the deaf child's psychological or even—as suggested by some—neurological development. Their legitimate fears in this regard should be allayed by recourse to an adequate description of personal development from within the wellsprings of the child.

The parents interacting with their child provide the necessary milieu for this development but they do not transmit vital components of personality or of intelligence the way a piece of information is passed on by language. They should be aware that for the first years of the child's life the healthy relating between parent and child is of paramount importance and that given a positive atmosphere and opportunity, deaf children will spontaneously engage in symbolic communication, even to the extent of constructing a limited conventional language.

While stressing the role and importance of a conventional language (whether ASL, some other manual language, or the natural language), all precaution should be taken to lessen the danger that language will be used to the detriment of personal relating. Any explicit focus on the learning of language is liable to distort adequate relating (cf. Cazden, this volume). During early childhood the proper function of language is to express the interaction of two persons, not merely to transmit information. At no time should parents or children experience language learning as an end in itself.

It is not unusual to define communication as a transmission of information. This view is patently one-sided in more than one sense. First, it stresses the one-directional act of sending or, reciprocally, of receiving something. Second, it refers to this something in terms of a given commodity, somewhat like the transfer of a box from one person to another. This kind of description may be appropriate for a rote memory type of knowledge, such as in telephone directories, where thousands of entries are collected in one source from which they are retrieved as the occasion demands. The operator who, over the phone, reads to the inquiring customer a particular number is quick to forget that number, just as people let go of a box when they hand it to another person. But this is communication in its most impoverished sense, stripped of its essential human components. We can justly call it storage and transfer of information. Often enough this transfer is much better accomplished by mechanical means without the potentially confusing effects of a human intermediary.

However, I would like to use the concept of communication primarily in a human-personal sense and differentiate its meaning along a personal I–you dimension. In its fullest sense communication has two vital components, an action component in the form of an interpersonal I–you encounter and a knowledge component. The knowledge component is one of the intentional goals of the encounter. Without it there can be an I–you encounter that is not really communication, such as a person helping a little child across the street, where the intention is an action, not the sharing of knowledge. Interaction of a less personal type is the situation of two or more people cooperating on a common purpose, e.g., supervisors and workers in a factory or players on a football team. Here the interaction and communication serves an extrapersonal goal, the making of an artifact or the winning of the game. The I–you component between the partners is absent: there are several "I"s relating to a common "it." The nonpersonal type of communication is most clearly illustrated by the telephone operator where a non-"I" (e.g., a computer) could easily substitute for the operator and the communication is purely technical. In this chapter I would like to discuss communication in the full sense of an intentional pairing of knowledge and personal relating and to relate this sense of communication to the development and education of profoundly deaf children.

One way of stressing the relational nature of knowledge would be to change the word *transmission* and substitute in its place the word *co-construction*. Then communication could readily be defined as a *co-construction of information*. In this manner information can no longer be treated as a preexisting given but is the product of an action; moreover, this action is not the fabrication of a solitary agent but the joint product of two or more persons relating to each other. One can observe this kind of communication at the earliest ages as infants and their caretakers interrelate. Through this interrelating the infants become conscious of the reality framework in which the relating partners live. This is not a one-sided process where the adult partner transmits information to a receptive child. We say that the child acquires knowledge of the world, but this is an active acquisition within an interpersonal context, in which the action of both sides is obligatory and the resulting knowledge bears the stamp of the participating individuals as surely as a certain composition belongs to Verdi or to Brahms.

Without doubt societal (or natural) language is frequently used in communicative interactions of child and others and increases in frequency with the age of the child. However, the relative amount of nonverbal communication, while difficult to assess, is probably much larger and more significant than is commonly assumed. Nevertheless, whatever may be the case with hearing children, the almost complete reliance on nonverbal means of communication in the case of many profoundly deaf children is obvious to anyone's observation and effectively discredits a language-based theory of communication and knowledge acquisition (Furth, 1978). The most astonishing feature of this nonverbal communication is its spontaneous nature. The adults may have no intention or awareness of teaching the children spontaneous expressions of feelings, interests, or gestures. Yet hearing children and to an even greater extent deaf children use them successfully in communication. There can be no question here of transmitting a ready-made pattern through formal instruction as perhaps there could be in the case of societal language. However, studies in language acquisition show that this apparent transmission necessarily is a component of personal relating. In short, symbolic communication—whether verbal or gestural—is an excellent illustration of the concept of co-construction as the active production of shared knowledge in the context of personal interrelating (cf. John-Steiner & Tatter, this volume).

The Education of Deaf Children

If this situation of co-constructing information is prototypical, it surely does not change at the age when children are ready to receive formal education. Unfortunately the traditional educational model of instruction conforms more closely to the transmission-of-information concept than to the co-construction concept. Not unlike the telephone operator in the above example, the teacher presents knowledge most typically in the form of a lecture, which literally means reading something which the students are required to memorize. This model is what can be called a *school for listening and learning*. Quite obviously the role of language in this type of school is vital. Hence the almost universal assumption that without the knowledge of societal language serious learning is unthinkable.

I should state more clearly what has been only implicitly suggested in previous remarks: developmentally, whatever makes for good communication also makes for good learning. This is of course no surprise when one considers that acquisition and sharing of knowledge are obligatory components of personal development, in a sense in which formal schooling or even societal language cannot be called obligatory. If I now put down three conditions that are conducive to good learning, they are the same ones that facilitate good communication. In order to differentiate the more traditional educational model from the one suggested here, I refer to the new model as a *school for thinking* (Furth & Wachs, 1974). At the same time I make it clear that general learning has two components, as does all knowledge: a specific content (which corresponds to learning in the strict sense) and a general structure or framework (which has to do with understanding or thinking).

Here are the three conditions conducive to good thinking and communication: First, the person is active in response to a certain internal challenge or conflict. This activity can take the form of exploration, trying out several possibilities, or asking questions where the important thing is not so much the answer but the articulation of a possibility that heretofore had not been considered as such (in other words, it is a question that results from the person's high-level thinking). Second, the person is sharing knowledge with others by taking their viewpoints into account, being responsive to the constructive criticism of other people. In this situation the motivation to improve knowledge and the motivation to share knowledge and be part of the knowledge community are two sides of the same coin. Finally, there is an inherent difference between the child–adult relation and child–child relation. The first one implies necessarily a unilateral relationship of a superior to an inferior. While mutual love and respect can make this relation a healthy one and avoid serious pitfalls, from a developmental viewpoint the peer relations of mutual equality are the more decisive ones. After all, the children's peers will be tomorrow's adult society and it is of this society that the developing child will have to be a full member.

Given these three conditions we can appreciate the dilemma facing the theory of education in general. Not surprisingly, the major problem for any form of school for learning is the problem of motivation. Technical, impersonal (I–it) communication always requires an external motivation, whether it is grades, rewards, punishment, persuasion, or public relations. In personal (I–you) communication, as in a school for thinking, there is no problem of motivation. Particularly with regard to deaf children, the situation is not as hopeless as a school for learning would imply. Deaf children may be quite deficient in the knowledge of society's language. But there is no reason to assume that they are therefore substantially impeded in communicating or thinking. There is one chief characteristic of mature behavior or thinking, namely, being autonomous; this means behaving or doing something the reason for which is within oneself and not primarily an imposition from outside. Notwithstanding appearances to the contrary, deaf children in general show an outstanding tendency toward autonomy. Not being able to imitate society's language or adult answers, they have no choice but to rely on their own resources when it comes to communicating and thinking.

This comment suggests practical applications. Deaf children provide educators with a remarkable opportunity to turn their classroom into a school for thinking where they can put into practice communication as co-construction of information. In fact, my contact and research with deaf children was the motivating occasion for my involvement in Piaget's theory of knowledge—which those familiar with his theory will recognize as underlying much of what is said in these remarks—and my further application of this theory to the notion of a school for thinking. I refer here to four books, two on deafness (Furth, 1966, 1973), the other two on general educational practice (Furth, 1970; Furth & Wachs, 1974).

What do I mean by a school for thinking? I have in mind a general attitude of open communication and encouragement of thinking, a clear message to the children that we respect them precisely as thinking persons, whether or not they know societal language, or indeed any particular content. I do not belittle the need for teaching societal language to these deaf children. There is room for rote learning and content learning. But these topics should not be pushed to such an extent or be presented in such a way that the thinking and communicating person is squashed. I suggest an overall atmosphere of intellectual and developmental health and take the strong viewpoint that language knowledge does not guarantee, nor does language ignorance preclude, this atmosphere.

Deaf children provide an ideal opportunity to put a constructive method of education into practice. The challenge of educators is not to let deaf children's poor knowledge of language become an excuse for neglecting the children's intellectual health. A constructive method in instruction implies both external and internal activity of the children that leads to insight and understanding. In the course of this thinking activity the children are motivated to communicate in the service of thinking. Research is needed to establish in which content areas, and to what extent, a predominantly activity- and discovery-oriented curriculum can be devised. Obvious examples are mathematics, logic, science, social roles, and aesthetics. But no amount of specific curricula is sufficient or can be a substitute for the overall atmosphere that will allow these curricula to function in the manner intended. An obligatory prerequisite in this respect is some form of what I called a school for thinking, where learning is treated primarily as an I–you relation of sharing knowledge, as a co-construction and not merely as transmission of information.

A knowledge of a language by itself will never assure the healthy personal development of the deaf infant. In this respect, what counts is not the particular oral or manual language but the quality of the relation within the family of the deaf child.

In short, deaf children's general healthy social and intellectual development confirms the crucial contribution, not of societal language as such, but of the twin psychological foundations underlying societal language: the quality of social relations, both interpersonal and societal, and the intellectual spontaneity of symbol formation.

References

Furth, H. G. Research with the deaf: Implications for language and cognition. *Psychological Bulletin,* 1964, *62,* 145–164.

Furth, H. G. *Thinking without language.* New York: Free Press, 1966.

Furth, H. G. *Piaget for teachers.* Englewood Cliffs, N.J.: Prentice Hall, 1970.

Furth, H. G. Linguistic deficiency and thinking: Research with deaf subjects, 1964–1969. *Psychological Bulletin,* 1971, *76,* 58–72.

Furth, H. G. *Deafness and learning: A psychosocial approach.* Belmont, Calif.: Wadsworth, 1973.

Furth, H. G. Denken ohne Sprache: Rückschau und Ausblick auf die Forschung mit Gerhörlosen. *Die Psychologie des 20. Jahrhunderts* (Vol. VII). Zürich: Kindler, 1978, pp. 992–1013.

Furth, H. G. *Piaget and knowledge* (2nd ed.). Chicago: University Press, 1981.

Furth, H. G., & Wachs, H. *Thinking goes to school: Piaget's theory in practice.* New York: Oxford, 1974.

Macmurray, J. *Persons in relation.* London: Faber, 1961.

11

Some Sociogenetic Determinants in Human Development Revealed by the Study of Severely Deprived Children

Tamotsu Fujinaga

Aim and Sources of the Present Study

This study aims to clarify some of the sociogenetic determinants in child development by means of cross-comparison among case studies of severely deprived children. Such studies are considered to afford evidence of great value in the attempt to determine whether certain aspects of behavior are dependent on sociogenetic determinants or on biogenetic ones.

Unsuitability of Feral Man and Wild Children as Data

Although the cases of the so-called "feral man" or "wild children" are quite widely known, they have not been accepted in the present study as data that could be relied on to render unimpeachable service. Many such cases have been reported and to a greater or lesser extent acquiesced to in the West. For example, the excellent biologist Carolus Linnaeus, in his famous book *Systema Naturae* (1775), which established the modern taxonomy of animals, proposed a special subcategory of humankind called *Homo ferus* (wild man). More recently, the anthropologist Robert M. Zingg has collected 35 cases of wild children in various countries (Singh & Zingg, 1942).

However, in the majority of such cases, the fact that such stories have met with any sort of credulity seems to the Oriental student of psychology to indicate at least some lack of critical judgment. Such legends, particularly regarding wild children, are rare in Japan and China, where the traditional pattern of belief may be seen as

Tamotsu Fujinaga ● Departments of Education and Psychology, Ochanomizu University, Tokyo 112, Japan.

a polytheistic-animistic view of nature in which a hard and clear boundary between the realm of humans and the realm of animals or other forms of perhaps less tangible life has not been enforced as it has been in the West. To the Oriental mentality, it was not regarded as terribly bizarre or unnatural that aged animals might be transformed into humans or that humans and animals could mate, let alone that a human baby could be raised by animals. Thus, perhaps because the subject has not traditionally stimulated emotional awe or doubt, the Oriental psychologist is culturally less prone to feel compelled to devote any scientific interest to subjects like wild children, such data being almost automatically relegated to the sphere of superstitious interpretation.

Basic Data—Severely Deprived Children

By categorically excluding such cases as lacking in proven reliability, we are left with the data on a number of famous cases of severely deprived children on which to base our study. These are the cases of Genie (Curtiss, 1977; Curtiss, Fromkin, Krashen, Rigler, & Rigler, 1974; Fromkin, Krashen, Curtiss, Rigler, & Rigler, 1974), Isabelle (Mason, 1942), Anna (Davis, 1940, 1947), Anne and Albert (Freedman & Brown, 1968), and P.M. and J.M. (Koluchova, 1972, 1976). The common features among these cases may be summarized as follows: First, the severe deprivation experiences of these children must be further characterized as multiple, or even total, with respect to the different types of deprivation, that is, maternal, stimulus, linguistic, social, and nutritional. Second, their deprivation periods were very long, exceeding four years at the least. Third, the follow-up studies on their prognosis were continued over a long period so that rather conclusive observations regarding the nature and extent of their deficiencies or recoveries could be made.

All of the cases mentioned above are quite well known, but one more case that provided valuable evidence in the present study deserves a rather complete description here in view of the fact that it has been reported heretofore only in one Japanese journal (Fujinaga, Saiga, Kasuga, & Uchida, 1980). From the following summary, it will be noted that this case also satisfies the above three conditions.

F.E. and G.E.—A Case of Severe Deprivation in Japan

In October 1972, a sister and brother, hereafter referred to respectively as F.E. and G.E., were rescued from their parents' extreme neglect and maltreatment in a small prefecture in Japan. A team of four Japanese researchers in various fields of psychology, led by the present author, have been conducting the follow-up study of this case for over eight years.

At the time of their rescue F.E. was 6 and G.E. was 5 years old, but they both measured 82 cm in height and weighed 8.5 kg. These figures represent a developmental level typical of no more than 1½-year-olds according to the Japanese norm. They were unable to walk and crawled instead. F.E. uttered only two jargon words the meanings of which were not understandable, while G.E. did not attempt to speak any words. Both appeared, mentally and physically, as if they were at the developmental level of 1½ years at best, with developmental quotients (DQs) of about 25 or 30, or the level of very severe retardation.

Two medical specialists on genetic defects were asked to examine them independently. In the opinion of these doctors, genetic and/or organic defects were not to be considered the main cause of retardation.

As a result, this severe case of developmental retardation was thought to be due to a complex of such factors as maternal, stimulus, linguistic, and nutritional deprivation. The children's father was unemployed and given to extreme indolence, causing their mother to earn what little money she could by a part-time job. Finally the family was able to receive a livelihood protection allowance, but they were still very badly off because there were eight children to feed. F.E. was the sixth and G.E. the seventh sibling. In addition, the father had a psychopathic personality and especially abused F.E. and G.E. on the excuse of their incontinence. The mother was a naive but otherwise ordinary woman, although quite heavily burdened by her large family. She was too tired from her work and from caring for the other children to look after F.E. and G.E. adequately, and in fact she resented them because they presented added burdens to her and were a cause of conflict between her husband and herself. Thus, she neglected them completely.

At first, the parents left them on their own on the wooden floor of the large empty room of a temple in which the family dwelt for nothing. When F.E. and G.E. were 4 and 3 years old, they began to crawl with difficulty and troubled their parents because of their incontinence. The parents enclosed them at night in a very small outdoor hut, a practice that continued for one year and 10 months. In the daytime, however, they were free to play in the large garden of the temple. Their elder sisters and brother mainly looked after them but, of course, in a very inadequate manner.

Summarizing the characteristics of this developmental retardation case, the following four points may be mentioned:

1. They had contact with the other siblings but almost no interaction with adults.
2. No attachment to any adult was found.
3. They were enclosed together for a long time, but nevertheless seemed to develop little attachment to each other. When rescued, the sister was taken to a children's home run by the prefecture and the brother to a baby home run by a Buddhist sect for about a month. They showed no signs of separation anxiety, nor did they express appreciable delight upon recognition at their reunion in the baby home.
4. The negative elements which had hindered the development of sensorimotor intelligence were not dominant factors.

Ever since the children were rescued and taken to the baby home, our project team has been investigating the remedial processes of the children's development by periodic testing, measurement, and naturalistic observation in terms of physical, cognitive, language, and socioemotional development in comparison with the control group children in the same baby home. Later they were transferred to a children's home founded by the same Buddhist order. They finished the nursery school in the same institution and entered normal classes of public elementary school two years behind their age mates. At this writing, F.E. and G.E. are 14 and 13 years old and attend the sixth and the fifth grades respectively.

Remedial education and follow-up study have been continued for the sake of the children's recovery by analyzing test results and building on inferences made with the aid of information from antecedent research. For example, we made every effort to provide remedial enrichment of their verbal environment and to supplement this with various forms of language instruction in anticipation of continuance of their language retardation. To this end, the methods of Luria and Yudovitch (1959) gave useful suggestions. At the present stage, our findings might be tentatively summarized as follows:

1. As for physical development, a high degree of plasticity was preserved, and a gradual catching up with the standard of normal development has been confirmed. Analyzing their rate of developmental velocity with respect to height and weight, it becomes clear that they are tracing a pattern of developmental phases similar to that of normal children, but concentrated into a telescoped time scale.

2. Regarding social development, interpersonal relations and affective interaction have attained almost complete smoothness. The children show few symptoms of antisocial behavior such as juvenile delinquency. Generally speaking, a proper course of development has been confirmed, although there yet remains an immature and asocial tendency in the boy's behavior pattern.

3. Study of the children's emotional development has revealed weak self-assertion along with defensiveness and dependency, features which may be signs of their immaturity on the one hand, or, on the other hand, may stem from the somewhat overprotective treatment given them at the home, nursery school, and elementary school out of pity for their unhappy infancies.

4. In the testing of language development, the children have lagged 3 to 3½ years behind the norm for children of their chronological ages on the psycholinguistic age (PLA) scale, of the Illinois Test of Psycholinguistic Abilities (ITPA) translated into Japanese. It seems very difficult for them to overtake the chronological standard. The main difficulties are found in what is called "internal language" (Vygotsky, 1962) or the domain of "elaborated code" (Bernstein, 1967).

5. As for cognitive development, at one time their IQ scores had reached the level of 80 to 90 points, but thereafter, a constant decrease has been observed. This pattern is attributable to the fact that the tasks encompassed by intelligence tests require more and more verbal and abstract abilities for problem solving as chronological age increases. At present, their IQs on the revised Wechsler Intelligence Scale for Children (WISC-R) are about 50–60 points. Their verbal IQs (VIQs) have uniformly been far lower than their performance IQs (PIQs). A low capacity in short-term memory has also been noted in both F.E. and G.E. These cognitive defects are quite marked; nevertheless, in daily life they encounter few problems thereby. Their social competence and daily communication ability are indeed better than one would expect. In addition, F.E. and G.E. both performed better than expected on the Standard Progressive Matrices, with the girl's score being in the 60th percentile, while the boy's was in the 40th percentile in comparison with their chronological standard. Without the loads of mnemonic capacity or verbal ability, their cognitive competences might be found to be unexpectedly high.

The Organicismic System

In the case record of F.E. and G.E., one of the findings we could never have anticipated was the rapid recovery of physical development. Because they had only attained a developmental level at best equivalent to that of a typical 1½-year-old Japanese child, the research team had little reason to hope that they would catch up to the normal range, but in fact they have been following the normal developmental course with amazing rapidity. The above observation leads to the impression that during deprivation the potentiality of development may be possessed in a state of what may be called *functional hibernation.* In attempting to cope with such phenomena conceptually, I subsequently postulated a highly self-regulative and totalistic structure that serves as the basis of human development. I refer to this structure as the *organicismic system.*

Direction of Development within the Organicismic System

It is an assumption of this position that facilitative information input from the environment will trigger the potential developmental tendencies of the system, causing it to begin or continue to progress through the normal course of development, a point that has already been suggested by Bower (1977). A second possibility occurs when there is insufficient facilitative input. The system will then behave in such a way as to maintain its present state of equilibrium maximally, that is, by hibernation (preserving the "organismic center"). Furthermore, if this system receives distortive information, a third course consisting of abnormal or deviated development will result. Rutter (1972, 1979), arguing along similar lines, stated that privation (lack) should thus be rigorously distinguished from deprivation (loss). From this viewpoint, adding distortion as a third possibility, altogether three developmental vectors can be distinguished.

With the present inadequate status of our knowledge, accurate prediction of the effects of these three vector influences is very difficult. However, in light of the alternatives, distortive information inputs might be expected to cause the worst defects in the organicismic system. If maximal status quo equilibrium can be ensured, lack of facilitative information might result in the phenomenon of interrupted development, but the organicismic system itself would retain its potentialities. The effect of deprivation—loss of facilitative information—might vary according to the state of the organicismic system (cf. Furth, this volume). If the basic equilibrium has already been acquired, deprivation can be reduced to simple privation, but if the necessary equilibrium has not yet been acquired, the severe frustration caused by deprivation might lead the organicismic system to a course of deviated development from which recovery, if possible, would be expected to be difficult.

Bower (1977), using cataracts as an analogy, argued that the disuse of a function causes the underlying neural structure of this function to disappear. However, cataracts are not an example of privation but rather of distortion; they do not actually prevent the transmission of information but rather inform of the inefficiency or uselessness of the visual stimulus inputs. Speaking generally, total lack of visual stimuli may cause the physiological structures for vision to become severely degenerated. But with regard to this function, it is impossible to discuss the effect of complete privation since there exist only the distortion effects; thus the validity of applying this analogy to human development may be open to question.

Among the types of information most facilitative to the organicismic system is sociogenetic information. F.E. and G.E. could not walk at all when rescued, but they began to walk within a week of their admittance to their child-care institutions. Some discussion of how this sudden progress might be explained is in order.

Accomplishment of the task of walking is not simply an automatic result of the maturational process; it also requires certain social stimulus input to the organicismic system. For example, babies who are not yet walking themselves nonetheless constantly watch the adults and elder siblings around them walking smoothly. Watching gives them the opportunity of modeling or observational learning preparatory to walking. Babies' mothers gladly encourage them to walk even a single step. Such interaction between mother and baby consists of various sorts of social exchange. Once the organicismic system is exposed to this social exchange process, potential walking ability first comes into bloom. On the other hand, if babies are not party to the appropriate social exchanges, walking ability may perhaps remain in the state of hibernation. This need for social stimuli would explain the failure of the sister and brother, F.E. and G.E., to begin walking until the time of their rescue.

The Critical Period Hypothesis

Another implication of this concept is concerned with the validity of the *critical* (or *sensitive*) *period* hypothesis. This hypothesis, of course, is important in recent developmental psychology. The critical period hypothesis states that the innate and autochthonous biological processes of development are predetermined for specific chronological ages. Some phases of these processes are considered to be especially important in the acquisition of certain traits or abilities.

However, given that human development is based on a highly self-regulative organicismic system as discussed above, the existence of completely predetermined periods critical to development and dependent on biological age is to be doubted. The phenomena of so-called critical periods may be nothing more than normal developmental phases occurring when the underlying organicismic system has already acquired the prerequisite equilibrium (readiness) and only awaits the appropriate facilitative information inputs. Such phases likely indicate the beginning of development of certain functions or characteristics.

Formation of Attachment

Attachment Formed after Rescue in Deprived Children

Intimately related to the critical period hypothesis is the formation of attachment (Bowlby, 1969). This problem was partially touched on above. However, a reexamination of the data supplied by the well-known studies of severe deprivation seems called for antecedent to drawing any valid conclusion.

The wide discrepancies among the data are truly worthy of astonishment. In Koluchova's (1972) case, P.M. and J.M. were found to form deep attachments to their foster mother. Genie showed affectional ties to her foster mother as well as to the researchers (Curtiss *et al.,* 1974). The case record of Isabelle by Mason (1942) included few apparent descriptions of her interpersonal relations, but the strong interest she showed in her acquaintances (e.g., Mrs. Mason's appraisal of her performance) firmly proved, in our eyes, the rapid development of affectional ties with the adults around her.

On the other hand, Davis's (1940) study of Anna revealed little attachment to anyone around her. The case of Anne (Freedman & Brown, 1968) also exhibited no affectional ties with others. Anne seemed to be enclosed in her autistic world and was never interested in other people. Her brother Albert, however, after two months in foster care, did show some affectional responses to his foster mother but still was quite indifferent to strangers.

Examining the latter cases exclusively, we may conclude fairly safely that a critical period for attachment formation exists in the child's early years. Nevertheless, in the light of the first cases cited it seems clear that such a conclusion must be rejected.

Our case seemed to offer data falling into an intermediate position. The sister, F.E., rapidly developed strong attachment to the nurse mainly in charge of her at the baby home. But her brother, G.E., formed merely shallow relationships with the adults around him, never forming specific attachment to his nurse. Thinking that this may have been due to a lack of rapport with the nurse, we felt compelled to direct that a different nurse be appointed to relieve her at this post. Fortunately enough, the new nurse took a liking to the boy and was able to foster in him strong affectional ties to herself.

Reexamination of the Data

Cases Developing Attachment with Some Prerescue Attachment and Appropriate Postrescue Treatment. P.M. and G.M., Isabelle, and Genie had all developed some level of mutual attachments with their mothers or fellow siblings before deprivation. P.M. and G.M. grew up normally to the age of 1½ years. Until then, they might have had some affectionate experiences with the caring adults. Moreover, they were enclosed together and developed strong attachments to each other. Upon rescue, they at first showed fear of strangers and communicated among themselves by means of private gestures.

Bower (1977) argued that attachment can be reduced to the formation of a style of interaction specific to a mother and her baby or to a pair of babies. According to this theory, the specific style of interaction exhibited by P.M. and G.M. would be describable as mutual attachment. Given such experience in combination with appropriate treatment after rescue, adoption into a warm-hearted home could lead them to establish firm attachment to their foster mother and the adults around them.

Similarly, Isabelle had lived in the same room with her mother since birth. Thus, her circumstances should not be viewed as severe or total deprivation, since there was intimate contact between mother and child. The mother perhaps had loved her baby and the baby had developed firm attachment to her mother. Isabelle's strong fear of strangers and separation anxiety on first being taken to the hospital may be taken as proof of her firm attachment to her mother. In addition, Isabelle and her mother communicated to each other with their own gestures—further indication of her attachment. Treatment at the hospital and by the researchers for Isabelle may well have been appropriate after admittance. From the first, it should be noted, she was sensitive to interpersonal relations, as exemplified by her interest in the baby in the next bed.

With Genie, the descriptions of the early environmental conditions under which she had been growing up are so few as to hardly permit inferences about her early relationship with her mother or about her developmental processes. The medical examination of her at 11 months of age had rated her as normal, but at 14 months of age possible retardation was first suspected. The report allowed the inference that Genie's early development and relationship with her mother were almost normal and that her early attachment to her mother had already been achieved. Further, the fact that Genie's mother acted to rescue her from her father's abuse additionally serves to reveal her mother's affection for her. From early on, Genie used a pointing gesture in seeking her mother's attention, suggesting that a specific means of communication between Genie and her mother had been formed—again, a sign of mutual attachment.

Having acquired this basis, Genie's adoption thereafter, with the wholehearted therapeutic efforts of the researchers, could facilitate her formation of affectionate ties to the persons in close contact with her.

In short, the above cases do not belong to a category of total neglect. Neglect came from the fathers alone; the mother–child ties were maintained.

Cases of Total Neglect with Abuse-Distortion Before and Inappropriate Treatment after Rescue. On the other hand, both Davis's case, Anna, and Freedman and Brown's cases, Anne and Albert, are typical instances of total neglect. From birth, they had been enclosed in a small room and pressed into their baby cribs. Anna's father had not been clearly identified, and Anne's and Albert's case record contains no description of their father. All their family members, including their mothers, either had little interest in them or actually hated them.

These children may have had little opportunity for interaction, or at least for affectionate interaction, with anyone else. Moreover, the treatment afforded them after rescue also seems to have been very inappropriate. They were taken to hospitals or infants' homes, after which they were transferred to other homes or to their families and then again to foster homes, one after another, and all within a short period. Thus they were not presented with the chance to develop attachment.

Such total neglect and abuse from the adults in charge does not indicate a lack of stimulus input for growth. Rather, such treatment serves to inform the neglected children of the uselessness or even harmfulness of interpersonal interaction with the adults around them and dissipates the intrinsic motivation for growth or the opportunity for modeling. This is, in other words, a case of distortive information inputs to the organicismic system.

Case of Parental Neglect but without Distortion before and with Appropriate Treatment after Rescue. In this sense too, our case of F.E. and G.E. seems to occupy an intermediate position. Although they had experienced little exchange with their father and mother, they did have some with their other sisters and brother. However, even in the absence of the hindering factor of parental abuse as distortive information input, social interaction with children only may be inadequate in the provision of facilitative information furthering the process of socialization. It can go no further than maintaining potentiality for growth, thus leading to a state of hibernation; it should be characterized, therefore, as a dearth of facilitative information input. As I mentioned earlier, F.E. and G.E. showed little separation anxiety when admitted to different institutions and little affective response of recognition at reunion. This behavior, taken with the fact that they had no specific means of communication, tends to prove that they had developed little attachment to each other, and, in spite of the undeniable existence of interaction with their fellow siblings to a certain extent, there is no reason to assume prerescue formation of attachment along the lines of that mentioned earlier.

Thus, attachment, for them, was a task that would have to be learned or developed from scratch. New attachment was anticipated to be facilitated by appropriate treatment, and this was indeed the case with the sister.

The brother did not achieve the formation of attachment as smoothly as the sister, but once his second nurse had taken charge, his attachment began to develop rapidly. Whether his failure at first in the socialization process was the fault of bad rapport with his original nurse or the result of the greater vulnerability of male children, as pointed out by Rutter (1979), has not been determined. However, it is certain that both children, once given the opportunity to form what were for them not just new but in fact their first attachments, were successful in this task.

Given the observation detailed above, one can hardly fail to see that application of the critical period hypothesis to attachment formation is of questionable validity. Indeed the main role in this process was undoubtedly played by the input of sociogenetic information by caring adults after rescue, under the probably necessary condition of lack of prerescue abuse-distortion.

Language Acquisition and Cognitive Development

It may be said that in recent developmental psychology the critical period hypothesis is regarded as more important in the area of language acquisition than in that of attachment formation (Lenneberg, 1967). In language acquisition, the discrepancies among the data on deprived children are as marked as was the case with attachment formation.

Language Acquisition in Children with Prerescue Attachment

Genie, whose case record is subtitled "Language Acquisition beyond the 'Critical Period'" (Fromkin *et al.*, 1974), first began to learn language at 13 years and 7 months of age, which is generally considered beyond the critical period for language acquisition. Certainly her progress was not as smooth as that of normal children. The researchers involved had to tax their ingenuity to develop her speech and written language abilities. She acquired vocabulary and semantic knowledge with relative speed, but her syntactic knowledge remained at a more immature level. Thus, in spite of the fact that Genie still exhibited marked imbalance, she could indeed learn something about language.

Neither the case of P.M. and G.M. nor that of Isabelle, in which the children

were rescued when they were at least a little beyond 6½ years old, involves infringe-
ments on the so-called critical period for language acquisition. Still, the progress in
language accomplished in these cases is simply amazing. By the time Isabelle was
about 8 years old, she had already acquired some 2,000 words and could produce
sentences of considerable complexity, with the prognosis that she would reach the
level normal for her age within a short time. It was concluded in the case of P.M.
and G.M. as well that they had attained the normal level of language development
in the seven years following their rescue. These four children all started out unable
to handle more than a few words but managed to progress favorably with their language development. Although Genie's developmental level was not yet quite satisfactory, the other three children are by now very likely completely normal. From the
data of these cases, therefore, it is clear that there exists no language acquisition
critical period, at least before the age of 7.

Language Acquisition in Children with Prerescue Distortion and Inappropriate Postrescue Treatment

Davis's report of Anna states that she was similarly discovered at about age 6
and had but few words; her language development thereafter was, by contrast, quite
unsatisfactory. When she was 9 years and 4 months old, her linguistic ability in both
production and comprehension was appraised at no more than the level normal for
2-year-olds. Her progress in language learning during the 2½ years after rescue was
but limited, and the researcher was led to conclude that in comparison with Isabelle,
Anna had had little linguistic competence from the beginning due to congenital
feeblemindedness.

Descriptions of language development in the case record of Anne and Albert
are not sufficiently detailed to allow conclusive remarks about their achievement, but
inferring from the facts that their speech was echolalic and that they were quite
indifferent to social interaction with others, attainment of reasonably normal language ability would not be expected. Even more than two years after their rescue,
their behavior patterns remained very autistic in nature.

The Critical Period Hypothesis of Language Acquisition and the Data

In the latter two cases, the data on the lack of progress made by the three children seems to support the critical period hypothesis in language acquisition. In short,
some data reject the validity of the critical period hypothesis while other data do not,
thus leaving us with the task of attempting to resolve this contradiction.

In studying the language acquisition process of F.E. and G.E., we were able to
uncover some relevant facts of great interest. As noted earlier, the development of
attachment to the caring nurse progressed smoothly with the elder sister, F.E. At the
same time, a rapid linguistic development also started which saw F.E. mastering at
least 17 words and becoming able to imitate phrases 3 words in length by the first
month after rescue, and two months later, she was able to form her own 2-word
sentences.

On the other hand, G.E. showed little success in forming attachment to his nurse
during approximately the first 6 months. During this period, G.E.'s progress with

language also went poorly, with the acquisition of vocabulary lagging behind that of his sister and with the use of apparently meaningless jargon persisting stubbornly. But once he began to show a healthy attachment to the second nurse, his language acquisition started to make great strides, finally catching up with that of his sister. From this observation came the suggestion of an intimate connection between the formation of attachment and language acquisition.

Attachment and Language Acquisition

At this juncture, Bower's (1977) communication theory of attachment comes to mind, namely, that attachment is the establishment of a special means of communication between mother and child whereby mutual understanding becomes possible. However, since this mutual understanding is peculiar to the particular mother and child involved, there arises in the child "stranger fear" toward others with whom understanding has not been established. At a later stage, when the more general means of communication—language—has been acquired and mutual understanding even with people met for the first time has become possible, such shyness toward strangers disappears.

Based on this theory, the formation of attachment and the development of language ability come to have a functional continuity as the acquisition of means of communication. Bruner (1975), too, recognized that a nonlinguistic communication forms and develops from the interaction between mother and child before the appearance of clear-cut linguistic forms and that the experience gained through intercommunication by this nonlinguistic means forms the foundation for the later acquisition of language. Thus it may be said that acquiring the nonlinguistic means of communication that accompanies the formation of attachment becomes the prerequisite readiness for the later acquisition of language (cf. John-Steiner & Tatter, this volume).

As I pointed out earlier, Genie, P.M., and G.M. underwent normal development, at least at the earliest stage, and may be assumed to have experienced the beginning of attachment formation. P.M. and G.M. were able to communicate between themselves by means of gesture; Genie had the pointing gesture and was able to understand the names of a few colors and other words. Isabelle was with her mother until the time of rescue, and along with the deep attachment formed between mother and child, they had developed a system of gesture language.

Taking the above into consideration, it may be seen that while these four children appeared at the outset to be utterly ignorant and unprepared with respect to language, this was just appearance and nothing more. P.M. and G.M., as well as Isabelle, had already obtained the prerequisite readiness necessary for language acquisition, but the next factor essential for development of language, input stimulus, was lacking, resulting in their linguistic ability being maintained in a state of hibernation. With Genie, however, since her father was extremely intolerant of noise, the girl was not allowed even to cry; thus, an additional factor was present in the form of the distortive developmental information that making sounds is harmful. Nevertheless, this complication does not seem to have had the effect of generally distorting her language ability; in spite of it, she had otherwise attained the readiness prerequisite to language acquisition. With these observations in mind, it begins to seem doubtful that the characterization of acquisition of language as taking place beyond the critical period is really appropriate in this case.

As we have already noted, the readiness needed for language acquisition, that is, attachment, was undeveloped in Anna as well as in Anne and Albert; furthermore, it was not properly developed even after rescue due to the inappropriate treatment afforded them. In such cases as these, the fact that language acquisition fails to occur is not in the least extraordinary, and it hardly seems necessary to seek for causes such as congenital feeblemindedness and the like.

In our case, the sister and brother studied lacked early interaction with adults; they mainly related to each other or to their fellow siblings. They exhibited neither mutual attachment nor special means of communication or interaction at the time of rescue. Here as well, one can notice the importance of interaction and social exchange with adults as a basis for language acquisition. F.E. and G.E. in essence started from zero in their acquisition of language after rescue.

The report that Genie, P.M., and G.M. were able after rescue to recall their experiences of abuse came as a great surprise. F.E. and G.E. had no memory of their lives prior to being rescued. Even when they were reunited with their mother, they failed to recognize her as anything more than a mere stranger. If one accepts the existence of a strong connection between memory and language, this fact would also tend to suggest that a latent language function had already been formed in P.M., G.M., and Genie, while in contrast, F.E. and G.E. were linguistically in a tabula-rasa-like state.

As mentioned earlier, F.E. and G.E. consistently attained scores on the ITPA equivalent to the norm 3 to 3½ years below their chronological ages. This fact, along with their poor short-term memory (STM) capacity and other factors, seems to indicate the lingering effect of the delayed start of language development. However, given the facts that they are still in the process of development and that the extent of their retardation is gradually lessening, one is inclined to view their future as promising.

Remarks on Chomsky's Theory of Language Acquisition

Chomsky (1965) postulated the existence of an inherent "language acquisition device," maintaining that the role of the various environmental factors is merely to activate this device. While a language acquisition device may well be inherent in humans, it seems difficult to say that that is all that is necessary for language development (cf. Prucha, this volume). At any rate, it would seem that the role played by interaction with adults as information input for the sake of sociogenetic development is far greater that that imagined by the Chomskians. Normally, such factors are universally available to children, so that their effect may be easily overlooked. In the cases of deprived children, however, their importance is clearly illustrated.

Remarks on Cognitive Development

Finally, a few remarks about cognitive development should be made. Our case, studied in Japan, was rather special in the fact that in comparison with the other cases there was little sensorimotor restriction. If, as Piaget (1952) maintains, the essence of intelligence is generated from operations, the possibility of the occurrence of cognitive retardation would be expected to be extremely slight in our case. Nevertheless, as stated before, after these children's IQ scores attained a peak level, they began to decrease steadily, and this decrease was most noticeable in verbal intelligence (cf. Schubert, this volume). Contrary to the Piagetian thesis, this finding seems to suggest, along with Vygotsky (1962) that thinking first shapes human intelligence upon encountering language. It seems, then, to paraphrase Vygotsky's general law, that sociogenetic input stimuli from caring, sharing adults are of vital importance.

References

Bernstein, B. Social structure, language, and learning. In J. P. de Cecco (Ed.), *The psychology of language, thought, and instruction*. New York: Holt, Rinehart & Winston, 1967.

Bower, T. G. R. *A primer of infant development*. San Francisco: Freeman, 1977.

Bowlby, J. *Attachment and loss* (Vol. 1): *Attachment*. London: Hogarth, 1969.

Bruner, J. S. The ontogenesis of speech acts. *Journal of Child Language*, 1975, *2*, 1–19.

Chomsky, N. *Aspects of the theory of syntax*. Cambridge, Mass.: MIT Press, 1965.

Curtiss, S. *Genie: A psycholinguistic study of a modern-day "wild child"*. New York: Academic Press, 1977.

Curtiss, S., Fromkin, V., Krashen, S., Rigler, D., & Rigler, M. The linguistic development of Genie. *Language*, 1974, *50*, 528–554.

Davis, K. Extreme social isolation of a child. *American Journal of Sociology*, 1940, *45*, 554–565.

Davis, K. Final note on a case of extreme isolation. *American Journal of Sociology*, 1947, *52*, 432–437.

Freedman, D. A., & Brown, S. L. On the role of coenesthetic stimulation in the development of psychic structure. *Psychoanalytic Quarterly*, 1968, *37*, 418–438.

Fromkin, V., Krashen, S., Curtiss, S., Rigler, D., & Rigler, M. The development of language in Genie: A case of language acquisition beyond the "critical period." *Brain and Language*, 1974, *1*, 81–107.

Fujinaga, T., Saiga, H., Kasuga, T., & Uchida, N. A case study of developmental retardation caused by early deprived environment. *The Annual Report of Educational Psychology in Japan*, 1980, *19*, 106–111. (in Japanese)

Koluchova, J. Severe deprivation in twins: A case study. *Journal of Child Psychology and Psychiatry*, 1972, *13*, 107–114.

Koluchova, J. The further development of twins after severe and prolonged deprivation: A second report. *Journal of Child Psychology and Psychiatry*, 1976, *17*, 181–188.

Lenneberg, E. H. *Biological foundation of language*. New York: Wiley, 1967.

Luria, A. R., & Yudovich, F. Ia. *Speech and the development of mental processes in the child*. London: Staples Press, 1959.

Mason, M. K. Learning to speak after six and one-half years of silence. *Journal of Speech Disorders*, 1942, *7*, 295–304.

Piaget, J. *La psychologie de l'intelligence*. Paris: Armand Colin, 1952.

Rutter, M. *Maternal deprivation reassessed*. Harmondsworth, Middlesex: Penguin, 1972.

Rutter, M. Maternal deprivation, 1972–78: New findings, new concepts, new approaches. *Child Development*, 1979, *50*, 283–305.

Singh, J. A. L., & Zingg, R. M. *Wolf-children and feral man*. New York: Harper & Bros, 1942.

Vygotsky, L. S. *Thought and language*. Cambridge, Mass.: MIT Press, 1962.

The Social Production of Language:
The State of the Art

Report from an Underdeveloped Country: Toward Linguistic Competence in the United States

Dell Hymes

There is nothing new in the goal of understanding language as a part of social life. What is new, as we near the end of the century, is the proliferation of activity toward that goal. Thirty years ago a paper on the meanings of kinship terms could count as a bridge between formal linguistics and social life and have a special designation, "ethnolinguistic," in its title. Today the scholarly world abounds with bridges and designations—"sociolinguistics," "ethnography of speaking," "pragmatics," "conversational analysis," "sociology of language," and relevant aspects of "semiotics," "ethnomethodology," "philosophy of language," and others. Yet work that has a useful bearing on the situation of a particular community or group is not common, and work that builds a truly social study of language, one that is concrete, yet comparative, cumulative, yet critical, is hard to find indeed. More of such work is beginning to appear; nonetheless, with regard to knowledge of itself in terms of language, the United States is indeed an underdeveloped country. There is a great deal of authority about language, both in linguistics and among savants of the media, but little knowledge directed toward the explanation, and even transformation, of the role that language has in our lives.

It would be valuable to be able to compare a variety of countries in regard to their conjunction of established disciplines, practical situations, and the life of lan-

Dell Hymes ● Graduate School of Education, University of Pennsylvania, Philadelphia, Pennsylvania 19104. This chapter is based on a lecture with the title "Toward Linguistic Competence," given at the Festival of the Social Sciences, held in Amsterdam in April 1975. The festival was organized by the late Alvin Gouldner, and I should like to dedicate the chapter to his memory. The text of the lecture, somewhat edited, was published in *Sociologische gids,* 1976, 76(4), 217–239, and I thank the editors of the journal for their interest in it. The present chapter is substantially revised. The organization has been somewhat changed, material added and omitted, and some individual points rephrased.

guage. What is taken for granted in the United States might well come into focus as particular, the result of a certain social history and certain valuations. The United States would come into focus as one kind of place, or set of places, alongside Nigeria, China, and other countries (cf. Berry, this volume). We are not far enough along to be able to ask, "Why is the United States the way it is?" because we have yet to realize that the United States is a certain way. I myself suspect that analysis ultimately will reveal the interaction of subtle forms of liberal hegemony with an identification of aesthetic and expressive elaboration, including skill in languages, with what is feminine, not masculine, a certain leveling of ideal masculinity to a good heart, open hand, and willing back. Be that as it may, I can try at least to broach some aspects of the present situation in terms of certain evident tasks, since these tasks relate to the intersection of the social sciences and linguistics in relation to sociopolitical trends.

The sociopolitical trends will be of concern in terms of their relation to problems of linguistic discrimination and inequality. These problems simmer now, but may boil, and in any case directly affect the degree to which the society achieves its professed goals. Prediction is risky—neither the left nor the right foresaw the left of the 1960s, and the 1970s did not much foresee the capitalist offensive represented so effectively so far by the Reagan administration. The best guess may be that the situation will change. If so, language practices and language rights may yet become central to the society. Explanations will be needed for the persistence of a large black underclass; policies will be needed toward a large immigrant work force that does not abandon its original languages; tensions will be felt between reality and ideology in a society that proposes equality in verbal interaction and the absence of verbal airs and at the same time increasingly separates those with a place within the secure economy from those without. Either social inequality must be verbally masked, the ideal of verbal equality must be abandoned, or a mixture of new verbal markers and displacement of inequality from the verbal sphere must come into being.

Even if there is only simmering, not boiling, and the country remains, so far as the major media can detect, simply linguistically a sort of indistinct mush, those of us who hold to some belief in a society better than that we now have should develop a well-grounded critique. What ideal or vision do we entertain in terms of language?

Two ingredients of a vision, I think, would be a kind of negative freedom and a kind of positive freedom. The negative freedom would be the absence of denial of opportunity due to something linguistic, whether spoken dialect or competence in writing and reading. The positive freedom would be the opportunity to find satisfaction in use of language—imaginative life and satisfying form. I unite these two kinds of freedom in my own mind in the notion of *voice*: the freedom to have one's voice— manner and matter—heard and the freedom to develop a voice worth hearing. A way to think of the kind of society in which one would like to live, linguistically, is to think of it in terms of the kinds of voices it would have.

If issues couched in terms of language come to the fore in the United States in ways not now expected, now is the time to build the knowledge needed to understand them when they arise. If the present condition of American society is not satisfactory, language may be a sphere in which to raise consciousness and direct critique. Something of the sort has been seen in connection with the women's movement in the last ten years. Claims of the connection between specific features and specific kinds of oppression may have been overstated or have implied assumptions about the general relation of language to thought and social life that require reflection, but language use, nonetheless, is inseparable from everyday interaction, and contentions about it cannot be ignored. One can identify a pronoun more easily than the controller of a corporate policy. Turns at talk are observed more easily than exchange of personnel among government agencies and the businesses the agencies ostensibly regulate. Discourse cannot ultimately change the gross inequities that make it rational for the centers and margins of power alike to combine in ecological destruction (Anderson, 1973), nor can it change the interests that find it reasonable to plan the destruction of us all; but discourse is at hand everywhere, and scrutiny of our own and of that of others is a lens that may sometimes focus light enough to start a fire.

Such a thought must seem vain, clutching at a straw, as against an analysis of modern society in terms of the state, multinational corporations, and the like. Perhaps it is. Still, no likely lever of change in American society is evident except immiserization, and rather than wait patiently for the worst to turn better, we may find scrutiny of language, literacy, and discourse productive of both knowledge and change.

Five Tasks

If one should try to do something about the language situation in the United States, how should one proceed? Five tasks can be singled out:

1. Remedy the degree to which the United States is a *terra incognita* with regard to quite elementary information as to varieties of language and values as to their use.

2. Study the processes by which something linguistic comes to be recognized as a problem.

3. Analyze the development of cultural hegemony through the language in the United States, historically and in comparative context.

4. Criticize the assumptions and practices of linguistics and the social sciences with regard to language.

5. Reshape the study of language in accord with the critique, not only as to what is done, but also as to who does it and for what ends.

Somewhat crudely reduced to parallel formulations:

1. What counts as a language?
2. What counts as a language problem?
3. What counts as proper use of language?
4. What counts as a contribution (about language) to linguistics, to sociology, etc.?
5. What will count in changing the above?

I shall suggest something about each of these five tasks in the following sections.

Task 1: Terra Incognita

Most people are likely to think of issues of language in terms of languages. There is much to be brought to attention simply as to the actual heterogeneity of the

United States in this regard. Most of us may think of Montana as a state of big sky and few people, but Beltramo (1981) has identified some 37 or so languages in varying degrees of use among its population: Cree, Chippewa, Atsina, Blackfoot, Crow, Teton, Assiniboine, Flathead, Kalispel, Kutenai, of American Indian languages; the French-Indian creole, Métis: French, English, Gaelic, German, Norwegian, Danish, Swedish, Finnish, Dutch, Polish, Czech (and Slovak), Serbo-Croatian, possibly Russian, Hungarian, Greek, Italian, Spanish, Basque, Hebrew, and Yiddish, of languages from Europe; Arabic; Chinese, Japanese, Korean, Miao (spoken by the recent immigrant Hmong), Vietnamese, and Lao (used as a *lingua communis* by Vietnamese with some other Asians).

The book to which Beltramo contributed, *Language in the USA* (Ferguson & Heath, 1981), is a major step toward making our language situation intelligible to us. Here I want to call attention to two considerations that are often overlooked in thinking about named languages. One concerns the true repertoire of language varieties present in a situation, and the other that aspect of language that has to do with attitudes and practices in its use. Understanding of each requires a common element, a mode of work that is ethnographic.

Varieties of Language

In a situation involving English and another language, most schools and scholars would assume that the number of elements (varieties of language) to be known is two. Often the true number is at least four.

In Native American communities, where the native language survives in a traditional form, there may also be a more widely used vernacular variety. A local vernacular English will be found besides a local standard English. The vernacular may play a socially significant role. Someone who has been away and returns may have to take up the "Indian English" again or be judged snobbish. This vernacular variety may show distinctive, creative adaptations of English material to phonological, syntactic, and semantic patterns that are Indian.

There are dozens of varieties of Indian English in the United States, but only very recently has there come to be any published analysis. A pioneer and important work is Leap's (1974), in which he shows that a double negative in Isletan English is not an error or borrowing of an error, but a way of maintaining in English a contrast between two kinds of negation (negation of the predicate and negation of an object) present in Isleta. (The difference is equivalent to "The fire is not burning" vs. "There is no fire.")

Varieties of English are distinguished not only by phonological and grammatical traits, but also by patterns that are poetic, or rhetorical, in nature. The characteristic voices of the older people of an Indian community may be colored not only by the native language in the narrow sense, but also by modes of expressing and replaying experience; relations in discourse, ways of segmenting and sequencing events, may maintain something of the centrality of narrative logic in the traditional way of life. Such characteristics of Indian use of English have gone almost unnoticed.

An example of a fourfold situation with regard to varieties of English and Indian language has been usefully depicted by Darnell (1971) for the Cree in the Canadian province of Alberta. Brandt (1970) presented a brief, clear picture of a Southwestern situation involving three languages (Indian, English, and Spanish), as is often the case in the Southwest, with degrees of command differing rather markedly among four generations (of approximately 20 years each). Voegelin, Voegelin, and Schutz (1967) presented a pioneering view of a state language situation with especial interest in the Indian languages. Leap (1981) is an indispensable guide to the general situation.

The importance of getting beyond language names to varieties is shown by a recent prize-winning study which analyzed the language development of Pima Indian children in Arizona. Their speech was interpreted in terms of norms derived from English-speaking children in Maryland. There was no information as to the variety of English spoken by the Pima, or indeed, locally around them in Arizona. Again, not long ago a comparison of the features of Choctaw, an Indian language of the Southeast, and English was prepared. The study was to be useful in schools with Choctaw children, pointing to differences between the two languages that might present special difficulties for them in learning English. The comparison was made between traditional standard Choctaw and standard English. The varieties of Choctaw and English known and used vernacularly by the children were ignored.

This kind of question arises with particular force with regard to Spanish. The main groups of Spanish speakers in the United States, Puerto Ricans, Cubans, and Chicanos, are organizationally and linguistically distinct. There is indeed a distinction to be observed between *Chicanos,* resident for some time in the United States, and *Mexicans*, recently arrived. The differences pose problems for practical programs. Not the least problem is attitude toward a standard language on the part of many users of Spanish and many Anglos. Some Puerto Ricans sympathetic to working-class problems may question whether maintenance of standard Spanish is in their interest or that of someone else. Teachers of Colombian origin may indict the Spanish of their Puerto Rican students. Native speakers of Spanish may do poorly in (standard) Spanish class in comparison with Anglo students. Anglo teachers who may have excused students in the past on the grounds of Spanish may be heard to tell Chicano children, "I used to think your trouble was that your language was Spanish. Now I see that you don't have any language at all." (I owe this example to Eduardo Hernandez-Che; cf. Ruskin & Varenne, this volume.)

The fact of the matter is that Chicanos may experience as many as four varieties of Spanish alone. In Austin, Texas, there is a local standard, *northern Mexican,* also called *Español formal, Español correcto, Español politico* (polite), *Espannñol bueno, Español bonito,* or *straight Spanish.* There are also *popular Spanish* (called also *Mejicano, everyday Spanish, Español, Español de East Austin,* or *Español mocho),* so-called *Spanglish* (also called *Tex-Mex, Español mocho, Español revelto,* or *Español mixtureado),* and *Calo* (also called *Pachuco talk, Barrio language, pachuquismos, Hablar al modo loco,* or *vato language).* (I owe this information to the research of Lucía Elías-Olivares.) A teacher may not accept the local standard as deserving classroom recognition, but consider Castilian, Colombian, or some other nonlocal variety the norm. If the local standard is accepted, the other varieties of the children's language experience still are likely to be ignored or condemned.

There is a great deal to be learned about the diverse and changing situation of Spanish. The state of sociolinguistic research into New World Spanish has been surveyed by Lavandera (1974) with critical observations. Hernandez-Chavez, Cohen, and Beltramo have provided an overview of Chicano language (1975). Craddock (1981) provided a useful introduction to New World Spanish generally, and Zentella (1981) to the specific situation of Puerto Rican Spanish.

The vernacular varieties of English used by black Americans have come to be better known, but the state of knowledge about language among them is perhaps no better overall. The full range remains obscure. For some black scholars, the question is why there has been so much attention to the variety associated with the streets and young adolescent males and so little to others. Why so much fascination with the ritual insults and obscenities of "playing the dozens," and so little attention to the eloquence of the preacher and minister or to the subtle use of "black" features by many of the middle class? (cf. the review articles by Mitchell-Kernan, 1972; Wright, 1975.) The impetus given by the civil rights movement and turbulence of the 1960s has not been sustained by systematic study, apart from a few individuals. (The state of studies of Black English has been surveyed by Abrahams & Szwed, 1975.) The recent decision of an educational suit in Ann Arbor on the basis of language brought judicial recognition of the existence of a variety of language, Black English, that could be defined linguistically, but the case itself is often misinterpreted. What was ordered was not instruction in a Black English variety, but workshops for teachers about the nature of Black English. The plaintiffs had not sought to base a case on language, but the judge found that language was the only grounds legally available to him. The law stated that equal opportunity could not be denied for reasons that included language. The law said nothing about denial of equal opportunity on grounds of class or economic status.

The decision was widely misinterpreted because of the division of opinion among black Americans themselves as to the status of Black English. Its general stigmatization has led many to reject it themselves. The conventional anthropological attitude of using the language of the community led some linguists in the 1960s to pioneer the use of Black English forms in written materials for classrooms, but this effort was taken as a threat by many blacks; unions in Philadelphia threatened to strike if such materials were introduced there. In the wake of the Ann Arbor decision, classrooms in the district in Philadelphia in which I live and work were forbidden to represent on the blackboard the nonstandard forms actually used by children in relating their experiences. All this is evidence, of course, that educated black people share with other educated Americans a view of writing that makes it almost something sacred (cf. Illich, this volume). What may be acceptable or tolerable in speech becomes a symbolic issue if represented materially in chalk or print. For every language situation, there is a need to know not only the range of varieties present in terms of linguistic characteristics, but also the range of varieties present in terms of modes or channels. Speech and writing are the obvious contrast, but reality is more complex. Speech and writing are not two homogeneous things, but merely names for modalities whose use is diversely shaped. One must discover the routines, genres, and functions of each. As recent work in urban classrooms by Susan Fiering and Susan Florio has shown, what counts as "writing" for the teacher may be only a portion of the kinds of writing in which children engage. A variety of uses for social interaction and personal expression can be seen if one looks.

In general, we have little accurate knowledge of where and what literacy is in our society. We have an image of what it should be, perhaps, but it would be hard to cite a careful profile of the life of literacy among any group of people. From the point of view of a child acquiring a way of life, the official literacy of the school follows its encounter with street signs, delivered newspapers and magazines, hubcap names that distinguish kinds of cars, Sunday school perhaps, brand names and advertisements on the breakfast table, and so on. A normal child would become literate to a degree without school, as a normal part of walking, eating, playing, being a Baptist, and the like. It would be useful to imagine the school as a trading post or mission, offering goods and practices to a community that already has something of the kind and would have, were the enclave not there. Classrooms are in the position of *adding* to experiences of literacy that children already have before they come to school and those that they develop as they grow, play, attend church, work, and become interested in kinds of objects and hobbies apart from school. It is important to know what the rest of life, outside of school, is telling children as to the nature and necessity of literacy. (See the important work of Heath, 1982, 1983, contrasting three groups in a region of South Carolina.)

The Ann Arbor decision may open an opportunity that all concerned have so far missed, because scholars and public alike associate the notion of *language* with the contents of a grammar and not with the ways in which the contents are actually organized for use. If language is legally protected, if equality of opportunity cannot be denied on grounds of language, then it matters very much to the future of the country how language is defined. Since 1967, a conception of participation in a speech community as consisting of more than knowledge of a grammar, as consisting as well of knowledge of appropriate use, has been advanced as a necessary basis for linguistics and sociolinguistics (Hymes, 1967). If this conception of what it means to know a language were to be adopted, then the cultural and social aspects of life that have been of concern to many blacks, Hispanics, and others would be brought within the scope of the stated law. The place of language in the life of the community would be understood as more than a matter of phonemes, morphemes, grammatical categories and constructions. It would be properly understood as involving varieties and modalities, styles and genres, ways of using language as a resource.

Black English itself, of course, is a matter of all these things. The studies that have been made in recent years show how important are certain ways of using language (see Whatley, 1981, as an introduction; the important book by Smitherman, 1977; Kochman, 1972; Mitchell-Kernan, 1972) and norms for appropriate contexts of use (cf. Abrahams, 1972; Hoover, 1978). Black English also points up a phenomenon for which the depiction of a language situation in terms of a set of languages, dialects, varieties, or levels of usage is inadequate. On the one hand, much the same linguistic features may be prejudicial to a working-class black speaker and not to a middle-class white. Lyndon Johnson could become president of the country with marked dialect features that would likely have disqualified a black. On the other hand, distinctive black style is acceptable, even applauded, in a case such as that of A. D. King, Sr.'s participation as a minister at the 1980 Democratic National Convention. There is a phenomenon here connected with the notion of *voice*. Certain voices are acceptable, even valued, in certain roles, but not others. A black minister, a British actor, an aged Indian leader, and perhaps some others have a niche in the public consciousness that involves role in a way distinct from a two-dimensional model of, vertically, levels of class-based norms and, horizontally, a range of situational styles varying with degree of self-consciousness. The study of community-wide change in language, such as the two-dimensional model reflects, is important, but it is too gross to catch the evaluations of speech and speakers that involve personification of role.

Varieties of language are so intimately involved with attitudes about and values related to their use that the discussion of black English inevitably broaches such questions. Before continuing, however, let me say something more about the United States from the standpoint of language varieties of European origin. Criteria for establishing types of national language situations have identified the United States as having *six* major languages: English, German, Italian, Spanish, Polish, and Yiddish (Ferguson, 1966, p. 321). Most work with regard to these and other immigrant languages (apart from English) has been concerned with their relation to their Old World counterparts. Studies have focused on survival and change of Old World features and on adoption of English features in adaptation to the New World environment. Relatively little has been done to identify the uses of varieties of these languages as part of the general verbal repertoires of the communities. Even the history of the use of German and other languages in bilingual schools and in churches in earlier generations is little known to the public at large, which falsely imagines immigrants from Europe in the past to have invariably adopted English promptly. Knowledge of such European-origin languages was well surveyed two decades ago by Haugen (1956), who is the source as well of the richest study of a single language (1953). Recent efforts to develop knowledge of the German language situation are reflected in Gilbert (1971), who has made an interesting comparison between German and French as well (1981). The maintenance of a number of languages through schools, newspapers, and churches has been surveyed by Fishman (1966). There is perhaps an increase in interest in maintenance now on the part of a good many people. In some urban centers and in some institutional contexts, at least, there is considerable bilingualism and multilingualism. New York City television stations offer programs in Spanish, Chinese, Korean, Japanese, Greek, Portuguese, and Italian, and there are at least five Spanish language stations in the country as a whole (New York Times, April 21, 1975, p. 59), as well as one Navajo one. The four-day 61st annual convention of the Apostolic Church of America at George Fox College in Newberg, Oregon, in July 1975 had dual sessions in English and Finnish for its 1,000 delegates from 52 churches across the country (The Portland Oregonian, July 5, 1975, p. B7). A multilingualism clipping service would no doubt accumulate a great many such facts. Despite all that has been done to Native American cultures and languages, 50 or 60 remain viable and are used in the home. Some 44 attract the current efforts of missionary linguists as having a "justified need for Bible translation" (Washington Star-News, December 21, 1974, citing the Conference on American Indian Languages Clearinghouse Newsletter, March 1975, *3*(2), p. 3). Information of this kind becomes known to residents of a locality, members of an organization, and specialists in a subject, but seldom goes further. Because of the isolation of such facts from one another the public allows us to continue to think of the country as blanketed by English, our particular bit of information being the odd exception.

We are pretty ignorant, by and large, of the sum to which the odd exceptions add up. Official statistics are of little or no use. According to the 1960 census, for example, there were only 1,200 native speakers of French in Louisiana, because it was presumed that a native-born American was a native speaker of English. Only the foreign-born were recorded as having a different mother tongue. The actual situation and the range of styles are indicated now in Tentchoff (1975). The 1960 census was discussed by McDavid (1966, p. 321). It would be one mark of success for a language-oriented movement if it succeeded in deepening the knowledge that the census and other government agencies provide and publish. There are of course considerable constraints of time, expense, and training governing what census takers themselves can do. Their inquiries and other records could be supplemented by detailed study in selected areas. (On the present situation, and improvements motivated by bilingual education, see the valuable overview of Waggoner, 1981.)

It is all too common, unfortunately, for official records and scholarly studies to rely on what people themselves say for information as to the languages they use and how often they use them. If there is one principle established in sociolinguistics, it is that people are often unable to answer such questions accurately. We are busy living our lives, not observing them, and often simply do not know all that we do or how often we do some part of it. Moreover, any answer to such a question about language is most likely a statement of identity. Self-report will tell about people's values, aspirations, current sociopolitical circumstances; but it cannot be relied on to tell what they do. If one were to take the answers to the census of India at face value, tens of thousands of speakers and even whole language communities would have to be assumed to have disappeared between one census and the next. As the Indian scholar L. Khubchandani has observed, the truth of the matter is that the communities are multilingual, circumstances change, and the variety of language which it seems most reasonable or advisable to name first may change.

Information as to the occurrence of a vareity can be accurate, of course, only in terms of the set of varieties found in a community. In multilingual situations, as in situations of a series of styles or registers, it is common for one to influence others. The attitude of members of the group may range from ignorance or shocked denial of any such influence to cultivation of the relationship as a stylistic resource. Code switching, in the narrow sense of use of a feature of one language in another, may be an ad hoc choice of the word that comes first to mind, an allusion to one's status or travels, a gesture to the interlocutor who shares that other language. The range of empirical possibilities is very great, and the relation between fact and popular impression quite loose. A few English words in another language may go unnoticed, may pass as sophistication, may spark a fear that the other language is being corrupted or is even in danger of being lost. It is the salient, detachable features of language—words—that most gain popular attention. The many and subtle ways in which languages can influence each other, through adaptation of grammatical categories, shifts in connotations, translation of phrasal patterns, and the like, are less apparent at the surface. And just as a few intrusive words may seem a symbol of loss, so a few remaining words may seem a symbol of maintenance. Just the ability to introduce a certain number of native language words on a public occasion may be symbolically meaningful and may count as use of the language.

In short, to describe the language situation of a community, to identify the varieties of language within its repertoire, is to do more than to enumerate a list. On the one hand, it is to discover the relations to each other of the members of a mutually contrasting set, a paradigmatic set in linguistic terms. On the other hand, it is to deal with a set of symbols whose significance cannot be inferred from linguistic facts alone, but must be discovered in the life of the community itself. Varieties and features of language, as organizations of linguistic signs, themselves become sociolinguistic signs, unities of form and meaning within a system. Their relations to each other are partly a matter of distribution, of allocation among topics and settings and purposes, and are partly a matter of sheer attribution of meaning in terms of the values and historical experiences of the people in question. The dimensions of contrast underlying these meanings can be discovered only through ethnographic inquiry.

We are used to thinking of varieties in connection with ethnic identity. There has begun to be sustained work on varieties in connection with occupational and institutional settings. O'Barr (1981), Cicourel (1981), and Cazden and Dickinson (1981) have introduced the law, medicine, and education in useful articles. Class has entered sociolinguistic analysis as an indispensable parameter of change, but has hardly begun to appear as a focus of inquiry in its own right. There is evidence to suggest that experiences with school and elsewhere leave many members of the working class (and others) with a sense that their lot in life is deserved and that language plays a great part in the process. Perhaps the appearance of equal opportunity to rise through education, joined with a process of selection and rejection that is mediated in great part by language, is essential to the stability of a society with democratic beliefs and a persistent hierarchy of wealth and power. Perhaps there is a functional need for stigmata of linguistic inferiority, such that if naturally occurring differences did not appear sufficient, others would be seized upon or even invented.

Differences of gender have been the focus of considerable attention in the past decade or so. Much remains to be worked out as to the actual relationships among verbal behavior, verbal stereotypes, features of language in the narrow sense, and features of the use of language, such as turn-taking, having the floor, symmetry and complementarity in styles of conversation, dependence of difference on setting and role, and so on. Most of the work has reflected middle-class and academic or professional settings. There is little information on the different attitudes and practices that may obtain in different ethnic groups, among different classes, regions, and religious traditions. Clearly men's and women's speech is too broad a contrast. There may well be two contrasting styles, associated with men and women primarily or often, but some work indicates that status and power may be basic to some features, such that they may be found in the speech of men occupying positions of low status or little power. The study of gender-related differences in speech could be a penetrating, leading edge of the general understanding of language in the country (cf. Phillips, this volume). The pursuit of the one focus could illuminate the relationships among all the various facets of linguistic diversity: ethnic, regional, occupational, and class. In the absence of a clear model of the society as a whole, the pursuit of one dimension as far as it can take us may be the best strategy for gaining a comprehension of the whole. Every ethnic and racial group, region, class, and most occupations have women members; every normal woman is a member of some ethnic or racial group, a resident of some region, of some class background, with experience of some kind of work, and so also is every normal man. Such a focus on kinds of person might best integrate in comprehensible fashion the attributes that measurement and models tend to separate.

Attitudes and Values

Let me select just one setting for attention here, that of the classroom. It is important to the life chances of children, and it is representative of the problem of knowledge. A key question in the classroom is what the teacher may make of the attitudes and values toward language use brought by the children.

Sometimes a situation is taken to be a question of knowledge of language when it is in fact a question of knowledge in the sense of appropriate uses of language. Children are assumed perhaps not to know enough English, not to know the right kind of English, or to be shy. Observing a school in central Oregon, Philips (1972) found that the Indian children did indeed talk less than other children in situations controlled by the teacher, but might talk just as much in other situations. A situation in which a single person commands everyone else's right to speak and can demand display of ability in performance goes contrary to the norms of the community from which the children come, where rights to speak are typically equal in public situations and where display of competence is typically self-initiated (and where public groups usually form a circle, rather than having one person in front facing the rest).

Notice that the difficulty is not one of a language other than English. The children come to school as native speakers of a variety of English. *It is the aspect of language, of membership in a speech community, governing how language is to be used that is in question.*

Of course, schools have long been aware of cultural differences, and there are many programs concerned with understanding them. What is often slighted is the "invisible" culture (to use Philips's term) of everyday interaction: the expression, through norms of speaking, of community values, of traditional rights and duties between persons, what Goffman has called the ceremonial sphere of deference and demeanor (1956). Teachers may be conscientiously respectful of explicit religious belief and practice yet may profane an unseen order vested in individuals.

Perhaps an adequate overall view of the ingredients of everyday interaction in this respect can be reached by combining Goffman's distinction with one made in a provocative, important study of politeness in language by Brown and Levinson (1978). Goffman distinguished between *deference,* or what is owed to the other, and *demeanor,* or what one owes to oneself. Both can be taken as involving respect, for the other and for oneself. Brown and Levinson built an extended comparative study on, in part, a distinction between two kinds of "face," positive and negative. "Negative face" is like Goffman's deference and is defined in terms of respecting the right of the other not to be intruded upon, impeded, and the like. "Positive face" has no direct equivalent in Goffman's distinction; it has to do with regard for another's usual wish to have some of his/her likes, preferences, and traits well regarded. We may associate it with Kenneth Burke's term for the heart of modern rhetoric, *identification.*

If we consider the way in which these three spheres contribute to the success or failure of interaction, we can say, roughly, that identification has to do with such things as establishing common ground (where one is from, whom one knows, what one does, what one likes, etc.), deference has to do with regard for the other's self-respect, and demeanor has to do with expectable regard for one's own. Failure in each respect might sometimes be characterized as "having nothing in common," "being rude," "losing one's cool." But interaction may fail, or pale, for a fourth reason, the lack of a contribution to the interaction, or of a contribution of interest, from one of the parties. One can find common ground, be polite and self-controlled, and still be too dull to bear. We glimpse here a logical possibility to be added to the intersection of Goffman with Brown and Levinson. Their categories give two spheres of concern for the other (identification, deference) but only one of concern for the self (demeanor). From another standpoint, their categories give two spheres of concern for respect, for avoiding insult and breach in the other and oneself (deference, demeanor), but only one for concern for what may unite and integrate, rather than maintain boundary (identification). The logic of the relationships points to a fourth category, concerned with what unites, integrates, and has to do with the self. Let us call it *expression,* the contribution one may be expected to make to the interest of what goes on. The four spheres can be shown thus:

	Union	Autonomy
Toward other	identification	deference
Toward self	expression	demeanor

    In attending to differences between classroom and community, we must not rely on broad dichtomies. It is not a matter simply of rich versus impoverished verbal environments, or of opposed orientations toward verbal meaning (elaborated and restricted), or of literate versus oral cultures. Such dichotomies are tempting, because we take what is familiar to us as academics, the classroom, as one pole and label what is not familiar "other." We have to deal with phenomena that are more various. In particular, the differences are not always aligned in the same way. In one case the salient difference may be ethnic, as between an Anglo and a non-Anglo orientation. In another, the difference may be saliently between two ethnic orientations, neither of which is Anglo (e.g., Jewish : Italian). Class orientations may sometimes be middle-class school and working-class parents, but also, sometimes, the other way around, with middle-class parents gradually dropping out of a school and community which is becoming too working class for them and for the way they want their children to be treated. *The dimensions of difference are various, they contribute to a plurality of types of situation, and dichotomies only obscure the complexity of the reality.*

    Clearly we must not rely on a simple assumption of making school and community match. In some communities the parents' expectation of school may be precisely that it is different from home in a specific way. Nor can the sensitiviy of teachers be expected to suffice. McDermott (1974, 1977) has analyzed interactions in a mostly middle-class first-grade in the New York area and has concluded that initial assignment to one of two reading groups on the basis of ethnicity-linked command of English leads to a stratification and emergence of differences that has an observable, ineluctable outcome. The advanced group, essentially "non-ethnic," had initial competence sufficient for confidence, and came to show an autonomous, minimally signaled, orderly sequencing of turns in reading, thus maximizing the teacher's use of time with the group for teaching of reading. In the other group, the teacher did not want to embarrass children by insisting on regular turns for those less proficient. The resulting process of volunteering and competing for turns allows some children tacitly to avoid being called on and directs much of the teacher's attention to interruptions and negotiations about turn-taking itself. The result is likely to maintain, if not increase, the initial stratification that is likely to be lasting. The causes will have been complex and likely not adequately recognized. The initial lack of command of English will be known, but not the contribution of stratification and norms of interaction.

One needs to include teachers among those who contribute to ethnographic knowledge of such situations, but clearly, the problem appears to be one of what happens in the classroom alone only because society, in effect, allows it to appear as such. A different complex of relations between classroom and community could exist. If literacy were a major social goal for all citizens, the society could be mobilized to ensure it. If the literacy of numbers of students is left to depend on turn-taking in reading groups, the invisible failure is that of the society. Other countries have been known to mobilize to ensure literacy. To let literacy depend on the outcome of a crowded classroom is an excellent way to perpetuate the class-linked differences in literacy which children bring to class. Perhaps an essential topic for research is the distribution in the society of the belief that literacy is the business of the schools, as against attitudes or practices that make it a matter of the home before, alongside, or with the school.

Task 2: Recognition of Problem

The preceding section focused on the language situation of the United States as a problem from the standpoint of someone motivated partly by a desire for knowledge as a basis for action and partly by a desire for general change in the place of language in the society. Questions of language have come to appear as problems in public life in a much more limited way. A fundamental task is to understand the circumstances that lead to recognition or definition of something as a problem for public attention. (On the difficulty of recognizing the existence of phenomena as a part of our society, because of social problems, see Szwed, 1973.)

The linguist Neustupný has outlined a systematic model of the scope of linguistic problems, ranging from correction in individual behavior to societal planning (in a paper given at the University of Pennsylvania in October 1973; see his book, 1979). Let us consider the latter pole. In Germany, the presence of guest workers *(Gästarbeiter)* is defined as a social problem, and funds are provided to study the linguistic adaptation of the workers and their children in Germany. In the United States the medical system depends in important part on thousands of doctors and interns whose native language is not English, but this has not been defined as a problem. Beyond the circle of top schools of engineering, faculties of engineering in the United States are drawn mostly from other countries. Native-born American engineers command too high a salary in engineering itself to be willing to teach. No problem is publicly identified here. Perhaps incidents will arise of difficulty of communication with hospital staff that will lead to public attention, perhaps not.

The development of what we know about language varieties has obviously not been the result of a systematic scholarly plan. There has been mobilization of ethnic and minority groups around questions of language. The emergence into national attention of the civil rights movement in the 1960s, as well as some riots, coincided with attention to Black English and funds for its investigation. Subsequently the mobilization of Spanish-speaking Americans led to support for bilingual education, defined generally but focused to a great extent on Spanish-language situations. The initial legal step, indeed, resulted from mobilization in San Francisco among Chinese citizens. In 1968 the United States Congress passed a Bilingual Education Act, establishing the right of children to be taught in their native language, and as a result of a suit brought on behalf of Chinese-speaking children in San Francisco (*Lau* v. *Nichols*), the Supreme Court affirmed the act (see Alcala, Rivera, & Thayer, 1974; Paulston, 1981). There is an effort among Native Americans, stimulated by Deni Leonard and others, to gain recognition for the language rights of Native American communities as a basis for their increased political and cultural autonomy.

Such mobilization and national action precedes knowledge rather than drawing upon it. The mobilization around language goes on with little systematic information on which it may draw or in terms of which it may be assessed. Laymen, social scientists, and linguists alike proceed largely on the basis of received attitudes and limited information. The elementary, most unifying goal is a place in schooling for a language other than English. That goal is itself hard to win in the United States, and among those who accept it, only some have in mind the further goal of community maintenance of a language other than English. Many who participate in bilingual education see it simply as a way to replace some other language with English (or, say, with French, as may be the case with Cajun and Creole in Louisiana). Few who participate have the opportunity to transcend the class-linked perceptions and prejudices about language that are part of the cultural stratification of the country. The institutionalized forms of English itself are part of the language problems of minority and ethnic groups, but there is little critical analysis of their role in cultural hegemony or of the total language situation (cf. Masemann, this volume).

There are three levels of aspiration, then, for the efforts at language-related mobilization: a place in schooling for a language not English; community maintenance of a language not English; and critical analysis of the total language situation of the country, including the place of standard English itself. Of these three, it is the third that would radically challenge the social order; the second is widely feared as doing so; only the first, minimal goal is at all strong, and it is increasingly under attack and threatened by lack of funding.

The availability of money is not itself a solution, insofar as it brings in its wake other problems. The money enters an institutional order. It may bring about vested interests, either in the existence of a certain class of persons needing to be helped, or in the restriction of employment and funds to persons of a certain background, many of whom may deserve and need employment, but few of whom may have had opportunity for the technical training required by the work to which they are assigned. An example of the first occurred in a school in Colorado, where the availability of funds for bilingual education led to appointment of a special aide, who visited classrooms, seeking children for the new program. The criterion was knowledge of Spanish; that is, knowing Spanish was defined as having a problem. One child selected for assignment to special education was the son of a professor at the University of Colorado. By dint of struggle, the father was able to have his son released from the remedial class. His son, of course, had no problem with language, or anything else in school; both English and Spanish were normally and fluently used in his home. Other children, with fathers less knowledgeable and positioned, might not be so fortunate. At a Georgetown Round Table in 1975 one participant plaintively asked, "Can anything be done to prevent bilingual education becoming a dumping ground?" He reported schools that were closing special classes for various difficulties and disabilities and transferring the children into classes for bilingual education, because money was available for that.

Sometimes funds have been obtained by members of a community on their own initiative, only to find a greater part of the funds going to supervening organizations, educational laboratories, and the like, who may actually exclude the advice of persons with knowledge of the subject. A major problem from one perspective, then, is the need for true community initiative and control. The major problem from the standpoint of sources of funds is likely to be fiscal responsibility and control. And of course the internal political life of any community is such that continuity of leadership may be interrupted, or leadership enlisted in the support of one view as against other strong views within the community. Community practices as to personal transmission of knowledge may not coincide with the institutional structure that comes from participation in larger political and bureaucratic life. What is smoothly running from a central point of view may be appalling in result closer to the ground.

It is recognized as a problem that knowledge of many of the languages of the United States, such as the Indian languages, has been almost entirely in the hands of persons not from the communities in which the languages are spoken or of which they have been a part. No solution to the language problems of such communities, indeed, can come without members of those communities playing a central part. At the same time scholars who are not members of those communities cannot simply turn over the problems to persons who are. There are too few who are, to begin with, and a certain bias of social position frequently accompanies the role of being the first linguistic specialist from one's community, just as a certain bias of social position frequently accompanies the role of being a professor from outside the community. The satisfaction that one older person takes in cooperating in lingusitic work may appear to a younger professional an affront, perpetuating the image of the native as only a source, not an analyst. There must be native analysts, but those who have been able to enjoy the status of a respected source of knowledge need not be disdained. Without the partnerships that included them, there would be no knowledge left for descendants of many of the Native American languages.

The worst case is when persons are hired for their ethnic identity and not their professional competence. It is no service to an ethnic group to right the wrong of past exclusion by associating it with shoddy work. The anti-intellectualism of many Hispanics and Native Americans is understandable, given past exploitation. When their principal claim on a newly won position is their access to knowledge that comes from their ethnic identity, they can hardly help but resent continued writing about such materials from others not of their background. Yet a world in which knowledge of a group was the exclusive property of the group and no other would be a compartmentalized, parochial world. Those who share an element of socialist aspiration cannot accept the easy solution of appointing the community, or its nearest representative, as arbiter. The community or its representative may be wrong, from the standpoint of some more general social and political position. It is a double standard if members of ethnic groups are granted a monopoly on knowledge of their own backgrounds, but not excluded from knowledge of other backgrounds. A fair challenge would be: If you do not want others to write about your language, or background, then don't write about anything else yourself. If non-Indians are not to write Indians or Indian languages, the Indian may not write about whites. To each his own, only. But the tensions of this situation will continue to reproduce themselves as long as there remains so great an inequity in the distribution of access to knowledge and the rewards of professional expertise. Someone like myself, in the middle of many such situations, gets angry in turn at the person who wants to deny any others the right to write and at the Anglo who doesn't understand why a non-Anglo would feel that way.

A widely recognized problem is the lack of local resources and help for communities that undertake some initiative about a problem of language. A less acknowledged problem is the fact that many local communities, and those nearby and willing and able to assist, inherit the generic ignorance and misconception of things linguistic that pervades American society. A minister living on a reservation for 30 years may invent his own way of writing the Indian language, but it may be inadequate. Teachers in an Indian-sponsored school may understand the importance and nature of cultural differences and may do everything they can to make the semester in which they have adult Indians for composition class a success for them, a basis on which they can go onward in education. Yet their background in English may include nothing that enables them to realize that difficulty with the articles in English is not a sign of inattention or lack of precision. They may never have encountered a Pole, Japanese, or Armenian holding a major academic position who has similar problems with English articles, and so may not realize that what appears simple has proven a subtle puzzle for many foreign-born speakers and linguists alike. Their insight into the native culture may include nothing about the language. They may prove to have taken for granted that the Indian language is simple, when in fact it has a morphological structure more complex by far than that of English. In short, good will and effort abound; elementary knowledge of language differences is nil.

Both locally and nationally, the desire and need to take action outstrips knowledge, not only knowledge not yet in hand that ought to be obtained, but also knowledge that has been shared in the linguistics community for generations and that has penetrated the wider world almost not at all.

The fundamental language problem, I believe, is the twin ignorance just described. Needed knowledge follows rather than precedes public action; the knowledge that we already have is little known. It does not seem to me possible that any mobilization around a particular issue of language or any accession of funds can be of much long-term value apart from a thoroughgoing conception of the needs in terms of knowledge and training of the country as a whole. It is as much a contribution to extend the sphere of linguistic common sense to include more of those who will act and decide as it is to extend the sphere of new knowledge. Both are essential to our future.

Greater public understanding may help as well to break the cycle of crisis first, research afterward. Distinctive varieties of English existed among black citizens for generations before they came to be defined as a problem during the 1960s; varieties of Spanish have existed among children in many schools before coming to be defined as an object of national concern; varieties of other languages exist that have not been defined as a public problem. A considered approach to the language situation of the United States as a whole as the fundamental problem may defuse individual issues a bit and gain ground on issues to come. Perhaps the next time that a school system is ordered to assign children bilingual classes, as happened in New York City with regard to Spanish in 1975, there will already exist, as there originally did not, research on the basis of which tests could be designed and administered fairly and accurately. No such research existed in the New York City case; yet the law required four separate tests, for speaking, hearing, writing, and reading, and what the law required was, willy nilly, done.

The need to break the cycle of action first, research afterward is especially evident in the case of bilingual education. It has come under attack before it has had much opportunity to discover what it might appropriately be, and the specific funds may be lost in block grants from the federal government. There is something to be said for the assumption that problems cannot be solved by throwing money at them (national defense seems to be considered an exception to that rule); but the need for practical programs and careful research grows with the increase in the Spanish-speaking population, the influx from Laos and Vietnam, and the persistence of a multitude of other language needs. One does not solve problems by papering them over either.

Social scientists and linguists who are not members of language minorities need to work to break the cycle of mobilization and action first, research second. Their contributions in research can be more valuable as background for policy than as sop and catch-up. There is much for them to understand in analyzing the cycle and changing it that is a contribution to the sociology of knowledge itself (I am indebted to Rolf Kjolseth for discussions of this issue). One should attempt not only to anticipate public consciousness and research support, but also to influence public consciousness through research. The best ground for such an effort, as suggested above, is a concern with the country as a whole. Such a concern challenges the various sciences of social life to transcend their own parochialism and to recognize the fundamental nature and unity of their subject matter in the sphere of language. The sociology of language tends to come as a congeries of topics—bilingualism, linguistic nationalism, standardization, pidginization and creolization, politeness, and so on. For the sake of a foundation for the understanding of language problems, we must deepen our ability to see particular topics as phenomena thrown up into salience by particular circumstances; we must see them as sharing fundamental dimensions with others. Particular constellations of phenomena must be seen as aspects of a single subject, the social organization of means of speech (cf. Wertsch, this volume). The choice that is among languages in one setting may be analytically part of the same semantic field as choice of pronoun in another; both may express degrees of intimacy or social distance. Choice of language in one setting may be analytically part of the same semantic field as choice of accent in another; both may express ethnic identification. And so on. The historical roots of a wide variety of language situations and problems about the world can ultimately be understood as diverse aspects of a single long-term process, the expansion of European mercantilism, colonialism, and capitalism (cf. Parker, this volume). The distribution of languages in Montana today is a reflex of the economic history of the state, region, and country.

Such an integration of our field of study unites the so-called micro and macro levels of the sociology of language. Our own scholarly forces are so meager that their unity is necessary if they are to have much impact. The unity is not a matter of numbers so much as it is a matter of conceptual strength. If in particular studies we cannot answer questions about general historical processes and social relationships, we can at least raise them. No study of the Quakers' special use of language should be conducted, for example, without at least raising the question of the consequences throughout religious life in Europe in the seventeenth century of the assumption that the individual could intepret the voice of God apart from a tradition; without at least asking the significance of the difference between mass and sermon as ritual organizations of language use; without at least wondering whether the experience of silently reading the word of God in the Bible did not encourage the practice of waiting in silence to hear God's voice; without at least a glance at Ranters, Levelers, Anabaptists, and others, and a wondering as to the way each chose to devise a liturgy and ministry, each choice implying some view of the role of language. And so for other topics.

The fundamental vantage point must be the question of what means of speech are available to a group and what meanings they find in them and give to them. Insofar as we are able to articulate a general foundation for understanding the place of language in social life, we will have a leverage that transcends particular cases and particular facts. Such a program declares an interest distinct from the interest of any particular group, but it is consistent with the interests of most. It is a necessary pole to the pole of practical work, justifying a claim to pursue knowledge as well as change.

Task 3: Cultural Hegemony through Language

It is probably through education—taken in its broadest sense, as schooling and instruction of all kinds—that the peculiar, latent, tacit American view of language most powerfully exercises cultural hegemony. To see this, to see that there is a characteristic American culture and policy in this regard, comparative analysis and systematic history are both badly needed.

One important aspect of the subject has been suggested by Fishman (1972, p. 195; 1974, p. 1714; cf. Fishman & Leuders, 1972):

> A true meeting of education and the sociology of language will enable *both* to discover why proportionately so many dialect speakers *do* and *did* seem to become readers and speakers of the standard language (and even of classical languages) in other parts of the world whereas so few seem to accomplish this in the U.S.A. today.

A related observation has been made by Charles Ferguson. In a trip to China in the fall of 1974, as one of a party of linguists, he was unable to discover any evidence of "reading problems"; it was difficult to convey the notion. The observation suggests that reading problems have to be understood partly as a *product* of American society and its particular history in education, rather than as an inevitable and natural circumstance (just as Margaret Mead's early fieldwork in Samoa indicated that "adolescence" was not an inevitable and natural problem, but a functon of a particular society).

The heart of the matter, I have suggested, is that language has been a central medium of cultural hegemony in the United States. Class stratification and cultural assumptions about language converge in schooling to reproduce the social order. A latent function of the educational system is to instill linguistic insecurity, to discriminate linguistically, to channel children in ways that have an integral linguistic component, while appearing open and fair to all. All have equal opportunity to acquire membership in the privileged linguistic network. If they fail, it is their fault, not that of the society or school (cf. Hymes, 1980; Stein, 1972).

What is usually left out of account, of course, is what the child brings to school in linguistic competence and community membership and what part of instruction in relation to this is instrumentally necessary for the acquisition of a national *lingua communis,* what part an instrument of class hierarchy.

I cannot demonstrate such an analysis. American scholarship has hardly addressed the facts of the matter. Language has been invisible to us as a problem for critical social science and educational history. Planning and policy about language have been thought of as something found in Belgium and Quebec, perhaps, where political mobilization around whole language identity has made public controversy. In the United States there has been neither a public agency signaled as responsible for a language policy, nor consciousness of policy. Amnesia toward the American past and passivity toward the American present, so far as language is concerned, seem characteristic of both American scholarship and the American public, except where the mobilization of Spanish speakers newly stirs concern. The widespread sharing of cultural assumptions about language has rendered their particularity almost invisible.

A first attempt at enumerating the assumptions would note the following:

1. Everyone in the United States speaks only English, or should.
2. Bilingualism is inherently unstable, probably injurious, and possibly unnatural.
3. Foreign literary languages can be respectably studied, but not foreign lan-

guages in their domestic varieties (it is one thing to study French spoken in Paris, another to study the French spoken in Louisiana).

4. Most everyone else in the world is learning English anyway, and that, together with American military and economic power, makes it unnecessary to worry about knowing the language of a country in which one has business, bases, or hostages.

5. Differences in a language are essentially of two kinds, right and wrong.

6. Verbal fluency and noticeable style are suspicious, except as entertainment (it's what you mean that counts) (cf. Lanham, 1974).

Notice that some of these assumptions would obtain, even if there were no language other than English in the United States. Class relationships would implicate language as an instrument of hegemony still.

We desperately need a critical social history of such assumptions and the associated practices regarding English and education. Leonard's (1929) early study of eighteenth century doctrines and Finegan's (1980) recent survey are useful guides. The literature of the women's movement makes some important contributions (e.g., Bodine, 1975). The studies that address the role of education in the country critically that I have seen do not seem to have much to say about language (Carnoy, 1972, 1974; Greer, 1972; Katz, 1968, 1971, 1975; Lasch, 1973; Useem & Michael, 1974). Studies made in other countries may be helpful in stimulating research in the United States (e.g., Bisseret, 1979, reviewed in Hogan, 1980; Snyders, 1965; cf. Roberts & Williams; Oppel; de Terra; Illich, all this volume).

What is amazing is that even the rather self-conscious and explicit implementation of a policy of *linguacide* (as an element of ethnocide) in the treatment of American Indians has not found a historian. Here are some excerpts from an official document (Atkins, 1888, pp. 17, 25, 26):

> These languages may be, and no doubt are, interesting to the philologist, but as a medium for conveying education and civilization to savages they are worse than useless; they are a means of keeping them in their savage condition by perpetuating the traditions of carnage and superstition . . . .
> To teach the rising generation of the Sioux in their own native tongue is simply to teach the perpetuation of something that can be of no benefit whatever to them . . . .
> I sincerely hope that all friends of Indian education will unite in the good work of teaching the English language only, and discourage in every way possible the perpetuation of any Indian vernacular.

Those comments were prompted by a dispute over the wish of some missionaries among the Sioux, who had translated the Bible and learned the language, to use the Indian language in the schools they had established. They were forbidden to do so. There are Indian people alive today who remember, indeed, being beaten for speaking their language in school as children. An old man at Umatilla reservation (Oregon) spoke a few years ago of a time when he and a schoolmate had had soap put into their mouths and their mouths taped shut for speaking their language. The schoolmate died. Sometimes a grandmother would let grandchildren think she knew no English so that they would have to use the Indian language to her, and so by individual resourcefulness she transmitted a knowledge of the language to another generation. These government and institutional policies, personal experiences, and family histories make a rich tapestry that has yet to find systematic voice. The efforts of Indian communities today to develop language programs and to determine language rights have received little systematic attenton as well (Leap, 1981, is an important exception).

The public school systems of urban centers are in need of social historians as well. Practice has gone far beyond instruction in a *lingua communis*. In New York City high schools, for example, it was required that one pass a speech test to graduate. The test included details of pronunciation: traces of phonetic habits from Yiddish, Italian, or regional or working-class English were grounds for failure. There flourished private tutors who taught students not how to speak well but how to speak to pass the high school graduation test by making the required recording correctly. (Until recently teachers themselves in Brooklyn had to pass a test of reading a word list without trace of influence from Yiddish or the like.)

These instances could be multiplied and should be. The systematic history that we need would show, probably, a widespread effort to eradicate linguistic diversity and implant uniformity down to the last colorless detail, bolstered by belief in the inferiority of varieties of language other than that officially enshrined in schools, by linguistic insecurity on the part of many educators themselves, and by a certain body of texts. But other strands would appear as well: writers of dictionaries and grammars who asserted the virtues of American as against British norms, for example, and had a good word to say for vitality as against mere correctness. One needs to continue the work of scholars like Leonard and Finegan, reading the leading texts, into the analysis of particular school systems and practices and to look for evidence of dispute that reflects divergent social background and aspiration. The new history of women in the country has shown that a great deal of past tension and struggle can be discerned. We need to know as fully as possible about past tension and struggle in the imposition of linguistic hegemony as well. The research that is needed would combine the techniques and perspectives of social history with the kinds of perception and question that arise within descriptive sociolinguistics and the ethnography of speaking. Such historical work can be seen as a diachronic counterpart of the work that is needed with regard to the present.

The topic of assumptions that support hegemony leads readily to the critique of disciplines, especially linguistics.

Task 4: Critique of Linguistics and Social Science

The work that is needed with regard to the present would consist of thoroughgoing analyses of language situations. A cadre of scholars for such work is hardly to be found. One can point to a few, and the number has gradually grown in recent years, yet it still is difficult to identify more than a handful of people engaged in linguistically informed research relevant to American life.

The difficulty is that such work requires command of skills that are partly linguistic and partly social, whatever the disciplinary origin of the investigator. Sociologists, psychologists, and even anthropologists today do not often learn how to notice a feature of speech, how to represent it so that its occurrence can be traced, how to calibrate what is particular or emergent in a text or discourse and what is common. A certain amount of linguistics is needed simply to perceive the relevant features of the data—that a pronunciation has altered, that a word order is reversed, that a grammatical category is surprisingly frequent or absent. Linguists today do not often learn how to notice features of social interaction, how to relate behavior to social relationships, activities, and institutions.

What one needs at the base of the enterprise is something neither social science nor linguistics now much provides. It is a social inquiry that does not abstract from verbal particulars, and a linguistic inquiry that connects verbal particulars not with a model of grammar or discourse in general but with social activities and relationships (cf. Dittmar, this volume). The social scientist lacks the observational skills and the linguist lacks the framework for making the connections. Introductory courses in either subject are usually going to lead away from the point of integration, rather than toward it. One is taught linguistics as if one were going on to study models of language abstracted from social interaction. One is taught social inquiry as if one were going on to do research in which relations among features of speech did not matter.

All this is not quite true. The study of language has evolved in many quarters into the study of discourse, to which people from many disciplinary backgrounds contribute. A good many linguists have broken away from the domination of formal models and investigate grammar with a wide variety of processes and kinds of explanation. A few linguists have launched efforts to use linguistic insight in the critical understanding of everyday life (Fowler, Hodge, Kress, & Trew, 1979; Kress & Hodge, 1979). It is increasingly accepted that linguistic elements should be analyzed and explained in terms of their *functional relevance,* meaning not their function within a grammar as such, but their relevance to the needs and interests of users of language in conveying and processing information, making discourse cohere, managing social relationships. These welcome developments tend to find generic psychological processes and assumed universal social requirements ready at hand, and have little to say about specific cultural patterns or institutional constraints. The initial inpetus of the ethnography of speaking, seeking to build an empirical base for comparative analysis of patterns of speaking, has not been much carried forward in anthropology, which sometimes seems ready to jettison its linguistic heritage altogether, rather than face the challenge of asking anthropological questions about language.

If we consider what is said in linguistics, discourse, and associated fields, it would be difficult to argue that there is a problem. The study of every imaginable level of linguistic organization is acknowledged. The relevance of the notion of language, and even of features of language, to social life and thought is nowhere denied, and in many places it is proclaimed. If we consider what research people are able to do and are being trained to do, it is a different story. It would be hard to point to a program or department in which the concerns of this chapter have a central place. Departments of linguistics are dominated by the prestige of formal theory. The very term *theoretical linguistics* is reserved for work concerned with the form of language in general. The greatest activity and support beyond this formalism appear to be in regard to discourse conceived as an area of cognitive science, where "cognitive" is restrictive in the sense of denoting general mental processes and certain kinds of meaning. There is some reawakening of interest in the issue to which Whorf left his name, that of the way in which patterns of language may cohere with patterns of cultural outlook. The specific circumstances of courtrooms, classrooms, medical interviews, psychiatric interviews, and the intrinsic interest of children as acquirers and users of language lead to a good deal of diverse work. Sociolinguistic models for empirical research into ongoing linguistic change have established themselves as a significant branch of the general field. But much of this work is conceived in terms of the experimental models of conventional psychology and sociology or as simply an adjunct to study of a particular language or established branch of linguistics (e.g., dialectology, historical linguistics). The peculiar combination of social theory, ethnographic perspective, and linguistic skills required by the thesis of this chapter is hardly to be found.

It would be helpful to this situation if social scientists were to abandon an attitude of laissez-faire toward linguistics and criticize it from the standpoint of sociology of knowledge and latent social function. Although a great variety of new activity goes on in a more tolerant general atmosphere in linguistics, nothing has arisen to replace or even challenge the assumptions of prestige and pride of place of so-called theoretical linguistics. It is an irony that ought to be widely shared that a linguist famous for his contributions to political life has shaped a linguistic climate in which the political has no place. Noam Chomsky's conception of linguistics can be seen as the bringing to perfection of the trend to focus on formal models, while investing formal models with the ultimate significance of being avenues to human mind and nature, the only general goal worthy of a linguist (cf. the analyses in Hymes, 1974, and Hymes & Fought, 1981; cf. also Slama-Cazacu; Prucha; Titone, all this volume). The unintended consequences of the success of this brilliant work were to disable linguists from the study of the social and to reinforce assumptions in American life prejudicial to understanding the place of language in it.

Recall the assumptions noted in the preceding section.

1. Only English. Chomsky assumed that the goal of insight into the general bases of human language could be achieved by intuitions as to one's own first language and could perhaps best be achieved by monolinguals. Most linguistic theory and analysis under his aegis focused on English.

2. Bilingualism is suspect. Focus on one's intuitions into one's own language again sets bilingualism aside as secondary. A necessary simplifying assumption of the theory is the ideally fluent speaker/hearer in a homogeneous speech community.

3. Learn literary standard. The variety of English in which Chomskian linguistics was conducted and to which it was addressed was essentially formal written English. Dialects and vernaculars are assumed to be superficial variations.

4. English is enough. See 1 and 3.

5. Right or wrong. Most Americans assume that there is a single standard, that grammars, dictionaries, or "best users" should be appealed to in case of doubt, that the problem of language today is change that makes it less precise, proper, cogent. Chomskian linguists were quick to apply a sign of exclusion, the asterisk, to sentences they judged impossible in English. The goal was initially taken to be to determine all and only the grammatical sentences of the language, on the analogy of logical decidability. The inability of linguists to agree on what was in and what was out, together with some evidence that education and training influenced their intuitions, became an Achilles' heel of the movement.

6. Fluency and style are suspect. Fluency is assumed, and style is not disparaged, so there may be no convergence here. On the other hand, a good many of the utterances set aside as ungrammatical prove acceptable in sufficient context, such as a poetic one; intonation, which is inseparable from the effect and acceptability of utterances, is ignored. There probably is thus a reinforcement of the tendency to assume that the written form of the language is "real" and normative. The invention of an account of the sound pattern of English that preserves the inherited orthography contributed to this effect. All in all, there has been a considerable reinforcement of the written standard as standard and exclusive concern.

A further reinforcement of traditional American culture is worth noting. The preceding generation of linguists in the United States, focusing on formal analysis of language structure, profoundly distrusted the teachings of schools about language and lay assumptions about things linguistic. One of the purposes of the movement which founded linguistics as an organized discipline in the United States was to challenge such views. Part of the impetus came from the critique of ethnocentrism in the anthropological wing, shaped by Boas and Sapir, and part from the lifelong convictions of Bloomfield, reinforced by his later adherence to a behaviorist psychology and positivist conception of science.

The generation of linguists associated with Chomsky attacked their predecessors as all of a piece, "structuralists," and in discrediting the approach, which came to be known as "neo-Bloomfieldian," they discredited its critical attitude as well. One particular tenet, the equality of all languages, was not questioned, but the insistence on the autonomy of the goal of linguistic theory and its independence of social considerations eliminated any basis for critique. The image of the maturing child acquiring creative fluency with minimal external influence might have made the circumstances of many actual children poignant, but left no ground for analysis, except to deplore social institutions. The possibility of a constitutive role for social institutions was not granted.

The Chomskian total rejection of the immediately preceding school of thought included an attack on its concern with phonology as starting point for analysis of language. (The misconceptions in this regard are analyzed in Hymes & Fought, 1981.) A part of this attack was a depreciation of training in the associated skills of hearing speech sounds accurately and recording them reliably. It is doubtful that more than a handful of leading grammarians today could transcribe anything actually spoken.

The Bloomfieldian school had accepted, through anthropology in part, an empirical, inductive approach to generalizations about languages stimulated by the experience of rash, false generalizations in earlier general linguistics, and it accepted some possibility of differences among languages being associated with insight into differences among ways of life, as well as being of value in their own right. (In this respect it represented a continuation of the outlook of Wilhelm von Humboldt and

J. G. von Herder, which I have labeled Herderian; Hymes, 1974, chapter 4.) The Chomskian frame of mind interpreted this approach as hostility to theory. Generalizations about language were thought to be near at hand; the differences among languages were thought to be superficial; ways of life were not considered. The link of the Bloomfieldians to ethnographic modes of work was dismissed either as due to a charitable desire to record dying languages or as the legacy of a crippling behaviorism. That an ethnographic mode of work might be necessary for certain kinds of knowledge about language was not considered.

Generic distrust of behavior and observation; reliance on intuitive insight and methodological authority; the view that the reality behind language that matters is universal mind and brain, not social life; the view that what matters is what is true of every language, not what has been made of linguistic means by particular people in history—all these ingredients of a Chomskian outlook discourage acquisition of the skills needed for the problems discussed in this chapter, discourage even contemplating such a program and often enough make the social order appear invisible. Social life appears unordered, and societal differences appear not as points of leverage for penetration of social reality but as indications that anything is possible.

The reinforcement of cultural assumptions and prejudices, together with the disarming of linguistics with regard to weapons with which to address serious problems of social life, cannot be said to have been intentional. It might be thought that the outcome would have been different had the Marxist intellectual tradition in the United States not suffered such dissolution after the Second World War. Not because of any specific Marxist propositions about language, but simply because of the Marxist postulate of social being as a determinant of consciousness and the example of Marx's critical disclosure of the taken-for-granted categories of political economy as not natural but products of a specific historical formation, such a background would have vaccinated many attracted to linguistics in the 1960s against the underpinnings and consequences of Chomsky's approach. Yet the revival of legitimate Marxist scholarship in recent years has left linguistics alone, or relied on references to British and continental thought. That Gramsci studied philology has been noticed, but not turned to account. The beginnings of a left critique of existing disciplines in the 1960s did not reach linguistics. Perhaps, indeed, it would not have reached that far. Linguists were prominent in the opposition to the Vietnam War, on the one hand, and the views of American Marxists about language and social life may not extend beyond those of their liberal colleagues. In any case, the challenge of thinking about language as problematic from a thoroughgoing sociohistorical standpoint has not been taken up.

The point to be reiterated is that use of linguistics must include a critique of linguistics. *Unexamined acceptance of existing forms of linguistics would be mistaken and misleading.* The diversity of opinion and interest that exists again in linguistic circles should not obscure the limitations with regard to the kinds of training and legitimate problem that dominate the subject. The dominance of the Chomskian school has been greatly loosened, but the ambience of the discipline continues to be shaped by it. The logic of linguistics' own development leads it to the study of discourse and, in discourse, to the study of the relationships among linguistic elements in styles—styles associated with persons, roles, activities, social life. How far that frontier will be crossed is uncertain. The pull of psychology and mind is strong, because there can be found explanations of a familiar kind, explanations in general human terms. What it would be like to find intellectual satisfaction in explanations that connect with social life and historically conditioned conjunctures is almost beyond imagination. The lack of academic employment increases the number of linguists working in practical circumstances, where social life comes into play, but that does not provide an intellectual framework or coherence for the experience.

A general sociolinguistics, uniting the various phenomena of language in social life in terms of the actual abilities of persons, the actual competence of speaker/ hearers, on the one hand, and in terms of actually existing communities, on the other hand, as a starting point for study—such a general sociolinguistics, integrating the skills of linguistics, ethnography, sociology, and social history and addressing the United States as a little-known country, might provide the framework and coherence that would gather the diverse threads and opportunities of the present time into a significant force.

The prospect of such an impetus coming from sociology and anthropology is not to be dismissed, but does not seem great. Sociologists have mostly studied language in ways that do not require linguistics—linguistic nationalism, language policy, language choice (societal or individual)—where one need only say that one language is different from another to have discussed language in general. Those using "language" as a category of critique today seem to have in mind an unending circle of critique and theoretical conversation, not discovery of the social world. The movement known as ethnomethodology makes an important contribution in its insistence that social science attend to its own dependence on the resources of language and of commonsense knowledge generally (cf. Cicourel, 1974; Kjolseth, 1972; Mehan, 1972; Turner, 1974a). Turner (1974b, p. 197) put it nicely: "A science of society that fails to treat speech as both topic and resource is doomed to failure." Insofar as ethnomethodology confronts concrete features of speech in social interaction, it is the major trend in sociology from which an adequate sociological linguistics can be hoped for. To say so is not to overlook its limitations. In its earlier phase its major motivation seemed sometimes to be to expose sociology, rather than social life and exploitation, and to reduce the modern world system (in Wallerstein's phrase) to transcribable encounters. The easy universalizing of Chomskian linguistics infected some of its assumptions about conversation. The reality of distinct, historically derived cultural traditions was washed away in a definition of problem in terms of the exigencies of a communication situation, taken as universal. The focus on selecting a next speaker, on managing verbal interaction over the telephone without access to the other's face, on what would be natural and necessary, seemed all too much an uncritical reflection of middle-class American experience. It may seem obvious that the person to speak first in a telephone call would be the person who answers the phone, but some European countries distribute the responsibility differently. It may seem obvious that face-to-face is the preferred stance for conversation, but the Mescalero Apache align themselves shoulder-by-shoulder for a heart-to-heart talk. And so on. What people do is in part a solution to a functional problem and in part a consequence of cultural meanings and definitions of situation.

However much may be hoped for from ethnomethodology's development, the fact remains that no sociology department, so far as I know, has hired a linguist to aid in training its students for research. Such knowledgeable integration of linguistics and sociology as occurs is due to valiant individual initiative (e.g., Aaron Cicourel, Joshua Fishman, Erving Goffman, Allen Grimshaw). As with other disciplines, the influence of linguistics seems to be felt more readily in analogy than in analysis. A purpose germane and inherent in sociology for controlling linguistic skills and verbal data hardly emerges.

The state of affairs in linguistics makes it unlikely that linguists are about to criticize sociology for not offering them help. If there is to be a substantial integration, it will have to come from sociologists determining that there are problems in language and about language that need to be addressed as sociology.

A variety of occasional work addressing language does come to sociological journals, but it is mostly imperceptive application of standard methods. Two loci of ideas about language do stand out: the work of the British sociologist Basil Bernstein and the theoretical interest in language and communication of Jürgen Habermas, as a development out of the Frankfurt school of critical Marxism. One can admire the independence and boldness of each, and there is merit and relevance in the work of each for the topic of this chapter, but neither singly nor collectively do they constitute an adequate sociological linguistics. As with much of ethnomethodology, a strict ethnography, comprising discovery of specific organizations of verbal means, is lacking, and with it a purchase on concrete situations. A comparative perspective on social types and cultural configurations is lacking. Each has an ingredient of critique, but imperfectly developed for our purpose.

Bernstein is known for his distinction between "elaborated" and "restricted" codes. His critical contribution is to insist that there is an organization of verbal means, socially constituted and cutting across the presumed homogeneity of a single "language"; to insist that theories of social order are incomplete in that they do not encompass such organizations of verbal means as essential to the processes by which society is maintained and changed; and to be prepared to assess socially organized "codes" as different in adequacy or orientation. Two things limit the contribution of Bernstein's work. Externally, his dichotomy has been variously reinterpreted outside Great Britain in ways that often quite mistake its original intent. Dichotomies are easily transplanted to categories of *us* and *them*, *white* and *black, native* and *immigrant,* and so on. Internally, his many insights have remained penned within a maintenance of his original dichotomy. There has been a retreat from overt linguistic marking of the contrast to an imputed difference in underlying orientation toward meaning, despite overt similarity. Thus, there is a restricted variant in everyone's speech. The ideal types posited by Bernstein no doubt correspond to aspects of reality, but not to enough of it. Linguistic ethnography is needed to discover the range of "code-orientations" in relation to family, class, institution, and setting. The sociological methods of Bernstein's funded research have belied his insights—questionnaire, interview, self-report, formal experiment. The ingredients subsumed under the original dichotomy have comparative, cross-cultural relevance, but only if freed from the dichotomy (in general, dichotomies are to be suspected in this field; cf. Hymes, 1974, pp. 39–41, 115). If he is right in suggesting that the orientation of the elaborated code is necessary for reflective analysis of social conditions and social change, his research has not traced the ingredients of this orientation in social life among the various classes of England. More recent work has suggested that middle-class orientations also have limitations and implicit channeling effects as preparation for certain kinds of occupations, and recent theoretical fomulations have suggested a considerably more dynamic conception of linguistic varieties. But the substantive work that would allow us to relate the ideas to social life is missing.

Critical theory, as developed by Habermas, seeks to discover in the sphere of symbolic interaction (cultural or communicative competence) a source of critical response to inequality and domination in modern society. The hoped-for transformation of the social order by a concentrated and aroused proletariat has been abandoned (cf. Clecak, 1974; Singer, 1974). The situation was described well by Habermas himself (1973, chapter 6, especially pp. 195–198, 241), who pointed out that the new focus of attention for Marxist theory is only a following in the footsteps of repressive forces themselves. Justification of the social order in terms of the idea of the free market has been succeeded by justification in terms of the purportedly neutral demands and benefits of science and technology. Yet belief in progress through these means is an illusion that serves to perpetuate actual irrationality and exploitation (cf. Anderson, 1973; Habermas, 1970, chapters 4–6, 1973, chapter 7; Schroyer, 1973). The revitalization of interest in ethnic and local identity throughout the world is perhaps a sign that many people have drawn some such inference. But it is not enough to consider the integration of the cultural dimension as the crucial problem of modern social theory, especially Marxian theory, and to recognize it as basic to any social transformation. How is one to get hold of the cultural (communicative) nuts and bolts of exploitation and alienation? And the postulation of a universal form of communicative competence, inherent in every attempt at discourse, is useful as a regulative ideal by which to criticize repressive speech situations but is of no help in comprehending specific structures of speech which are what their participants want them to be. There must, presumably, be some state of the world that the perspective would accept as worth working toward. Any such state of the world would be characterized by some form of social order, and any form of social order would entail a limitation of the ideal of unrestricted turns at talk in the pursuit of consensus. The universal ideal provides no criterion for preferring or understanding the various specific organizations of speech events which any society will have (cf. Hymes, 1980, chapter 2, for further comment on Bernstein and Habermas).

No one would be so rash as to claim more than a crude inkling of the dimensions and dynamics of the life of language in the United States. What (to pick one town) is the state of language in Florence, Oregon? What has it been, what is it becoming, what should it become? The questions may seem foolish. One takes states of language for granted as transparent, until and unless someone makes them a problem not to be ignored. Only then one may realize that some do not use language as others do, and that the others think they should "learn standard English" or "tell the truth."

If someone should want to know about the forces that produce migration, marriage, mobility, or any of a number of aspects of the distribution of people and kinds of people, someone in a sociology department would likely be able to be helpful. So also for almost any aspect of American life. Hardly so for language. Most social theory, even critical theory, reasons about language with a prior reason: language is essential; its potentialities are great. One may compare language to money, or other things to language. But hardly a sociologist is able to articulate social theory with linguistic facts, so as to be able to characterize the state of language, say, in Florence, let alone able to go and find out whether the characterization holds. Nor is there indication that sociology programs, even those emphasizing a perspective to which language is important, plan to require linguistic training of their students or to offer the kind of linguistic training they want themselves. Such knowledgeable integration of sociology and linguistics as occurs is due to the valiant efforts of a few individuals. This is not to make a plea for any school of linguistics, and, indeed, one theme of this book is that sociologists should not admire and emulate linguistics so much as criticize and help to correct it. Social scientists should make use of linguistic tools for purposes of their own. The point here is that social scientists need elementary command of linguistics in order to recognize some of the essential characteristics of linguistic problems. The proper analogy is not to linguistics for the sake of writing a grammar or contribution to formal linguistics, but rather to linguistics for the sake of learning a language when, as an adult, one is past the point at which such a thing can be done unconsciously, or for the sake of interpreting a text whose meaning one needs to know. The proper expectation is not of some kind of structural magic, but of preparation to see, as one would need to learn the elements of music in order to understand someone else's accomplishment and one's own response. The catch in all this is that the elements of linguistics may have to be reconstituted by social scientists themselves or sought out in anthropological niches. A linguist may so subordinate the elements of language to a current understanding of purely linguistic theory as to obscure and omit what a student of uses of language needs. Social scientists must come to see linguistics itself as sometimes a linguistic problem.

Language is a unity of diversity *par excellence,* a configuration of common understandings and individual voices. As universal resource, it presumably shares in each community's reproduction of its organization, tensions, satisfactions, way of life. Insofar as communities differ, they presumably differ somewhat in their usage of speech and in the kinds of personal competency they encourage and discourage, require and neglect. What things are said and can be said, how things are said and can be said, presumably is an integral part of the fabric of the community. If one wanted to maintain that fabric, one presumably would want to maintain certain whats and hows of saying. If one wanted to change that fabric, rend it or open it to a different orientation, one presumably would have to change certain whats and hows of saying. Saying, indeed, might be an aspect of life most within the power of persons in the community to change.

If one considers, then, that the sphere of symbolic interaction is crucial to social theory and that within that sphere lie means essential to social change, both from the standpoint of possible levers of change and from the standpoint of desirable levers of change (thinking of desirable change as personal as well as institutional, that "the educator must himself be educated," as Marx put it in one thesis on Feuerbach), then the absence of a sociological linguistics, able to address the place of speech, is perhaps the greatest linguistic problem of all, for social science and for society.

Task 5: Reshaping the Study of Language

There is reason to think that some reshaping of the study of language will occur in the next decade or so, simply through the logic of the long-term history of the subject. Linguistics as a distinct academic field is only some 50 years of age in the United States. It grew out of the background of a study of language distributed among a variety of fields, distinct departments of language, anthropology, philosophy; it crystallized around a distinct methodology of its own for the study of structure and created a new general science of the several levels of linguistic structure; now that the levels wholly internal to language have been developed to the point at which the organization of language in discourse is the frontier and now that members of a number of other disciplines have learned enough of linguistic method to contribute, the half-century monopoly has been effectively broken. Linguistics will continue to be the home of the study of structure internal to language and of particular languages perhaps, but the larger field of linguistics will embrace contributions from many disciplines.

Such reshaping could occur without any contribution to the problems discussed in this chapter. Two sources of alternative seem possible. One is sociology, inasmuch as it is the discipline among the social sciences in which problems of society are most likely to be defined. If sociology were to discover the problems of this chapter as problems, much might be accomplished. The other source of an alternative is the recurrent mobilization of members of groups affected by language situations. Perhaps American Indian languages, for example, will never have the sustained attention they need and the academic recognition they deserve until "Indians" become a "problem" about language. There is a great deal to be done generally, simply in terms of the motives that lead people to wish to preserve components of the diversity of language in the country and to understand and deal with the processes that affect their languages and them. As argued earlier, however, this source is an intermittent and often premature one.

Moreover, ethnic lines of demarcation are not themselves a sufficient mapping of the country. Some of the uses of language associated with Black English, for example, may be shared across class lines with whites who have similar relationships to employment, authority, and power and who have similar verbal needs. We are largely ignorant of what is black and what is working-class about such phenomena.

Institutional studies will contribute much, but they tend to be focused on what is seen as a problem by the profession concerned, whether doctor, lawyer, or other. Good research is independent of that perspective and may indeed be motivated by concern for the problem of the client or patient. Still, there is as yet little work that answers Nader's (1973) call for "studying up" as well as "down" in our society.

All of these lines of interest may contribute to the solution of the problem posed, but only, I think, if the problem is posed in its general terms and has a disciplinary and extradisciplinary base united. The scholar must take the conceptual lead, not merely follow after crisis and funds. At the same time, the members of communities affected by situations must be participants in the development as well. A general sociological linguistics that excluded them might be an intellectual solace, but in the practical world it would probably be mainly a resource for the administration of things as they are. The task of general scope is one of intellectual understanding and disciplinary skills, on the one hand, and of cooperation across institutional boundaries, on the other. (For reflections on this task in regard to education, see Hymes, 1980.)

Such work would broach a truly general study of the language situations of the United States. It would begin to constitute a true sociolinguistics. The central assumption would be that every social group, activity, or relationship may give rise to characteristic verbal means. Of any facet of the society, one would be prepared to ask:

1. What is involved in talking like an X?
2. What is involved in talking to do Y?

That is, what is the verbal concomitant of being, or being seen to be, a certain kind of person or position? What is the verbal concomitant of doing, or being considered to do, a certain kind of activity, work, or purpose? What is the distribution of such verbal styles in the society? Who has access to which style and who lacks it? Who has commitment to which? What are the consequences for institutional outcomes, genuine culture, personal identity, and integrity? What would be a rough assessment of the linguistic health of the society? What costs and benefits result from the present distribution of linguistic abilities, the present institutionalization of values, beliefs, and attitudes, regarding features and uses of language?

(I have in mind the possibility that for many Americans, particularly perhaps males in certain occupations, much of their daily speech is not a satisfaction or genuine expression of identity, but a kind of verbal passing. Where, for whom, and about what is there verbal expressivity that is satisfying or rewarding? Uses of language that are felt to be integral to the self?)

Such an approach requires overcoming the separation between questions of language and questions of value that has characterized the development of modern linguistics in the United States (perhaps in a way similar to the situation of modern economics). Values have been taken as obvious, taken for granted, or else excluded on principle, so far as linguists themselves are concerned. The uses of language have been postulated as everywhere essentially equivalent, rather than being investigated. Indeed, one of the central tenets of the liberalism of modern linguistics has been the essential equivalence in use of all languages studied by linguists, despite the abundant empirical evidence to the contrary. Some even think it the mark of a radical to denounce attention to differences of this sort. Inequality in speaking is to be overcome, it seems, by denying that it exists. I cannot explain this deep-seated hostility on the part of even cultural materialists toward facts that one would think a Marxist would be the first to see, except as a projection of a professional bias (all languages are equal in the sight of linguistics) and a reaction against the prejudices of the society at large, prejudices which do equate difference with inferiority. But I cannot see any way for a science of language to contribute to the transformation of a situation of linguistic inequality that it does not recognize as existing. I see no possibility of a truly social science of language on the basis of this attitude, an attitude that I would call militant, not radical. For it is essential to this attitude that social shaping of verbal means and abilities is denied. Amidst all the costs of inequality and exploitation, language is privileged, on this view, and remains unscathed.

There is a grain of truth in this view. The potentialities of language are great. It is a resource capable of transcending situations to a degree; it is a resource more within the control of people than many others. These possibilities of language should be developed politically. But the militant view of equality does not see a need for development; it sees a need only for an end to prejudice. Reality is different. Langage, verbal means, like other resources of human life, become shaped to specific ends. Their adaptation to some purposes lessens or precludes their ready adaptation to others. They carry something of their history with them. The great poetry of one variety cannot be the great poetry of another. *It is utopian (in the negative sense) to imagine as an ideal for communicative competence and language a state of society in which anyone can say anything to anyone in any way, a state in which there are no constraints on communication and language.* Social life, social order, would be impossible. What one can do, thinking in terms of aspirations, is to envision the costs and benefits of different forms of social order, including the costs and benefits of different forms of communicative, linguistic order. I apologize for the obviousness of what I have just said. My excuse is that it is a point of view which has almost no support within the practice or theory of lingustics today.

These issues of background and domain assumptions, then, pose great obstacles to the development of the sociolinguistics that is needed.We have far to go to gain acceptance of the fundamental assumptions of a socially constituted linguistics:

- That verbal means and the social matrices in which they exist are interdependent
- That the organization of verbal means must be viewed from the vantage point of social matrices
- That one must discover ways in which verbal means are organized by virtue of social matrices (using *social matrices* here as a general term for activities, insitutions, groups, etc.)

It is here that the linguistic competence we need may be dependent on the contribution of social scientists. The term *linguistic competence,* indeed, is used in two ways in my title. On the one hand, it refers to the object of study of a true sociolinguistics: the actual linguistic abilities of definite persons in a definite social life. On the other hand, it refers to the abilities that scholars must have, if they are to be able to study such competence. "Toward linguistic competence," in this sense, refers to efforts toward a cadre of scholars competent to undertake such work.

The nature of the needed competence can be seen from the implications of the assumptions just stated.

The elements and relationships analyzed in linguistics are seen to be but a part of the verbal means (and, indeed, communicative means) employed in the conduct of social life. The organization of these means as a whole cannot be grasped within ordinary grammar. The paradigmatic and syntagmatic dimensions of language find their full scope in what Ervin-Tripp has called "rules of co-occurrence" and "rules of alternation" (see discussion in Hymes, 1974; pp. 59, 201); these two types of rules govern the organization of verbal means in the speech styles and in discourse and the organization of the use of such styles in situations. The true scope of a socially constituted study of language is thus the study of speech styles within culturally constituted ways of speaking.

Grammar in the usual sense contributes analysis of many of the *resources* of speech styles, but not all. The grammar of *discourse* has additional properties. Two crucial properties are these: (1) a speech style involves selection and grouping of features across the usual levels of linguistic analysis, coordinating them in a novel way independent of such levels; (2) a socially significant speech style often involves only a portion of the occurring features.

Now, the grammarian is used to seeking total accountability at each level of analysis—all of the message form is referable to phonological elements and relationships, to morphological elements and relationships, to syntactic and semantic elements and relationships. This kind of accountability can be pursued to a fair degree in abstraction from social context. It is not possible to pursue accountability of speech styles in abstraction from social context. And much of the interest, both in formal properties and in meaning, of speech styles may lie in the relations among social contexts, not in the relations of the linguistic features themselves. It is possible that linguists, given their usual training and outlook, will find the study of speech styles, of discourse grammar, neither feasible nor interesting. They may pursue it to a point, but when its social foundation becomes both unavoidable and a major part of what there is to study, they may draw the line. One sees evidence of such a line now.

This restriction may be overcome, and the linguistic skills needed for a true sociolinguistics may become adequately available in response to the social and political mobilization of groups within the country—yet such groups may have little basis on which to consider what kind of linguistics, if any, they may profitably have. The restriction may be overcome if social scientists work to develop the subject. Here the most promising prospect, I think, is the confluence of sociology, as a discipline in which the empirical study of American society is most developed and in which critical perspectives are considerably developed, on the one hand, with the work in the ethnography of speaking, which so far has been mostly limited to other societies. Let me conclude with a few further comments on the contribution of this last field.

The ethnography of speaking has gone through two stages. The first stage has been the development of the perspective itself, drawing on ideas of Sapir and Jakobson, so as to make the case for the qualitative study of the patterning of verbal means beyond grammar and for the cross-cultural relativity of the role and meaning of language. In other words, the first concern has been to make the case for a discipline based on the social constitution of language with respect both to structure and function.

The second stage has been the undertaking of field studies explicitly devoted to these two questions of structure and function of means of speech. It is striking that until the last decade cross-cultural differences in this regard had been virtually ignored. It is a rare ethnography from which one can learn much explicitly about such matters. The usual comparative guides and collections are virtually useless.

The third stage has several tasks: (1) to go beyond accumulation of case studies to comparative-typological work; that is, to sharpen terminology and dimensions of description, so as to place them within a generalized framework; (2) to apply the generalized framework to our own society, as part of the development of social theory; and (3) to apply the principles of a critical, reflexive perspective to its own work.

References

Abrahams, R. The training of the man of words in talking sweet. *Language in Society,* 1972, *1*(1), 15–30.

Abrahams, R., & Szwed, J. Black English: A review of the work. *American Anthropologist,* 1975, *77,* 329–335.

Alcala, C. N., Rivera, B., & Thayer, B. The legal significance of *Lau* vs. *Nichols.* In J. Reichert & M. Trujillo (Eds.), *Perspectives on contemporary Native American and Chicano educational thought.* Davis, Calif.: D. Q. U. Press, 1974, pp. 90–111.

Anderson, E. N., Jr. The life and culture of ecotopia. In D. Hymes (Ed.), *Reinventing anthropology.* New York: Pantheon, 1973, pp. 264–283.

Atkins, J. D. C. *Correspondence on the subject of teaching the vernacular in Indian schools, 1887–88.* Washington, D.C.: Government Printing Office, 1888.

Beltramo, A. F. Profile of a state: Montana. In C. A. Ferguson & S. B. Heath (Eds.), *Language in the USA.* New York: Cambridge University Press, 1981, pp. 339–380.

Bisseret, N. *Education, class language, and ideology.* London: Routledge and Kegan Paul, 1979.

Bodine, A. Androcentrism and prescriptive grammar: Singular 'they,' and sex-indefinite 'he,' and 'he or she.' *Language in Society,* 1975, *4*(2), 129–146.

Brandt, E. On the origins of linguistic stratification: The Sandia case. *Anthropological Linguistics,* 1970, *12*(2), 46–50.

Brown, P., & Levinson, S. Universals in language usage: Politeness phenomena. In E. N. Goody (Ed.), *Questions and politeness.* New York: Cambridge University Press, 1978.

Carnoy, M. (Ed.). *Schooling in a corporate society: The political economy of education in America.* New York: McKay, 1972.

Carnoy, M. *Education as cultural imperialism.* New York: McKay, 1974.

Cazden, C. B., & Dickinson, D. K. Language in education: Standardization versus cultural pluralism. In C. A. Ferguson & B. Heath (Eds.), *Language in the USA.* New York: Cambridge University Press, 1981, pp. 446–468.

Cicourel, A. Ethnomethodology. In T. A. Sebeok (Ed.), *Current trends in linguistics* (Vol. 12). The Hague: Mouton, 1974, pp. 1563–1605.

Cicourel, A. V. Language and medicine. In C. A. Ferguson & B. Heath (Eds.), *Language in the USA.* New York: Cambridge University Press, 1981, pp. 407–429.

Clecak, P. *Radical paradoxes: Dilemmas of the American left, 1945–1970.* New York: Harper & Row, 1974.

Craddock, J. R. New World Spanish. In C. A. Ferguson & B. Heath (Eds.), *Language in the USA.* New York: Cambridge University Press, 1981, pp. 196–211.

Darnell, R. The bilingual speech community: A Cree example. In R. Darnell (Ed.), *Linguistic diversity in Canadian society.* Edmonton: Linguistic Research, 1971, pp. 155–172.

Ferguson, C. A. National sociolinguistic profile formulas. In W. Bright (Eds.), *Sociolinguistics.* The Hague: Mouton, 1966, pp. 309–324.

Ferguson, C. A., & Heath, S. B. (Eds.). *Language in the USA.* New York: Cambridge University Press, 1981.

Finegan, E. *Attitudes towards English usage.* New York: Teachers College Press, 1980.

Fishman, J. A. *Language loyalty in the United States.* The Hague: Mouton, 1966.

Fishman, J. A. *The sociology of language.* Rowley, Mass.: Newbury Hourse, 1972.

Fishman, J. A. The sociology of language. In T. A. Sebeok (Ed.), *Current trends in linguistics* (Vol. 4). The Hague: Mouton, 1975, pp. 1629–1784.

Fishman, J. A. & Leuders, E. What has the sociology of language to say to the teacher? (On teaching the standard variety to speakers of dialectal or sociological varieties). In C. B. Cazden, V. John, & D. Hymes (Eds.), *Functions of language in the classroom.* New York: Teachers College Press, 1972, pp. 67–83.

Fowler, R., Hodge, B., Kress, G., & Trew, T. *Language and control.* London: Routledge, and Kegan Paul, 1979.

Gilbert, G. (Ed.). *The German language in America.* Austin: University of Texas Press, 1971.

Gilbert, G. French and German: A comparative study. In C. A. Ferguson & B. Heath (Eds.), *Language in the USA.* New York: Cambridge University Press, 1981, pp. 257–272.

Goffman, E. The nature of deference and demeanor. *American Anthropologist,* 1956, *58,* 473–502.

Greer, C. *The great school legend: A revisionist interpretation of American public education.* New York: Basic Books, 1972.

Habermas, J. *Toward a rational society: Student protest, science, and politics.* Boston: Beacon Press, 1970. (Translated by Jeremy J. Shapiro from essays in *Technik und Wissenschaft als 'Ideologie',* 1968, and *Protestbewegung und Hochschulreform,* 1969, Frankfurt: Suhrkamp.)

Habermas, J. *Theory and practice.* Boston: Beacon Press, 1973. (Translated from *Theorie und Praxis.* Frankfurt: Suhrkamp, 1971, 4th edit., with an additional chapter by John Viertel.)

Haugen, E. *The Norwegian language in America: A study in bilingual behavior.* Philadelphia: University of Pennsylvania Press, 1953. (Reissued, Indiana University Press, 1969.)

Haugen, E. *Bilingualism in the Americas: A bibliography and research guide.* (American Dialect Society, no. 26). University, Ala.: University of Alabama Press, 1956.

Heath, S. B. What no bedtime story means: Narrative skills at home and school. *Language in Society,* 1982, *11*(2), 49–76.

Heath, S. B. *Ways with words.* New York and Cambridge: Cambridge University Press, 1983.

Hernandez-Chavez, E., Cohen, A. D., & Beltramo, A. F. (Eds.), *El lenguaje de los Chicanos.* Arlington, Va.: Center for Applied Linguistics, 1975.

Hogan, D. Review of N. Bisseret. *Language in Society,* 1980, *9,* 393–398.

Hoover, M. R. Community attitudes toward Black English. *Language in Society,* 1978, *7,* 65–87.

Hymes, D. Models of the interaction of language and social setting. In J. Macnamara (Ed.), Problems of bilingualism. *Journal of Social Issues,* 1967, *23*(2), 8–28.

Hymes, D. *Foundations in sociolinguistics.* Philadelphia: University of Pennsylvania Press, 1974.

Hymes, D. *Language in education: Ethnolinguistic essays* (Language and Ethnography series). Washington, D.C.: Center for Applied Linguistics, 1980.

Hymes, D., & Fought, J. *American structuralism.* The Hague: Mouton, 1981.

Kress, G., & Hodge, R. *Language as ideology.* London: Routledge and Kegan Paul, 1979.

Katz, M. *The irony of early school reform: Educational innovation in mid-nineteenth century Massachusetts.* Cambridge, Mass.: Harvard University Press, 1968.

Katz, M. *School reform: Past and present.* Boston: Little, Brown, 1971.

Katz, M. *Class, bureaucracy, and schools: The illusion of educational change in America.* New York: Praeger, 1975.

Kjolseth, R. Making sense: Natural language and shared knowledge in understanding. In J. A. Fishman (Ed.), *Advances in the sociology of knowledge: Vol. 2. Selected studies and applications.* The Hague: Mouton, 1972, pp. 50–76.

Kochman, T. *Rappin' and stylin' out: Communication in urban Black America.* Urbana, Ill.: University of Illinois Press, 1972.

Lanham, R. A. *Style: An anti-textbook.* New Haven: Yale University Press, 1974.

Lasch, C. Inequality and education. *New York Review of Books,* May 17, 1973, pp. 19–25.

Lavandera, B. On sociolinguistic research in New World Spanish. *Language in Society,* 1974, *3*(2), 247–292.

Leap, W. On grammaticality in Native American English: The evidence from Isleta. *International Journal of the Sociology of Language,* 1974, *2,* 79–80.

Leap, W. American Indian languages. In C. A. Ferguson & B. Heath (Eds.), *Language in the USA.* New York: Cambridge University Press, 1981, pp. 116–144.

Leonard, S. A. *The doctrine of correctness in English usage, 1700–1800* (University of Wisconsin Studies in Language and Literature, 25). Madison, Wisc.: University of Wisconsin 1929. (Reprinted, New York: Russell and Russell, 1962.)

McDavid, R. I. [Comment]. In W. Bright (Ed.), *Sociolinguistics*. The Hague: Mouton, 1966, p. 321.

McDermott, R. Achieving school failure: An anthropological approach to literacy and social stratification. In G. D. Spindler (Ed.), *Education and cultural process: Toward an anthropology of education*. New York: Holt, Rinehart & Winston, 1974, pp. 82–118.

McDermott, R. The cultural context of learning to read. In S. F. Wanat (Ed.), *Issues in evaluating reading*. Arlington, Va.: Center for Applied Linguistics, 1977, pp. 10–18.

Mehan, H. Language using abilities. *Language Sciences,* 1972, *22*(October), 1–10.

Mitchell-Kernan, C. Signifying and marking: Two Afro-American speech acts. In J. Gumperz & D. Hymes (Eds.), *Directions in sociolinguistics*. New York: Holt, Rinehart and Winston, 1972, pp. 161–179.

Nader, L. Up the anthropologist: Perspectives gained from studying up. In D. Hymes (Ed.), *Reinventing anthropology*. New York: Pantheon, 1973, pp. 284–311.

Neustupný, J. *Post-structural approaches to language: Language theory in a Japanese context*. Tokyo: University of Tokyo Press, 1979.

O'Barr, W. M. The language of the law. In C. A. Ferguson & B. Heath (Eds.), *Language in the USA*. New York: Cambridge University Press, 1981, pp. 386–406.

Paulston, C. B. Bilingualism and education. In C. A. Ferguson & B. Heath (Eds.), *Language in the USA*. New York: Cambridge University Press, 1981, pp. 469–485.

Philips, S. Participant structure and communicative competence: Warm Springs children in community and classroom. In C. B. Cazden, V. John, & D. Hymes (Eds.), *Functions of language in the classroom*. New York: Teachers College Press, 1972, pp. 370–394.

Schroyer, T. *The critique of domination: The origins and development of critical theory*. New York: Braziller, 1973. (Paperback, Boston: Beacon Press, 1975.)

Singer, P. Review of Clecak, 1974. *New York Review of Books,* 1974, *21*(12), 20–24.

Smitherman, G. *Talkin' and testifyin':* The language of Black America. New York: Houghton, Mifflin, 1977.

Snyders, G. *La pedagogie en France aux XVIIᵉ et XVIIIᵉ siecles*. Paris: Presses Universitaires de France, 1965.

Stein, A. Educational equality in the United States: The emperor's clothes. *Science and Society,* 1972, *36*(4), 469–476.

Szwed, J. F. An American anthropological dilemma: The politics of Afro-American culture. In D. Hymes (Ed.), *Reinventing anthropology*. New York: Pantheon, 1973, pp. 153–181.

Tentchoff, D. Cajun French and French Creole: Their speakers and the question of identities. In S. DeSesto & J. Gibson (Eds.), *The culture of Acadiana: Tradition and change in South Louisiana*. Lafayette, La.: University of Southern Louisiana, 1975.

Turner, R. (Ed.). *Ethnomethodology*. London: Penguin, 1974. (a)

Turner, R. Words, utterances and activities. In R. Turner (Ed.), *Ethnomethodology*. London: Penguin, 1974, pp. 197–215. (b)

Useem, E., & Michael, L. *The education establishment*. Englewood Cliffs, N.J.: Prentice Hall, 1974.

Voegelin, C. F., Voegelin, F. M., & Schutz, N. W. The language situation in Arizona as part of the Southwest culture area. In D. Hymes (Ed.), *Studies in Southwestern ethnolinguistics*. The Hague: Mouton, 1967.

Waggoner, D. Statistics on language use. In C. A. Ferguson & B. Heath (Eds.), *Language in the USA*. New York: Cambridge University Press, 1981, pp. 486–515.

Whatley, E. Language among Black Americans. In C. A. Ferguson & B. Heath (Eds.), *Language in the USA*. New York: Cambridge University Press, 1981, pp. 92–107.

Wright, R. Black English (review article). *Language in Society,* 1975, *4,* 185–198.

Zentella, A. C. Language variety among Puerto Ricans. In C. A. Ferguson & B. Heath (Eds.), *Language in the USA*. New York: Cambridge University Press, 1981, pp. 218–238.

13

Descriptive and Explanatory Power of Rules in Sociolinguistics

Norbert Dittmar

Introduction: Methodological Crisis in Sociolinguistics

Important sociopolitical and programmatic statements in the late sixties and early seventies gave rise to the hope of intellectuals, academicians, and teachers that sociolinguistic analysis would help to solve crucial communicative problems concerning the social use of language codes and subcodes. Whether they were deceived by abstract (algebraic) linguistics or were participants in the worldwide students' movement, they carried great expectations into the field of sociolinguistics.

Bernstein asked the fundamental question, whether subcodes, mostly generated by social class, determine equality and inequality in society. Fishman broadened this question to the whole scale of languages and their varieties which are distributed in coexistent and diglossic relations, reflecting the dominant and the dominated, the superior and the inferior status. Labov (1972c) considered the question "Why does anybody say anything?" the fundamental sociolinguistic problem. Labov noted that sociolinguistic methods have inevitably to do with discourse analysis. Under the heading of this question, a large variety of sociolinguistic problems could be faced by research, including norms and social values of vernaculars, dialects, sociolects, standards, and registers; adequacy of language varieties; pragmatic functions of discourse types; and symmetry and asymmetry in communication. Authors have focused on the most socially relevant problems and underlined with emphasis that *application* should be the research guideline of the field. (It was no accident that issues in language planning came up abundantly in the very early seventies.) Furthermore, Hymes, being most fascinated by all these exciting tendencies, wrote in 1973: "The final goal of sociolinguistics, I think, must be to preside over its own

Norbert Dittmar ● Department of Linguistics, Free University of Berlin, 1000 Berlin 33, Federal Republic of Germany.

liquidation" (Hymes, 1973, p. 324). What has been left from this hopeful perspective nearly a decade later?

Those who have been working inside the new discipline for years are faced with disillusionment and the ruins of original dreams. As unfortunately true as this might be, a critical (and inevitably theoretical) account of the present state of the art could initiate a cautious reflection on the fundamental aims and methods of sociolinguistics—if one is inclined to admit that the following points, which are now more or less called into question, were at one time unquestioned fundamentals in the field:

1. The "heterogeneity" of urban language as studied by Labov, Wolfram, Cedergren, and others seems to be still quite homogeneous if one considers the underlying static concepts of situation, style, type of interaction, type of relationship between communicative behavior and extralinguistic variables that have been used in these studies. Erickson (1971), Giles and Smith (1979), and Milroy (1980) have shown that things are much more complicated.

2. The "speech community" cannot be defined by "a uniform set of attitudes towards language which are shared by almost all members of the speech community" (Labov, 1972a, p. 146); there is considerable doubt that the representative sample of a given population can be called a "representative group" of the whole speech community. There are good reasons to believe that the speech community has more to do with "social and interactional networks" (Gumperz, 1976; Milroy, 1980; Ryan, 1979).

3. It seemed for several years that the "variable rule methodology" could solve most of the descriptive problems that have to be accounted for by an analysis of variation. Since the distinction between functional and semantic equivalence has been introduced, there has been quite an exasperated debate over this issue (Lavandera, 1979; Thibault, 1979).

The discussion of technical methodology has become a topic of its own scientific relevance, concerned with technical details, linguistic and statistical adequacy, and the like (Kay & McDaniel, 1979; Klein, 1974; Romaine, 1980). But there is a more general question underlying the technical ones: How can we get access to the social meaning of linguistic structures? Are variable rules the right tool for getting the relevant information about the *social meaning* of language behavior?

4. One of the basic concepts of large-scale sociolinguistic, but also of microlinguistic, analysis has been (and still is) the concept of *diglossia*. Diglossia has been defined on the basis of the sociological construct of domains (Fishman, Cooper, & Ma, 1971) and evaluated by speaker judgments on their use of two languages in different domains and situations. The distribution of languages or language varieties (based on speakers' subjective evaluations) has been used as an indicator of their stability or instability. There is evidence that the concepts of domains and diglossia as they stand now cannot grasp the more subtle problems of "real communicative behavior" in different situations (Centro de Estudios Puertorriqueños, 1980) and that, given conditions of a certain economic power and the social prestige of varieties, *low-prestige varieties cannot survive in any known type of diglossia* (Eckert, 1980).

If we look at recent papers on sociolinguistic description and explanation, we realize a tendency toward reflection on technical and analytical tools (Kay &

McDaniel, 1979; Klein, 1974; Lavandera, 1982; Sankoff & Labov, 1979) and socio-logical explanation (Bourdieu, 1979; Giles & Smith, 1979; Milroy, 1980). There are very few new empirical and original studies, compared with the decade between 1965 and 1975. The enthusiasm of the empirical work in the first phase of the new para-digm seems to have been left behind; the question now is: *Quo vadis, sociolinguistica?* The fact that methodology is more thoroughly considered may reconcile those who were skeptical from the beginning about a quick solution to the problems of sociolin-guistic analysis by behavioristic practices (Encrevé, 1982; Laks, 1980; Romaine, 1980). There are two consequences concerning this current state of affairs in socio-linguistics to which this article must respond:

1. The adequacy of sociolinguistic methodology must be scrutinized in three respects: (a) What kinds of rules do we need or are we aiming at? (b) Inter-ested as we are in *social meaning,* how do we cope with *linguistic meaning?* (c) What are the *quantitative* and *qualitative* relations between varieties of a language? Where do language varieties (German *sprachliche Existenzfor-men*) start and where do they leave off?
2. To what *end* are we doing sociolinguistic research and in what adequate sociological framework can we embed the widespread details of linguistic variation? How can we account for social change?

These questions can be subdivided into many particular problems that shall be dis-cussed in the next paragraphs. But before I start with the discussion of the collection of questions concerned with rules, theories, notions, and explanations, I would like to add a more general point—a moral, normative, ethical, and speculative one; take it as you please.

I have no doubt that we can find technical solutions in sociolinguistics to descrip-tive problems of variation. But I am sceptical about our evaluation, interpretation, understanding of variation, stratification, inequality, and vitality in language. The predominant questions most often raised are the following: How well does the data obtained fit the proposed model? Can the features of variation be incorporated in a "scalogram analysis"? To what extent do social stratification, ethnic diversity, and rapid progress of urbanization *explain*—as correlates of linguistic differences—the facts of variation?

To my knowledge, there are almost no studies on the *adequacy* of codes or sub-codes for a set of communicative needs. And I do not know of any studies concerned with the "feeling of well-being" in a language or language variety. We do, however, know a lot about *prestige* or *stigmatization* of varieties. Yet very little or nothing is known about the vacillating feelings people have in identifying themselves or being identified with a given variety.

Investigations state, for example, that urban language is as complex as the whole process of industrialization and modernization; code switching and levels of accommodation are necessary in order to cope with the diversity of spoken varieties; the great range of different market and public places in a city, for example, requires the change of verbal repertoires and register flexibility. For some time now, we have been asking about architecture: What building or housing style would fit a given environment adequately? In sociolinguistics, such a question is rarely picked up.

More attention should be given to the question: How well or how poorly does one feel with one's language variety in a certain environment? How is group identification expressed by language codes or subcodes? This is the question of fundamental communicative needs. And if this is to be more than just an empty slogan, we have to investigate more closely whether there are some average communicative gratifications relating the speechlessness in supermarkets and the rhetorics of advertising, the poor conversation in medical care or other consultations and the chitchat in street corner bars.[1]

Some Basic Assumptions about Sociolinguistic Methodology

Taking into account the above criticism, I offer the following theses which can be considered orientation lines for my subsequent argumentation:

1. Sociolinguistic description of communicative behavior cannot be done from a point outside meaningful interaction. Comprehending always presupposes comprehension. Mere technical procedures superimposed from outside or according to categories external to interactive behavior must fail if they neglect the deeper interpretive and hermeneutic framework of descriptive procedures.

2. χ^2 tests of reliability, samples, frequencies, probabilities, factor analysis and other sophisticated tools never can decide *how valid findings are, how right and justified they may be.* There is no technical guarantee that we will understand what we observe in real life by means of our *human experience* and *social competence.* (This argument will be substantiated below).

3. The comparability of languages and varieties is not only a technical problem of meaning-identical forms, but beyond that of sameness or difference in *social-psychological* content. Each language code or subcode must be seen as a unique existential linguistic form with particular social-psychological connotations attached to it.

4. There is a difference between a natural science and a social science model in linguistics. Whatever may be achieved in linguistics, there will be no exhaustive explanation of communication without a deep understanding of the social back-

---

[1]In the original version of this chapter, I included an additional section entitled "Some Remarks on the Historical Genesis of Sociolinguistics." There I gave an account of the differences between Schleicher's natural science and Steinthal's social scientific approach in the middle of the nineteenth century. I am arguing that the dichotomy in linguistics which separates a natural science and a social science model can be traced back to the origins of linguistics in the last century (for a detailed account, see M. Lang, 1977.)

I tried to follow the evolution of linguistics as a science, focusing mainly on the orientation of the discipline toward either natural or social science.

In order to remain within the prescribed length requirements of this chapter, I excluded the "historical" section from the version to be published, although I think that the historical arguments are quite interesting. Those readers who would like to have the unshortened version of my chapter should write to me at the following address: Fachbereich Germanistik (FB 16), Freie Universitat Berlin, Habelschwerdter Allee 45, 1000 Berlin 33, Federal Republic of Germany.

ground. And this understanding will not be possible without looking at human *actions* in socializing and learning situations and everyday behavior in the communicative dynamics of daily life cycles. The roots of heterogeneity are found in the cycles of everyday communicative situations and routines. Otherwise, how could we explain "why anybody does say anything" (Labov, 1972b, p. 207) (fundamental pragmatic sociolinguistic question), why language varieties emerge, persist, or die (change), or why linguistic differences are maintained in connection with identity differences. It will be shown that we need a more radical concept of heterogeneity than we have had up to now.

The following section will deal with theoretical aspects of sociolinguistic rules. First, types of rules will be distinguished on a purely theoretical basis. Second, existing rule models will be evaluated under the headings of the theoretical outline. Third, the adequacy of the given models will be discussed.

What Do and What Should Rules Really Account for?

Everybody agrees that there are *rules* for behavior, *but* there is broad disagreement about (1) how they should be formulated; (2) how they account for behavior (Do they account for *all* or only a *few* cases? Do they reflect internal or external states?); and (3) on what basis they describe regularities (Are they based on ego or alter observation? Do they reflect objective data or intuitions?). There are other questions connected to these; too many problems are involved in the issue to mention them all.

If we look seriously at sociolinguistic rules, we cannot be satisfied with merely writing linguistic ones. Their nature has to reflect the social part of behavior. Dealing first with the social aspect of behavior, I distinguish between behavior of human beings and behavior of natural matter (material). The latter can be manipulated by the researcher from outside in the sense that under identical and controlled conditions the outcome of an experiment would always be the same and therefore is predictable. Human beings cannot be manipulated by sociology in this way for at least two reasons. (1) As *actors* in a social context, they may have some unpredictable effect on the experiment. (2) Experiments with human beings are an intervention in the unique, unrepeatable cycles of social life. The resulting dichotomy of natural science and social science has been stated most explicitly and lucidly by von Wright (1971):

> The systems ("fragments of the history of a world") which experimental science studies can be manipulated by an outside agent. This agent has learnt to reproduce the initial states of the systems under conditions where they would not otherwise originate. From repeated observations he then gets to know the possibilities of development inherent in the system. The systems which social scientists study cannot, as a rule, be manipulated by outside agents. Instead, they can be manipulated by agents inside. This means that predictions about the systems' development can, within the limits of human "know how," be made to come true, but can also be made to come false. (p. 164)

This statement establishes a clear distinction between material and social science. In trying to find an explanandum for the outbreak of the First World War, von Wright wrote:

> Let the suggestion be that the cause of the outbreak of the First World War was the assassination of the Austrian archduke at Sarajevo in July 1914. . . . Here we have a given *explanandum:* the outbreak of the war, and a proposed *explanans:* the shots at Sarajevo. The critical historian's task would be to test the explanation for (factual) correctness. The philosopher's task is to investigate the conceptual nature of the mechanism connecting the *explanans* (the "cause") with the *explanandum* (the "effect"). *How* then did the assassination cause the outbreak of the war? Surely it did not do this in literally the same way as a spark makes a barrel of gunpowder explode. The simile may after all be highly misleading and the mechanism at work in the two cases completely different. In both cases there are intermediate links between cause and effect which must be made clear before we understand the connection. In the case of the Sarajevo incident—but not in the explosion incident—these links are, typically, *motivations* for further actions. . . . The example can be generalized. The explanation of events in history (e.g., the outbreak of a war) often consists simply in pointing out one or several earlier events (e.g., an assassination, a breach of treaty, a border incident) which we regard as its "contributory causes." If the anticedents are called *explanantia,* then *explananda* and *explanantia* in such historical explanations are indeed logically independent. What connects them, however, is not a set of general laws, but a set of singular statements which constitute the premises of practical inferences. The conclusion which emerges from the motivation background given in these premises is often not the *explanandum* itself, but some other, intermediate event or action—in our example the Austrian ultimatum—which enters into the motivation background of yet another practical inference with another intermediate conclusion—say Russia mobilizing her army—and so forth through a number of steps, until eventually we reach the *explanandum* itself. (pp. 139–142)

Von Wright explained what he meant by "motivations for further actions" by reconstructing the underlying actions of the "war parties" and came to the following conclusion:

> To call the shots at Sarajevo a cause of the 1914–1918 war is a quite legitimate use of the term "cause"—only we must remember that we are not now speaking about human causes and nomic connections. And to call the explanation "causal" is also quite in order so long as we do not assimilate it to explanations which fit the covering law model. To call the explanation "teleological" would certainly be a misnomer, although teleology essentially enters into the practical inferences which link the *explanans* to the *eplanandum.* When, *faute de mieux,* I call it quasi-causal this does not imply any value judgment or imperfection of it as an explanation. I use the term because the explanation does not depend for its validity on the truth of general laws. (p. 142)

Explanations by means of "practical premises" are called by von Wright "quasi-causal explanations" and they are represented by the scheme shown in Figure 1. Similar schemes were developed earlier by Toulmin (1958, p. 94). The real causes of social events are therefore—in the long run—not understandable without *reconstructing the human actions.* This insight led von Wright to differentiate between two kinds of norms (rules):

> It is important to distinguish between norms which regulate (enjoin, permit, or prohibit) conduct and rules which define various social practices and institu-

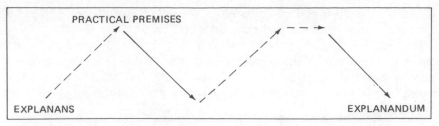

Figure 1. Quasi-causal historical explanation. (Based on Wright, 1971, p. 143.)

tions. Both are called "norms" or "rules." ... Norms of the first kind tell us *that* certain things ought to or may be done. Norms of the second kind tell us *how* certain acts are performed. Often, but not in all cases, a norm of the second kind is needed in order to make compliance with a norm of the first kind possible. (p. 151)

In recent theoretical and philosophical essays the distinction to which von Wright referred is generally known as the difference between *regulative rules* and *constitutive rules* (cf. Searle, 1969, sections 2.4 and 2.5). A complete discussion of different types of rules which can explain social behavior can be found in Collett (1977).

The most lucid recent account of the issue involved in rules and social behavior is Eglin's (1980).

According to types of rules, Eglin (pp. 7–17) distinguishes three kinds of sociology:

1. Positivistic sociology (regulative rules)
2. Semantic sociology (constitutive rules)
3. Interpretive sociology (rules of instructions).

A regulative rule has the following form:

(i) If X then Y [or] If x then y.

The sentences in (i) are models of the conditional statements typically found in deductive theorizing. The form contaning the capital letters represents the high-level, abstract, theoretical, "universal" proposition. The small-letter form depicts the low-level, concrete, empirical, "singular" hypothesis derived from such theorizing. ... In sociology, these matters are the abiding concern of the experimental study of small groups [and the] characteristics of sociology-on-the-natural-science-model. (pp. 7–8)

"Universal" and "singular" statements are linked by "corresponding rules" which establish the connection between "abstract" and "concrete" concepts. Concerning the establishment of correspondence rules and theoretical concepts as outcomes of human activities, Eglin considers them to be "institutional facts":

The theoretical concepts in regularities are institutional facts (Y,Q). ... while the theoretical terms of science and positivistic sociology have no necessary relationship to categories that are meaningful to the population being studied, they are nevertheless meaningful, their meaning frequently being only partially determined ... to the community of scientists using them. ... Insofar as constitutive rules say what some *activity* counts as in some context they typically embody more than is contained in the positivist's correspondence rules and operational definitions. (pp. 9–11)

It is in this sense "that positivistic sociology's object of explanation, the regularity, is underlain by one or more constitutive rules" (Eglin, 1980, pp. 9–11).

If regulative rules describe behavior with and through categories that are attached to it from outside the dynamic process, they fail to grasp those factors that essentially *constitute* behavior loosely. So-called institutional facts are therefore accounted for by constitutive rules, which have the general form

> (ii) In context Z, x counts as Y.
>
> Constitutive rules . . . tell what it is bits of the brute world count as in terms of some human institution, given some context. (Eglin, 1980, pp. 11–12)

Searle had already stated in 1969 that "'institutions' are systems of constitutive rules. Every institutional fact is underlain by a (system of) rule(s) of the form 'X counts as Y in context C'" (pp. 51–52). As an example of a constitutive rule, Eglin (p. 12) cites:

> (iii) In the game of cricket (Z), hitting-the-ball-full-pitch-across-the-boundary-line (X) counts as "a six" or "six runs" (Y).[2]

These rules turn the brute facts into institutional facts of our specific social context: mere behavior becomes socially and culturally meaningful action. These rules (for example, those for football) are partially constitutive ones. But it is held in general that constitutive rules *determine* other rules (see Searle 1969, p. 69).

Are constitutive rules the ideal solutions for the description and explanation of institutional facts? At first glance and according to the recent philosophical literature, they are. But in one way, Searle's constitutive rules are similar to Chomsky's regulative rules: they do not take into account the specific social context that constitutes—beyond the universal meaning—the specific interpretation of constitutive rules. Thus, the expression in (ii), "in context Z," is left open for any specification. In order to make sure that his constitutive rules for a promise apply, regardless of numerous intervening contextual conditions, Searle has to establish a kind of "wall" against the misinterpretation of the constitutive rule.[3] Just as Chomsky could not account for the variability of the speech community by introspection, Searle was unable to account for the context-dependent meaning of promises by mere intuition. The contextual information that is necessary for any interpretation of meaning is the key to understanding, to the operation of "finding out what one means." According to this context-dependent understanding (Garfinkel & Sacks, 1970), constitutive rules are *indexical* and *have to be interpreted:* Garfinkel wrote that "a common understanding, entailing as it does an 'inner' temporal course of interpretive work, necessarily has an operational structure" (1967, p. 31). Taking this statement into account, Eglin proposed "to characterize the operational structure of interpretive work . . . as the reading (giving and receiving) of instructional interpretations or, simply, of *instructions*" (Eglin, 1980, p. 15).

---

[2]Excellent concrete examples for rules of this type will be found in White (1943, pp. 14–35).

[3]"Defective" or elliptically formulated promises are excluded; elements that are irrelevant for the promise are not considered; the promise has to be expressed by a "grammatically well-formed sentence"; "normal input and output conditions obtain"; etc.

The third type of rule to be considered here has the form of instructions which can be formulated as follows (Eglin, 1980, p. 15):

> (iv) Find any lower-case letter to be Z, and see that in context Z, x counts as Y.

An example would be, loosely put (p. 15),

> (v) See that what's-going-on-here (c) is a quarrel (Z), and hear, in the context of the quarrel (Z) utterance (x) as an insult (Y).

In (v) we have two unknowns, namely, *c* and *x,* which are linked to a constitutive rule. Thus, (iv) and (v) are *instructions* for the interpretation. Instructions enable us to interpret what has been meant by meaningful (communicative and other) actions beyond the *mere given information.*

Whereas positivistic sociology measures social behavior according to principles of natural science with regulative rules, and semantic sociology according to actor-centered meaningful intentions with constitutive rules (being constructed by inspection for universal contexts), instructions tell actors (speaker/hearers) respectively

> how particular behaviors (utterances) are to be taken (heard) *in the very course* of enacting (uttering) the particular, that is, without coming out and saying so in so many words. (Eglin, 1980, p. 17)

Garfinkel and Sacks (1970) called this phenomenon "reflexivity."

In conclusion:

1. *Regulative rules* describe activities and behaviors which take place independently of them (the activity is logically independent of the rule); they are behavioristic rules (Searle, 1969; Wittgenstein, 1958).
2. *Constitutive rules* generate new forms of behavior and regulate activities, the existence of which is *logically dependent* on the rules; they are universal-context rules and describe unilaterally the intention-oriented semantic aspects of the actor perspective according to the intuition of the researcher (for further details, see Streeck 1980b).
3. *Instructions* are context-sensitive rules and descibe actions as "displays of meaningful items" (Eglin, 1980, p. 17) in reflexive interactions; in this sense, they deal with interactive meaning, that is, with the effects of *intended meaning* on the *understanding* by the hearer (the *interpretive result*).

Before I look at *sociolinguistic rules* in the next section, I have to clarify one point which will be crucial for the following discussion: Do we have to look at *social* and *linguistic* rules from different points of view? Or would the structure of linguistic rules, insofar as *linguistic* behavior is part of *social* behavior, be similar to the structure of social rules? Accepting without reservation the position held by Labov (1972b) that (1) "the student of his intuitions, producing both data and theory in a language abstracted from every social context, is the ultimate lame (p. 292) (science is substituted to constitutive rules) and (2) "language is a form of social behavior" (p. 292), I do not see a reasonable way to separate the two kinds of behavior. If "the fundamental sociolinguistic question is posed by the need to understand *why anyone says anything*" (Labov 1972b, p. 207), I consider the social to be an integral part of linguistics.[4]

At this point, I would like to emphasise three points which form a basis for the following discussion:

1. There is no substantial difference between *social* and *linguistic* rules.
2. Whether we think that the practical interpretive work of everyday life should be called instructions (Eglin) or maxims (Clarke, 1977), it should be clear that *both* are the *fundamental subject matter of sociology*.
3. Chomskian rules follow the natural science paradigm. They are an illustration of regulative rules.

Rules in Sociolinguistics

In this section, I will discuss common sociolinguistic rule models. By "common," I mean that they have been applied for years and are still in use today. I distinguish three groups of rules:

> Type I. Rules for grammatical variation
> Type II. Rules for variation in (lexico)semantic concepts
> Type III. Rules of "interactive" meaning

These three groups are differentiated according to the following dimensions: (a) the linguistic level of description; (b) the type of rule (qualitative vs. quantitative; sequencing vs. classificatory; behavioristic vs. mentalistic; regulative vs. constitutive); (c) the relationship between social context and linguistic actions (social facts are incorporated into the rules; correlation of linguistic and social factors; social and linguistic facts converge in rules); (d) the reflection of the speaker and the hearer perspectives, respectively, in rules (assumption of symmetry/asymmetry between production and interpretation, etc.).

I have only listed the most salient features. Others could be added. Of course, rule groups can be established on the basis of quite different criteria. The most pertinent criterion for my classification is linguistic level. But we will see that other criteria are linked to this distinction. The following presentation is nontechnical; it deals with presuppositions and implications of the models, not with their mechanical handling; the latter is taken for granted. I will, however, quote the relevant technical literature.

---

[4]That there are confusions about the "linguistic" or "social" character of rules can be shown by Chomsky, who considered *generative* rules as entirely and only linguistic, and David D. Clarke, who hoped to "be able to tell whether the rules . . . which produce all and only the acceptable behavior sequences in an abstract 'Behavior Grammar' do describe the generative processes of the social actor *in vivo*" (Clarke, 1977, p. 68).

Rules of Type I

The purely regulative rules of this paradigm deal with *grammatical variation*. They follow the form of conditional statements well known in deductive theorizing:

(i) If A, then B.

Models for this type of rule are found in all introductory texts. According to (i), the rule of a Chomsky grammar has the general form

(ii) $A \rightarrow B/X \relbar Y$
If A occurs in the context of X and Y, then replace it with B.

The four rule schemata which attempt to cope with grammatical variation are all based, although not dependent, on generative-transformational rules. They differ according to principles of *comparability* of items and devices for *ordering* speakers.

The most conservative version is that of *coexistent grammars*. Chomsky's famous corollary of the "ideal speaker/hearer living in a homogeneous speech community" (1965, p. 13) is withdrawn. The speech community is conceived of as heterogeneous and is divided into varieties with a set of common and distinctive rules. First, each variety must be (generatively) described on its own. Second, its specific other-than-linguistic feature (geographical or social distance, etc.) must be specified. Third, shared and nonshared rules among several varieties of a language must be identified. This concept has been suggested by (among others) Chomsky (1964), Loflin (1969), and Kanngiesser (1972).[5]

This approach is mainly theoretical. Two varieties which have been separately described in their entirety have never been compared. There are no explicit criteria for a systematic comparison. The reference to the need for social categories is mere lip service. This position, then, belongs to traditional "autonomous" linguistics and is, with regard to variation, no more than *formal extension*.

The second model of variation that has been used by many scholars is that of *implicational scales*. It shares the view of the coexistent model that varieties should be distinguished by qualitatively (and not quantitatively) different rules and that social factors play a role only insofar as they have to explain that which cannot be explained by autonomous linguistics. As illustrated by Table I, varieties are isolated by their shared and nonshared features. Their minimal definition is that they differ in at least one feature.

> An implicational anaylsis is a binary relation between linguistic features and language varieties (dialects, styles, etc.) so selected and so arrayed in order, as to result in a triangular matrix. (DeCamp, 1971, p. 33)

If the value of any desired point of intersection of the matrix, the product $F \times V$, is 1, then this implies that any value above or to the left of this value is also 1. A value of 0 implies that every value below or to the right of it is likewise 0 (Dittmar, 1976, p. 153). Thus, implicational scales result in some kind of continuum which makes it

---

[5]A recent account of this approach was given by Bierwisch (1976), who tried to attach to each rule in a grammar a set of connotations which speakers of social groups attribute to their application.

Table I. The Principle of Implicational
Analysis

Varieties	Features				
	F_1	F_2	F_3	F_4	F_5
V_1	1	1	1	1	1
V_2	1	1	1	1	0
V_3	1	1	1	0	0
V_4	1	1	0	0	0
V_5	1	0	0	0	0

possible to isolate a scale of varieties that share a common set of features and are distinguished by another set of features. By distinctive feature I mean simply relevant result of a rule operation.

The problem with implicational scales is illustrated by Table II. Forty-eight Italian and Spanish immigrants learning German without explicit teaching (undirected learning) were ordered implicationally by 11 rules (for details of the analytical procedures, see Klein & Dittmar, 1979, and Dittmar, 1980). The dashes indicate nonapplication of the rule. The numbers represent the frequency of a rule occurrence in a well-defined corpus. The learning varieties of the 48 speakers were first described by 100 probabilistically weighted context-free rules (see Klein & Dittmar, 1979). No clear-cut boundaries between different varieties could be established. We got a very transitional variety continuum. In order to account for varieties as discrete comunicative-existential forms *(Existenzformen)* reflecting different social experience, I tried to rank the speakers in an implicational ordering according to application and nonapplication of rules. Out of about 100 rules, I could apply only 11 in this procedure. Other rules follow quite different implicational patterns, and there is no known mathematical way to describe how to project different implicational orderings on only one scale that will result in the overall ordering of the speakers. Although my procedure had the advantage of allowing me to distinguish 8 varieties by application and nonapplication of rules[6] (criterion: complexity of linguistic structure) and by statistical group means of application frequencies (the first three rules in the scale), I have to say that the analysis is not satisfying for the following reasons:

1. There are exceptions to the pattern (boldface in the table). How can this be interpreted?

2. The criterion for ordering is *rule production* (application vs. nonapplication). The ordering would, of course, be different if we took receptive competence into account. The scale does *not* reflect *active* and *passive knowledge* of the speakers.

3. First, speakers are ordered according to features of linguistic production.

---

[6]As you can see, there are some exceptions to the general patterns indicated by "circles." I discussed this issue in more detail in Dittmar (1980).

Then, reasons must be found to account for the differences. This procedure is, in the long run, an unsatisfactory scientific crutch:

- The effects of the situation, self-consciousness, and identity of speakers for every instance of application of nonapplication are overlooked.
- The linear ordering is a construct. There will be internal variation for each speaker of a variety. The ordering assumes a systematicity that does not correspond to real communicative behavior. Thus, the scales inevitably lead to idealization.
- The grouping of speakers together according to some shared linguistic features is arbitrary. How can the homogeneity of people who speak the same variety be based on constructed criteria external to their behavior, normative self-evaluation, and communicative networks?

Grouping speakers without knowing the details of their background of social values and norms is possible as an idealistic construction, but it is not an adequate reconstruction of social reality. Last but not least, the reverse method would be more appropriate: grouping speakers together according to their shared social values/ norms and communicative networks and *then* looking for the linguistic reflection of their group membership.

The best-known model accounting for grammatical variation is the *variable rule model* developed by Labov (1972b) and mathematically adjusted by David Sankoff (Cedergren & Sankoff, 1974). Variable rules are at present the dominant tool for describing variation; they have been applied in innumerable studies all over the world. They are quantitative accounts of transitional stages of the distribution, evolution, or loss of rules in language acquisition, variation, and change. They describe "productive competence" (cf. Cedergren & Sankoff, 1974) in its variable application of rules under different social conditions and speaker-internal states. They operate on data-based corpora of actual language production with well-known statistical principles in the sense that they account for the proportion of rule application within a defined text passage out of all possible applications in the same environment. The borderline case of a variable rule is the "categorical" rule: a rule that always applies or does not apply at all. In this regulative rule model, language variation is the dependent and social categories the independent variable. Their relationship is formally expressed by correlations. The whole rule model is based on what I call the *semantic paradox: whereas differences in meaning imply different social life-styles, social meaning can only be discovered if differences in linguistic meaning are excluded.* The fundamental corollary of the Labovian paradigm is the assumption that *social meaning* corresponds to and is equivalent to "a set of alternative ways of 'saying the same thing'" (Labov 1972b, p. 94), that is, different forms that denote the same referent. This alternation of forms referring to identical linguistic meaning has been called by Pierrette Thibault (1979) *functional equivalence.* The Bloomfieldian warning, "Don't touch semantics, *it's psychology,*" is also the fundamental rule of Labovian sociolinguistics. Variable rules are behavioristic tools in Bloomfield's sense: only the linguistic surface, not the underlying knowledge of language, only "conventional uncon-

Table II. Implicational Scale-Ordering of 48 Adult Learners Illustrated on 11 Syntactic Rules[a]

Group/learner variety	Informant	S with subject	NP is a pronoun	S without V	VP is a V	VP consists of				S is a		
						ADV-L	Mod +V	CopV	Aux +V	NOM-CL	ATT-CL	Aux +Mod
I: V_1	01 SP-35	27	12	78	15	—	—	—	—	—	—	—
	02 IT-08	53	10	79	21	—	—	—	—	—	—	—
	03 SP-21	42	26	64	36	—	—	—	—	—	—	—
	04 SP-25	50	35	69	31	—	—	—	—	—	—	—
	05 SP-02	56	43	58	42	—	—	—	—	—	—	—
	06 IT-09	64	40	54	40	—	—	—	—	—	—	—
	07 SP-04	55	26	43	57	—	—	—	—	—	—	—
	08 SP-22	72	32	51	49	—	—	—	—	—	—	—
	Mean	*53*	*28*	*63*		—	—	—	—	—	—	—
II: V_2	09 SP-12	65	27	35	65	5	—	—	—	—	—	—
	10 SP-09	58	46	24	76	2	—	—	—	—	—	—
	Mean	*61*	*37*	*30*		—	—	—	—	—	—	—
III: V_3	11 SP-14	62	37	26	71	—[b]	3	—	—	—	—	—
	12 IT-23	34	28	38	24	6	2	—	—	—	—	—
	13 T-12	56	49	49	42	8	9	—	—	—	—	—
	14 IT-13	65	42	54	45	4	1	—	—	—	—	—
	15 IT-26	57	67	22	70	4	8	—	—	—	—	—
	16 IT-32	64	52	27	68	6	5	—	—	—	—	—
	Mean	*56*	*46*	*36*		—	—	—	—	—	—	—
IV: V_4	17 IT-24	59	29	45	52	6	—[b]	2	—	—	—	—
	18 SP-30	72	43	30	65	—[b]	1	4	—	—	—	—
	19 IT-28	55	39	34	60	5	2	4	—	—	—	—
	20 IT-29	55	47	31	66	2	1	2	—	—	—	—
	21 IT-18	63	39	34	55	4	10	1	—	—	—	—
	22 SP-18	61	53	28	69	5	1	2	—	—	—	—
	23 IT-25	67	66	27	48	3	2	23	—	3[b]	—	—
	24 IT-05	72	48	29	58	8	3	9	—	—	—	—

25 IT-15	63	41	18	60	8	11	11	—	—	—	—	—
26 SP-15	59	40	13	67	4	4	6	—	6[b]	—	—	—
Mean	*63*	*45*	*29*									
V: V_5												
27 SP-36	65	42	28	57	12	14	—[b]	1	—	—	—	—
28 SP-08	45	31	39	52	1	1	7	1	—	—	—	—
29 IT-07	60	51	32	58	4	1	6	3	—	—	—	—
30 SP-01	62	47	33	40	3	15	11	1	—	—	—	—
31 SP-13	72	51	21	66	1	4	8	1	—	—	—	—
32 SP-17	91	75	15	50	1	2	31	2	—	—	—	—
Mean	*66*	*50*	*24*					*2*				
VI: V_6												
33 IT-16	50	31	25	65	9	2	5	3	3	—	—	—
34 SP-26	67	40	34	54	5	1	5	6	2	—	—	—
35 SP-06	61	61	13	55	4	6	15	11	3	—	—	—
36 IT-20	70	62	9	69	13	9	5	8	1	—	—	—
37 IT-02	74	70	12	50	5	7	23	8	2	—	—	—
38 IT-33	77	61	10	26	1	10	39	5	8	—	—	—
39 IT-06	82	76	4	47	6	4	21	24	1	—	—	—
40 IT-22	84	89	5	55	8	2	23	14	3	—	—	—
41 IT-31	95	87	—	40	14	15	18	37	3	—	—	—
Mean	*73*	*64*	*12*					*12*				
VII: V_7												
42 IT-10	73	71	8	52	12	5	20	15	4	1	1	—
43 SP-29	76	70	1	34	7	7	24	23	1	1	1	—
44 SP-31	85	62	3	44	9	2	28	18	—[b]	2	2	—
45 SP-24	85	88	2	52	2	11	11	24	1	1	1	—
46 SP-19	94	83	—	43	8	9	21	27	5	1	1	—
Mean	*83*	*75*	*3*					*21*				
VIII: V_8												
47 SP-11	95	83	—	11	5	3	24	59	3	2	2	3
48 IT-01	100	96	—	17	18	8	12	57	12	3	3	3
Mean	*98*	*90*	*0*					*58*				

[a]Abbreviations: S, sentence; NP, nominal phrase; V, verb; VP, verbal phrase; ADV-CL, adverbial clause; Mod, modal verb; CopV, copulative verb; Aux, auxiliary; NOM-CL, Nominal clause; ATT-CL, attributive clause; V_i, variety.
[b]Indicates an exception to the pattern.

scious" language use, not conscious, socially motivated, stylistic choices, are the object of (socio)linguistic description. Very often, the early articles one writes reveal some determinants of weltanschauung, and in his 1963 article "Social Motivation of a Sound Change," Labov pointed out what "useful properties" a linguistic variable should have (Labov 1972a, p. 8). They are not described here, because they are not central to my argument, but the comments Labov gives on his useful properties of a linguistic variable are interesting in connection with the above-mentioned critical point:

> There are a few contradictory criteria, which pull us in different directions. On the one hand, we would like the feature to be salient, for us as well as for the speaker, in order to study the direct relations of social attitudes and language behavior. But on the other hand, *we value immunity from conscious distortion,* which greatly simplifies the problem of reliability of the data. (Labov 1972a, p. 8)

This brief outline leads us to the following conclusion: Variable rules deal with different forms of identical linguistic meaning. Alternative forms of "saying the same thing" reveal *social meaning.* Only those structures that are performed below speakers' consciousness carry social meaning. By this definition, conscious stylistic choice, for example, for social reasons or purposes, is excluded from social meaning. Social meaning is more or less confined to phonological and morphological variation. I think that this is a poor perspective for sociolinguistics at this point in history.

Variable rules are generative rules, with the addition of quantitative devices. The structure of a variable rule is:

$$(iii)\ X \rightarrow \langle Y \rangle /\ \left\langle \begin{array}{c} \text{[feature A]} \\ \text{[feature B]} \\ \cdot \\ \cdot \\ \cdot \end{array} \right\rangle \underline{\quad\quad} \left\langle \begin{array}{c} \text{[feature P]} \\ \text{[feature Q]} \\ \cdot \\ \cdot \\ \cdot \end{array} \right\rangle \text{[feature Z]}$$

$$\left\langle \begin{array}{c} \text{[feature I]} \\ \text{[feature J]} \\ \cdot \\ \cdot \\ \cdot \end{array} \right\rangle$$

where X is replaced by Y in accordance with the quantitative weighting through variable constraints, and each pair of angled brackets contains a list of features (bundles of features or subcategories) that can occupy a certain position in the structural description. In analogy to "more" and "less" relations ($>$ and $<$), variable constraints are given between angled brackets, whereas the feature Z, which occurs between square brackets, only stands for an obligatory feature, which makes the application of the rule obligatory. (Dittmar, 1976, p. 138). For an exploration of technical details, the reader is referred to Labov (1972b, pp. 65–129), Cedergren and Sankoff (1974), and Dittmar (1976). For the present purpose, it is important to know that variable rules are generative rules with quantitative weighting that are correlated with social categories like social class and profession. Apart from the numerous technical (mathematical and linguistic) inadequacies of variable rules,[7] I will, in conclusion, present some arguments why, although they are highly technical tools, variable rules are neither adequate nor explanatory devices for a sociolinguistic theory:

1. Besides being regulative rules (see above), variable rules are *behavioristic* devices; semantics, linguistic knowledge (for example, receptive competence), linguistic awareness, variation due to interactional forces, and the like are excluded from the rule formation.

2. Languages and varieties (codes and their subcodes) appear as a continuum of quantitative transitions which does not show clear-cut boundaries between standard and subcodes although speakers in a speech community have a social awareness of these boundaries.

3. Variable rules are limited to the description of those parts of language production which are automatic, below consciousness, and not reflected in speech. They cannot account for different productive and interpretive communicative strategies because intention, underlying meaning, and pragmatic aims of communication are not considered in the analysis.

4. In order to define the linguistic variable, it is necessary that its function and meaning be the same, instance for instance, for a defined context. The method assumes that deviations from the once defined functions according to discourse and process of interaction are not tolerated. Thus, variable rules are context-sensitive in a restricted sense; specific local discourse-dependent variations in the meaning of a variable in a defined context cannot be accounted for.

5. Variable rule methodology prescribes a procedure separating linguistic and social aspects by avoiding pragmatic factors. The linguistic variable is quantified separately from its social meaning within a corpus. The structural unit in the corpus is quantified in abstraction and isolation from its possible different social and pragmatic function in the course of verbal interaction. Methodologically, then, global interactions between sets of linguistic features and sets of social features are correlated, without looking at the specific local interaction of a meaningful linguistic fact and a meaningful social fact at any point in discourse.

In addition to these points, there are some arguments giving evidence that variable rules have mere descriptive, but not explanatory, power. They are discussed in detail in Romaine (1980), and are not repeated here.

The critical points I raised in the preceeding paragraph cannot be eliminated by way of mere technical solutions. In his excellent and sophisticated account of linguistic variation, Klein (1974) proved that (1) the contextual features of a linguistic variable are not constraints with effects independent of each other, but interact to a certain degree; and (2) social factors do not affect the contextual constraints of a linguistic variable in a uniform way; that is, it is not likely that the constraints

---

[7]See, among others, Kay and McDaniel (1979), Kelin (1974, pp. 135–148), Lavandera (1982), and Romaine (1980). Questions which are discussed in this chapter were discussed in depth by Romaine (1980) from a point of view of *theory of science*. I think that her arguments and my arguments complement each other and converge in many respects.

affecting the application or nonapplication of a rule for speakers of the upper class will have the same effect on rule application for speakers of the lower class. The two technical inadequacies of variable rules are illustrated in detail in Klein (1974, pp. 145–152).

Avoiding the disadvantages of variable rules, Klein devised a *variety grammar,* a syntactic model based on generative rules which describes syntactic variation by means of probabilistically weighted rules. A well-known application of the model is illustrated in Klein and Dittmar (1979). The undirected second language learning of 48 Spanish and Italian immigrants learning German is described by about 100 context-free syntactic rules. The descriptive problems which variable rules could not overcome (despite David Sankoff's important improvements) have been solved by Klein in the following way: Variation is described by rule blocks. Every block of rules has the same symbol on the left. The symbol on the left side is expanded to the right side of the arrow by different alternative expansions. Table III illustrates the working principle of variety grammar. It shows the evolution of the second language learning process progressing from the less complex variety 1 to (V_1) to the more complex and correctly used variety 6 (V_6). The probabilities reflect rule acquisition and reweighting of the rules. Each of the five rules has a fixed context attached to it. Thus, the problem is avoided of different contextual constraints having interdependent influence on rule application or nonapplication. The second difficulty with variable rules, the assumption that contextual constraints have the same function for different social categories or subcategories, is solved in variety grammar, too. The solution can be easily explained by looking at Table III. Let us assume that V_x is a lower-class variety (LC) and V_y is an upper-class one (UC). Then, for any NP emerging in the corpus of either LC or UC, we examine which of five rules has been applied. First the frequencies are calculated and then the probabilities. The comparison of the class-specific use of varieties is carried out for the whole noun-phrase block (every syntactic category of a rule has its fixed context), covering for the possibility of contextual constraints on any given linguistic variable. As we can see in Table III, the different probabilistic weightings of the rules show their distinctive use for six varieties.

Among the advantages of variety grammar, I will briely mention that whole syntactic profiles of varieties can be described—not only single, isolated variables.

Table III. Fragment of a Variety Grammar: Five NP Rules Describing Varieties of Six Second Language Learners[a]

	Variety					
Rule	V_1	V_2	V_3	V_4	V_5	V_6
1. NP → N	0,9	0,6	0,3	0,2	0,2	0,2
2. NP → DET N	0,1	0,3	0,3	0,3	0,3	0,3
3. NP → DET ADJ N	0	0	0	0	0,4	0,4
4. NP → DET N ADJ	0	0,1	0,3	0,4	0	0
5. NP → DET N ADV	0	0	0,1	0,1	0,1	0,1

[a]Abbreviations: NP, nominal phrase; N, noun; DET, determiner; ADJ, adjective; ADV, adverb. (Based on Klein & Dittmar, 1979, p. 92.)

Linguistic descriptions with variety grammar, like variable rules, are correlated with social factors.

I believe that variety grammar is a powerful, elegant, and flexible tool for describing variation at the present state of technical progress. But in spite of its practical descriptive handling of varying linguistic structures, it cannot cope with the five critical points I mentioned above. I do not deny that it serves well for producing an inventory of varying structures. Nevertheless, it cannot provide deeper explanations. Do the different patterns simply coexist? Or are they distributed in some kind of diglossic relationship? How did the varieties emerge historically and what are the social values interwoven with and reflected in them? What discourse function do they have and what is their communicative status? Variety grammar offers technical solutions superior to those of variable rules. But it does not provide sufficient explanations for the critical questions mentioned above. Indeed, rules of variety grammar cannot give satisfactory explanations because of their status as regulative rules.

Rules of Type II

In this section, I will be concerned with culturally determined semantic variation. This is the field of *ethnosemantics*. Anthropologists dealing with ethnosemantics investigate the different terminology cultures have for kinship, colors, plants, animals, and so forth. They look for the shared knowledge of these terms and approach their research objective with inductive methods. Their aim is a classification of cognitively different concepts. Rules for the denotative use of terms (lexemes) are categorical (qualitative) according to the fact that anthropologists try to find out under which conditions a given term names a given object. Insofar as they look for the *underlying meaning* of the term, they are interested in *constitutive rules* which specify in which context a given object x counts as an institutional fact y.

> A semantic rule states, for example, that "mother," as an American kinship term, denotes that class of objects having the simultaneous features, "first generation above ego," "female," "lineal.". . . This can be rewritten as:

> (iv) In the context of the semantic domain of American kinship terms, the collection of feature components, "first generation above ego," etc. counts as the taxonomic category conventionally labelled as "mother." . . .

One can abstract from this to

> (v) In domain (k), etic fact(s) (m) count as emic fact(s) (M). (Eglin, 1980, p. 21)

Statement (v) is a constitutive rule, belonging to the domain of semantic sociology. "The rules of (ethno-)semantics are constitutive, for acting in accordance with them constitutes performing minimally adequate referential (or propositional) acts" Searle, 1969, p. 24).

If constitutive rules are essential properties of semantic sociology, ethnosemantics must also be included under this heading. Ethnosemantics is concerned with the intuitions of speakers in a speech community regarding which terms for things (and which speech acts) are appropriate and which are not. People have a competence for judging the appropriateness of terms, things, speech acts. The judgment is the observable part of the unobservable intuitions. Anthropologists assume that informants share intuitions on appropriateness which are semantically encoded. Thus, an investigation of a semantic concept in a culture also reveals the cognitive categories of that culture (cf. Greenfield, this volume). According to Goodenough (1964), ethnosemantics tries to explain cultural diversity where "a society's culture consists of *whatever it is one has to know or believe in order to operate in a manner acceptable to its members, and do so in any role that they accept for any of themselves."*

Anthropology deals more or less with lexical semantics, assuming the existence of a domain in which a term (word) can be applied according to a semantical rule, called *signification.* The signification is a symbol standing for something in the outer world; the inherent components of its meaning which make up the *denotatum* can be isolated. In this respect, ethnosemantics follows the pattern of *componential analysis.* In terms of componential analysis, the referential sense of *boy* is

(vi) Boy (x) = Male (x) & Non-adult (x) & Human (x). (Clark & Clark, 1977, p. 415)

In order to establish semantic rules, three steps must be taken: (1) the relevant data must be elicited; (2) the gathered data must be arranged in some kind of taxonomy; (3) the end product of the analysis is a group of semantic rules. The data gathering procedure makes it necessary to *abstract from pragmatics.* Although context-specific referential meaning should be established, it can only be inferred from context-independent responses to questions in interviews. Ethnosemantics is, therefore, faced with a problem of "contextedness."

It is a truism to say that meaning varies with context. How can ethnosemantics cope with social variation of referential meaning? Tyler (1969) demonstrated that the ethnosemantic enterprise will, in the long run, be a failure:

> Note also that if rules of use are to incorporate contextual features, it is not even possible to formulate rules unless contexts are finite. It does not need demonstration to prove that the total physical surroundings or context of any utterance are never exactly the same on two different occasions. Thus, contexts cannot be finite. This is the paradox of the contextual theory. Since the notion of context violates the idea of rule, we cannot properly speak of meaning as a rule of use. (p. 75)

The second problem of ethnosemantics is the taxonomy of components reflecting the structure of inherent meaning of lexical items. What is the appropriate set? How can informants establish equivalences between nonidentical contexts in order to judge whether these and no other components are relevant to a lexeme for its use in different contexts?

This is a problem involving the interaction of the researcher and the informant (how can they come to an agreement on specific meanings?) and the imaginative ability of the informant to establish equivalencies between nonidentical contexts.

As I tried to demonstrate in the second section of this chapter, constitutive rules fail to account for particular contexts, context variation and discrepancies between imagined context meaning and real context meaning. We need instructions in order to understand the particular context-based meaning. I must therefore, state once again that regulative rules depend on constitutive rules and that the latter, at least, depend on instructions. By means of analogy, semantic sociology depends on interpretive sociology, which can give us the necessary instructions for understanding.

In summary, ethnosemantics is not able to overcome the following four problems:

1. The abstraction from pragmatics: What place has a certain action in a series of biographical and other actions?
2. Context-specificness: What is really *done* and *understood* in a concrete context?
3. Interactive agreement between ethnographer and informant: How can they arrive at shared knowledge?
4. Establishing equivalences between nonidentical contexts: How is social order interpreted as same or different by competent members of a community?

The four problems raised here can only be solved within the framework of interpretive sociology. As such, a sociological ethmethodology offers the concept of *indexicality* for problems 1 and 2, and the concept of *accomplished social order* for the difficulties mentioned under 3 and 4. Garfinkel (1967) used the term *indexical* for utterances whose

> sense cannot be decided by an auditor unless he knows something about the biography and the purposes of the speaker, the circumstances of the utterance, the previous course of the conversations, or the particular relationship of actual or potential interaction that exists between user and auditor. The expressions do not have a sense that remains identical through the changing occasions of their use. (p. 40)

For ethnomethodology, then, the main problem is: "Given indexicality, how is social order possible?" (Eglin, 1980, p. 40).

Social order is considered to be the accomplishment of societal members; the way it is accomplished can be reconstructed by means of the *documentary method of interpretation:*

> treating an actual appearance as "the document of," as "pointing to," as "standing on behalf of," a presupposed underlying pattern. Not only is the underlying pattern derived from its individual documentary evidences, but the individual documentary evidences, in their turn, are interpreted on the basis of "what is known" about the underlying pattern. Each is used to elaborate the other. (Garfinkel, 1967, p. 78)

Interpretive sociology is, in its present state, little more than a program; but there are already substantial empirical investigations which illustrate its principles on the basis of a variety of different data. One of the best overviews on theory and methods can be found in Schenkein (1978).

Rules of Type III

Recall the model of an instruction (where individual lowercase letters stand for brute facts, uppercase for institutional facts):

(vii) Find any lowercase letter to be Z, and see that in context Z, x counts as Y.

An example of this rule is (v) on p. 233.

The formulation of such rules is at present hard to find. The most striking and elaborate example is that of Sacks, Schegloff, and Jefferson (1978), who tried to formulate rules for "a simplest systematics for the organization of turntaking for conversation." The rules the authors give for turn-taking account for innumerable empirical observations. They are qualitative rules of instruction which give an exhaustive account of the turn-taking possibilities participants have in a conversation. These rules are both universalistic and context-sensitive. The rules for turn-taking have the form described below (details or definition of terms are not given):

> The following seems to be a basic set of rules governing turn construction, providing for the allocation of a next turn to one party, and coordinating transfer so as to minimize gap and overlap. For any turn:
>
> 1.   At initial turn-constructional unit's initial transition-relevance place:
>   (a) If the turn-so-far is so constructed as to involve the use of a "current speaker selects next" technique, then the party so selected has rights, and is obliged, to take next turn to speak, and no others have such rights or obligations, transfer occurring at that place.
>   (b) If the turn-so-far is so constructed as not to involve the use of a "current speaker selects next" technique, self-selection for next speakership may, but need not, be instituted, with first starter acquiring rights to a turn, transfer occurring at that place.
>   (c) If the turn-so-far is so constructed as not to involve the use of a "current speaker selects next" technique, then current speaker may, but need not, continue, unless another self-selects.
> 2.   If, at initial turn-constructional unit's initial transition-relevance place, neither 1 (a) nor 1 (b) has operated, and, following the provision of 1 (c), current speaker has continued, then the Rule-set (a)-(c) reapplies at next transition-relevance place, and recursively at each next transition-relevance place, until transfer is effected. (Sacks *et al.*, 1978, pp. 12–13)

I cannot comment on the details of the rule formation. On the one hand, rules reflect what people do; on the other hand, they seem to be followed whether a speaker in a concrete conversation takes the turn or loses it. The rules are formulated in such a way that they have components for both universal and local application. The principles underlying the rule formulation and the view of social interaction are explained in detail by Streeck (1980b). I think that a good understanding of the methodology may be achieved by carefully reading the explanations given by the authors themselves. I quote passages which give a deeper insight into their principles:

> The turn-taking system is a local management system, then, in the sense that it operates in such a way as to allow turn size and turn order to vary, and be under local management, across variations in other parameters, and while achieving the aim of all turn-taking systems—the organization of "*n* at a time"—and the aim of all turn-taking organizations for speech-exchange systems—"one at a time while speaker change recurs."
>
> The turn-taking system under examination can be further characterized for the kind of local management system it is. The character and organization of the rules that constitute the system as a local management system themselves determine its more particular organization in not only allowing and/or requiring turn size and turn order to vary, but in subjecting their variability to the control of the parties to the conversation for any conversation. It is, therefore,

among local management systems, a "party-administered system. . . . For conversationalists, that turn size and turn order are locally managed (i.e., turn-by-turn), party-administered (i.e., by them), and interactionally controlled (i.e., any feature being multilaterally shaped), means that these facets of conversation, and those that derive from them, can be brought under the jurisdiction of perhaps the most general principle particularizing conversational interaction, that of "recipient design." With "recipient design" we intend to collect a multitude of respects in which the talk by a party in a conversation is constructed or designed in ways which display an orientation and sensitivity to the particular other(s) who are the coparticipants. In our work, we have found recipient design to operate with regard to word selection, topic selection, the admissibility and ordering of sequences, the optons and obligations for starting and terminating conversations, and so on, which will be reported in future publications. It is a major basis for that variability of actual conversatins that is glossed by the notion "context-sensitive." By "the particularizing operation of recipient design on turn size and turn order," we are noticing that parties have ways of individualizing some "this conversation"; their collaboration in turn allocation and turn construction achieves a particular ordering of particular-sized turns and turn-transition characteristics of the particular conversation at the particular point in it. In evolving a machinery by which turn organization is subjected to recipient design in a workable way, turn taking, abstractly conceived, is adapted specifically for conversation. (Sacks *et al.*, 1978, pp. 41–43)

I think that the turn-taking rules describe in some ideal way the universal and the local, the constitutive and the instructive parts of behavior. They account for *interactive meaning,* the mutually intelligible product of interaction processes. In these respects, they are powerful descriptive devices. But whether they really explain social order and its constitution in the reality of daily social order and its constitution in the reality of daily social life will be discussed in the next section where I will briefly deal with the sociological component. In this section, I have discussed advantages and disadvantages of regulative, constitutive, and instructive rules in sociolinguistics.

It is evident from our discussion in the section on what rules account for that instructions have the highest level of explanatory adequacy for social interaction. We will see that this can only be true if idealization is removed from the rules and if the dynamic parameters of society are taken into account.

Sociology in Sociolinguistics

In the preceding sections of this chapter, I have reflected on the adequacy of the sociological component in sociolinguistics. I compared rules within sociology and I came to the conclusion that the explanatory power of rules in sociology fits into an implicational pattern:

(viii) Regulative rules ⊃ Constitutive rules ⊃ Instructions

This means that regulative rules depend on constitutive rules and the latter on instructions. The rules on the left can explain little, those on the right enable us to explain more.

Recall that in interpretive sociology, as outlined by Garfinkel (1967), *recipient design* is a fundamental term.

> With "recipient design" we intend to collect a multitude of respects in which the talk by a party in a conversation is constructed or designed in ways which display an orientation and sensitivity to the particular other(s) who are the co-participants. (Sacks *et al.*, 1978 p. 43)

That means that the (verbal) interaction process produces some social order, and to some extent, this order follows *universal* and *particular* rules which vary from context to context (cf. Berry, this volume). Briefly stated and in a very simplified form, this means that *social order is produced in a microcosm of daily interactions in different situations and (more or less institutionalized) contexts.* Verbal interaction and social order are produced in a mutual (reciprocal) process: they influence one another; they are mutually embedded in each other. One assumption of interpretive sociologists is that self-regulatory social interaction processes produce a social world of orderliness. I agree with the fact that social order is constituted, to a fundamental degree, on the microlevel of interaction and daily life. There is some output of inter-active meaning telling you every day in your specific interactions "how to do it." But where do routines come from? Which historical and social conventions do they reflect? How do they change and can they change? It is a corollary of ethnomethodology not to look at traditional sociological categories and constructs like *social class* and *prestige*. It is argued that assuming the social reality of such categories obscures the unadulterated perception of discourse and interaction, since researchers superimpose their constructed social categories (e.g., social class) on verbal behavior and code it with preconceived attitudes. The results of such research would be biased. *Before* such categories are established, the mere interactional process (what really goes on) has to be described. In opposition to this, "correlational sociology" maintains that there are universal categories determining the social life in communities. One of these is social class. If there is variation in social patterns, it can be explained by class differences. The methodology is this: people are classified according to social class indicators (e.g., years of schooling, income, profession, etc.; indicators vary according to the theoretical background); they are observed in certain contexts and situations; their behavior is coded with respect to salient class-specific features; these must *differentiate* between people because, otherwise, if there are *no* differences, the research is not interesting. Features of behavior and indicators of social class are constructed and coded independently of one another.[8] Each of the two sides is calculated separately and then correlated. The relationship between the two sets of indicators is expressed by correlation coefficients. The most famous example of such a correlational study in sociolinguistics is Labov (1966). Linguistic differences in phonetic production are explained by differences in social class structure. Language is the dependent variable and social structure is the independent variable. Numerous studies have been done following this paradigm of Labovian methodology (Oevermann, 1972; Neuland, 1975; cf. Osser, this volume).

---

[8]Ethnomethodologists have convincingly shown that this "ideal" procedure is not in fact followed in practice.

Abstracting from the particular concept of social class (it is one social category among others in the correlationalist framework), I think that there are good reasons for the assumption that categories, factors, and social conditions exist as *antecedents* of actions and concrete behavior in the sense that they *predetermine* and historically canalize the social adequacy of behavior by the imposition of institutional norms and values. These external institutional norms and values constitute the frames for daily routines and actual behavior. Within the boundaries of these frames, I think that broad variation of different conduct—in the sense of interpretive sociology—is possible. I will give a simple example. Table manners in their actual execution may differ infinitely from context to context. Apart from this variation, which makes context-sensitive interpretations essential, there are, however, some recurrent indicators of social identity which give an outsider insight into the milieu the participants come from. In his recent book, Bourdieu convincingly showed the truth of this view (Bourdieu, 1979). Because society can change socially and historically, social differences in institutions, social milieu, culture, and ethnic and indigenous population as *superstructures* of institutional and private life must be taken into account. The stigmatized or prestigious phonetic variants produced by a member of the society tell us something about his/her presumed social background, although we must examine each instance to see whether these variants have interactive relevance and of what nature, according to differing persons, situations, and contexts. There are no constant patterns of daily routines and interactions which are reproduced as a result of some biological program. The frames of behavior will change according to changes in institutional (i.e., economical, social, juridical) norms and values. Before I try to formulate some kind of synthesis between the behaviorist and the interpretive sociological approaches, I will briefly mention that the explanatory power of *social class* (in the classical operationalization of this category) has been considerably weakened.

Hager, Haberland, and Paris (1973, pp. 185–222) have shown that the definition of social class changes fundamentally according to the ideological position of a bourgeois or Marxist research perspective. Giles and Powesland (1975) ad Ryan (1979), among others, have given evidence that lower class language behavior will *not* change simply because the social class structure is changed. As a result of closed *interactional* networks in neighborhoods of social groups, social norms and speech styles persist in urban and rural milieus because they are maintained on the basis of an affective and *obligatory exchange system*. Transactions of goods and services govern long-term relationships between members of a neighborhood, thus reinforcing closed contact and a shared set of norms among them. In her recent application of the *net work theory*, Milroy (1980) has shown that a speech community must be defined on the basis of shared social values and norms within the group networks and *not* on the basis of grouping together randomly distributed people. Thus, criteria for defining *social class* are to some extent arbitrary. (For another criticism of this view, held by Labov, see Dittmar, 1975.) It seems that stigmatized varieties persist because of the affective cohesiveness of groups, which overrides the social class effect. Still another aspect has been criticized by Bourdieu (1979): Introducing the notion of *linguistic market,* Bourdieu objected to social class theory since it does not distinguish between an assemblyline worker who earns 3,400 francs and a salesperson in a fashion shop who earns the same amount. He argues that the salesperson needs a higher level of verbal ability for his/her job and that s/he will be more skilled verbally than the assembly-line worker. Therefore, we must determine the position of the speaker in the linguistic market that accounts for the "symbolic value" and "symbolic capital" that a speaker has in a capitalist society. The term *symbolic capital* is derived from a theory dealing with the *relations of symbolic power*. I cannot go into the important critical questions raised by Bourdieu. However, from the critical aspects I have mentioned it should be clear that *ideology* with respect to social values, speech norms, table manners, and so on, plays some role in society (cf. Phillips, this volume). In general, this is overlooked by both social class sociologists and by ethnomethodologists (the latter assuming that there is some self-regulatory social world which is more or less untouched by institutional ideologies).

At first glance, there seems to be no way of reconciling "macro- (correlationalist) sociology and micro- (interpretive) sociology. If we examine both paradigms more closely, we realize that we are involved with some kind of *sociological paradox: the constitutional processes of social order can only be revealed by scrutinizing in depth daily social interactions on the micro level using the documentary method of recipient design; however, they can only be understood by taking into account the broader underlying macrostructure of societal values, norms, and ideologies that have their materialistic and historical source in the sociopolitical actions of human beings and are unavoidable presuppositions and preconceived knowledge of any contextual interpretation.*

In the light of this paradox, I think that macro- and microsociology are necessarily complementary fields. Social order and social structure should be described and explained by means of a multilevel form of analysis. Such an integrated approach does not exist at present, although Fishman (1972) tried to formulate a first synthesis. The methodology of multilevel analysis in sociolinguistics should follow four principles which appear to require a dialectical procedure:

1. Proceed from the pragmatic to the "lower" (semantic, syntactic, morphological, phonetic) level.
2. Document as far as possible the interaction processes under investigation according to the principle of recipient design.
3. Proceed hierarchically in rule formation: establish constitutive rules on the basis of instructions and regulative rules on the basis of constitutive rules.
4. On a concrete and an abstract level of analysis, try to establish the major social and historical forces which explain the interactional and institutional facts discovered in your analysis in terms of norms and values.

In this model, pragmatic conditions determine the specific function of phonetic variants in discourse. Their function (and meaning) is dependent on interactional effects. The interpretation of interactions and communication processes is linked to a reconstruction of major sociohistorical forces and their reflection in institutional values. Regulative rules are understandable only in the light of constitutive rules and instructions; that is, there is a relation between universal and local principles. From this perspective, the microorganization of social interaction can be reconstructed in its functioning on a documentary level of first order analysis and socially evaluated and completed on a macrolevel of historically legitimized constructs of second order analysis. No preconceived social categories must be selected in the macroanalysis. They should be meaningful for the specific sociohistorical background of the investigation (cf. Parker, this volume).

Beyond the Narrow Scope of Current Sociolinguistics

In the preceding parts of this chapter I have shown that present sociolinguistic research is dominated by two major approaches, the correlationalist approach and the conversationalist approach. The correlationalist paradigm is confined to regulative rules, social constructs external to the process of interaction, static description, and a restricted concept of social meaning. It tries, nevertheless, to explain linguistic variation with categories which are derived from some understanding of the sociohistorical background of the society (the ideological bias is not discussed here; cf. Hymes, this volume).

Interpretive sociology departs from the principle of recipient design and works with instructions, that is, rules which formulate universal aspects of interactional processes and at the same time account for local variation. They try to grasp social order on a microlevel, without applying preconceived sociological constructs to the analysis from the outset. In contrast to behavioristic sociology, we can call this approach *natural sociology,* with reference to its principle of using the smallest possible set of analytical categories.

In the preceding section, I argued for an integrated approach combining both methodologies. Instead of trying to present an exhaustive account of methodological questions and a list of urgent research topics, I would like to conclude this article by making some suggestions that might be useful for further sociolinguistic research.

1. Research should be legitimized by application. Fieldwork could serve to sensitize people to language diversity, minority problems, and communicative tolerance. The people concerned should *gain* through research.

2. Social meaning should no longer be restricted to phonological and morphological variants of the same referent. Sociolinguistic analysis should be extended to syntactic and semantic variation. The studies could be exploratory and renounce statistics and a sophisticated method of "semantic equivalents" (there is no applicable theory of "paraphrase"; see E. Lang, 1977). It would even be worthwhile to look at the specific semantic properties and the stylistic range of a certain variety which distinguish it from other ways or varieties of communication. I think that communicative strategies, whether consciously or unconsciously performed, should not be excluded from analyses, because they represent the underlying concepts of surface features of social meaning.

3. It is time to describe and to explain the *social genesis* of speech variation, verbal routines, attitudes, stigmatization of varieties, linguistic inequality, and the like. A high standard has been reached in technical synchronic descriptions of variation. However, the purely technical debate on quantitative methods of describing variation now being pursued is moving farther and farther away from any meaning-

ful application in research. Pragmatic questions should be brought well to the fore: *why* people behave and communicate the way they do, *why* these and not other sociolinguistic identities are acquired, *why (and when) people feel comfortable or uncomfortable in their variety of daily communication. There should be more in-depth research on the contribution of speaking a certain variety in a given society to well-being in overall social behavior. Such research is possible only if we use our data not simply to support an interesting theory, but as documents and arms for improvements in communication.*[9]

4. Many studies have focused on cross-class variation of comparable level items. This method excludes many substantial differences between varieties. It would be worthwhile to investigate in greater detail the whole range of syntactic, semantic, and stylistic properties of *one* variety or sociolect and to know more about the social and cultural values that are attached to it. Satisfactory methods for cross-sectional comparisons must be developed. The broad range of different social meaning could be investigated with more modest requirements with respect to comparability.

5. I will mention one last point. The question of whether we are right or wrong in linguistic description can be decided to a certain degree, but by no means definitely through sociolinguistic studies. Romaine (1980) has effectively shown that this claim held by Labov cannot be maintained. Following von Wright (1971), I am convinced that, in the long run, it will not be formal criteria like tests of significance (χ^2) and factor analysis, which will pronounce judgment on the adequacy or correctness of our analysis, but rather our understanding of the results in the light of our historical human experience.

Some parts of this chapter have been critical, some even polemical. It was not my intention to say that variable rules or componential analysis should *not* be employed. But I hope to have shown that sociolinguistics must go *beyond* the mere description of recurrent rule application in a well-defined corpus. The description of surface phenomena by regulative rules is the most accessible, but also the most behavioristic part of the sociolinguistic enterprise. *Sociolinguistic explanation* has to come to grips with: (1) the wide range of *social meaning* of linguistic structures including semantic and pragmatic variation; (2) the individual and social genesis of variation, that is, the *acquisition* process of sociolinguistic diversity; and (3) what it means "to follow a sociolinguistic rule": context-sensitive constitutive rules (instructions) should be found out for different social functions of language use.

Acknowledgments

I wish to express my gratitude for the great help I received from Janet Wheelock and Flora McGechan in correcting my "Interlanguage English" and typing the manuscript. Both contributed considerably to the improvement of the manuscript.

[9]As some Catalan and French sociolinguists point out, there is a *sociolinguistics of the center,* writing theories and looking at universal principles in sociolinguistic variation, and there is, opposed to it, a *sociolinguistics of the periphery,* doing research with the perspective of improving the rights and the linguistic situation of the minorities.

References

Bierwisch, M. Social differentiation of language structure. In A. Kasher (Ed.), *Language in focus.* Dordrecht, Holland: D. Reidel, 1976, pp. 407–456.

Blom, J. P., & Gumperz, J. J. Social meaning in linguistic structure: Code-switching in Norway. In J. J. Gumperz & D. Hymes (Eds.), *Directions of sociolinguistics: The ethnography of communication.* New York: Holt, Rinehart & Winston, 1971, 407–434.

Bourdieu, P. *La distinction: Critique sociale du jugement.* Paris: Editions de Minuit, 1979.

Cedergren, H. C.. & Sankoff, D. Variable rules: Performance as a statistical reflection of competence. *Language,* 1974, *2,* 333–355.

Centro de Estudios Puertorriqueños. Social dimensions of language use in East Harlem. J. Attinasi, P. Pedraza, S. Poplack, S. Pousada (Eds.), *Language Policy Task Force 7,* Working paper, New York, 1980.

Chomsky, N. Comments for Project Literacy meeting. *Report of the Second Research Planning Conference Held under the Auspices of Project Literacy.* Chicago, August 6–8, 1964, pp. 1–8.

Chomsky, N. *Aspects of the theory of syntax.* Cambridge, Mass.: MIT Press, 1965.

Clark, H. H., & Clark, E. V. *Psychology and language.* New York: Harcourt Brace Jovanovich, 1977.

Clarke, D. D. Rules and sequences in conversation. In Collet (Ed.), *Social rules and social behavior.* Oxford: Basil Blackwell, 1977, pp. 42–69.

Collett, P. (Ed.). *Social rules and social behavior.* Oxford: Basil Blackwell, 1977.

De Camp, D. Implicational scales and sociolinguistic linearity. *Linguistics,* 1971, *73,* 30–43.

Dittmar, N. Sociolinguistics: A neutral or a politically engaged discipline? *Foundations of Language,* 1975, *13* (2), 251–265.

Dittmar, N. *Sociolinguistics: A critical survey of theory and application.* London: Edward Arnold, 1976.

Dittmar, N. Ordering adult learners according to language abilities. In S. Felix (Ed.), *Second language acquisition.* Tübingen, West Germany: Gunter Narr, 1980.

Dittmar, N. Soziolinguistik: Ein Forschungsüberblick. *Studium Linguistik,* 1982, *12,* 20–52.

Eckert, P. Diglossia: Separate and unequal. *Linguistics,* 1980, *18,* 1053–1064.

Eglin, P. Talk and taxonomy. *Pragmatics and beyond* (Vol. 8). Amsterdam: John Benjamins B. V., 1980.

Encrevé, P. A propos du "marché linguistique." In N. Dittmar & B. Schlieben-Lange (Eds.), *La sociolinguistique dans les pays de langue Romane.* Tübingen, West Germany: Gunter Narr, 1982, pp. 97–104.

Erickson, F. The cycle of situational frames: A model for microethnography in urban anthropology. Paper read at Midwest Anthropology Meeting, Detroit, 1971.

Fishman, J. The relationship between micro- and macro-sociolinguistics in the study of who speaks what language to whom and when. In J. B. Pride & J. Holmes (Eds.), *Sociolinguistics.* Harmondsworth, Middlesex: Penguin Books, 1972, pp. 15–32.

Fishman J. A., Cooper, R. C., & Ma, R., Bilingualism in the Barrio. *Language and Science Monographs,* 1971, *7.*

Garfinkel, H., *Studies in ethnomethodology.* Englewood Cliffs, N.J.: Prentice-Hall, 1967.

Garfinkel, H., & Sacks, H. On formal structure of practical actions. In J. C. McKinney & E. A. Tiryakian (Eds.), *Theoretical sociology.* New York: Appleton-Century-Crofts, 1970.

Giles H., & Powesland, P. F. *Speech style and social evaluation.* New York and London: Academic Press, 1975.

Giles H., & Smith, P. M., Accomodation theory: Optimal levels of convergence. In H. Giles & P. M. St. Clair (Eds.), *Language and social psychology.* London: Basil Blackwell, 1979, pp. 45–65.

Goodenough, W. Cultural anthorpology and linguistics. In D. Hymes (Ed.), *Language in culture and society.* New York: Harper & Row, 1964.

Gumperz, J. J. *Social network and language shift* (Working Paper 46). Language Behavior Research Laboratory, Berkeley, 1976.

Hager, F., Haberland, H., & Paris, R. *Soziologie und Linguistik: Die schlechte Aufhebung der Ungleichheit durch Sprache.* Stuttgart: J. B. Metzler, 1973.

Hymes, D. The scope of sociolinguistics. In R. W. Shuy (Ed.), *Report of the twenty-third annual round table meeting on linguistics and language studies.* Washington, D.C.: Georgetown University Press, 1973, pp. 313–333.

Kanngiesser, S. *Aspekte der synchronen und diachronen Linguistik.* Tübingen, West Germany: Niemeyer, 1972.

Kay, P., & McDaniel, Ch. K. On the logic of variable rules. *Language in society.* 1979, *8,* 154–187.

Klein, W. *Variation in der Sprache: Ein Verfahren zu ihrer Beschreibung.* Kronberg: Scriptor, 1974.

Klein, W. & Dittmar, N. *Developing grammars: The acquisition of german by foreign workers.* Heidelberg/New York: Springer Verlag, 1979.

Labov, W. *The social stratification of English in New York City.* Washington, D.C.: Center for Applied Linguistics, 1966.

Labov, W. *Sociolinguistic patterns.* Oxford: Basil Blackwell, 1972. (a)

Labov, W. *Language in the inner city: Studies in the Black English Vernacular.* Philadelphia: University of Pennsylvania Press, 1972. (b)

Labov, W. Some principles of linguistic methodology. *Language in Society,* 1972, *1* (1), 37–120. (c)

Laks, B. Differenciation linguistique et differenciation de sociolinguistique francaise. Thèse de 3ème cycle de linguistique, Paris, 1980.

Lang, E. Paraphrasenprobleme I: Über verschiedene Funktionen von Paraphrasen beim Ausführen semantischer Analysen. *Linguistische Studien* 42, Reihe A, Arbeitsberichte, Academie der Wissenschaften der DDR, Zentralinstitut für Sprachwissenschaft, Berlin, 1977, pp. 97–756.

Lang, M. Sprachtheorie und Philosophie: Zwei wissenschaftshistorische Analysen. *Osnabrücker Beiträge zur Sprachtheorie, Beihefte 1,* Osnabrück, 1977.

Lavandera, B. Le principe de réinterpretation dans la théorie de la variation. In N. Dittmar & B. Schlieben-Lange (Eds.), *La sociolinguistique dans les pays de langue Romane.* Tübingen, West Germany: Gunter Narr, 1982, pp. 87–96.

Loflin, M. D., Negro nonstandard and standard English: Same or different deep structure? *Orbis,* 1969, *18* (1), 74–91.

Milroy, L. Language and social networks. *Series language and society 2.* Oxford, 1980.

Neuland, E. *Sprachbarrieren oder Klassensprache? Untersuchungen zum Sprachverhalten im Vorschulalter.* Frankfurt am Main: Fischer, 1975.

Oevermann, U. *Sprache und soziale Herkunft: Ein Beitrag zur Analyse schichtenspezifischer Sozialisationsprozesse und ihrer Bedeutung für den Schulerfolg.* Frankfurt am Main: Suhrkam, 1972.

Romaine, S. The status of variable rules in sociolinguistic theory. Unpublished manuscript, University of Birmingham, 1980.

Ryan, E. B., Why do low-prestige varieties persist? In H. Giles & R. St. Clair (Eds.), *Language and social psychology.* Oxford: Basil Blackwell, 1979, pp. 145–157.

Sacks, H., Schegloff, E., & Jefferson, G. A Simplest systematics for the organization of turntaking for conversation. In J. Schenkein (Ed.), *Studies in the organization of conversational interaction.* New York: Academic Press, 1978, pp. 7–55.

Sankoff, D., & Labov, W. On the uses of variable rules. *Language in society.* 1979, *8,* 189–222.

Sankoff, G. *The social life of language.* Philadelphia; University of Pennsylvania Press, 1980.

Schenkein, J. (Ed.). *Studies in the oganization of conversational interaction.* New York: Academic Press, 1978.

Schuchhardt, H. *On sound laws: Against the neogrammarians* (T. Venneman & T. H. Wilbur, Eds. & trans.). Frankfurt: Athenäum Verlag, 1972, pp. 39–72. (Originally published, 1885.)

Searle, J. R. *Speech acts: An essay in the philosophy of language.* Cambridge: Cambridge University Press, 1969.

Streeck, J. Speech acts in interaction: A critique of Searle. *Discourse Processes,* 1980, *3*(2), 133–153.(a)

Streeck, J. Review of 'Schenkein, ed. Studies in the organization of conversational interaction.' *Journal of Pragmatics,* 1980, *4,* 401–411. (b)

Thibault, P. Style, sens, fonction. In N. Dittmar & B. Schlieben-Lange (Eds.), *La sociolinguistique dans les pays de langue Romane.* Tübingen, West Germany: Gunter Narr, 1982, pp. 73–80.

Toulmin, S. *The uses of argument.* Cambridge: Cambridge University Press, 1958.

Tyler, S. A. A formal science. In Tyler, S. A. (Ed.), *Concepts and assumptions in contemporary anthropology.* Athens, Ga.: University of Georgia Press, 1969, pp. 65–80.

von White, W. F. *Street corner society: The social structure of an Italian slum.* Chicagee: University of Chicage Press, 1943.

Wright, G. H. *Explanation and understanding.* Ithaca, New York: Cornell University Press, 1971.

Wittgenstein, L. *Philosophical investigations* (2nd ed., G. E. R. Anscombe, trans.). Oxford: Basil Blackwell, 1958.

14

Theoretical Prerequisites for a Contemporary Applied Linguistics

Tatiana Slama-Cazacu

The aim of this paper is to advance some theoretical prerequisites that I consider necessary for the development of a contemporary applied linguistics. I have defined applied linguistics as

> the collection or reelaboration, classification and systematization through specific research of linguistic facts and priciples of language functioning required by practical goals: i.e., discovering practical solutions in specific situations. (Slama-Cazacu, 1981, p. 18)

An applied linguistics should emphasize the *human* dimension of language: that language is a human phenomenon which occurs in concrete settings. An applied linguistics should answer practical questions whose solutions are implicit in the character of practical human goals. These specific goals have often been ignored because they conflict with dominant trends in linguistics (particularly those of the last three decades) and because the scope and objectives of contemporary applied linguistics have been widely misunderstood.

A contemporary applied linguistics must take into account the following: (a) the interrelationship between human reality and concrete reality, that is, the real setting in which language functions; (b) the importance of human psychology; psychology should be considered a unitary, complex, and organized whole, from which neither rational-intellectual nor affective-motivational components can be omitted; (c) the uniqueness of the human psyche, which cannot be separated from the reality in which it exists and in which it is essentially determined, that is, its sociohistorical context; (d) practical problems such as the improvement of language education together with the optimization of communication and related human activities involving language.

Tatiana Slama-Cazacu ● Laboratory of Psycholinguistics, University of Bucharest, Bucharest, Rumania.

The components of a contemporary applied linguistics are not artifically inferred from linguistic and psychological theories but are logically derived from the goals and processes necessary for *language use.*

Language is essentially human. It is intimately interwoven with the concrete conditions of practical life. This thesis, formulated as an indisputable truth, necessitates an analysis of its implications and logical consequences. These are:

1. The theoretical foundations of applied linguistics and the methodological corollaries derived from them should be elaborated within the context of language as a human phenomenon.

2. The psychological aspects of production and perception, including the practical conditions for language use and language acquisition, should be conceptualized within an integrated theoretical framework. Such a framework views the human being as unitary, active, and socially determined.

3. An adequate psycholinguistic approach should correspond to the real peculiarities of a human communication model, in which specific interaction occurs between language and human subject.

Applied linguistics emphasizes the selection, description, and specific elaboration of language facts for particular practical purposes. Psychology and psycholinguistics bring to applied linguistics possibilities of interpreting phenomena, furnishing explanations, and providing solutions (as linguistic facts and psychological idiosyncrasies are integrated in the moment of communication).

Principles of Linguistic Foundations in Applied Linguistics

In addition to collecting facts through its own methods, applied linguistics should use linguistic data for processing, interpretation, and transposition into metalanguage and proper linguistic theory. By *linguistic theory* I mean (a) a systematization and classification of linguistic components, (b) the corpus of knowledge on the history of different languages, and (c) the linguistic tools for comparative studies. The need for a linguistic theory is present whenever materials have to be elaborated, as in language teaching, translation, creating programs, constructing computer codes or models, and machine translation and automatic documentation, to name but a few.

The Need for an Adequate Linguistic Theory

It is obvious that there must be linguistic foundations for an applied linguistics. However, the essential question is whether any linguistic theory or classification system could be employed *tale quale,* irrespective of the methods used to acquire data.

At the moment, there is neither a single nor an ideal linguistic theory. For instance, I do not consider useful for applied linguistics those theories that rely on the concept of language as (a) detached from the contingencies of human reality, (b) an "autonomous entity" (Hjelmslev, 1959), or (c) connected with an "ideal speaker/listener" (Chomsky, 1965). Such theories, which analyze language outside its concrete determinations, its role in communication, and its social context, are of no value in applied linguistics.

Generally speaking, the classification criteria for the typical model of language found in traditional grammars or in modern linguistic theories have been established without due regard for accurate investigation of all the aspects of language-as-lived. Most linguistic theories have been elaborated without taking into account the concretization of language in the act of communication and especially in oral communication (which is the most frequent form of language use). Even when the sociogenesis of language is openly recognized, the logical consequences are rarely followed through (cf. Slama-Cazacu, 1959/1961).

In the fifties, linguistic theory was predominantly influenced by information theory and related attempts at formalizing an "objective," quantitative basis for linguistics. The meaning dimension was completely overlooked (with consequences persisting on into the seventies in transformational-generative analyses of syntax isolated from semantics). Writers of this persuasion conveniently ignored the role of interpretation as a function of context, bringing forth extremely negative consequences (e.g., the theory and practice of machine translation and applied computational linguistics). An exaggerated logicalness focused on constructed language instead of real language (which was considered to be "impure" because of its contact with the variability of human reality).

Early transformational-generative grammar advocated the separation of semantics and syntax. This separation contributed to a false rupture in relations between these two language levels, resulting in confusion and stagnation in various areas of applied linguistics. Even when attempts were made to reunite syntax and semantics while emphasizing the latter, new problems and questions emerged which have yet to be resolved. For example, if the dichotomy of competence/performance remains, contradictory but equally justified questions arise: Does semantics reflect what Chomsky calls "competence"? Or are pragmatic aspects of performance being introduced into formal description?

Most theories simply do not take into account the realities of applied linguistics and do not serve applied linguistics' goals, a point which can be illustrated by numerous examples of situations in which these theories or the data supplied by them neither were verified by practice nor produced results that were significant (cf. Nemser & Slama-Cazacu, 1970).

This brief overview leads us to the conclusion that, first, an applied linguistics requires language facts collected *ad hoc* for its specific concrete aims or careful selection of already existing facts within linguistic corpora. Second, current theories should undergo a judicious selection as a function of the practical goals of applied linguistics. Third, it becomes obvious that an applied linguistics should elaborate a general theory of its own, one that also allows for theoretical principles peculiar to each language or language-specific domain (cf. Berry, this volume).

Some Principles for a Linguistic Theory in Applied Linguistics

The specific theories of applied linguistics are yet to be elaborated. Thus, I have confined myself to the task of outlining the prerequisites to which they should comply. Particulars will be derived from these general theoretical principles.

Language as Concrete Phenomenon. Components of language may be considered as concrete phenomena which issue from particular life settings and general communication, reflecting specific psychological features and contents. Should applied linguistics maintain Saussure's distinction between the concept of language as an abstraction *(langue)* and language as *parole,* then it should operate at the level of *parole.* Organizations, regularities, and constants which were considered to be part of *langue* are found in *parole,* too. However, in this paper, I will use the term *language* (rather than *parole*) because the questions here are relevant to the original Saussurian concept of *langue,* and I also wish to stress the fact that linguists themselves must develop such a theory instead of leaving this task to other specialists, who would work with *parole.* Furthermore, any abstract model or *in abstracto* approach to language should be recognized as having a restricted value for an applied linguistics, as these approaches can only serve limited ends (e.g., machine translation and some computational linguistic applications).

Language as Dynamic. Language may be viewed as dynamic and thus in a process of continuous change (both at the lexical-semantic level and at the grammatical-phonematical level). Sounds undergo variations, and meaning is a flexible category subject to general dynamics. Meanings also undergo modifications in the individual's development as they are acquired. Stability should only be evaluated by reference to a given register or individual context. Unity within variety, constancy in relation to variation, diachrony within synchrony and vice versa are corollaries of this theoretical principle. These corollaries would play a fundamental role in applied linguistics.

Language as Totality/Whole. Language may be viewed as a total system or whole in which all of the components or levels are interdependent.[1] Hence, language has systematic or structural features with properties for organization from which rules are derived.[2] According to the second principle language as dynamic, there is continuous movement or dynamic structuring (Slama-Cazacu, 1959/1961).[3] For example, sounds do not occur *in abstracto* or as isolates, but as part of an ensemble (within the linguistic and social context).

Language as Manifestation of Various Forms. Language is a phenomenon which is manifested through various hypostases, or forms (written, oral, monologue, or dialogue). These forms must be recognized when models of language are constructed; any detailed linguistic theory should specify them because they have important consequences.

Language as One Aspect of Human Manifestations. Language is inextricably related to all the other manifestations of being human; hence, the necessity for psychological and psycholinguistic perspectives in applied linguistics. Attention should also focus on the sociogenetic relation between language and thought.

[1]This is one reason, among others, that Chomskian theories of a syntax isolated from semantics are not suitable for applied linguistics.

[2]The stress placed on rules in the analysis or teaching of language is not a logical consequence of the mentalistic transformational-generative linguistics exclusively (as maintained by Malmberg, 1971, p. 8); it can have also a structural origin.

[3]It is not enough to assert that meaning is taken into consideration; it is also necessary to emphasize the contextual effects at the semantic level, namely, that determinism is not of the linguistic context alone, but more of the broader social context.

Language and the Ensemble. Language may be viewed as a phenomenon in which the general principle of "determination through the ensemble" or "through the context" is manifest (Slama-Cazacu, 1956, 1959/1961). Language is influenced by linguistic, situational, and social contexts (see Figure 1). This principle is derived from the general rule of language functioning in communication, viz, the relation between coercion and freedom—social constraint or norms plus creativity or individual initiative. This relation, however, is limited by the first vector, which allows adaptation to the particular.

Language as Pluridimensional. Because language components are complex, pluridimensional phenomena, their essential characteristics are liable to be lost if we use a linear approach. The meaning of a word is a complex category which includes polysemy both at the levels of denotation and connotation. In language, the whole represents more than the sum of the component parts. This gestalt principle must, however, be integrated within a dynamic conception with a sociogenetic emphasis (Slama-Cazacu, 1959/1961; cf. Titone, this volume). The dystaxies (correlates of lexical polysemy) represent a strategy in language use that implies more than a supersegmental accumulation of intonation: it implies nonverbal elements and even cues alluding to the implicit context.

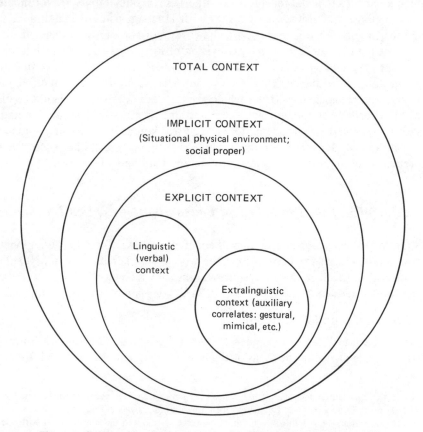

Figure 1. Contexual levels of communication (Slama-Cazacu, 1973a, p. 82).

Metalanguage of Linguistics as Reflection of Psychosocial Reality. Any systematization or naming (metalanguage) of language data is a reflection of a psychosocial reality—a reality which stems from a particular practical circumstance (register or style related to a given social stratification or social setting or to a given activity). Therefore, there can be no single description of a language—there cannot even be a single norm, established either *in abstracto* (without specifying its derivation from the language used by a certain social stratum) or as a function of a certain context.

Present-Day Metalanguage of Linguistics. From what I have said above, the need arises to consider the metalanguage of linguisics as a working tool which cannot be arbitrarily established. It must express real units which reflect the "chunking" *(découpage)* of the continuum that corresponds to the experience and mental elaborations of a member of a given sociolinguistic community. Linguistics cannot be identified with mathematics. Mathematical models can ignore a psychological reality whereas linguistic models cannot. Language is strictly a human phenomen and, thus, preeminently psychological. The artificial imposition of mathematical symbols on psychological reality leads to constructs of limited practical utility. "Metalinguistic units" (Slama-Cazacu, 1972b) must correspond to psychological units in order for applied linguistics to avoid this problem; otherwise, artificial units are formulated as a metalanguage which does not overlap with language-as-lived. Such a metalanguage for language-as-it-is-in-reality is, however, not yet known in linguistics.

Consequently, the *découpage* or division of any linguistic system into various units must take into account the psychological modalities of processing and storing language facts in a manner that avoids the discrepancy between (meta)linguistic units and psychological ones (from which they actually derive and should be discovered). The terminology identifying them and aiding in their classification and systematization should also be adequate for each real language.[4] Imposing a nomenclature that is not derived from the reality of language itself is of no relevance theoretically, in linguistics, or practically, in applied linguistics.

Principles of the Psychological Foundations of Applied Linguistics

Given that language is a human phenomenon, it is natural that an applied linguistics acknowledge the person, together with his or her particular psychological characteristics. In effect, this necessitates taking into account psychological data, and all the results derived from that data, within the domain of applied linguistics.

Linguistics and Psychology

Malmberg (1971, p. 6) exaggerated when he said that "twentieth century linguistics . . . has placed in the focus of the linguist's interest, the role and functioning

---

[4]Slama-Cazacu and Dutescu-Coliban, 1980. It has been noticed, for instance, that the terminology used for classifying the errors made in English by Rumanian speakers was not adequate because it had in view exclusively the syntax-dominated English linguistic system and did not fit either with the categories or the morphologically oriented base language (Rumanian) or with the metalanguage known from school years by Rumanian students.

of language as a mechanism of human communication." His affirmation accords with only one part of linguistics. However, it is true that after diverse attempts at collaboration between psychology and linguistics (often marked by distrust and labeled "psychologism," cf. Slama-Cazacu, 1968/1973a, 1972a) structural linguists (especially in the Linguistic Circle of Prague, largely due to the influence of Jakobson and Bühler, 1934) began to underline the necessity of studying language *functioning* (cf. Prucha, this volume).

On the other hand, the principal linguistic trends (especially the transformational-generative grammar of the 50s and 60s) were actually moving away from the functional aspects of language in theory and methodology. Blind trust in these linguistic theories led to nothing but frustration for those who attempted to adopt these elaborations in applied linguistics. It was more than a decade before it was generally understood that no modern linguistic theory was adequate for applied linguistics and that linguistics alone is not sufficient. As strange as it may seem, the idea of a positive relationship between linguistics and psychology was not sufficiently clear even to those who discussed this parallel. Much time was wasted before it was recognized that linguistics alone is insufficient for applied linguistics.

It was necessary to stress the link between linguistics and psychology[5] until the connection was clearly understood. It was not sufficient simply to proclaim the connection, since the claim itself was no guarantee of immediate conformity to the principles of scientific psychology. An adequate model of psychology for applied linguistics requires the concept of human being as concrete individual, living in a social context. In addition, numerous fundamental problems demand clarification, not only in the areas of language learning and language teaching, but also in other areas of applied linguistics where psychological processes occur. Hence, no solutions to the problems of applied linguistics can be found without an adquate psychological perspective. Placing the human being—the user and learner of language—as the predominant concern for applied linguistics necessitates the appeal to psychology.

Early attempts to establish the connection between applied linguistics and psychology were sporadic. These attempts were usually inspired by behaviorism or were tied to a traditional psychology of language behavior (even when the new term *psycholinguistics* appeared in the title; cf. for example, the bibliography in Rivers, 1964). The majority of these cases referred exclusively to the teaching of language.

Official recognition of these ideas developed gradually and materialized almost timidly. One particular instance was the invitation of psychologists and psycholinguists to the first international meeting of applied linguistics (1964). The inclusion of sections on the psychology of language and the subsequent promotion of psycholinguistics through the creation of the International Commission on Psycholinguistics in the Association Internationale de Linguistique Appliquée (AILA) confirmed this recognition.

A clear reflection of the official position of psychology/psycholinguistics among

---

[5]Chomsky manifested a special and contradictory interest in psychology and psycholinguistics (utilizing concepts which apply to these domains and even calling linguistics a branch of cognitive psychology). Yet the ensemble of his theory, his methodology, the sense given to diverse concepts (e.g., competence/performance and the concept of the ideal speaker/listener) at the base of his conceptions contradict psychology as a modern science.

specialists in applied linguistics was evidenced in the orientation of the plenary report at the third congress of the AILA (1972) by Corder. Corder and others again affirmed at the fourth congress that the learner should be central. Slama-Cazacu (1978) summarized the events of these congresses by noting the tacit consensus that psychology was a necessity for applied linguistics. It also became apparent that an appropriate psychology should be made available to applied linguistics.

Delineating General Principles of Psychology for Applied Linguistics

In modern scientific psychology, the psyche is not referred to in general or abstract terms, the psyche evolves into a structural organization (the person) in a certain state, at a certain moment, profoundly determined by the social context. In keeping with this approach, the following psychological principles can contribute to resolving diverse and detailed aspects of applied linguistics (see Slama-Cazacu, 1968/1973a).

Human as Concrete. Humans are determined by reality, in contrast to that ideal abstract entity or artificial construct of some trends in traditional psychological theory.

Human as Totality. The whole human being, including his or her consciousness and thought, participates in all communication. The study of this totality cannot but assist applied linguistics in resolving its diverse practical problems. Scientific psychology does not accept the hypertrophy of one aspect (e.g., the unconscious) of human reality as acceptable normal datum. Language and communication cannot be separated from the totality of the language user.

Interrelationships. There are interrelationships between social determinism, on the one hand, and psychological and physiological processes on the other (as in the functioning of the cerebral cortex, the articulatory organs, and the auditory system). For example, it is not possible to resolve the problem of strenuous simultaneous translation by isolating the knowledge of a foreign language from the functioning of the individual's perception capacity, short term memory, attention, and emotions and the general tonus of the central nervous system.

Sociogenesis. Social determinism plays an important role in the development and activity of the psyche. The human context is a social context in which each individual influences the others and is influenced by them. In this process, thought and language are developed as the individual adapts to the demands of communication and assumes the transmission of knowledge within society.

Dynamism. The human being is a dynamic, active being in the process of continual transformation. This process confers extraordinary flexibility and plasticity, permitting reflection and voluntary action on the self, others, and the natural environment.

Need for Scientific Methodology and Terminology. Scientific methodology in psychology is based on facts rather than sterile speculation. Generalizations must be founded on collected data (especially through observation and experiments) which are enhanced by experimental techniques (such as tape recordings, eliciting reactions, etc.) and mathematical data analyses. A psychological terminology must also be sought which corresponds to the principles outlined above and which aims, primarily, at a proper and adequate definition of the contents of older psychological terms.

In summary, these six principles characterize a *humanistic integrative psychology* (see Slama-Cazacu, 1959/1961, 1968/1973a) emphasizing the complex reality of the human psyche (which is a socialized structure dominated by consciousness).

In light of these principles, behavioristic and neobehavioristic mechanistic psychology (which cannot explain the complexity of specifically human processes), as well as the individualistic or egocentric conceptions (where biogenesis dominates to the exclusion of sociogenesis), is not useful for applied linguistics. It is useless in language teaching to introduce a "psychology of learning" into a "teaching model of language" (Nehls, 1975, p. 75) as long as this learning model is not adequate for the task.

Another area of concern in the relationship between applied linguistics and psychology is the psychologist's attitude toward applied linguistics. Although the potential contribution psychology has to offer applied linguistics is acknowledged today, psychological research specifically devoted to this area is scarce. A similar situation exists in psycholinguistics. Often experiments have been conducted within artificial or contrived settings that do not correspond to the complex situations that applied linguistics serves, such as language teaching in the classroom.

Generally speaking, applied linguistics specialists, lacking interdisciplinary training, have not always been sufficiently competent to demand the necessary psychological research. This problem has been compounded by psychologists who did not always focus on the practical aspects of language in natural or concrete social settings, that is, language *as it is* in reality.

If problems confronting applied linguistics are to find their resolution in psychology, then an adequate conceptual framework of the human psyche is the only effective psychology for applied linguistics. The data, methods, and explanations in applied linguistics depend on the general psychological model or theory.

Psycholinguistics and Applied Linguistics: Which Psycholinguistics?

The contributions of psychology and psycholinguistics to applied linguistics may be viewed as a relationship between the general and the particular. Applied linguistics should include general psychological principles of learning, perception, and so on, considered as human psychological events. These principles are not assumed *tale quale*, but in applying them it becomes obvious that they are psycholinguistic realities. They illustrate the link between individuals and the real concrete phenomenon called language. Thus the integration of linguistics and psychological theories suitable for contemporay applied linguistics is attained by the psycholinguistic approach. Psycholinguistics can offer the required psychological data directly processed and adapted to the specific goals of applied linguistics. Hence, *inter alia,* the usefulness of psycholinguistics for applied linguistics is established.

The Need for an Efficient Theory in Psycholinguistics

In applied linguistics literature, the distinction between psychology and psycholinguistics is not always made explicit. We might say that the contribution of psychology has been gradually replaced by that of psycholinguistics or that the very development of psycholinguistics in the last two decades is evidence of the efficiency of the psycholinguistic orientation for applied linguistics (cf. Nemser & Slama-Cazacu, 1970). The name *psychoinguistics* was more frequently mentioned and understood as auxiliary to applied linguistics (cf. Rosenberg & Koplin, 1968).

The usefulness or necessity of a collaboration between psycholinguistics and applied linguistics is generally accepted. However, the use of psycholinguistics in applied linguistics presupposes a well-defined attitude on the part of the users. Several essential ideas call for clarification: (1) Because there is no single psycholinguistics, the adoption of an approach should be accompanied by knowledge of the specific underlying theory. (2) The applied linguistics user should state clearly those requirements to be met by psycholinguistic theory. (3) The title psycholinguistics does not guarantee applicability to applied linguistics. Similarly, studies that are not labeled psycholinguistics may be useful to applied linguistics. (4) It is not possible to resolve applied linguistics problems by resorting to a realistic psycholinguistics for one phenomenon and, for another phenomenon, to abstract phenomena and artificial psycholinguistic theories which ignore the social impact or the language-as-lived perspective.

These various aspects must be integrated into a functioning whole or general system of psycholinguistic interpretation. Because they are interdependent, all solutions offered by psycholinguistics will be connected with solutions to other problems. Reciprocal references (not necessarily through analogy) are essential in addressing the need for a coherent integration of psycholinguistics and applied linguistics.

From the outset, one must clarify (1) what an applied linguistics requires from psycholinguistics and, consequently, (2) why some psycholinguistic trends cannot be of use to applied linguistics.

Criticism of Some Psycholinguistic Theories

A psycholinguistic theory includes a set of problems and a corpus of interpretations, but unless it copes with the concrete reality of life and people involved in social relations it is not useful in practice. Similarly, a theory cannot be useful if human beings are not viewed as active, creative, and transforming. Theories that imply rigid mechanisms in which reactions would be viewed as those of programmed organisms inexorably predetermined by biological templates or that suggest a functional pattern in which data offered by social life would be inserted and molded are of no value (see the nativistic psycholinguistic assumption in transformational-generative grammar).

Theories that do not locate language (in the sense of the French term *langage,* i.e., the ensemble of psychological processes involved in language functioning) in the social context are useless to applied linguistics. A similar judgment is conferred on theories that ignore the reality of communication or human beings as integrated in a social context: such theories are in disagreement with the aims of applied linguistics. However, these negative traits figure in two significant trends in psycholinguistics that originated in America (and have influenced psycholinguistics on other continents): the behavioristic psycholinguistics and the psycholinguistics based on transformational-generative linguistics. Obviously, if applied linguistics is to avoid failures, it must establish fundamental criteria and confront psycholinguistic theory and methodology with the reality within which applied linguistics must operate.

Psycholinguistics is not a single trend or school of thought but a field. It should develop further as an autonomous entity, not as a branch of psychology or a branch of linguistics. Psycholinguistics is a tributary of different trends in the basic sciences; however, older psychological concepts have infiltrated modern trends in applied linguistics and have been falsely identified as recent developments in psycholinguistics.

Two important trends in psycholinguistics no longer in vogue are the behavioristic and transformational-generative approaches. A third trend is gaining ground—the contextual-dynamic approach (which will be discussed below).

American psycholinguistics was born early in the fifties. Its foundations were in behavioristic psychology and thus it was almost synonymous with behavioristic learning theory. This mechanistic outlook, which also permeates neobehaviorism, was unable to explain the richness of rational, conscious, integrative facts and context related language and communication; however, it did contribute to broadcasting American psycholinguistics. Interestingly, the first definition of psycholinguistics remains basically valuable. Unfortunately, the assimilation of psycholinguistics into behaviorism generated its initial attack by nonbehaviorists. Early adoption of psycholinguistic trends into applied linguistics was usually confined to the audio-lingual method of foreign language teaching, which involved repetition of pattern drills and memorizing dialogues which lead to a mechanical acquisition that was fraught with problems. It was a time-wasting and absurd attempt to store a language repertoire which was either reduced or else too large to be learned as such.

The second trend, transformational-generative grammar in American psycholinguistics, which also extended to other continents, came as a reaction to behavioristic psycholinguistics. It exerted a lesser influence on applied linguistics, because it did not focus initially on practical aspects and also because it was more difficult to assimilate; thus, teachers of foreign languages were left more or less to their own devices. A psycholinguistics which resorted to a linguistics that analyzed the utterance outside communication and social context and that developed a theory and methodology based on the ideal speaker/listener with inherited capacities was inherently contradictory to the very objectives of applied linguistics. Neither experimental evidence nor classroom reality appeared to validate the hypotheses of transformational-generative linguistics.

These early trends in psycholinguistics severed unconfessed distinctions between psychological and linguistic foundations. They led, on the one hand, to the prevailing influence of transformational-generative grammar and rejection of the behavioristic psychological foundation of psycholinguistics and, on the other hand, to the gradual restriction of transformational-generative grammar to psychology. The result took the shape of a transformational-generative antibehavioristic theory.

Without a comprehensive awareness of the development of psycholinguistics in other countries, Carroll (1971), after asserting that the "first generation" of psycholinguistics was behavioristic psycholinguistics—which was true in America—and that the "second generation" was the transformational-generative-biased psycholinguistics, forecast the advent of a "third generation." The third generation would resume the problems raised by the first generation, which would result in a "creative renaissance" of the "learning theory" approach and, consequently, a "triumphant" behaviorism in psycholinguistics.

My Views of Psycholinguistics: Contextual-Dynamic Psycholinguistics

Actually, the third generation is recognized by some authors (e.g., Titone, 1975, 1977) as the cognitivist psycholinguistics. However, others follow the line expressed here. This line—contexual-dynamic psycholinguistics—meets with some outlooks and results generated in language teaching (Prucha, 1972; Titone, 1975), social psychology, and, more recently, American sociolinguistics. It differs from transformational-generative, behavioristic, and cognitivistic psycholinguistics in that it has a unitary and consistent character and has not overlooked underlying aspects that the others have.

Contextual-dynamic psycholinguistics has been broadly defined for almost thirty years (see Slama-Cazacu, 1959/1961, *et passim*). It has a clear-cut and consistent outline, has been tested through practical applications, and can be supported today as a theory which meets contemporary trends in applied linguistics. The theory is called a *contextual-dynamic* psycholinguistics to distinguish it from other trends. A summary of its basic principles follows.

This psycholinguistic model postulates that the essential point in the definition of the human use of language is communication. A relationship is established between one or several emitters (E) and one or several receivers (R): a *social relationship*. Communication includes the *context* (or situation, broadly speaking), the *partners,* the *information* they encode/decode, the *message* which carries the latter, and the *code* used to construct the message. Communication is influenced by three factors: its function, the existence of relationships, and its social nature. The fundamental form in which language occurs is a dialogue or bilateral communication. (This relationship is reversible; see the double arrows in Figure 2).

Oral communication is the most frequent form of communication; thus, the Es and the Rs are usually both present. This social situation has important consequences on the form of the message as well as its reception. The form of the message can consist of mixed elements, both verbal and nonverbal. (Refer to the concept of *mixed syntax,* Slama-Cazacu, 1968/1973a, 1976, 1977.) The message can be received by the auditive and visual channels simultaneously.

In this model, communication cannot be detached from the context in which emission and reception occur. In every act of communication there is always a context. This context consists of various inseparable levels: (1) the linguistic whole in

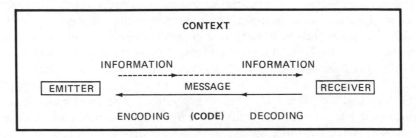

Figure 2. The act of communication (Slama-Cazacu, 1973a, p. 52).

which a word finds its true meaning; (2) the extralinguistic context (1 and 2 together form the *explicit context*); (3) the setting itself, (4) the psychological state of Es and Rs, and (5) the social context (3, 4, and 5 form the implicit context). The social context includes the relationship between the partners, the code itself, and the special social community (Slama-Cazacu 1970). Examples of the special social communities include the microgroup, the social ambiance of the moment of communication, the professional community, and the general social milieu.

Special features of this model are: (1) the link between the partners, (2) their integration within the contexts that determine them, (3) the relation of any message with the interlocutors, and with the contexts. These relationships are reflected by one of the most important processes occurring during communication: the adaption to the partner. This is part of the general law of "adaptation to the context" (Slama-Cazacu, 1956). E organizes the message by using explicit cues or alluding to what is supposed to be known by R. Thus, E organizes the message expecting a correct and complete decoding by R. R interprets communication acts and their results by reference to various contextual levels, including the presupposed, or implicit, context. The dynamic-contextual model considers both the dynamic aspects of the act of communication and its contextual features (Slama-Cazacu, 1972–1973, 1968/1973a, 1973b).

The methodological goal of this psycholinguistic theory is to detect structurings together with their characteristics of organization. Thus, messages are seen as sequences, and learning as a dynamic process consisting of steps (the gradual acquisition of elements influencing each other). One must be able to see diachrony even in a section operated in synchrony. A second goal is the detection of all the aspects (such as gestures, etc.) that are to be found in any concrete act of communication and the detection of all the reciprocal influences in the succession of contextual levels including each other.

These aspects cannot be ignored by any science or field that deals with the act of communication, the functioning of language, learning repertoires, and strategies of social adaptation to the various contextual aspects and levels.

Language teaching is influenced by social contexts; thus, teaching within the social context is a requirement directly derived from this model. This model provides a scientific foundation and concrete aids for the elaboration of teaching materials in applied linguistics settings.

References

Bühler, K. *Sprachtheorie*. Leipzig: Fischer, 1934.

Carroll, J. B. *The American heritage word frequency book*. Boston: Houghton Mifflin, 1971.

Chomsky, N. *Aspects of the theory of syntax*. Cambridge, Mass.: MIT Press, 1965.

Corder, S. P. *Problems and solutions in applied linguistics*. Presidential address presented at the third congress of the Association Internationale de Linguistique Appliquée, Copenhagen, 1972.

Hjelmslev, L. *Essais linguistiques*. Copenhagen: Nordisk Sprog-og Kulturforlag, 1959.

Jakobson, R. *Essais de linguistique générale* (2 vols.). Paris: Editions de Minuit, 1963, 1973.

Malmberg, B. The applications of linguistics. In G. Perren & J. Trim (Eds.), *Applications of linguistics*. Cambridge: Cambridge University Press, 1971.

Nehls, D. Überlegungen zum Aufbau eines Didaktischen Sprachmodels für dem Fremdsprachen Unterrichts. *International Review of Applied Linguistics*, 1975, *13*, 51–68.

Nemser, W., & Slama-Cazacu, T. A contribution to contrastive linguistics (A psycholinguistic approach: Contact analysis). *Revue Roumaine de Linguistique*, 1970, *15*(2), 101–128.

Prucha, J. Verbal communication in the classroom. *International Journal of Psycholinguistics*, 1972, *1*(2), 23–38.

Rivers, W. *The psychologist and the foreign language teacher*. Chicago: University of Chicago Press, 1964.

Rosenberg, S., & Koplin, J. (Eds.). *Developments in applied psycholinguistics research*. New York–London: Collier–Macmillan, 1968.

Slama-Cazacu, T. Principe de l'adaptation au contexte. *Revue Roumaine de Linguistique*, 1956, *1*, 79–118.

Slama-Cazacu, T. *Langage et contexte: Le problème du langage dans la conception de l'expression et de l'interprétation par des organizations contextuelles*. The Hague: Mouton, 1961. (Originally published in Rumanian, 1959.)

Slama-Cazacu, T. The power and limits of social context of language behaviour. *Cahiers de Linguistique Théorique et Appliquée*, 1970, *7*, 31–41.

Slama-Cazacu, T. *La psycholinguistique: Lectures*. Paris: Klincksieck, 1972. (a)

Slama-Cazacu, T. Sur les rapports entre unité psychologique et unités linguistiques au niveau phonétique. *Cahiers de Linguistique Théorique et Appliquée*, 1972, *9*, 1–13. (b)

Slama-Cazacu, T. Sur le concept 'socio-psycholinguistique.' *Bulletin de Psychologie* (Special issue: *Psycholinguistique*), 1972–1973, *26*, 246–251.

Slama-Cazacu, T. *Introduction to psycholinguistics*. The Hague: Mouton, 1973. (Originally published in Rumanian, 1968.) (a)

Slama-Cazacu, T. Is a 'socio-psycholinguistics' necessary? *International Journal of Psycholinguistics*, 1973, *1*(2), 93–104. (b)

Slama-Cazacu, T. Nonverbal components in message sequence. The "mixed syntax." In W. McCormack & S. Wurm (Eds.), *Language and man*. The Hague: Mouton, 1976.

Slama-Cazacu, T. Le concept de 'syntaxe mixte': Recherchers autour d'une hypothèse. *Etudes de Lingusitique Appliquée*, 1977, *27*, 114–123.

Slama-Cazacu, T. 'Hidden psycholinguistics,' or 'The purloined letter and psycholinguistics (Chronicle). *International Journal of Psycholinguistics*, 1978, *5*(3), 75–82.

Slama-Cazacu, T. Sur l'object de la linguistique appliquée. *Revue Roumaine de Linguisitique*, 1981, *18*(1), 5–20.

Slama-Cazacu, T., & Dutescu-Coliban, T. The first hierarchical system of errors in the acquisition of English by native speakers of Romanian. In R. Grotjahn & E. Hopkins (Eds.), *Empirical research on language teaching and language acquisition*. Bochum, West Germany: Brockmeyer, 1980.

Titone, R. *The glossodynamic model: A humanistic approach to language behaviour and language learning*. Paper presented at the fourth congress of the Association Internationale de Linguistique Appliquée, Copenhagen, 1975.

Titone, R. *Il linguaggio nella interazione didattica*. Rome: Bulzoni, 1977.

Select Bibliography

Editor's Note. Because Professor Slama-Cazacu's works deserve to be more widely known outside of Rumania and a circle of dedicated admirers, I have included a short, select bibliography of some of her writings other than those included among her references.

Slama-Cazacu, T. *Communicarea in procesul muncii*. Bucharest: Ed. Stiintifica, 1964.

Slama-Cazacu, T. Problèmes psycholinguistiques posés par les messages verbaux employés dans l'automation. *Revue Roumaine de Linguistique*, 1964, *9*(2), 119–130.

Slama-Cazacu, T. La méthodologie psycholinguistique et quelques-unes de ses applications. *Revue Roumaine de Linguistique*, 1965, *10*, 309–316.

Slama-Cazacu, T. La linguistique appliquée et quelques problèmes psycholinguistiques de l'enseignement des langues. *Cahiers de Linguistique Théorique et Appliquée,* 1968, *5,* 221–246.

Slama-Cazacu, T. Psycholinguistics and contrastive studies. In *Zagreb Conference on English contrastive projects (1970).* Zagreb: Institute of Linguistics, 1971, pp. 188–225.

Slama-Cazacu, T. L'approche psycholinguistique est-elle necessaire pour l'enseignement des langues?
Contact, 1971, *17,* 17–29.

Slama-Cazacu, T. Un problème actuel de l'enseignement des langues et l'approche psycholinugistique:
La rencontre des deux systèmes. In *Proceedings of the XVIIIth International Congress of Applied
Psychology (1971).* Brussels: Editest, 1971.

Slama-Cazacu, T. La régularisation: L'un des universaux de l'acquisition de la langue. *Cahiers de Linguistique Théorique et Appliquée,* 1973, *1,* 63–69.

Slama-Cazacu, T. Aspectos convergentes (y divergencias fortuitas) de la sicolinguistica y de la sociolinguistica. In O. Uribe Villegas (Ed.), *La sociolinguistica actual.* Mexico: UNAM, 1974.

Slama-Cazacu, T. Topicality of psycholinguistics. *International Journal of Psycholinguistics,* 1975, *2,*
67–81.

Slama-Cazacu, T. Applied psycholinguistics: Its object and goals. In G. Nickel (Ed.), *Proceedings of
the IVth International Congress of Applied Linguistics* (Vol. 1). Stuttgart: Hochschulverlag, 1975.

Slama-Cazacu, T. (Ed.). *The psycholinguistic approach in the Romanian–English Contrastive Analysis Project.* Bucharest: University Press, 1975.

Slama-Cazacu, T. Psycholinguistics and applied linguistics. *International Journal of Psycholinguistics,*
1976, *3,* 79–94.

Slama-Cazacu, T. The role of social context in language acquisition. In W. McCormack & S. Wurm
(Eds.), *Language and man.* The Hague: Mouton, 1976.

Slama-Cazacu, T. *The dialogue in children.* The Hague: Mouton, 1977. (Originally published in Rumanian, 1961.)

Slama-Cazacu, T. Le concept de 'syntaxe mixte': Recherches autour d'une hypothèse. *Etudes de Linguistique Appliquée,* 1977, *27,* 114–123.

Slama-Cazacu, T. Psycholinguistique. In *Grand Larousse de la langue française* (Vol. 7). Paris: Larousse, 1978.

Slama-Cazacu, T. Psycholinguistics (in Romania). In A. Rosetti & G. Golopentia-Eretescu (Eds.),
Trends in Romanian linguistics. Bucharest: Editura Academiei, 1978.

Slama-Cazacu, T. *Psicolinguistica aplicada ao ensino de linguas.* Sao Paulo: Pioneira, 1979

Slama-Cazacu, T. The place of applied linguistics in the system of sciences. Applied linguistics in relation to 'linguistics.' *Revue Roumaine de Linguistique,* 1980, *25,* 153–160. (Originally published in
Rumanian, 1978.)

Slama-Cazacu, T. *The dialogue in children.* The Hague: Mouton, 1976. (Originally published in
Rumanian, 1961.)

Slama-Cazacu, T. Psycholinguistique. In *Grand Larousse de la langue française* (Vol. 7). Paris: Larousse, 1978.

Slama-Cazacu, T. Psycholinguistics (in Romania). In A. Rosetti & G. Golopentia-Eretescu (Eds.),
Trends in Romanian linguistics. Bucharest: Editura Academiei, 1978.

Slama-Cazacu, T. *Psicolinguistica aplicada ao ensino de linguas.* Sao Paulo: Pioneira, 1979.

Slama-Cazacu, T. The place of applied linguistics in the system of sciences. Applied linguistics in relation to 'linguistics.' *Revue Roumaine de Linguistique,* 1980, *25,* 153–160. (Originally published in
Romanian, 1978.)

Slama-Cazacu, T. Circular relation between fundamental an applied research in linguistics. *Cahiers de
Linguistique Théorique et Appliquée,* 1980, *17,* 2–7. (Originally published in Rumanian, 1977).

15

Second Language Learning: An Integrated Psycholinguistic Model

Renzo Titone

Slow but steady progress has been made in the last few years in the attempt to clarify some basic modalities and factors specific to second language learning. Theory and research have undergone deep cross-fertilization, with the result that students of the problem have begun to see through a few important aspects of the process of learning a second language as consecutive to the acquisition of the first language. While research steadily and strenuously blazes new trails, theories come and go as has been wont to happen in the brave new world of psycholinguistics.

The chief objective of this paper cannot consist of a review of the multifarious and floating proposals of both recent research and theory; such a task would demand hundreds of pages. I aim solely to sketch out what I consider to be the essential point at issue: namely, the path to a comprehensive or integrated theory of second language learning. Such a theory is viewed in terms of a holistic model of language behavior and language learning, capable of broad transfer potentialities. And, it must be noted, unbiased theoretical speculation as well as psycholinguistic investigation are involved.

A Holistic Model of Language Behavior and Language Learning

Mechanistic and Cognitive Models of Language Behavior

The quick passing away of five—to my reckoning—generations of psycholinguistics is indicative of a deep-seated state of dissatisfaction on the part of most students concerned with the psychological problems of language, However, this succession of varied theories during such a short period of time (1954–1980) has at the same time been characterized by a constant flow of progress: ever closer approximation to a realistic and comprehensive concept of language.

Renzo Titone ● Department of Psychology, University of Rome, 00185 Rome, Italy.

Briefly, the stages of this theoretical evolution are:

- *Stage 1.* The wedding of a structural-taxonomic concept of language with a behavioristic-empiricistic view of verbal behavior (Bloomfield/Skinner)
- *Stage 2.* A rationalistic generative-transformational explanation of language combined with a cognitive (mentalistic) interpretation of human behavior (Chomsky/Miller)
- *Stage 3.* A generative-semantic reinterpretation of language processing branching out into anthropological and pragmatic connotations of communicative behavior ("communicative competence") (post-Chomskians–Chafe/ Hymes)
- *Stage 4.* The social (sociocentric) contextualization of language and the social functions of linguistic messages (Leontyev/Slama-Cazacu/Rommetveit/ Halliday)
- *Stage 5.* The attempt to recapture the total personality (behavioral, cognitive, affective, ego-dynamic dimensions) of the speaker/hearer in communicating and learning to communicate (Titone 1970, 1981; cf. John Steiner & Tatter; Dittmar, this volume)

The five stages are placed in a progressive order of theoretical development, based on the successive "falsification" (Popper, 1959) of inadequate hypotheses.

Mechanistic and cognitive models have held key positions in this scientific warfare, but they are far from being the final winners. Stages 4 and 5 are acquiring momentum.

A Personological View of Language and Speech

The solution that I wish to submit to earnest examination is the development of a synthetic approach to language learning, the *holodynamic model.*

The starting point of the holodynamic model of language learning is the recognition that language behavior, far from being a linear series of one-level operations, is basically a *stratificational and hierarchical system of dynamic structures.* Such a unified multiplicity implies the simultaneous and overlapping involvement of very different operational levels. I believe that language behavior is a very important specification of *personality dynamics* viewed in concrete contextual organization,[1] and, as such, it cannot be reduced to a mere system of verbal habits (Bloomfield) or even to a system of cognitive processes (Chomsky). Such a reduction would be tantamount to admitting the possibility of speaking without a speaker or of hearing without a hearer, in other words, acts of communication which lack a pertinent and competent Actor. Therefore, language behavior, like all behavior, postulates an adequate concept of personality as the ultimate root and source of incoming and outgoing processes. A comprehensive view of personality structure does not do away with but rather implies the intra-action and inter-action of cognitions and habits.

---

[1] I am in full accord with Slama-Cazacu's thesis about the importance of totality in language events (1961, pp. 10, 15, 43).

This integrated view of language behavior and learning includes the coexistence and cooperation of three distinct levels, namely:

1. Personality structure and dynamics in a contextual perspective
2. Cognitive processes
3. Operant conditionings

These three variables are in essence mutually dependent and integrated on a dynamic level (which means that integration is not a state but a continuous process, a dynamic equilibrium, never entirely achieved, as is typically evident in the case of individual bilingualism). The assembling of three different levels does not entail a mere juxtaposition of three theories; rather, all three levels are the essential constituents of one unified theory of language behavior and language learning.

At this point I should make it clear that the holodynamic model is consistently grafted on a humanistic approach to psycholinguistics. Just to recall some of the characteristic features of humanistic psychology as related to language, I quote from Floyd W. Matson (1971, p. 9):

> This recognition of *man-in-person*, as opposed to *man-in-general*, goes to the heart of the difference between humanistic psychology, in any of its forms or schools, and scientific psychologies such as behaviorism. . . . This emphasis upon the human person, upon the individual in his wholeness and uniqueness, is a central feature of the "psychology of humanism."

But there is an important corollary without which this personalistic emphasis would be inadequate and distorted. That corollary is the recognition, to use Rank's (1936) phrase, that "the self needs the other."

The names of the spokesmen of psychological humanism are well known: Martin Buber and his philosophy of dialogue, Ludwig Binswanger's, Viktor Frankl's, and Rollo May's existential psychology, Abraham Maslow, Gordon Allport, Carl Rogers, Erich Fromm, Henry A. Murray, Joseph Nuttin, and others.

Personality is the cornerstone of this psychological outlook. Personality as defined by Allport (1965), among others, is "the dynamic organization within the individual of those psychophysical systems that determine his characteristic behavior and thought" (p. 28). And further, "the individuality of man, the future-pointed thrust of his living, and the systematic interlacing of his key qualities, are the central features of his personality" (p. 21).

But personality is not reducible to mere individuality. Personality is an *open* system, that is, a *relational* system. For this emphasis on the relational nature of human personality I am especially indebted to the Belgian psychologist Nuttin for his idea of the structure of personality (Nuttin, 1953, 1968). The relational theory of personality starts from the assumption that the human being is not only internally structured but necessarily related externally, namely, ordered in accordance with, and dependent on, the world (physical, social, cultural). "Personality," wrote Nuttin,

> is a mode of functioning involving essentially two poles: the *Ego* and the *World*. The Ego is the total of the individual's functions and psychological potentialities; the World is the intrinsic object of the Ego. Indeed psychological function-

ing—i.e., perception and behavior in general, including motivation—necessarily implies an object as the intrinsic reference point of the process itself. This functioning, therefore, cannot but locate itself within a structure implying an intrinsic and active reference of the Ego to a World of objects. This world of people and objects is not only situated *in front of* the Ego but constitutes the very *content* of personalized psychological life. This amounts to saying that, from a functional point of view, a personality cannot exist but within the framework of a structure transcending the physical-psychological organism, in other terms, within an *Ego-World structure.* (1968, pp. 205–206)

Personality is then conceived as an *open system* in Bertalanffy's sense (1950). In this perspective, the process of communication takes on a new meaning and significance: verbal behavior is first of all the fundamental expression of the individual and social personality of each human being.

This idea is the deepest core and the very source of *language as communication and expression.* Human communication is the very marrow of personality, and language as a species-specific power (the *Sprachfähigkeit* mentioned by von Humboldt) is essentially and operationally connected with *human* personality.

The holodynamic model of language behavior is but a logical application and development of a humanistic assumption about man and his relation to the world through language. It implies, furthermore, that first language acquisition and second language learning each represent a particular mode of existence, a definite way of self-assertion in front of the world, a symbolic act of recognition of the Existent. This principle denies radically the possibility of language learning as mere rote (robot) learning; it involves, on the contrary, conscious and motivated action through the whole of the process of acquisition.

I will now discuss the basic constituent structures of language behavior according to the holodynamic model.

The Deep Structure of Language Behavior

Communicating and the ability to communicate verbally are surface aspects rooted in profound layers of the individual's personality. The verified existence of such layers disproves the validity of the Chomskian dichotomy of competence and performance.[2] In other words, it is necessary to postulate a hierarchical structure of operational levels in human behavior and learning in order to account for all types and tokens of language events.[3]

---

[2]Chomsky (1965, p. 3 and *passim*). The Chomskian dichotomy shows numerous faults among which are (1) a sterilely abstract and generic view of language devoid of its physical, psychological, social, and cultural constraints and correlates and of its evolutionary features; (2) an overrationalistic concept of language which ignores its motivational, imaginational, and emotional functions (a theory of language as a code, not of speech as behavior); (3) an undue reduction of linguistic and psycholinguistic study to the analysis of competence as heterogeneous to performance; (4) an unjustified reduction of linguistic competence to the sphere of grammar to the oblivion of semantic processes as intrinsic to verbal symbolization (cf. Chafe, 1970); (5) ignorance of the complex hierarchical articulation of the processes intrinsic to competence, the latter to be seen as linguistic "strategy."

[3]The present model should not be confused with the "cybernetic model," which shows a seeming resemblance to mine as laid down in Miller, Galanter, & Pribram (1960).

The three following levels seem to have sufficient explanatory power for our purpose.

The Tactic Level.[4] This is the appropriate *ordering* of each single language act with respect to all verbal antecedents and consequents. Ordering is seen here as the actual result of language programming: the finished product or concrete verbal performance. Tactics are necessarily contextualized.[5] The following, therefore, can be considered as tactical operations:

1. Decoding and Encoding Performance. Obviously, listening and speaking, or reading and writing, presuppose the acquisition or formation of sets of specific verbal habits, habits related to (1) auditory/visual input (perceptional habits) and (2) articulatory/graphic output (motor habits).

2. Neural Cortical/peripheral Coordination and Integration. Outward language performance presupposes the correct and satisfactory functioning of neural endings and cerebral centers presiding over both perception and articulation.

3. Verbal Feedback. Language behavior as a self-regulatory system is endowed with self-control devices and mechanisms which connect input and output flows uninterruptedly. Feedback is the very basis of tactical coordination

The Strategic Level. The order nature of single language performance requires the action of ordering or programming mechanisms which are not directly observable, but strictly mental in their nature. The mind of the speaker/hearer is responsible for the meaningfulness and grammaticality of each speech act and for its connection with the communication situation (pragmatic framework). Tactics, therefore, presuppose strategy. Strategic operations would include:

1. Rule-making (Nomothetic) Processes. The impact of cognition on empirical language data takes the forms of inductive generalization and of categorization. Phonological, morphological, syntactic, and lexicosemantic rules are not the result of mere induction from sets of language instances; they are the internal elaboration of language data as raw material on the basis of mental schemata and categories. This explanation goes counter both to the empiricist view (Skinner) and the rationalist-innatist hypothesis (Chomsky); it is basically a dualistic concept which synthesizes experience and conceptualization.

2. Selective Processes. The verbal act implies a selection of distinct molecular elements (sememes + morphemes + phrases + sentences) which go to make up discourse. They are the building blocks of speech constructs.

3. Programming Processes. The ordering of molecular elements into molar structures requires definite programming mechanisms capable of building larger units of speech. This, discourse construction, the choice of stylistic variants, and more

---

[4]The terms *strategy* and *tactics* are used here in analogy with military parlance. "In military usage, a distinction is made between *strategy* and *tactics*. *Strategy* is the utilization, during both peace and war, of all of a nation's forces, through large-scale, long-range planning and development, to ensure security and victory. *Tactics* deals with the use and deployment of troops in actual combat" *(The Random House Dictionary of the English Language).*

[5]The idea of *context* as basic to language as communication has been thoroughly developed by Slama-Cazacu (1961, pp. 209–216). Context is much more than linguistic environment or the communicative situation. Contexts are all the surrounding elements which make speech acts understandable.

particularly, adjustment of each speech act to specific types of situation (contextualization) are typical programming operations designed to give order, unity, and purpose (significance) to verbal encoding and decoding in actual instances of communication between humans.

4. *Conscious Self-regulatory Processes (Cognitive Feedback).* Proprioceptive and control mechanisms are reflected principally on a conscious level in the human communicator. Here the speaker/hearer becomes aware (or is at least virtually aware) of what goes on in the flow of speech and how language works. S/He is, therefore, also capable of self-correction and self-criticism.

The Ego-dynamic Level. All psychological and linguistic activities ultimately stem from and flow back to the self of the communicating person. The subject of responsibility, the center of accountability in human behavior, is the individual self or the *ego* (not only in the psychoanalytic sense).

To think that a behavioral model can be complete by simply restricting itself to a cybernetic structure (tactics + strategy) is to posit an acephalous organism, a beheaded body. In *human* communication, the cybernetic concept must be subsumed under a personological concept. It is indispensable, therefore, to admit a conscious, directing, and unifying agent: the individual speaker's *self* operating on a higher level and controlling all subordinate activities (tactics and strategy).

The channels of the ego's dynamics are manifold. The following list is only a tentative scheme that certainly needs further articulation and development.

1. *The Existential Experience of the Speaker/Hearer.* Personal experience is the very stuff and marrow of expression, whether verbal, iconic, or other. The whats, the hows, and the wherefores of life are reflected, although in divers fashion, in the content and form of human language. This is true of the poet no less than of the man in the street.

2. *World-Perception (Weltansicht).* The individual's immediate outlook on reality and his ultimate view of life and the world—his philosophy of life—determine to varying extents his style of expression. There is a language or *speaking policy,* flexibly adjusted to the varying circumstances of life situations, which characterizes each individual. To speak or not to speak, to speak thus or not thus, to listen or not to listen are parts of a behavioral policy dependent on the way life and each life instance are concretely envisaged.

3. *Attitudes.* Personal, sociocultural, linguistic attitudes—as cognitive-affective sets—may be related to both the substantial content of expression and the reaction or standing of the receiver. A message is chiefly a stimulus and a response conditioned by the affective tones of its cognitive content. Perhaps only in scientific or technical expertise may attitudes be kept aside or paraded.

4. *Affective Components.* Feelings and emotions are rarely absent from verbal expression, although sometimes they are seemingly so. At times, they are primary connoters, as in poetry. In many cases, if latent, they can be rather easily detected. In particular instances, language sounds can carry a symbolic value or emotional appeal, of which Rimbaud among others was a great master.

5. *Unconscious/Conscious Sources of Verbal Messages.* Depth psychology can bring powerful illustrations to this point. From Freudian psychoanalysis to existential analysis, there is abundant evidence of how far and how deeply speech can mirror

the buried ghosts of the human soul, no matter how dark such a mirror sometimes may be.

6. Communicative Intentions, Volitions, and Decisions. Communication takes place only when awareness of speech conditions is followed by the intention to speak *(intentio loquendi)* and this, finally, by the decision to speak. Conative or decisional processes affect the all-or-none, the why, the what, and the how of actual communication. This is the final step, as internal antecedent of the speech act, before the incarnation of thought into words. Unfortunately, decisional procedures have been underrated in contemporary psychology; they represent, however, an extremely important factor antecedent to all human behavior, including communication and expression (cf. Thomae, 1960). But above all these processes hovers one distinctly human state:

7. Linguistic Self-awareness. The human speaker/hearer is conscious of his/her *self as a communicating agent.* Linguistic competence to the highest degree is equal to the ability of total self-perception and self-control of the verbal actor. This is the summit of ego dynamics. But it should be clearly pointed out in this respect that linguistic self-awareness is not to be identified with self-centered or narcissistic monologism. Soliloquy and monologue are not the norm of human speech. Since communicating implies interpersonal contact, linguistic self-awareness is essentially *dyadic consciousness,* that is, the perception of one's verbal interactions affecting people and the world (cf. Smith, Giles, & Hewstone, this volume).

This last remark brings me to the necessity of underlining the point that my personological concept pivots on the idea of an *open personality,* which is ready for and capable of vital exchanges, giving and taking, and is communicative and interactive. Accordingly, all the states and processes belonging on the ego-dynamic level are both centripetal and centrifugal, afferent and efferent, finalized to a constant search for equilibrium between the ego and the world. The communicating ego is not an insulated monad; it is rather a concretely contextualized agent.

The Surface Structure of Language Behavior and Language Learning

If we visualize the deep sources of linguistic behavior as stratified from bottom to surface, we can lay ego-dynamics on the lowest (deepest) layer; next would come strategy; and last, close to the surface, tactics. The performance of communication as a surface process stems immediately from the tactical level; it is, in fact, the actualization or prolongation of the total of tactical operations. Let us define a few concepts relative to the surface aspects of language behavior.

Language Mastery. Mastery can be defined as the *acquired ability to symbolize, to express, and to communicate experience by means of a system of verbal symbols.* Obviously, we start here from the assumption that speech is characterized by three intrinsic and overlapping functions; symbolization, expression, and communication. These are not separate functions but rather mutual implications; all three are constantly actualized in every act of speech, although with varying emphasis. Indeed symbolization is a class of functions including, as a rule, expression and communication. On the other hand, communication (objective transmission of information) includes expression (subjective manifestation of individual states of mind).

Consequently, this specific set of abilities should be the target of language learning. However, communication remains the dominant (concretely inclusive) function of language behavior. Therefore, a consideration of the nature of this function boils down essentially to the analysis of the constituent elements of *language behavior as communication* and language learning as *learning to communicate*. The elements of the communication process are well known: source, transmitter, situation, code/message, channel, receiver, destination, feedback, noise. A more modern view of verbal communication rightly emphasizes two oft-neglected elements, namely, situation and feedback.

Situation. Linguistic output is subject to certain constraints: *context perception* (the type of message construction is defined by the structure of a particular situational context), *verbal pertinency* (the choice of words and structures must conform to the demands of a concrete situation).

Feedback. The destination's perception of the source gives rise to a basic control mechanism which operates on the tactical level (acoustic feedback), on the strategic level (cognitive feedback), and on the ego-dynamic level (linguistic consciousness).

The act of communication takes the form of an automatic chain of events because the total process results from the coordination and integration of all intermediate steps and centers into a compact, unified behavioral system, that is, a linguistically operating structure. External coordination of vocal elements on the tactics level issues from the internal coordination of programming rules on the strategic level, and finally both levels are unified into vertical control exerted by the Ego.

Language learning, therefore, implies the acquisition of psycholinguistic abilities of reception and production on all three levels, but especially the ability to *coordinate* all three levels effectively so as to generate a well-integrated verbal behavior, different from schizophrenic verbal acts, which typically lack basic consistency and unity.

Figure 1 summarizes in simpler terms the essentials of the holodynamic model from the point of view of second language learning and teaching.

Language Acquisition and Language Learning: Child versus Adult Styles of Second Language Learning

If the holodynamic model has a transfer validity, it must be applicable both to the analysis of language acquisition and language learning as different and distinct

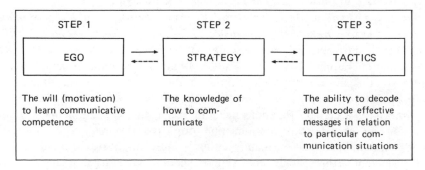

Figure 1. The holodynamic model.

processes and to the specification of age and situation contexts. No doubt an analytic model like the holodynamic one can become the basis for the construction of an operational model, that is, a teaching method appropriate to the needs of different classes of learners.

Language Acquisition versus Language Learning: Similarities and Differences

In the discussion of the similarities and differences between first language acquisition and second language learning, one important criterion is often dismissed or glossed over: age and the time distance between the two consecutive processes. In other words, it may be safely stated that the child learning two languages simultaneously (early simultaneous bilingualism) does not differentiate the two processes: it is just one basic linguistic code being learned, although with growing internal differences. If, on the contrary, the child—or more likely the adolescent or adult— acquires the second language when a significant time period, say, three or four years, has elapsed since the acquisition of the first one, most likely, newly intervened conditions of a psychological and social nature will more or less heavily condition the second learning process. Age, therefore, is a most complex factor, involving physical, emotional, and cognitive growth, along with the possession of more differentiated learning strategies naturally or educationally acquired. The issue, therefore, is better worded if one speaks of difference between *early* language acquisition and *late* language learning.

There have been several studies in recent years which have discussed whether a person learning a second language employs the same process and factors as a person learning his/her first language. Taylor (1974) does not believe in the different influence of physiological factors, and argues that the psychological learning strategies involved seem similar, although he accepts, somewhat contradictorily, that cognitive maturity possibly makes some difference. Ervin-Tripp (1974) fell into the above-mentioned fallacy by not distinguishing accurately between age levels when she examined first and second language learning with children aged 4 through 9. Children learning their first language and children learning a second language at an early age may in fact show large process similarities. A very recent position taken by Macnamara (1976) would deny the existence of any differences even between child learning and adult learning, but his counterarguments are rather weak. This position was preceded by theorists in the past who tended to identify the two processes in all respects; hence the literal interpretation of the so-called natural method of language teaching advertised at the end of the 19th century. Some other theorists think that the process of second language learning is altogether different from the child's language development in the mother tongue. Yet a solid body of opinion points toward only a partial identification of the two processes: there seem to exist differences (of a major nature) as well as similarities (of a more general character) that should be taken into account in teaching (Titone, 1964, pp. 18–19).

There are several critical differences when we consider language acquisition in infancy and later learning in adolescence or adulthood. First, second language learning is what we make it, whereas first language acquisition is rarely planned or controlled. A second difference lies in the nature of reinforcement control: in second language learning we must rely solely on such weak reinforcers as a nod, a smile, a little approval, a grade, or remote success in the profession, whereas the infant acquiring his mother tongue is conditioned and supported by primary reinforcers, such as food, affective relations with his parents and the need to communicate in vital matters, in one word, the urge to survive (cf. Fujinaga, this volume). A third difference derives from the fact that the student learning a second language begins with a highly articulate verbal repertory. This may be an asset as well as a liability in that the two systems may partly coincide or find mutual support, but often they actually conflict, as contrastive analysis has pointed out. The fourth difference lies in the nature of discrimination learning. The second language learner does not follow a gradual process in attaining the ability to discriminate sounds or structures, since, unlike the infant, he has had extensive discrimination training and is essentially faced with the task of concept attainment as a process of transfer of earlier discriminative behaviors. Antecedent language learning represents an important premise for all successive learning. A fifth difference depends on the higher development of cognitive structures in the older learner's mind that may enhance conscious assimilation of the language and those that Harold E. Palmer (1964) used to call "studial capacities." A sixth difference is connected to the learner's degree of social development and cultural fixation which either may create in him/her positive attitudes vis-à-vis the foreign culture or may determine negative attitudes (chauvinism, nationalism, racism, etc.).

Of course, these general differences are underlined by individual differences with children or adults in the same process or at the same age. Consequently, arguments favoring an individualized approach to language instruction are growing in number and strength.

On the contrary, the very fact that both categories of learners are *human* learners confirms the existence of universals of language learning; this should not be ignored in considering the total picture of the learning situation. The holodynamic model indeed underlines the reality of an identical basic structure of the personality of the language learner, no matter what age or personal and social conditions may be. No language learning or acquisition takes place unless the following conditions apply: the child or adult is intrinsically motivated or feels justified in the effort of starting the learning process (ego-dynamic level); s/he is able to comprehend and elaborate the rules governing communication and verbal expression (strategic level); s/he decides to exert enough effort to master the instrumental skills of decoding and encoding language messages as signs and as contents (tactic level). The degrees of involvement and perfection in the operations in these three levels may differ by age and aptitude, but the three categories of operations are all necessary for communicating and learning to communicate. Hence, no teaching method would be complete without trying to work on all levels.

Important Factors in Second Language Learning

The dearth of longitudinal studies on success in language study does not allow for universally valid conclusions on the factors underlying achievement. However, a few safe statements can be made about what appear to be the most important factors in successful language learning, especially in the classroom environment:

Motivation. The primary factor according to various investigations (summarized by Burstall, 1975) is motivation. Specific motivational factors would be:

Integrative versus Instrumental Motivation. The combination of the results of different research data leads to the conclusion that both the utilitarian value of the achievement of proficiency in the foreign language and the tendency to self-identification with the members of the foreign linguistic community are—together or separately—a key to success in foreign language learning.

Contact with the Foreign Culture. It seems that those individuals endowed with empathic capacity develop a greater desire to study a foreign language, particularly as a spoken code, if they are brought into contact with the foreign country through visits.

Socioeconomic Factors. Positive attitudes toward the foreign language and culture seem to be correlated with higher socioeconomic status, perhaps due to greater parental support and encouragement in approaching new school experiences.

Sex Differences. Sex differences in achievement favoring girls have been evident in several studies, although these may be limited to children of lower socioeconomic status; results may be different and favor boys, particularly on the secondary school level, once language proficiency is perceived as having a payoff value.

Classroom Situation. The small school seems to foster achievement, due to an atmosphere characterized by cooperative behavior among pupils and closer contact between teacher and pupils.

Teacher–Pupil Interaction. Teachers' high expectations and positive attitudes toward the foreign language and culture, no less than their enthusiasm for the project, seem to be clearly correlated with pupils' success.

The Presentation of Material. Methods of presenting language learning material should vary according to the stage of learning reached, the nature of the material itself, and the ability, maturity, and modality preferences of the learner. Multisensory modalities and devices inducing active pupil participation have a positive effect as well.

Linguistic Aptitude. The second major factor for success in language learning, according to—albeit limited—experimental data is linguistic aptitude. Carroll (1960, pp. 13–14) has repeatedly emphasized the role of linguistic aptitude. He has found that it consists of at least four identifiable variables (1961, Chapter 4):

1. *Phonetic coding:* the ability to code auditory phonetic material in such a way that this material can be recognized, identified, and remembered over a period longer than a few seconds
2. *Grammatical sensitivity:* the ability to recognize the grammatical functions of words in sentence contexts
3. *Rote memorization ability:* the ability to learn a large number of associations in a relatively short time
4. *Inductive language learning ability:* the ability to infer linguistic forms, rules, and patterns from new linguistic content itself with a minimum of supervision or guidance.

Linguistic aptitude, as defined by Carroll, characteristically operates on the strategic and tactic levels, while motivational variables belong to the sphere of the ego.

Time. Another important variable is the total amount of time spent actively in the learning situation (Carroll, 1963). The reason is that language learning is basically a developmental process very similar to maturation: the entire organism is deeply involved in a process of transformation and organization of communication abilities at various layers of the human personality, as indicated by the holodynamic model. This explains why a longer period of time devoted to language instruction, when started at as early an age as possible, will bring better results. However, it may be suggested, according to the present writer's speculations, that while children will benefit from a more *extended* period of time in order to be able to digest new behavioral materials like language skills, adults will be able to profit from more *intensive* courses due to their higher degree of transfer ability, as experience has proven.

An Integrated Perspective on Second Language Learning Strategies: A Modular Model

The integration of ego–strategy–tactics is dependent on a process of assimilation which tends to incorporate a language behavioral system into the communicator's personality. This assimilation process—common to both first language acquisition and second language learning—can be described as a series of phases or learning units, each consisting of a set of well-defined activities aimed at the fixation of specific verbal habits or rules. Since such units necessarily include rather large portions of content and usually extend over sufficiently long periods of time, we can name them *macromathemes* (a *matheme* is a minimum learning unit).

Learning as guided by teaching takes on in the case of adult learners a characteristic systematicness. The belief that adults cannot learn a second language without systematic instruction is now supported by several interesting studies on adult learning (Krashen & Seliger, 1976; Krashen, Seliger, & Hartnett, 1976). *Systematic* instruction should not be confused with *formal* instruction: the former implies careful planning of situations, materials and procedures, and the latter restricts work to the rational or notional level, as in the case of traditional teaching of formal grammar. A great deal of confusion has arisen in methodological debates from the lack of a precise distinction between the two types of approach. The teacher ought to keep in mind that systematicity goes hand in hand with concreteness and practicality. Systematicity is a principle of intellectual economy: it makes for fast and effective learning without wasting an excessive amount of time and energy; it is synonymous with *programming*.

Now, programming effective learning can be carried out in a variety of modes. What seems to be recommended on the basis of a three-level model (the holodynamic model) is a teaching–learning process consisting of flexible modules ensuring the gradual assimilation (internalization) of coordinated levels of verbal skills and capacities.

We can define *modular teaching–learning* as any instructional process characterized by *cyclical reversibility* and *spiral development*.

Teaching is modular when it is characterized by reversibility and interchangeability of instructional roles and phases. This means that the position of each phase can be changed or reversed according to particular needs. It may be useful or necessary accordingly to go back and forth along the basic stages of learning in order to clarify, reorganize, strengthen, and expand the essential constituents of language competence.

Teaching is modular if instructional roles are reversible. The teacher offers initiating stimuli to the learner's responsiveness, but he in turn becomes a respondent by taking up contingently the role of the learner, and so forth. Both the teacher and the student are alternately stimulators and reactors.

Teaching is modular if each phase is present while each of the others is being developed. Development of each phase takes place in a spiral manner and is virtually endless (open-ended learning).

The cyclical nature of modular teaching is an overall characteristic of this process, inasmuch as phases and roles are not linearly juxtaposed but unfold, one out of the other, after some sort of generative process. Each phase is more like a germinal molecule pushing toward greater development, not like a fenced-in monad or a completely self-contained unit. Learning is therefore a developmental process working through differentiation and integration; it is in a profound sense a *biological continuum;* it is not an accumulation of disjointed building blocks.

References

Allport, G. W. *Pattern and growth in personality*. New York: Holt, 1965.

Bertalanffy, L. von. The theory of open systems in physics and biology. *Science,* 1950, *3,* 23–28.

Burstall, C. Factors affecting foreign-language learning: A consideration of some recent findings. *Language Teaching and Linguistics: Abstracts,* 1975, *8*(1), 5–25.

Carroll, J. B. Foreign languages for children: What research says. *The National Elementary Principal,* 1960, *39*(6), 13–20.

Carroll, J. B. The prediction of success in intensive language training. In R. Glaser (Ed.), *Training research and education*. Pittsburgh: University Press, 1961.

Carroll, J. B. A model of school learning. *Teachers College Record,* 1963, *64,* 723–733.

Chafe, W. L. *Meaning and the structure of language*. Chicago: University of Chicago Press, 1970.

Chomsky, N. *Aspects of the theory of syntax*. Cambridge, Mass.: MIT Press, 1965.

Ervin-Tripp, S. Is second language learning like the first? *TESOL Quarterly,* 1974, *8,* 111–127.

Krashen, S. D., & Seliger, H. W. The essential contribution of formal instruction in adult second language learning. *TESOL Quarterly,* 1976, *8*. (Cited in Macnamara, 1976.)

Krashen, S. D., Seliger, H. W., & Hartnett, D. Two studies in adult second language learning. *Kritikon Litterarum,* 1976. (Cited in Macnamara, 1976.)

Macnamara, J. First and second language learning: Same or different? *Journal of Education,* 1976, *158,*(2), 39–54.

Matson, F. W. Humanistic theory: The third revolution in psychology. *The Humanist,* March–April 1971, *9,* 14–26.

Miller, G. A., Galanter, E., & Pribram, K. *Plans and the structure of behavior*. New York: Wiley, 1960.

Nuttin, J. *Tâche, réussite et échec*. Paris: Presses Universitaires de France, 1953.

Nuttin, J. *La structure de la personnalité*. Paris: Presses Universitaires de France, 1968.

Palmer, H. E. *Principles of language study*. London: Longman, 1964.

Popper, K. R. *The logic of scientific discovery*. London: Hutchinson, 1959.

Rank, O. *Will therapy*. New York: Knopf, 1936.

Slama-Cazacu, T. *Langage et contexte*. The Hague: Mouton, 1961.

Taylor, B. P. Towards a theory of language acquisition. *Language Learning,* 1974, *24,* 23–35.

Thomae, H. *Der Mensch in der Entscheidung*. Munich: J. A. Barth, 1960.

Titone, R. *Studies in the psychology of second language learning*. Zürich/Rome: PAS, 1964.

Titone, R. *Psicolinguistica applicata*. Rome: Armando, 1970.

Titone, R. (Ed.). *Avamposti della psicolinguistica applicata* [Strongholds in applied psycholinguistics]. Rome: Armando, 1981.

16

Using Language: A Sociofunctional Approach

Jan Prucha

There are some questions which, in my opinion, are of importance for any explanation of the sociogenesis of language: Why is the use of language so variant in human conduct? Why are linguistic products so differentiated in form and content? What causes bring about the fact that the development of an individual from early childhood to late adulthood is characterized by an increasing variability in the linguistic messages s/he can produce as well as comprehend?

These questions might sound trivial, because differentiations in using language—that is, immense varieties of texts operating in human communication—are simply accepted as quite natural and therefore problem-free. Such questions are usually not subject to scientific debates—though there do exist certain disciplines (for instance, psycholinguistics or sociolinguistics) which, de facto, describe and explain the varieties of language use.

In the present chapter, I will try to offer one possible answer to these questions, namely, that the real existence of language (its use by an individual as well as its functioning in society as a whole) is substantially bound up with social needs. All linguistic reality (system, process, product) serves social needs (objectively existing purposes), and these needs are the causes of an imense variety of language use and great diversity of linguistic messages.

Thus, explaining the functioning of language will mean, in this chapter, explaining how using language is determined by certain extraindividual and extralinguistic purposes, that is, by social needs. I refer to this approach as *sociofunctional*.

With this basic statement, two elaborations will be examined: (1) the role of social needs in coming into the world of using language and (2) how social needs, as determinants of language behavior, have been ignored in most psycholinguistic theories.

Jan Prucha ● Institute for Educational Research, Czechoslovak Academy of Sciences, Prague 1, Czechoslovakia.

Social Needs as Evolutionary Power of Using Language

The problem of the development of human language and language communication has two basic aspects: the ontogenetic and the phylogenetic. Certain explanatory theories exist for both—for instance, the ontogenetic aspect is dealt with by Vygotsky (1934/1962; cf. Wertsch, this volume). However, I am concerned with phylogenesis, because if we want to explain the sociogenesis of language and language communication in contemporary society, we must ask *why* communication has arisen in its existing form.

One answer has been derived from traditional Marxist linguistics; however, I deem it unsatisfactory. It suggests that the historical origins of language and language communication can be seen as a linking of sequential determinants. These are:

Collective work (using tools)
↓
Social interaction
↓
Evolution of thought
↓
Evolution of language (and
other social sign systems)

This anthropogenetic conception of the origin of human language has been based on the theory of historical materialism and is supported at present by a sizable literature (see Serebrennikov, 1970). In this connection reference is often made to Engels' statement that "work created Man."

A well-argued contemporary version of this idea of sequential determinants has been offered by the Italian Marxist Rossi-Landi (1975). Rossi-Landi differentiates two basic modes of human social development:

1. The production and circulation of goods (in the form of commodities)
2. The production and circulation of sentences (in the form of verbal messages)

This differentiation is based on the theory of the anthropogenetic character of work:

> Man is the result of his own work, and it is through such work that he has
> progressively severed himself from the other animals. One of the most important
> aspects of this theory is that everything that has value (and therefore, as we
> shall see, everything that has meaning) is always a product of human work. . . .
> All social sign systems also have meaning and value as products of human work.
> (Rossi-Landi, 1975, p. 6)

It is apparent, however, that a theory of sequential determinants gives only a limited explanation of the causes leading to the development of language and language communication. Other Marxists (e.g., A. A. Leontiev, 1963) earlier pointed out the incompleteness of this theory. They suggested that Engels's statement about the role of work should not be taken literally. It is better seen as a figurative expression.

It seems more appropriate to explain the development of language and language communication not as a *result* or *consequence* of collective work, but rather as a *condition* or *instrument* for the realization of cooperative work (cf. Williams, this volume). Rossi-Landi also recognized this inversion of conventional Marxist wisdom by noting that "there would be no division of labor without the existence of some form of communication; communication, however, would not arise without the division of labor" (1975, p. 71).

Here again, though, we can pose the questions: What existed, then, at the beginning? What was the real cause or power through which language communication came into existence (together with cooperative work)?

Such questions have very rarely been dealt with in Marxist linguistics. There is even a body of Marxist opinion which suggests that it would be incorrect to formulate such questions. For example, Pimenov (1978) asserts (in relation to phylogenesis of language): "Thus, if we speak about natural historical process of anthropogenesis, it is impossible to explain, *what was at the beginning*. Such a formulation . . . appears non-dialectic and, therefore, false" (p. 8).

On the other hand, Marx presented certain explanations regarding the question of "what was at the beginning." He referred to social needs, that is, needs existing in a primeval society that caused interaction, collective work, and, interdependently, the development of language and language communication.

This idea is acceptable because it seems to be the key for an explanation of the evolution of language as well as for the variety of language communication which now exists. Marx's idea about needs has been maintained also by Rossi-Landi (1975).[1] He stated that any act of human communication fulfills certain "programs" by means of social sign systems, whether verbal or nonberval:

> *Communication is the execution of programs.* Learning to execute the programs, one learns to communicate and become part of the process of "social reproduction." . . . Man becomes part of programs which then determine his behavior in an *automatic, i.e., unconscious way* for the rest of his life. (1975, p. 27)

Rossi-Landi used the term "program" in the sense of "aim" or "the end for which one works."

I am of the same opinion: all of linguistic reality (whether individual or societal), its origin, development, and present-day functioning, is determined by certain purposes, programs, or aims. These can generally be called social needs.

What evidence exists, however, to support the thesis that social needs have caused an evolution of language and language communication? There is, of course, a lack of direct evidence, because the matter involves an immense depth of time. We have only indirect evidence at our disposal, based on paleontologic remains. For example, the remains of *Australopithecus africanus* have been dated to a period 2.5 to 5.0 million years ago; there is evidence to indicate that these hominids used tools and had a social fabric (cf. Montagu, this volume). As A. A. Leontiev (1963) deduced, the work of highly developed hominids was cooperative from the very beginning; this implies that the communicative signals were social (serving collective

---

[1]See my review of Rossi-Landi's book (1978).

needs). "Therefore, there was a need for a development of such means of communication which would function not only as signals about events but which would become means of the *social regulation* of behavior" (p. 46).

Again, however, a question arises: What were the social (communicative) needs of prehistoric (wo)men? Here, also, we have at our disposal only indirect evidence and speculation. We can assume certain things about communicative needs in prehistoric society from the content of communication in present-day primates and other groups of social animals. Hediger (1961) has found that the communication of most social animals is concerned with five main types of events: warning of predators, courtship and territory, mother–child contact, social structure and cohesion, and announcement of food.

Campbell (1971), speculating on findings related to the increase in brain size of primates and early humans, has differentiated several types of phenomena stimulating communicative needs in prehistoric society: the use of stone tools, well-organized social hunting, intercourse as a result of the division of labor, and birth of myth and ritual. For example, "socially organized hunting would have required shared concepts of aims and methods, of animal species, plants, tools, geography and time. A more complex environment came with more complex perception" (p. 17).

In summary, it can be said that social needs (in the sense just illustrated) are supposed to be a cause of the evolution of language and language communication. We can reason thus: if social needs have operated as a decisive determinant for the evolution of language and language communication in the history of humankind, it is probable that they are also functioning at present. If this is so, social needs would be reflected in present-day theories about language and language behavior. How social needs—or social factors in general—are taken into account in psycholinguistics will be discussed in the next section.

Social Needs in Psycholinguistic Explanations of Language Behavior

In spite of its relatively short period of existence, psycholinguistics has developed as a discipline revealing a great diversity of theoretical explanations and methodological procedures (cf. Dittmar, this volume). This diversity has spread so much that even several independent schools inside psycholinguistics have arisen. Though their theoretical bases are sometimes radically opposed, they all have something in common, which, in my opinion, is a serious obstacle, namely, an insufficient recognition (and in some cases simple neglect) of the social factors involved in language behavior.

This neglect generally arises when language behavior is interpreted:

- As a process determined by factors stemming exclusively (or predominantly) from an *individual* only
- As an *isolated* activity removed from a complex of other activities accompanying language behavior
- As a *causeless* activity elicited through no external need or purpose

It seems natural to wonder why these approaches have persevered in psycholinguistics. The main reason seems to be that psycholinguistics (despite some endeavors to develop it as a really autonomous discipline) is, in fact, deeply rooted in individual psychology and/or structural (as opposed to functional) linguistics, in which questions of extraindividual and extralinguistic determinants of language behavior are simply (and studiously) avoided. Early criticisms of this avoidance can be seen in Vološinov (1929/1973).[2]

A number of contemporary examples illustrating this avoidance of social factors could be introduced. I shall mention only the following one as typical: the theory of speech perception as represented in the book *Language and Speech* (Carterette & Friedman, 1976). Some 17 researchers present their explanations of various aspects of speech perception and speech production, from phonetic coding to sentence comprehension to neurolinguistic models. The variety of data, theories, hypotheses, and research methods related to perception of speech is imposing indeed. Nevertheless, after finishing the reading of some 500 pages of the volume, one must ask: Is the picture of speech perception and speech production presented a realistic one? The answer is, unfortunately, no, because the respective processes have been explained as if they were performed by an entirely isolated individual who exists without dependence on an external world, and who behaves verbally without external purposes, aims, or needs. In other words, language behavior has been treated *pars pro toto;* a part has been taken for the whole—the way in which the organism transforms, organizes, and structures information arising from the social world was entirely ignored.

It is quite obvious that any human being perceiving or producing speech—in any of the immense number of situations occurring in real life—is always acting in settings of extraindividual dependencies which influence his activities. Therefore it is quite natural to call for a theory of language behavior which would incorporate determinants (variables) of the social setting. The following part of this chapter is intended to support this view, called *sociofunctional approach.*

The most fruitful arguments for a sociofunctional approach in psycholinguistics arose from a reaction to the Chomskian theory of language and linguistic competence. The Norwegian Rommetveit (1968) has presented theoretical and experimental criticism, arguing that any communicative act is always embedded in some extralinguistic situation and that it is therefore impossible to explain language behavior adequately if the social setting is not considered. He has postulated a radical reorientation in psycholinguistics; instead of examining an ideal speaker–hearer with his sentence in vacuo, one should study acts of language behavior embedded in a social setting.

Similar criticism and suggestions for such a reorientation have been expressed by other researchers (e.g., A. A. Leontiev, 1969; Slama-Cazacu, 1973; Working Group Social Psychology of Language, 1969). Their arguments are typically based on findings concerning changes in language behavior in different communicative situations (see Ageev, 1972; Moscovici, 1967).

What is essential for this reorientation is that social context or social situation

---

[2]"In point of fact, the speech act or, more accurately, its product—the utterance, cannot under any circumstances be considered an individual phenomenon in the precise meaning of the word and cannot be explained in terms of the individual psychological or psychophysiological conditions of the speaker. *The utterance is a social phenomenon*" (Vološinov, 1973, p. 82).

must be incorporated into the study of language behavior. Any explanation of language behavior which does not reflect social factors can be held as incomplete. As a consequence, a new (if aesthetically ugly) term has appeared: *psychosociolinguistics*. This term seems to reflect appropriately the changes in psycholinguistic thinking.[3]

A similar alternative has recently been suggested by Salzinger (1979). He recognizes the fact that language behavior always occurs in a context and can only be understood in a context. He argues for a new, more complex theory of language behavior called *ecolinguistics:*

> This approach . . . is based on the assumption that language behavior is best studied in representative situations in which we are likely to obtain representative samples of the behavior to which we want to extrapolate. . . . An ecolinguist is naturally interested in measuring the relative amount of control that particular parts of the environment exert over the emission of particular classes of language behavior. (p. 126)

Undoubtedly, the variables of the situations in which language behavior occurs are both physical and social. Though psycholinguistics has been less concerned with examining the influence of social variables on language behavior, a large amount of relevant data regarding communication and functional stylistics has been developed in social psychology (see Prucha, 1972b).

The two disciplines mentioned represent, at the same time, the two basic approaches which can be (and actually are to some degree) applied in explaining the role of social context in language behavior:

1. Coming from the known conditions and variables of a communicative situation, the effects of the changes of contextual variables on language behavior (texts) are studied. This approach (typical of social psychology of cmmunication) makes it possible to measure the effectiveness of situational stimuli in gaining control over language behavior (which is also the aim of econlinguistics).

2. Coming from the known (ascertained) characteristics of texts and their specific distribution and differences in classes of texts, one can infer the extralinguistic determinants involved in the selective process of text production (just such as an approach has been developed by Doležel, 1969).

A sociofunctional approach also has serious implications for developmental psycholinguistics. For instance, Palermo (1971) has shown that the results of child language acquisition studies which are conducted in a laboratory setting are not fully valid, because the laboratory-derived data do not reflect the relationship between the contextual stimuli and the language behavior observed.

With the controversy regarding approaches and the need for a reorientation in mind, I am convinced that psycholinguists now have to answer the question: How do we evolve a general strategy for investigating language behavior?

Critical arguments against the nonsocial approach have been sufficiently numer-

---

[3]The term, however, can be seen as redundant if "what would be called SOCIO-PSYCHOLINGUIS-TICS is actually PL (psycholinguistics) proper, which takes into consideration the real situation of communication, the real facts to be found in it, the determinants in action, those which cannot be left aside in any analysis of a fact of message without great danger of distorting the results" (Slama-Cazacu, 1973, p. 99).

ous and persuasive; it is now necessary to begin to create constructive alternatives. The first matter which calls for solution is the clarification of social context, social setting, and social determinants in respect to language behavior.

Unfortunately, one has to admit that the concept of social context remains rather unclear, its meaning more guessed than defined. It is often tacitly assumed that some social determinants actually influence language behavior, but a suitable taxonomy of the determinants has not yet been formulated. On the other hand, some of the manifestations of socially influenced language behaviors have been already studied in other disciplines (see Dittmar, 1976; Prucha, 1972a, 1976; Robinson, 1972; Wertsch, 1978).

What are social determinants as such, and how do they control language behavior? The task can be delimited by formulating the problems:

1. To identify and describe all relevant extraindividual factors influencing particular types of language behavior, in order to clarify the essential content of the phenomenon called *social determinants*
2. To ascertain which of the social determinants are primary and which are subsidiary
3. To ascertain which determinants operate in all types of language behavior and which operate in specific types only
4. To investigate how social determinants—defined according to points a, b, and c—function in particular developmental stages of language behavior in life and how social determinants operate in respect to the ontogenesis of language behavior

Psycholinguists nowadays need not carry out extensive new explorations to be able to answer these problems. On the contrary, the answers could be productively gleaned from the great amount of data already collected in various disciplines dealing with language communicaton (pragmalinguistics, sociolinguistics, semiotics, etc.). What, in my opinion, is now necessary is a *synthesis:* not only to produce new findings, but also to compare, to classify, and to evaluate the information already available. Making syntheses in the field of psycholinguistics ought now to be accepted as a normal, useful procedure, as valuable as original investigations (cf. Smith, Giles, & Hewstone, this volume).

In conclusion, I would like to express some postulates concerning the first of the named problems: What is the relevant content of social determinants? On the empirical level, this question could be formulated as: From what objective sources should information on social determinants influencing language behavior be extracted?

I think two presumptions can be accepted here:

1. Any form of languange behavior has to be viewed in the framework of other human activities. Thus, a starting point for an identification of social determinants of language behavior lies in a description and analysis of human activities. It should be kept in mind that not only are activities which accompany language behavior relevant; we must also realize that language behavior often serves as a prerequisite for the realization of other human activities.

Although there are promising signs (e.g., the chapters of this volume), it seems apparent that there still exists no systematic explanation of language behavior in the framework of other human activities.

2. Any act of language behavior is caused by certain purposes existing in supraindividual, social reality. The purposes can be called social needs. Generally speaking, social needs can be understood as certain states of individuals, social groups, or whole societies, which represent the relation between present conditions of existence and the necessity for making certain changes leading to further development. In this sense, social need is a prerequisite of any activity of an individual or a society—as something which elicits the motives for activity (A. N. Leontiev, 1975).

From this vantage point, the social determination of producing language behavior can be viewed as:

| Social context | Individual's consciousness | Act of language behavior | Product of language behavior (text) |

SOCIAL NEEDS → MOTIVES → COMMUNICATIVE → FUNCTIONAL
                                    GOALS   CHARACTERISTICS

Thus, the interpretation of language behavior as a component of other human activities, a component which is aimed at fulfilling certain social needs, is, in my opinion, a way of stimulating further progress in the theory and methodology of psycholinguistics. Apparently, psycholinguists must now begin to explain the purposefulness of language behavior: that real power which becomes a cause of language behavior. In other words the traditional paradigm of psycholinguistics, which focused on problems of *how* people behave verbally and *what* they verbally communicate, should be completed by examining *why* they verbally behave (cf. Dittmar, this volume).

Though this statement seems self-evident, it is surprising that questions of purpose (need, function) remain to a great degree unanswered in psycholinguistics. The exploration of what language behavior is when it is used for certain purposes has for too long been skirted.[4] However, something has reason for its existence only because some purpose is served by it—and this is true of language behavior as well. The sociofunctional approach to the study of language and human conduct seems viable in light of this truism.

References

Ageev, V. S. Situational variants of speech parameters. In A. A. Leontiev & T. V. Rjabova (Eds.), *Psycholinguistics and teaching Russian as a foreign language.* Moscow: Moscow University Press, 1972, pp. 180–199.

Campbell, B. The roots of language. In J. Morton (Ed.), *Biological and social factors in psycholinguistics.* London: Logos Press, 1971, pp. 10–23.

---

[4]Robinson (1972, pp. 38–42) has cleared up the roots of the unpopularity of problems concerning function (purpose) in psycholinguistics. At the same time, he has argued for a functional approach considering it "the growth point for investigations in the next decade" (p. 36).

Carterette, E. C., & Friedman, M. P. (Eds.). *Language and speech.* In *Handbook of perception* (Vol. VII). New York: Academic Press, 1976.

Dittmar, N. *Sociolinguistics.* London: Edward Arnold, 1976.

Doležel, L. A framework for the statistical analysis of style. In L. Doležel & R. W. Bailey (Eds.), *Statistics and style.* New York: American Elsevier, 1969, pp. 10–25.

Hediger, H. The evolution of territorial behavior. In S. E. Washburn (Ed.), *The social life of early man.* Chicago: Aldine, 1961, pp. 34–37.

Leontiev, A. A. *Origin and initial development of language.* Moscow: Publication House of Academy of Sciences, 1963.

Leontiev, A. A. *Psycholinguistic units and the production of the speech utterance.* Moscow: Nauka Publishers, 1969.

Leontiev, A. N. *Activity, consciousness, personality.* Moscow: Politizdat Publishers, 1975.

Moscovici, S. Communication processes and the properties of language. In L. Berkowitz (Ed.), *Advances in experimental social psychology* (Vol. 3). New York: Academic Press, 1967, pp. 225–270.

Palermo, D. S. On learning to talk: Are principles derived from the learning laboratory applicable? In D. I. Slobin (Ed.), *The ontogenesis of grammar.* New York: Academic Press, 1971, pp. 41–62.

Pimenov, A. V. On relation of speech to other forms of human activity. In E. F. Tarasov, J. A. Sorokin, & N. V. Ufimceva (Eds.), *Psycholinguistic and sociolinguistic determinants of speech.* Moscow: Linguistic Institute, 1978, pp. 4–25.

Prucha, J. *Soviet psycholinguistics.* The Hague: Mouton, 1972(a).

Prucha, J. Psycholinguistics and sociolinguistics—separate or integrated? *International Journal of Psycholinguistics,* 1972, *1,* 9–23. (b).

Prucha, J. (Ed.). *Soviet studies in language and language behavior.* Amsterdam: North-Holland, 1976.

Prucha, J. Review of *Linguistics and Economics* by F. Rossi-Landi. *Linguistics,* 1978, *206,* 88–90.

Robinson, W. P. *Language and social behaviour.* Harmondsworth, Middlesex: Penguin Books, 1972.

Rommetveit, R. *Words, meanings, and messages.* New York: Academic Press, and Oslo: Universitets-forlaget, 1968.

Rossi-Landi, F. *Linguistics and economics.* The Hague: Mouton, 1975.

Salzinger, K. Ecolinguistics: A radical behavior theory approach to language behavior. In D. Aaronson & R. W. Rieber (Eds.), *Psycholinguistic research: Implications and applications.* Hillsdale, N.J.: Lawrence Erlbaum, 1979, pp. 109–130.

Serebrennikov, B. A. (Ed.). *General linguistics.* Moscow: Nauka Publishers, 1970.

Slama-Cazacu, T. Is a 'socio-psycholinguistics' necessary? *International Journal of Psycholinguistics,* 1973, *2,* 93–104.

Vološinov, V. N. *Marxism and the philosophy of language.* New York-London: Seminar Press, 1973. (Originally published in Russian, Leningrad, 1929.)

Vygotsky, L. S. *Thought and language.* Cambridge, Mass.: MIT Press, 1962. (Originally published in Russian, Moscow, 1934.)

Wertsch, J. V. (Ed.). *Recent trends in Soviet psycholinguistics.* New York: M. E. Sharpe, 1978.

Working group Social psychology of language. In J. Janoušek (Ed.), *Experimental social psychology.* Prague: Institute of Psychology, 1969, pp. 274–337.

17

New Horizons in the Study of Speech and Social Situations

Philip M. Smith, Howard Giles, and Miles Hewstone

Introduction

The tireless study of human conduct by social scientists is predicated on the well-founded assumption that regularities in human behavior can be detected, described, and explained. Sociolinguistic studies of speech in its social context demonstrate this well, with a great variety of research showing how variations in speech can be systematically related to speaker characteristics and to facets of the situation (e.g., Ervin-Tripp, 1969; Hymes, 1972; Labov, 1972; Trudgill, 1978). We have argued elsewhere (Smith, Giles, & Hewstone, 1980), however, that preoccupation with the linguistic side of the sociolinguistic endeavor has fostered a casual and sometimes rather naive use of social variables in explanations for linguistic variation. In particular, Giles and Hewstone (in press) expressed serious misgivings about the way that the concept of *situation* has been employed in sociolinguistics. They drew attention to what they called the "taxonomic" approach to the definition of social situations, an approach that emphasizes the static, objective features of situations and neglects the dynamic nature of social interaction and its consequences for speech. Proponents of this kind of approach strive to create lists and taxonomies of influential situational variables on the basis of commonsense assumptions about how to operationalize situations in meaningful ways, usually without checking these assumptions empirically, or checking them only by referring to the very data that their taxonomies are meant to explain. Moreover, taxonomists provide few suggestions as to how elements of situations combine to influence behavior and tend to ignore the ongoing or unfolding nature of social interaction.

In this chapter, we take our examination of research approaches to the relation

Philip M. Smith ● Department of Psychology, University of British Columbia, Vancouver, British Columbia V6T 1W5, Canada. ***Howard Giles*** ● Department of Psychology, University of Bristol, Bristol BS8 1HH, England. ***Miles Hewstone*** ● Maison des Sciences de l'Homme, Paris, France.

between speech and situation somewhat further. Besides reviewing some examples of the taxonomic approach, we will also briefly consider the symbolic interactionist perspective. Symbolic interactionists, far from neglecting the dynamic nature of interaction, assign pride of place in their explanations to participants' own interpretations of their immediate situation, and how these interpretations are influenced by and reflected in speech. In stark contrast to the taxonomists, they tend to emphasize, perhaps too strongly, the importance of factors that emerge during the course of interaction and neglect the influence exerted by the stable background features of situations and the role of cross-situational stabilities in social perception processes.

We will argue that a powerful model of situational influences on speech should not only afford prominence to the role of cognitive processes that mediate between situational stimuli and their interpretation (an emphasis that is implicit in the symbolic interactionist perspective), but must also attend to the details of such processes. Furthermore, such a model should account for the influential role of both stable and emergent facets of situational input. Later in the paper, we will review some theory and data from contemporary psychology that are consistent with the idea that individual knowledge about different facets of situation is organized in networks of cognitive schemata about settings, events, episodic structure, cause–effect relations, and people, their characteristics, dispositions, behaviors, and so on. These schemata constitute the basis of people's interpretive skill, enabling them to integrate both stable and emergent facets of incoming situational information in producing inferences. We will also argue that a model of interpretive processes, although certainly a necessary component of any attempt to explain the influence of situational variation on speech, is not in itself sufficient. Just as one has to account for the relation between interpretations of situations and their objective counterparts, so one has to explore the relation between action and interpretation. The prediction of action given a situational interpretation is neither simple nor direct, for the same inference will have quite different implications for two different people depending on their goals, individual and social characteristics, and which aspects of their self-concepts are salient in the situation. Our aim in this chapter is to contribute to the development of a general theoretical framework within which more specific and powerful models of the relation between speech and situational variation than those presently available can be developed.

The Taxonomic Approach

The taxonomic approach to situations assumes its most sophisticated form in the writings of those concerned with explaining patterns of linguistic variation in terms of generic behavioral categories such as codes and patterns of pronunciation. Central to this approach is the idea that speakers possess a "speech repertoire" (Ervin-Tripp, 1969; Gumperz, 1964) which allows them to select from among a plurality of linguistic possibilities for producing essentially the same messages, using different languages or dialects, vocabularies, and a host of other segmental and nonsegmental stylistic tactics. As Hymes (1972) stated:

> No normal person, and no normal community, is limited to a single way of speaking, to an unchanging monotony that would preclude indication of respect,

insolence, mock seriousness, humor, role distance, and intimacy by switching from one mode of speech to another. (p. 38)

An early theoretical contribution relevant to the analysis of situation-related variation is the concept of *diglossia* (Ferguson, 1959), which relates to the use of two languages or dialects in bilingual or bidialectal societies, each serving functions with different status connotations. Use of the low (L) variety is most often confined to the home, everyday activities, and familiar relationships, whereas the high (H) variety is often acquired later in the socialization process and is reserved for use in educational and bureaucratic contexts. To cite an example that illustrates the concept, consider the use of Spanish by Paraguayans when speaking in the more formal contexts of public life and their shift to Guarani within the privacy of the home.

Research on diglossia stimulated at least two developments on the original theme in order to cope with more complex sociolinguistic environments. The first of these involved a more refined specification of the classes of situations, or *social domains,* that would elicit H or L varieties. Fishman (1972) proposed an analysis in terms of five general social domains: family, neighborhood, religious, educational, and occupational. He noted for example that the bilingual Mexican-American in the United States might use Spanish while talking with people at home, in the neighborhood, and at church, and English might be spoken for educational and occupational purposes. The second development to have emerged from research on diglossia involved the extension of the concept to embrace instances of *polyglossia,* or multi-code switching, as well as the simpler phenomena of two-code choices (Platt, 1977). For instance, ethnic Chinese in Malaysia have a speech repertoire that might include two varieties of each of three different languages, each used in different situations, including Hokkien, Cantonese, formal Malaysian English, colloquial Malaysian English, the official standard Malay (Bahasa Malay) and Bazaar Malay (Bahasa Pasar; cf. de Terra, this volume).

Other developments have been concerned with applying similar types of analysis to monolingual environments (e.g., Ervin-Tripp, 1969), so that taxonomies emerged to relate more specific situational characteristics (e.g., the age of the person addressed) to more specific speech variables (e.g., the minutiae of grammatical form). For example, Hyme's influential taxonomy, captured in his SPEAKING mnemonic (Hymes, 1972), concentrated attention primarily on three components of situational input, namely *setting* (which locates the interaction), *participants* (the specific characteristics of the interactants), and *ends* or *purposes* (the extended objectives of interaction). Subsequent taxonomies differ in terms of which elements of situations feature most prominently. For instance, Ervin-Tripp (1969) and Yamamoto (1979) provided situation hierarchies with a view to formulating rules for *social grammars,* specifying the particular speech patterns considered appropriate for certain situations. Giles and Powesland (1975) stressed the salience of the characteristics of the *person addressed,* whereas Brown and Fraser (1979) and Argyle, Furnham, and Graham (1981) opted for the preeminence of the *purpose* of interaction in determining the speech patterns produced. Brown and Fraser's model of social situations and speech is probably the most comprehensive and explicit exemplar of the taxonomic approach to date, and for this reason we will devote the next section to a brief but detailed exposition of its main features. Their model illustrates well the tension between the desire to quantify situations in terms of objective parameters and the need to rely on psychological assumptions in order to calibrate these parameters.

Brown and Fraser's Model

Brown and Fraser (1979) distinguished between two major facets of situations; the *scene* in which speech is produced and the *participants* of interaction. Scene is determined in their model by the setting of the interaction (including time, locale, and bystanders) and by its purpose. For Brown and Fraser, "purpose is the motor which sets the chassis of setting and participants going" (p. 34) and is the crucial determinant of linguistic behavior. Purposes are seen to inspire the selection of culture-specific kinds of "activity types" (Levinson, 1978) such as buying, selling, and chatting, and the selection of particular subject matter: that is, both the style and the content of interaction. It is somewhat unclear just how Brown and Fraser envisage the interaction of setting and purpose in the creation of scenes. On the one hand, they point out that some configurations of locale, time, and bystanders are heavily inbued with cultural significance which may exert normative constraints on activity types and hence presumably on purposes as well. Churches on Sundays and kitchens at mealtimes are good examples. On the other hand, it is evident that determined efforts to achieve preordained purposes may at times override the normative salience of the immediate setting: hecklers flout social convention at public meetings; people in courtrooms sometimes speak out of turn. The most straightforward resolution of this apparent antagonism is to postulate that purpose and setting are co-determinants of activity, which is essentially what Brown and Fraser signify when they classify both facets under the single rubric of *scene*. Moreover, they observe, not all possible combinations of setting, activity type, and other components of situations are equally probable, so that particular settings and specific purposes typically coincide in recurrent scenes.

Turning to consider the participants of interaction, Brown and Fraser draw attention to the evidence for speech correlates of stable personality characteristics and transient emotional states, as well as of larger social category memberships (see Scherer & Giles, 1979). Besides these largely situation-independent factors, however, the *relationships among* participants influence speech. For example, people who like each other display more verbal productivity and self-disclosure, and less silent pausing, then those who are not mutually attracted. Occupational and social roles may be reflected in asymmetrical patterns of address, as in the case of teacher–pupil relationships. Thus, should the affective, role, or status relationships among interlocutors change during interaction, one would expect this change to be reflected in speech (cf. Harris, this volume).

Although the burden of explanation for speech variation rests in Brown and Fraser's model, as it does in other approaches that we have mentioned, mainly on objective parameters like those of setting and participant characteristics, several features of their analysis indicate that they are keenly aware of the need to know more about the psychological processes that mediate participants' awareness of these factors. For example, the key concept of purpose is explicitly psychological, and they

point out that "an understanding of the nature of the scene, as viewed by participants, is essential in order to detect and interpret many of the markers that appear
in their speech" (1979, p. 54). Hence, "we would do well to pursue lines of research
that could get at the actor's-eye-view of the situation" (pp. 56–57). Furthermore,
they observe that "codes are not simply passively marking but are in large part creating the situation" (p. 48). Finally, although they advocate research aimed at the
development of a taxonomy of situations, it is a taxonomy based on participants'
representations of them, such as might be discovered by ethnography (p. 58). From
these points, it can be seen that despite the taxonomic character of their model,
Brown and Fraser would clearly sympathize with the aims of this paper.

Exemplars of the taxonomic approach have enjoyed a large degree of success in
their efforts to relate objective situational parameters to speech variation, without
having had explicitly to consider the mediating role of psychological processes. However, it is evident that taxonomists must rely heavily on assumptions about these
processes in delineating even the most elementary classification of situational variables. Decisions about the classification of scenes as formal or informal, or the characterization of interlocutors in terms of relative status and group membership, are
predicated on (usually) tacit assumptions about the significance of these parameters
to the speaker population under scrutiny. The component of situational taxonomies
that best illustrates the implicit deference to psychological considerations is purpose
or goal, a motivational concept. Purposes cannot be considered properties of situations in the same sense as settings or participants; at best they are situation-depen-
dent. However, we have already had occasion to note that not all situations are
equally goal-inspiring, and that goals which antedate situations may result in coun-
ternormative behavior. These considerations cannot be reconciled within a framework that treats purpose as a facet of situations. Another area in which taxonomists'
psychological assumptions inform their models has to do with the way in which facets
of input are thought to combine to produce the observed behavior. In fact, taxonomists have been preoccupied with articulating the individual components of situations and have had little to say on this subject, although it is evident that a model of
situational influence on speech must address the problem of how incoming information is integrated. A final observation on the shortcomings of taxonomic models
is that they have generally overlooked the dynamic, emergent qualities of the situations in which most speech is produced. Brown and Fraser, for example, alert us to
the possibility that changes in the relationships among interlocutors during interaction may produce changes in speech, yet it is difficult to see how even a very sophisticated classificatory system for situational variables would be helpful in predicting
emergent changes like these. Symbolic interactionism, a perspective that we will consider briefly below, recognizes the need for a dynamic view of interaction, although
it too falls short of attempting to specify the processes underlying this dynamism.

The Symbolic Interactionist Perspective

O'Keefe and Delia (1982) have presented a very brief assessment of some of
the key working hypotheses shared by the founders and descendents of the Chicago
school of symbolic interactionist sociology (see Manis & Meltzer, 1978), whose

interest in speech stems from the desire to account for how meaning is conveyed in speech, rather than from an interest in speech variation itself. Adherents of this theoretical orientation, based substantially on the writings of G. H. Mead and H. Blumer, advance the view that human society is only possible through, and indeed is realized in, the process of continual interaction among people. Furthermore, the vast majority of interaction involves the use of shared systems of symbolic reference, such as spoken language. For symbolic interactionists, the effective use of language in interaction (i.e., communication) entails the ability to detect and remember how it has been used by others, that is, the possession of interpretive skills. Moreover, the effective use of language requires of interactants knowledge in excess of that necessary for the production of speech itself: it requires knowledge of how to modulate linguistic choices in accordance with variation in situational factors in order to preserve meaning and convey intent. This implies the presence of corresponding interpretive competence. Symbolic interaction is thus seen to depend on participants' interpretations of actions-in-context, interpretations which are in turn reflected in participants' choice of linguistic (and other) action.

The fundamental problem facing interactants is that of negotiating a definition of the situation itself, in order that interpretations of subsequent phases of the interaction will be grounded in similar sets of assumptions on behalf of all participants. Without this "architecture of intersubjectivity," as Rommetveit (1974) has termed it, misunderstanding would be the rule and communication the exception, rather than the other way around. All aspects of the situation are potentially subject to overt negotiation. However, shared beliefs about the meaning of setting, participants, and their interrelationships enable people to forgo much of this explicit work and simply to encode their tacit assumptions in the form of routine strategies that do not attract comment unless they indicate incompatible definitions of the situation. In this way, interaction can progress beyond a preoccupation with the immediate situation to focus on issues of wider relevance.

It should be evident even from this thumbnail sketch of one theme from the symbolic interactionist tradition that it assigns great importance in the analysis of situational influences on speech to the participants' interpretations of their circumstances, and not to objective situational parameters. Furthermore, great stress is placed on the importance of speech, both as an emergent and influential facet of situational input and as a medium of response. These sensitivities have informed a number of empirical analyses of aspects of speech in interaction, including topics of conversation (Handelman, 1975), prosody in interethnic meetings (Gumperz, 1977), and code switching among bilinguals and multilinguals (Kendall, 1980; Parkin, 1974; Scotton & Ury, 1977). However, this perspective has not yielded specific treatments of the concept of situation and its relation to speech to rival those of the taxonomists, nor has it resulted in an explicit concern for the processes underlying interpretation. Furthermore, O'Keefe and Delia (1982) have pointed out that the emphasis on the fluid, emergent qualities of ongoing interaction has led to the neglect of cross-situational stabilities in people's interpretive processes and, we would add, of the role of noninteraction facets of situations in the production of inferences. Such considerations would constitute an additional set of constraints on the variety of interpretations and strategies generated in interaction, over and above the unique qualities of particular interactions. Finally, the symbolic interactionists, like the taxonomists, fail to distinguish between the cognitive processes underlying the interpretation or comprehension of situational input and the motivational processes with which these interpretations interact to produce action (cf. John-Steiner & Tatter, this volume). However, their explicit recognition of the mediating role of interpretation and of the dynamic nature of interaction have stimulated our own thinking along these lines, which is why we have included them in our review. We hope that these emphases will encourage a fuller appreciation of the significance of theory and data from psychology, some of which we will consider in the next section, that contribute to our understanding of how situations are construed by the people who are in them.

The Organization of Situational Knowledge

Throughout our lives, we accumulate experience with configurations of environmental stimuli—people, places, objects, events—in the form of schematized knowledge. This knowledge constitutes people's understanding of the contingencies that obtain among different facets of reality. Investigating and theorizing about the acquisition and organization of knowledge are among the most distinctive hallmarks of psychology as a division of scientific labor, and these activities have a long and distinguished history in the discipline. It is with some trepidation and great humility therefore that we offer the following sample of a few contemporary contributions to our understanding of how situational knowledge is organized, in the hope that it will stimulate the reader to undertake a more thorough examination of the research in this area.

Of course, any attempt to grasp fully the nature of the schematization process without consideration of schematic acquisition in ontogenesis—as the individual reconstitution of social, historical realities—would likely result in adult-centered or behaviorist model of the individual, language, and society. It would, however, take us too far too afield from the immediate aim of this chapter to attempt such an analysis. In regard to the developmental acquisition of schemata, the reader is hereby referred to the seminal works of Piaget (1929), Werner and Kaplan (1963), and Vygotsky (1962), as well as to Wertsch (this volume) and the many discussions of developmental phenomena throughout this volume.

For the present purposes we can simply note the work of Bindra (1976), who has elaborated a comprehensive model of individual cognitive processes, in which knowledge about the identity and attributes of objects is integrated with knowledge about the spatial and temporal relations among them to yield *situational schemata*. Bindra argued that cognitive schemata develop on the basis of our ability to detect positive and negative correlations among different facets of the environment. Repeated experience with these environmental contingencies leads to the establishment of neural representations of them, such that incoming information from one facet of a situation (a particular locale, for example) will lead to inferences about what to expect and what not to expect from other facets (activity types, for example). Initially discrete and tentative, these representations of objects, attributes, locales, episodes, and so on, become progressively more interconnected via the mechanisms of learning, until they comprise a network of schemata that enables the individual (1) to integrate diverse sources of situational information, both simultaneous (synchronic) and sequential (diachronic) in arriving at interpretations; (2) to generate full-blown inferences about a variety of parameters on the basis of only partial or minimal incoming information; and (3) to anticipate how the situation will unfold and how it might respond to the individual's own actions. The outcome of these interpretive processes influences, but does not wholly determine, the selection of goals and strategies by means of which to achieve them, the issue to which we shall return in the next section.

Although the details of how schematic organizations develop and operate must remain vague in this chapter, we note simply that Bindra's model provides at least one example (and there are others) of a systematic account of how situational information might be cognitively represented and integrated. The model also deals explicitly with the integration of both stable and emergent features of unfolding situations. Schemata pertaining to the sequence and significance of activity develop in the same way as do representations of time and locale, for example. A model of interpretation based on the activation of cognitive schemata can also account for variations in the rapidity and clarity with which inferences are generated, variations which will in turn have important implications for the nature of activity generated in response. Successive stimulus inputs can either constrain the range of interpretations by augmenting excitation at a focal point in the network or broaden it by stimulating nonoverlapping parts. Some configurations of information may thus seem completely unambiguous and amenable to only one interpretation, others may generate a whole range of interpretations, and still others may pose severe interpretive problems because they are so novel.

Many investigators have done more detailed research on specific aspects of situational knowledge, whose results are generally compatible with the generic model envisaged by Bindra, although they vary considerably in the completeness and consistency of the individual models they espouse. Mandler (1978) has drawn attention to the importance of memory organizations for spatial configurations, such as the arrangement of furniture in a room ("scene schemata"), and temporal configurations, such as the sequence of events in a story ("event schemata"). Even very young children have been shown to acquire schemata for familiar scenes and event sequences, which distort the interpretation of incoming information in the direction of making it seem more consistent than it actually is with a schema that it activates. Schank and Abelson (1977) have developed the idea that recurrent and commonplace combinations of setting and participants evoke widely shared "scripts" or expectations about the sequence and type of activity likely to unfold therein (e.g., restaurant scripts, getting-up-in-the-morning scripts). Heider (1958) and others (Ajzen, 1977; Michotte, 1963; Tversky & Kahneman, 1980) have demonstrated that people are also possessed of cause–effect schemata that enable them to predict the probable outcomes of particular situational configurations and to infer causes from effects. Bain (1973) has shown the interrelationships of the "inner" and "outer" faces of schematic processes by charting the developmental regularities between the general body schema and configurations of aesthetic expression. These studies offer a potential mine of information to taxonomists who may be interested in validating their intuitions about situational knowledge. A great deal of research has also been done on the perception of people, their characteristics and behaviors, and how these are integrated with other aspects of inputs (see Schneider, Hastorf, & Ellsworth, 1979, for a review of person perception processes). For example, research on our "implicit personality theories" about the coincidence of personality characteristics, models of the processes underlying the integration of information in impression formation (Anderson, 1965; Kaplan, 1971; Wyer & Carlston, 1979), and studies of stereotypes about the personality, attitudinal, and even physical concomitants of membership in various social groups (McCauley, Stitt & Segal, 1980; Tajfel, 1981a) produce results that are generally consistent with a schematic model of situational knowledge.

So are several models that have been developed in social psychology to account for the ways in which we arrive at conclusions about the causes and reasons for people's behavior and the extent to which responsibility for people's actions is attributed to characteristics of the actor (such as his/her knowledge, ability, and disposition), to particular characteristics of the situation, and to combinations of the two (Hewstone & Jaspars, 1982; Kelley, 1971; Reeder & Brewer, 1979). With respect to the role of particular types of behavior in people's definitions of the situation, research has been carried out on the ways in which various aspects of speech itself influence impressions and attitudes in a wide variety of situations (see, for example, Giles & Powesland, 1975; Giles, Robinson, & Smith, 1980; Ryan & Giles, 1982). This work has encouraged us, like the symbolic interactionists, to stress the importance of speech both as an influential component of incoming situational information and as a vehicle of response to that situation (Giles & Hewstone, in press; Smith *et al.*, 1980). Research is also being conducted into the connotative and affective dimensions along which relations among people, situations, and combinations of the two are construed (Argyle *et al.*, 1981; Delia, O'Keefe, & O'Keefe, in press; Forgas, 1980; Wish, 1978). For example, the formality/informality of a situation seems to be a very important abstract dimension along which most situations can be ordered.

Despite our concern to generate interest in the details of cognitive processes among sociolinguists, we ought not lose sight of the fact that construal processes themselves remain intimately linked to objective parameters of situations. The significance of our reconsideration of the situation concept, then, is not that it somehow frees the analyst from the task of empirical description, but that it makes the calibration of situational parameters in formulas for linguistic variation dependent on their psychological significance. We need more detailed investigations of individuals' and groups' situational schemata before we can generalize confidently about the importance of objective situational parameters and how they combine to influence interpretation.

Goals, Self-presentation and the Generation of Action

Many social scientists who have considered the relation between situation and behavior have confined their attention to behavior in recurrent and culturally significant contexts, such as those considered most frequently by taxonomists. This limitation has given rise to a functional model of behavior in situations, echoed implicitly by all of the taxonomists that we mentioned above, but most explicitly taken as a point of departure by Argyle *et al.* (1981), who proposed that

> situations emerge within a culture because they have the function of enabling people to attain goals, which are in turn linked to needs and other drives . . . all other features of situations can be explained in terms of facilitating the attainment of these drive related goals. (p. 10)

The functional model claims that there is bound to be an almost isomorphic relation between the perception of situations and the perception of goals to be attained within them, arising as a consequence of either the drive-inducing/drive-reducing potential of the situation, or the seeking out of situations in which to satisfy particular drives. Indeed, Argyle *et al.* (1981), like Brown and Fraser (1979), regard goals as properties of situations, rather than as individual aspirations arising from motivational processes.

Perhaps because we are concerned with action generated in unfamiliar and unanticipated situations, as well as in familiar ones, we do not share the functional point of view. We agree that virtually every situation, familiar or not, can evoke strong inferences as to its purpose and the best means to achieve it, as we discussed in the last section. However, we argue that these situation-induced expectations are not always compatible with the achievement of goals that antedate particular situations, goals whose salience will temper and sometimes completely overrule implicit situational demands. For this reason, we do not believe that a model of situational influence on speech can be based solely on a model of interpretive processes. For example, two interviewees may have virtually identical interpretations of an interview with a sociolinguistic researcher, yet the speech of one who is concerned to make a favorable impression will be different from the speech of one who is indifferent and in a hurry to leave. Of course, our actions are not always informed by clearly defined prior goals, and we often rely heavily upon immediate situational information to provide an idea of what we ought to do and how we ought to do it. It is equally true that in some cases our obsession with achieving a goal or conveying an impression is so great that our actions appear to be highly unconventional. In general, action is probably seldom wholly subservient to either the normative demands of the situation or the demands of self-presentation, but results form a compromise between these two sources of pressure.

Up to this point, we have dwelt exclusively on individual cognitive processes, and we have noted that the implications of interpretation for speech and other kinds of action vary according to individual goals and characteristics. Much more research must be done to discover the ways in which these processes of inference and goal-directedness interact in specific circumstances to influence speech. In the remainder of this section, however, we will turn our attention to motivational processes that operate as a consequence of the fact that individuals often act as members or representatives of larger social groups and select strategies of interaction that serve to reflect and establish these aspects of their identities (Tajfel, 1981b; Turner & Giles, 1981). Significant portions of our self-concepts derive from the knowledge that we belong to various social groups, ranging from the small-scale and transient (such as groups created in social psychological laboratories for experimental purposes: e.g., Asch, 1956; Billig & Tajfel, 1973) to the large-scale and long-term (such as national, ethnic, and racial groups). Each of these memberships entails normative demands pertaining to actions in at least some situations, although groups vary in the pervasiveness of their influence and the clarity of their aims and functions. Given that the normative demands of self-presentation and goal achievement exerted by various aspects of individual and group identity may well be incompatible and even contradictory when taken all at once, they clearly cannot all be brought to bear on the individual in each and every situation.

Turner (1982) elaborated a model of the self-system that helps to clarify how we conceive of its articulation with interpretive processes in the production of action. He distinguished two subsystems of the self-concept which together account for the variety of ways in which a person sees him or herself vis-à-vis others. The personal identity subsystem comprises idiosyncratic, unshared conceptions of oneself, concerning aspects such as temperament, body image, and personal tastes. The social identity subsystem is comprised of self-conceptual organizations held in common with others, such as party political affiliations and racial and regional loyalties. It seems reasonable to propose that these subsystems can be conceived of as poles defining a continuum that embraces the totality of the self-concept, from purely idiosyncratic aspects of self-construal to those which are held in common with members of the most inclusive groups with which one identifies. Some aspects of the identity system would seem constantly to be in transition between the personal and the social realms of the self-concept, while other aspects are more or less static. Turner likened the system to the musical technology of an orchestra:

> It has overall coherence and organization which produces a sense of unity and consistency and yet structurally and functionally its parts are highly differentiated. They are apparently able to function relatively independently of each other. Thus, in any given situation a different part or combination of parts of the self-concept could be at work with the subjective consequence that different self-images are produced. (Turner, in press)

If the self-concept is the orchestra, then the fluctuating self-images are homologous with the sounds that the orchestra makes at any particular moment: "Different situations tend to 'switch on' different conceptions of self so that social stimuli are construed and social behavior controlled in the appropriately adaptive manner" (Turner, in press).

In addition to whatever may be the influence exerted on a person's speech style and vocabulary by task-related norms associated with salient aspects of personal and social identity, research in social psychology indicates that people are constantly comparing themselves with others on dimensions related to their self-esteem (e.g., Festinger, 1954; Suls & Miller, 1977; Tajfel, 1981a). People strive to maintain a self-image with evaluatively positive connotations by choosing to compare themselves to those with whom they compare favorably and sometimes reinterpreting unfavorable comparisons in terms that place them in a positive light. We suggest that this preoccupation with the maintenance and enhancement of self-esteem will exert a major influence on people's choice of speech strategies in most situations, whether primarily personal or primarily group aspects of identity are salient. Indeed, research has already been carried out to determine when intergroup comparison processes result in divergent speech strategies (Giles & Johnson, 1981; Giles, Bourhis, & Taylor, 1977). In short, the need for positive self-esteem may be a superordinate goal that underpins our choice of self-presentation strategies across situations.

Summary and Conclusions

We admit that we have been overly ambitious in attempting to cover so much ground in so short a space. While it has not been possible to do justice to any of the several models that we have reviewed, we can only hope that by our omissions we have not seriously misrepresented the work that has been cited. In this chapter, we have tried to illustrate some deficiencies in sociolinguistic accounts of the relation between speech and situations and to suggest ways in which theory and data from contemporary psychology might help to correct these (cf. Slama-Cazacu; Titone, this volume). This critique and subsequent suggestions are based on the conviction that if we are to progress in our understanding of how situations influence speech, we must (1) explicitly recognize the role of cognitive processes in mediating between the objective parameters of situations and interpretations of them; (2) attend to the details of these processes (see also Giles & Ryan, 1982; Roloff & Berger, in press); and (3) recognize the significance of an analytical distinction between the cognitive processes underlying interpretation and the motivational processes with which they interface in the production of speech and other forms of action.

Our emphasis on cognitive processes should not be taken as an excuse for neglecting the measurement and description of situational parameters, just as an interest in the meaning of speech cues does not preclude their measurement and dscription. But at present far more energy goes into the operationalization and manipulation of situational variables than into research aimed at discovering how these variables figure in the construal of situations. Thus, explanations of speech variation in terms of simple constructs like formality, for example, rely at best on intuitions about how to manipulate any of dozens of objective parameters in order to produce situations with formal connotations. More seriously perhaps, very little sociolinguistic attention has been directed at the role of self-presentation processes in interaction with situational factors in influencing speech. Giles and his colleagues have stressed the importance of social comparison processes, interpersonal attraction, and group identity in influencing tactics for achieving associative and dissociative goals with others, but little headway has been made in measuring the linguistic vehicles whereby this is achieved and in describing how the choice of vehicles varies across situations. We hope that this chapter will stimulate the research necessary to make the advances we are confident can be achieved. We also hope that the psychological constructs and theory outlined, albeit briefly, in the foregoing discussion will prove to be helpful tools along the way.

Acknowledgments

We wish to express our thanks to Colin Fraser, Cheris Kramarae, Nick Pidgeon, and Peter Robinson for their helpful comments on an earlier draft of this paper.

References

Ajzen, I. Intuititve theories of events and the effects of base-rate information on prediction. *Journal of Personality and Social Psychology,* 1977, *35,* 303–314.

Anderson, N. H. Adding versus averaging as a stimulus combination rule in impression formation. *Journal of Experimental Psychology,* 1965, *70,* 394–400.

Argyle, M., Furnham, A., & Graham, J. A. *Social situations.* Cambridge: Cambridge University Press, 1981.

Asch, S. E. Studies of independence and conformity: A minority of one against a unanimous majority. *Psychological Monographs,* 1956, *70*(Whole No. 416).

Bain, B. Toward a theory of perception. *Journal of General Psychology,* 1973, *89,* 157–296.

Billig, M, & Tajfel, H. Social categorization and similarity in intergroup behaviour. *European Journal of Social Psychology,* 1973, *3,* 27–52.

Bindra, D. *A theory of intelligent behavior.* New York: Wiley and Sons, 1976.

Brown, P., & Fraser, C. Speech as a marker of situation. In K. R. Scherer & H. Giles (Eds.), *Social markers in speech.* Cambridge: Cambridge University Press, 1979.

Delia, J. G., O'Keefe, B. J., & O'Keefe, D. J. The constructivist approach to communication. In F. E. X. Davis (Ed.). *Comparative human communication theory.* New York: Harper & Row, in press.

Ervin-Tripp, S. Sociolinguistics. In L. Berkowitz (Ed.), *Advances in experimental social psychology* (Vol. 4). New York: Academic Press, 1969.

Ferguson, C. A. Diglossia. *Word,* 1959, *15,* 325–340.

Festinger, L. A theory of social comparison processes. *Human Relations,* 1954, *7,* 117–140.

Fishman, J. A. The relationship between micro and macrosociolinguistics in the study of who speaks what language to whom and when. In J. B. Pride & J. Holmes (Eds.), *Sociolinguistics.* Harmondsworth, Middlesex: Penguin Books, 1972.

Forgas, J. *Social episodes: The study of interaction routines.* London: Academic Press, 1980.

Giles, H., & Hewstone, M. Cognitive structures, speech and social situations. *Language Sciences,* in press.

Giles, H., & Johnson, P. The role of language in ethnic group relations. In J. C. Turner & H. Giles (Eds.), *Intergroup behaviour.* Oxford: Blackwell, 1981.

Giles, H., & Powesland, P. *Speech style and social evaluation.* London: Academic Press, 1975.

Giles, H., & Ryan, E. B. Prolegomena for developing a social psychological theory of language attitudes. In E. B. Ryan & H. Giles (Eds.), *Attitudes towards language variation: Social and applied contexts.* London: Arnold, 1982.

Giles, H., Bourhis, R. Y., & Taylor, D. M. Towards a theory of lanugage in ethnic group relations. In H. Giles (Ed.), *Language, ethnicity and intergroup relations.* London: Academic Press, 1977.

Giles, H., Robinson, W. P., & Smith, P. M. (Eds.). *Language: Social psychological perspectives.* Oxford: Pergamon Press, 1980.

Gumperz, J. J. Linguistic and social interaction in two communities. *American Anthropologist,* 1964, *66*(supplement no. 6), 137–153.

Gumperz, J. J. Sociocultural knowledge in conversational inference. In M. Saville-Troike (Ed.), *28th Annual Round Table Monographs on Language and Linguistics.* Washington, D.C.: Georgetown University Press, 1977.

Handelman, D. Components of interaction in the negotiation of a definition of the situation. In W. C. McCormack & S. A. Wurm (Eds.), *Language and man: Anthropological issues.* The Hague: Mouton, 1975.

Heider, F. *The psychology of interpersonal relations.* New York: Wiley, 1958.

Hewstone, M., & Jaspars, J. Intergroup relations and attribution processes. In H. Tajfel (Ed.), *Social identity and intergroup relations.* Cambridge University Press, 1982.

Hymes, D. Models of the interaction of language and social life. In J. J. Gumperz & D. Hymes (Eds.), *Directions in sociolinguistics.* New York: Holt, Rinehart & Winston, 1972.

Kaplan, M. F. Context effects in impression formation: The weighted average versus the meaning change formulation. *Journal of personality and social psychology,* 1971, *19,* 92–99.

Kelley, H. H. Causal schemata and the attribution process. In E. E. Jones, D. E. Kanouse, H. H. Kelley, R. E. Nisbett, S. Valins, & B. Weiner (Eds.), *Attribution: Perceiving the causes of behavior.* Morristown, N.J.: General Learning Press, 1971.

Kendall, M. B. Radical grammars: Interplays of form and function. In H. Giles, W. P. Robinson, & P. M. Smith (Eds.), *Language: Social psychological persepctives*. Oxford: Pergamon Press, 1980.

Labov, W. *Sociolinguistics patterns*. Philadelphia: University of Pennsylvania Press, 1972.

Levinson, S. *Activity types and language* (Pragmatics Microfiche 3.3, DI). University of Cambridge, Department of Linguistics, 1978.

Mandler, J. M. *Categorical and schematic organization in memory* (Center for Human Information Processing (CHIP) Technical Report 76). University of California, San Diego, 1978.

Manis, J. G., & Meltzer, B. N. *Symbolic interaction: A reader in social psychology* (3rd ed.). Boston: Allyn and Bacon, 1978.

McCauley, C., Stitt, C., & Segal, M. Stereotyping: From prejudice to prediction. *Psychological Bulletin,* 1980, *87,* 195–208.

Michotte, A. *Perception of causality*. New York: Basic Books, 1963.

O'Keefe, B. J., & Delia, J. Psychological and interactional dimensions of communicative development. In H. Giles & R. St. Clair (Eds.), *Recent advances in language, communication and social psychology*. Hillsdale, N.J.: Erlbaum, 1982.

Parkin, D. Language switching in Nairobi. In W. H. Whiteley (Ed.), *Language in Kenya*. Nairobi: Oxford University Press, 1974.

Piaget, J. *The child's conception of the world*. New York: Harcourt & Brace, 1929.

Platt, J. T. A model for polyglossia and multilingualism (with special reference to Singapore and Malaysia). *Language in Society,* 1977, *6,* 161–178.

Reeder, G. D., & Brewer, M. B. A schematic model of dispositional attribution in interpersonal perception. *Psychological Review,* 1979, *86,* 61–79.

Roloff, M. E., & Berger, C. R. (Eds.). *Social cognition and communication*. Beverly Hills, Calif.: Sage, in press.

Rommetveit, R. *On message structure*. London: Wiley, 1974.

Ryan, E. B., & Giles, H. (Eds.). *Attitudes towards language variation: Social and applied contexts*. London: Arnold, 1982.

Schank, R. C., & Abelson, R. P. *Scripts, plans, goals and understanding*. Hillsdale, N.J.: Erlbaum, 1977.

Scherer, K. R., & Giles, H. *Social markers in speech*. Cambridge: Cambridge University Press, 1979.

Schneider, D. J., Hastorf, A. H., & Ellsworth, P. C. *Person perception* (2nd ed.). Reading, Mass.: Addison-Wesley, 1979.

Scotton, C. & Ury, W. Bilingual strategies: The social functions of code-switching. *International journal of the Sociology of Language,* 1977, *13,* 5–20.

Smith, P. M., Giles, H., & Hewstone, M. Sociolinguistics: A social psychological perspective. In R. St. Clair & H. Giles (Eds.), *The social and psychological contexts of language*. Hillsdale, N.J.: Erlbaum, 1980.

Suls, J. M., & Miller, R. L. *Social comparison processes*. Washington, D.C.: Hemisphere, 1977.

Tajfel, H. Social stereotypes and social groups. In J. C. Turner & H. Giles (Eds.), *Intergroup behaviour*. Oxford: Blackwell, 1981(a).

Tajfel, H. *Human groups and social categories*. Cambridge: Cambridge University Press, 1981(b).

Trudgill, P. (Ed.). *Sociolinguistic patterns in British English*. London: Arnold, 1978.

Turner, J. C. Towards a cognitive redefinition of the social group. In H. Tajfel (Ed.), *Social identity and intergroup relations*. Cambridge: Cambridge University Press, in press.

Turner, J. C., & Giles, H. *Intergroup behaviour*. Oxford: Blackwell, 1981.

Tversky, A., & Kahneman, D. Causal schemes in judgements under uncertainty. In M. Fishbein (Ed.), *Progress in social psychology*. Hillsdale, N.J.: Erlbaum, 1980.

Vygotsky, L. *Thought and language*. Boston: MIT Press, 1962.

Werner, H., & Kaplan, B. *Symbol formation*. New York: Wiley, 1963.

Wish, M. Dimensions of dyadic communication. In S. Weitz (Ed.), *Nonverbal communication* (and ed.). New York: Oxford University Press, 1978.

Wyer, R., & Carlston, D. *Social cognition, inference and attribution*. Hillsdale, N.J.: Erlbaum, 1979.

Yamamoto, A. Communication in culture spaces. In W. McCromack & S. Wurm (Eds.), *Language and society: Anthropological issues*. The Hague: Mouton, 1979.

18

Language as the Instrument of School Socialization: An Examination of Bernstein's Thesis

Harry Osser

An assumption shared by many educators is that language is somehow a crucial factor in a child's education. There are a number of basic research questions that have been raised which refer to the role of language in school. They include: (1) How is language related to school learning? and (2) How are a child's language performances related to success or failure in school? The observer only has to spend a small amount of time in school settings to realize that language is pervasive there. The children are told through language what to do, when to do it, how to do it, and when to stop; further, they are verbally praised or punished for their performance. The extent to which they understand, or fail to understand, what the teacher has said is also available to the teacher through the evaluation of the questions the children ask, as well as the answers they provide to questions. In fact, the language of the classroom is even more complex, for not only does the teacher inform the child and thereafter test the child's comprehension of the content of school subjects, but, in addition, the child is told *who* and *what* to be, or in other words, what forms and expressions of social-cognitive competence are valued by the teacher.

No one has yet made an inventory of the language demands made on children in school; however, the minimal language demands must include listening to the teacher and asking and answering questions to offer proof of attention to the lesson. The child's answers may take the form of mere repetitions or simple paraphrases of what the teacher has just said, or the child, perhaps uncommonly, may offer an original answer or pose a novel question to the teacher. Language in the classroom is pervasive because it is valued there as the principal means of socializing, or resocializing, children into the appropriate forms of behavior and skills judged to be

Harry Osser ● Faculty of Education, Queen's University, Kingston, Ontario K7L 3N6, Canada.

required by all members of society. It is also the central means of reaffirming certain values and skills already available to some elite subgroups.

Language and Educational Failure

Conventional contemporary thought on the topic of educational failure is that it is primarily a function of the child's linguistic skills. Bisseret (1979) placed this characterization in historical perspective. She argued that academic inequalities have, in the past, been interpreted variously as functions of inherited "aptitudes" or "abilities"; that is, that school failure reflects fundamental intellectual deficiencies. Interpretation of school failure, especially that of lower class children, she suggested, was changed in the 1960s by substituting alternative theories of linguistic and cultural differences across social groups. She credited Bernstein with being "one of the first researchers to have broken with the dominant ideology by demonstrating the existence and importance of linguistic factors in scholastic success, thereby demonstrating the limits of the theory of aptitudes" (p. 90).

Any examination of the roles language plays in educational failure and success must consider the work of Bernstein, because it represents the most widely discussed theory and body of empirical research on the possible causal connections between the social class background of children, language performance, and the production of rates of educational failure. His research is organized around these two major themes: (1) linguistic codes and (2) knowledge codes (Bernstein, 1971, 1973, 1975).

Linguistic Codes

In his discussion of language and socialization in the family, Bernstein (1971) argued that with respect to the ways in which parents attempt to control their children, there exist two distinct family types. The first is the *positional* family, in which the children are controlled in terms of status. In this type of family, usually lower class, the parents focus on the general characteristics of the child, such as sex and age. Parents in the second family type, the *person-oriented* family, which is most commonly middle-class, focus on *particular* characteristics of the child, those that are *specific* to him/her. In the positional family, the child's identity is thrust upon him/her; in the person-oriented family, the child has some authority in shaping his/her own identity. The communicative consequences are that in the person-oriented family, the parents' social control strategies involve making the principles, reasons, and motives behind their own and others' actions explicit, so that the language used in such families is qualitatively different from that of positional families, in which parents tend to control their children by issuing orders, rather than by offering detailed explanations. Bernstein suggested that the distinctive forms of social control are communicated through the use of an elaborated code in the case of the person-oriented parents and a restricted code by the positional parents. Bernstein argued that the linguistic code typically employed by parents in the course of socialization becomes the child's own preferred code.

Theoretically, the parents' use of an elaborated code should orient the child to the use of context-free language, whereas parents use of a restricted code would usually result in the child's using relatively context-bound speech. The restricted code speaker will only be able to communicate with those with whom s/he shares many assumptions, experiences, and meanings. The elaborated code user is less dependent on shared knowledge. The two linguistic (or sociolinguistic) codes are presumed to provide access to different *orders of meaning*. A restricted code gives access to *particularistic* orders of meaning, in which, for example, principles of action remain implicit and therefore are less available to reconsideration and change. By contrast, an elaborated code gives access to *universalistic* orders of meaning so that principles can be made explicit and are thereby open to change. The educational significance of the different modes of social control in the two family types and their correlative linguistic codes is, according to Bernstein, as follows. The school is predicated on an elaborated code, with its associated universalistic order of meaning. A prerequisite for school success is for the child to have access to a linguistic code that will make available a universalistic order of meaning, and a restricted code, by definition, does not allow this. The child who has been socialized in such a manner that his/her predominant linguistic code is a restricted one (typically a child from a lower-class family), will fail in school relative to the performance of middle-class children there.

Empirical Evidence on Linguistic Codes

The empirical evidence provided by Bernstein's (London-based) research team to support the concept of class-related linguistic codes that is at the heart of his theory typically takes the common form that speakers of middle-class background tend to use *more* of a certain kind of language form than speakers of lower-class background. The differences are never absolute. What the data commonly display is that *both* groups use the same linguistic items (e.g., complex noun groups), but one group uses them more frequently than the other. Bernstein nevertheless argued for a sharp contrast between the two underlying modes of speech, which he calls restricted and elaborated codes. The meaning of differences in relative frequency in the use of linguistic items must be understood. Suppose that in five minutes of speech a lower-class child uses simple pronouns most of the time (he, she, it, etc.) and just once uses a complex noun group (e.g., the very old man). This pattern proves that s/he does know how to use complex noun phrases, not that s/he does not. The empirical work shows only what appear to be rather minor differences in relative frequency of some grammatical items. However, if these differences continue to be found, they will merit some attention. What would have to be explained is *why* lower-class children do not frequently use linguistic forms which they clearly know (cf. Dittmar, this volume).

New Developments in Research

Over the past few years, the study of the connections between language and education has been invigorated by reformulating some of the Bernstein group's basic research questions and procedures. Essentially, the newer lines of research have been built on an examination of the constituents of the child's communicative or interactional knowledge. In such studies, the child, irrespective of social class background, is seen as an *active* partner in conversations with adults, whether they be teachers or parents. The basic research questions are: (1) what are the connections between social class, language usage (including planning functions), and school performance? (2) what are the similarities and differences between the communicative demands on the child at home and at school? and (3) what is the appropriate research strategy to uncover the layers of the child's communicative competence? Mehan (1980) provided the context for the discussion of these questions by stating: "To participate effectively in the classroom, students must, indeed, accumulate a stock of academic knowledge. Students must also learn that there are interactionally appropriate ways to cast their academic knowledge" (p. 137). Many contemporary studies are organized around the latter topic of communicative competence (cf. John-Steiner & Tatter, this volume).

Studies in Communicative Competence

Collett, Lamb, Fenlugh, and McPhail (1981) have argued that Bernstein's theory, or at least some of its crucial features, has not received any empirical support. An example is Bernstein's claim that use of the restricted code has direct consequences for the user's ability to communicate efficiently. Collett *et al.* also proposed that Bernstein and his co-workers "have merely relied on the assumption that an investigation of differences in the speech styles of the two classes, will, in itself, be sufficient to indicate their cognitive and communicative abilities" (p. 312). Collett *et al.* designed a study in part to test the hypothesis that differences in speech styles may have insignificant communicative consequences. In this study, lower- and middle-class children 10–11 years of age were cast in the role of instructor or receiver in a communication task. The results indicated that whereas there were significant social-class-related differences in the formal properties of the children's speech, there were no consequent effects on communicative efficiency. Collett *et al.* commented on this finding:

> The fact that there is no necessary relationship between the structure of speech and its communicative functions, is not entirely surprising, especially when one considers that speech is always the property of one individual, whereas communication is inevitably the property of at least two people. It is possible to describe the structure of speech according to some scheme or other, but a full understanding of its communicative properties must necessarily wait upon the analysis of what the speech does to, or for the listener. . . . He builds upon the content of what he is given, filling in gaps and making explicit what is often implicit. Because communication is a joint activity, it cannot, by definition, be exposed by an analysis of individual activity. Only by externalizing the impact of speech, by requiring a listener, say, to follow instructions, and then examining his performance, can we begin to explore the relationship between the characteristics of speech and the characteristics of communication. (p. 318).

Toft and Kitwood (1980) also suggested that much of the research carried out by Bernstein's group was based on a speech model that failed to acknowledge the interactional nature of verbal communication. Toft and Kitwood argued further that the application of the results of speech samples produced under experimentally controlled conditions to everyday life is imperfect. To avoid procedural and interpretive flaws, they used speech obtained through informal interviews with adolescents of different social class backgrounds. The participants had been invited to discuss their values by presenting accounts of typical incidents in their recent experience and to provide information about the grounds of their actions and decisions. The study was predicated on a conception of the person as perceptive, constructive, and active, which corresponds to the theoretical stance of Prucha, Slama-Cazacu, and Titone (this volume). An attempt was made to minimize the asymmetries of power and status that are common features of the typical experiment. The expectation was that a friendly and informal conversation would take place, as similar as possible to some kinds of interaction in everyday life.

The language samples were analyzed using 16 categories derived from Bernstein's theory. Significant social class differences were observed in only three of these categories. Toft and Kitwood suggested that the observed differences were quite limited and were not obviously associated with the speaker's communicative competence. In further discussion, they suggested that it is possible to draw two inferences from their results. One is that their categories of analysis emphasizing the *structure* of language are insufficiently sensitive to social class differences, which might show up more clearly if their model were more closely linked with function. The other is that lower-class adolescents have much richer linguistic resources than is implied in much of the work associated with Bernstein's theory.

Speech-planning Functions and Social Class Membership

MacWhinney and Osser (1977) tested Bernstein's hypothesis that significant differences should exist between lower- and middle-class speakers with respect to verbal planning for explicit symbolization. The method chosen to explore verbal planning functions was to examine the various hesitations and dislocations that occur in speech. Bernstein (1962; see also Hawkins, 1973) examined the silent pauses in the speech of lower- and middle-class adolescent boys. He found, in part, that lower-class boys spent less time pausing, which suggested that they were spending less time planning, presumably because the speech sequences they were producing were heavily precoded and therefore highly accessible. Instead of looking at a single type of hesitation, MacWhinney and Osser examined 13 categories of hesitation phenomena in the speech of children who, according to Bernstein's theory, would be likely to take up either the elaborated or restricted code as their primary mode of communication. They found no evidence of difference in verbal planning functions between the two social class groups, although sex-related differences were observed (cf. Phillips, this volume).

Language Use, Social Class of Speaker, and Educational Success

Wells (1977) has investigated the relationships between language use, social class, and educational success. His basic speech data were spontaneous speech of 32

3-year-old children recorded in their homes. He argued that if one follows Bernstein's theoretical position—namely, that as a result of their primary socialization at home, children develop preferences for using their language resources for different purposes—then "recordings made of spontaneous speech in the home should serve only to magnify whatever differences there may be between children from different home environments" (p. 13). The transcripts were analyzed by using a set of functional categories developed by Tough (1977). Wells assessed the educational success of 20 of these children by testing their reading performance at the end of their first year at school. The results of the analyses indicate that there was no clear-cut relationship between language use and either social class membership or educational success after one year of schooling.

In his discussion, Wells expressed his reservations on the common practice of generalizing about children' habitual use of language from speech samples that are restricted and nonspontaneous:

> Although the external features of the situations may have been the same for each child, there is no certainty that each child's perception of the task demands was the same. Nor can it reasonably be inferred that, because a child did not choose to use language for a particular function within a particular interview situation, he cannot, and does not do so, in other situations where the relationship between the communication partners is different. (p. 18)

Whereas Wells did not dispute the contributory role to a child's success in the educational system of the use of language for complex purposes, he argued: "But I do question the assumption that such uses of language are important, and, as such, are central to skill in communication" (p. 20). In his view, the predominant communicative skill is to be able to collaborate with another person "in the joint construction of a shared reality" (p. 20). Successful communication can only be understood by examining the speech of conversational partners. What he suggested is the necessity of developing some measures of the interrelatedness of the utterances of both participants.

Wells suggested that

> those who wish to show that the language of lower-class children is different, will always find evidence to prove their point, but it does not follow that such differences necessarily put these children at an educational disadvantage— unless they trigger off expectations that all too easily become self-fulfilling (p. 22).

Wells finally argued that the most promising way to study the contribution of language to educational success is to examine the collaboration and negotiations which take place between participants in a dialogue (cf. Harris, this volume).

Adult–Child Interaction at Home and at School: The Bristol Group

A great deal of energy has been invested over the past 20 years in the investigation of the connections between language, social class, and educational disadvantage, especially focusing on the presumed differences between the language of home and school. However, there have been few systematic attempts to develop naturalistic data obtained in both settings (cf. Cazden, this volume). The group at Bristol University is trying to fill this gap. Wells and Montgomery (1981) started with the analysis of texts of particular conversations, with the intention of identifying "styles of interaction" which may be related to larger issues, such as what the differences may be between the "language of the home" and the "language of the school" and the different opportunities these two interactional contexts provide for children to develop control of the resources of linguistic communication.

One of the questions Wells and Montgomery pose is: "Can some of the differences between children in the rate of their initial language learning, for example, be accounted for by differences in the quality of the linguistic interaction they experience?" (p. 229). In an earlier study, Ellis and Wells (1980) found that speech addressed by adults to more rapidly developing children was significantly different in a number of ways from that addressed to slow developers; in particular, it contains a larger number of acknowledgments of the child's contributions as well as of the joint activities of child and adult.

In a study of two conversations between mothers and their 2-year olds, Wells, Montgomery, and MacLure (1979) found that two styles of interaction were distinguishable in that whereas the first mother encouraged her child to take on an autonomous role in the conversation, the second mother retained control of the discourse by making initiating moves herself, thus casting the child in the role of respondent. The first child's contributions to the conversation were found, not surprisingly, to be linguistically more mature than the second child's; such a difference might well be related to the opportunities made available by each mother's style of interaction. Such comparisons suggest a way of studying the learning that takes place through language use at home and at school and of investigating the different degrees of success achieved by different children in both language and academic development.

Wells and Montgomery did not find a sharp discontinuity in their various studies between the interaction styles of home and school. They argued that the major differences were not in the style of discourse itself, but in the type of information being exchanged and how it relates to the child's experience. They found that much of the talk at home for example, arises out of the child's immediate activities and interests, whereas the content of classroom exchanges is directly related to the curriculum, over which the child has very little control.

Question and Answer Sequences

Two other members of the Bristol group, MacLure and French (1981), raised these questions: (1) How far is it feasible to suggest that classroom encounters with language are a new and strange experience to the novice pupil? (2) In which *specific* ways may the language of teacher and pupils be seen as aligned or unaligned with that of parents and their children? (3) At what level do school and home language, irrespective of social background, have properties in common?

MacLure and French elected to study the organization of question and answer sequences because they saw them as central to classroom interaction. The issue here is how questions are handled by the participants in each setting.

It is commonly accepted that question-answer sequences in school tend to have a three part structure, consisting of

   I.   TEACHER: (*Question*)
   II. PUPIL: (*Answer*)
   III. TEACHER: (*Evaluation*)

This question–answer structure is also commonly found in the home data.

   I.   MOTHER: What's that?
   II. CHILD: Boat.
   III. MOTHER: A boat, yes.

It can be reasonably claimed that the three-part question structure is not unfamiliar to children starting school.

An associated feature of questions and answers in the classroom is that they are typically *pseudoquestions,* that is, the questioner is asking the respondent for a display of knowledge already available to the questioner, for example, "Who is the president of France?" It turns out that this conversational strategy is also very common in adult–child talk in the home during the preschool years. The proportion of pseudoquestions is, however, much higher in the school data. A second difference in question–answer sequences in the home and at school noticed by MacLure and French is that child-initiated questions are much more frequent in the home.

Children's Strategies for Answering Questions

MacLure and French discovered that a possible answering strategy for the child was to identify an item presented in the teacher's question as a superordinate term for a class of items and to select his answers in terms of their membership in that class. For example,

   TEACHER: What is the squirrel looking for?
   CHILDREN: Nuts.
   TEACHER: Paul, what sort of nuts?
   PAUL: Acorns.
   TEACHER: Yes. Any other nuts, Karen?
   KAREN: Coconuts.
   TEACHER: Not coconuts, no.
   CHILD: Hazelnuts.

There is evidence in MacLure and French's data that preschool children operate at home with the same abstract categorization procedure to come up with answers.

It appears that by the time children enter school, most are familiar, to some degree, with the pseudoquestioning techniques and the associated conversational formats. They may also be equipped with strategies for answering their teacher's questions when they are uncertain of their information. MacLure and French conclude that there does not seem to be any fundamental discontinuity with regard to questioning and answering between the language of the home and that of the school.

Conversational Structure at Home and at School

Sequences involving questions and answers in home and school settings comprise only a part of the complex structuring of interaction, and given this limited and partial analysis of home and school interactions, only a few tentative conclusions can be drawn. It appears that children do *not* enter a culture of unfamiliar interactional routines when they enter school. There does appear to be much continuity in the nature of home and school interaction despite differences in the two settings. Many of the interactional demands in school will be familiar to children of all social backgrounds. The differences across the interactions in each setting consist of relative frequency of types in the two settings, as well as the asymmetry of the participants' contributions to the interactions.

Summary of Research on Linguistic Codes

The results of many recent studies of children's language clearly do not corroborate the social-class-related language differences previously observed by members of Bernstein's Sociological Research Unit. It would appear that data generated by this group may well be artifacts of the research procedures used, rather than representative samples of lower-class children's speech. Interesting new questions are being raised and useful research strategies developed; however, there are still relatively few significant studies of the sociolinguistic resources of children from different social backgrounds (see also Dittmar, 1976).

Knowledge Codes

The second theme in Bernstein's work is summarized in this statement: "It has always been clear to me that the class structure affected access to elaborated codes through its influence upon initial socialization into the family *and* through its fundamental shaping of both the organizational structure and contents of education" (Bernstein, 1971, p. 241). His argument is that the lower-class child's chance of academic success is reduced by the manner in which the *educational knowledge code* is structured. This term refers to the three basic message systems of the school. These are: (1) *curriculum*, or what counts as valid knowledge; (2) *pedagogy*, or the way such knowledge is transmitted; and (3) *evaluation*, or what counts as acceptable realizations of that knowledge. In this argument, Bernstein has clearly allotted the responsibility for lower-class children's academic failure to the school and the ways in which its educational knowledge code is biased against children whose predominant linguistic code is a restricted one. Bourdieu (1974) offered a smiilar argument: "To penalize the underprivileged, and favour the most privileged, the school has only to neglect in its teaching methods and techniques, and its criteria when making academic judgements, to take into account the cultural inequalities between children of different social classes" (pp. 37–38; cf. Maseman, this volume). In specifying this differentially distributed knowledge, Bourdieu focused on language:

> By acting as if the language of teaching, full of allusions and shared understanding, was "natural" for "intelligent" and "gifted" pupils, teachers need not trouble to make any technical checks on their handling of language, and the student's understanding of it, and can also see, as strictly fair, academic judgments, which in fact perpetuate cultural privilege. (pp. 39–40)

Bourdieu was obviously arguing that it is the *teacher's* language, rather than the child's, that takes too much for granted.

Empirical Evidence Concerning Knowledge Codes

There are relatively few studies of how knowledge is transmitted in school, and fewer still that bear a direct relationship to the study of the interconnections between language usage, social class membership, and educational attainment. There are, however, some studies of teacher and student language which do illuminate the three aspects of the educational knowledge code, namely, curriculum, pedagogy, and evaluation. Barnes (1969), for example, has studied language used by secondary school teachers. He found that in using certain words, they often assume that the student has access to knowledge that, in fact, he or she does not necessarily possess. Barnes offered an illustration of the pedagogical practices of a teacher:

> In trying to explain "city-states," the teacher seems unable to escape from language equally unfamiliar to children: "complete in themselves," "ruled by themselves," "supported themselves," "communicate," "tended to be." City-states is typical of the concepts which teachers are enough aware of to "present" to pupils; the other phrases exemplify the language of secondary education, which this teacher was so unaware of that he used it to explain the former, . . . In learning such essential concepts as "tendency," which form part of no specialization, the child is given no support from school, which tacitly assumes that he comprehends them. Children whose home life does not support such language learning may feel themselves to be excluded from the conversation in the classroom. (p. 55)

In another study, Keddie (1971) provided an example of a teacher's biased evaluation procedures. In a lesson which Keddie observed, the children were shown a slide of the fetus in the womb. A boy in a "C" ability group asked about the fetus: "How does it go to the toilet, then?" Keddie relayed this as an example of the children's questions to a group of teachers, one of whom said that the boy must have been joking. Keddie's comment about the teacher is: "At the least, he implies that these questions are not appropriate to the business of learning, and it is likely that his response is to the pupil's language, and has a social class basis" (p. 158). It does appear that the teacher was responding to the style of language and the child's status as a "C"stream student, rather than to the concept he was formulating.

Summary of Research on Educational Codes

Bernstein's theories of the transmission of knowledge and of the roles that the curriculum, pedagogic practices, and school evaluative procedures play in controlling the lower-class child's academic performance, as well as Bourdieu's parallel theoretical statements, are attempts, on a grand scale, to explain lower-class children's relative school failure. The broadness of the arguments makes them difficult to pin down empirically, thus accounting in part for the scarcity of studies that directly test the connections between the performance of lower-class children in school and the forms taken by the school's knowledge code. The empirical research of both Barnes (1969) and and Keddie (1971) suggests that the consequences of the child's predominant linguistic code in school learning can only be fully understood by referring to the character of the school's (or the teacher's) knowledge codes. Analysis of the manner in which each of the three message systems impinges on the classroom performances of children from different social backgrounds should yield valuable information on some of the causal relations between classroom language use of both teachers and children and the latter's educational attainments.

In conclusion, schools, according to Bernstein, are predicated on the use of an elaborated code and, as a consequence, the lower-class child *must* fail in school, unless, in the course of being resocialized, s/he adopts its sociolinguistic values. Remarkably, these views have not led to many studies of how lower- and middle-class children *actually* use language in school. This is one area where we have to make progress. We need more studies of children's and teachers' classroom communications that will permit us to understand in detail how the teacher's use of the curriculum, pedagogic practices, and evaluative procedures in the classroom relates to the judgment that the child is failing or succeeding there (cf. Hymes, this volume). This is an ambitious proposal, but its implementation could lead to substantial progress in our comprehending some of the complex relations between language, social class, and educational performance.

References

Barnes, D. *Language, the learner and the school,* Harmondsworth, Middlesex: Penguin Books, 1969.

Bernstein, B. Linguistic codes, hesitation phenomena, and intelligence. *Language and Speech,* 1962, *5,* 31–46.

Bernstein, B. *Class, codes and control* (Vol. 1). London: Routledge and Kegan Paul, 1971.

Bernstein, B. *Class, codes and control* (Vol. 2). London: Routledge and Kegan Paul, 1973.

Bernstein, B. *Class, codes and control* (Vol. 3). London: Routledge and Kegan Paul, 1975.

Bisseret, N. *Education, class language and ideology.* London: Routledge & Kegan Paul, 1979.

Bourdieu, P. The school as a conservative force. In J. Eggleston (Ed.), *Contemporary research in the sociology of education.* London: Methuen, 1974, pp. 32–46.

Collett, P., Lamb, R., Fenlaugh, K., & McPhail, P. Social class and linguistic variation. In M. Argyle, A. Furnham, & J. A. Graham, *Social situations.* Cambridge: Cambridge University Press, 1981, pp. 312–318.

Dittmar, N. *Sociolinguistics: A critical survey of theory and application.* Birkenhead, Great Britain: Edward Arnold, 1976.

Ellis, R., & Wells, G. Enabling factors in adult-child discourse. *First Language,* 1980, *1,* 46–62.

Hawkins, P. The influence of sex, social class, and pause-location in the hesitation phenomena of seven-year-old children. In B. Bernstein (Ed.), *Class, codes and control* (Vol. 2). London: Routledge and Kegan Paul, 1973, pp. 235–252.

Keddie, N. Classroom knowledge. In M. F. D. Young (Ed.), *Knowledge and control.* London: Mac-Millan, 1971.

MacLure, M., & French, P. A comparison of talk at home and at school. In G. Wells, A. Bridges, P. French, M. MacLure, C. Sinha, V. Walkerdine, & B. Woll, *Learning through interaction.* Cambridge: Cambridge University Press, 1981, pp. 205–239.

MacWhinney, B., & Osser, H. Verbal planning functions in children's speech. *Child Development,* 1977, *48,* 978–985.

Mehan, H. On competent students. *Anthropology and Education Quarterly,* 1980, *11,* 132–152.

Toft, B., & Kitwood, J. M. An exploratory study of adolescent speech using measures derived from Bernstein's theory. *Research in Education,* 1980, *23,* 44–56.

Tough, J. *The development of meaning.* London: Unwin, 1977.

Wells, G. Language use and educational success: An empirical response to Joan Tough's *The development of meaning. Research in Education,* 1977, *18,* 9–34.

Wells, G., & Montgomery, M. Adult-child interaction at home and at school. In P. French & M. MacLure (Eds.), *Adult-child conversation.* London: Croom Helm, 1981, pp. 210–243.

Wells, G., Montgomery, M. M., & MacLure, M. Adult-child discourse: outline of a model of analysis, *Journal of Pragmatics,* 1979, *3,* 337–80.

19

The Rise of the Vernaculars in Early Modern Europe: An Essay in the Political Economy of Language

Ian Parker

Language and labor are outer expressions in which the individual no longer retains possession of himself *per se,* but lets the inner get right outside him, and surrenders it to something else. For that reason we might just as truly say that these outer expressions express the inner too much as that they do so too little. (Hegel, 1967, p. 340)

The production of ideas, of conceptions, of consciousness, is at first directly interwoven with the material activity and the material intercourse of men, the language of real life. Conceiving, thinking, the mental intercourse of men, appear at this stage as the direct efflux of their material behavior. The same applies to mental production as expressed in the language of politics, laws, morality, religion, metaphysics, etc. of a people. Men are the producers of their conceptions, ideas, etc.—real, active men, as they are conditioned by a definite development of their productive forces and of the intercourse corresponding to these, up to its furthest forms. . . .

    From the start the "spirit" is afflicted with the curse of being "burdened" with matter, which here makes its appearance in the form of agitated layers of air, sounds, in short, of language. Language is as old as consciousness, language *is* practical consciousness that exists also for other men, and for that reason alone it really exists for me personally as well; language, like consciousness, only arises from the need, the necessity, of intercourse with other men. . . . Consciousness is . . . from the very beginning a social product, and remains so as long as men exist at all. (Marx & Engels, 1970, pp. 47–51)

Instead of producing something common to all that we call language, I am saying that these phenomena have no one thing in common which makes us use the

Ian Parker ● Department of Economics, Scarborough College, University of Toronto, West Hill, Ontario M1C 1A4, Canada.

same word for all,—but that they are *related* to one another in many different ways. And it is because of this relationship, or these relationships, that we call them all "language." . . . [We] see a complicated network of similarities, overlapping and criss-crossing: sometimes overall similarities, sometimes similarities of detail. (Wittgenstein, 1953, pp. 31–32).

Introduction

A sociogenetic orientation toward language and human conduct assumes a concern with the relations between language and economy and thus inevitably poses the theoretical question of the possibility of an economics, or a political economy, of language. This chapter will examine the rise of the vernaculars in late medieval and early modern Europe and its relationship to contemporaneous developments such as the extension of commerce; the spread of paper, printing, literacy, and lay education; the emergence of absolutist nation-states; Protestantism; and the spread of humanism. In so doing, it is intended to cast light on certain linguistic aspects of the transition from feudalism to capitalism and to provide some historical perspective on such theoretical issues in sociogenetic linguistics as the relations between linguistic and political-economic change, the role of specialized languages in reproducing monopolies of knowledge, and the implications of linguistic imperialism and colonialism.

Yet some theoretical consideration of the relations between language and economy would appear to be a necessary prelude to such an economic-historical exploration. The next section, therefore, will briefly survey the treatment of language within economics and will suggest some elements that appear to be of importance in the articulation and development of the political economy of language, as a context for the historical discussion that follows.

On the Economics of Language

Economists on Language

Despite its strategic importance in a number of interrelated theoretical-historical spheres, the economics or the political economy of language is in many respects still in its infancy as an integrated field of investigation. Stress must be placed on the word "integrated" in the preceding sentence. Considerable attention has been paid by social anthropologists, cultural historians, literary theorists, and linguisticians, particularly historical linguists and historians of particular languages, to problems which bear on the development of the economics of language. Yet in terms of what is implied by the "sociogenesis" of language, remarkably little work has been done from an economic or political-economic standpoint in tracing the historical and theoretical interdeterminations of language and economy or of linguistic and political-economic systems.

There are powerful reasons for this neglect. Not all of these stem from the character of disciplinary specialization that has been both a cause and an effect of the economic and linguistic centrifugal pressures related to the historical articulation of the division of labor within the social sciences. The tracing of that process would itself be an important element in a fully developed economics of language. Perhaps even more significant are the formidable methodological difficulties present in any investigation of the relations between language and economy: (1) the dangers of oversimplification, premature closure, or reductionism, of giving insufficient attention to the full range of mediations and processes of reciprocal causation and mutual determination involved, or of assigning an unjustified privileged "causal" or "explanatory" status to some elements, political-economic or linguistic, in the field, at the expense of others; (2) the radical uncertainty concerning the relative weight to be attached to strictly incomparable types of evidence drawn from different realms of discourse; and, at base, (3) the possible implication that such an investigation is central both as origin and as end of a self-reflexive historical materialist epistemology. The enterprise thus involves major methodological difficulties as well as potentially considerable returns.

In view of the potential returns from analysis of the economics of language, however, the limited amount of systematic exploration of the field by economists is still perhaps surprising. A brief survey of economists' writings on the subject should suggest, both by its content and by its brevity, the relative neglect language has experienced as a sphere of economic enquiry. Fraser's (1947) study, *Economic Thought and Language,* is an important contribution to economic methodology and contains some valuable insights into economically determined processes of "semantic subreption" in certain basic categories of economic thought and discourse, but its principal concern is with the language of economics, rather than with the economics of language. In addition to Machlup's (1972) study of the production and distribution of knowledge in the United States, his work on economic semantics, for example, demonstrates a deep concern with the economic significance for scientific inquiry of the uses of particular terms, but his writings in the area do not generally treat the existence of a well-defined language system as in itself economically problematical.

The methodological writings of economists like Stanley Jevons and Roy Harrod raise a number of issues related to the economics of language, although the relationship between their logical-linguistic analyses and their economic contributions is at best implicit. Similarly, while Keynes's *Treatise on Probability* (1973) is an important source with respect to certain problems in the economics of probability and language (most notably in its emphasis on probability as involving the *propositional* logic of partial belief, which in contrast to other economic approaches to uncertainty permits—indeed necessitates—an integral role for language in the *production* of probability judgments), it plays virtually no explicit role, with the exception of a minor footnote reference in the *General Theory* (1964, p. 148), in Keynes's economic writings. Virtually all of G. L. Shackle's writings have an implicit or explicit epistemological concern, related to a sensitivity to the temporal dimension in the formation of expectations and decision under conditions of uncertainty, although language *per se* receives limited explicit attention.

The Austrian school of economists, including Carl Menger himself and more particularly Hayek (1963) and Ludwig von Mises, have expended much labor on problems of epistemology and communication under conditions of uncertainty, but most of their major economic writings do not reflect (except perhaps implicitly) a fusion of the linguistic and economic strands of their thought. Some mathematical economists, most notably Hurwicz (1973) and Marschak (1963, 1968; Marschak & Radner, 1972), have devoted considerable attention to general models of certain stylized communication processes in economic systems. The direct relevance of these models to the economics of language, however, is severely curtailed by the restrictiveness of the assumptions they require to generate determinate results, although Marschak's (1963) theorem on the optimal degree of "fineness" or capacity for distinction in a communication channel is still of considerable heuristic value in providing insight into the economic forces which underlie processes of lexical articulation and refinement.

The foregoing inventory, with three significant exceptions considered below, constitutes a reasonably complete catalogue of economists' contributions to the study of the interrelations between language and economy. Three features of the catalogue are worth noting: first, the brevity of the list, even with a generous stretching of definition to include many of the contributions as having a "linguistic" aspect; second, the separation which exists for a number of these economists between their "linguistic" studies and their principal "economic" works; and third, the fact that virtually without exception these works have been consigned to the margins of mainstream economic thought, notwithstanding the pervasive importance of language as the primary medium of communication in all historical economic systems.

It is arguable that apart from the methodological difficulties and pressures toward disciplinary specialization that militate against investigation of the economics of language, the very pervasiveness of linguistic phenomena in all economic systems has conferred a sort of invisibility that accounts for their relative neglect by economists. Yet it is also distinctly possible that the invisibility may be indicative of a systematic predisposition, or incapacity, in the language of mainstream economics itself. In Robbins's (1952, p. 16) now classic formulation, which treats economics as a subfield of the logic of choice, "economics is the science which studies human behavior as a relationship between ends and scarce means which have alternative uses." Tastes, technology, property rights, and resources are here assumed to be given and well defined. The primary concern is with the efficient allocation of resources through marginal adjustments *within a given system,* guided by the "ratios of valuation" generated by a costless implicit or explicit price system, rather than with the determinants or preconditions of system reproduction and transformation in space and over time. Such a conception of the economic process tends to privilege what Georgescu-Roegen (1974, pp. 60–94, 330–345), himself an eminent mathematical economist, has criticized as excessively "arithmomorphic" modes of analysis, and a focus on phenomena whose relationships can be more or less readily reduced to quantitative form. Merleau-Ponty (1967, p. xxviii) has noted a methodologically problematical linguistic aspect of this bias in his observation that "the numerical determinations of science are schematically patterned upon a constitution of the world which is already made before them" (cf. Kvale, this volume). Of even more direct significance than this metatheoretical difficulty is the fact that language does not enter into the choice or valuation process as it is modeled within mainstream neoclassical economic theory, and that the marginalist apparatus falters in relation to the indivisible or *systemic* character of communications systems generally and of language in particular.

It is hence not accidental that the three political economists who have contributed most to the development of the economics of language have all been sensitive to the systemic character of economic processes, concerned with historical processes of structural economic transformation, and preoccupied with a wider range of communication processes than those of the price system alone. Boulding's works, for example, perhaps especially *The Image* (1966), have illuminated the range of processes of ecological competition, symbiosis, and parasitism that characterize political-economic activity and consistently emphasize the linguistic-epistemological dimension of economic systems and processes.

Marx's writings contain numerous brilliant asides on the economics of language, although with the exception of certain brief discussions, particularly in the earlier works, of the relations between language, ideology, and the mode of production, his observations are expressed primarily in aphoristic rather than systematic form. Nonetheless, his basic dialectical-materialist standpoint, with its emphasis on the integrated and many-sided character of human activity and on the social and material determination of consciousness, is eminently conducive to investigation of the economics of language, as Williams (1977, pp. 21–44) has suggested in a subtle and brilliantly commonsensical analysis of language as practical consciousness.

The third political economist who can be said to have made a major contribution to the economic theory and history of language is Innis (1946, 1952, 1964, 1972, 1980). His later works on the history of communications in western civilization constitute in part a path-breaking exploration from a historical materialist standpoint of the interdeterminations of political economy and language, as a central element in his investigation of the role of communications in the historical development and decline of empires. Innis's overall project remained unfinished at his death in 1952, and virtually inevitably, in an original historical study conducted over a relatively short period of time on such a vast spatial and temporal scale, his works contain some errors of historical fact and judgment. Notwithstanding these limitations, Innis's studies represent a major advance in theoretical and historical understanding (Parker, 1977, 1980). The notions of "forces of production" and "relations of production" and of "economic base" and "superstructure" developed by Marx have hindered as well as helped much subsequent Marxist analysis, to the extent that such analysis has tended toward a nondialectical and ahistorical separation of terms in each dyad, and the consequences for the Marxist analysis of language have been acute. Innis's mode of analysis, by its emphasis on the fact that communication *is* production, on the social-material determination of communications patterns and processes, and *particularly* on the determinative influence of the *forces* of ideological reproduction in the development of the relations of production, gives an extended theoretical-historical content to the materialist notion of the *dialectic* between the forces of production and the relations of production, and thus contributes to an annihilation of the reifying tendencies inherent in the dichotomization of economic base and superstructure that have generated the mechanistic and voluntarist fallacies in some strains of Marxist thought.

The foregoing brief survey should suggest that while the economics of language has been effectively ignored within mainstream economics, political economists, most notably Marx and Innis, have made significant theoretical-historical contributions to the articulation and development of the field. The next section will sketch some working assumptions that have informed my analysis of the rise of the vernaculars.

Language and Economy

The first presupposition of the analysis concerns the centrality of language in all human social-economic activity, whether one conceives of mankind as *Homo sapiens, Homo faber,* or *Homo ludens:* as Benveniste (1971, p. 25) has argued,

> the emergence of *Homo* in the animal series may have been helped by his bodily structure or his nervous organization, but it is due above all to his faculty of symbolic representation, the common source of thought, language and society. . . . This symbolizing capacity is at the basis of conceptual functions. . . . Actually, the symbolizing faculty in man attains its supreme realization in language, which is the supreme symbolic expression, all the other systems of communication—graphic, gesticulatory, visual, etc.—being derived from it and presupposing its existence.

Benveniste's discussion requires extension at one point. The origins of language are necessarily obscure, and John Blacking, in a brilliant speculative analysis of "dance, conceptual thought, and production in the archeological record" (Sieveking, Longworth, & Wilson, 1976, pp. 3–13), has suggested that a prelinguistic process of "generalized sensori-motor communion" may have constituted the social basis for the emergence of human conceptual thought and language, a conclusion not inconsistent with the results of research on ethology, kinesics, and proxemics (cf. Montagu, this volume).

Notwithstanding this qualification, the hegemonic position which Benveniste assigned to language among modes of symbolic representation would appear to be warranted by the development of an articulated transpersonal social memory which it preeminently enables. The spatial-temporal extension of social knowledge permitted by language at the same time involves an increase in the role of "indirect" or reported experience relative to "direct" experience in human conceptual capacity and social-economic activity. This fact is of considerable importance for economic theory, since it suggests that in all economic systems individuals in their actions necessarily rely to a substantial extent on information and propositions which they can at best indirectly verify and that the role of such information and the consequent difficulties of verification will assume greater importance in systems involving greater degrees of specialization and division of labor, larger scale, and greater spatial extent and mobility, all of which tend to increase the volume of information in the system. The potential for the development of "monopolies of knowledge" (Innis, 1964, 1972) is thus inherent in the social character of language itself.

Cornforth (1971, pp. 309–332, 342–344) has emphasized a further, socially constitutive aspect of language, in noting that

> such a basic human institution as *property* could not be established without the use of language. . . . The language of property, the "legal expression" of the relations of production, without which those relations fall apart and vanish and human association would become unworkable, is of profound importance for the formation of all human relations, of all relations between persons, without exception.

Yet language is not only a medium of *social* communication, but also one of the principal forces of individual consciousness. Cassirer (1953, pp. 280–281) has described the process of conceptual abstraction as follows:

> [We] do not simply seize on and name certain distinctions that are somewhere present in feeling or intuition; on the contrary, on our own initiative we draw certain separations and connections, by virtue of which distinct individual configurations emerge from the uniform flux of consciousness. . . . Before any contents can be compared with one another and ordered into classes according to the degree of their similarity, they themselves must be defined as contents. But for this a logical act of *postulation* and *differentiation* is required, which will provide certain intervals in the continuous flow of consciousness, which in a sense will halt the restless coming and going of the sense impressions and create certain stopping places. Hence the original and decisive achievement of the concept is not to compare representations and group them according to genera and species, but rather to form impressions into representations.

Cassirer's formulation, with its roots in Kant's thought, exhibits a somewhat static bias and perhaps overemphasizes the conscious, logical, and inherently determinate nature of "the concept." As Vygotsky (1970, p. 125) has argued regarding the dialectic of thought and word, in terms which render problematical Alexander Pope's (1963, p. 153) definition of *wit* as "what oft was *Thought,* but ne'er so well *Exprest"*:

> The relation of thought to word is not a thing but a process, a continual movement back and forth from thought to word and from word to thought. In that process the relation of thought to word undergoes changes which themselves may be regarded as development in the functional sense. Thought is not merely expressed in words; it comes into existence through them. Every thought tends to connect something with something else, to establish a relationship between things. Every thought moves, grows and develops, fulfills a function, solves a problem.

Nonetheless, Cassirer's emphasis on language as providing reference points, or "stopping places," is a central element in the process of production of thought or meaning described by Vygotsky. It is in this context that language, as a means of reproducing social-economic relations while simultaneously expanding the conceptual capacity of individuals within an economic system, can be said to constitute a necessary medium for the development of all economic systems (cf. Wertsch, this volume).

The first presupposition relates to language as a "category common to all stages of production" (Marx & Engels, 1970, p. 129). Yet language historically is enmeshed in a *particular* network of communicative media and processes and in a particular social-economic formation. This factor assumes significance in that language is not simply a preexisting system or set of lexical tokens and grammatical rules which is instantaneously and costlessly available to new entrants to the language community, but rather involves all economic systems in time- and resource-consuming processes of social language reproduction and individual language learning, with the further consequence that the specific historical conditions of language reproduction determine its distribution and extent. The linguistic core of a social-economic system, which may be taken to include spoken, written, and mechanically reproduced language(s), is reproduced in relation to a complex of language-transmission media and processes: by the family, by schools and other specialized loci of language and literacy training, and in the very exercise of linguistic capacities in the interdependent spheres of social intercourse, political and economic life, religion, and "literature," broadly defined. These spheres in turn are determined in character by the overall development of the economic system, so that the historical character of the linguistic core is *mediately* determined, in the process of its reproduction, by the social-economic formation, at the same time that the language so produced constitutes a necessary condition of overall system reproduction (cf. Williams, this volume).

A second significant aspect of the socially reproduced and inductively learned character of language is that *as experienced* it is not simply a countably infinite set of *potential* propositions, but rather a *finite* number of historically produced expressions, some of which (by virtue of frequency of repetition, a conviction as to their "truth," or the social context of their expression) have for social-economic reasons assumed a privileged status or degree of social valorization. Hector (1966, p. 13) has noted with regard to the emergence of formularies in England before the thirteenth century, in relation to demands posed by the quantitative increase in administrative activity, that

> routine procedures inevitably produce routine documents. When once a satisfactory way of saying something has been devised it is not usual for men of business to seek gratuitously for new ways of expressing it. For the administrator the standardized formula has the double advantage of consistently presenting the same sort of information in the same way and of enabling much of the mechanical labour of writing to be delegated to humbler workers, competent to copy but not to draft.

Distinct but related factors underlie phenomena such as the emergence of religious liturgical traditions and the utilization of formulaic elements in oral poetic composition (Lord, 1960), which also involve different forms of increased economy or control of time in the process of linguistic production.

One implication of the privileged status necessarily acquired by certain expressions or forms of expression is that language learning is not simply the acquisition of a technique of communication or an "instrument of production" (Stalin, 1972, p. 6); it is also in an essential way a process of mythological or ideological reproduction, with the possibility of bias which that implies. A second implication is that the appropriate concept of language as an economic phenomenon requires inclusion not only of "technical" levels (phonemic, morphemic, lexical, grammatical, and semantic), but also of the level at which language is directly constitutive of social mythology (cf. Stein, this volume). At all of these levels the social distribution of access to and control over different spheres of the language system can be investigated, and the question of the relation of language to political-economic power can properly be posed.

The final presupposition of this chapter is that there *are* meaningful analogies between certain economic and linguistic processes that permit the direct metaphoric extension of economic concepts into the linguistic field—the distance between metaphor and model being less than is supposed in some versions of positivism—but that such extension, if it is to be productive, depends on a simultaneous recognition of the limits of the analogies. Of all of the limits, perhaps the most basic involves the difference between language and the price system as systems of social valuation or determination of social values. At the core of a fully developed price system is a universal equivalent form of value, or money, in terms of which the "values" of all commodities can be expressed, so that the relative values of all commodities can be determined as *quantitative* ratios, given their prior, *qualitative* identity as "commodities." No such general index for the quantitative determination of relative values exists within the sphere of linguistic activity, which rather relies on the establishment of qualitative distinctions and the tacit or explicit association of the *differentiata* with ultimately "moral" categories or value hierarchies (including socially accepted canons of mathematical and scientific "proof"). The paradoxical nature of the communicative power of the money form of the commodity in the exchange process is strikingly suggested in the apostrophe to monetary gold in Shakespeare's *Timon of Athens,* which influenced Marx (1961, pp. 136–141) in his early economic studies:

> O thou sweet king-killer, and dear divorce
> Twixt natural son and sire!
> . . . Thou visible God!
> That solder'st close impossibilities,
> And makest them kiss! That speak'st with every tongue,
> To every purpose!

In short, while "money talks," it can do so only because it is "omnilingual," or "inarticulate"; in contrast, "language creates values," but it can do so only by the articulation of qualitative distinction or difference. From another perspective, the value of the metaphor of linguistic "exchange" is limited by the difficulties of determining the precise nature of the *quid pro quo,* although the juridical or linguistic activity of courts in resolving contractual disputes should suggest that the sphere of economic exchange itself is not devoid of problematical aspects in this regard.

Notwithstanding the care that must be taken in directly applying economic categories to the linguistic sphere if one is to avoid crude forms of "economics imperialism," certain extensions of this type appear to be useful, indeed even necessary. In particular, the notion of language activity as a process of "production" of meaning, involving the creation and communication, distribution, or dissemination of knowledge or information (despite the obvious difficulties of measuring "meaning"), enforces a concern with the similarities and differences between linguistic and other spheres of production that is of importance not only for the economics of language but for economics generally, given the growing empirical importance of the service sector and of what Machlup (1972) has called the "knowledge industry" in technically advanced economic systems. For related reasons, the notion of the "reproduction" of language in space and over time, provided that reproduction is not understood as simply replication, draws attention to the time- and resource-consuming nature of the activities required for the maintenance of language in all social-economic formations, to the economic or material preconditions of language reproduction, and to the role of changes in these material conditions in the diachronic transformation of language.

Analogies drawn from the sphere of commodity circulation can also have certain heuristic value as applied to linguistic phenomena, although for reasons suggested above they are among the most conceptually treacherous. At a basic level, the "circulation," communication, or diffusion of information frequently occurs more rapidly or in greater volume within than between linguistic communities, in part because of costs of translation, just as the existence of different currency areas privileges internal as opposed to external trade, although the difficulties in developing the theory of "optimal currency areas," while considerable, are slight in comparison with those of a theory of "optimal language areas."

Shell (1978) has carefully traced certain formal similarities between metaphorization itself and economic representation and exchange. Derrida (1972) has played on the various (French) senses of the *usure* (erosion, wear, erasure, usage, usury) of coins as a metaphor for the effacement of the specificity of words in the process of linguistic circulation, in developing his critique of the notion that metaphysics can somehow be separated from its metaphoric roots. It is also common and intelligible to speak metaphorically of the "debasement" of the language or (more significantly) of the "devaluation" and "revaluation" of particular terms, expressions, propositions or texts, as a way of indicating changes in the "currency" of particular forms of language. Metaphor becomes catachrestical, however, in certain writings intent on establishing the "homologies" between linguistic and economic phenomena, to the extent that the quest for similarity forecloses adequate attention to differences. Thus, Rossi-Landi (1975, p. 6) has written: "I will maintain that when goods circulate in the form of commodities they 'are' messages; and that when sentences circulate in the form of verbal messages they 'are' commodities." Inverted commas notwithstanding, the above formulation and related attempts to theorize in terms of "constant linguistic capital," "variable linguistic capital," and "linguistic surplus value," or in terms of the homologies between "use value" and the "signified," "exchange value" and the "signifier" (Baudrillard, 1972), ultimately tend to obscure at least as much as they reveal, for reasons outlined above and in Jameson (1972).

A final economic metaphor which is of considerable importance for the economics of language, in part because of its range of application and its susceptibility to various types of measurement, is that of *capacity*. Of course, it is not possible to establish a single-dimensional quantitative measure of *the* capacity of a language, a language speaker, or a text, as one might be able to say, "The capacity of this paper mill is 100,000 tons of paper of given quality per year." Yet languages do appear to differ in their inherent expressive capacities, as Hockett (1954, p. 122) has argued in his modified version of the Sapir–Whorf hypothesis: "Languages differ not so much as to what *can* be said in them, but rather as to what it is *relatively easy* to say." Moreover, the acute difficulties of precisely translating certain poetic works provide a degree of justification for Pound's (1961, p. 34) somewhat stronger position: "The sum of human wisdom is not contained in any one language and no single language is CAPABLE of expressing all forms and degrees of human comprehension." Such differences do not warrant the crude ranking of languages as innately superior or inferior, particularly when such rankings are taken to imply a corresponding racial hierarchy (Pulgram, 1958, pp. 139–156). Yet such differences as do exist—at the syntactic level, for example (as in the different weights of ordination and inflection or the range and frequency of use of verb tenses and voices in various languages), or at the lexical level (insofar as different "densities" of words in particular spheres of reference affect the capacity for economical lexical distinction)—do appear subtly to promote different habits of expression and different characteristic modes of thought, in ways which define as they reflect the cultural and political-economic history of the system in which they are embedded (cf. Greenfield, this volume).

At the lexical level, languages differ significantly in the "richness" of their vocabulary, or potential capacity for distinction. English (in part because of its combined Germanic and Romance roots) has about 240,000 words, French about 93,000, and Latin about 51,000 (Wolff, 1971, p. 17), although such crude aggregate comparisons require qualification in relation to the small proportion of the "potential lexical capacity" of a language that is normally utilized or even understood by most members of a language community and the specific areas of particular languages where ambiguity, polysemia, and limited articulation occur, a significant instance being the word *language* itself in English (Rossi-Landi, 1975, p. 17). Such differences often assume importance, even apart from the influence of asymmetric political-economic power (as with military conquest and occupation), in defining the structure of competition between languages in the various spheres of language use in situations of linguistic interpenetration within a single social-economic formation and in determining the nature of lexical borrowing, particularly if such borrowing accompanies the introduction of new cultural-economic elements. The presence in Swahili of the Arabic *ktb* ("book") complex and the specific combination of Bantu and Arabic roots in Swahili number terms constitute significant instances of the process.

A further dimension of the capacity of a language is given by the territorial or spatial extent of the area within which it can be spoken and/or understood, or alternatively (and distinctly) by the number of fluent speakers of the language, both of which indexes can in principle be refined through analysis of the distribution of types and levels of competence among members of the language community, individually and by urban–rural and class divisions. This dimension, insofar as there are elements of increasing returns to scale within language systems, is of considerable importance for the political economy of language, particularly as it conditions and reflects the relations between language development and phenomena such as trade, migration, and conquest. In the Inca empire at the time of Pachacutec, for example, the difficulty for imperial administrators of communicating in local languages resulted in a concentrated program by the emperor to "extend the use of the Quechua tongue throughout the Empire" (Flornoy, 1958, p. 177). A major element in this systematic process of imperial centralization was the imposition of a standard vernacular, a fact not unrelated to the increase of fluency in Russian in Eastern Europe in the period since World War II (cf. deTerra, this volume).

The preceding discussion has sketched some theoretical considerations that appear relevant to an examination of the historical relations of language and political economy in the late medieval and early modern period. The investigation of the next section is intended in turn to contribute to the further development of the economics of language.

The Rise of the Vernaculars

In Western Europe between the thirteenth and eighteenth centuries a number of interrelated developments occurred in the social use of language, which for convenience may be termed *the rise of the vernaculars*. In several senses, however, this designation could be misleading, and it is hence necessary to specify these senses at the outset. If by "the vernacular" we mean the spoken language of everyday life and the written and other forms of language dependent on it, then at least one vernacular exists in all human societies, and the notion of a "rise" might thus appear otiose. What is intended, rather, is a focus on the extension of vernacular language activity in certain spheres of language use relative to Latin, the growth of effective sentiment in favor of *popular* vernacular languages in opposition to sharply different *ruling-class* vernaculars, and the tendencies toward standardization of the vernacular within larger scale political-economic units at the expense of regional vernacular dialects.

The second sense in which the designation could be misleading stems from the connotation of uninterrupted advance implicit in the term *rise*. Although in long-run historical terms this connotation is not inappropriate, it could tend to divert attention from the unevenness of the process of extension of the vernaculars in different spheres, periods of relative or absolute retrogression or recession of vernacular use, and the intensity of linguistic competition (including systematic repression of the vernaculars) at certain times and places. Finally, the element of arbitrariness in the focus on the period from the early thirteenth to the late seventeenth century should be acknowledged: from one standpoint the appropriate starting point might be as early as the period of the barbarian incursions into the western Roman Empire; and the end of the seventeenth century by no means marks the supplantation of Latin in all spheres, perhaps most notably in the area of theological, scientific, and other scholarly writings.

Yet the thirteenth century opened in the wake of that period of substantial political-economic development and cultural growth from the tenth to the twelfth centuries which had produced many of the institutional and cultural foundations of subsequent medieval development (Bautier, 1971; Lopez, 1967). In particular, the revival of the ancient classics and of jurisprudence and the growth of new intellectual centers had contributed in the linguistic sphere to an increase in the importance and range of Latin use (Haskins, 1970; Southern, 1964). Conversely, by the end of the seventeenth century, although Latin had not been displaced in all spheres—and was not to be in some until the nineteenth century or later—most of the characteristic aspects of the subsequent linguistic realignments involving the relative contraction of Latin can, *in nuce,* already be discerned. The following consideration of the rise of the vernaculars in the medieval and early modern period is intended to comprehend the foregoing qualifications.

It must also be conceded that there are certain unavoidable speculative elements in any examination of the economic history of language at such a temporal distance, even apart from the potential for oversimplication or reductionism inherent in any survey such as the present one. Most obviously, our knowledge of the spoken vernaculars and of spoken Latin is mediated by the particular written representations of the spoken tongues which have survived, so that linguistic biases associated with the historical conditions of written production and conservation imply that the types of surviving document on which judgments regarding the development of the spoken languages are based are not necessarily representative, in a statistical sense. Moreover, the imperfect and changing correspondence between phonetic signs and phonemic referents, as well as the elements of orthographical, lexical, and syntactic conservatism associated with the written tradition, involve a distinct but varying and uncertain distance between spoken language and written language in any time and place, a distance which may be inversely associated with the level and extent of literacy (Zengel, 1968, pp. 296–304). Finally, for the medieval and early modern period there are still considerable gaps in our systematic knowledge of general political-economic and language development, particularly in their quantitative aspects, so that analysis of the interdependence of quantitative and qualitative changes in these spheres contains an inevitable conjectural element, which may be reduced on occasion but rarely eliminated. Independently of the scarcity of data, the interpretation of the data that do exist involves numerous potential pitfalls: use of the ratio of signatures to marks on legal documents as a measure of literacy, for example, on the assumption that this proportion is lower than that of "readers" to "non-readers" and higher than that of "writers" to "non-writers" (Lockridge, 1974; Schofield, 1968), depends on the relation between reading and writing instruction in primary educational curricula, and presupposes that a constant and negligible proportion of nonreaders will learn to write just their signature for prestige reasons. Notwithstanding these genuine difficulties, however, enough is known to permit a reasonably confident characterization of certain basic aspects of the rise of the vernaculars between the thirteenth and seventeenth centuries.

As a prelude to that discussion, however, it is worth recalling certain aspects of the linguistic history of republican and imperial Rome, which are of importance in themselves and insofar as they provide the basis of many of the ideological justifications for use of the vernacular in the early modern period. In particular, the powerful influence of Greek language and culture on Roman thought and education generated responses not unlike those to Latin in early modern Europe. Roman advanced education centered on rhetoric was not conducted in Latin until the first century B.C., and the introduction of Latin instruction was resisted by the aristocracy as reducing barriers to entry to rhetorical competence. For patriotic reasons, Cicero, as a fluent Hellenist who had studied from 79 to 77 B.C. in Athens, attempted in his rhetorical and philosophical works "to create in Latin a technical language that could be used to 'popularize' Greek thought" (Marrou, 1964, p. 340), and as late as the early sixth century A.D., Boethius, whose works were highly influential in Western European literate thought in the eleventh and twelfth centuries, was inventing Latin equivalents for technical Greek terminology. Complaints regarding the "poverty" of Latin relative to Greek were not infrequent (Melmoth, 1786, pp. 6–7); there was a substantial translation industry of Greek works into Latin; a large number of Roman works were written in Greek; in the eastern empire, the wide diffusion of and deference to Greek meant that the diffusion of Latin was limited, in contrast to the western empire, where Latin use was actively promoted and widespread; and Paulinus's complaint in the early fifth century A.D. regarding the costs of bilingualism is a forerunner of similar ones in the early modern period: "To have to learn two languages at once is all right for the clever ones and gives excellent results; but for an average mind like mine such dispersion of effort soon becomes very tiring" (Marrou, 1964, p. 351). Latin versions of the Greek New Testament and the Old Testament, particularly Jerome's fourth-century translation based on the Hebrew scriptures in preference to the Greek Septuagint, were an attempt to meet the needs of non-Greek-speaking Christian communities, as the term *vulgate* itself suggests (Chaytor, 1967; Kenyon, 1975; Knowles, 1962; Laistner, 1966; Marrou, 1964; Pulgram, 1978; Robinson, 1954; Sandys, 1964). These facets of the linguistic experience of Rome and the arguments developed by Roman writers in favor of the Latin vernacular and against the hegemony of Greek were in turn to be adapted by early modern defenders of the vernaculars against the hegemony of Latin.

The question of when Latin ceased being spoken—or alternatively put, when the Romance vernaculars became sufficiently distinct from Latin that they can no longer be described as Latin—involves a subjective element. Migliorini (1966) has noted with regard to the emergence of Italian that divergences between written and spoken Latin had already increased under the emperors, as had the intensification of class divisions; while Vinogradoff (1968, p. 13) has spoken of the period of the breakup of the western empire in terms of "the Romanization of the provinces and . . . the barbarization of Rome." Depending on the criteria used, the development of independent Romance vernaculars can be said to have occurred sometime between 500 and 800 A.D.: by an edict of the Council of Tours (813), the increasing inability of commoners to understand the Latin sermons at Mass was officially acknowledged in the requirement that sermons should be translated *"in rusticam romanam linguam aut theotiscam,* 'into the rustic Roman or German tongue'" (Hall, 1974, p. 105).

In contrast to the growth of the primitive Church, from the time of Constantine, for the most part,

> Christianity spread by the addition of masses of men, not by the conversion of particular people. . . . Generally speaking, the acceptance of Christianity was . . . an affair of state, in which kings and other leaders, moved no doubt by missionaries and, as time went on, acting under the influence of the Pope, carried their subjects with them or imposed their will upon alien social groups. (F. M. Powicke, in Crump & Jacob, 1948, p. 29)

It was in this period that the Church became the preeminent agent of Western Europe in the conservation and reproduction of learning and literacy, in part as a result of the emphasis on monastic literacy and manuscript production laid down about 526 A.D. in the Benedictine *Rule,* which was adopted almost universally throughout western Christendom (Laistner, 1966, pp. 91–95).

Concern for the decline in clerical learning and the demand for well-trained administrators led Charlemagne in 781 to institute educational reforms under the direction of Alcuin which had the effect of raising the standard of clerical Latin, increasing the gap between Latin and the vernaculars, and enhancing the clergy's virtual monopoly of knowledge (Pirenne, 1951, pp. 137–154). Thompson (1963) has demonstrated that lay literacy was by no means unknown in Western Europe before 1300, particularly in Italy, where Latin-trained professional laymen (teachers, lawyers, notaries, scribes, and physicians) performed many activities relatively neglected or in clerical hands in northern Europe, and where reasonably literate nonprofessional laymen existed from at least the tenth century onward. Yet given the limited evidence of lay literacy uncovered by Thompson's concerted efforts, it is difficult to avoid the conclusion that literacy declined between the fourth and the tenth centuries (Hall, 1974, p. 102) and that the clerical orders during this period represented an increasing and preponderant proportion of the literate population of Western Europe.

The extent of monastic determination of which texts were to be reproduced, the ecclesiastical distrust of most "pagan" works, and the limited resources for copying, following the disruptions and destruction of the barbarian invasions, resulted in the permanent disappearance of a large body of classical writings and the effective oblivion for centuries of a number of manuscripts preserved in monasteries where they remained virtually unnoticed until the conscious expeditions of search and recovery undertaken by humanists like Poggio Bracciolini (1380–1459) during the Renaissance (Reynolds & Wilson, 1978, pp. 108–124).

The extension of papal activity between the pontificates of Leo IX (1049–1055) and Innocent III (1198–1216), which saw the decisive break between eastern and western Christendom, the assertion of the independence of the Church from secular political control, and internal centralization of authority, developed in relation to the active assertion of the papal right to make ecclesiastical appointments, the increase of cathedral schools and the rise of the universities, the consolidation and articulation of canon law, the stricter enforcement of clerical celibacy after 1123, the exercise of more direct papal control over the monastic orders, the development of the curia and papal chancery, the strengthening of the fiscal structure of the Church, the accumulation of property, and the increased emphasis on the sacred function of Latin. Gregory VII (1966, p. 148) wrote to Wratislaw of Bohemia on January 2, 1080, explaining his prohibition of divine service in the Slavic vernacular: "It is evident to those who consider the matter carefully that it has pleased God to make Holy Scripture obscure in certain places lest, if it were perfectly clear to all, it might be vulgarized and subjected to disrespect or be so misunderstood by people of limited intelligence as to lead them into error."

Ullman (1968, pp. 52–53) has noted the unduly neglected importance of the Latinized Bible, as "the one book with which every literate person was thoroughly familiar," in facilitating the diffusion of Roman law ideas and contributing to the "theocratic-descending thesis of government": "What needs stressing is that the Bible in its Latin shape was held to have contained not only the truth itself, but the Truth in Latin. The divine word was written and spoken in Latin." The increased sanction of Latin, in contrast to the declaration of the Synod of Frankfurt in 794 that "God is worshipped, and man's prayers heard when his demands are just, in every language" (Wolff, 1971, p. 118), placed contradictory demands on the Church. In the relations between clergy and laity, a contradiction was evident between the demand for exclusivity and maintenance of the purity of the faith and the demand for effective communication of the word of God, which involved recourse to the vernaculars, as the emergence of the preaching orders in the thirteenth century suggests. Internally, Latin was an essential educational, legal, administrative, and theological medium, particularly given the territorially and linguistically catholic nature of the Church, but the rapid growth of clergy numbers, limitations of clerical Latin education, and the incessant pull of the vernaculars implied deficiencies in the Latin competence of the clergy, especially among the lower orders (Coulton, 1940).

In the thirteenth and early fourteenth centuries, by a number of criteria, the Church may be said to have reached a zenith of relative power and influence. During the fourteenth-century tenure of the papacy at Avignon (the so-called Babylonian Captivity, from 1309 to 1377, that preceded the Avignonese Schism), papal financial administration and fiscal centralization were further articulated and Church finances were in a sounder state than those of most heavily indebted secular rulers. Further, the hierocratic argument regarding the supremacy of the spiritual over the temporal sword that had been refined under popes from Gregory VII through Innocent III (1198–1216) to Boniface VIII (1294–1303) in his unsuccessful struggle with Philip the Fair of France over taxation of the clergy, continued as an ideological weapon of the papacy (Smalley, 1965, pp. 15–43). A discernible quickening of ecclesiastical intellectual life had occurred by the twelfth century incidental to the recovery in the West of many classical texts and commentaries imported from Byzantium and (still more significantly) from Iberian and southern Italian Arabic sources, to the translation of these texts, particularly those of Aristotle, from Arabic and Greek into Latin, and to the growth of cathedral schools and the emergence of the early universities, which constituted the beginning of a shift in the center of gravity of learning and education from the rural monasteries to the towns. Church councils, particularly the Fourth Lateran Council of 1215, stressed the necessity of expanding the basic educational program of the Church. Scholastic philosophers, perhaps most notably the Dominican Thomas Aquinas (1224/5–1274), developed a partially successful synthesis of Aristotelean and Christian thought which contributed to the legitimization of the study of the ancient classics.

Yet by the thirteenth century a number of political-economic developments had already begun to occur which would subsequently strengthen the position of the vernacular languages relative to Latin. According to J. C. Russell's estimates (Cipolla, 1977, p. 36), the population of Western Europe rose between 1000 and 1340 A.D. from about 24 million to about 51.5 million, a substantial rate of increase under preindustrial conditions, although the extended demographic consequences of the Black Death after 1348 meant that the estimated population in 1450 was still only about 37 million. The population was predominantly rural and agrarian until well past the end of the seventeenth century, but from the tenth century onward a perceptible growth of commerce and a corresponding growth and differentiation of urban economic activity occurred, which by the mid-fourteenth century had had a sufficient impact on the structure of social-economic relations that Lopez (1976) has argued that it may properly be described as a "commercial revolution."

The relatively self-contained manorial village of the tenth century was gradually but increasingly involved in commercial activity, and the role of towns as administrative, ecclesiastical, educational, craft-industrial, trading, and financial centers expanded, as did their relative autonomy from the countryside. The increase in commercial economic activity was accompanied by the absolute and relative concentration of wealth, by pressures for the commutation of feudal obligations into cash payments, by a growing recognition of the limitations inherent in subinfeudation, and by a significant increase in the demand for literate individuals to meet the growing requirements of administration, law, and commerce. Many of the above-noted developments in the Church during the period are a reflection of and a response to these changes, particularly given the active involvement of the monasteries in agricultural innovation and trade. Yet as early as the twelfth century, there is evidence that the educational capacity of the Church was insufficient to meet the growing demand for lay literacy, even apart from the irrelevant components and gaps in the ecclesiastical curricula relative to the needs of commercial life in particular. Lay schools independent of Church control, which had existed for some time in Italy, began to develop in other parts of Europe: in Ghent in 1191, despite ecclesiastical protests against infringement of their educational prerogatives, the Countess of Flanders stated that "if anyone suitable and capable wants to open a school in the town no one can prevent him" (Wolff, 1971, p. 141). While Latin was still generally taught in such schools, in many of them at least some of the instruction was in the vernacular (cf. Illich, this volume).

A distinct but related development, associated with the political centralization and administrative expansion of countries like England and France, was the declining relative importance of the clerical orders in secular administration. In the words of J. R. Strayer (Thrupp, 1964, p. 107): "The multiplication of the number of lay officials is one of the striking phenomena of the thirteenth century." By the fourteenth century, the monopoly of knowledge of the Church had significantly weakened: "Secular governments were catching up. A literate laity in the upper reaches of society and the growth of vernacular cultures undermined the status of 'clergy'" (Smalley, 1965, p. 35).

It should be emphasized that this shift toward the literate laity was not everywhere simultaneously accompanied by a shift toward the increased utilization of the vernaculars in official documents, although that was the eventual outcome. The continuing high status and more spatially extensive comprehensibility of Latin relative to the vulgar tongue, the inherent, economically intelligible conservative tendencies of written administrative traditions, the maintenance of reasonable standards of Latin competence among the laity, and technical change in administrative procedures (as in the use of formularies) permitting the delegation of mechanical tasks to less educated clerks lower in the administrative hierarchy, all contributed for a time to the retention of Latin. Yet it appears probable that the shift in administrative control reduced barriers to, and ultimately increased the demand for, subsequent introduction of the vernaculars in certain spheres of official language use, and thence generally.

A third factor which contributed to the rise of the vernaculars in a number of important respects was the development of vernacular oral and written poetry, and later prose, during the Middle Ages. While Shelley's claim that "poets are the unacknowledged legislators of the world" is perhaps that of an interested party, in the present case (if only by default) the claim appears to have some merit. The troubadors, minstrels, trouvères, and minnesänger, wandering poet-musicians or residents at a particular feudal court, were an important element in the cultural life of the Middle Ages, as entertainers, as bearers of news of distant events, and as articulators of the mythology of chivalry to their courtly audiences. From the standpoint of the present essay, one of their most important legacies stems from their early development of a *public, secular* sphere of refined vernacular use. The patronage of feudal courts was important to their existence and exerted a powerful direct influence on the poetry they produced, and in turn they contributed to the reputation of the courts. The growth of Provençal poetry, which exerted a decisive influence on poetic development in Italy, was not unrelated to the largesse of the counts of Toulouse, and the defeat of the Count of Toulouse in the Albigensian Crusade (1208–1227) resulted in the virtual disappearance of an active poetic tradition. The fall of the Hohenstaufen dynasty by 1272 was similarly reflected in a decline in the vernacular poetry which court support had fostered (Holzknecht, 1923).

The importance of such vernacular literature consists partly in its reflection and development of "national" consciousness, sense of history, and pride (as in the epics and romances) and partly in its exploration and delineation of the individual experience of consciousness (as in the lyrics). Yet it was also important in indicating and extending the expressive capacity of the vernaculars, or in developing consciousness of and pride in the languages themselves. Moreover, vernacular poetic production enabled and necessitated the translation of Latin concepts into the vernacular and constituted one of the principal processes for the importation and domestication of lexical borrowings. Finally, the core texts, those recognized as somehow capturing the "essence" of the language, contributed in their diffusion over time and space, along with other political-economic forces, to the displacement of regional dialects and the standardization of the vernaculars.

Long before the widespread diffusion of such core written vernacular texts as those of Dante, Petrarch, and Boccaccio in Italy, Luther's modified High German translation of the Bible and other writings in Germany, Rabelais's works and Calvin's *Institution Chrétienne* in France, the works of Chaucer and later Shakespeare and the King James Bible in England, and Cervantes's *Don Quixote* in Spain, the minnesänger were developing a transdialectal compromise "Dichtersprache" in twelfth- and thirteenth-century Germany, as had the troubadours of southern France (Chaytor, 1967, p. 44). The oral character of such poetic production implied the possibility of the diffusion of the articulated vernacular across class lines and irrespective of literacy. Other forms of oral vernacular linguistic activity—sermons (Owst, 1965), vernacular religious plays and cycles, the interpenetration of regional dialects fostered by urban commercial-economic relations—also contributed to the extension of vernacular expressive capacities and to the homogenization or increased comprehensibility of vernacular dialects over wider areas. The development of oral vernacular expressive and spatial range reinforced and was reinforced by the adoption of orally produced forms in written vernacular discourse. Gybbon-Monypenny (1965, pp. 230–244) has argued convincingly, for example, that poets of the Spanish *mester de clerecía* of the thirteenth to the fifteenth centuries, despite their use of formulas of direct address to an audience, were composing for a literate *readership,* and that they "were simply following a convention derived from their models, and did not expect their works to be performed by *juglares.*" Bakhtin (1968) has documented the powerful strain of folk vernacular culture that informs the peculiarly Rabelaisian element of Rabelais's sixteenth-century vernacular masterworks.

The cumulative effect of these processes in the economic, political, and cultural spheres over time was to provide the basis for the general extension of the vernaculars in Western Europe into virtually all areas of language use by the seventeenth century. There are significant differences among the patterns of transition in different countries, related to differences in their political-economic and linguistic history, as well as similarities traceable in part to the common action in many of them of a number of interdependent developments: the processes of political centralization and class realignment associated with the emergence of "absolutist states" (Anderson,

1979), the growth of Protestantism, the spread of humanist ideas, and the transformation of the forces of linguistic production represented by the invention, rapid spatial diffusion, and quantitative expansion of printing utilizing moveable type. Both the similarities and the differences among countries are of historical and theoretical importance.

One important common element in the political-economic and linguistic history of all of the countries of Western Europe throughout the period from the thirteenth to the seventeenth century was the existence of numerous distinct local or regional dialects within each major language area—dialects that were the product of centuries of reasonably self-contained internal development and that (even in virtually adjacent regions) often posed sufficient barriers to transdialectal expression or comprehension that some scholars have suggested that it is almost more fruitful to regard them as distinct languages. Dialectal divisions, together with transport limitations and localistic fiscal structures, reflected and reinforced political and economic decentralization or fragmentation and particularism, and thereby indirectly strengthened the competitive position of Latin as a transvernacular medium of political, economic, and cultural communication. While such dialectal divisions assumed particular importance in Germany and Italy, they were of significance in the other countries as well. Further common elements resulted from the general influence of widespread medieval Latin models in the religious, legal, administrative, and cultural spheres on vernacular language forms, in the process of vernacular articulation and development; from the diffusion processes stemming from the cosmopolitan enrollments of major medieval centers of higher learning; and from the adoption or adaptation of particularly vigorous or politically powerful vernacular cultural traditions (such as those of France from the eleventh to the fourteenth century, and of Italy from the fourteenth century onward) within other countries, exemplified by the use of French as a literary medium by northern Italian writers in the thirteenth century (Rickard, 1974, p. 66), by Chaucer's debt to his French and Italian models (Muscatine, 1966), and by the pervasive diffusion of Italian humanistic thought, particularly in the sixteenth century.

In Italy, political divisions, maintained by the power of and competition between individual city-states and by the separation of north from south by the papal states, contributed to the continuing strength of regional dialects. Dante's remarkable Latin *De Vulgari Eloquentia,* written about 1304, early in his exile from Florence, involved an attempt to identify a language which could serve as a unifying standard vernacular. This "illustrious vernacular" would be "courtly," since "if we Italians had a court, it would be spoken at court"; as it is, "our illustrious language wanders about like a wayfarer, . . . seeing we have no court" (Dante, 1904, p. 61). Dante's interest in an Italian literary vernacular emerged in the context of a history of use of the written vernacular in commercial documents as early as the middle of the twelfth century (Auerbach, 1965, p. 292). The rise of Dante's Florentine or Tuscan dialect, to the point where by the sixteenth century it had become the written vernacular standard, was aided by the diffusion throughout Italy of the vernacular works of Dante and his trecento Tuscan successors, Petrarch and Boccaccio, especially with their printed publication in the early 1470s and their valorization in works like Pietro Bembo's pro-vernacular *Prose della Volgar Lingua* of 1525.

In the fourteenth century, many city constitutions and statutes were translated into or written in the vernacular, although Latin remained the language of public correspondence, and in 1414 use of the vernacular became obligatory in the *tribunali commerciali* of Florence (Migliorini, 1966, pp. 130–132; Pulgram, 1958, pp. 59–62). In the fifteenth century, the rise of humanistic studies, stimulated by patronage and the recovery of classical Latin and Greek learning that began well before the westward flight of Greek scholars with the fall of Constantinople in 1453, resulted in the translation of Greek classics into Latin and into the vernacular; in the growth of philological sophistication, evident in the demonstration by Lorenzo Valla (1406–1457) that the so-called Donation of Constantine, held to establish the legitimacy of the papacy, was fraudulent; and in the devaluation of current Latin, as a "degenerate" form of the "purer" Latin of the classical writers, which was taken as the standard of emulation.

Kristeller (1969, pp. 14–15, 473–493) has emphasized that it would be unwise to overestimate the decline in vernacular use that accompanied the growth of humanism or to associate the humanists with Latin alone, in contrast to "popular" vernacular writers, noting the numerous vernacular writings and translations by humanists and the at least partly symbiotic relationship between vernacular and neo-Latin literature: "When the vernacular definitely won out in the sixteenth century, it had already absorbed the characteristic achievements of humanism, in style, terminology, literary form, and subject matter. Otherwise it could not have replaced Latin." Establishment in the sixteenth century of the fourteenth-century Tuscan vernacular as the standard for literary Italian was facilitated by the widespread diffusion, prestige, influence, and distance from contemporary dialectal rivalries of the earlier Tuscan poets, and ratified by the publication in 1612 of an Italian dictionary by the Accademia della Crusca, founded in 1582 and a forerunner of the Académie Française. The process by which standard Italian emerged, as well as the absence of political unity, implied a gap between written Italian and the spoken vernaculars that persisted into the twentieth century: "The language of Italy receives precocious stability, precisely because it is addressed to a closed circle of men of letters. . . . [t]he Italian tradition is born as, and for centuries will remain, the language of an oligarchic minority" (Devoto, 1978, p. 231).

In France, the establishment of a national standard vernacular in the sixteenth century was integrally related to the extended historical process, dating from the election in 987 of Hugh Capet, Duke of Ile-de-France, as King of France, by which the political centralization of France, centered on Paris as capital, was gradually achieved. Linguistically, the two broad language groups of northern and southern France, the *langue d'oïl* and *langue d'oc* or Occitan, both included numerous regional dialects; politically, the Capetian kings were initially less powerful than a number of the princes who were nominally their vassals. Nonetheless, by the eleventh century, if the power of the monarchy (supported by the Church) was still limited, Paris was identifiably the capital of France.

The twelfth and thirteenth centuries witnessed a strengthening of the position of Paris, and correspondingly of the Francien dialect, as a consequence of the location there of the royal court, law courts, the University of Paris, and the nearby religious center of Saint-Denis; the geographically and linguistically central position of Paris relative to northern France and Norman England; the growing acceptance of the vernacular as a poetic medium; and elimination of the Occitan vernacular poetic tradition following the Albigensian Crusade (Cohen, 1973, p. 87; Rickard, 1974, pp. 46–54). By 1250, a French translation of the entire Bible had been completed within the University of Paris that formed the basis of Desmoulin's *Bible Historiale* (1295), which circulated widely among the aristocracy in the succeeding centuries (Berger, 1967); after 1254, French was even occasionally used for royal chancellery documents.

While Francien French was increasingly accepted as the literary vernacular of all of France between the fourteenth and sixteenth centuries, Latin or local languages were still used, especially in the south, for administrative purposes, until the sixteenth century. Recognition of the value of a standardized vernacular as an instrument of political centralization led to a series of royal edicts from 1490 onward, culminating in the Ordonnances of Villers-Cotterets of 1539, which directed that all court proceedings and legal documents were to utilize French exclusively, thereby eliminating the use of both Latin and regional languages (Rickard, 1974, p. 88; Wartburg, 1969, pp. 144–145). In the realm of letters, translations of the classics from the fifteenth to the seventeenth century resulted in a large importation of vocabulary and even affected syntax, while the growing stress on pure classical Latin under Italian humanistic influence undermined the position of Latin: "Its very new-found purity rendered it unsuitable for everyday use" (Rickard, 1974, p. 89; Rickard, 1976).

Diffusion of Protestant doctrines from 1519 onward was met by attempts at repression of heresy and of vernacular religious writings, as in the burning of Lefèvre d'Etaples's vernacular translation of the New Testament at Meaux in 1525 and the institution of censorship, but the publication of Calvin's *Institution Chrètienne* in 1541 (based on the Latin version of 1536) necessitated orthodox responses in the vernacular and produced the linguistic background to the religious civil wars of the latter part of the century. Outside the religious sphere of language use, however, defenses of the vernacular like those of du Bellay in 1549 accompanied the growing use of French in literature, the production of Latin–French and French–Latin dictionaries, efforts at orthographical standardization, and increased concern with French grammatical structure, culminating in the foundation of the Académie Française in 1635 as a central linguistic authority. By the end of the seventeenth century, "rigid codification and a fixed and hierarchical vocabulary" (Rickard, 1974, p. 106) and the corresponding widening of the gap between the written and spoken vernacular paralleled the development of absolutism under Louis XIV.

In Germany, the pattern of linguistic development exhibited significant differences from that of Italy and France. The vernacular poetic literary development of the twelfth and thirteen centuries was followed by the development of vernacular administration, stimulated by Eike von Repgow's translation of the *Sachsenspiegel*, a book of common law, into Low German about 1222, followed rapidly by the production of High German versions. Increase in the numbers and importance of the relatively uneducated lesser nobility in the thirteenth century, the weakening of imperial centralized power, capacity limits of Latin formularies, and the costs of maintaining Latin scribes contributed to the emergence before 1300 of some vernacular legal writs. With the growing strength of burghers in the towns, German languages had supplanted Latin in many urban chanceries by 1300, and in most of the others by 1350.

The political fragmentation of Germany, particularly from the later thirteenth century onward, fostered and was reinforced by the continuation of regional dialectal variations, most notably between Low German dialects and High German dialects, and the development of independent, particularistic legal-administrative traditions. Such centrifugal linguistic tendencies were partly offset in the north by the widespread adoption by the mid-fourteenth century of the written Low German of the commercial and legal center of Lübeck as the vernacular standard of the Hanseatic League, although Latin was utilized in German Hanseatic urban chancery documents as late as the close of the fourteenth century (Waterman, 1966, p. 112). The rising power of the High German area relative to the Hansa led to the gradual northward spread of High German as the language of urban official documents from as early as the mid-fourteenth century onward, until by the beginning of the seventeenth century it had even been adopted as the language of local administration in Hamburg.

The displacement of Low German by High German in the north, however, occurred earlier in administration than in the schools, where Low German was utilized in some regions until the latter third of the seventeenth century: "The upper classes and the educated were the first to change to spoken High German. The use of High German in the north was clearly associated with class interests, which then expressed themselves in a contempt for Low German" (Lockwood, 1976, pp. 78, 125–126).

The interpenetration of northern and southern German dialects, in the fluid linguistic situation created especially from the twelfth century onward with the colonization of eastern Germany by settlers from the older areas, had produced a compromise dialect in the east-central regions which became the basis of the imperial written chancery language at Prague under Charles IV (1347–1378) and of the chancery language of Saxony and Silesia in the fifteenth century. Knowledge of the Saxon chancery language increased outside Saxony with the diffusion of Saxon cultural developments, particularly after 1480 with the introduction of Saxon features into the Mainz chancery language used in printing ordinances of the Imperial Diet (Chambers & Wilkie, 1970, p. 39). The fifteenth-century extension throughout much of Germany of familiarity with a standard compromise written vernacular was accompanied by the partially countervailing diffusion of Roman law in a relatively pure form, as a critical element in an imperial strategy of legal centralization and standardization (Vinogradoff, 1968).

The extension of the compromise written vernacular, together with the heritage of German mystic thought and lay devotion (Ozment, 1971), the political ambitions of princes, and the capacity of the printing industry (Eisenstein, 1979), contributed to the rapid diffusion of Luther's writings, including his German New Testament of 1522 and his German Bible of 1534, the language of which was consciously modeled on the German of the Saxon chancery. In turn, Luther's writings contributed to a sharpening of the linguistic gap between Protestant and Catholic regions: "In the Protestant parts Luther's language was authoritative. But his language only became familiar to the majority of his readers after they had learnt it" (Lockwood, 1976, p. 113). The spread of Roman law, on the other hand, together with the penetration into Germany of Renaissance humanist ideals, strengthened a virtually complete Latin monopoly of German university instruction until after Thomasius's vernacular lectures at the University of Leipzig in 1687. Moreover, the political fragmentation and economic disorganization and devastation of the Thirty Years War (1618–1648) adversely affected German cultural-linguistic development and contributed, along with the prestige of seventeenth-century French culture and the use of Romance languages from the time of Charles V (1519–1556) by the Hapsburg court and the German aristocracy, to the widespread adoption of French even as the language of the home among segments of the German bourgeoisie (Waterman, 1966, pp. 137–138).

Even with the impetus given to vernacular development in Germany by the Reformation, the articulation of German as a literary language did not occur until the eighteenth century: as late as 1691, more Latin than German titles were published in Germany (Blackall, 1959; Lockwood, 1976, p. 131). Maintenance of a range of linguistic hierarchies in different regions and spheres of language use, involving the cultural-economic dominance of groups characterized by differential access to Latin, non-Germanic vernaculars, and German vernaculars spoken by a minority within particular regions, contributed to the maintenance of political-economic particularism and sharp social hierarchical divisions in Germany well past the end of the seventeenth century.

The most decisive event in the political-economic history of language in England was the Norman Conquest of 1066, which resulted in the imposition of a French-speaking feudal ruling class whose vernacular would remain the dominant language of the aristocracy for over three centuries. Although Ireland and England had developed centers of ecclesiastical Latin learning from the fifth to the eighth centuries that provided the base for missionary and educational activity on the continent from the late sixth century onward, and had experienced a monastic revival in the tenth and eleventh centuries that recouped some of the ground lost during the Scandinavian incursions following 781, the spoken and written vernacular likely played a more prominent role in Anglo-Saxon and Anglo-Danish religious, cultural, and political-economic life than in most of Europe (Adamson, 1946; Laistner, 1966). The conquest not only resulted in a centralization and standardization of pre-Norman English feudal relations, a process facilitated by William the Conqueror's displacement of the Anglo-Danish aristocracy and distribution of territories among his chosen vassals; it also significantly weakened the position of the English vernacular, insofar as familiarity with French (or Anglo-Norman) as the language of the aristocracy began to penetrate other classes, and as Latin displaced English as the written language of law and administration.

It is not the case that English simply ceased to be spoken at some point after the Conquest, as certain scholars once held. It is likely more correct to say that between 1100 and 1300 the majority of the lower classes were effectively illiterate and unilingual English speakers, not infrequently possessing a smattering of French; that merchants, master craftsmen, and the aristocracy became more or less bilingual over time in English and French, with a higher proportion of English unilingualism at the lower end of the social scale and a higher, but secularly declining, proportion of French unilingualism at the upper end of the scale; that the lower clergy were more or less bilingual in English and Latin; and that the upper clergy were not infrequently trilingual. Yet the conquest did weaken the position of the standard West Saxon literary dialect, which declined significantly by the end of the twelfth century and was supplanted by regional dialects in written English works, while Anglo-Norman became the dominant literary language of England after 1200 (Wilson, 1943).

The loss of Normandy to the French in 1204 under King John (1199–1216) reduced, although it did not eliminate, the numerous direct ties between the Anglo-Norman aristocracy and the Continent, as nobles were forced to choose between their French and English holdings during the first half of the thirteenth century. Notwithstanding the influx and preferment of French nobles under Henry III (1216–1272), who married Eleanor of Provence in 1236, considerable evidence suggests that as early as the latter part of the thirteenth century, even among some of the aristocracy French was becoming less "a mother tongue inherited from Norman ancestors" and more "a cultivated tongue supported by social custom and by business and administrative convention" (Baugh, 1957, pp. 154–187).

Even in this form, the cultural and political-economic importance of Anglo-Norman French should not be underestimated. Between about 1300 and 1327, French was introduced and rapidly supplanted Latin as the principal language of documents of the Privy Seal Office, and English was not used until about 1422, although it had effectively displaced French by about 1437. French was the language in which the business of the law courts was conducted (although proceedings were recorded in Latin), even after 1362, when Edward III ordered that proceedings be in English. French was used in the wills, accounts, and personal correspondence of members of the merchant class as well as of the aristocracy into the fifteenth century. It was only in 1422 that the London brewers began to keep their records in English, since the king had begun to use English in his informal correspondence and more brewers read and wrote English than French or Latin. English did not supplant French in the operative parts of parliamentary statutes until 1489 (Helen Suggett, in Southern, 1968; Baugh, 1957; Hector, 1966).

The extension of spoken and written English during the fourteenth and fifteenth centuries was not unrelated to the effects of the Hundred Years War (1337–1453) in increasing antipathy toward French. Likely of even greater significance was the displacement of French by English as the language of grammar-school education, a practice which spread rapidly after 1349 in the wake of the Black Death until by 1385 it was quite general, and which had the consequence of seriously weakening the link between literacy and knowledge of French. Related to these developments and the growing importance of London as the political and economic center of England was the emergence of the East Midlands dialect spoken at London as the standard of English, particularly written English, by the fifteenth century, although regional rustic dialects provided a source of humor for Shakespeare and remained important as spoken vernaculars long after his time.

Translations of passages from the Bible into English had occurred in the Anglo-Saxon period, although Abbot Ælfric in 992 had expressed misgivings concerning his translations, "lest peradventure the pearls of Christ be had in disrespect." The first English translations of the entire Bible were the two persecuted Wyclifite versions, the second of which was completed about 1400. These editions were produced by the Lollards as a means of increasing lay access to the Scriptures and were in many respects an anticipation of the concerns which motivated the wave of sixteenth-century vernacular translations that were stimulated by Reformation thought and by Erasmus's Greek New Testament of 1521. Among these translations were Tyndale's banned New Testament (1525) and Pentateuch (1529) and Coverdale's Bible of 1535, based on Tyndale's (Robinson, 1954, pp. 128–145). The Henrician Reformation established the Coverdale Bible and the vernacular liturgy in England.

The rise of English in certain spheres required the extension of the expressive capacity of the language, and involved substantial lexical and stylistic importation. The period from 1250 to 1400 during which English began to displace French was also the period with the highest rate of borrowings from French, while the sixteenth and seventeenth centuries in which English effectively displaced Latin were characterized by a massive importation of Latin neologisms and humanistically influenced stylistic development. Elton (1965, pp. 287–288) remarked of early sixteenth-century English prose that "one need only compare the Latin writings of Sir Thomas More with his English prose to see how superior in subtlety, though often inferior in vigor and originality, the learned language still was." By 1500, English was already being commonly used for a widening range of official documents, and the period from 1500 to 1650, when the Cromwellian Protectorate required English for all official documents except international communications, witnessed a steady recession of Latin use, though the Restoration brought back Latin with the monarchy, and Latin was not finally eliminated in certain traditional official spheres until 1733. The nature and vigor of vernacular development in England by the early seventeenth century may be related to a range of interdependent political-economic factors including: England's separation from the continent, the linguistic distance of English from Latin, the early development of a relatively strong monarchical government centered on London, the implications of trilingualism in reducing the relative power both of Latin and of Anglo-Norman, the establishment of a Protestant state religion, a level of literacy that was likely higher than that of any other country in Europe with the possible exception of the Netherlands, the higher proportion of virtually exclusively vernacular literacy in England, the degree of fluidity of class lines in England relative to much of Europe in the early modern period, and the mediated impact of humanistic studies on English cultural development.

The rapid diffusion of printing throughout Europe from 1450 onward had a number of implications for the development of the vernaculars. Although some manuscript production was being conducted on a mass production basis before the advent of printing, the printing of books on paper dramatically increased the number and degree of standardization of texts available at a fifth to an eighth of the cost of parchment manuscripts, thereby significantly increasing the relative access to texts of less wealthy literate individuals. In the *incunabula* period of printing, Latin printed works predominated: of some 24,000 non-Greek works printed in Europe before 1500, over 77% were in Latin, most of these being religious or classical works, with just under 23% in vernaculars. Native vernacular works ranged, however, from 17.5% of the total printed in Italy to 19.7% in the German-speaking area, 24.4% in the Low Countries, 29.3% in France, 51.9% in Spain, and 55% in Great Britain (Hirsch, 1967, pp. 133–134). This pattern reflected the nature of the demand for books, the wider, transvernacular market open to Latin works, and the initial scarcity of printable vernacular works relative to the preexisting stock of Latin works for which a known demand existed. Yet the proportion of vernacular works printed rose steadily, if not continuously, until by the end of the seventeenth century vernacular books predominated in the aggregate in Europe. Their influence was supplemented by the growth of printed vernacular newspapers, pamphlets, and broadsheets for which no major Latin counterpart existed. Printers contributed actively to orthographical and dialectal standardization, as a means of extending their internal market. Translations of classical works into the vernacular reduced the necessity of learning classical languages in order to gain an acquaintance with classical and Latin religious thought and in the process contributed to the expansion of vernacular expressive capacity: of over 5,000 works printed in English between 1475 and 1560, about 16.6% were translations (calculated from Bennett, 1969, pp. 277–319). The extension of printing involved a major transformation in the mode of linguistic production, which contributed to the alteration of the relations between Latin and the vernaculars, oral and written traditions, Church and State, and language and thought.

Conclusion

The foregoing chapter has involved an attempt to outline certain aspects of the linguistic revolution that accompanied the transition from feudalism toward capitalism and to suggest some of the probable mutual interdeterminations of linguistic and political-economic change in medieval and early modern Europe. It has emphasized developments in the mode of linguistic production, rather than focusing explicitly on issues such as the role of language in the reproduction of social classes, in part because of constraints of space, and in part because of a conviction that historically grounded class analysis requires attention to the dialectic between the mode of linguistic production and the constitutive determination of class relations. The implicit theme of the essay has been that linguistic development cannot be adequately understood without reference to the underlying material conditions of language reproduction, and conversely, that an understanding of the development of language, as the primary medium of social communication, is an essential element in the understanding of political-economic change.

Acknowledgments

I would like to express my gratitude to Margaret Ferguson, Nita Krevans, John Munro, Patricia Parker, David Quint, Abraham Rotstein, Tom Walkom, and Andrew Watson for their help in the production of this essay, while at the same time absolving them of any responsibility for its commission.

References

Adamson, J. W. *'The illiterate Anglo-Saxon'*. Cambridge: Cambridge University Press, 1946.
Anderson, P. *Lineages of the absolutist state*. London: Verso, 1979.

Auerbach, E. *Literary language and its public in late Latin antiquity and in the middle ages.* London: Routledge and Kegan Paul, 1965.

Bakhtin, M. *Rabelais and his world.* Cambridge, Mass.: MIT Press, 1968.

Baudrillard, J. *Pour une critique de l'économie politique du signe.* Paris: Gallimard, 1972.

Baugh, A. C. *A history of the English language.* New York: Appleton-Century-Crofts, 1957.

Bautier, R. H. *The economic development of medieval Europe.* London: Thames and Hudson, 1971.

Bennett, H. S. *English books and readers: 1475 to 1557.* Cambridge: Cambridge University Press, 1969.

Benveniste, E. *Problems in general linguistics.* Coral Gables, Fla.: University of Miami Press, 1971.

Berger, S. *La Bible française au moyen age.* Geneva: Slatkine Reprints, 1967.

Blackall, E. A. *The emergence of German as a literary language: 1700–75.* Cambridge: Cambridge University Press, 1959.

Boulding, K. *The image.* Ann Arbor, Mich.: University of Michigan Press, 1966.

Cassirer, E. *The philosophy of symbolic forms* (Vol. 1). New Haven, Conn.: Yale University Press, 1953.

Chambers, W. W., & Wilkie, J. R. *A short history of the German language.* London: Methuen, 1970.

Chaytor, H. J. *From script to print.* New York: October House, 1967.

Cipolla, C. (Ed.). *The Fontana economic history of Europe: The middle ages.* London: Collins/Fontana, 1977.

Cohen, M. *Histoire d'une langue: Le français.* Paris: Editions Sociales, 1973.

Cornforth, M. *Marxism and the linguistic philosophy.* New York: International Publishers, 1971.

Coulton, G. G. *Europe's apprenticeship.* London: Thomas Nelson and Sons, 1940.

Crump, C. G., & Jacob, E. F (Eds.). *The legacy of the middle ages.* Oxford: Clarendon, 1948.

Dante Alighieri. *A translation of the Latin works* (A. G. Ferrers Howell, trans.). London: J. M. Dent and Sons, 1904.

Derrida, J. La mythologie blanche. In *Marges de la philosophie.* Paris: Minuit, 1972.

Devoto, G. *The languages of Italy.* Chicago: University of Chicago Press, 1978.

Eisenstein, E. *The printing press as an agent of change* (2 Vols.). Cambridge: Cambridge University Press, 1979.

Elton, G. R. *Reformation Europe: 1517–1559.* London: Collins, 1965.

Flornoy, B. *The world of the Inca.* New York: Doubleday, 1958.

Fraser, L. M. *Economic thought and language.* London: Adam and Charles Black, 1947.

Georgescu-Roegen, N. *The entropy law and the economic process.* Cambridge, Mass.: Harvard University Press, 1974.

Gregory VII. *The correspondence of Pope Gregory VII.* New York: Octagon, 1966.

Gybbon-Monypenny, G. B. The Spanish *mester de clerecía* and its intended public. In F. Whitehead, A. H. Diverres, & F. E. Sutcliffe (Eds.), *Medieval miscellany.* New York: Barnes & Noble, 1965.

Hall, R. A., Jr. *External history of the Romance languages.* New York: American Elsevier, 1974.

Haskins, C. H. *The renaissance of the twelfth century.* New York: World, 1970.

Hayek, F. A. *The sensory order.* Chicago: University of Chicago Press, 1963.

Hector, L. C. *The handwriting of English documents.* London: Edward Arnold, 1966.

Hegel, G. W. F. *The phenomenology of mind.* New York: Harper & Row, 1967.

Hirsch, R. *Printing, selling and reading 1450–1550.* Wiesbaden: Otto Harrassowitz, 1967.

Hockett, C. F. Chinese versus English: An exploration of the Whorfian theses. In H. Hoijer (Ed.), *Language in culture.* Chicago: University of Chicago Press, 1954.

Holzknecht, K. J. *Literary patronage in the middle ages.* Philadelphia: George Banta, 1923.

Hurwicz, L. The design of mechanisms for resource allocation. *American Economic Association, Papers and Proceedings,* 1973, *63,* 1–30.

Innis, H. *Political economy in the modern state.* Toronto: Ryerson, 1946.

Innis, H. *Changing concepts of time.* Toronto: University of Toronto Press, 1952.

Innis, H. *The bias of communication.* Toronto: University of Toronto Press, 1964.

Innis, H. *Empire and communications.* Toronto: University of Toronto Press, 1972.

Innis, H. *The idea file of Harold Adams Innis.* Toronto: University of Toronto Press, 1980.

Jameson, F. *The prison-house of language.* Princeton, N.J.: Princeton University Press, 1972.

Kenyon, F. G. *The text of the Greek Bible.* London: Duckworth, 1975.

Keynes, J. M. *The general theory of employment, interest and money.* London: Macmillan, 1964.

Keynes, J. M. *A treatise on probability*. Cambridge: Royal Economic Society/Macmillan, 1973.

Knowles, D. *The evolution of medieval thought*. New York: Random House, 1962.

Kristeller, P. O. *Studies in renaisance thought and letters*. Rome: Edizioni di Storia e Letteratura, 1969.

Laistner, M. L. W. *Thought and letters in Western Europe*. Ithaca, N.Y.: Cornell University Press, 1966.

Lockridge, K. A. *Literacy in colonial New England*. New York: Norton, 1974.

Lockwood, W. R. *An informal history of the German language*. London: André Deutsch, 1976.

Lopez, R. S. *The birth of Europe*. London: Phoenix House, 1967.

Lopez, R. S. *The commercial revolution of the middle ages*. Cambridge: Cambridge University Press, 1976.

Lord, A. B. *The singer of tales*. Cambridge, Mass.: Harvard University Press, 1960.

Machlup, F. *The production and distribution of knowledge in the United States*. Princeton, N.J.: Princeton University Press, 1972.

Marrou, H. *A history of education in antiquity*. New York: New American Library, 1964.

Marschak, J. The payoff-relevant description of states and acts. *Econometrica*, 1963, *31*, 719–725.

Marschak, J. Economics of inquiring, communicating, deciding. *American Economic Review*, 1968, *58*, 1–18.

Marschak, J., & Radner, R. *Economic theory of teams*. New Haven, Conn.: Yale University Press, 1972.

Marx, K. *Economic and philosophic manuscripts of 1844*. Moscow: Foreign Languages Publishing House, 1961.

Marx, K., & Engels, F. *The German ideology*. New York: International Publishers, 1970.

Melmoth, W. (Ed.). *The letters of Pliny the consult* (Vol. 1). London: J. Dodsley, 1786.

Merleau-Ponty, M. *The structure of behavior*. Boston: Beacon Press, 1967.

Migliorini, B. *The Italian language*. London: Faber and Faber, 1966.

Muscatine, C. *Chaucer and the French tradition*. Berkeley, Calif.: University of California Press, 1966.

Owst, G. R. *Preaching in medieval England*. New York: Russell and Russell, 1965.

Ozment, S. E. (Ed.). *The reformation in medieval perspective*. Chicago: Quadrangle, 1971.

Parker, I. Harold Innis, Karl Marx and Canadian political economy. *Queen's Quarterly*, 1977, *84*, 545–563.

Parker, I. Innis, Marx, and the economics of communication. In W. R. Melody, L. Salter, & P. Heyer (Eds.), *Culture, communication and dominance*. Newtown, N.J.: Ablex, 1980.

Pirenne, H. *Histoire économique de l'occident médiévale*. Bruges: Desclée de Brouwer, 1951.

Pope, A. *The poems of Alexander Pope*. London: Methuen, 1963.

Pound, E. *ABC of reading*. London: Faber and Faber, 1961.

Pulgram, E. *The tongues of Italy*. New York: Greenwood Press, 1958.

Pulgram, E. *Italic, Latin, Italian: 600 B.C. to A.D. 1260*. Heidelberg: Carl Winter, 1978.

Reynolds, L. D., & Wilson, N. G. *Scribes and scholars*. Oxford: Clarendon, 1978.

Rickard, P. *A history of the French language*. London: Hutchinson, 1974.

Rickard, P. *Chrestomathie de la langue française au quinzième siècle*. Cambridge: Cambridge University Press, 1976.

Robbins, L. *An essay on the nature and significance of economic science*. London: Macmillan, 1952.

Robinson, H. W. (Ed.). *The Bible in its ancient and English versions*. Oxford: Clarendon, 1954.

Rossi-Landi, F. *Linguistics and economics*. The Hague: Mouton, 1975.

Sandys, J. E. *A history of classical scholarship* (Vol. 1). New York: Hafner, 1964.

Schofield, R. S. The measurement of literacy in pre-industrial England. In J. Goody (Ed.), *Literacy in traditional societies*. Cambridge: Cambridge University Press, 1968, pp. 311–325.

Shell, M. *The economy of literature*. Baltimore: Johns Hopkins University Press, 1978.

Sieveking, G. de G., Longworth I. H., & Wilson, K. E. (Eds.). *Problems in economic and social anthropology*. London: Duckworth, 1976.

Smalley, B. Church and state, 1300–77: Theory and fact. In J. Hale, R. Highfield, & B. Smalley (Eds.), *Europe in the late middle ages*. London: Faber and Faber, 1965, pp. 15–43.

Southern, R. W. *The making of the middle ages*. New Haven, Conn.: Yale University Press, 1964.

Southern, R. W. (Ed.). *Essays in medieval history*. London: Macmillan, 1968.

Stalin, J. V. *Marxism and problems of linguistics.* Peking: Foreign Languages Press, 1972.

Thompson, J. W. *The literacy of the laity in the middle ages.* New York: Burt Franklin, 1963.

Thrupp, S. (Ed.). *Change in medieval society.* New York: Appleton-Century-Crofts, 1964.

Ullman, W. *A history of political thought: The middle ages.* Harmondsworth, Middlesex: Penguin Books, 1968.

Vinogradoff, P. *Roman law in medieval Europe.* New York: Barnes & Noble, 1968.

Vygotsky, L. S. *Thought and language.* Cambridge, Mass.: MIT Press, 1970.

Wartburg, W. V. *Evolution et structure de la langue française,* Berne: Editions A. Francke, 1969.

Waterman, J. T. *A history of the German language.* Seatttle: University of Washington, 1966.

Williams, R. *Marxism and literature.* Oxford: Oxford University Press, 1977.

Wilson, R. M. English and French in England. *History,* 1943, *n.s. 28,* 37–69.

Wittgenstein, L. *Philosophical investigations.* Oxford: Basil Blackwell, 1953.

Wolff, P. *Western languages: A.D. 100–1500.* London: Weidenfeld and Nicolson, 1971.

Zengel, M. S. Literacy as a factor in language change. In J. A. Fishman (Ed.), *Readings in the sociology of language.* The Hague: Mouton, 1968.

20

The Impact of Informatics on Social Sign Systems

Roy Williams

Complexity in Sign Systems

Very high levels of complexity have been reached in the social sign systems used in the late twentieth century. Because of this complexity, the systems are very difficult to alter, and they tend to take on a life of their own. They have been termed "pseudo codes" (Williams, 1976) because they seem to take on the characteristics of organic codes—that is, stability across time and space.

Codes

First of all, we must look at the characteristics of codes themselves. *Codes* are opposed, in the present usage, to *sign systems;* that is, *codes* include classifications of physical and biological relations, as opposed to *languages* or *sign systems,* which are confined to human activity. (Of course, one must point out that the understanding of codes takes place through human language.)

Inorganic Codes. These are the most basic levels of *articulation,* in an extended sense of the way in which Rossi-Landi (1977) used the term. He described an articulation as a level of complexity of the combination of elements into units, which in turn are the elements to be combined into the units of the following articulation. The elements and units of inorganic codes are stable and the combination of elements is highly predictable—at least in relation to other articulations. The units are also highly uniform.

Organic Codes. These are the following articulations to inorganic codes. They are characterized by the self-reproduction and self-maintenance of the elements into units—organisms. Organisms do not present the same uniformity as do inorganic

Roy Williams ● Communication Department, University of South Africa, Pretoria 0001, South Africa.

combinations, and the units themselves are not as stable. The organism dies, but the *life form,* that is, the pattern of combinations of elements, is stable and is propagated across time and space, according to internally stored codes within the organism.

Behavior at this level is reasonably predictable, and in animals it can be very complex. But that too remains resonably automatic, or instinctual. It is useful for the argument that follows to reformulate this idea in terms of Prodi's (1979) analysis of behavior and meaning. One would then say that the organism's *reading* of its environment remains stable and also that its *behavior* is predictable, given certain elements in the environment that it is in a position to read. It will be useful to quote at some length from Prodi, because his work is not necessarily well known. He defined the elementary semiotic situation as that in which two

> material objects, A & B, are linked in a situation whereby, on coming together, they form a complex A-B. Object A moves randomly and collides with an indefinite number of objects without establishing any link with them. Only when it meets B does it react in a specific manner. (p. 1)

He went on to elaborate at length, but importantly he said:

> Reading is always governed by parameters, and is always subjective. *A* reads its environment from the viewpoint of its own structure, which is what enables it to react with *B.* . . . reading is a particular process, because A reacts only with B. However it is also a general process, because it can react with all B's. (p. 2)

He started at the molecular level, which is why he included the fact that A and B form "a complex A-B." For our purposes, the more general notion, that A reacts in a specific manner, is better. Using this scheme, we can reformulate the notion that behavior is instinctual by saying that both reading and behavior are predictable and that reading itself *is* activity—or a form of behavior—since reading entails the recognition of select elements of the environment as significant for that organism. Reading is then an active process, which is only separable from behavior in abstraction. This is very much the same line of thought as that of von Uexküll (1979), who maintained that the primary framework for analyzing behavior should be that stimuli are *elicited* by actions and not that actions are the *result* of stimuli.

Sign Systems

The next articulation is that of sign systems, as opposed to codes (see Figure 1). There is a continuity between sign systems and codes in that activity is the basis of readings at both levels. The discontinuity is that *work* is present, which means that "appetite (or desire) is held in check" (Rossi-Landi, 1977, p. 37). And that means, using Prodi's terms, that both readings and the behavior that is tied in with particular readings can be held in check while alternatives are tried out. In Prodi's words,

> Significance is realised in the process which links reader and sign . . . [via] a translation chain: a series of operations which links, by the fact of being translated, two structures each of which signifies the other. The reading machine can, once it reaches a certain degree of complexity, reconvert the semiotic contact with these things into traces: it is capable of memorising. In a subsequent stage, it can employ these traces to produce internal material states, which are taken as translational reactions with things: these are hypotheses. (1979, pp. 7–8)

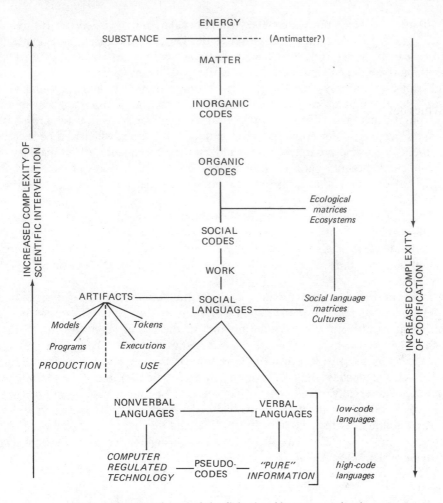

Figure 1. Scheme of some of the dialectics of languages and codes.

This ability to separate readings from behavior is what makes work possible: that is, the ability to abstract from a stereotyped reaction to readings and the immediacy of need satisfaction. Such work, at the crudest level through trial and error, allows new and changed readings and need satisfactions to develop. (This development also, logically, allows new needs to develop, but that is not part of the argument at this point.) What is important is that the ability to alter readings and behavior should not be confused with the erroneous belief that readings and behavior can become nonstereotyped altogether.

Behavior and readings merely settle into new stereotypes, or perhaps one should use a different term and say new *routines*. These in turn become increasingly fixed or automatic—stable across time and perhaps communicated to others as well—as they are habitually carried out (cf. Greenfield, this volume).

This process leads to a very specific conception of human behavior and meaning—that it is by definition not confined to a particular, and phylogenetically limited, set of stereotypes, since these can be set aside. On the other hand, stereotypes or routines cannot be set aside for too long. The so-called existential vacuum in which everything is contingent is neither desirable nor possible in the long run if there is to be physiological and psychological stability. Using computer terminology somewhat metaphorically, we can say that the human brain can program, erase, and reprogram, but it cannot put aside—or even continue to change—programs for any length of time. Such a situation would be consistent with madness, which can be seen as the absence of stable programs. This could be the consequence of the inability to maintain stable programs and/or the unwillingness to maintain any of the programs that the person knows, that is, those programs that the person has been in a position to read and to carry out.

From this conception of human behavior and meaning it follows that sign systems allow by definition for changes in behavior not only through trial-and-error in activities but also through hypothesizing new readings and behaviors, that is, through planning new programs or, as we will say, through *program design* (cf. Schubert, this volume).

Program design in turn becomes more and more complex, and I will argue that very complex systems tend to develop into systems that are very difficult to change at all. That is, although they are the product of the use of languages in program design, they eventually take on the characteristics of codes. Their potential for change, even by those who developed the systems in the first place, is greatly diminished. Such pseudocodes seem to take on a life of their own and to be reproduced according to internally stored codes. They seem to be autonomous life forms with remarkable ability to outlast the individuals who work within them, who seem to come and go much as the cells of organisms live and die and are replaced with little or no effect on the life form. The life forms survive, as characterized in the book *The Selfish Gene* (Dawkins, 1976).

The Dialectics of Social Sign Systems

Between pseudocodes and the most elementary social sign systems lie the variations of social reproduction, which will be explored in this section. Figure 2 is an attempt to outline *all* social sign systems on a flowchart—a rather ambitious task perhaps. In the scheme, differences between matrices of social sign systems, or cultures, are accommodated by different emphases in the strengths and/or directions of the vectors and by variations in the importance of particular elements on the charts—or even the absence of some of the elements.

This scheme has many elements to it, but it is essentially trichotomous. The three constituents are: *material social reproduction,* which is comprised of routine practices of nonverbal sign systems for the transformation of material; *sign systems* (i.e., verbal exchange and exchange of exchange or monetary systems), which inform these routine practices; and *coding functions,* which regulate sign systems. Particular coding functions materialize in programs for work as the ideological commitments of particular ideological institutions (cf. Kvale, this volume). Such institutions

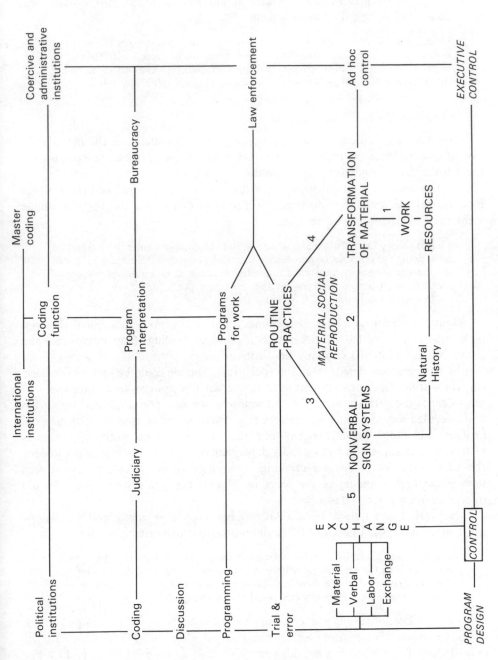

Figure 2. An outline of social sign systems.

embody forms of control over social reproduction as a whole. This idea is in line with Rossi-Landi's (1978) analysis, which uses the three terms *modes of production, sign systems,* and *ideological institutions,* and in which he summed up the dialectical interrelationship among the three elements.

> Usually intermediate sign systems are carriers of the structures of the mode of production, permeating them with the ideological institutions, which then serve to justify it. But a well-timed political work can use sign systems to permeate the dominant mode of production with new ideological values. (p. 64)

Material Social Reproduction

The primary element in the dialectics of social reproduction is the *transformation of material* or, more extensively defined, *material social reproduction.* This element is the sine qua non for social reproduction as a whole.

In this analysis material social reproduction will be distinguished from all the other elements of social reproduction. It will be given definitive status for all the other elements. But we must remember that

> even to satisfy immediate material needs, individuals must unite in groups, and by so doing put other social processes into action at once; and the material goods themselves are not all consumed immediately, even at an elementary stage of social development, but rather for the most part put aside . . . for later consumption. (Rossi-Landi, 1978, p. 49)

Material social reproduction is confined in this scheme to nonverbal sign systems, although as we have said before behavior and readings (and thus verbal and nonverbal sign systems) can only be distinguished in abstraction. In terms of the Base–Superstructure debate, material social reproduction could be seen as the Base. But the distinction drawn here between nonverbal sign systems and other sign systems defines the primary area of social reproduction in a particular and somewhat more detailed way. Specifically, the area of production and consumption of material artifacts is included, but exchange of all kinds is excluded, since exchange is seen as historically subsequent to and logically dependent on production. This is not to deny the actual unity of production–exchange–consumption, but it is a necessary step toward the understanding of the ways in which exchange systems regulate and inform nonverbal sign systems.

Nonverbal sign systems are a relatively new area of research, and it is worthwhile to mention Rossi-Landi's (1978) definition, that they are sign systems

> which are *not in the least verbal* because founded upon codes which have nothing to do with the articulated sounds constituting the code of verbal sign systems, or that are distinguished from these because they are not originally systems of sounds, but rather systems of other objects. (p. 59)

And on the relation between nonverbal sign systems (NVSS) and verbal sign systems (VSS) he wrote: "The central point is that we are dealing with NVSS which are not only distinct from VSS, but are also *not reducible to them*" (1977, p. 17). For example,

> the exchange of commodities, as with every type of exchange, is already a nonverbal sign system, which becomes more complicated, and reaches higher levels

of abstraction with the institution first of coins, and later of money. The structures of this non-verbal sign system are reflected in language. (1978, p. 61)

As a last example, let us look at the work of von Uexküll (1979), which allows us to see how meaning and action are reciprocally related, even though action should be regarded as primary. Von Uexküll's scheme is opposed to the traditionalist view of the psychology of perception, namely, that perception is to some (large) degree passive in that it is a response to stimuli. He argued convincingly that the paradigm should be reversed: stimulus and readings are produced by the activity of the organism; meaning is created by action. In his own words,

> behaviour has as its primary function the production of signs for communication of the organism with itself. . . . Signs are therefore strictly subjective phenomena of the organism, whose receptors are affected by the effects of its own behaviour. (1979, pp. 7–8)

This view accords with Prodi's model. At both the cellular level (Prodi) and the animal level (von Uexküll), activity is primary and provokes reaction in the environment, which subsequently causes sensory information to flow back to the organism. Significance in this way is established by action. This theory corresponds closely to the idea that one has to change the world in order to understand it.

Transcribing this model into the language of nonverbal and verbal sign systems, one might say that action is primarily in terms of nonverbal sign systems, and meaning is formed as a derivative of what happens when nonverbal sign systems are employed in action. And, of course, action can, subsequent to the formation of meaning, be elicited by sensory information. The scheme is also applicable to the use of verbal behavior itself as behavior which stimulates the formation of meaning. Vector 5 (in Figure 2), between nonverbal and other sign systems, is bidirectional, but nonverbal sign systems remain the basis.

At this stage we must stress, with Rossi-Landi, that the primacy of nonverbal sign systems does not mean that they are somehow presocial or nonsocial. All sign systems are social by definition. Even at the most primitive level, artifacts contain signs, and every usage "is converted into a sign of itself" (Barthes, 1967, p. 42). This usage is to some extent at least a sign of the social relations of its production and use, although as the sign system increases in complexity, these social relations become less and less apparent in the artifact itself. (This idea will be expanded later.)

More important is the fact that the genesis and the later development of nonverbal sign systems are socially mediated or even determined. In Figure 3 the vectors show the intial development of material social reproduction. In the first place, resources are used for work. This use, of course, implies a selection from the products of natural history, and at the most basic level this selection takes place by trial and error. The transformation of material, abstracted from the immediacy of need satisfaction, leads to the formation of nonverbal sign systems. Because these are part of the social relations (albeit, strictly speaking, at the level of social codes, initially in anthropogenesis), and because they enter into the ongoing process of reproducing social relations, they tend to be repeated habitually, that is, according to their success in terms of the transformation of material.

In this way the material base for social reproduction is established and the nonverbal sign systems become institutionalized as *routine practices*. (In the long run

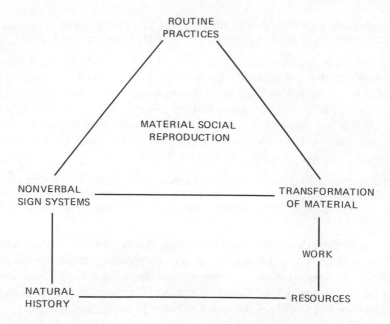

Figure 3. The basis of material social reproduction.

these routine practices are only adopted in relation to prevailing social relations.) These change the transformation of materials and the pool of the products of natural history from which the selection of resources is made. Selection in this way becomes selection as such—an active process—and once again is dependent on the prevailing social relations. In this way a natural history, that is, a systematic human interpretation of natural phenomena, begins (cf. Wertsch, this volume).

Material social reproduction also produces waste and by-products. These are not initially incorporated in any useful way into the transformation of materials, but as the consumption of natural resources progresses, they are incorporated into the flow, because resources become scarcer and/or because wastes become damaging to the producers themselves and to the pool of resources.

This process completes the cycle of material social reproduction. Routine practices, instead of the immediacy of need satisfaction, start to determine the transformation of material. Minimally, this means that adustments occur in social relations. Ultimately, it entails the creation of new *wants* in the individual sense, as well as new *needs,* that is, new necessary aspects of the transformation of material. These wants can rightfully be termed needs, since the new system of social reproduction, which both consists of and (perhaps forcefully) maintains social relations, will require new immediacies of satisfaction (cf. Prŭcha, this volume). This is the beginning of *social* history, which becomes an increasingly important force as it develops inertia in time and in complexity: in time, because of the self-evident validity of tradition and in complexity because more complex systems are increasingly difficult to change and/or to replace, both as systems and as changes in individual work.

The scheme (see Figure 2) has three main loci of control: program design, control of exchange, and executive control. We have already said that initial developments in nonverbal sign systems come about through trial and error. Later developments are dependent on the establishment of significant abstractions of sign systems from material social reproduction.

The primary abstraction, which is within material social reproduction, is from the immediacy of need satisfaction. It is the beginning of the matrix of social sign systems which one can call *culture,* in the sense that artifacts are produced that are the products of work and the above abstraction. It is in this sense that one can comprehend the apparent contradiction between different types of artifacts of cultures (especially early ones): on the one hand, tools for further work and on the other hand, artifacts which seem to be so far removed from the sphere of productive work that they seem to be merely aesthetic. But it must be remembered that *all* artifacts are, from the beginning, consequent to the initial abstraction from the immediacy of need satisfaction. It is this common abstraction, which is a *major* characteristic of both kinds of artifacts at this level, that renders their production in one and the same society both possible and comprehensible.

The next abstraction is that of material exchange. It is possible, at least logically, to remain for a moment in the realm of *use* value as such. That is, suppose that people with their artifacts, in a chance meeting, come to exchange their artifacts. At this level, it is an exchange of material goods, for use. But as Rossi-Landi (1977) has pointed out, included in the production of an artifact is a program for use; that is, the exchange is *also* an exchange of sign systems—albeit only nonverbal ones. And, since routine practices also include social relations, the exchange of material goods entails the (potential, at least) exchange of social relations as well.

The exchange of goods leads to the establishment of social relations between the people of the various groups who exchange goods. These wider social relations are dependent on, and can also strongly influence, the primary abstraction of material exchange, that is, that of *exchange value.* Social relations lead to the production of goods *for exchange,* which obviously influences the primary area of material social reproduction.

We have said that there are three loci of control, and we have already mentioned program control. The area of exchange and of the interaction between material social reproduction and exchange is a major area of control, and its importance develops with the development of material social reproduction, which is simultaneous with the development of exchange itself and the development of the production of exchange value.

This development in turn involves a definite change in the complexity of social relations. At the stage prior to the development of exchange, another locus is dominant—that of executive control. In its simplest form this locus is merely the ad hoc control of material social reproduction directly through control of the transformation of material and also through the control of routine practices. The control of access to resources is also important here, for instance, the access to (wo)men. When exchange becomes an important part of social reproduction, the producers of goods must abstract from the production of use value to the production of exchange value. And almost by definition that exchange is not wholly under their control; that is, social relations and the modes of control become more complex. The differential hierarchy of those who control material social reproduction and those who actually carry it out becomes accentuated. This differentiation is the beginning of a clearly discernible division of labor into intellectual and manual, and at the same time it necessarily involves an increase in the size of groups under a unitary control structure. In other words, it involves a logical increase in the amount of power and control invested in the controlling group/elite.

This discussion brings us to the point at which we must enlist the help of Sohn-Rethel (1978). He raised the central question of the "network of relations by which society forms a coherent whole," and called this network the "social synthesis" (p. 4). Clearly, in a primitive society one can envisage the social synthesis being merely the direct production of goods for consumption. The proximity of production and consumption and the absence of any sort of exchange constitute the social synthesis.

On the other hand, in societies based on commodity production, the social synthesis is precisely the *exchange abstraction,* and as Sohn-Rethel said, "the abstraction does not spring from labour, but from exchange as a particular mode of social relationship" (p. 6). This concept can best be illustrated by reference to some of the examples given by Sohn-Rethel. He started with the forms of social control in which exploitation was based on "unilateral appropriation as opposed to the reciprocity of exchange" (p. 24). He cited the example of the appropriation of surplus value from the Nilotic peasants by the servants of the pharaoh and said that the collected produce was then placed under the sole authority of the pharaoh himself.

All this is changed, and the exchange abstraction comes into its own, when the

> social power has lost this personal character, and in its place is an anonymous necessity which forces itself upon every individual commodity owner. The whole of the hierarchical superstructure of the Egyptian society has disappeared, and the control over the use and disposal of things is now exercised anarchistically by the mechanism of the market, in accordance with the laws of private property, which are in fact the laws of the separation of exchange and use. (p. 25)

This central separation, or abstraction, is that in order for exchange to function, "the physical condition of the commodities, their material status, must remain unchanged" (p. 25). He added: "The salient feature of the act of exchange is that its separation from use has assumed the compelling necessity of an objective social law."

Let us return to the general theme of the loci of control. We can say that the personal and largely ad hoc control exercised prior to commodity production is replaced by what appears to be an objective social law. That is, it appears that the control over the use and disposal of things is now exercised anarchistically by the mechanisms of the market. But we have already said that the existence of the separate realms of the production of exchange value and the exchange itself—a development which is only a matter of increasing complexity over time—necessitates a separation of the producers from those who carry out the exchange.

This separation in turn merely shifts the locus of control from the direct control over material social reproduction to the control over material social reproduction via the control of exchange. Thus, while it is true that the *nature* of the control changes from a personal one to one that appears to be the control of objective laws, the *locus* of control can remain much the same. The same people or group who previously controlled material social reproduction directly could now control the exchange process, and thus material social reproduction too. It is a less direct control, but this change can be attributed to the necessity of the increasing complexity of the forces of material reproduction. This discussion leads us to the hypothesis that control over material social reproduction of increasing complexity *has to be* control of increasing indirectness. The development in the conditions of material production is what changes the nature of the social relations, but at the same time it does not necessarily change the locus of power and control, but merely their breadth of distribution.

Complexity in Sign Systems

Before we continue the exploration of the abstractions of commodity exchange, we must look at the levels of complexity in sign systems themselves, the systems that will be the carriers of the social synthesis. Thereafter we will return to the question posed by Sohn-Rethel, namely, that "not only analogy, but true identity exists between the formal elements of the social synthesis and the formal elements of cognition" (1978, p. 7).

To start with, complexity is seen from two points of view, which must be kept in mind simultaneously, namely, the complexity which is a formal characteristic of a particular sign system and the complexity which is a complexity of *reading,* and subsequently using, a sign system, that is, the way in which a sign system is complex for particular groups of people at a point in history. These two types of complexity will, later in the analysis, have implications for the control over social reproduction. I will argue that control is developed and maintained both by the increasing complexity of sign systems themselves and by the increasing complexity of the reading of those systems by particular groups of people.

Verbal Sign Systems. I have already said that the abstraction from the immediacy of need satisfaction is what makes possible both work and the development of verbal and nonverbal sign systems, as opposed to codes.

Verbal sign systems have peculiar characteristics: they can be seen as information systems. As such, they are "indifferent to the material of the signs that compose them" (Barthes, 1967, p. 13). Their sign content overshadows other uses, leading to the somewhat paradoxical situation that their only use is in exchange. Verbal sign systems consist almost exclusively of sign material, as opposed to nonverbal sign systems, which consist of material artifacts and are only in small part composed of material which has sign content. Thus, although verbal sign systems are logically subsequent to nonverbal sign systems and are always related to them, they do "enjoy a certain measure of independence, which allows them to develop *also* according to their own laws" (Rossi-Landi, 1978, p. 62; cf. Nadin, this volume).

To put it crudely, this independence enables one to "lift off" the sign elements and structures from nonverbal sign systems, to rearrange them, and then to try to impose this new arrangement on the elements of nonverbal sign systems and material social reproduction. In this way language can be used extensively to reprogram routine practices—directly and/or via reprogramming programs that are already in verbal form. Thus a parallel cycle develops alongside that of material social reproduction (not shown in Figure 2), in which the three elements are the transformation of information, verbal sign systems, and routine practices within verbal sign systems. This cycle is part of exchange in general and is the basis of program design.

As soon as *work* is part of program design, and design is no longer mere trial and error, programming develops. This change influences routine practices through *programs for work,* which are the equivalent, for verbal sign systems, of routine practices. Such planned programming, which is characteristically conscious and reflective, in contrast to the largely ad hoc reprogramming possible within nonverbal sign systems alone, depends on three factors: the extent to which behavior is instinctive (which is very small), the extent to which one set of routine practices can be changed to another without excessive personal and/or systems stress, and the extent to which the development of material social reproduction enables people to gain control of the material conditions for social reproduction. Of course, the third factor is the most important, but it could be said that as the so-called developed countries progress toward the end of the twentieth century, the importance of the second factor is increasing.

Verbal sign systems incorporate, at this point in the argument, three levels of abstraction: (1) abstraction from the immediacy of need satisfaction, (2) abstraction from the use of a particular artifact to the use of that artifact in general, and (3) abstraction from the material of the sign itself.

A fourth abstraction, that of quantitative sign systems, entails an indifference to the material *and the content* of the sign system and consists solely of *form.* Quantitative sign systems, which are a development within verbal sign systems, are above all internally consistent, and this consistency, together with the high degree of abstraction, makes them ideally suited for control and predictability, the so-called instrumental use of sign systems. These features lead to the claim that sign systems, such as those of science and monetary exchange, are instrumental sign systems and are value neutral in themselves.

Nonverbal and Verbal Sign Systems. At this point the connections between nonverbal and verbal sign systems must be examined. Both culminate, at the highest level, in sign systems that are quantitative.

The similarities have been masterfully outlined in "Linguistics and Economics" (Rossi-Landi, 1977), and for details the work itself must be consulted. At issue here are the levels of complexity, or articulations, of the two sorts of sign systems and the fairly exact parallels between them. In brief, the development of complexity in nonverbal and in verbal sign systems progresses from the simplest use of individual elements—words and sentences in one case, simple tools in the other—to combinations of these elements which involve further levels of abstraction. The first of these (as far as our argument is concerned) is the combination of sentences into syllogisms, representing a set of verbal signs which is in large part indifferent to its use and to the user. It remains valid (or not) regardless of the speaker. In nonverbal sign systems the parallel is the opposition of elements in simple machines, which at the most basic level may be just two tools or artifacts working in opposition to one another to produce a joint effect. The action of a boat with oars is one of Rossi-Landi's examples.

At a more complex level, such combinations (both nonverbal and verbal sign systems) involve sets of elements which are so internally consistent and almost completely independent of the people who use them that they are at the level of automated machines or very complex verbal texts. Thus the sign systems reach a level at which their use is almost completely abstracted from the particular needs or wants of the user. The system "goes its own way," or "takes on a life of its own," and we have reached the level of pseudocodes referred to in the first section.

Pure Information. At the level of pseudocodes, sign systems, both verbal and nonverbal, are articulated primarily in quantitative terms—the mathematics of science and the computerization of automated manufacture, as well as of information handling. (The latter is an interesting conceptual hybrid of verbal and nonverbal systems.)

I have outlined the many levels of abstraction that this articulation involves. But there is one further aspect that needs unpacking: objectivity. In the section on Sohn-Rethel's conception of the social synthesis, the commodity abstraction was said to operate successfully because "the salient feature of the act of exchange is that its separation from use has assumed the compelling necessity of an objective social law" (Sohn-Rethel, 1978, p. 25).

It is in fact a general characteristic of pseudocodes that the codification in terms of quantitative signs involves such a high level of abstraction that the sign systems—and even to some extent their use—seem quite simply to be above personal characteristics. If one regards only the *form* of such systems, this is in fact true. But it is *not* true of the genesis and maintenance of the *use* of such a system which is, precisely, the result of personal and *non*objective forces.

This distinction is, however, very difficult to discern. In the process of arriving at such a level of abstraction and making a set of signs work in terms of quantitative data, any signs of the persons who worked to produce the set of signs, and/or the sets of social relations involved in the conditions that made the work possible, have been erased from the final product, the set of pseudocodes. One can say, in an ironic sense, that this represents "purified" or "pure" information.

Let us take up Sohn-Rethel's concern with the exchange abstraction once again. The appearance of the laws of exchange as objective social laws is made possible because of the highly abstract nature of the exchange form. But the *level* of abstraction, precisely, is nonobjective, because it is at the level of pure information that the vast majority of people are lost. They can neither comprehend nor influence what is going on as a whole, and it is precisely as a whole that complex systems work (cf. Parker, this volume).

In this way the control of exchange, and thereby the control of material social reproduction, is confined to a small elite. This phenomenon seems, at first glance, to be at variance with the initial effect of the introduction of commodity exchange: namely, that the personal control over social reproduction (as in Sohn-Rethel's example of the pharaoh) is replaced by the control of the marketplace. That is, the origins of commodity exchange in society appear to be a liberation from both the *nature* and the *extent* of control previously exercised by a small elite over material social reproduction. The growth of the petite bourgeoisie is invariably a very enthusiastic one. But the appearance of liberation is deceptive. The very means of their supposed liberation, the exchange system, very soon becomes so complex that control of material social reproduction (via exchange this time) returns to the hands of the controlling elite—and perhaps the very same controlling elite at that.

The key to understanding how this deceptive liberation of commodity exchange turns out to be a return to control in a different form, and also turns out to be largely beyond the understanding and hence influence of the majority of people, is supplied by Sohn-Rethel (1978). He wrote:

> While exchange banished use from the actions of marketing people, it does not banish it from their minds. . . . Thus in speaking of the abstractness of exchange we must be careful not to apply the term to the consciousness of the exchanging agents. They are supposed to be occupied with the use of the commodities they see, but occupied in their imaginations only. It is the action of exchange, and the action only, that is abstract. The consciousness and the actions of the people part company and go different ways. (pp. 25–26)

In this way a series of abstractions is built up. The act of production becomes abstract as it becomes production for exchange and not for use. The link between production and consumption, which at an earlier stage was simpler and thus comprehensible, is now interrupted by an exchange abstraction of increasing complexity. This is true in two ways: the sign systems of exchange become more complex in themselves, and as they do so they have to be constantly readjusted in terms of world markets, inflation, and so forth. The constant change in a sign system of high complexity makes it, almost by definiton, more complex to read—to understand—for the majority of people. This double incomprehensibility abstracts the sign system from the actions *and* the consciousness of the agents. In such a situation the people must accept that the *sign system* (as opposed to the act of exchange) is objectified—or alienated—from their actions and their understanding. The act of exchange, which is already an abstraction in fact, becomes even more abstract when the objective social laws themselves become incomprehensible. In this sense one can speak of an objective social *necessity,* as opposed to laws, and we have come to the stage where the release from the immediacies of need satisfaction has turned into a new immediacy of the satisfaction of objective (social) needs.

Control

Once such complexity is reached in sign systems, we can refer to them as pseudocodes. The particular pseudocodes which are produced and put into operation control material social reproduction via this high level of abstraction. In Figure 2, I have used three loci of control: those of exchange, executive control, and program design. The last of these is obviously involved in the production of sign systems both at the level of programming and the level of *coding.* Coding refers to the *overall* program design, which affects a whole set of programs for work. The ideas of free trade or parliamentary democracy are examples.

At the level of programs for work, there is a further articulation into hardware, software, and division of labor (see Figure 4). *Hardware* includes the machinery for the transformation of material; *software,* the organizational structure—the programs for what you do with the hardware at your disposal; and the *division of labor,* the so-called career structures and job demarcation. Together they make up the programs for work, which inform routine practices and also arise out of routine practices.

Routine practices are the point at which control factors of program design and of executive control meet. The latter can exercise control over day-to-day processes. For instance, people, hardware, and software can be selectively removed from routine

Figure 4. The constituents of programs for work.

practices on an ad hoc basis. This selection can be developed into an institutionalized form of executive control, in which case it amounts to law enforcement. But the element of ad hoc control can always remain in operation alongside law enforcement. It is quite possible to maintain a reasonably respectable law enforcement operation together with arbitrary bannings of particular people's participation in particular sectors of social reproduction. And such executive control can also function at the level of programs for work, for example in the banning of particular organizations.

The same spectrum is present in program design. The laws which are enforced need be no more than edicts issued in an ad hoc manner. But they can, and very often do, fall under a separate, political institution responsible for program design. This may be a representative body, a nominated body, etc. To the extent to which it is truly representative of the forces operative in society, it reaches some form of legitimation, or even participation. Program design on the basis of consensus is also a possibility.

The various forms of program design are tied up with the flow of information. In what could be termed an *authoritarian* system, only enough information is allowed to circulate to allow people to act in some coordinated way. The best example of this type of system is the military, in which there is a close tie between obedience and the minimal amount of available information. People are given only enough information to *act* on, but not enough to decide for themselves whether such action is justifiable in terms of broader moral, political, or other parameters.

If enough information is allowed to circulate for people to decide about their actions, then the field of *discussion* about program design—both in itself and in its social implications—comes into its own, and it soon becomes institutionalized in various media. Two peculiar phenomena arise in such a situation, namely, *public opinion* and *public debate*.

This circulation of information usually operates only within a host of qualifications; that is, certain people are not allowed to participate on the basis of general categories or ad hoc bannings. For example, there is a restriction on membership of Nature Conservation boards in South Africa which excludes "the insane, the criminal, and Blacks." Other restrictions are on the information about programs and the body of facts on the basis of which programs were developed, as well as on the circulation of information about what is happening as a result of the application of particular programs.

At the same time, another sphere of discussion about program design must be kept in mind, that of *private debate*. This is not restricted to those directly involved in program design but also involves those who have a knowledge about such activities, meet in separate groups to discuss such proposals, and try to influence decisions. This obviously occurs whether public debate exists or not. A good example is the secret Afrikaner Broederbond organization in South Africa, which is able to wield considerable political, religious, and cultural power without any of its debates being made public. In the same breath one should also mention that private agreements are made in the business sphere which have wide implications, for instance, cartels. As a hypothesis for further consideration one could say that it is quite possible that even within highly complex and multifaceted—and multimedia—public debates, which include parliaments and a free press, the hidden influence of private debates could be far more important than that of public debates.

A further development of program design is the separation of *program interpretation* from design. This is still closely linked to program design, but can take independent form, in the judiciary, for instance. Included in program interpretation are interpretation at the macro level, in the form of a legal system, and interpretation at the micro level, in the form of the interpretation of rules by the bureaucracy.

A third factor can influence program design, namely, *master codings*. That is, apart from the influence of interpretation of programs on the one hand, and the influence of coding functions on the other, design can also be influenced in an even more general fashion by master codings—coding functions that are articulated by the operations of organizations transnationally.

Informatics

I have outlined the dialectics of social reproduction in general terms. The social synthesis has been pinned down to the exchange abstraction, which makes the sphere of exchange the most important locus of control. This is because the exchange abstraction is determinant of material social reproduction, which is at the center of social reproduction, and because it is the locus of a highly complex sign system in which every action in a commodity producing society is caught up. This abstraction, in fact, has an exact parallel in abstractions in thought, and the latter has developed on the basis of the former. Sohn-Rethel has argued this at length, and his work must be consulted for details. He argued that the development of systems of monetary exchange, because they involve the necessary abstractions, pave the way for the development of abstract thought:

> Time and space, rendered abstract under the impact of commodity exchange, are marked by homogeneity and emptiness of all natural and material content, visible or invisible. The exchange abstraction excludes everything that makes up history, human and even natural history. . . . Time and space thereby assume the character of absolute historical timelessness and universality which must

mark the exchange abstraction as a whole and each of its features. (1978, p. 49)

Of the exchange abstraction he said: "It determines the conceptual mode of thinking peculiar to societies based on commodity production" (p. 23). In modern societies this idea has its clearest articulation in the abstractions of science. Once again the necessity of *objectifying* the sign system of science must not be allowed to confuse the issue of the so-called objectivity of science and applied science. For just as the complexity of exchange systems, together with complexities resulting from continual change in the system, serves to restrict the size of the elite which can exercise control over exchange, so too the complexity of science functions for control.

The realm of science is within the realm of program design. Scientific research and development are concerned with producing and improving programs for work. When the complexities of the pseudocodes of modern science come to inform program design and debate, participation in any real sense is minimized. This effect is even more apparent when one takes into account that such public debate is framed in the terms of the economic viability of scientific applications—a twofold operation of pseudocodes. The extreme case of such restricted control over social reproduction is the space race. One could even argue that in this case the complexity itself produces such awe in the minds of the public that they foot the bill for the pure research of the large aerospace companies. Space research is pure research by very powerful companies who could afford to finance their own research but who, in the name of the space race, get their research fully subsidized by public funds. The results of the research are theirs alone; no royalties accrue to the public from the use of these results.

The Information Revolution

In the late twentieth century, the advances of science, mainly as spin-offs from the research of the space race, have produced what is called the *information revolution,* the sphere of *informatics,* the set of information-based activities which have the potential to alter radically present practices in most sectors of society.

The general trends of informatics in terms of social reproduction can be said to be the increase in information-handling capacity and the flow of information, which allows for the increasing hardwaring of tasks, that is, the increased automation of all sorts of production.

In order to understand what happens in such an extraordinary situation, the traditional opposition between capital and labor will be reexamined. I have said, with Sohn-Rethel, that the commodity abstraction is the crux of the social synthesis and that exchange is the most important locus of control, especially when it is coupled with the framework of modern science. These relationships can also be described as the control over social reproduction via pseudocodes, including those of exchange systems and science. If the control over material social reproduction is seen as control *via* such systems, it can be described as control via information systems as such. Information systems include the information itself, the process of encoding use values into exchange values, and, of course, the social relations that make this process possible. In this sense one can rephrase the opposition as that between information and labor instead of capital and labor. This is a way of overcoming the dilemma of how one includes informatics in "capital." Does one speak of "information capital"? The term does seem to be logically viable, but remains a little awkward. Instead, we can include both economic and scientific sign systems in the term "information." This definition should make the opposition clearer, since it is an opposition between those who control information about social sign systems and those who control their own labor.

If we return to Figure 2, we can locate the opposition between information and labor. I have said that the crux of material social reproduction is routine practices and that these are informed by programs for work. If labor, in the sense of those directly involved in material social reproduction, wishes to exercise control over material social reproduction and thus over its own social reproduction as a whole, it has few options. The most often recommended—the "proper channel"—is via participation in program design and discussion. What is more often successful, in terms of tangible results, is the organization of labor into unions. Unionization can have a direct effect on routine practices, and can push further up the chart to programs for work, influencing choices of hardware, software, and demarcations. Unfortunately, this influence is often limited to demarcations. An example is the protracted dispute on Fleet Street, involving notably the *Times,* in which the transition to electronic typesetting and editing, as well as the transfer of the typesetting to the journalists themselves, is being opposed by those who were previously responsible for those tasks.

It is, of course, possible that the organization of labor can at the same time pursue control via the control over programs for work *and* via control over the parliamentary process. The close liaison between the Labour Party and the unions in the United Kingdom is a good example of this.

The above dispute at the *Times* is an example of the hardwaring of tasks previously performed by skilled or semiskilled workers. Their jobs are being replaced by machines that are operated by fewer people at higher (and other) skill levels, machines that have a large component of information technology. Information handling, the work of numerous clerks throughout bureaucracies and the administration of industry, has for years now been slowly taken over by computerized systems. More recently, the advances in capability and the decrease in costs of chips (micro integrated circuits) have made possible the increased automation of a large variety of industrial and manufacturing processes.

The results are that large numbers of people are in danger of being made redundant, with little prospect of other employment. At the least, present employment levels in some sectors can be maintained, but only for those already in employment. The new technology enables present staffing levels to be frozen at the same time as allowing substantial increases in production. New entrants to the job market are the hardest hit. (See Association of Scientific, Technical and Managerial Staffs, 1979; Mather, 1981.)

These trends affect the developed world most. But other aspects will affect the developing nations, especially those involved in the assembly of goods for foreign multinationals. The Counter Information Services (CIS) report (1979) outlines the extent of foreign assembly of parts—cases in which parts are made in the host country, shipped to, say, Singapore, and assembled there and the final product is shipped back to the host country. This might seem to be an expensive way of assembling products, but the low cost of such "highly disciplined"—which inevitably means non-unionized—workforces in such countries makes it economically viable. However, it has recently been reported that in the United States, for instance, the advances in informatics will reduce the number of components to be assembled to such an extent that assembly will no longer be a labor intensive task. This change will bring home much of the assembly.

Here we have a good example of the increase in information at the expense of labor. It is representative of a general trend in the pattern of control. When labor and routine practices become hardwared in this way, the control of labor over material social reproduction is diminished. For example, using the new electronic media it is possible for the junior management of a newspaper to put out an abbreviated edition in the absence of the rest of the staff.

This kind of development allows the material sign systems to be developed to levels of complexity of pseudocodes; they take on a life of their own and seem to be maintained and reproduced according to internally stored codes. Once in operation, it is exceedingly difficult to alter them. Therefore, if labor is not consulted beforehand, in the planning stages, it does not really matter what labor thinks later on. There will be no way they can change the program; they can only refuse to operate the machines at all. But that tactic is often not effective, because such machines are built to be dependent on as few operators as possible and some of the new applications, like the digital telephone exchanges, are virtually maintenance free (see Mather, 1981).

The locus of control thus shifts substantially toward the area of program design and the scientific-technological elite, or as some have termed it, the information-industrial elite. Design of programs for work is confined to a small group of experts. For the rest, what is left is only the carrying out of predetermined routine practices. The ability to change and reprogram routines, which is at the basis of work in the beginning of sociogenesis, has been transformed into reasonably stereotyped performance of socially necessary tasks. Phylogenetic determinism is replaced by social determinism.

The Cultural Sector

Our discussion now turns to the connection between the scientific-technological and the cultural sectors. The cultural sector is at present being integrated into the economic one, under the control of very large multinational companies. Mattelart (1979) has outlined in detail the way in which multinationals have come to be involved in cultural production—the production of educational and entertainment programs. Their ability to do this on a worldwide scale is the product of their dominance of the hardware development and sales of the new information technology. This new technology is mass-marketed, but in a way that differs substantially from previous mass-marketing; that is, the cost of the hardware that is being developed and made available is now actually reduced *in real terms,* simultaneous with increases in capacity. That means that contrary to previous economies of mass-marketing, where the size of the turnover allowed a reduction in the profit on individual items (this loss was more than recouped by the increase in the number of units sold), the present mass-marketing reduces the selling price of the item to below what it previously cost to produce the item. Even in very large-scale marketing, profits will be less than in the previous mode.

That, however, is only half the story. The same companies that are now producing the hardware, which is becoming exceedingly attractive in consumer pricing, are already heavily involved in the production of software. And the sales of software are very lucrative. If a momentum of changing fashion can be maintained in such products, where the best program is always the next one, the software market will become open-ended. It is even conceivable that the hardware could be provided virtually free, and Mattelart cited some cases in which large numbers of television sets were provided at no cost in order to facilitate later sales of software. A medium like television is not only a channel for the sale of educational and entertainment programs, but is also one of the best channels ever for marketing a wide range of products via advertising (preferably in color).

In the United Kingdom, for instance, this shift from hardware sales to software is threatening public broadcasting (the BBC). In the early seventies the public expenditure on license fees for television was less than one third of what was spent on sets. But the early eighties will see the total saturation of the color television market in the United Kingdom.

As far as license fees are concerned, alternatives must be sought. The BBC is reported to be taking an interest in pay-TV experiments (Porter, 1981). But for the manufacturers, who are tied in through parent companies with the progam makers (see Mattelart, 1979), software will have to replace hardware as the major area for exploitation. Porter gave the example of films:

> In future, feature films will be released first to cinemas, followed by the sale of prerecorded video cassettes, by sales to cable casters, and finally, when all these markets are exhausted, by release for broadcasting, whether by satellite or terrestrial, when they may be video recorded in the home. (p. 38)

He left out, of course, the most important of the new gadgets, the videodisc. The videodisc has no recording facility, as the record player for music has none. It is being sold at a price which is less than half of the price of a video recorder, and one wonders whether the development cost of a videodisc was not perhaps *more* than the cost of a video recorder—that is, that its pricing is a deliberate ploy to encourage the purchase of playback-only video equipment.

In this sense the cultural sector becomes very closely tied to the economic sector. It is the channel for marketing par excellence, via animated color advertising in every home, and also a channel for increasing expectations for the consumption of commodities. Entertainment exports—even without advertising—create an aura of technologically induced happiness around those who are successful in terms of commodity consumption. The ultimate in this regard is the technological vision (dream or nightmare?) of the fully computerized home, in which all activity is so well planned that the only work one has to do is to push a series of buttons at the right time. And with the impact of the information revolution it should be possible for many or all of those involved in information-based activity (which apparently is already a substantial portion of the workforce) to be employed solely at home, via an information link.

Thus, not only will most people be freed from all noninformational work, but they will not even have to interact directly with people as far as their work is concerned.

Human-to-human interaction would be substantially displaced by machine-mediated interaction. This scenario is, of course, applicable only to those in information-based activity. The implications are that the gap between information and labor could increase dramatically. The most enthusiastic proponents of the information revolution claims that it will improve the lot of all people. If, as the above line of thought suggests, the gap between information and labor increases, the improvement will be very one-sided.

The Informatics Potential

It is possible that the technical advances could be utilized in different ways, specifically oriented toward alternative scenarios. To appreciate these, we must first look at the characteristics of informatics.

In the long run, all costs should decrease dramatically for hardware, although software is likely to remain relatively expensive. Barron and Curnow (1979) have written in detail about trends for the future. For our purposes, we need say only that as software becomes hardware—that is, as programs become part of the manufactured circuitry and are not later loaded into memories—it is possible for some software to benefit from the same economies of scale and manufacture from which hardware is benefiting. Hardware costs will continue to fall. A report by the Organisation for Economic Co-operation and Development (OECD) (1973, p. 34) said: "The cost of raw computing power has declined by an order of magnitude every four years, and there is no reason to believe that this trend will not continue." And Barron wrote that "as a completely semiconductor product, although speculation on the long term cost is difficult, there would seem to be little reason why it should (i.e., an electronic typewriter) cost more than a pocket calculator does today" (1979, p. 146).

This means that electronic display, which should be the major display mode for all information by the end of the decade, will be very cheap as soon as the cathode ray tube of the television set can be replaced by solid-state flat-screen displays. Digitally processed television, already in use within studios, allows virtually any manipulation of the image one could think of. Digital use in transmission is still a few years off.

The next aspect of informatics to be discussed is line cost. In the first place, as all information and data become encoded digitally for manipulation and transmission, a *single* system becomes possible for carrying and storing all data, entailing obvious economies of scale. More problematic are the new carriers. Satellites are reducing data traffic tariffs markedly for both traditional telecommunication traffic and private traffic. The Satellite Business System in the United States is operational, providing private receiving and transmitting facilities for businesses. Direct broadcasting satellites with small (1 m) receivers are being heralded as the answer to broadcasting problems, but at present signal dispersion is still not under control, and many nations object to the potential pollution of their airspace.

Much higher carrying capacity is available through optic fibers, in the order of 1,000 times the capacity of present satellites, but the cost of replacing the millions of miles of existing telecommunications cables, together with the cost of replacing switching centers, will delay the cost benefits from reaching the public for many years.

The combination of falling computing and display costs with static (in real terms) line costs means that utilization of informatics potential must concentrate on the former. This type of use can be characterized as the use of the *intelligent terminal,* a terminal with display facility, limited processing facility, and a reasonable (but small) memory.

Private networks, both in-house locally and transnationally, use such systems. Wider applications are now being tried experimentally in various videotex systems. These use the television set for display and both the broadcast and telephone-line facilities for transmission. The leading systems at present are Telidon in Canada, Antiope in France, and Prestel in the United Kingdom.

Videotex could, at least in the broadcast mode, be used as a virtually free medium. The failure to do so in the United Kingdom is a good example of the inability of institutional practices to utilize new technological potential for the public. This is due to the inertia of their operations, which are bound by the inertia of routine practices at the level of pseudocodes, as well as the inertia of tradition. Elsewhere, I have detailed this nondevelopment (Williams, 1979b).

One of the main obstacles to full utilization of the new media is that present institutional practices operate in a very centralized way. To some extent the ability of the new media to increase this centralization is being opposed. For instance, the plans of Radio Luxembourg to set up a European-wide television channel via the Franco-German satellite have met with initial resistance, but the matter has not yet been settled. In Japan there is some opposition to the use of Direct Broadcasting Satellites (DBS) as these would interfere with the regionalized nature of broadcasting. One should not read too much into this apparent opposition, however, for such information exchange is already extensively centralized, and what seems to be the target of opposition is one form of centralism instead of another.

More to the point is the failure of cable television to take off, despite the fact that it has been technically possible for years. Mattelart (1979) has rightly attributed this to the fear of losing centralized control of the media.

In general terms, one can see informatics as increasing the potential for centralized control, as well as the opening up of media and networks for wide and varied usage. This potential is at present confined to the former, and there is no reason to be optimistic about the latter. In terms of Mattelart's analysis, which agrees with this premise, the most likely scenario is that the economies of scale of informatics will be capitalized on by those at present dominating hardware—and, increasingly, software—markets.

Exchange of cultural and educational material will be subsumed under the synthesis of commodity production even more than is the case at present (cf. de Terra, this volume). The potential exists for a reversal (even if only a slow one) of this trend to begin, with the development of a multitude of channels and material originators. This would allow some disentanglement of communication exchange from the overwhelming social synthesis of commodity exchange. But at present it would seem unrealistic to try to separate the "superstructure" of culture from its dominance by the social synthesis of commodity exchange, a dominance operative in equal force over the "base" of material social reproduction.

References

Association of Scientific, Technical and Managerial Staffs (ASTMS). *Technological change and collective bargaining.* London: Author, 1979.

Barron, I., & Curnow, R. *The future with microelectronics.* London: Pinter, 1979.

Barthes, R. *Elements of semiology.* London: Cape, 1967.

Counter Information Services (CIS). *The new technology* (CIS report no. 23). London: Author, 1979.

Dawkins, R. *The selfish gene.* London: Oxford University Press, 1976.

Madden, J. C. *Videotex in Canada.* Ottawa: Department of Communication, 1979.

Mather, B. The electronic working environment. *Intermedia,* 1981, *9*(1), 33–37.

Mattelart, A. *Multinational corporations and the control of culture.* Sussex: Harvester, 1979.

Organization for Economic Co-operation and Development (OECD). *Computers and telecommunication.* Paris: OECD, 1973.

Porter, V. The hardware-software connection. *Intermedia,* 1981, *9*(1), 38–39.

Prodi, G. *Le basi materiali della significazione.* Milan: Bompiani, 1977.

Prodi, G. *Formation of meaning in phylogenesis.* Paper presented at the 2nd International Congress of Semiotic Studies, Vienna, June 1979.

Rossi-Landi, F. *Linguistics and economics.* The Hague: Mouton, 1977.

Rossi-Landi, F. Sign systems and social reproduction. *Ideology and consciousness,* 1978, *3,* 49–65.

Sohn-Rethel, A. *Intellectual and manual labour.* London: Macmillan, 1978.

von Uexküll, Th. *J. von Uexküll's doctrine for a synthesis of signs and behaviour.* Paper presented at the 2nd International Congress of Semiotic Studies, Vienna, June 1979.

Williams, R. *Social control and institutionalised education.* Unpublished thesis, University of Stellenbosch, S.A., 1976.

Williams, R. *Ideology and complexity.* Paper presented at the 2nd International Congress of Semiotic Studies, Vienna, June 1979. (a)

Williams, R. *Multichannel telecasting: UK introduction of Videotex.* Unpublished thesis, Central London Polytechnic, 1979. (b)

21

The Semiotic Processes of the Formation and Expression of Ideas

Mihai Nadin

Several peculiarities of a semiotic nature add themselves to the numerous contradictory characteristics of our epoch. Although language continues to exercise a dominant role in sociocultural processes, a variety of other sign systems (such as those of art, of social and political forms of ceremonial, of new rites imposed by the media of communication or the artificial media connected to computer technology) tends to occupy a role comparable to that of the language called natural. These other sign systems even limit language's sphere of action. The credibility crisis language is going through and the imposition of these new sign systems (some strictly normative) in sociocultural practice are two phenomena which are evidently connected. The resurrection of interest in semiotics is in turn explainable in this context. Although belief in language as a means of communication has declined, the objective process of social development is characterized by an accentuated semiotization. The relationship of the human subject, as an individual and as a social being, to the object in its varied forms of existence (including the subject as object) is more and more mediated through *signs*. Instead of direct action on the labor object (raw material, processed material, nature), mediated action is imposed, at the beginning through tools and machines and at present through action algorithms. Education, culture, and political practice are coming through less directly; mediation takes place through signs, and practice becomes a matter of *interpretation*. The consequences of this process of semiotization—as a form of (wo)man's alienation corresponding to a new stage of his/her evolution—are difficult to anticipate. The legitimacy of semiotic research, in direct connection to the process of semiotization, is obvious under the premise of the philosophical establishment of this research, but not as an additional step in the direction of transforming all that exists into signs and semiotic processes. This prem-

Mihai Nadin ● Liberal Arts, Rhode Island School of Design, Providence, Rhode Island 02903, and Center for Semiotic Research, Brown University, Providence, Rhode Island 02912.

ise should not be taken for granted or regarded as a bagatelle. The affirmation that anything can be interpreted as a sign system (which is true in principle but not relevant) becomes efficacious only after it has been shown exactly how the sign is produced and what its defining relationship is regarding the object for which it stands and its interpretant (generic, hence infinite). This is the aim pursued by the text that follows, the object of which is precisely the presentation, explanation, and interpretation of sociohistorical processes which bring about the constitution of the *idea* (itself interpretable as a sign—very complex, of course—representative for a particular society and moment of its development). To carry out this objective, several elements of semiotics (sign, semiosis, meaning, semiotic field, etc.) will be introduced progressively without being elaborated upon (although a consensus regarding their definition is far from having been reached). The references can aid the interested reader in furthering his/her knowledge.

The simplest representation of a *field*—a concept coming from physics and algebraic typology—can be found, like so many other things, in Lewis Carroll's *Alice in Wonderland:*

> "I wish you wouldn't keep appearing and vanishing so suddenly, you make one quite giddy."
> "All right," said the cat: and this time it vanished quite slowly, beginning with the end of the tail, and ending with the grin, which remained some time after the rest of it had gone.
> "Well! I've often seen a cat without a grin," thought Alice; "but a grin without a cat!"

The field is a "grin without a cat," be it the magnetic field (visualized by iron filings around the poles of a magnet), the electromagnetic field (around a wire through which electricity is transported), the gravitational field, or human fields of action at distance (the ethical, aesthetic, ideological, and psychological fields, etc.; Hartmann, 1948; Lewin, 1939; Nadin, 1981).

The semiotic field can be more precisely defined only on acceptance of a definition of sign; otherwise, the grin ceases to refer to a cat—that is, to semiotics as a scientifically founded discipline—and eventually remains only a metaphor. Throughout this chapter, the definition of *sign* utilized will be the one given by Peirce: "A sign is . . . something which stands to somebody for something in some respect or capacity" (1960, 2.228). The sign, then, is the unity of the three elements: object, sign *per se* (which Peirce also called *representamen*), and interpretant, a unit understood in the dynamic sense (realized in semiotic processes or, as they are also called, *semioses*). The sign, as a unit around which the semiotic field is constituted, actually fulfills two functions: communication and signification. These functions—which in the reality of the semiotic field are impossible to separate—are made evident in semioses. All signs participate in the reality of the semiotic field and are of necessity interpreted in this field. The field is not a mental construct substituting for the reality of the sign and its action (fulfillment as meaning, for instance), but is precisely the medium in which signs associate or disassociate, in which meaning is constituted, in which semiotic interaction is carried on between different sign systems (of language, of art, of religion, of norms, of science, etc.). It is probably in this sense that Rossi-Landi's (1979, p. 358) affirmation regarding sign as "the center of a network of social relations" can be understood (cf. Williams, this volume).

The signs of a society (related to the mode of grouping) and of the persons in it—as well as the motives (direct, indirect, conscious, subconscious and unconscious, psychological, logical, etc.) behind this grouping—are not simply generated by this society; they represent a given framework as well as the object of present and future action. Social coming-of-consciousness is *par excellence* semiotic without being reduced to expression in doubly articulated language (man's most complex system of signs). The confirmation of social existence in space and objective time—whose semiotic representation is one of place and moment—is mediated through signs. In the actual semiotic field, man disappears "beginning with the end of the tail" (in other words, his concrete materiality), "and ending with the grin," with what we shall call his *ideas* (in the broad sense). We can therefore continue asking ourselves how they are formed, how they are expressed, and what interaction in the semiotic field exists between ideas (pertaining to one domain or to many different ones).

No matter which type of semiotics defines them, signs can only be material, individual, and concrete—hence spatially determined—whereas ideas, inexpressible without the intermediary of signs, can be only general, abstract, and spiritual—hence temporally determined. This paradoxical condition stems from the condition of the sign itself, which cannot be justified as such except in relation to another sign. Any set of signs, incidental or necessary, can be considered a unit between a repertory (the inventory of the signs of the set, also spatial) and sign operations (semioses, hence successions), the idea expressed being a distinct semiotic set enhanced in a context. The transition from *something* of the condition of space (the sign) to something else of the time condition (idea) is basically the fulfillment of meaning and its repeated retroaction on the sign it brings about.

Obviously, when discussing ideas—the subject so much disputed by traditional philosophers—we must ask ourselves whether they truly find their origin in linguistic activity (as it is insistently affirmed in our day), whether the signs participating in their constitution are merely those of speech (writing, in this concept, itself determined by speech), or whether other things participate in one way or another in the process of forming and transmitting ideas (Nadin, 1980). The role played by speech in the communication of ideas is incontestable. But as far as the formation of ideas is concerned, things are not so simple. In fact, the signs of speech—in their concreteness, materiality, and individuality—are in principle the same as any other sign; that is, spatial.

Humans not only express themselves to (enter into contact with) one another through their sign system, but also "listen" to themselves. They are both emitters and receivers. Signs succeed themselves in a series of self-controlled sequences. Communication at the level of nature (a subject approached by zoosemiotics) does not cease even when the natural condition becomes predominant. Subverbal, unarticulated language (at the signal level of smell, touch, taste, etc., or language of a kinesic or proxemic type) participates in the definition of sensations directly, as well as through specification of context. The interrelationship of articulated language and unarticulated subverbal languages shows up at the level of predominantly natural activities (the life cycle as a natural cycle) as well as at the level of predominantly sociocultural activities. When the sign of speech becomes a sign of language, the process deepens. The concrete sign (written, stabilized) participates in the definition of the abstract. The succession of individual signs is metamorphized into the sign of the general (supersign). The materiality of expression supports the spirituality of the idea. We do not dispose of a system of signs in the way a person disposes of some machine or elements to be assembled. Humans are sign and language—an intuition which confers on Peirce's semiotic system a surprising opening in the sense that (wo)man occupies a place in the network of social relationships and is identifiable through these relationships. Signs, communication, and signification complete themselves reciprocally and can never really be separated—their separation being a common error in today's semiotics. In speech, for example, the sequence of signs emitted cannot be separated from their speaker as in the case of kinesic or proxemic systems. (Humans are, themselves, part of the sign.) Not even writing changes the human condition of being part of the sign, but permits its progression from the individual (the one who writes) to the general (interpretant, "reading" species). Writing is always less concrete, poorer, more impersonal than speech. The meaning conferred through writing is brought about, however, through a process of generalization, of reindividualization; that is, writing is read (and this means it is heard, seen, felt, smelled, etc.). In short, it inversely travels the route that led from speech to writing, from the concrete to the abstract. Another important aspect connected to the fact that humans are themselves a sign (language, in particular) results from the semiotic analysis of generative mechanisms. On the one hand, we have the finite reality of signs and on the other, the practically infinite reality of ideas. In view of this phenomenon, the question arises regarding the source of ideas as well as that of the relation between signs and the meanings that can be expressed by them. The most troubling representation (hence, idea) that we owe to signs is that of the future. Presensing (premonition) is the natural form of the diffuse perception of time: a perception that can be immediate or less immediate and that is extended not from *now* to *what was* (stored in the memory or not) but to *what might be* (a sign of danger, for instance, on the level of nature). The subsigns participating in these representations are indexical (and therefore imply iconic elements). Speech makes premonition and feeling explicit, but not wholly so, transforming accumulated signs (past) into signs of the possible (future), in the sense that it points to the fact that any past was once a future. Monoarticulated speech (signaling), as well as ideographic writing, is located at the pragmatic-affective level. The idea is constituted precisely on surpassing this level. The prospective force of articulated speech, as well as that of writing, reflects the generative capacity of signs (I repeat: humans are themselves sign and language).

While dualism is the source of some of the weaknesses of Chomsky's conception, it should be pointed out that his model, based on the opposition of competence and performance, permits the approach of language learning, as well as that of generative mechanisms, the latter participating in the elaboration of ideas. The sign of language—whose object is always the uttered sign (with the object in (wo)man's interior and reconstructed in its ideality)—represents the dialectic unity of the phonetic and the semantic units that are obviously contradictory, interdependent (one does not exist without the other), asymmetric (the first determines the second), and autodynamic (the retroaction of the semantic on the phonetic determines the evolution and refinement of the sign as a whole). The learning of language is not reducible to the memorization of expressions (Skinner, 1957); the interaction of stimuli and responses is unable to explain the creative nature of human language (the formation of ideas, for instance), although this interaction plays an undeniable role. In fact, (wo)man is not born free of experience nor free from the evolutionary cycle of his/her species. Speech (and later writing) was not the result of evolution from natural to sociocultural communication but the moment when society and culture were founded: "The birth of speech does not exist more in humanity's prehistory than in the life of the child. Speech has no origin, it is origin (Ursprung)" (Buytendijk, 1965, p. 121). So linguistic performance is the realization of competence—a result not of learning but of living, of practicing language, of existence as language; that is, of the fact that (wo)man does not dispose of language but *is* language at a certain level of his/her evolution (individual on one hand, as a species on the other).

Ideas—to return to the subject of this study—once expressed with the aid of signs, in turn become signs. Thus the process goes on, often in connection to (wo)man's direct experience but also to his/her stage of evolution. An idea expressed in a complicated linguistic form has a high degree of correctness but is rarely attested in the use of language. The explanation of the discrepancy between *correctness* and *attestation* lies in the fact that out of the infinite totality of enunciations generated by the linguistic mechanisms belonging to our *competence,* only a finite part, belonging to *performance,* is used. We know how to read, but reading competence is carried out in finite performance (which is all the more restricted through selective reading: literature, professional texts, newspapers, financial texts, etc.). Aesthetic competence involves an even more complicated problem: partial competences—including specialized scientific ones—which are denied in the very act of performance. Linguistic performance is of necessity repeatable. Aesthetic performance, of necessity, undergoes continuous change, not only in the act of creation, but also in the act of reception. The fact that linguistic determinations are among the most important should not lead us to reduce everything to verbal language. Nonlinguistic forms of communication which participate in social processes, especially forms of signification (presupposing semiotic systems of codification and decodification that are among the most complicated in direct relation to the meanings instituted), give evidence of the mechanism in which the realization of competence in performance takes place.

Research on generative and learning mechanisms (in particular the creative types—which are not only aesthetic or aesthetically relevant—and those of understanding—again not only in art nor concerning aesthetic values) in humans and in animals prove that humans are the only known beings capable of manipulating (of mastering in generative and learning processes) infinite languages. The mechanisms taking part in the formation and communication of ideas are of infinite creativity (a finite repertory of signs called the alphabet generates an infinite collection of finite series called *sentences*).

Since the brain does not reach completeness of thought without speech, thought itself cannot be carried on without the support of signs (sometimes sequential, sometimes configurational) which (wo)man reads as meanings in the "book" of his/her environment (natural, social, cultural, etc.). Perception of the world is a condition for knowing and understanding it. The language of the world is not verbal, but is articulated at the level of the elementary sensations (Merleau-Ponty's "participative perception") that the world occasions and which (wo)man perceives at the semiotic—hence cultural—level as stabilized meanings. If the word is the body of the idea, then the word itself has another body which is the sign system of the world in which (wo)man exists. Speech does not escape the senses, but neither does it automatically reflect them. Between the senses and speech—hence between nonverbal and verbal languages—numerous influences play a role. Words obviously have a richer content of knowledge than perceptions; speech—a social phenomenon *par excellence*—adds to sensorial information intellectual information capable of reflecting not only the present but also the absent: genus, cause, future. That this concept is not necessarily arrived at in non-European cultures reflects the fact that languages do not participate passively in the establishment of culture; they are also components of the latter and live in its reality as a dynamic factor.

On the basis of historic (however limited direct sources are) and systematic arguments, the evolution of the word—from the univocal to the ambiguous or vice versa—can be brought into discussion. The same analysis can be completed (and it is relevant only to the extent it has been completed) by determining the evolution of art or of specialized languages (the latter, being more recent, lend themselves to the analysis in question). Nevertheless, it is proven fact that systems of univocal signs can participate in the production of ideas only to a small degree. Polysemy is a gradual acquisition and reflects the principle of retroaction of meaning on the sign (particularly of significance on the significant). Philosophy and literature (and the arts in general) become possible only at a certain level of language development, hence from a certain level of social development. The philosopher, for example, resorts to *common* speech (verbal language) but uses it in an *uncommon* way: metasemically, metaphorically, metaphysically; therefore, categorically. Ancient philosophy is still so metaphoric that it can be read as literature. Modern philosophy (post-Heidegger) shows how *relations* (which it points out and dwells on) have absorbed the *related*. The crisis of language—actually the reflex of the fact that the limitation of any philosophy is the language expressing it—has aroused an attempt at liberation from the word (but not from meaning) pursued in the reality of formalizations, themselves unrealized outside of adequate interpretation (the complementarity of model—interpretation as an axiom of analytical philosophy). It is no less true that the process we define also corresponds to a change in the functions of philosophy and in its role. It is a social system's most abstract form of *retroaction* (feedback); the meaning it proposes consequently influences not only the signs of value but also value itself. The heuristic content of the metaphors of philosophy (and of the myths through which it is constructed and reflected) is intertwined with expressive content.

The history of philosophy—as one of the histories of production and communication through the signs of ideas—records the step-by-step progress from connotation to denotation without the danger of the establishment of an artificial language (a so-called philosophical language) manifested in any way. The idea sets itself up as a unity between the intellectual force of concepts and the emotional force of morphosyntactic constructions. The distance between the verbal significant (implying subverbal and paraverbal significants, the super segmentals of language, for example) and the significance of the idea—hence the distance between sign and meaning of the idea—is maximum in relation to all other forms of semiotic expression. The distance is itself a parameter of the evolution from nature to culture (society, in particular) and, within the framework of culture, from one stage to another. The lengthening of the distance is not a criterion *per se* of human progress (hence not a criterion of social progress) but certainly one of progress of the semiotic system of culture. The sign is arbitrary in relation to the idea it embodies. The idea rejects individuality and institutes the general, essential meaning which knowledge revealed in the order of nature or thought. In expression of the idea, rational rigor (the degree of necessity at the semantic and syntactic level) is animated by the expressivity of the semiotic system; that is, it bears the distinctive mark of its immediate interpretant. Ideas express the implicit will to be expressed (what Marcuse, 1964, called "the imperative quality" of thought). The appearance of supertemporality of ideas (what is expressed in the Platonic model of the universe of ideas) stems precisely from the sense of revelation (in the idea) of a content that was, is, and will be noticeable.

The apparent supertemporality of the idea stems from the mechanism of its formation, communication, and realization (what I call the instituting of meaning). Essentially, this is a question of sign processes that develop like Markov processes: the influence of the past is limited to the value from which it started out. (A *Markov process* describes an aleatory evolution which, starting out from a moment *t*, depends only on the state of that moment *t* and not on the way that state was reached.) The appearance of a certain sign in a certain sequence that participates in expressing an idea (qualitatively, things stand the same with the "sequences" of art) is due to the idea's *heredity*, that is, to what extent at moment *t*, when it is expressed, does the sign in question participate in the constitution of the idea.

The isomorphism between the structure of the semiotic processes of forming ideas (in the complex context of social existence) and the structure of the idea itself reflects the idea's processive realization in time. Each idea is the result of choice in a certain paradigm, a result which acquires its determination (realization as meaning) through insertion in a context. The idea is itself a sign which is communicated (predominantly information value) or is realized in processes of signification (interpretation and specification of meaning in one context or another and always in the historical context, hence in the framework of time). Transition from the level of competence (infinite) to that of peformance (finite) is not the same on the individual level (the person as a concrete identity) and the social level (the person as a member of a species subject to historical, economic, and spatiotemporal determinations). In relation to the biophysical component, the role of the social component in producing and communicating ideas at the collective level (groups, strata, classes, etc.) is greater. It can be said that human society, like the human brain, is a black box, but a less complex one. Therefore, algorithmic models of the formation of social ideas have greater relevance than those concerning individual ideas. It is true, however, that ideas are not born under the mark of anonymity, even though in the process of their realization they earn their independence from the one who produced them and become, through continuous (self-)perfection and (self-)refinement, the ideas of a time, of a class, of a society. This process of anonymization is also reflected onto the semiotic condition. It seems that works of art tend to single themselves out more and more, becoming signs of the author projected on the background "sign of an epoch." Other examples can be given, the significance of the process being of interest from the perspective of the transformation of signs of a certain quality (symbolic, for example) into another type of sign (indexical, for example) unequivocally referring to an author.

The idea is on the order of the possible (which in Peirce's system corresponds to Firstness); the concept (category) is on the order of necessity (Thirdness in Peirce's system); the jump from one state to another is made by transition through reality (Secondness). Thus arises the need to define semiotically the forms through which these transitions actually take place (Nadin, 1982). Therefore, we shall analyze the sociogenesis of writing and speech in order to determine what is communication and what is signification.

The object for which the *written sign* stands is the *sign of speech*. But writing came a relatively long way before reaching this semiotic condition. In prelinguistic forms, graphic representation had its object in reality—the representation of the absent—since what is present need not be represented (no necessity exists in this sense). The direction impressed on visual representation is from past to present. What must be retained is the originating tendency of distancing in respect to the present, the direct. Initial representations have only a communicative function; in particular, they retain information about the absent that is not seen (heard, felt, smelled) for future relationships between (wo)man and his/her environment. Codification appears later, on the level of signification. The image belongs to nature; that which is communicated is the way of seeing it (more precisely, of perceiving). Hence the attitude regarding it is implicit. The execution of the written sign is not its realization as information—as in the case of pictographic representations—that is, not *how something is written* but *what it means,* that is, *what is the meaning of what is written.* Again, we find ourselves before a problem of applying competence/performance criteria in the sense that a relatively small number of signs (the alphabet and the respective punctuation and diacritical marks) participate in the infinite competence of writing. Pictographic representations precede double articulation but do not disappear together with it, evidencing instead a new meaning.

If the material of thought is words (see also Wald, 1979) and all that pertains to them from the other forms of human language, the stabilization of thought comes about with the stabilization of signs—of writing, that is. The present loses its impact of immediate action; the sensible is rationalized; what we read is no longer the colors and forms of nature, but colors and forms charged with meaning. No written word has ever reached the surface without being "uttered" and "heard"—that is, without being "sensed." The reality of meaning stems from the ratiosensory establishment of language. It is not accidental that spatial establishment (in village-type settlements) and the establishment of language in writing, also of a spatial nature, are synchronous (cf. Leroi-Gourhan, 1964). Also not accidental is the great moment of Greek philosophy in the temporal context of "alphabetization." Socrates, as the philosopher of the way of thinking and discovering truth through the dialogue, defends oral culture. Heuristics and maieutics are essentially oral, presupposing the philosopher's physical presence. Aristotle belongs to culture, to writing. Plato, situated between the two, can thus observe and express the consequences of writing:

> I cannot help feeling, Phaedrus, that writing is unfortunately like painting; for the creations of the painter have the attitude of life, and yet if you ask them a question they preserve a solemn silence. (1937, p. 278)

As one of the first philosophers of writing, Plato cannot yet observe that writing is not simply the transcription of thoughts (of the words *through which* and *in which* (wo)man thinks), that ideas are formed differently in writing than in speech, that writing represents a qualitatively new semiotic system in which meanings are formed and communicated through a mechanism once more mediated in respect to the system of reality. Through writing arises the possibility of communicating and signifying at the same time (cf. John-Steiner & Tatter, this volume).

The history of culture has recorded numerous attacks against writing, culminating in Marshall McLuhan's (1964) philosophy: alphabetic cultures have uniformized, fragmented, and sequentialized the world, generating an excessive rationalism, nationalism, and individualism. Here we have—in a succinct list—the indictment made of "Gutenberg's galaxy." Commenting on *A Passage to India* by E. M. Forster, McLuhan quotes and draws his own conclusion:

> Rational, of course, has for the West long meant "uniform and continuous and sequential." In other words, we have confused reason with literacy, and rationalism with a single technology. (p. 30)

The consequence of these attacks—as much as they can be judged from the historical perspective—has nevertheless not been the abatement of writing or of its influence. In the same vein, the need to proceed to an oral-visual culture has been idealistically suggested (in addition to McLuhan, Barthes', 1970, plea can be cited), since through its globality and synchronism, such a culture seems more faithful to human conscience than is the analyticism and sequentiality of alphabetic writing.

What is actually the opposition between the phonetic, sequential system and the ideographic, global one? The two great cultures of humankind give evidence of the following opposition: one is a great analytic, discursive (rhetorical, at the extreme) culture; the other is a great synthetic, configurative (dialectic, at the extreme) culture. The meaning instilled in the first case is based on the *additive* mechanism; in the second it is based on an *integrative* mechanism. One can thus understand why alphabetic writing—although more simple and stabilized—is really more difficult than ideographic writing. The effort to abstract that which it implies (and in fact contains) obliges the reader of the alphabetic text to run the enormous cultural distance separating the graphic sign from its referent in order to determine meaning. The reader of the ideographic text has the advantage of the concreteness of the representation. We have referred in both cases to the reader formed in the spirit of one or the other of the cultures mentioned. When confronted with a way of writing different from that in whose spirit he has been educated (culturally formed), the human subject must "invent" this writing step by step (not an easy task), because every language integrates its own history. Research undertaken in recent years shows that at a certain stage, aphasia brings on a regression from alphabet to image reading as design, as pictographic, iconic reading. Letters lose their identity. Ideas crumble like buildings shaken by an earthquake. What is still perceived is the similarity to concrete things. The decline from the abstract to the concrete is a sociocultural accident taking place against the background of a natural accident which psychologically and linguistically has not been researched with much care.

The tendency to abstract and the tendency toward hermetic discourse (an expression of excessive chiseling at the sign, that is, of oversoliciting the representamen) are semiotically relevant to the integral condition of communication and signification. The mystification (masking, hiding) of the represented object, that is, the establishment of a vague meaning which only "strong" contexts can point out, is, in the semiotic sense, a return to the origin of speech and language. The above observation obliges us to present a few more words of explanation. It is known that the oldest preserved cave drawings are indexical signs of an oral context rather than representations of hunting scenes (even though they are often interpreted as such). The magical value of the first representations (likewise the ideological field instituted by the proposed meaning)—representations that codify messages intended to be secret, addressed to the initiated—is the necessary reference in analyzing later hermetic expression (including today's). The manifestos of hermeticism of all types represent an ideological rather than an ontological justification. The transition from speech to writing is in fact the transition from the pragmatic-affective level to the intellectual-rational level. It takes place in the context of the evolution from syncretic to analytical logic and is made concrete by substituting categorical epistemy for mythomagical epistemy. These affirmations concern the semiotic universe of European cultures (and their later extensions), an observation which imposes itself here due to the distinction proposed in the foregoing pages. The cultures of the Far East are characterized by language's tendency to *represent* and not to *explain*. There, logic has a predominantly dialectic nature:

> An analysis of concepts, a sharing of themes and definitions are not necessary, and sometimes even an impediment. The examples are those which most often stimulate adhesion. (Elders, 1966, p. 392)

The analytical structure of logical thought is actually formed in the sentence structure of speech, which is fundamentally different in the two cultures referred to. The imperative energy of the act of expressing confers on the Chinese language, for example, a continuous state of birth (speech in the act). It should be pointed out here that there is a level from which it becomes possible to speak (express oneself) about one's language, and this level corresponds to entities without referential meaning (phonemes in the familiar case of doubly articulated language). To speak about visual, kinesic, proxemic, or paralinguistic language in the terms of these languages is only partially possible (imitations, for example, rarely attain the level of self-evaluation and never the level of generality). Metalanguage can be descriptive, prescriptive, or explanatory. In the concept of Indian grammaticians, for example, linguistic metalanguage refers only to the form of language but not to the concrete individuality constituting its object, so that it does not pertain to knowledge. The preeminence of the act in oriental culture is reflected by the central position the verb occupies. Concentration around the verb orients thought toward the relationship between *condition* and *conditioned*. In this logical universe—semiotically, perfectly determined—definition is a cognitive act of primarily pragmatic value. The relationship between index and indicated (index in the sense strictly determined by Peirce's definition) is predominant and not that given by the hierarchy of genus in the universe of the logic of Indo-European languages.

The experience of logic characteristic of European cultures (under the distinctive mark of classical Greek philosophy) shows that the main instrument of categor-ical thinking is the noun. It is freer than the verb (tied to the forms it specifies), more stable, capable of reflecting identity, invariance, and the universal. The logic founded on this premise is oriented toward the search for unity between species and genus. European writing and oriental ideographic writing have each participated in this pro-cess of defining logic, being complementary from the historical perspective. Recalling not only the history of knowledge but also history *per se,* we can say that the Euro-pean Occident achieved the meaning of knowledge and world control while the Ori-ent achieved self-knowledge and self-control. It would be utopic—but also practical (with vast historical, social, ideological, political, etc., implications)—to imagine a world uniting these meanings.

The isomorphisms between the intimate structures of living matter and the structure of language can lead to the suggestion that cultural models (semiotic expression of complex ideas) permit the discovery of natural laws. This idea is appar-ently situated in the extension of animism. But as "Savage Thought" (Lévi-Strauss, 1962) tends to equate nature and culture, "Civilized Thought" tends toward the opposite direction. The progress, still in its initial stages, made possible by modern science should not lead us to make hasty generalizations. The dissolution of thought in speech is one extreme; the withdrawal of thought from speech is another.

The nucleus of communication is dialogue. But to carry on dialogue does not necessarily mean putting two people (consciences) into relation but two semiotic structures showing up in social reality:

> In communication, meanings are transmitted not from one person to another but from one sign to another from the minds of the same persons.... The essence of the act of communication is to modify the signs that bear a given meaning. (Hörmann, 1972, p. 179)

Communication on the level of nature (between animals, for instance) is nondialog-ical, nonarticulated, and unhistoric. Signaling (for danger, presence, etc.) awaits no response. Speech, hinting at the absent—hence, situations beyond the perceptual horizon—at the future, at essence or law, is a self-regulating semiotic system. In this sense, any act of speech is a dialogue with the self, continuous interrogation. In writ-ten communication, dialogue is established with difficulty, presupposing presence precisely to preserve the temporal nature of the idea taking shape in dialogue. In reality, signs are born (produced) under the mark of dialogue: to stand for an object (as sign) means to stand for someone (interpretant). Dialogue is founded on the real-ity of language's second articulation (cf. Martinet, 1939). It is difficult to say whether dialogue created double articulation or whether double articulation is the cause and explanation of language's capacity for dialogue. It is certain, however, that the continuous ascension of meaning from the reflection of individual appropriation of things to the discovery of ever more general properties (in the metaphoric energy of the representamen) is achieved in dialogue-type semiotic processes. Writing—which was intentionally analyzed before dialogue—represents a weakening of dia-logue on the one hand and the attempt to free dialogue from the imperative of co-presence on the other. On one side we have postponement of the response (or its suppression), and on the other, projection of the question over time, that is, a kind of projection of doubt in the semiotic field. But writing is not possible outside the semiotic field.

It must also be pointed out that writing, as a symptom of undermining dialogue, has a social connotation, too. By its nature, dialogue is democratic, inviting confrontation, knowledge, and self-knowledge. Anyone who analyzes history from the perspective of this semiotic truth will observe that the forms of governing through writ have been nondemocratic (despotic) by nature (cf. Illich, this volume). But writing in respect to other prior forms of expression (pictographic, ideographic writing, etc.) is more democratic than the latter in the sense that it is more widely accessible and has become a social asset. Contemporary audio-visual forms which impose themselves as alternatives to writing (communication systems) affect dialogue even more. Neither radio nor television, speeches nor cybernetic information systems, have openings to dialogue; their effectiveness makes them necessary media. The lack of dialogue—which semiotics not only observes but also explains in its specific terms—causes the message to become predominantly pragmatic-affective ("hot"), this too being a symptom of an attempt to surpass the rational. Sometimes, in escaping from dialogue's critical control, even alphabetic writing tends toward a system of signs that are no longer intended to be uttered, purged of any sensible content, sufficient in themselves. This characteristic explains the word-processing systems in which content becomes secondary to the signs utilized to express it.

Is it true, as Whorf (1963) and others believe, that "a change of language . . . transforms our conception of the Cosmos"? In other words, is the semiotic system of language a means of knowledge or even its content? The logically possible answers are located between the extremes of absolute objectivity and absolute subjectivity. From the gnoseological perspective, languages are pertinent to relativity. We live not only in nature but in a social environment. We live in our sign system, and our solidarity with it manifests itself in the semiotic retroaction in which we participate (and which is aesthetic, ethical, logical, epistemological, etc. by nature). Things do not circulate in thought; the idea is not a conglomerate of things. Concepts are formed at the level of the meanings and not at that of signs, whose arbitrariness grows in proportion to our operative and memorative capacity (individual and social). The experience accumulated in language is sociocultural but placed in the species's semiotic field.

The sign negates the object. More precisely, semioses simultaneously represent the unity between object and its sign(s) as well as their opposites in the semiotic field. Unity guarantees recognition, a process in which the interpretant subsign is implicit. Opposition explains the inexhaustibility of semioses, endlessly stimulating the continuation of refinement of the sign and thus of meaning instillment. Objects are concrete, phenomenal, individual. Signs tend to be abstract, essential, general. Growing distance—recorded in the history of culture between sign as sign (representamen) and its meaning (respectively, between significant and significance from the perspective of de Saussure's concept)—is only a measure of the semiotic field. The tension between sensorial perception (of fundamental signs) and rational understanding in which the human sign of speech takes part (implying fundamental signs) explains the semiotics of the absent as a semiotics specific to man. The signal is as the thing: It communicates directly. The sign, rejecting the object, communicates indirectly; its form of fulfillment, called signification, means the institution of sense and its progressive achievement. The signal means acceptance of things as they are and adaptation to them. The sign sets up negation as a specific human attitude and radically differentiates (wo)man's indirect connection to his/her environment from the direct contact between animal and nature. The most exact definition of the sign is a *mediator*.

The negation it contains causes meaning to be irreducible to sensorial content, and, likewise, acts of thought to be inseparable from sensorial acts; the negation is fulfilled in the contradictory reality of meaning. Disposing of many sign systems and capable of realizing the difference between natural and artificial signs, (wo)man is in the condition of semiotic perpetual motion. The quantity of information produced is greater than what is received. *Information-added* (to adapt here Marx's concept of value-added) is characteristic of human creativity. However seductive this image might be, it does not release us from the elementary obligation of scientific caution. It must always be pointed out that information-added, as exemplified by some scientific hypotheses, artistic images, or philosophical systems, is relative; that is, it stems either from the ability to generalize (which the senses do not directly have but which they acquire through *rationalization*, that is, through the system of memory that participates in the double articulation of speech) or the ability to abstract. It would be naive of us to believe that information can be produced from nothing; the same goes for meaning. Information-added is not the consequence of communication—the process in which what is transmitted remains relatively the same (affected of course by the mechanisms inherent in transmission)—but of signification. The relative autonomy of signs regarding objects begins together with the formation of meaning, continues with its achievement, and is brought to fulfillment (an inexhaustible process) in the retroaction that meaning exercises on the sign as such. The formation (constitution) of meaning is demonstrated by the diversity of languages as well as by the interpretant's (partial) ability to switch from one language to another (and, in the case of speech, from one tongue to another). The achievement of meaning cannot be understood without taking polysemy into account, the simultaneity representative of ideas (meanings) being historical proof that this must be true. Finally, the retroaction of meaning on sign (especially on the linguistic sign) is evidenced by the appearance of the second (phonematic) articulation. This must be understood within the semiotic field.

Meaning has an infralogical dimension (where differentiation takes place) and a logical dimension (where identification takes place). Identical ideas are thus constituted in different ways at the (relative) end of the signification processes. There is no meaning without sign, but the sign, as representamen, does not block the way of meaning toward logic; it represents the access to rational foundation. Signification presupposes a morality of meaning, that is, the need to keep signs near things, to maintain their connection, and to relate meaning not only to signs but also to the objects that those signs stand for. Peirce's ethical warning about the use of signs must be understood in this respect. The autonomy of thought in relation to sign systems (especially the verbal sign) has as a fundamental consequence the retroaction of meaning on the sign (respectively significance on the significant, in de Saussure's semiology), one of the best known forms being polysemy. It can consequently be characterized as the condition of a sign (*word* in particular) in which a new idea is formed. If signs were to renew themselves at the rate at which ideas appear, especially in this epoch, we would live in an insupportable semiotic universe. The bombardment of new signs would bring about a decline from culture into nature and the need to adapt to signs as signals. Nevertheless, the universe of signs is actually in relative expansion. The axiom of signification is precisely the transition from the finity of signs to the infinity of meanings, retroaction having the effect of optimization. The sign expresses on the one hand and forms on the other; that is, it has a specific analytical force (any sign is the "resumé" of its object from a certain perspective) in opposition to the synthetic force that it develops. The sign ideally "recreates" the object from the ideological perspective which it explicitly or implicitly represents. The myth generalizes individual experience (is a *sui generis* algorithm of human action), while art—sometimes utilizing similar signs—individualizes the general. The recourse is analytical in the first case and synthetic in the second. Certain sciences (or branches of science) are predominantly analytical (a fact expressed by the laws of mechanics, chemistry, zoological, typology, anatomy, etc.); others are synthetic (mathematics, *par excellence*). The mechanism of signification and the way in which its synthetic and analytical dimensions interact are evidenced in complex sociocultural processes. Communication is represented by the semiotic processes of the recovery of information codified in signs and signification and by the processes of carrying out information-added (scientific, aesthetic, political, social, etc.), which is not always necessarily in connection to information *per se*. Signification is not only cognitive-rational but also pragmatic-affective. *The final products of semioses are not signs but meanings in relation to signs* (cf. Wertsch, this volume). Interactions between (wo)man and the system of signs s/he participates in as an integral part have undergone enormous diversification through the course of history and promise to continue undergoing diversification. Therefore, under the condition of the intense semiotization of contemporary social and practical life, it is impossible to ignore the way this interaction takes place. The semiotic process of the formation of ideas is only one aspect of this interaction.

References

Barthes, R. *L'empire de signes*. Geneva: Skira, 1970.

Buytendijk, F. J. J. *L'homme et l'animal*. Paris: Gallimard, 1965.

Elders, L. Les rapports de la langue et de la pensée japonaise. *Révue Philosophique de la France et de l'Etranger*, 1966, *3*, 391–406.

Hartmann, R. S. *Can field theory be applied to ethics?* Unpublished dissertation, Northwesern University, 1948.

Hörmann, H. *Introduction à la psycholinguistique*. Paris: Larousse, 1972.

Leroi-Gourhan, A. *Le geste et la parole* (Vol. 1). Paris: Albin Michel, 1964.

Lévi-Strauss, C. *La pensée sauvage*. Paris: Gallimard, 1962.

Lewin, K. Field theory and experiment in social psychology: Concepts and methods. *American Journal of Sociology*, 1939, *44*, 868–896.

Marcuse, H. *One-dimensional man: Studies in the ideology of the advanced industrial society*. Boston: Beacon Press, 1964.

Martinet, A. Un ou deux phonèmes? *Acta Linguistica*, 1939, *1*, 94–103.

McLuhan, M. *Understanding media*. New York: McGraw-Hill, 1964.

Nadin, M. The logic of vagueness and the category of synechism. *The Monist*, 1980, *63*(3), 352–363.

Nadin, M. *Zeichen und Wert*. Tübingen: Gunther Narr Verlag, 1981.

Nadin, M. Consistency, completeness, and the meaning of sign theories: The semiotic field. *American Journal of Semiotics*, 1982, *1*(3), 79–98.

Peirce, C. S. *Collected papers* (C. Hartshorne & P. Weiss, Eds.). Cambridge, Mass.: The Belknap Press of Harvard University Press, 1960.

Plato, *Dialogues* (B. Jowett, trans.). New York: Random House, 1937.

Rossi-Landi, F. Signs and bodies. In S. Chatman, U. Eco, & J.-M. Klinkenberg (Eds.), *A semiotic landscape*. The Hague: Mouton, 1979, pp. 356–359.

Skinner, B. F. *Verbal behavior*. New York: Appleton, 1957.

Wald, H. La parole et la structure logique de la pensée. In S. Chatman, U. Eco, & J.-M. Klinkenberg (Eds.), *A semiotic landscape*. The Hague: Mouton, 1979, pp. 372–374.

Whorf, B. L. *Language, thought, and reality* (J. B. Carrol, Ed.). Cambridge, Mass.: MIT Press, 1963.

22

Psychoanalytic Anthropology and the Meaning of Meaning

Howard F. Stein

> Nothing but the truth is good enough, and . . .
> any truth, if it is genuine, is good enough for
> every man. (La Barre, 1959, p. 689)

Introduction

People never merely act. They mean something by their acts. They ascribe meaning to their deeds. Even their fatuous denials that "I didn't mean anything by it" or "It doesn't mean anything" protest about that hidden or unconscious meaning to which their acts might attest. Meanings govern relationships—from dyads to families to cultures and international diplomacy. Meaninglessness in turn refers to the loss or inadequacy of particular meanings or systems of meanings. The connotation of the word *meaning* often subsumes such terms as purpose, intentionality, significance, creativity, transcendence, ineffability. One speaks of finding, losing, appreciating, recognizing, rejecting, searching (etc.) for meaning, as though the referent of meaning were experienced to lie outside the self, occupying an objective reality distinct from the self.

Meaning is not experienced as an act or process of attribution (which is to say, an active verb); rather it is experienced as an attribute of the world (which is to say, a noun), self-evidently tangible to all who will see. We speak of meaning as though it were an ontological given or a property of life to be recovered, rather than an epistemological problem. Our very language belies the quality, or character, of meaning: we speak of "grasping" or "comprehending" the meaning of something. We say that something "possesses" meaning, and that the meaning of something is

Howard F. Stein ● Department of Family Medicine, University of Oklahoma Health Sciences Center, Oklahoma City, Oklahoma 73190.

"manifest," "intrinsic," or "inherent." Likewise, when we lose meaning, we go through a process of mourning, feeling that without our cognitive schema life (not merely ourselves) is meaningless, that we are empty, abandoned, bereft.

Furthermore, meaning is something we defend hotly and over which we wage wars. Provisionality, tolerance, and the spirit of play vanish when such systems of meaning as ideologies, values, beliefs, and attitudes meet and clash. It is as though one's own system of meaning must be immutable, necessary, and true. One has a stake in that particular meaning, as though one's very life depended on it. Meaning thus takes on the character of a massive defense—but against what, and for what? We act as though meaning were something we could not live without—but what is that "something"? When we talk about meaning, what are we talking about? In short, what is the meaning of *meaning?*

The problem of meaning—from proximal concerns to ultimate concerns—takes us immediately to consideration of symbolism and language, vehicles through which meanings are represented and expressed. But symbolism and language are only a beginning, since symbol and language are but way stations or repositories of that elusive substance, meaning. However, the very fact that the symbol is so often, and so tenaciously, held to *be* the thing leads one to inquire, "What are symbolism and language *for?*" hence, "What is thought *for?*" We must explain the plausibility of meaning in the human animal. In turn, I think, we can explain what culture is for and thereby what it "is."

I propose that a *psychoanalytic human biology,* another way of saying a psychoanalytic anthropology, is essential to account for human meanings, regardless of the size or complexity of the social unit. A sociogenetic model of meaning that omits psychodynamic and psychogenetic levels amounts to stagecraft without dramaturgy. Human relationships exist only inasmuch as participants ascribe meanings to them. Among the behavioral and social sciences, psychoanalysis is unique in its "preoccupation . . . with the purposes and symbolic content of thought" (La Barre, 1968a, p. 85), which makes of it an indispensible tool with which to interpret if not decode the meaning of meanings. A psychoanalytic anthropology is necessary to complete, which is often to say, explain, such widespread paradigms as "symbolic interactionism," "symbolic anthropology," "ritual studies," "cognitive anthropology," "situational analysis," and the like. These paradigms become "wrong" only because they prematurely impose final meanings or structures on symbol systems. The composer Gustav Mahler put it well when he insisted that the most important part of the music is not in the notes. Psychoanalysis, as contrasted with other explanatory systems, derives its explanations by listening attentively to the individual rather than by imposing meanings on him (e.g., classifications). The frequently encountered criticism that psychoanalysis imposes meanings or would deprive people of their meaning systems is a favorite ploy that reveals more about the accuser than about psychoanalysis. Paradoxically, only by its steadfast insistence on value neutrality toward the patient can psychoanalysis help the patient transcend those absolutistic values that have kept him a prisoner of his own fears. Psychoanalysis cannot discern or impose what is not there. La Barre wrote:

> Psychoanalysis was the first and still is the only psychology to take seriously the whole growing human body as a place to live in and to experience—for . . . the

emotional predicaments of this body-experiencing profoundly shape adaptive personality, the historic character of groups, and human institutions alike. Psychoanalysis is the first psychology to preoccupy itself with the symbolic *content* and *purpose*, as opposed to the mere modalities and processes, of thinking. It is the first authentically human as opposed to animal psychology. It is naturalistic, rather than experimental. (1972, pp. xii–xiii)

I owe a word to the reader about my own epistemology. In this work I will sharply distinguish between unconscious fantasy (and its products) and reality. Indeed, I will go so far as to suggest that the greatest impediment to human adaptation and evolution is the human proclivity to confuse realms, to be unconsciously motivated to blur the distinction between the internal and external environment. In these antipositivistic times, many scholars are given to reject the very possibility, let alone the necessity of a reality principle—that is, that there is an implacable That Which Is (La Barre, 1972), the physical universe of which we are a part, yet which is separate from our perceptions, needs, and wishes. Clearly, if there is no reality principle, there can be no reality testing, since there is nothing to test. One colleague, commenting on my assertion that projection is a ubiquitous, but faulty, guide to reality, said, "One man's projection is another's hard fact." Another colleague argued: "It would be interesting to have the author define reality except as the perceived world; there ain't no such thing as reality independent of an observer." (One is tempted to reenact Bishop Berkeley's reply to David Hume!)

Relativistically, of course, the *fact* of perception cannot be impugned: it must be meticulously described. But the truth value of all perceptions cannot be equated. A paranoid may well be convinced that the rays of the sun are persecuting him/her, but unless we enter into collusion with the paranoid's delusion, we must accept that one thing that the sun cannot do is persecute. The approach that I take in this chapter is the humbling recognition that we have vested unconscious interests in not perceiving reality undistorted. Tolstoy once wrote of God that "God is my desire." One must say the same for reality: Reality "is" as we desire it to be. Our cultural disquisitions about reality are as much autobiographical as are our theological maunderings about God. The distinction between subjective and objective, however tentative, is one of the finest aspirations (certainly not achievements) of the human odyssey.

"Go, go, go, said the bird: human kind cannot bear very much reality," wrote T. S. Eliot in "Burnt Norton," the first of *Four Quartets* (1944, p. 14). In the flight from reality, humankind takes refuge in the cultural time that lures us with the promise of gauzy sameness. Again, Eliot (1944, p. 13):

> Time present and time past
> Are both perhaps present in time future,
> And time future contained in time past.
> If all time is eternally present
> All time is unredeemable.

Near the end of the fourth quartet, "Little Gidding," Eliot vowed (1944, p. 59):

> We shall not cease from exploration
> And the end of all our exploring
> Will be to arrive where we started
> And know the place for the first time.

—hitherto "not known, because not looked for" (p. 59). Such knowledge will be "a condition of complete simplicity (Costing not less than everything)" (p. 59).

In his mystical quest, Eliot sought theological redemption beyond time, from (biological) time. A psychoanalytic anthropology can speak only of the redemption *of* time. The end of our exploring is to know the one place in which we have been eternally imprisoned in timeless repetition compulsions, and to know for the first time the place where we started: in the neotenic, familial, universal condition of childhood whence we fashion defensive culture to protect us.

.   For the remainder of this chapter, I shall ask the reader to accompany me (with Alice) down the rabbit hole to the labyrinth of symbolism and meaning. I hope to demonstrate that what one finds disorienting and frightening in Wonderland is systematically related to what we discern in the workaday world. I shall first discuss the human biology of symbolism, then inquire into the effect of symbolization on human adaptation, and conclude with some thoughts on the transcendence of meaning. (For excellent overviews of the relationship between psychoanalysis, psychiatry, and anthropology, see Boyer, 1978; Devereux, 1978, 1980; DeVos, 1974; Dundes, 1976; Kluckhohn, 1944; La Barre, 1958, 1978a; Lewis, 1977; Paul, 1980; Róheim, 1950; Sapir, 1949; Spiro, 1978.)

Toward a Human Biology of Symbol and Meaning

In his celebrated essay on symbolism, Whitehead (1927/1959) wrote that "the human mind is functioning symbolically when some components of its experience elicit consciousness, beliefs, emotions, and usages, respecting other components of its experience. The former set of components are the 'symbols,' and the latter set constitute the 'meaning' of the symbols" (pp. 7–8). To this definition, one only need add that consciousness is not necessary for symbolic process to occur (e.g., the dream). The essence of symbolism is the *representation* of meaning.

The fallibility of symbolism is that it is unconsciously used to misrepresent both the inner and outer worlds (Whitehead, 1927/1959, pp. 4–5). We often experience symbolic reality as though such mediations were in fact direct knowledge. Properly speaking, these misrepresentations (e.g., causality, misplaced concreteness, extrapolation, distortion) can legitimately be called illusions only when they are motivated but quickly modifiable, but must be labeled delusions when the misperception is both motivated and obdurate to change. The referent of a delusion has the quality of an imperative: what is perceived must be as it is perceived. In delusions, shared or idiosyncratic, the symbolic equation is rigid: the flag must *be* the nation, the word or wish must *be* the thing or deed, whiteness (in Western culture) *is* purity, and so on.

Yet the compelling power of a symbol lies both in the conscious associations made to it and in what is omitted. What is *not* said (together with the missing affect) becomes the key to why the symbol-as-rigid-compromise is necessary at all. Such symbolism is a built-in closed system of meaning designed to prevent the return of the repressed—which is to say undisguised—meaning. It is a closed system in the sense that the underlying forbidden fantasy or conflict may indeed populate an entire universe with meanings and referents that represent and avoid the underlying issues.

Its symbolism is thus rigidly tethered, undergoing constant fortification and revision as each previous symbolic symptom becomes inadequate to the task of defense (cf. Nadin, this volume).

Because the underlying fantasy issues can only be couched, never obliterated, a careful fantasy analysis (cf. Boyer, 1979; deMause, 1977, 1979) of material from folklore to newspaper copy can reveal what the psychic editor is trying valiantly to conceal. Such signaling defenses as "It was just a dream," "It is only a story," or "This is a folktale," typically mark or qualify dangerous unconscious material by distancing it from the self, by disqualifying its unconscious significance. Personal or cultural meanings possess the character of a surface structure which the ego uses to defend against the underlying unconscious meaning or deep structure (cf. Paul, 1980). Thus the paranoid—or paranoid culture—is vigilantly on the lookout for "enemy aliens" when he is in fact projecting his hatred onto them. The more the surface structure is elaborated or bowdlerized with associations, the more the fearsome material from the deep structure threatens to erupt into consciousness. The ego is preoccupied with warding off these latter associations; by compulsively "remembering" a symbolic set of substitute associations, we are able to "forget" (repress) our painful past.

Sperber, however, argued that

> none of the many explicit, implicit, and unconscious associations of "symbols" are meanings; the perception of a symbol is not mentally replaced by the representation of an associate, as it would be if symbolic associations were semantic relationships; rather, associations are extensions of symbols and equally open to interpretation. (1979, p. 61; see also 1975)

What, one might ask, prevents a symbol from being mentally replaced by an associate? I would reply that it is the very unconscious meaning of the symbol that prohibits such a free association. Already in his early writing, Freud (1892–1893/1953, p. 122) referred to "distressing antithetical ideas" that run counter to (conscious) intentions, the result of which conflict was the dramatic conversion reaction in which the body symbolized the conflict itself. The human world is literally peopled by a Turnerian "forest of symbols" at the conscious level so that one does not have to face affectively what the symbols mean. The symbol is thereby split off from its source so that the representation does not re-present to the person what he is afraid to face.

"Associations are extensions of symbols," rather than windows on underlying meanings, *only* when such associations are under strictly conscious control—which is rare. That is why associations obtained even outside the orthodox psychoanalytic setting reveal what the speaker would prefer to conceal, for they point, both in patches and omissions, to the referent of the symbol. Forgetting, so-called slips of the tongue, and jokes are examples of this phenomenon in everyday discourse. DeMause has developed a technique of fantasy analysis by which even daily newspapers can be analyzed for their unconscious themes (1977).

Symbolism and meaning are not mere cognitive or semantic functions, but deeply affective ones (DeVos, 1975); we therefore need a psychoanalytic semiotics (Dundes, 1976). The degree to which symbols and meanings are emotion laden is attested to both by the resistance of the patient to underlying meanings and by the overwhelming yet liberating force of recognition and conviction (insight) that occurs precisely when the original symbol is indeed *replaced* by its progenitor. The recovery of the (overdetermined) meaning of a symbol, idea, fantasy, or behavior lies in the analysis of the resistance to truly free associations and in the gradual reconstruction of memory traces that lie behind screen memories. One must go further: as the original trauma is restaged and the forbidden fantasy confronted, its myriad symbol symptoms lose their possessive hold. One can choose what to do with them rather than be driven by them. Symbols can be replaced, decathected, revised, even discarded, because what they were designed to avoid has at last been recovered.

As an aside, one must comment that much of contemporary symbolic anthropology's compulsive negation of the importance of affect in cognitive and semantic processes and categorization makes it unlikely that the meaning of symbols will be discovered by a method that is itself a defense against unconscious meaning (cf. Devereux, 1967; Spiro, 1979; Harris, this volume). What is true for an obsessive patient's denial and isolation of affect applies equally for a methodology widely embraced in anthropology. One cannot hope to find what one is loath to seek. Stated differently, one can discover only those meanings which one's defenses permit. Spindler (1978) expressed the fear of a "psychologized anthropology," as though one had to be sure beforehand of what the data would reveal about (wo)man. In revealing language, Spindler expressed disapproval of the tendency to "bring the abstracted culture concept down to a grubby level of individual motivation, thinking, and emotion" (p. 16), as though some tribal separation of the pure and the filthy were in danger of being violated.

Anthropology, with its penchant for the safer realms of disembodied cognition, symbol, behavior, and the like, is certainly not alone in its aversion to affect. In fact, it shares the ethos of American culture in its sanitizing of Freudian psychology. Ego psychology, with its emphasis on adaptation, the environment, innate strivings for mastery, and a certain "optimism," has been warmly received by American society just as it has been influenced by society. The downplaying of the vicissitudes of the instincts and of Freud's philosophical pessimism makes ego psychology quite at home (see Brody, 1976). The self-psychology of Heinz Kohut and his followers (who have contributed much to our knowledge of narcissism) has likewise been enthusiastically received. At the 1980 meeting of the American Psychoanalytic Association, Kohut concluded his brief address with the rhetorical question "What if man is simply not an animal?" (quoted in Malcolm, 1980). The cultural domestication of the id is the denial, or at least minimization, of (wo)man as an animal. One might say that the chain of symbolic associations in mainstream anthropology, in one influential school of psychoanalysis, and in American culture are identical! The analysis of cultural as well as individual symbolic associations leads to human familial childhood as the repository and source of life's meanings (cf. Stein, 1978a,b).

Human communication and symbolization are a Janus-faced creature. On the one hand, the newborn uncompleted baby is not rigidly programmed instinctively for behavior in the uncertain world. Thus, through symbols, (wo)man can learn, revise, discard, and try out ideas in Einsteinian "thought experiments" before testing them in action. On the other hand, the very vulnerability and hence exploitability of infancy can, mediated by poor early parenting and trauma, lead to a rigidity in symbol investment and ritual behavior that rivals gene-directed "instinctive" behavior in "lower" animals. Thus, symbols and the interpersonal sharing of symbols can be profoundly adaptive *and* profoundly counteradaptive. Symbols can be used in the playful spirit of as-if provisionality and inquisitiveness or in the dogmatic spirit of the quest for certainty and security. In the latter regard, official science is as culpable as are magic and religion. Consider, for instance, that Watson and Crick identified their model of DNA as a "central dogma," or that in 1976 a group of geologists, now some 200 strong, founded the International Stop Continental Drift Society to oppose plate theory, or at least to protest the uncritical acceptance of the theory as proven fact (Tierney, 1981). Even in science, "it might be" often becomes "it must be" (necessity).

Because symbolization is concerned simultaneously with what goes on both inside and outside the epidermis, and thereby frequently confuses realms, it is often difficult to know whether an act or idea occurs in response to inner anxiety or to outer reality. Although both types of responses result in a homeostasis of sorts, their consequence for survival are far different. In this regard, I find the well-known distinction made by Gordon Allport between autoplastic and alloplastic modes of behavior too clear-cut since the categories are not mutually exclusive. One acts upon the outer world based on internal premises and fantasies about the world. Because human communication is primarily, even overwhelmingly, phatic (expressing an emotion), even our efforts at mastery in the world are governed by the unconscious fantasies which our behavior implements. Characteristically, the wondrously complex metacommunication in which we convey to one another our inner states (in disguise, to be sure) does not liberate us from endocrine system or childhood; instead, it articulates and organizes those inner states, employing as camouflage the official reasons we use to justify our actions.

I emphasize that this use of symbolism is far from limited to the so-called expressive forms such as religion or art. As Mumford (1972) has shown, technics is inseparable from aesthetics or art. Anthropologists have long concentrated on the purely instrumental or practical (survival) dimension of artifacts. Yet *homo faber* has from the outset been *homo ludens*. Tools are also, even primarily, toys—which is to say, symbols—with which one can play. Now, if technics is always partly aesthetics, phatic symbolism would seem to be an inherent part of tool making and tool use (cf. Montagu, this volume).

Tools and symbols alike (and tools as symbols) are means by which (wo)man extends him/herself from his/her body outward into the world. Take words, for instance, as tool-like extensions of thought. McLuhan wrote that the word

> was the first technology by which man was able to let go of his environment in order to grasp it in a new way. Words are a kind of information retrieval that can range over the total environment and experience at high speed. Words are complex systems of metaphors and symbols that translate experience into our uttered or outered senses. They are a technology of explicitness. By means of translation of immediate sense experience into vocal symbols the entire world can be evoked and retrieved at any instant. (1964, p. 64)

Through these extensions, s/he can first imagine new modes of living, and then implement these instrumentally—for instance, the bridge where there was once only a river (Hall, 1977). But (wo)man can also wildly overextend him/herself, extrapolating from the *"temporarily adaptive and relevant"* (La Barre, 1978b, p. 59) infantile behaviors and modes of experience onto the physical environment. The formerly effective, because stage-specific, magical and religious habitus may be pathetically inappropriate in one's attitude toward the physical and larger social world. Yet they survive because the individual projectively or transferentially experiences the present in terms of the regressed-to past: for example, (wo)man invests tribe and nation with the wished-for mother love of infantile need.

Omnipotence of thought was once a reality that worked, for one was once symbiotically tied, first physically and later psychologically, to the maternal object of one's desire. Wish was once command (magic), then humble plea (religion). What began as effortless omnipotence (Silverberg, 1949) in early symbiosis is succeeded by omnipotence by proxy, which is to say omnipotence borrowed from a human, mythic, or supernatural figure (Rado, 1969), after considerable self- and object-differentiation has occurred. In both cases, world is an extension of wish. Little wonder that meaning should become reified, that the fallacies of misplaced concreteness and causality should be rampant, or that thought is confused with substance (e.g., animism).

Linking homeopathic magic (e.g., metaphoric thinking) with talking, and contagious magic (i.e., metonymic thinking) with walking, La Barre wrote that

> symbolic effigy-magic over-extrapolates the real powers we learned from symbolizing in speech: the symbol is considered to be the thing. Likewise, contagious part-for-whole magic illegitimately over-extrapolates our personal experience of the nature of organism: the feces and sputum are *no longer functionally part* of our enemy's organism, and they are never part of one's own.
>
> Hence, while walking and talking *do* give us new powers, they do *not* preserve the omnipotence that we once knew in the womb or in infantile management of mother and that we think we still have in any discrepancy between wish and world. Old adaptations are seductive precisely because of their experienced power. We must sometimes *unlearn* old adaptations to make new ones. (1978b, p. 61)

I would only add that there is an important feedback relationship between magical thinking and magical doing, so to speak. The newly acquired power of an infant's motility and coordination, and likewise the improvement of adult techniques for mastery in the environment (say, the internal combustion engine over the horse-drawn carriage), are readily used to confirm the omnipotence of thought. The feedback can likewise proceed in the reverse direction: energized by new attainments, the regressed ego (or national ego) with its labile and voracious boundaries, hurls itself into fantasy-driven reality to achieve or consume even more. The sinister compulsion of nationalism to devour orally and expel anally everything that obstructs its need for infinite *Lebensraum* is but a single, though sufficient, example this feedback between symbolic and motoric magic. Perhaps also, this ontogenetic pairing of the two categories of magic explains the close association of symbol with ritual which many thinkers have noted. The locomotor eroticism of ritual can only self-intensify character structure and social structure alike. Ritual "'confirms' the reality of myth: compulsive act coerces obsessive belief" (La Barre, 1975, p. 18).

In the oral stage of development, both in terms of "zone" or orifice and dominant "mode" of relating to others (Erikson, 1963), what is shortly to become the power of the word or language is already the power of the wish. Developmentally, words have substance, as the saying goes, because the wish and fulfillment which language and symbols were later to represent were originally tangible, substantial. Words are as much extensions of as they are successors to primitive modes of power, control, classification, and so on. Language summons reality into being, just as the preverbal wish and cry magically brought the mother. "Let there be . . . And there was!" is the universal equation.

Symbols (e.g., words, signs, language) are *hypercathected,* or overinvested in, because developmentally, *the flesh became the word.* The mother's touch and breast, coordinated with infant's mouth, eyes and hands, are the powerful precursors of the word. In the New Testament, the Gospel According to St. John begins with the words: "In the beginning was the Word, and the Word was with God, and the Word was God. . . . And the Word was made flesh among us." One could not find a more striking instance of omnipotence, omniscience, and omnibenevolence—which is to say, the awesome, hence reluctantly relinquished, power of the preverbal now dimly recollected in words. Of course, in the beginning was the mouth, not the word; but although the infant *could* not associate a word with the experience, the memory trace (theologized, to be sure) of "In the beginning was the Word" gives the whole show away. In the narrow sense, the Biblical passage presents to us in distilled form the synthesis of Christological mysticism and Platonism, within which eternal essences and pure forms abound in the flesh. Yet this passage is universally apposite to the experience of all children—and to the adult who magically or religiously invokes omnipotent beings, or who psychotically "becomes" one him/herself.

Likewise, *supernatural* (from deity to anima to mythic hero) is a universal category, because we originally experience our bodies and our caretakers to be more than human. It too is an extension, an extrapolation by an adult whose neotenic childhood and early object relations confirm his theology. Theology is always "true," although the theologian mistakes what its subject is: autobiography. One's epistemology and ontology—which is to say, one's premises about the nature of knowledge and life's meaning—are likewise autobiographical statements about how one's ego has inwardly structured and outwardly represented one's psychosocial development. Internalization is essential to meaning and symbolization—and to the subsequent misidentification of what the problem is, where it is located, and how to deal with it. Discussing "neurotic defences as elaborations and combinations of the responses of animals to situations of threat," Rycroft (1970, p. 137) formulated a psychoanalytic human biology, that is:

> anxiety as a specific form of vigilance, neurotic anxiety as a special form of anxiety which arises as a by-product of the tendency of man to internalize his environment, and defences as responses which can be evoked by internal as well as external stress. (p. 138)

Moreover, as DeVos wrote, the human solutions to the problem of anxiety—the defenses—are rooted in preverbal, presymbolic functions which humans share in common with the most primitive cell biology:

> (1) Intake, (2) exclusion, that is boundary protection of contents, and (3) expulsion. At the earliest stage of ego development, we find these three basic mechanisms at work, often defined as the mechanisms of introjection, denial, and projection. Traces of these basic mechanisms can persist in almost unmodified

form in adult behavior. For the most part, however, the early forms of these
mechanisms become transmuted through maturation in the course of human
socialization. When they persist in their more primitive forms, they can result
in certain characteristic forms of mental illness. (1980, p. 105)

Through repression, the original conflict or forbidden fantasy is replaced by an
acceptable compromise symbol (Boyer, 1979; Freud, 1900/1953; Jones, 1948; La
Barre, 1969; Paul, 1980). Yet the safety conferred by the symbol (except for those
arrived at by sublimation; see Devereux, 1971) is both temporary and illusory, for
now the symbol must constantly be reaffirmed through ritualization that shores it up
to prevent the imminent danger from resurfacing. In the long run, the repression-
derived symbol is a symptom, the defense itself a displaced adversary that weakens
and must be paralleled if not succeeded by still another defense. The Judeo-Christian
tradition, for instance, does not possess a meager one or two exemplary myths rationalizing away sadistic, filicidally motivated circumcision. There are literally
hundreds of them, ranging from official sacred texts to oral literature—even to modern medicine (Menninger, 1938). The persistent cycle of decompensation, disorganization, and reorganization of individual and group psyche (Devereux, 1980, pp. 80–
81) is the sacred culture which (wo)men are loath to relinquish; for fear of pain, we
incur even greater pain for ourselves and others.

One of the most crucial yet most difficult life tasks is to accept that our words
are not only potentially remarkable tools of communication and mastery, but that
they are mere words, not reality itself. One sure indicator of maturity is the *relative*
decathexis of language, that is, the divestment from speech of a hallucinatory quality
(Hippler, 1977; Sarnoff, 1976). In order to accept the provisional nature of symbols,
one must be able to discriminate between the self (with its boundaries) and symbols
which the self might use, to be able to lose symbols and meanings without feeling a
loss of self. Thus, one would not be strait-jacketed *by* symbols—warden and prisoner
in one.

Navigating the difficult channel between the Scylla of infantile omnipotence
and the Charybdis of infantile vulnerability (e.g., annihilation, separation, castration)—these mediated by parenting figures with their own unresolved fantasies and
conflicts—the child and later adult goes into the world incapable of knowing what
his/her competencies might be and what his/her real threats are. As La Barre noted:
"We perceive *everything* through glasses colored by personal and persistent cultural
pasts. We don't know the now because we so stubbornly refract it through the
immortal past's prism" (personal communication, September 20, 1980). The spec-
tacle of cultural variation is indeed edifying, but should not deceive us into mistaking
local variations for the themes whose universality in precultural human nature is
played out in human symbols and meanings (Bidney, 1947; Devereux, 1980; La
Barre, 1954/1968b, 1972; Spiro, 1979). All cultural creations are attempts to grap-
ple with human neotenic and familial biology. The abiding meanings of humankind's
symbolized "collective realities" lie in the mere fact of human childhood.

Culture, Projective Environment, and Adaptation

Unpopular as it is to argue in a culture and in an anthropology dominated by a
pseudorealistic outlook on the function and origin of culture, every culture must not

only face, but is in fact built from (at least) three interrelated nodal issues in the human organism and family: (1) integrity, change, drives, and mortality in the body; (2) attachment, symbiosis, annihilation, separation, abandonment, loss, individuation, differentiation, and dependency in relation to the mother; and (3) submission, rebellion, overthrow, restitution, and identification in the oedipal/counteroedipal struggle. These are conventionally dismissed as a kind of "icing on the cake"; I propose instead that these constitute the essence of the "cake of custom" by which reality and realistic issues in adaptation, social control, and the like are *mediated*.

Devereux (1942) has proposed that systems of multiple mothering are one interpersonal and organizational means of dealing with problems of dependency, loss, and abandonment. Jones (1924/1964) proposed the plausible but knee-jerk rejected hypothesis that matrilineal forms of social structure, with attendant splitting between roles of biological father and mother's brother, are one way of dealing with the universal Oedipus. A psychoanalytic ecology suggests that the most influential environments in human inner homeostasis and outer adaptation are the internal environment and the early emotional field of family object relations. This does not say that the outer environment is irrelevant, but states more precisely how it is relevant experientially: more as projective target for primitive fantasies and unresolved conflicts than as cause of culture, family relations, and fantasies (Stein, in press).

As a result, this model reverses the causal sequence of the prevalent Whiting (1961), Kardiner (1939), and Fromm (1970) models. The best learned lessons of history, geography, and sociology derive from early object relations (particularly the mothering objects), are in all probability preverbal (Stein, in press; Winnicott, 1967), and are only subsequently symbolized in acceptably impersonal group form. Such outer symbolic, mythic, and ritual forms, as secondary-elaboration compromise formations, allow the individual (as they are continually reinvented and revised by the individual) to pretend that history, geography, literature, and the like are not "really about me" but something real and distinct "out there" that is somehow compelling of its own accord. Culture is thus in large measure a camouflage, distortion, projection, and displacement of inner onto outer, experienced and rationalized (by anthropologists as well as tribalists) as though the source and location of the experience were the outer world.

Cultures are thus "mutations" (La Barre, 1971) whose "psycho-speciations" (deMause, 1977) create "average expectable environment(s)" (Hartmann, 1939/1958), which come to be symbolically represented by "culturally constitutionally behavioral environment(s)" (Hallowell, 1955) mediated by "culturally constituted defense mechanisms" (Spiro, 1965). One speaks of one's culture as an objectified *it*, a *Ding an sich*, so as not to disclose oneself. In fact, culture is more precisely a "group-fantasy," which deMause defined as "a set of shared unconscious assumptions, quite unrelated to any 'objective' reality, about the way it *feels* to be a member of a historical group at a particular time in history" (1977, p. 11; cf. Parker, this volume).

In what I discern to be the earliest use of the notion of group fantasy, La Barre wrote:

> It is true that group fantasy confines and delimits our private psychoses, but if the culture of the group comes to resemble a psychosis itself, by a kind of *folie à deux* to the nth degree, then the group is worse off than when it started. In

this unconscious and unwitting way, all social groups are in the long run either
therapeutic, that is adaptive to a real world, or anti-adaptive. Man is like an
existentialist spider who spreads out a moral net of symbolism over the void out
of his own substance—and then walks upon it. But the final safety of the net
depends always on the integrity and the soundness of the postulated points of
reference to a real physical world. (1962, p. 67)

How sound, one wonders, can that "net" be if—as is common in culture—reality is
not experienced as distinct from fantasy, and, in more advanced cultures where the
distinction has been made, its members have historically shrunk from accepting that
fact? Cannot delusions—false fixed ideas—be the basis for a group "norm" as readily as they are departures from it? (Cf. Illich, this volume.)

La Barre wrote that "worldview is . . . a function of ego differentiation and consequent psychosexual maturation. Similarly, cultural institutions roughly manifest
degrees of hallucinosis in their epistemological grounds" (1975, p. 21). Likewise,
Devereux noted that

man tends, in one way or another, to see reality as a projection of psychic forces.
(1980, p. 282)
    The *fact* is that the primitive acts realistically most of the time; the *trouble*
is that he does not *know* that he is acting realistically when he bandages a
wound but unrealistically when he tries to cure an illness by offering a sacrifice.
(1980, p. 227)
    So-called advanced cultures, which differentiate sharply between reality
and fantasy on the *logical* level, continue *in practice* to take collective fantasies
for reality and sometimes to take reality for fantasy. (1980, p. 139)
    In psychological illness *the external world is structured at the expense of
the ego's structure;* the organism as a whole is kept functioning at the expense
of the ego-functions; the world and the organism are made *emotionally* compatible at the expense of realistic, logical compatibility. This, to my mind, is the
true definition of psychological illness [and, likewise, the definition of the der-
eistic side of culture and of social movements]. (1980, p. 81)

It is the collective realities of childhood (based on universals of neoteny and
family, together with parental attitudes—as contrasted with child-rearing practices;
see Devereux, 1951/1969, 1980; Hartmann, Kris, & Loewenstein, 1970) that give
rise to compelling "collective representations" from religion to history (Durkheim,
1912/1961) and social structures that simultaneously dramatize and disguise early
conflicts. Koenigsberg wrote that "cultural ideas, beliefs and values may be viewed
. . . as an institutionalization and social embodiment of primal human phantasies"
(1975, p. viii). What can liberate us from both cryptoenvironmentalism and reduc-
tionistic ecological thinking is to propose rather than assume that groups *might*
derive part of their social structure, role functions, and symbolisms (etc.) from an
accurate assessment of the social and natural worlds.

The next issue would be in demonstrating where, how, and why these (and only
these) are under the sphere of the conflict-free ego. Just as our assessment of the
individual includes a discernment of ego strengths and id/superego-dominated areas
of the personality, an assessment of the group dynamics of culture or society includes
a discernment between its areas of reality testing and distortion (including those
areas in which it is only spuriously "adapted" to reality, e.g., radical ethnomedical
empiricism in which a local herb or drug—for instance foxglove—"works," but the

native population does not know why or ascribes magical explanation to its action). A group's theology, cosmology, mythology, folklore, official history, ethnomedical beliefs, and the like provide a marvelously rich Rorschach and Thematic Apperception Test—designed by those who interpret it!—that reveals the group's core conflicts and their basis for apperception of the world.

Rather than posit that a group designs its culture to make itself adaptive to the environment (subsistence, social control, etc.), it is far more likely and intellectually productive to propose that groups adopt selective aspects of the environment to weave into their dominant (albeit changing) group fantasy about social relations and the universe. Environment is perceptually conformed by personality, not the reverse. Moreover, deMause has boldly proposed that "primitives did not adapt their personalities to their harsh environments—they migrated to harsh environments because they matched their inner life" (1977, p. 262).

Historical groups, the anthropologist's "cultures," thrive on the very ambivalence they cannot rid themselves of; in purporting to dig out of the psychosocial problems that plague them, they dig only deeper, becoming entrenched by the very machinery (group defenses) they use to extricate themselves. Group entropy is the outcome of culture history, a symbolic inbreeding that assures obsolescence when deprived of its own protective bubble—one that is eagerly transported to new environments (e.g., migration, modernization, urbanization) and by which are fashioned new lives from old. Such entropy is clearly evidenced in "more of the same" types of behavior, governed by obsolete—perhaps, never useful in reality testing—premises (cf. Watzlawick, Beavin, & Fisch, 1974).

Culturally, if the inner space is sacred, then the outer space is profane. Consequently, a host of ingenious tribal, ethnic, or national boundary-maintaining devices are developed (Barth, 1969) to shore up the distinction between inside and outside. Ironically, the vigilance that upholds this distinction is founded on the confusion of what is psychically inside for what is outside. I hold, moreover, that the repetitive action on this faulty premise is the essence of ritualization. Not a social category of behavior (e.g., religion vs. subsistence activity), ritual is characterized by the psychological quality that infuses a private or social activity, one which makes of that act a necessity impelled from within the psyche to solve inner anxiety that is attached to (projected on) the real world. Attitudes and conduct that were once appropriate to the infant and toddler's experience of the world (e.g., merging, summons, placation, worship, obedience, etc.) are altogether useless in relation to recalcitrant, implacable Nature. Ritual solutions only postpone, and never solve, the encounter with social and physical reality.

Social scientists are fond of saying, echoing Malinowski (1954), that people resort to magicoreligious (ritual) behavior when, under stress, traditional knowledge and technique are insufficient to explain or handle a situation. What they omit is that the spurious "success" of ritual manipulation or exhortation (etc.) rules out the learning of ego-derived techniques or ideas that would make their behavior more consequential in coping with reality, which would in turn reduce inner anxiety. It is insufficient to say that magic begins where science (however "primitive") ends, or that magic declines with increased control over the environment. Rather, it is necessary to say that the capacity for science begins where the need for magical thinking diminishes. Such outer conditions as stress or stimulus or inner cognitive conditions as uncertainty or ambiguity are themselves insufficient to account for the reaction to them (Devereux, 1955; La Barre, 1969, 1972).

In his epochal study *Religion and the Decline of Magic,* Thomas remarked that

> in England magic lost its appeal before the appropriate technical solutions had been devised to take its place. . . . The change which occurred in the seventeenth century was thus not so much technological as mental . . . the emergence of a new faith in the potentialities of human initiative. (1971, pp. 656–657, 661)

A change in parent–child relations permitted the emergence of a greater scientific (realistic) orientation to the world from a largely magicoreligious (persecutory, dependent) past. Unlike science, ritual fans the flames of the anxiety it temporarily purports to extinguish. Ritualization mistakes both the source and the remedy for the problem.

One may distinguish between ritual and other types of patterned, repetitive, recurrent sequences, on the basis of whether the act is performed in the service of adaptive reality testing or in the service of assuaging anxiety whose source is the psyche but which is obdurately experienced as coming from without. The dynamic content or meaning makes the decisive difference in determining whether the repetition is coerced, compulsive from within, or adaptive to a reality perceived through the anxiety-free sphere of the ego.

Following psychoanalytic thinking, I take ritual to be the enactment of a symbolic statement about "something else" in which (1) that "something else" is inaccessible to the consciousness of the participant and (2) the iteration of that statement resists change, or, if it does change, becomes for however long it is used, a regimen that must not be questioned by participants. Ritual, then, is a way of *not* communicating about something directly while re-presenting it in disguise (as in a screen memory of a dream).

Ritual is closed-system thought and action. It *ipso facto* cannot be adaptive *to* reality, since the mythic thought and its performance replace reality with myth. Ritual thus not only consists of distortive thought but is delusional thought put into deed. Ritual is thus a behavioral system of *actions of reference* that confirm the belief about the nature of reality *(ideas of reference)* by acting it out. A crucial dynamic factor in ritual is the need for constant repetition, whether idiosyncratic or in regularized group enactments. Whatever it is that has been alleviated symbolically can never be resolved so long as it is managed exclusively at the symbolic-ritual level rather than at the deeper level of its unconscious meaning to the communicant.

Of course, to the participant, the meaning *is* the ritual—just as, to the snake phobic, the snake *is* the adversary. To the participant, the symbol is not a symbol, it is reality. Likewise, the enactment of the ritual is absolutely essential so that the belief be confirmed by sensate experience—a daydream in which one is the central character. Far from deepening our awareness of self and reality, ritual narcotizes that awareness. What a symbol is used for, not what it purportively is (an epistemologically erroneous Jungianism or existential cop-out), determines its clinical status.

Far from ritualization being selected for as an adaptive response toward the attainment of "practical outcomes" (Kiefer and Cowan, 1979), it is in fact danger-ously maladaptive. The reality to which we are adapting, under the influence of rit-ual, is a timeless dreamworld made in the image of our anxieties, conflicts, and wishes. The very ritual process which we use to defend us against the unknown (our-selves and reality) makes us even more vulnerable and helpless, for the simple reason that we use symbolism to misdefine the problem and ritual to solve the wrong prob-lem. We remember in order to forget; the fact of memory (symbol) is inseparable from the act (ritual) of remembering. And just as screen memories are substitute recollections, likewise are screen actions substitute behavior and "screen symptoms" (Devereux, 1953) substitute pathology—in each case a symbolicoritual disguise for the underlying problem that itself is only encountered safely masked.

It is no wonder that the ritual process among groups is identical to the vicious cycle of psychopathology among lone neurotics or psychotics. Every new, erroneous solution becomes a new problem for which yet another ritual must be devised, further removing the participant from the source of the need for the ritual in the first place. The context upon which ritual is ultimately dependent is the unconscious, which is to say the unresolved childhood present in the adult who is now equipped to act on the old premises. In role relationships, the mere fact of complementarity, stability, or homeostasis is, by itself, an inadequate criterion for assessing the health or nor-mality of an individual, familial, or cultural system.

To argue, for instance, as Boyer (1979) has done, that just as dreams help sta-bilize the individual, so folktales help stabilize societies is to be technically correct while not saying enough. The complementarity of dream, folklore, myth, and religion may well together supply sufficient outlets for the representation and discharge of inner conflicts that the inner and interpersonal (ego-syntonic and culture-syntonic, respectively) balance is rigidly defended. As a consequence, painful unconscious material and reality itself are censored from providing necessary feedback for adap-tation about the self, the object world, and the natural world.

We frequently err in thinking of adaptation as a noun, that is, a static state, rather than as a verb, or, as Devereux (1980) suggested, a process of and capacity for "continuous readjustment." Hardesty (1972) has made the same point in arguing for a generalized human ecological niche as contrasted with a fixed, rigid niche. Not unexpectedly, the study of other human systems has led to a similar conclusion: for instance, family studies. The distinction between rigidity and flexibility is one of the diagnostic hallmarks for differentiating between pathological and healthy families (Beavers, 1976; Speer, 1970). Speer (1970) has challenged the use of homeostasis as a criterion of family health and has proposed the diagnostic as well as descriptive distinction between "morphostasis" and "morphogenesis." Like dysfunctional cul-tures, pathological families are characterized as steady states, closed systems, whose disturbance in orientation is severe and whose members have a frightened stake in confusing the "map" with the "territory" (Korzybski, 1933). What Ferreira wrote of "family myth" is especially cogent to the student of culture:

> The term "family myth" refers to a series of fairly well-integrated beliefs shared
> by all family members, concerning each other and their mutual position in the
> family life, beliefs that go unchallenged by everyone involved in spite of the

reality distortions which they may conspicuously imply. . . . the family myth "explains" the behavior of the individuals in the family while it hides its motives. (1963, pp. 55–56)

To maintain the myth is part of the struggle to maintain the relationship. (1963, p. 60)

This very struggle and the attendant myths that attempt to justify the relationship, however, are themselves plausible only because of the separation anxiety that underlies it. The fear of being alone, itself based on a chilling feeling that one is indeed separate if not empty, leads to the flight from separation, to the denial of separateness. Herein lies one of the powerful—yet rarely acknowledged—underpinnings of culture and of the panicky quest for a restoration of that symbiosis in cults and movements when one experiences the collective womb which he has taken for granted to be now disintegrating. Levi-Strauss wrote that "the one real calamity, the one fatal flaw which can affect a group of men and prevent them from fulfillment is to be alone" (1968, p. 40).

In the early classic and popular book *Escape from Freedom*, Fromm (1941) argued that the lure of totalitarianisms lay in participants' flight from individuality and responsibility into collectivity. Yet the fear of separation is not itself a fixed given, but is the pathological outcome of the inability of early object relations to facilitate transition from symbiosis to separation-individuation (Mahler & Pine, 1968; Mahler, Pine, & Bergman, 1975). Pathological homeostasis, expressed simultaneously at individually, familially, and societally interlocking levels, reflects the terror of realizing one's *biologically* distinct selfhood. In the attendant flight into group collectivity, one merges with the group self—and thereafter anxiously defends the delusion of security.

Summarizing a tenet of anthropology, Barkow wrote that "it is well accepted that culture was the environment to which natural selection adapted us, and that as selection for cultural capacity proceeded, it made possible the further elaboration of culture" (1977, p. 413). Reproductive success, or "inclusive fitness," is the final biological criterion of cultural adaptability. This seems to me to take a dangerously short-term view of adaptive success, since what might lead in the immediate future to a glut of progeny might be attained at the price of more restricted knowledge of the real world. And it is the latter which is the final measure of success. Given a culturally relativist model of adaptation, one might be compelled to conclude that the Catholic Church, not Galileo Galilei and his circle of heliocentrists and their descendants, was the most adaptive, since at least in official ideology, the Church's worldview prevailed, and its adherents most likely outreproduced post-Galilean scientists. (It was only in 1981 that the Church reexamined Galileo's trial.)

Culture is too broadly credited with adaptation, when it should be more carefully combed for its adaptive and counteradaptive elements. A properly psychoanalytic human biology would suggest that long-term adaptation occurs where reality testing, object love (which is to say, the capacity to cherish another person who is experienced as separate from one's needs and cherished *for* their separateness), and reproductive success coincide—or at least approach one another. To bequeath to the future not only one's children but one's motivated ignorance (and theirs) as well is to bequeath an evolutionary cul-de-sac. Those who measure *any* type of success only according to group standards omit any assessment of the group standards themselves. Alas, a considerable portion of the reality we studiously seek *not* to understand is ourselves; and until we understand ourselves, we simply will not even know that the environment to which, in large measure, we are (spuriously) adapting is but the one we have spun from our fantasies.

In his deservedly celebrated essay on the Balinese cockfight, Geertz (1972) introduced Bentham's notion of *deep play* to the Balinese passionate participation in their sport. He wrote:

> Bentham's concept of 'deep play' is found in his *The Theory of Legislation*. By it he means play in which the stakes are so high that it is, from his utilitarian standpoint, irrational for men to engage in it at all. If a man whose fortune is a thousand pounds (or ringgits) wages five hundred of it on an even bet, the marginal utility of the pound he stands to win is clearly less than the marginal disutility of the one he stands to lose. In genuine deep play, this is the case for both parties. They are both in over their heads. Having come together in search of pleasure they have entered into a relationship which will bring the participants, considered collectively, net pain rather than net pleasure. Bentham's conclusion was, therefore, that deep play was immoral from first principles and, a typical step for him, should be prevented legally.
>
> But more interesting than the ethical problem, at least for our concerns here, is that despite the logical force of Bentham's analysis men do engage in such play, both passionately and often, and even in the face of law's revenge. (p. 15)

I would like to see in the concept of deep play a metaphor for culture itself, the kind of "playing with fire" (Geertz's heading for the above section) that leads to what might be called *reality's revenge*. That is, people become so passionately committed to a belief system, so literally get in over their heads, that what they are convinced is mankind's only way becomes, in fact, maladaptive. The stakes that are so high are the shared defenses of identity that even anthropologists come to defend as "culture." A psychoanalytic investigation into what (wo)men, seeking pleasure and repeatedly finding pain, invest in it *for,* takes us in a direction different from that of Geertz.

Transcendence of Meaning

In this chapter I have explored *meaning* as a symbolized system of defenses that profits (wo)man by giving him/her a "soul" at the price of losing knowledge of him/herself and the world. It is true that (wo)man cannot live by staples ("bread") alone, yet his/her meanings substantially impair his/her abilities to love or work—even as they inspire him/her to labor in behalf of his/her fantasies. The problem lies not in the word *meaning,* just as misplaced concreteness is not a necessary attribute of symbolism; the problem lies in how and for what end they have been *used* over human history. Becker wrote that

> depression can illustrate beautifully the primarily symbolic nature of human striving: man will make a last-ditch attempt to sustain life-meaning and a positive identity, even if it means denouncing himself. "I have failed: *ergo* I am

evil" substitutes for a thought that most people will not entertain: namely, the possibility that *"Life has no meaning."* (1962, p. 144)

Conventionally, we tend to think of meaning as a solution to life's problems rather than *being the problem itself.* We celebrate our collective compulsion neuroses and externalize them as tribal totems. They are not something to transcend, but something we reverence, immutable and eternal. We defend our defenses, and thus perpetuate those underlying conflicts and distortion-ridden fantasies which these defenses re-present to us in our elaborate symbolic disguises. Symbolic-ritual solutions must fail in our adaptation to reality, for they comprehensively misrepresent both the inner fantasy and our apperception of outer reality.

Those seeking the peace of mind of inner homeostasis devote their lives to the denial of the reality principle. They ask: "Which meaning system ought I embrace?" and "Which ideology ought I believe?"—not recognizing that belief and meaning are themselves the problem. We act as though one system *must* possess superior value to another, and that therefore, we must choose. Perhaps *not to choose at all* is preferable. As Freud asked: "Am I obliged to believe every absurdity? And if not, why just this one?" (1957, p. 48). Is it possible that the reintrojection of what we have originally extrajected is everywhere, regardless of content, our universal human idolatry? If, as Freud said, it is only repression that makes the instincts monstrous, then does not the goal of a psychoanalytic species-therapy consist in the reclamation of human biology from the archaic superego, the recovery of mortal time from frozen timelessness? Where *superego* was, there might ego be.

Rycroft has suggested that

> far from modern man having lost a true sense of identity, it may well be that as his external supply of idealized father-figures is being diminished by the dis-illusioning effect of scientific knowledge he is being forced to become aware of himself in terms of his capacity to love, without recourse to the supports of religion or morality, which . . . is ultimately a defense against infantile ambiv-alence. (1960, p. 87)

In a sublime passage, Devereux linked art, sublimation, object relations, and maturity:

> 1) Art is a sublimation and not an ordinary defense.
> 2) The impulses and wishes perpetuated by art are the same as those that actuate the normal, the neurotic, the compulsive rebel, and the inhibited Puri-tan. However, these impulses are neither distorted, not [*sic*] negated, nor are they permitted to erupt in the form of a brute, almost subcortical discharge. They are . . . discharged in such a manner that there occurs a kind of "feed-back" that automatically increases: a) The ability to mobilize and to discharge affect; and b) The technical proficiency of achieving a *disciplined* discharge. . . . Moreover, the technique of the discharge implies creative outgoing communi-cation, receptivity, and *object relations*—three processes which presuppose, and are uniquely characteristic of, maturity. (1971, pp. 220–221)

It is not surprising that the capacity for great art (and the capacity to appreciate such greatness), reality testing, and the ability to love a distinctly other human being are three expressions of the same maturity of ego development. In *Music as Meta-*

phor, a work deserving wider attention, Ferguson (1960) distinguished between genuine and spurious use of musical metaphor in terms of how it illumines or falsifies the human experience that is represented.

Meanings, values, worldviews, symbols—these are only as good as they are true to what they represent. Just as the capacity for uncorrected distortion lies in childhood and in the relationships that exploit the vulnerabilities of psychosexual-psychosocial development, so also in childhood and early object relations lies the capacity for faithfulness to the unconscious and to reality. The fateful issue for every generation of parents and children anew is whether parents will be able to solve their conflicts for themselves and thereby need less to inflict them on the next generation— or whether they will need their children as living symbols of their anxiety and narcissism. Imprisoning (wo)man in the false security of what s/he needs to believe as immutably true, the dire importance of defensive symbols robs (wo)man of what s/he might become. Enticing him/her with tales of superhuman heroism and supernatural power, devotion to his/her symbols denies him/her the dignity that only an adult human mortal can attain: One who knows what s/he knows and what s/he does not, what s/he can do and cannot, and who finds in such knowledge, mastery, and humility sufficient recompense for leaving behind childhood's fancies.

At the conclusion of his epochal essay *Symbolism,* Whitehead (1927/1959) wrote:

> The art of free society consists first in the maintenance of the symbolic code; and secondly in fearlessness of revision, to secure that the code serves those purposes which satisfy an enlightened reason. Those societies which cannot combine reverence to their symbols with freedom of revision, must ultimately decay either from anarchy, or from the slow atrophy of a life stifled by useless shadows. (p. 88)

Hard-won insight is freedom's master tool, yet one which as readily doubts itself as it applies itself to life. Through insight into how symbols come to be, hence what they "are," one comes to accept them for the vehicles they are—and to need less to clutch them as essences. In a profound sense, insight offers people as species a meaning beyond meaning, because insight must—in order to be insight—be metacultural. It cannot be prescribed or codified, for that would put an end to the process that insight is. Nor can it be made easy: without the crucial affect, insight is but a compulsive's emotionally sanitized verbiage.

To transcend our recurrent crises of meaning demands that we transcend culture and the distorted childhoods that perpetuate it and its paranoid-schizoid systems of meaning. The psychodynamically genuine solution to the problem is paradoxical: not flight *from* psychic pain, which only assures its perpetuity, but the experiencing of what can only be called curative pain. As Winnicott long ago wrote, what is required is "to re-experience this intolerable anxiety on account of which defences were organized" (1962, p. 238). With Sartre, most contend that hell is other people. The beginning of integration is the humbling recognition that hell is myself. Therein lies the promise of a liberation that properly belongs to all humankind: a human species that, first having had the courage to face itself, encountered reality face to face and lived.

References

Barkow, J. H. Conformity to ethos and reproductive success in two Hausa communities: An empirical evaluation. *Ethos*, 1977, *5*, 409–425.

Barth, F. (Ed.). *Ethnic groups and boundaries*. Boston: Little, Brown, 1969.

Beavers, W. R. A theoretical basis for family evaluation. In J. M. Lewis, W. R. Beavers, J. T. Gossett, and V. A. Philips, *No single thread: Psychological health in family systems*. New York: Brunner/Mazel, 1976.

Becker, E. *The birth and death of meaning*. New York: Free Press, 1962.

Bidney, D. Human nature and the cultural process. *American Anthropologist*, 1947, *49*, 375–399.

Boyer, L. B. On aspects of the mutual influences of anthropology and psychoanalysis. *The Journal of Psychological Anthropology*, 1978, *1*, 297–320.

Boyer, L. B. *Childhood and folklore: A psychoanalytic study of Apache personality*. New York: The Library of Psychological Anthropology, 1979.

Brody, B. Freud's analysis of American culture. *The Psychoanalytic Review*, 1976, *63*, 361–377.

deMause, L. The psychogenic theory of history. *The Journal of Psychohistory*, 1977, *4*, 253–267.

deMause, L. Historical group-fantasies. *The Journal of Psychohistory*, 1979, *7*, 1–70.

Devereux, G. Social structure and the economy of affective bonds. *The Psychoanalytic Review*, 1942, *29*, 303–314.

Devereux, G. (Ed.). *Psychoanalysis and the occult*. New York: International Universities Press, 1953. (Reprinted, 1970.)

Devereux, G. Charismatic leadership and crisis. In W. Muensterberger & S. Axelrad (Eds.), *Psychoanalysis and the social sciences* (Vol. 4). New York: International Universities Press, 1955.

Devereux, G. *From anxiety to method in the behavioral sciences*. The Hague: Mouton, 1967.

Devereux, G. *Reality and dream: Psychotherapy of a Plains Indian*. New York: New York University Press, 1969. (Originally published, 1951.)

Devereux, G. Art and mythology: A general theory. In C. F. Jopling (Ed.), *Art and aesthetics in primitive societies*. New York: E. P. Dutton, 1971.

Devereux, G. The works of George Devereux. In G. D. Spindler (Ed.), *The making of psychological anthropology*. Berkeley, Calif.: University of California Press, 1978.

Devereux, G. *Basic problems of ethno-psychiatry*. Chicago: University of Chicago Press, 1980.

DeVos, G. A. Cross-cultural studies of mental disorder: An anthropological perspective. In S. Arienti (Ed.), *American handbook of psychiatry* (2nd ed.). Vol. 2: *Child and adolescent: sociocultural and community psychiatry* (G. Kaplan, Ed.). New York: Basic Books, 1974.

DeVos, G. A. The dangers of pure theory in social anthropology. *Ethos*, 1975, *3*, 77–91.

DeVos, G. A. Ethnic adaptation and minority status. *Journal of Cross-Cultural Psychology*, 1980, *11*, 101–124.

Dundes, A. Projection in folklore: A plea for psychoanalytic semiotics. *Modern Language Notes*, 1976, *91*, 1530–1533.

Durkheim, E. *The elementary forms of the religious life*. New York: Collier, 1961. (Originally published, 1912.)

Eliot, T. S. *Four quartets*. London: Faber and Faber, 1944.

Erikson, E. H. *Childhood and society* (revised ed.). New York: Norton, 1963.

Ferguson, D. N. *Music as metaphor: The elements of expression*. Minneapolis: University of Minnesota Press, 1960.

Ferreira, A. J. Family myth and homeostasis. *Archives of General Psychiatry*, 1963, *9*, 55–61.

Freud, S. A case of successful treatment by hypnotism. J. Strachey (Ed.), *Standard edition* (Vol. I). London: Hogarth Press, 1953. (Originally published, 1892–1893).

Freud, S. The interpretation of dreams. In J. Strachey (Ed.), *Standard edition* (Vols. IV & V). London, Hogarth Press, 1953. (Originally published, 1900.)

Freud, S. *The future of an illusion*. New York: Anchor, 1957.

Fromm, E. *Escape from freedom*. New York: Farrar and Rinehart, 1941.

Fromm, E. *The crisis of psychoanalysis*. New York: Fawcett, 1970.

Geertz, C. Deep play: Notes on the Balinese cockfight. *Daedalus*, 1972, *101*, 1–37.

Hall, E. T. *Beyond culture*. Garden City, N.Y.: Doubleday/Anchor, 1977.

Hallowell, I. *Culture and experience*. Philadelphia: University of Pennsylvania Press, 1955.

Hardesty, D. L. The human ecological niche. *American Anthropologist, 1972, 74,* 458–466.

Hartmann, H. *Ego psychology and the problem of adaptation*. New York: International Universities Press, 1958. (Originally published, 1939.)

Hartmann, H., Kris, E., & Loewenstein, R. M. Some psychoanalytic comments on 'culture and personality.' In W. Muensterberger (Ed.), *Man and his culture*. New York: Taplinger, 1970.

Hippler, A. E. Cultural evolution: Some hypotheses concerning the significance of cognitive and affective interpenetration during latency. *The Journal of Psychological Anthropology, 1977, 4,* 419–438, 455–460.

Jones, E. The theory of symbolism. In *Papers on psychoanalysis*. Baltimore: Williams and Wilkins, 1948.

Jones, E. Mother-right and sexual ignorance of savages. In *Essays in applied psychoanalysis* (Vol. 2). New York: International Universities Press, 1964. (Originally published, 1924.)

Kardiner, A. *The individual and his society*. New York: Columbia University Press, 1939.

Kiefer, C. W., & Cowan, J. State/context dependence and theories of ritual. *The Journal of Psychological Anthropology, 1979, 2,* 53–83.

Kluckhohn, C. The influence of psychiatry on anthropology in America during the past one hundred years. In J. K. Hall, G. Zilboorg, & H. A. Bunker (Eds.), *One hundred years of American psychiatry*. New York: Columbia University Press, 1944.

Koenigsberg, R. A. *Hitler's ideology: A study in psychoanalytic sociology*. New York: Library of Social Science, 1975.

Korzybski, A. *Science and sanity*. Lancaster, Pa.: The International Non-Aristotelian Library, 1933.

La Barre, W. The influence of Freud on anthropology. *American Imago, 1958, 15,* 275–328.

La Barre, W. Religions, Rorschachs, and tranquilizers. *American Journal of Orthopsychiatry, 1959, 29,* 688–698.

La Barre, W. Transference cures in religious cults and social groups. *Journal of Psychoanalysis in Groups, 1962, 1,* 66–75.

La Barre, W. Personality from a psychoanalytic viewpoint. In E. Norbeck (Ed.), *The study of personality*. New York: Holt, Rinehart & Winston, 1968. (a)

La Barre, W. *The human animal*. Chicago: University of Chicago Press, 1968. (b) (Originally published, 1954.)

La Barre, W. *They shall take up serpents*. New York: Schocken, 1969.

La Barre, W. Materials for a history of studies of crisis cults: A bibliographic essay. *Current Anthropology, 1971, 12,* 3–44.

La Barre, W. *The ghost dance: The origins of religion*. New York: Dell, 1972.

La Barre, W. Anthropological perspectives on hallucination and hallucinogens. In R. K. Siegel & L. J. West (Eds.), *Hallucinations: Behavior, experience and theory*. New York: John Wiley and Sons, 1975.

La Barre, W. The clinic and the field. In G. D. Spindler (Ed.), *The making of psychological anthropology*. Berkeley: University of California Press, 1978. (a)

La Barre, W. Psychoanalysis and the biology of religion. *The Journal of Psychological Anthropology, 1978, 1,* 57–64. (b)

Levi-Strauss, C. *Race and history*. Paris: UNESCO, 1968.

Lewis, I. (Ed.). *Symbols and sentiments: Cross-cultural studies in symbolism*. London: Academic Press, 1977.

Mahler, M., & Pine, F. *On human symbiosis and the vicissitudes of individuation*. New York: International Universities Press, 1968.

Mahler, M., Pine, F., & Bergman, A. *The psychological birth of the human infant: Symbiosis and individuation*. New York: Basic Books, 1975.

Malcolm, J. The impossible profession—II. *The New Yorker,* December 1, 1980, pp. 55–152.

Malinowski, B. *Magic, science, and religion*. New York: Doubleday/Anchor, 1954.

McLuhan, M. *Understanding media*. New York: McGraw-Hill, 1964.

Menninger, K. A. *Man against himself*. New York: Harcourt, Brace, 1938.

Mumford, L. Technics and the nature of man. In M. Krazenberg & W. H. Davenport (Eds.), *Technology and culture: An anthology*. New York: New American Library, 1972.

Paul, R. A. Symbolic interpretation in psychoanalysis and anthropology. *Ethos*, 1980, *8*, 286–294.

Rado, S. *Motivational psychodynamics: Motivation and control*. New York: Science House, 1969.

Róheim, G. *Psychoanalysis and anthropology*. New York: International Universities Press, 1950.

Rycroft, C. Review of *The quest for identity* by A. Wheelis (London: Gallancy, 1959). *International Journal of Psychoanalysis*, 1960, *41*, 87.

Rycroft, C. *Anxiety and neurosis*. Baltimore: Penguin, 1970.

Sapir, E. Cultural anthropology and psychiatry. In D. Mandelbaum (Ed.), *Culture, language and personality: Selected essays*. Berkeley, Calif.: University of California Press, 1949.

Sarnoff, C. *Latency*. New York: Jason Aronson, 1976.

Silverberg, W. V. The factor of omnipotence in neurosis. *Psychiatry*, 1949, *12*, 387.

Speer, D. C. Family systems: Morphostasis and morphogenesis, or is homeostasis enough? *Family Process*, 1970, *9*, 259–278.

Sperber, D. *Rethinking symbolism* (A. L. Morton, trans.). Cambridge: Cambridge University Press, 1975.

Sperber, D. Comment on *The female Lingam* by G. E. Ferro-Luzzi. *Current Anthropology*, 1979, *21*, 61.

Spindler, G. D. Introduction to part I. In G. D. Spindler (Ed.), *The making of psychological anthropology*. Berkeley, Calif.: University of California Press, 1978.

Spiro, M. Religious systems as culturally constituted defense mechanisms. In *Context and meaning in cultural anthropology*. New York: Free Press, 1965.

Spiro, M. Culture and human nature. In G. D. Spindler (Ed.), *The making of psychological anthropology*. Berkeley, Calif.: University of California Press, 1978.

Spiro, M. *Gender and culture*. Durham, N.C.: Duke University Press, 1979.

Stein, H. F. Aging and death among Slovak-Americans: A study in the thematic unity of the life-cycle. *The Journal of Psychological Anthropology*, 1978, *1*, 297–320. (a)

Stein, H. F. The Slovak-American 'swaddling ethos': Homeostat for family dynamics and cultural continuity. *Family Process*, 1978, *17*, 31–45. (b)

Stein, H. F. Historical understanding as sense of history: A psychoanalytic inquiry. *The Psychoanalytic Review*, in press.

Thomas, K. *Religion and the decline of magic*. New York: Scribner's, 1971.

Tierney, J. Against the drift. *Science 81*, 1981, *2*, 92–94.

Watzlawick, P., Beavin, J., & Fisch, R. *Change: Principles of problem formation and problem resolution*. New York: Norton, 1974.

Whitehead, A. N. *Symbolism: Its meaning and effect*. New York: Capricorn, 1959. (Originally published, 1927.)

Whiting, J. W. M. Socialization process and personality. In F. L. K. Hsu (Ed.), *Psychological anthropology: Approaches to culture and personality*. Homewood, Ill.: Dorsey Press, 1961.

Winnicott, D. W. The theory of the parent-infant relationship: Further remarks. *International Journal of Psychoanalysis*, 1962, *43*, 238–239.

Winnicott, D. W. The location of cultural experience. *International Journal of Psychoanalysis*, 1967, *48*, 368–372.

23

Dialectics, Ethnography, and Educational Research

Morris A. Okun, Elizabeth C. Fisk, and Elizabeth A. Brandt

Introduction

Dissatisfaction with current approaches to research in educational contexts has lead to a search for new direction—both methodologically and theoretically. Recent trends in educational research suggest that a dialectical *theoretical orientation,* as outlined by Riegel (1979), can offer useful guidelines for formulating substantive research questions and generating the scope and structure of theoretical concepts relevant to studying educational settings. At the same time, ethnography, the method of inquiry of sociocultural anthropology, promises to provide a compatible *valid organon* (Rychlak, 1976) or set of basic principles for conducting educational research on topics of interest to dialecticians. Further, by conducting educational ethnographies within Riegel's dialectical framework, researchers will be in sync with the actors in the social scenes under investigation, since it appears probable that students learn ethnographically and think dialectically.

Dialectics is concerned with the study of actions and changes (Riegel, 1976a), seeking the essence of a phenomenon which can be disclosed only by conducting an extensive and concrete study. Recently, there has been an upsurge of interest among developmental psychologists in the perspectives provided by a dialectical orientation (e.g., Huston-Stein & Baltes, 1976). Baltes and Cornelius, (1977) have suggested that this movement reflects the mutual focus of developmentalists and dialecticians

---

Morris A. Okun ● Department of Higher and Adult Education, Arizona State University, Tempe, Arizona 85287. *Elizabeth C. Fisk* ● Department of Higher and Adult Education, Arizona State University, Tempe, Arizona 85287. *Elizabeth A. Brandt* ● Department of Anthropology, Arizona State University, Tempe, Arizona 85287. This chapter was facilitated by an award (NIE-C-400-78-0061) made by the National Institute of Education to the Department of Higher and Adult Education, Arizona State University. The views expressed in this chapter are the authors' and do not necessarily reflect the views of the National Institute of Education.

on process and change. With the introduction of dialectics into American developmental psychology by Riegel (1973) and Rychlak (1976), advocates have called for
a theoretical framework grounded in the dialectical interactions between the changing individual and the changing world (Wozniak, 1975).

Riegel (1976a) has suggested that education is an area ripe for the application
of dialectics inasmuch as one of the functions of education in postindustrial societies
should be to enhance the capability of individuals to cope with the accelerated rate
of change (Toffler, 1974). Within the dialectical orientation, the teacher is viewed
as an intermediary between the student and society. To accomplish their objectives,
teacher and learners should engage in encounters inducing dialectical thinking
(Okun, Fisk, & Toppenberg, 1978).

A fundamental issue has been raised concerning whether dialectics provides a
method for understanding change. Baltes and Cornelius (1977) disputed Riegel's
(1976a) claim that the empirical translation of dialectical questions requires the formulation of unique research methods. Instead, they argued that it is important to
view dialectics as a theoretical orientation as opposed to a way of coming to know
truth (e.g., valid organon; Rychlak, 1976).

In summarizing their position, Baltes and Cornelius (1977) stated:

1. Dialectics may best be regarded as a perspective or an orientation in the
   sense of a metaphor. It is not an acceptable procedure or prescriptive method
   for knowledge generation in the empirical sciences.
2. Viewing dialectics as an orientation and not as a mehod in the empirical
   sciences leads to a refutation of any monolithic method of research implementation. (p. 131)

Consistent with this view is Kvale's (1977) assertion that in employing the dialectical orientation to study interacting human beings, it is possible to use a wide
array of research methods. We agree inasmuch as a pluralistic approach to methods
is consistent with the multiple views of reality associated with the dialectical
approach (Meacham, 1975). Nonetheless, we contend that a certain genre of
research method, the ethnographic mehod of sociocultural anthropology, may be
more useful than others as a vehicle for conducting educational research derived
from a dialectical orientation (Lourenço, 1976). Ethnography represents a particularly viable valid organon for dialectical inquiries since ethnography and dialectics
share many underlying assumptions.

In the next section, an overview of the dialectical orientation will be provided,
followed by a review of the major tenets of ethnography. Subsequently, ethnography
and the dialectical orientation will be compared. In the concluding section of the
chapter, a rationale will be provided for conducting educational research from a dialectical framework and using an ethnographic approach.

Overview of Dialectics

There are many historical roots and meanings of dialectics (Hook, 1957). Several diverse theories based on dialectical perspectives have been formulated within
the social sciences (Baltes & Cornelius, 1977). Our specific focus is on the dialectical

orientation to human development proposed by Riegel (1973). Five major issues are considered: (1) dialectics and change, (2) dialectics and development, (3) dialectics and cognitive operations, (4) subjects and objects, and (5) dialectics and dialogues.

Dialectical Changes

Riegel viewed human development as consisting of short-term situational changes, long-term developmental changes, and their interaction. The basic tenet of Riegel's theretical orientation is that development is the result of synchronization of progressions along four interdependent, but unique, dimensions: (1) inner-biological, (2) individual-psychological, (3) cultural-sociological, and (4) outer-physical. A corollary notion is that individuals have a reciprocal relationship with their world; that is, as the individuals act to change the world, they change it in ways that ultimately change themselves.

The environment and the individual both take on active roles. Additionally, the individual's development is codetermined by other active organisms. Development itself lies neither in the individual alone nor in the social group but in the dialectical interactions of the two. The individual is viewed as an organized totality, a system of parts in interaction, such that each part derives its meaning from the whole (cf. Wertsch, this volume).

Dialectics and Development

The impetus for development occurs when there is a lack of coordination between two dimensions. These contradictory conditions, or *crises,* are viewed as an opportunity for growth. Moreover, the dialectical view assumes that asynchrony between the dimensions is ever-present (except for momentary periods of synchronization) and that contradiction is both inherent in nature and mind and essential for development. Thus, although the individual strives for synchronization, it is inevitable that the individual will respond to contradictions arising from the continuous changes in the relations among the various dimensions interacting in developmental progressions. Balance is a fleeting achievement as the individual engages in actions elicited by the interplay of inner and outer forces. As soon as the individual completes a developmental task, new questions and doubts arise in the individual as well as in society.

Thus, the dialectical view rejects the notion of stable traits and balanced equilibriums. Instead, the individual, as well as the world, is seen as process, that is, as being in a *ceaseless flux.* Development does not consist of incremental gains but, rather, progresses in dialectical leaps. Riegel (1979, p. 23) suggested "that the dialectical orientation integrates open and closed systems, allowing for information accumulation which leads to internal reorganization."

Simultaneously, knowledge influences and is influenced by the individual's activities (Wozniak, 1973). The concept of praxis highlights the codeterminous nature of activity and knowledge (Rappoport, 1975). In dialectics, the aim is to accomplish change through praxis. The criterion of knowledge is the praxis that it leads to.

In sum, developmental changes are the result of the complex interplay of a host of forces operating on (and being operated on by) an active individual. The changes

represent qualitative syntheses of quantitative inputs and are genuine transformations, yielding successively different, emergent forms.

Dialectics and Cognitive Operations

Riegel (1975a) proposed that an individual at any cognitive developmental level
may directly progress to dialectical operations, reaching thereby a "mature" stage
of thinking. That persons may reach dialectic maturity without ever passing through
the (Piagetian) period of formal operations implies interindividual variation at the
general level of maturity and intraindividual variation at the level of functioning
within specific contexts. The course of development is both nonlinear and multidi-
rectional (Riegel, 1976c). Although the process of development has no definite end
point, mature cognitive development is characterized by tolerance for, and appreciation of, contradiction (Wozniak, 1975). Problem *finding* involves discovering many
general questions from ill-defined problems (divergent thinking). In contrast, problem *solving* typically involves discovering one specific acceptable answer to one well-
defined problem (convergent thinking; Mackworth, 1965). For dialectics, it is more
important to find out how challenges are recognized and how questions are asked
than how problems are solved and how answers are given.

Subjects and Objects

In focusing on the developmental interdependence of organism and environment, individual and society, Riegel (1975b) argued for subject–object interpenetration as opposed to subjct–object alienation. In the context of the psychological experiment, the paradox emerged that the objects of the experiments came to be known
as the subjects. Consequently, the subjects' individual and social qualities were minimized (although they refused to "disappear"; see, e.g., Weber & Cook, 1972).

Dialectics stresses the interdependence of the observing subject and the observed
phenomenon, of observation and active interpretation. Thus, the study of development must acknowledge the participatory role of the subject and the reciprocal relationship between investigator and subject (Basseches, 1980). Riegel (1975b) suggested that investigators and subjects engage in a collaborative enteprise in which
the emphasis is on lived experiences and directed actions instead of experientially
empty performances.

Riegel also criticized psychologists for failing to pay adequate attention to
meaning and context. Reacting to the efforts of researchers to *eliminate* meaningfulness as a source of *error* variance, Riegel (1979) commented:

> Meaning is not something that can be added later to the system analyzed;
> rather, it is the most fundamental topic. Strictly speaking, it is the only topic
> for any inquiry by human beings of human beings. (p. 3)

The focus on meaning requires acknowledgment of its relationship to context (Mishler, 1979 cf. Slama-Cazacu, this volume). Currently, camps within sociolinguistics,
cognitive sociology, and cognitive psychology emphasize the context dependency of
language, knowledge, learning, meaning, and action (see Garfinkel, 1967; Jenkins,
1974; Labov, 1972). Contrary to other developmental orientations, the dialectical

perspective brings meaning in context to the fore. Riegel (1979) put the matter this way:

> By disregarding the contextual implications, psychologists, thereby have brought themselves into the unfortunate position of having eliminated meaning from their consideration, that is, those aspects that ought to be of greatest interest in their analysis of language acquisition and use. (p. 71)

The dialectical view seeks to take into account the multiple views of the various aspects of realty and their organization (Meacham, 1975). Psychologists are encouraged to unravel the complex interaction of historical and sociocultural factors on the course of development (Riegel, 1977). The development of universal laws requires studies of the inner and outer dialectics and their interaction with psychological processes. Such laws will be based on research emanating from sociological, anthropological, and biological, as well as psychological, traditions. In addition, dialectics is the concrete analysis of concrete conditions. Understanding a phenomenon requires analysis of internal contradictions and differences manifested under varying social and historical conditions.

Dialectics and Dialogues

The study of dialogues was singled out by Riegel (1979, p. 109) as representing an exemplary topic for the investigation of dialectical development and change (cf. Cazden, this volume). In terms of methodology, the study of dialogues forces a departure from the subject–object alienation prevalent in psychological and educational research. In research on dialogues, both speakers are concurrently subject and object and the researcher is examining the outer dialectics between the individual and social conditions. By emphasizing "performance" dialogues between individuals instead of internal operations by noninteracting individuals, it should be possible to construct a theory of the dialogues of human development.

A theory of dialogic interaction embraces dialectical principles if successful communication is viewed as reflecting a thesis–antithesis–synthesis process. From this perspective, the original statement represents a thesis. The reply modifying the original utterance denotes an antithesis. The second statement by the initial speaker, taking into account the message of the second speaker, constitutes a synthesis. Typically, conversations are prolonged as thesis and antithesis are elaborated. The dialogue is imbued with a reflective character, that is, the thesis provides the stimulus for, and is an anticipatory response to, the antithesis. On the other hand, the antithesis alters the thesis and permits synthesis at a higher level.

In an unsuccessful dialogue, speakers may fail to assimilate the other person's statements and/or accommodate their own. Consequently, there is no *progression* of viewpoints. To coordinate a dialogue, then, requires the active participation of both individuals in the roles of listener and speaker. According to Riegel (1979),

> the synchronization or transformational coordination of their actions with their overt speech acts as well as the synchronization of both speakers' statements in the alternations of a successful dialogue represent the fundamental basis of individual and social developments. (pp. 97–98)

Understanding contradiction is an important ingredient in developing a meaningful interpretation of dialogue (Freedle, 1975). The dialectical orientation, with its emphasis on the internal contradictions of all elements and relations, is well suited to analyzing the contradictory aspects of dialogues (Harris, 1975). In terms of analyzing dialogues at a symbolization level, symbol use is triggered by contradiction (Bateson, 1972). For example, a teacher may nominate student A to respond to a question but then may quickly "close out" the student by rescinding the turn and allocating it to student B (Mehan, 1978). Here, the teacher is signaling to student A, "Calling on you is not an opportunity for you to speak; instead it's an opportunity to demonstrate that you have nothing to say." The symbolic meaning of the communication is a synthesis of the contradictory aspects of the message (Bateson, 1972). The tension in contradictions is dialectical because elements in the dialogue both deny and presuppose each other (Harris, 1975).

Thus, dialectics contends that to understand the phenomenon of dialogues, it must be investigated in its multiple aspects. Contradictions are manifested in the thesis–antithesis–synthesis process. Dialectics also places an emphasis on the multiple sources of data provided by communication acts, including their symbolic aspects. Finally, dialectics accepts conflicting and interdependent conceptions and encourages pluralistic views.

Riegel's dialectical framework receives additional support from some recent developments within the physical sciences. The Belgian Nobel laureate Ilya Prigogine has shown that the orderliness of biological systems, which used to be an exception to the gradually increasing disorder in the universe predicted by the Second Law of Thermodynamics, is now the general case, and physical systems in equilibrium are the exception. Prigogine showed that systems far from equilibrium have special properties. They are self-organizing. Random fluctuations in an open system which exchanges energy or matter with the outside may reach a point at which they will drive the system to an entirely *new* order (Prigogine, 1976, 1980). Information systems and human systems are self-organizing structures which exchange energy with the environment. Prigogine's work has had great success in dealing with problems in physical and biological chemistry, in modeling urban traffic flows, and in complex ecological systems. Prigogine stressed that any nonequilibrium system will have fluctuations. They may be damped by the system, but if they exceed a certain size, they will instead drive the system to a new structure. This is true at both the individual and the societal levels. The dialectic between the mass and the minority takes on a new meaning when viewed through Prigogine's (1976) theory. Similarly, the theory provides a model for viewing individual development and change.

Ethnography as Valid Organon

Sociocultural anthropologists have developed a distinctive approach to research usually termed *ethnography*. While ethnography with its many variants is difficult to define by a set of precise characteristics, it can be described by referring to prototypical examples of research carried out under that rubric (Sanday, 1979). In prototypical ethnography, lone anthropologists journey to small, isolated communities in unfamiliar parts of the world where they take up residence for an extended period of time. The ethnographers' purpose in their chosen setting is to describe the way of life of the people in as much detail as possible. Through this description, they hope to reveal the nature of a particular culture. Culture, the central concept in sociocultural anthropology, is complex, composed of several interrelated systems including at least technoeconomic, social-structural, and the ideational systems (Kaplan & Manners, 1972). Variants of ethnography can be recognized in terms of preferred data collecion techniques and theoretical stance. For example, cognitive anthropologists emphasize the ideational subsystem of a culture, whereas materialist anthropologists are primarily interested in the study of the technoeconomic system.

Although the ethnographers may lack specific hypotheses to test or a strictly formulated data collection procedure to follow, they bring along an often implicit list of the aspects of culture usually described in a completed ethnography, a set of analytical categories normally found in an ethnographer's vocabulary, and a concern for certain broad questions about culture which they know will be discussed with colleagues when they return from the field.

Without a prescribed sequence of steps to follow in developing their cultural description, ethnographers nonetheless engage in a set of customary activities (Pelto & Pelto, 1980). These activities or *field work* include participant and nonparticipant observation, informal and formal interviews, document analysis, and various "unobtrusive measures" (Webb, Campbell, Schwartz, & Sechrest, 1966). Although original, often highly specialized techniques have been developed by inventive ethnographers, these never supplant the more basic components of field work.

The data collected during fieldwork are recorded in voluminous field notes which are later coded and analyzed to produce a final product, an *ethnography*. The ethnography will include narrative accounts of events and series of events along with a discussion of the meanings of these events to the members of the community. Also included will be more analytic treatments of various topics which seem to capture what is distinctive about the culture observed.

Ethnography evolved as an approach to research through the study of nonindustrial communities, but, increasingly, anthropologists have turned their attention to their own urban cultures. At the same time, the lack of syncretism in modern industrial societies has caused anthropologists to focus on particular settings and activities (Bromlei, 1980). Ethnography of education is currently one of the fastest growing subfields of ethnography in the United States (see collections of recent work in Gilmore & Glatthorn, 1982; Green & Wallet, 1981; Roberts & Akinsanya, 1976; Spindler, 1982). This area of study has been promoted on the one hand by educators who recognize a need for more longitudinal, qualitative, and open-ended research after decades of disappointment with narrow, experimental, quantitative research and on the other hand, by anthropologists who acknowledge the central importance of education within a culture as well as the practical necessity of doing research which will be financially supported.

However, the adoption of the label *ethnography* to refer to recent qualitative research in education and other applied fields has sometimes reflected overenthusiasm for, rather than an understanding of, ethnographic research (Brandt, 1982; Rist, 1980; Wolcott, 1975). Too often, researchers have merely adopted one or more fieldwork techniques or forms of presentation which, when divorced from the tradition in which they emerged, take on at least a different if not an ineffectual function.

The ethnographic research tradition represents neither a loose collection of techniques nor a single unified methodology. Rather, ethnography can be seen to stand as a cover term for a developing valid organon for research in sociocultural anthropology, where *organon* is considered as a set of basic principles about how valid knowledge can be acquired (Bacon, 1620/1960; Rychlak, 1976). As organon, ethnography embodies the epistemological base of an important brand of qualitative research. If the fieldworkers' techniques are used in ways inconsistent with these epistemological assumptions, the research is not ethnography. Although the extensive catalog of specific techniques which has been developed and adapted by sociocultural anthropologists reveals much about the epistemological assumptions of the researchers, it is not the techniques themselves which give ethnography its distinctive character. Most if not all of these techniques are also used by other disciplines. Ethnographers are encouraged to use a wide variety of techniques within a single study, to invent new techniques, and to borrow unashamedly from other disciplines. There is an implicit understanding, however, that all procedures will be used in accordance with the ethnographic organon.

Until recently, research methodology was not a common topic of discussion among sociocultural anthropologists, and ethnographies included only very general descriptions of the procedures used by the researchers. However, the lack of explicit attention to methodology was not recognized as a problem because the community of researchers shared an implicit organon which they asserted by saying they were "doing ethnography."

Currently, however, because of the demand for ethnographic studies in applied areas such as education and because of the participation of anthropologists on multidisciplinary research teams, many attempts have been made to explicate ethnography both for collaborators outside the anthropological community and for anthropologists themselves who are conducting research in situations distressingly different from the familiar prototypical cases (Erickson, 1979; Heath, 1982; Wax & Wax, 1980; Wilcox, 1982). Anthropologists and nonanthropologists who are extending the uses of ethnography have a need to understand ethnography as organon.

It is as an organon that we suggest ethnography as potentially appropriate for research in dialectics. In this section we will discuss four basic principles of the ethnographic organon. Then we will consider the degree of fit between these principles and the tenets of dialectics.

Subject–Object Interdependence

For any given cultural situation, ethnography values not only the interpretation proposed by the researcher but also the insider's interpretations offered by the participants. It seeks to learn about reality from the point of view of the participants. This position has long been taken by those anthropologists who focus on the ideational subsystem of culture (Geertz, 1973). Recently the "new ethnography" influenced by symbolic interactionism (Blumer, 1972) and cognitive sociology (Goodenough, 1971) has placed renewed emphasis on meanings in cultural analysis. Because people are seen to operate at the level of meanings, to be meaning-makers, objective descriptions of events in a community become trivial without discussion of their interpretation by members of that community (cf. Nadin, this volume).

Ethnographers have borrowed from linguistics the terms *emic* and *etic* to refer to the insider and outsider interpretations, respectively. *Emic* is taken from the term *phonemic,* which refers to the categories of speech sounds considered as distinct by native speakers of a given language, while *etic* comes from *phonetic,* referring to the researcher's system for describing (by standardized scales of measurement for physical properties) all possible variation in speech sound in any language (Pike, 1967). Linguists realize that both phonemic and phonetic descriptions are necessary to make valid and useful statements about language. In the same way, ethnographers recognize both native and researcher perspectives as essential to valid knowledge about a culture.

The ethnographer strives to establish and maintain rapport with participants, particularly key informants. Members of the community under study have been explicitly recognized as co-investigators (Hale, 1972). In educational ethnography, there has been a recent emphasis on collaborative investigation with joint input from teachers and outside researchers (Florio & Walsh, 1976; Griffin, 1980; Smith & Geoffrey, 1969). The common humanity of the co-investigators is stressed and reciprocity is actively pursued, with the onus on the ethnographer to "give back" as well as to "take out." Ethnographers attempt to avoid treating the subjects as objects and try to respect them as experts in their setting.

Further, an anthropologist usually takes on the role of participant observer, attempting to combine in one individual the perspectives of insider and outsider. To be effective in these dual roles, participant observers must maintain a "dialectic" tension between their own emic and etic perspectives (Wax, 1971).

The inclusion of both insider (emic) and outsider (etic) perspectives implies an assumption of the validity of multiple interpretations of the same reality. In line with this assumption, the ethnographer goes on to document the perspectives of participants with varying roles and statuses within the same setting. Multiple sources of data are exploited to "triangulate" any one bit of knowledge about the setting. Ideally, multiple emic and etic interpretations are overlayed to provide a "thick" description (Geertz, 1973) of the same cultural scenes. Because ethnographers value and seek out multiple views, they learn to tolerate and even value a high level of ambiguity during the course of the fieldwork (cf. Berry, this volume).

Holism

The second basic epistemological assumption of ethnography as organon is that cultural phenomena must be studied holistically. Ethnographers study all of a way of life. If they focus on one aspect of a culture such as child-rearing or religious practices, that aspect is always studied in context and all other aspects of the culture are related to it. The holism advocated in ethnography is very broad, applying not to a single system such as the sociostructural, technoeconomic, or ideational systems but to the whole set of such interacting systems that comprises the culture (Kaplan & Manners, 1972). None of these systems reveals its true nature unless it is viewed in interaction with all the rest. Because of its holistic nature, ethnography has been called an "omniscience" (Erickson, 1979, p. 59) or a "super discipline" (Bromlei, 1980, p. 5).

The holistic approach of ethnography leads to other principles for gaining valid knowledge. First, it motivates the effort to achieve triangulation of multiple data sources and data collection procedures, since the researcher with access to "multiple outcroppings" (Webb *et al.,* 1966) of the same phenomenon is better able to tap its position within the entirety of the interacting systems of the culture. Because ethnographers study systems, they advocate unobtrusive and nonreactive research techniques which result in a minimum of interference with the totality of the systems. Ethnographers try to blend with the environment as much as possible and merely select rather than manipulate or control phenomena of interest. Nature is seen as the inducer, and the researcher is seen as the transducer (Willems & Rausch, 1969).

Third, the naturalistic approach of ethnography leads to contextual relativity within a single ethnography but a search for universals through cross-cultural comparison. An ethnographer obtains, through a labor-intensive, time-consuming process, a thick, rich, elaborate description of a single culture which becomes the basis for statements about cultural phenomena. These statements are made with specific reference to the contexts in which they were studied; the meanings of cultural phenomena are seen to change with each context (Mishler, 1979). For example, even if the same child-rearing practice were to be found in a wide variety or even in all cultures, its significance might vary radically when seen within the overall working of each culture.

This concern with contextual specificity in ethnography, however, is balanced by the cross-cultural, comparative perspective of ethnology. Ethnologists seek universals through systematic comparison of ethnographies. They search for patterns of behavior, taking into account the full range of local factors. Generalizations emerge from the comparison of descriptions and interpretations across a wide array of settings (Cronbach, 1975). In this way, the ethnologist moves from the concrete to the abstract, from the specific to the general, from working hypotheses to universal laws. In the search for universal knowledge about culture, ethnography and ethnology are complementary. They embody the "dialectic of the universal and the particular" (Bromlei, 1980, p. 14). Each presupposes the other. Detailed, contextually relative statements from ethnography are essential for, and trivial without, the ethnologic effort in cross-cultural comparison.

Finally, the principle of holism leads to an appreciation of qualitative, narrative reporting as a nonreducible aspect of data storage and presentation (Hymes, 1978). Respect for narration comes from a desire to describe thickly "slices of life" which reflect the total culture and represent data in which all subsystems within the culture are revealed in interaction. In recent years, this desire for "whole" pieces of cultural data has led to the utilization of videotape and film as a supplement to firsthand narrative accounts.

Focus on Process and Change

By the preference for firsthand observation and detailed description of events, ethnography reveals its focus on process rather than simple input–output covariation. There is a major interest in *how* things happen—in sequences and patterns of activity within a single event and in regular cycles of events. The activity of the community is seen as ongoing and interlocking. Although ethnographers take slices of activity for more thorough analysis, they try to fit these slices into the overall fabric of activity. For this reason, they maintain a residence for an extended period of time and may return to the setting periodically to collect historical information, including, especially, life histories of individuals within the community.

This longitudinal information aids in the understanding of process and change. Although much of a ethnographer's interest is in establishing regular, recurring patterns, information about change and adaptation over time is seen as especially significant in revealing the underlying nature of the culture. Cultural change, considered as qualitative (or structural) change in the complex system that comprises a culture, is an important topic in ethnology (Foster, 1962; Steward, 1955). The search for universals, therefore, involves attention to sociohistorical as well as cross-cultural analysis. Constitutve ethnography, a new brand of educational ethnography largely in the tradition of symbolic interactionism and ethnomethodology, stresses a more dynamic view of culture as an ongoing process rather than an accomplished fact (Mehan, 1978, 1980). Continuous change is considered the *sine qua non* of *in vivo* situations.

Open Inquiry

A fourth basic principle of the ethnographic organon is the preference for an open-ended, self-generating sequence of research activities. In contrast to a prestructured, closed approach to research, ethnography does not begin with preconceived ideas about the gamut of techniques that will be used throughout the course of the research effort or about all the aspects of the ongoing cultural scene that will be investigated.

Although ethnographers are open-minded, they typically enter the field with a general theoretical orientation, general analytic (etic) categories, and research questions. On the basis of their own research, they generate more specific conceptual categories and hypotheses. As the concepts and hypotheses take form, they suggest the direction for continuing data collection. The developing hypotheses become the bases for decisions about where to look next, whom to talk to, what questions to ask, and what data to record.

Because it is so open-ended, ethnography is also self-correcting (Dawson, 1979). Field-workers seek contradictions to and negative instances of their developing conceptual framework. They state their current hypotheses, find contrasting data, and then formulate new hypotheses that take into account both the original hypotheses and the contrasting cases. Through the use of multiple data sources, ethnographers try to resolve apparent contradictions and achieve a higher level of synthesis. In this way, preliminary concepts and hypotheses are refined and expanded. Although analysis is a continual process, ethnographers experience breakthroughs as they gain insight into the latent structure of a phenomenon.

Just as the full research plan cannot be anticipated, the nature of the final product is also open. There is no logical end to the open-ended, self-generating process implied by the ethnographic organon, but whenever it stops—usually for external reasons—a product (i.e., an ethnography) appropriate for that point in the study can be devised.

The validity of the ethnography generated can be tested by the ability of the researcher to use it to predict events and to act as a culturally competent person in the social scene studied. It is also possible for the ethnographer to assess his or her analysis of the culture by sharing it with natives and obtaining feedback. Such validation is an acid test of knowledge since it depends on the ratings of the experts— the members of the culture. When a contextually grounded cultural analysis "works," it is likely to affect the actions of the participants, because they will readily be able to discern the concepts generated and their implications.

The final ethnography, however, does not attempt to provide final answers to research questions. Instead, its goal is the "enlargement of the universe of human discourse" (Geertz, 1973). In fact, the whole sequence of fieldwork, analysis, and write-up might be thought of not as an effort to answer questions conclusively but as an exercise in posing increasingly refined questions.

Compatibility of Dialectics and Ethnography

The central contention of this chapter is that ethnography and dialectics are well matched. Table I delineates 12 attributes of ethnography as valid organon and notes those principles of dialectics as a theoretical orientation which correspond to the attributes of ethnography. This table was constructed to provide support for the position that ethnography and dialectics are compatible. Inspection of this table indicates that *ethnography as a valid organon and dialectics as a theoretical orientation appear to be in synchrony. Ethnography offers dialectics a way of coming to know truth* (i.e., a valid organon), and *dialectics offers ethnography a general framework for guiding inquiries* (i.e., a theoretical orientation). However, there have as yet been no educational ethnographies which explicitly use Riegel's dialectical orientation. Thus, it is possible that a merger of the ethnographic research method with Riegel's dialectical orientation will lead to "high-yield" educational research (cf. Dittmar, this volume).

Students as Dialectical Ethnographers

In concluding this chapter, we hypothesize that by conducting ethnographies within the Riegelian dialectical framework, researchers will be in harmony with the participants in educational settings. Students and instructors carrying out their daily school-related activities seem to engage in ethnographic inquiries and dialectical thinking.

Observational data from a wide array of contexts suggest that individuals use ethnographic techniques naturally to acquire valuable survival information (Hymes, 1978). This is especially true of situations where there is an unequal distribution of power. Members of minority groups and women who are engaged in interaction with actors in more powerful positions often come to be better informed about appropriate structures, events, and behavior patterns than the elite are about those of the less powerful. Clearly, members of minority groups are expected to acquire the cultural patterns of the dominat society. Interaction across social and ethnic boundaries is necessary for such acquisition to take place. Classrooms can be considerd contexts

Table I. A Comparison of Ethnography as a Valid Organon and Dialectics as a Theoretical Orientation[a]

Attributes of enthography as a valid organon	Principles of dialectics as a theoretical orientation
Ethnography is committed to a holistic, comprehensive interpretation.	In dialectics, development is viewed as being determined by the complex interplay of four dimensions.
The ethnographer tries to learn reality from the participants' point of view.	Dialectics emphasizes the multiple views of the various aspects of reality and their organization.
The ethnographer seeks to describe and interpret multiple perspectives holistically.	Dialectics contends that to understand a phenomenon, it must be investigated in its multiple aspects.
The ethnographer has an interest in cultural change as qualitative change.	Dialectics is interested in discontinuous changes: quantitative changes which lead to qualitative changes.
Ethnography emphasizes hypothesis generation and category discovery.	Dialectics gives a high priority to posing problems and raising questions.
Ethnography is process-oriented.	Dialectics views the person as being in perpetual process; equilibrium is fleeting.
Ethnography views the sociohistorical context as critical.	In dialectics, the study of human behavior must consider the social and historical aspects of a given situation.
The ethnologist uses ethnographies as the basis for developing universals.	Dialectics seeks the essence of a phenomenon through concrete studies.
The ethnographer provides thick description through labor-intensive and time-consuming work.	Dialectics calls for extensive studies to uncover the phenomenon.
The ethnographer adopts an insider-outsider stance.	Dialectics emphasizes the interdependence of observing subject and the observed phenomenon, observation and active interpretation.
The ethnographer and the participants are co-investigators.	In dialectics, the researcher and participants are encouraged to engage in collaborative endeavor.
The ethnographer's ability to act as a native is the ultimate test of knowledge acquisition.	In dialectics, the criterion of knowledge is the praxis it leads to.

[a]There are many different branches of ethnography and dialectics. Some main aspects are delineated in this table. We present somewhat simplistic conceptions because our purpose is to compare ethnography with dialectics. In constructing this table, we drew extensively on discussions of naturalistic inquiry and dialectics by Guba (1978) and Kvale (1976), respectively.

for such "cross cultural" interaction (Florio, 1980, cited in Green, 1981) through which students must learn the dominant "school" culture of their teachers.

In a sense, students acquire their knowledge of school culture ethnographically; that is, through participant observation, they learn the meanings, norms, and patterns of life in the classroom (Sevigny, 1981). In a recent naturalistic study of a college classroom, Fisk (1981) noted that students seemed to be acting like participant observers in order to learn how to succeed in the course (cf. Kvale, this volume). They carefully observed the interaction in the classroom and interviewed other students about their perceptions of the instructor, the other participants, and the course demands. They especially valued certain "key informants" who had been the instructor's students before. Students analyzed all available documents, such as course schedules, blackboard writings, texts, and friends' lecture notes, and they took various "unobtrusive meaures" of the physical and temporal setting. For example, they considered the significance of rearrangements of furniture and of allotments of time for different activities.

The college students required triangulation of multiple expressions of information before they would accept it as legitimate. For example, just because an assignment appeared on a course schedule, it was not taken seriously until it was presented verbally by the instructor in class and confirmed as essential in conversation with other students. Repetition of information in various contexts from different sources increased authority. This preference for multiple sources of information was most evident during times of high demand and uncertainty but was always present to some extent in student strategies. The skillful use of triangulation and of ethnographic techniques of data collection may be the mark of both the competent student in a classroom setting and the researcher studying that setting.

By conducting classroom studies as ethnographers, researchers will be better able to interpret the ongoing activities they observe and to discern how students learn the rules for and make sense of their schooling experience. This theoretically based focus on how school processes are established and learned will extend while remaining consistent with recent classroom research carried out from the perspective of symbolic interactionism (Blumer, 1972) by cognitive sociologists and sociolinguists (see, for example, collected studies in Cicourel, Jennings, Jennings, Leiter, MacKay, Mehan, & Roth, 1974; Green & Wallet, 1981; Wilkinson, 1981). Mehan has termed this research "constitutive ethnography" (1978) and has linked it with the theoretical orientation of social constructivism because of its concern for the "principle that social structures and cognitive structures are composed and reside in the interaction between people" (Mehan, 1981, p. i.).

Such a sociogenetic position further considers students and teachers as "practical reasoners" (Cicourel, 1973; Cook-Gumperz, 1975) who, unlike scientific or logical reasoners, deal heuristically and practically with the world as it exists in its full complexity. Practical reasoners, concerned with their need to act in the world, constantly define and redefine indexical or prototypical concepts (Rosch & Mervis, 1975) and always consider specific phenomena in context. In one recent study of how teachers interpret their students' behaviors, Mehan, Hertwech, Combs, and Flynn (1981) observed that "instead of attending to behavior in isolation, teachers are attending to actions in context which includes the student, the task, the lesson, and the situation in which the action transpires" (p. 22).

The thinking of practical reasoners like teachers and students can be further illuminated if it is considered as dialectical in nature. Lourenço (1976) observed that dialectical thinking occurs as individuals carry out everyday activities, and Basseches (1980) found evidence that students think dialectically about their educational experiences. He conducted a study designed, in part, to ascertain students' thinking as they analyzed their educational activities. Protocol analysis of open-ended interviews with 18 freshman and seniors indicated that an average of seven "dialectical schemata" were used by the students. Although the evidence to date must be considered preliminary, there is a basis for contending that students act as ethnographers and think dialectically.

This chapter has raised questions and posed problems which could serve to initiate a dialogue among educational researchers, ethnographers, Riegelian-oriented dialecticians, and others. Such a dialogue could generate the methodological and theoretical guidelines needed to facilitate a fruitful redirection of research in educational contexts.

References

Bacon, F. *The new organon and related writings.* Indianapolis, Ind.: Bobbs-Merrill, 1960. (Originally published, 1620.)

Baltes, P. B., & Cornelius, S. W. The status of dialectics in developmental psychology: Theoretical orientation versus scientific method. In N. Datan & H. W. Reese (Eds.), *Life-span developmental psychology: Dialectical perspectives on experimental research.* New York: Academic Press, 1977.

Basseches, M. *An empirical study of dialectical thinking: What it contributes.* Paper presented at the meeting of the American Psychological Association, Montreal, September 1980.

Bateson, G. *Steps to an ecology of mind.* New York: Ballantine, 1972.

Blumer H. Symbolic interaction. In J. P. Spradley (Ed.), *Culture and cognition: Rules, maps, and plans.* San Francisco: Chandler, 1972.

Brandt, E. A. Popularity and peril: Ethnography and education. *International Review Journal of Philosophy and Social Science,* 1982.

Bromlei, I. V. On peculiarities of the ethnographic study of the contemporary world. *Soviet Anthropology and Archeology,* 1980, *18,* 3–31.

Cicourel, A. V. *Cognitive sociology: Language and meaning in social interaction.* London: Penguin, 1973.

Cicourel, A. V., Jennings, S. H. M., Jennings, K. H., Leiter, K. C. W., MacKay, R., Mehan, H., & Roth, D. R. *Language use and school performance.* New York: Academic Press, 1974.

Cook-Gumperz, J. The child as practical reasoner. In M. Sanches & B. G. Blount (Eds.). *Sociocultural dimensions of language use.* New York: Academic Press, 1975.

Cronbach. L. J. Beyond the two disciplines of scientific psychology. *American Psychologist,* 1975, *30,* 116–127.

Dawson, J. *Validity in qualitative inquiry.* Paper presented at the meeting of the American Educational Research Association, San Francisco, April 1979.

Erickson, F. Mere ethnography: Some problems in its use in educational practice. *Anthropology and Education Quarterly,* 1979, *10,* 182–188.

Fisk, E. C. *A microethnography of a lecture/lab college class* (Working paper on literacy). Tempe, Ariz.: Department of Higher and Adult Education, 1981.

Florio, S., & Walsh, M. *The teacher as colleague in classroom research.* Paper presented at the meeting of the American Educational Research Association, San Francisco, 1976.

Foster, G. M. *Traditonal cultures and the impact of technological change.* New York: Harper & Row, 1962.

Freedle, R. Dialogue and inquiry systems: The development of social logic. *Human Development,* 1975, *18,* 97–118.

Garfinkel, H. *Studies in ethnomethodology.* Englewood Cliffs, N.J.: Prentice-Hall, 1967.

Geertz, C. *The interpretation of culture.* New York: Basic Books, 1973.

Gilmore, P., & Glatthorn, A. A. (Eds.), *Children in and out of school: Ethnography and education.* Washington, D.C.: Center for Applied Linguistics, 1982.

Goodenough, W. *Culture, language and society.* Reading, Mass.: Addison-Wesley Modular Publications, 1971.

Green, J. L. *Contexts in classrooms: A sociolinguistic perspective.* Unpublished manuscript, University of Delaware, 1981.

Green, J. L., & Wallet, C. (Eds.). *Ethnography and language in educational settings.* Norwood, N.J.: Ablex, 1981.

Griffin, G. A. *Interactive research and development: Process, product, and consequences.* Unpublished manuscript, Teachers College, Columbia University, 1980.

Guba, E. G. *Toward a methodology of naturalistic inquiry in educational evaluation.* Los Angeles: Center for the Study of Evaluation, 1978.

Hale, K. A new perspective on American Indian linguistics. In A. Ortiz (Ed.), *New perspectives on the Pueblo.* Albuquerque, N.M.: University of New Mexico Press, 1972.

Harris, A. E. Social dialectics and language: Mother and child construct the discourse. *Human Development,* 1975, *18,* 80–96.

Heath, S. P. Ethnography in education: Defining the essentials. In P. Gilmore & A. A. Glatthorn (Eds.), *Children in and out of school:* Ethnography and education. Washington, D. C.: Center for Applied Linguistics, 1982.

Hook, S. *Dialectical matrialism and scientific method.* Manchester, England: Special supplement to the Bulletin of the Committee on Science and Freedom, 1957.

Huston-Stein, A. C., & Baltes P. B. Thory and method in life-span developmental psychology: Implications for child development. In H. W. Reese & L. P. Lipsett (Eds.), *Advances in child development and behavior* (Vol. 11). New York: Academic Press, 1976.

Hymes, D. H. *What is ethnography?* (Sociolinguistic Working Paper No. 45). Austin, Tex.: Southwest Educational Development Laboratory, 1978.

Jenkins, J. J. Remember that old theory of memory? Well forget it. *American Psychologist,* 1974, *29,* 785–795.

Kaplan, D. & Manners, R. *Culture theory.* Englewood Cliffs, N.J.: Prentice-Hall, 1972.

Kvale, S. Facts and dialectics. In J. F. Rychlak (Ed.), *Dialectic: Humanistic rationale for behavior and development.* New York: Karger, 1976.

Kvale, S. Dialectics and research on remembering. In N. Datan & M. W. Reese (Eds.), *Life-span developmental psychology: Dialectical perspectives on experimental research.* New York: Academic Press, 1977.

Labov, W. The study of language in its social context. In W. Labov (Ed.), *Sociolinguistic patterns.* Philadelphia: University of Pennsylvania Press, 1972.

Lourenço, S. V. The dialectic and qualitative methodology. In J. F. Rychlak (Ed.), *Dialectic: Humanistic rationale for behavior and development.* New York: Karger, 1976.

Mackworth, N. J. Originality. *American Psychologist,* 1965, *20,* 51–66.

Meacham, J. A. A dialectical approach to moral judgment and self-esteem. *Human Development,* 1975, *18,* 159–170.

Mehan, H. Structuring school structure. *Harvard Educational Review,* 1978, *48,* 32–64.

Mehan, H. The competent student. *Anthropology and Education Quarterly,* 1980, *11,* 131–152.

Mehan, H. *Social constructivism in psychology and sociology.* Unpublished manuscript, University of California, San Diego, 1981.

Mehan, H., Hertwech, A., Combs, S. E., & Flynn, P. J. Teachers' interpretations of students' behavior. In L. C. Wilkinson (Ed.), *Communicating in the classroom.* New York, Academic Press, 1981.

Mishler, E. G., Meaning in context: Is there any other kind? *Harvard Educational Review*, 1979, *49*, 1–19.

Okun, M. A., Fisk, E. C., & Toppenberg, L. W. Implications of Riegel's dialectic approach for adult instruction. *Human Development*, 1978, *21*, 316–326.

Pelto, P. J., & Pelto, G. H. *Anthropological research: The structure of inquiry* (2nd ed.). New York: Cambridge University Press, 1980.

Pike, K. *Language in relation to a unified theory of the structure of human behavior*. The Hague: Mouton, 1967.

Prigogine, I. Order through fluctuation: Self-organization and social system. In E. Jantsch & C. H. Waddington (Eds.), *Evolution and consciousness*. Reading, Mass.: Addison-Wesley, 1976.

Prigogine, I. *From being to becoming: Time and complexity in the physical sciences*. San Francisco: Freeman, 1980.

Rappoport, L. On praxis and quasirationality. *Human Development*, 1975, *18*, 194–204.

Riegel, K. F. Dialectic operations: The final period of cognitive development. *Human Development*, 1973, *16*, 346–370.

Riegel, K. F. Toward a dialectic theory of development. *Human Development*, 1975, *18*, 50–64. (a)

Riegel, K. F. Subject-object alienation in psychological experiments and testing. *Human Development*, 1975, *19*, 181–193. (b)

Riegel, K. F. The dialectics of human development. *American Psychologist*, 1976, *31*, 689–700. (a)

Riegel, K. F. From traits and equilibrium toward developmental dialectics. In W. Arnold (Ed.), *Nebraska Symposium on Motivation*. Lincoln: Uniersity of Nebraska Press, 1976. (b)

Rigel, K. F. Dialectical operations of cognitive development. In J. F. Rychlak (Ed.), *Dialectic: Humanistic rationale for behavior and development*. New York: Karger, 1976. (c)

Riegel, K. F. History of psychological gerontology. In J. F. Birren & K. W. Schaie (Eds.), *Handbook on the psychology of aging*. New York: Van Nostrand-Reinhold, 1977.

Riegel, K. F. *Foundations of dialectical psychology*. New York: Academic Press, 1979.

Rist, R. C. Blitzkrieg ethnography: On the transformation of a method into a movement. *Educational Researcher*, 1980, *9*, 8–10.

Roberts, J. I., & Akinsanya, S. K. (Eds.). *Schooling in the cultural context: Anthropological studies in education*. New York: David McKay, 1976

Rosch, E., & Mervis, C. B. Famiy resemblances: Studies in internal structure of categories. *Cognitive Psychology*, 1975, *1*, 573–605.

Rychlak, J. F. The multiple meanings of 'dialectics.' In J. F. Rychlak (Ed.), *Dialectic: Humanistic rationale for behavior and development*. New York: Karger, 1976.

Sanday, P. R. Ethnographic paradigm(s). *Administrative Science Quarterly*, 1979, *24*, 527–538.

Sevigny, M. Triangulated inquiry: A methodology for the analysis of classroom interaction. In J. Green & C. Wallet (Eds.), *Ethnography and language in educational settings*. Norwood, N.J.: Ablex, 1981.

Smith, L. M., & Geoffrey, W. *The complexities of an urban classroom*. New York: Holt, Rinehart & Winston, 1969.

Spindler, G. (Ed.). *Doing the ethnography of schooling*. New York: Holt, Rinehart and Winston, 1982.

Steward, J. H. *Theory of culure change*. Urbana, Ill.: University of Illinois Press, 1955.

Toffler, A. The psychology of the future. In A. Toffler (Ed.), *Learning for tomorrow: The role of the future in education*. New York: Vintage, 1974.

Wax, M. L., & Wax, R. H. Fieldwork and the research press. *Anthropology and Education Quarterly*, 1980, *11*, 29–37.

Wax, R. *Doing Fieldwork: Warnings and advice*. Chicago: University of Chicago Press, 1971.

Webb, E. J., Campbell, D. T., Schwartz, R. D., & Sechrest, L. *Unobtrusive measures: Nonreactive research in the social sciences*. Chicago: Rand McNally, 1966.

Weber, S. J., & Cook, T. D. Subject effects in laboratory research: An examination of subject roles, demand characteristics, and valid inference. *Psychological Bulletin*, 1972, *77*, 273–295.

Wilcox, K. Ethnography as a methodology and its application to the study of schooling: A review. In G. Spindler (Ed.), *Doing the ethnography of schooling*. New York: Holt, Rinehart and Winston, 1982.

Wilkinson, L. C. (Ed.). *Communicating in the classroom*. New York: Academic Press, 1981.

Willems, E. P., Raush, H. L. *Naturalistic viewpoints in psychological research*. New York: Holt, Rinehart & Winston, 1969.

Wolcott, H. Criteria for an ethnographic approach to research in schools. *Human Organization*, 1975, *34*, 111–127.

Wozniak, R. H. *In-context research on children's learning as a basic science prophylactic: Or true purity doesn't need to wash*. Paper presented at the meeting of the American Psychological Association, Montreal, August 1973.

Wozniak, R. H. A dialectical paradigm for psychological researh: Implications drawn from the history of psychology in the Soviet Union. *Human Development*, 1975, *18*, 18–34.

24

The Quantification of Knowledge in Education: On Resistance toward Qualitative Evaluation and Research

Steinar Kvale

Introduction

The Pythagoreans insisted that everything is numbers. Modern education involves a related assumption: evaluation of pupils' learning and educational research findings must be expressed in numbers—as grades and statistics—in order to be considered really real.

Unfortunate by-products of a dominating quantification of knowledge are, however, well known. Negative social and educational effects of grading have for many years been pointed out in educational literature, but with little effect on grading practices (Thorndike & Hagan, 1977). Negative effects of the domination of quantitative research methods have been pointed out for the disciplines of psychology (Koch, 1959), sociology (Filstead, 1970), and educational research (Karabel & Halsey, 1977), but again without marked consequences for research practice.

In recent years there have been trends toward an increased use of qualitative methods, involving qualitative evaluation of pupils and qualitative research methods, such as interviews and participant observation. The use of qualitative methods often counters resistance. A teacher who gives a qualitative evaluation of a pupil's performance is typically greeted by the pupil or his parents with, "But what is the grade?" And an educational researcher who uses a qualitative approach is likewise greeted by colleagues with, "But where are the statistics?"

The concern of this chapter is why educational evaluation and research must be expressed in a quantified language in order to be taken seriously. The interrelationship of methodological and social reasons that quantitative approaches have pre-

Steinar Kvale ● Institute of Psychology, University of Aarhus, Aarhus, Denmark.

vailed in education will be analyzed in four sections. Following a discussion of the reciprocity between qualitative and quantitative methods, I will describe some of the unfortunate consequences of the quantitative hegemony. I will then question the common justifications for quantification in educational evaluation and research: business employment practices and natural science research. I will end the analysis by centering the privileged status of quantified knowledge in a broad context of bureaucratic, technological, and capitalist concerns. Two conclusions are derived from my line of argument: first, that the usual opposition between quantitative and qualitative methods is a side issue, one which has been made a core issue by external social interests and second, that quantitative methods tend to dominate within bureaucratic systems where simplicity and legitimacy have priority over deeper understanding and the desire to effect social change.

A Reciprocal Relation between Quantitative and Qualitative Methods

A parallel analysis of the relation between quantitative and qualitative methods within two different fields such as educational evaluation and educational research will be speculative. A comparison of methods within evaluation and research will nonetheless make visible tendencies which have not been fully recognized within one area or the other. Evaluation and research both involve a methodical collection and analysis of information. Evaluation of knowledge obtained serves the function of making decisions in specific situations, decisions which may be of considerable importance for the individual pupil. Research aims at more generalizable knowledge and usually does not have any direct consequence for the research subjects. Evaluation is usually based on the re-production of established knowledge. Research aims at the production of new knowledge. However, the distinction between evaluation and research collapses in a total systems evaluation where educational or other social systems are evaluated in terms of more general concerns (cf. Okun & Fisk, this volume).

The issue of the present analysis is whether there is any characteristic of educational knowledge that necessitates quantitative methods having a privileged status within evaluation and research. It should be noted that the quantitative and qualitative aspects of an investigation cannot be absolutely separated. Within social research, however, it is common to speak of quantitative and qualitative methods, of quantitative and qualitative material, and it is in this common usage that the terms quantitative and qualitative are understood in this discussion.

Evaluation: Multiple-Choice Tests and Essays

Multiple-choice tests involve an extreme but typical form of quantitative evaluation. The evaluation process proceeds mechanically by counting the number of correct answers, a process which may be left to a computer. A point which is often missed, however, is that the formulation of these questions and response alternatives involved qualitative decisions. An example of a qualitative evaluation is a judgment of an essay as passed or failed. This placement on a nominal scale may also be accompanied by an oral or written argumentation for the final judgment.

Those subjected to a strict quantitative evaluation often experience it as mechanical and superficial, as not coming to grips with the variety and depth of their own achievements. Such reactions against quantification may come from pupils subjected to multiple-choice tests and from teachers confronted with a quantification of their teaching abilities. In summary, educational evaluation involves quantitative as well as qualitative aspects. Restriction to only the quantifiable aspects yields a one-sided and superficial picture of the content and process of evaluation.

Research: A Quantitative and Qualitative Analysis of Interviews on Grading

The relation between quantitative and qualitative methods in educational research is exemplified by an investigation in which 30 pupils were interviewed about the effects of grading on social relations and learning in high school (Kvale, 1980). The total interview material of more than 700 typewritten pages was subjected to a *quantitative scoring procedure,* the purpose being to provide structure for the complex material. The quantitative scoring was conducted at *surface level,* that is, at a level corresponding to the interviewees' self-understanding. A *qualitative content analysis* of the same material also included a deeper, more critical reading "between the lines" of the interview. The relationship of the quantitative and qualitative approaches to the interview material was illustrated by four *meeting points.*

Qualitative Presuppositions for a Quantitative Scoring: Defining Competition. The quantitative scoring presupposed a categorization of the pupils' descriptions of the effects of grading. The attempt to obtain a reliable quantitative scoring of the qualitative interview material necessitated precise qualitative definitions of the different grading behaviors. Thus the original homogeneous category of "competition for grades" was differentiated into more or less related categories of comparison by grades, envy about grades, individualization, "fair play" competition, and "destructive" competition. In summary, the quantitative scoring procedure augmented the qualitative precision of the meaning of the grading behavior.

A Quantitative Contribution to a Qualitative Interpretation: Displacement of Wheedling. Pupils' statements about grading behavior pertaining to themselves or to other pupils were quantified. The scores suggested that some forms of grading behavior were consistently attributed to other pupils and denied for the pupils themselves. This displacement tendency appeared most conspicuously for *wheedling,* that is, currying favor and playing up to the teachers.

As Table I shows, among the 20 pupils who described currying favor in order to improve grades, none admitted to engaging in wheedling, and 10 said quite directly that they did not wheedle themselves. Among the 20 pupils there were 16 who reported that the other pupils wheedled, and one who stated that no wheedling took place at all.

A conclusion based on this quantitative analysis would suggest that currying favor is something others do. This quantified person-displacement of wheedling was the starting point for a qualitative content analysis. Wheedling was something pupils hesitated to mention and, when they touched on the subject, the descriptions were often characterized by conspicuous pauses and reservations. The form and content of the statements were interpreted as pointing to wheedling as a taboo phenomenon,

Table I. Occurrence of Wheedling

	Yes	No
Self	0	10
Others	16	1

one which was subjected to deeper qualitative interpretations in relation to the psychoanalytical defense mechanisms of denial, projection, and rationalization.

In summary, there tends to be a reciprocal relation between quantitative and qualitative methods. Hence it may be arbitrary in a specific research situation which method first points out a tendency that can be further investigated through the other.

A Quantitative Main Finding in a Qualitative Material: Amount of Speech and Grade Point Average. In one interview, the following exchange was reported:

> INTERVIEWER: You mentioned earlier something about grades, can you tell anything more about that?
> PUPIL: That they are often unjust, because they, very often—very often—are only an expression of how much one talks, and how much one follows the opinions of the teacher.

The pupil obviously expressed a quantified hypothesis: the more a pupil talks, the better the grade. For the total interview material, a relationship was found which could be interpreted as an indirect confirmation of the pupil's "speech-quantity" hypothesis. One of the most interesting findings in the qualitative interview material was strictly quantitative; that is, for the 30 pupils a correlation was found between amount of speech, as measured in number of typewritten pages per interview, and a pupil's grade point average ($.68$, $p < .001$). In summary, a qualitative analysis of an interview statement brought forth a quantified hypothesis which could indirectly be supported by a quantification of the total interview material.

A Quantitative Increase and a Qualitative Leap: From Denial to Confirmation of Competition. From a purely quantitative viewpoint one might expect that the more often a form of grading behavior was confirmed or disconfirmed by a pupil during an interview, the more certain the quantitative scoring could be. In some cases, however, problems with a quantitative scoring on the level of a pupil's own understanding could arise, as in the following statement from a boy:

> INTERVIEWER: Does it influence the relationship between the pupils that the grades are there?
> PUPIL: No, no—no, one does not look down on anyone who gets bad grades, that is not done. I do not believe that; well, it may be, that there are some, who do it, but I don't.
> INTERVIEWER: Does that mean there is no competition in the class?
> PUPIL: That's right. There is none.

Following the procedures for quantitative scoring, this statement had to be scored as indicating nonoccurrence of competition; that is, the pupil insisted that he did not experience competition. A more critical qualitative content analysis led to the opposite conclusion because the boy who introduced the phenomenon of looking down on pupils with bad grades first denied that it occurs, then repeated the denials.

At a certain point in the quantitative increase of denials that competition occurs a qualitative leap occurs. Further denials appear as confirmation. As Shakespeare would have it, "The lady doth protest too much, methinks."

This example points to a principal limitation of quantification of qualitative interview material. It would be foolhardy to give an exact quantitative measure of how many "no's" are needed before they mean a "yes." To decide when a quantitative increase in negatives turns around and becomes the qualitative opposite, it is necessary to do a critical qualitative interpretation of a statement (pauses, intonation, stylistic formations, etc.). In summary, for a complex taboo phenomenon—in this case, the denial of competition—an exact quantitative scoring appears in principle impossible.

Conclusion

Qualitative methods are conventionally used in exploratory pilot studies; whereas the "real" scientific results of an investigation are reported in quantitative form. The above analysis suggested two points. First, there was no fixed order of qualitative and then quantitative methods in identifying a phenomenon and testing a hypothesis. The taboo of wheedling first appeared in the quantitative scoring and was supported by the qualitative analysis, whereas the order was reversed in the speech-quantity hypothesis.

Second, it appears to be impossible to conduct an analysis of denial of competition in a purely quantitative form. It was simply not possible to quantify the number of disconfirmations which were required to decide when a qualitative leap had occurred and the denials had become a confirmation. For many pupils, wheedling and competition are taboo phenomena. They are types of conduct which are in conflict with their social norms and self-concepts. They find themselves forced to "play the game" in order to maximize their "grade profit." They are understandably reluctant to discuss their behavior. Hidden phenomena such as these constitute part of what has been termed the "hidden curriculum." These are difficult to quantify. Only some limited aspects of such phenomena lend themselves to quantification.

A third point may be added: that other issues concerning grades required quantitative methods. In a subsequent questionnaire study with several hundred pupils the general extension of grading behaviors was investigated, as well as the relationships between grading behavior, grades obtained, and social backgrounds.

In conclusion, the examples discussed suggest that neither quantitative nor qualitative methods have any scientific priority when it comes to obtaining knowledge about an educational issue. Quantitative and qualitative methods are reciprocal aspects of the process of describing the extension and understanding the content of the effects of grading on the social relations and learning in school. The common contrasting of quantitative and qualitative methods appears as a side issue, one which hampers the development of educational research.

Retroactive Effects of Quantification of Knowledge

The relation between quantification and knowledge can be conceived as being purely external; I mean this in the sense that quantification does not influence the knowledge which is quantified any more than a thermometer influences the temperature it measures. An alternative conception will be argued here, namely, that there exists an internal relationship between measurement and knowledge in educational evaluation and research. Pupils and scientists are purposeful human beings and their learning or research is influenced by their intentions and goals. When a goal involves quantification (either grade point average or statistical analysis) such requriements may "react" and shape the knowledge which is acquired or presented. Two possible retroactive effects of strict requirements of quantification shall be discussed here: First, *selection* of what knowledge is acquired and second, the *transformation* of the knowledge obtained.

Evaluation: Fragmentation and Surface Knowledge

Pupils who want to reach the top of the educational hierarchy pay strict attention to knowledge as measured by examinations. Investigations of the effects of grading show that for a large number of pupils the grade point average is the major goal (Becker, Geer, & Hughes, 1968). Knowledge as a means of understanding the world and oneself tends to be of minor importance. Obviously grades further an instrumentalism whereby learning is primarily an activity which should pay off with respect to the grade point average.

The importance of grades as a goal of learning may lead the pupils to *select* knowledge which will be measured at examinations and to neglect all knowledge which is not required reading. Learning may be reduced to a rote learning of well-established and generally accepted knowledge, whereas a critical attitude toward what is learned becomes too risky in that it may negatively influence the final grade.

The character of knowledge also may be *transformed* by the grades. This retroaction on the acquisition of knowledge is probably most conspicuous in multiple-choice tests. Some empirical investigations suggest that multiple-choice tests further a fragmented and superficial learning at the expense of a more critical and deeper understanding (Balch, 1964; Kirkland, 1971). In summary, grades are not a neutral measurement. They tend to react upon the learning process through a selection and transformation of what is learned. The social retroactive effects of grading, found in the interviews reported above, will be discussed at a later point.

Research: Surface Knowledge and a Qualitative Self-censorship

The strict requirements of quantification of scientific knowledge have contributed to the development of techniques of measurement at the expense of clarification and interpretation of the meaning of phenomena. The result is that the statistical, hypothesis-testing phase of research has acquired priority at the expense of an exploring phase of hypothesis development.

The strict requirement of quantification demands that those aspects of social reality which readily lend themselves to quantification be *selected* for scientific research and that difficult quantifiable phenomena be neglected. In a stronger form of quantitative retroaction on knowledge, the phenomena to be researched are themselves *transformed* to a quantifiable mode. This is seen in case of laboratory rote learning of nonsense syllables (Kvale, 1977a). In order to transform complex social phenomena from natural situations to quantifiable data, methical instructions usually require the observers to focus on abstracted pieces of behavior, to limit their interpretation to surface meanings, and to avoid deeper interpretations (e.g., Bales's method for observing behavior in small groups and Cartwright's method for content analysis of texts; see Kvale, 1976a). The price of an exact quantification of these phenomena is their fragmentation and isolation from their social context.

In the quantitative analysis of interviews discussed above it was necessary to limit the interpretation of meaning to a surface level. But when the analysis of the interview material is restricted to quantitative scoring with high intersubject reliability, the total result is superficial. It hardly reaches any hidden curriculum. For example, it would be easy to obtain high intersubject agreement on the number of "no"s and "not"s in the denial statements, but it is impossible to obtain an equally high agreement on the interpretation of the meaning of a statement as being the opposite of what was said. Whereas it was possible to state that the relation between speech quantity and grade point average was a finding with a probability of less than $\frac{1}{1000}$, it would be of doubtful value to give probability statements for qualitative interpretations.

It should be emphasized that quantitative methods are not in themselves superficial. A multivariate analysis may bring forth hidden structures; for example, intelligence coefficients are based on systematic analysis of various dimensions. The superficiality pointed out above is one that follows from absolute requirements that scientific knowledge be formulated in a quantitative language, regardless of the subject matter investigated or the purpose of the investigation.

Decisions about whether the results of an investigation constitute scientific knowledge are made by editors of journals, research councils, appointment committees, and, for student research, examination committees. There are hardly any explicit rules demanding that scientific knowledge be quantified. In some research milieus, however, there appears to be an unwritten law. It is difficult to document the precise requirements for quantification of scientific knowledge. Many social researchers recognize, however, that quantitative research is conventionally seen as synonymous with scientific research. Karabel and Halsey (1977) postulated the general tendency for official institutions to give priority to quantitative research. Their postulate is based on a study of sociological research which showed that the probability of an investigation using quantitive methods was highest in articles acknowledging financial support.

The expectation that the more statistics there are in an article or research project, the larger the chance of acceptance contributes to a *qualitative self-censorship* among scientists. Scientists, too, learn to play the game because emphasizing quantification pays off with respect to financing and publication. Qualitative self-censorship does not necessarily effect the research process itself. When it comes to presenting the results, however, qualitative aspects may be suppressed or deemphasized. The result is a distorted picture of research: the "dirty" qualitative aspects of a research process are washed away leaving the "pure" quantitative data for public presentation.

Arguments for the Quantification of Knowledge

In the two preceding sections, the reciprocity between quantitative and qualitative methods and some unfortunate by-products of a dominating quantification of educational knowledge have been noted. The question to be raised at this point is: Why do quantitative methods have such a privileged position within educational evaluation and research?

Evaluation: Grades and Employment

The purpose of educational measures is to obtain information in order to make decisions, particularly concerning pupils (Thorndike & Hagan, 1977). Educational textbooks and reports from official committees often mention the unfortunate by-products of grading practices and then proceed to detail the external reasons why grades are necessary. The main arguments for retaining grades in school today are not that they further learning, but rather, at least in Scandinavian countries, that they are needed for selection purposes, especially by private businesses which need the best possible information on the work power they will employ.

External legitimation of grading of that type is not without problems. For example, the correlations reported between grades at the end of formal education and later occupational success are generally close to zero (Kvale, 1972, 1977b). Moreover, according to Scandinavian studies, employers tend to rely less on school grades than on a general evaluation based on level of education, job experience, recommendations, and particularly impressions from a personal interview.

Grades are nonetheless important in certain milieus. In the public bureaucracy, and particularly in the educational system, grades may be decisive for a pupil's future career. The necessity of grades then stems primarily from the educational system itself and not directly from external requirements. On the contrary, for employment in private business, a qualitative evaluation of predominantly qualitative material is considered more relevant than a grade point average. The usual argument for grades tends to be based on a *pedagogical myth* about employment practices in private business.

Research: Quantification and Natural Science

Quantitative methods have a dominant position in social science research. For example, a goal of American psychology has been to arrive at mathematical laws for behavior (Koch, 1959). A textbook on developmental psychology maintains that "the degree to which the observations can be quantified (translated into numbers) is often a good index of the maturity of science" (Mussen, Conger, & Kagan, 1979, p. 13). An article on market research is more categorical: "Quantitative research which does seek scientific explanation can be referred to simply as the scientific approach" (Calder, 1977, p. 355). And concerning the methodological empiricism within educational research, Karabel and Halsey (1977) have pointed to the tendency to confuse empirical method with statistical method and to neglect those problems that do not readily lend themselves to quantification.

The requirement that scientific knowledge be quantified appears to be self-evident in social science today. Textbooks seldom give arguments in support of the claim that the subject matter of social research—human actions in a social world—requires quantitative methods to be regarded as scientific. If a synonymization of science with quantification is argued at all, it is often pointed at the natural sciences which are alleged to be based on quantitative methods. Quantitative methods are important to the natural sciences, but quantification is not the absolute criterion of science. Geology, biology, and zoology make use of descriptive and qualitative methods. The works of Darwin and Lorenz could be cited in this regard.

The "parade discipline" of a positivistic philosophy of science—physics—has in previous eras been dominated by a mechanical, quantitative world view. In this century, however, with the advance of the theory of relativity and nuclear physics, qualitative descriptions and interpretations have again come to the fore. Physicists such as Bohr and Heisenberg distanced themselves from the positivistic interpretation of physics as early as half a century ago (Brandt, 1973). Whereas quantification is an important methodological means in natural science research, any legitimation of synonymizing science with quantification by pointing to the natural sciences is a *positivist illusion*.

Social Interests in the Quantification of Knowledge

When the traditional arguments for the quantification of educational knowledge provide little validity, it becomes necessary to seek other reasons for the domination of quantitative methods. Toward this end some specific and general social interests in educational knowledge will be discussed. The goal is not to reduce a pedagogical inquiry to ideology and sociology but to investigate the possible influences of social interests on the constitution of educational knowledge.

Evaluation: Socialization and Selection

The retroactive effects of grading on social relations and learning in school are rarely noted in official educational curricula today. The Jesuits who introduced the grading system in European schools in the 16th century were less inhibited. The Jesuits were quite explicit in stating that grades were desirable because they encouraged discipline, competition, and diligence (*Ratio studiorum,* 1887, § 39). In his analysis of Jesuit education, Durkheim (1977) suggested that it was in the interest of the Jesuits of those days to further a superficial learning of the classical Greek and Latin texts. In limiting the pupils to the style and grammar of the classical texts, they would spare them the underlying pagan allures. Strong competition for grades was a sure means of keeping the pupils' eyes on the letter, rather than the meaning, of the prose (cf. Illich, this volume).

Today such possible social and cognitive retroactive effects of the quantification of knowledge in grades are seldom officially formulated as desirable. Whenever it is suggested that grades be abolished, conservative politicians and employer representatives may, however, argue for retaining the grades by pointing to desired social effects like discipline, competition, and instrumental motivation; that is, the pupils learn through grading of learning in school that it pays to work, that extra effort will be rewarded.

This argument leads to the "employer paradox." The employers argue in official committees for retaining in school the grades which they have little regard for in their own employment practices. This paradox can be explained by the employers' insight into the socializing effects of grading and their correspondence to the qualification requirements of business.

The common arguments for grades today are not their retroactive effects but their future application as a means of selection. As mentioned earlier, it remains a pedagogical myth that grades are generally necessary for employment in business. In business it is decisive to find the right man for the right job, and qualitative procedures have a central role in the selection procedures. Within bureaucratic institutions, as in some ministries and in the educational system, it is of primary importance to make simple decisions based on formal rules. These rules must appear legitimate. Hence, standardized grading and the resulting differentiation of pupils constitute a legitimate bureaucratic means of selection. In this respect, a grading system with a one-dimensional scaling of pupils and job applicants represents a bureaucratic stroke of genius.

It may be inferred that in institutions where simplicity and *legitimacy* of decisions are primary, formal quantitative methods will dominate, whereas in institutions where *efficiency* of the decisions made is important, quantitative *and* qualitative methods will be subordinate to substantive judgments.

Research: Prediction and Control

It seems apparent that the positivist emphasis on quantitative studies of isolated data supported the empiricst conception of social reality as consisting of social atoms connected by external, quantitative relations (Kvale, 1976a). This conception is in agreement with Comte's emphasis that a positivist science should limit itself to the immediately observed facts and should forgo any deeper interpretation of the essence of the social phenomena.

The dominating position of quantitative methods in current educational research is less likely due to such retroactive effects than to the future application of educational knowledge. It thus behooves me to discuss some possible user interests. Educational researchers who want their research to influence politicians and public opinion often find that a quantified knowledge has the strongest impact. Karabel and Halsey (1977) characterized educational research in Great Britain as "political arithmetic." The social democrats particularly emphasize quantitative research which would document the existing social inequality in the educational system and, at the same time, would be the data base for subsequent educational planning.

Within certain areas of social research, particularly of the behaviorist tradition, the prediction and control of behavior have been a major research interest. Quantitative methods should serve this technical interest. Gallup's opinion research is a well-known example of the predictive efficiency of quantitative methods. Market research is an applied field of social science with a research interest in predicting and controlling consumer behavior. Quantitative methods (questionnaires, etc.) are used to a large extent in studies of consumer behavior. Less attention has been given the fact that market research also involves qualitative methods (Dichter, 1960). Qualitative methods (in-depth interviews, etc.) are necessary in order to obtain a deeper understanding of why consumers buy commodities and, particularly, of how consumers can be effectively manipulated to buy certain goods through product design and advertising. It appears paradoxical that this applied form of social research whose survival depends on its ability to predict and control consumer behavior, has found it necessary to use qualitative methods which behaviorists insist are unscientific.

Behaviorism, of course, is not a unitary research tradition. Skinner (1959), for example, distanced himself from the formal depiction of scientific method as irrelevant to much actual research practice. In fact, he challeged the dominating position of statistical method in experimental research. The usual mechanical application of statistics hampers a flexible and exploring use of experimental method, according to Skinner. His view on the theories of learning may also pertain to the common use of statistical methods—their function is to create an imaginary world of law and order and thus to console us for the disorder we observe in behavior itself. The positivist bureaucratization of science has also been described this way: "Psychology was unique in the extent to which its institutionalization preceded its content and its methods preceded its problems" (Koch, 1959, p. 783).

Market research likewise is not unitary with respect to attitudes toward quantitative and qualitativ methods. Lower level managers often want extensive quantitative data in order to legitimize their decisions and thereby to have an alibi if things should go wrong. Upper level managers, who themselves have the responsibility for the future of a company, may be more open to qualitative methods with creative and new interpretations. One market researcher has formulated this tendency thus: "Those who really want the help of an investigation in order to solve concrete issues are more susceptible to consider a qualitative investigation, whereas the 'alibi-seekers' rather choose quantitative studies" (Osiatynsky, 1976).

It seems that in situations where the primary interest is in providing decisions with *legitimacy,* quantitative methods dominate. In situations where the primary interest is *efficiency* of behavior control, quantitative and qualitative methods are put on the same level—their application depending on the nature of the phenomena to be investigated and the purpose of the investigation.

Excursus: The Glorification of Qualitative Methods

The crux of the present analysis has been the privileged position of quantitative methods as a barrier against qualitative methods in educational evaluation and research. The analysis has, in a sense, given undue emphasis to the negative aspects of quantitative methods in comparison to qualitative methods. In order to counteract an eventual methodological or political glorification of qualitative methods, some common negative features of qualitative measures will be briefly commented on.

While grades may involve a pseudoexactness, qualitative evaluations of learning can consist of standardized expressions and gratuitous statements. While grades may have oppressive effects on social relations in school, the often vague qualitative statements may open a subjective partiality or nepotism is selection committees. This eventuality is excluded if the outcome is based on a one-dimensional grade point average. Methodologically, qualitative research is often of low quality, with long interview excerpts or case descriptions either uninterpreted or serving as a pretext for speculative constructions. Criteria for reliability and validity of qualitative interpretations are seldom discussed, although the reflections on method developed within phenomenology and hermeneutics will likely provide a frame of reference for clarification of qualitative methods (Giorgi, 1975; Kvale, in press).

Political biases also enter this picture; that is, in some milieus there is a peculiar linking together of qualitative methods with the so-called progressive attitude and quantitative methods with the so-called reactionary attitude. These biases are peculiar in that it is absurd to conceive of the manipulation of consumer behavior through qualitative market research as progressive. Similarly, it is unreasonable to brand statistical research documenting social discrimination in the educational systems as reactionary.

The landscape becomes rather murky when the dismissal of quantitative methods comes from so-called Marxist groups. These groups have a way of overlooking the fact that a Marxist theory of knowledge presupposes a dialectical relation between quantitative and qualitative aspects of inquiry (Cornforth, 1971). Marx's own research involved qualitative and quantitative studies, including a questionnaire on working conditions in factories. In order to work for social reforms, it was necessary to obtain exact and reliable knowledge about the social conditions of the workers (*Marx-Engels Werke XIX,* 1957).

In summary, it appears meaningless to give quantitative or qualitative methods preferred methodological or political status. A cult of qualitative methods will only be a negative counterpoint to the synonymization of scientific method with statistical method. In this analysis, I have tried to argue that the opposition of quantitative and qualitative methods is a side issue. The very fixation on issues of method has been the preferred battlefield of a positivist philosophy of science and has detracted from social interests in knowledge.

Bureaucracy, Technology, and Capitalism

A technical research interest in control over objectified prcesses will now be discussed in relation to the more general contexts of bureaucracy, technology, and capitalism. It should be noted that the discussion does not concern individual bias or interests of teachers and scientists. The concern is with consequences of an institutional bias toward the quantification of knowledge.

Bureaucratic interests in quantitative knowledge as a means of formalizing and legitimizing decisions have been pointed out above. Bureaucracies are characterized by pertinent impersonality, anonymity, written communication, formalized procedures of decision, simplicity, and stability. Method, therefore, has priority over content. And quantification *per se* counts more than what is quantified. In bureaucracies it is less important to understand and change social reality than it is to administer and legitimate the given social reality. Giving quantified knowledge a privileged position contributes to a standardized model of social reality, one which can be easily administered by the given rules. In order to provide a frictionless bureaucratic administration, an attempt is made to eliminate social phenomena such as uncertainty, ambiguity, contradiction, and conflict. It is these very phenomena which are essential in a dialectical approach to understanding social reality in order to bring about radical change. Whereas grades have been characterized as a bureaucratic stroke of genius, it is tempting to characterize positivism as a scientific bureaucracy.

A variant of a bureaucratic understandng of knowledge is found in the current *technologizing* of knowledge (Kvale, 1976b). The focus on quantified data reflects and furthers a technological organization and computerization of the human raw material. In contrast to the bureaucratic necessity for simplicity, stability, and legitimacy, a technological paradigm is more open to complexity, flexibility, and efficiency.

A further context for explaining the dominance of quantified knowledge may be found in the *logic of the capital* (cf. Parker, this volume). Within a capitalist economy, knowledge has obtained a commodity character. Whereas the use values of commodities are qualitatively different, their exchange values may be compared quantitatively through their exchange equivalent, money. The quantification of knowledge in educational evaluation and research is one means of furthering an exchange value conception of knowledge. Moreover, the use of grades as rewards for learning in school tends to further an instrumentalism in line with the subsequent rewarding of work with money. In other words, grade learning socializes to wage labor (Kvale, 1981).

The contextualizing of a dominant quantification of knowledge in education to bureaucracy, technology, and capitalism is tentative; it remains to be worked out whether the relations pointed out are limited to a surface level or are expressions of more substantial functional relations. That there may be a substantial social reality involved is suggested in the works of Weber (1947), who pointed to the general bureaucratization of capitalism as a condition for the modern extension of the examination and grading system. Today the capitalization of knowledge is treated in as different approaches as the bourgeois human capital theories of education (e.g., Blaug, 1968) and in existential and Marxist analyses of education, such as Freire's (1973) critique of the banking model of education.

The relations between the contexts invoked here to explain the privileged position of quantitative methods in education remain to be worked out. Whereas for a bureaucratic system the importance of quantification is as a method and not as a goal, to a capitalist system quantification is less important as a method but all decisive by the final quantitative goal—profits of the invested capital. And it is possible that the often apparently inefficient quantification of educational knowledge may socialize to the logic of the capital; everything which exists can be measured and exchanged in money.

Conclusion

The main results of the analysis of the domination of quantitative methods will be summarized separately for an internal educational level and an external level of social interests in educational knowledge, acknowledging the interrelatedness of the two levels.

On an *internal educational level* there appears to be no reason to give quantitative methods of evaluation and research any privileged position. The common opposition of quantitative and qualitative methods is a side issue; the choice of quantitative or qualitative method is, rather, a concrete issue to be decided in relation to the subject matter and purpose of an evaluation or investigation. By dismissing the conception of a quantitative-qualitative dichotomy as synonymous with a scientific-unscientific dichotomy, a systematic reflection on criteria of qualitative methods becomes important. And by relieving quantitative methods of the not uncommon function of "scientific ritual," an open and creative use of quantitative methods may be developed. What remains as a substantial methodological issue after dismissing the quantitative-qualitative polarity is whether evaluation and research should be conducted according to formal methods or what degree formal methods should be abandoned.

The dominant position of quantitative knowledge in education and the subordinate position of qualitative knowledge have in the present analysis been attributed to *external social interests* in educational knoweldge. Different social interests in educational knowledge were discussed, for example, the selection procedures in public bureaucracies and private business and the more general contexts of bureaucracy and capitalism. A tentative conclusion may be formulated thus: In social systems where simplicity and legitimacy of decisions are of primary importance, quantitative methods will have a privileged position; whereas in social systems with an interest in obtaining deeper understanding and efficient change of social phenomena, the issue of quantitative and qualitative methods will be subordinated the use value of knowledge.

References

Balch, J. The influence of the evaluating instrument on students' learning. *American Educational Research Journal*, 1964, *1*, 169–182.

Becker, H., Geer, B., & Hughes, F. *Making the grade*. New York: Wiley, 1968.

Blaug, M. (Ed.). *Economics of education*. London: Penguin Books, 1968.

Brandt, L. W. The physics of the physicist and the physics of the psychologist. *International Journal of Psychology*, 1973, *8*, 61–72.

Calder, B. J. Focus groups and the nature of qualitative market research. *Journal of Marketing Research*, 1977, *14*, 353–364.

Cornforth, M. *Materialism and the dialectical method*. New York: International Publishers, 1971.

Dichter, E. *The strategy of desire*. New York: Doubleday, 1960.

Durkheim, E. *The evoluation of educational thought*. London: Routledge and Kegan Paul, 1977.

Filstead, W. H. (Ed.). *Qualitative methodology*. Chicago: Markham, 1970.

Freire, P. *Pedagogy of the oppressed*. London: Penguin Books, 1973.

Giorgi, A. An application of phenomenological method in psychology. In A. Giorgi, C. Fischer, & E. Murray (Eds.), *Duquesne studies in phenomenological psychology II*. Pittsburgh: Duquesne University Press, 1975, 82–103.

Karabel, J. & Halsey, A. H. (Ed.). *Power and ideology in education*. New York: Oxford University Press, 1977.

Kirkland, M. C. The effects of tests on students and schools. *Review of Educational Research*, 1971, *41*, 303–350.

Koch, S. Epilogue. In S. Koch (Ed.), *Psychology: A study of a science* (Vol. 3). New York: McGraw-Hill, 1959, pp. 729–788.

Kvale, S. *Prüfung und Herrschaft: Hochschulprüfungen zwischen Ritual und Rationalisierung*. Weinheim: Beltz, 1972.

Kvale, S. Meanings as data and human technology. *Scandinavian Journal of Psychology*, 1976, *17*, 171–180. (a)

Kvale, S. The psychology of learning as ideology and technology. *Behaviorism*, 1976, *4*, 97–116. (b)

Kvale, S. Dialectics and research on remembering. In N. Datan & H. W. Reese (Eds.), *Life-span developmental psychology: Dialectical perspectives in experimental research*. New York: Academic Press, 1977, pp. 165–189. (a)

Kvale, S. Examinations: From ritual through bureaucracy to technology. *Social Praxis*, 1977, *3*, 187–207. (b)

Kvale, S. *Spillet om karakterer i gymnasiet: Elevinterviews om bivirkninger af adgangsbegrænsing*. Copenhagen: Munksgaard, 1980.

Kvale, S. What is learned by measuring learning in grades? Unpublished manuscript, Aarhus Universitet, Psykologisk Institut, 1981.

Kvale, S. The qualitative research interview: A phenomenological and a hermeneutical mode of understanding. *Journal of Phenomenological Psychology,* in press.

Marx-Engels Werke XIX. Berlin: Dietz Verlag, 1957.

Mussen, P. H., Conger, J. J., & Kagan, J. *Child Development and Personality.* New York: Harper & Row, 1979.

Osiatynski, A. Tillämpning av psykologiska kunskaper i näringslivet. In J. Arndt & A. Friman (Eds.), *Industriel marknadsføring.* Stockholm: Liber, 1976, pp. 47–59.

Ratio studiorum et institutiones scholastica societatis Jesu. Berlin: Hoffmann, 1887.

Skinner, B. F. A case history in scientific method. In B. F. Skinner, *Cumulative record.* New York: Methuen, 1959, pp. 76–100.

Thorndike, R. L., & Hagan, E. P. *Measurement and evaluation in psychology and education.* New York: Wiley; 1977.

Weber, M. *Wirtschaft und Gesellschaft.* Tübingen: Mohr, 1947.

25

The Sociogenesis of Social Sciences: An Analysis of the Cultural Relativity of Social Psychology

John W. Berry

In recent years, social scientists have been increasingly engaged in disciplinary intro-spection in an attempt to comprehend the nature of their enterprise. One dimension of this activity has been to relate the evolution of one's discipline to historical con-texts, such as the economic, military, or social characteristics which have influenced a discipline over the course of time. For example, in psychology, Buss (1975) has reviewed "the emerging field of the sociology of psychological knowledge," and more recently (Buss, 1980), he has brought together a number of authors concerned with similar ideological and historical analyses (e.g., Danziger, 1980).

A second dimension has been the relation of various social science disciplines to national and political characteristics of a society. This approach has been the dom-inant form of the question in political science and sociology (see, for example, Cairns, 1975; Kumar, 1979; Lamy, 1976; Social Science Federation of Canada, 1978), where an interest in contemporary power relations takes precedence over concern for historical origins.

Yet a third dimension is that of the cultural relativity of social sciences; it has been argued (for psychology, for example, by Berry, 1978) that the discipline is so culture-bound and culture-blind that, as it stands now, it should not be employed as is in other cultures. We need to take three important steps: (1) major cultural decen-tering (away from Euroamerican theory and method), (2) recentering the discipline within the cultures of interest, and (3) an integration of the various societal psy-chologies in order to move toward a truly universal psychology (see also Jahoda, 1979; Triandis, 1978; cf. Okun & Fisk, this volume).

John W. Berry ● Department of Psychology, Queen's University, Kingston, Ontario K7L 3N6, Canada.

Although the historical and national dimensions of the topic are equally socio-genetic, my focus in this chapter will be the cross-cultural comparative dimension, that is, the cultural relativity issue. Although I have analytically separated the general issue into three sets of sociogenetic factors, we will find that they are interrelated—that there is little chance that a psychology bound to an alien culture can be relevant to national needs or can bear much relation to their local historical experience. Finally, I will center on the argument which has taken place in the discipline of social psychology; this is where my interest and experience lie, and such a restricted focus should make the topic more manageable.

A Preliminary Framework

Three points need to be made in order to develop a preliminary framework. The first is that contemporary social psychology is a discipline that is very much associated with a particular society. When one considers the number of social psychologists, their research funding and productivity, and their general impact on the field, it is difficult to escape the conclusion that social psychology, as we know it, is something which is largely an American phenomenon. Although statistics might be useful here (for example, is 90% or 95% the correct proportion of the world's social psychologists in the United States?), analytical evidence is just as important. Moscovici (1972, p. 19) has argued persuasively that social psychology was largely developed in the United States, taking "for its theme of research and for the contents of its theories the issues of *its own* society." More recently, Berry (1974, 1978), Faucheux (1976), Jahoda (1979), Kalin and Gardner (1981), Pepitone (1976), and Triandis (1977) have made similar observations and interpretations, so that I take it as established that social psychology is largely social psychology in the United States.

The second point is that there is an important distinction to be made between the *what* and the *how* of the discipline, that is, between the content, and the theory and method employed. Although there is an obvious interplay between the content and the theory and method of discipline, for analytic purposes it is useful to consider them separately. This distinction was impiled by Moscovici in the quotation above and was further developed by Berry (1976). For many researchers in social psychology, their theoretical and methodological perspectives emerge from the content areas or problems with which they work; at the same time, research questions which receive priority are often those which are congruent with local ideology. For example, Sherif and Sherif (1969, p. 222) have noted that the emphasis in American political culture is clearly on the individual; this is held to account for the individualist emphasis in American social psychology, in contrast to a collectivist one. Another commentator (Hofstede, 1980, p. 32) has found that "American theories fit American value patterns" in a large study of workers' values in forty nations.

A third preliminary point is that there are three legitimate goals, or levels of research, in cross-cultural work which need our attention (Berry, 1969, 1979a). At one level, we see the transportation of current psychological knowledge in order to test its applicability in other cultural systems *(imposed etic);* at the second level, we seek out new psychological knowledge from a point within other cultural systems *(emic);* at the third level we compare the psychological knowledge acquired from these first two activities, and then integrate them into a more general (*derived etic* and eventually a *universal*) psychology which is applicable to more than one cultural system.

These three points may be brought together into the preliminary framework in Figure 1. The distinction between the what (content) and the how (theory and method) of social psychology provides the basic horizontal and vertical structure of the framework. The three goals or levels of cross-cultural research are indicated within each dimension. Because I am writing from a Canadian perspective, the present approach of social psychology in the United States is represented by the "imported" lines.

Since the ultimate goal of science is the production of general statements about all relevant phenomena, using appropriate theoretical and methodological tools, I take it that the social psychology we all wish to develop is universal both in its content and in its theory and methods; this ultimate social psychology is indicated in the lower right sector of the framework, where all social psychological phenomena are included within a comprehensive theoretical system.

In sharp contrast to this universal social psychology is the kind indicated in the upper left sector. Here, social psychology is imported from the United States to another society and is used to study topics which are central to the established literature using extant theories and methods; we can refer to this as social psychology *in* another society, with little regard to what is actually happening there or to how it may best be studied.

An emerging antidote to doing social psychology *in* another society is to develop the discipline from within, to create a social psychology which relfects the local reality (Berry, 1974; Berry & Wilde, 1972; Enriquez, 1979; Kumar, 1979; Moscovici, 1972; cf. Schubert, this volume). The numerus societal (or indigenous) social psychologies *of* various societies are indicated in the central sector of the framework. Of course what United States social psychology does now in the United States is included here and is entirely appropriate. But clearly the two problems are its importation and use *in* other societies and its masquerading as the universal social psychology; this double error is what we face at the present time.

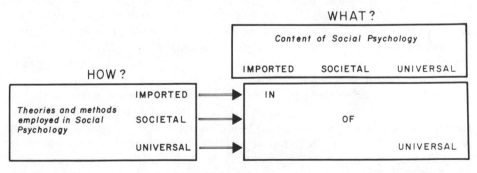

Figure 1. Preliminary framework for considering the cultural relativity of social psychological knowledge.

The other sectors in the framework will be described in the following sections, where we will attempt to put some flesh on this skeleton. These are all problematic and involve a mismatch between content and theory, such as employing imported theory or methods to study local phenomena.

Imported Social Psychology

In Canada, as in so many other societies, the materials available for teaching and research in social psychology are largely "made in the U.S.A." In physics or even in experimental psychology, this may not pose much of a problem, although even this benign view has been debated by Symons (1975), as well as by Crutchfield and Krech (1962, p. 12), who argue that "the scientist—like every other person—is a member and product of his society. Certainly no psychologist can escape this influence, no matter what his experimental problem, and no matter how thick and sound-proof are the walls of his laboratory cubicle." However, especially in the social sciences, the uncritical use of the imported product directs us to commit a number of errors.

For one, we incorrectly identify our own social phenomena by either ignoring local societal issues which are important or by assimilating them to the version which exists in the imported literature. These errors of omission and commission abound in social psychology *in* Canada. With respect to errors of omission, phenomena associated with our ethnic pluralism (for example, intergroup relations and linguistic and multicultural phenomena), with our regionalism, and with our political, economic, and cultural dependency have with few exceptions been ignored (Berry, 1974; McLeod, 1955).

With respect to errors of commission, when they occur, they frequently are identified with apparently similar phenomena in the United States (such as equating French Canadians or Canadians from the West Indies with U.S. blacks); numerous examples are documented by Alcock (1978) and Sadava (1978). Such attempts to insert "appropriate Canadian examples" (Wrightsman, 1977, p. viii) into a ready-made (in the U.S.) social psychology are insulting to all (but particularly to students and researchers) in these other societies.

Another error occurs when we employ imported theory (and methods) to study and explain local phenomena. For example attempting to understand multiple inter-group relations in the Canadian ethnic mosaic by the mainstream–minority American concept would have been fruitless (Berry & Kalin, 1979; Berry, Kalin, & Taylor, 1977); in Canada we simply do not have a single mainstream to which minorities relate one by one in neat dyadic interactions.

To take another example, in unpublished thesis research, which I recently had a chance to review, it was predicted that the self-esteem of non-European immigrant students to Canada would be lower than that of native-born students; this expectation was based entirely on the U.S. literature with black and Chicano children. However, lower self-concept was not found, and the author squirmed to explain why his Canadian findings did not fit the American theory; nowhere did he attempt to relate his results to the idea of support for self-concept of ethnic group members which is available in multicultural societies (Berry, 1979b; Murphy, 1969).

In summary, it is not difficult to find examples of mismatch between phenomena and theory when social psychology is done *in* another society. This situation has been likened to the use of a blueprint to help understand a piece of machinery. Errors exist when one mismisidentifies either the machine or the blueprint, but also when one uses an inappropriate blueprint for the machine being examined. To continue the analogy:

> The blueprint which we use to help us understand the machine must bear some resemblance to it. Our social science concepts and assumptions are often mere copies of those developed and employed in other societies: to import them uncritically for our special purposes may lead us to serious errors. If our blueprint were printed elsewhere, how can we hope to make sense of the complex machinery we see here? One way to resolve the inconsistency between the machine and the blueprint is to make the machine match the blueprint; this we are in danger of doing. The other is to discard the present blueprint, and make a new one based upon the machine as it is; this is what I hope we will be able to do. (Berry, 1974, pp. 137–138)

Societal Social Psychologies

Making new blueprints to match the local phenomena requires the construction of societal social psychologies *of* a particular society. As we have seen, this is precisely what has happened in the United States, and it is what is required in other societies who wish to understand themselves. That social psychology from the United States does reflect society in the United States has been pointed out by a number of oservers (e.g., Sampson, 1977).

More generally, as we have seen, Crutchfield and Krech (1962, p. 12) believe that this situation is basic to all science; it is not limited to dominant scientific communities. Again turning to Hofstede (1980, p. 182), we see that his analyses demonstrate a link between one particular value dimension (uncertainty avoidance) in a society and the type of theory which is preferred in a society: "In high uncertainty avoidance countries, scholars look for certainties, for Theory with a capital T, for Truth. In low uncertainty avoidance countries, they take a more relativistic and pragmatic stand and look for useable knowledge."

Thus, we should accept as normal the existence of a match between societal characteristics and social psychological content, theory, and method; this match clearly exists in the one well-developed example that we have available. The situation that is abnormal is the resistance, in many quarters, to the drive to establish other societal social psychologies. We hear that they are unnecessary, that they are nationalistic, and that they are too limited; but they are also potentially threatening to those who are well trained in *the* social psychology and who may require a degree of relearning and retooling in order to reduce their ethnocentrism and to maintain their credibility. In addition, of course, these societal social psychologies *of* a people and their society are more likely to be accurate and useful, and so deserve a life of their own for reasons quite apart from the innuendo in the above caricature of a debate.

Universal Social Psychology

One other criticism of the development of numerous societal emphases is that there is no end, and no resultant, which may be used *generally* to the social psychologist. This issue is not a problem for those who wish to remain culturally encapsulated (e.g., an American doing American social psychology in America); but it is a problem to those who wish to see social psychology become a more comprehensive and generally applicable discipline.

Taking our lead from comparative (cross-cultural) psychology, we may adopt as a goal the incorporation of phenomena from all cultural groups, and we may employ a general scheme of comparative integration in order to pursue it. I have argued (Berry, 1978, 1979a) that psychology is both "culture bound and culture blind." The movement toward societal analyses will reduce the culture-blind nature of our discipline; the cultural context of our behavior will be drawn into our research as we try to understand its local basis. The movement toward a universal social psychology will reduce the culture-bound nature of our discipline; the winnowing of behaviors and their theoretical interpretations across cultures will reveal which are local and which appear in all societies and are, hence, universal characteristics of all mankind. Indeed, it must be emphasized that it is only if we pursue simultaneously the universal goal and the local analyses that the full import of such indigenous efforts will be realized. For without the pursuit of the eventual universal integration, the use of a societal social psychology (albeit a more appropriate one) merely replaces an imported ethnocentrism with a local one.

While subscribing to the need for a less culture bound and culture blind social psychology, writers vary in their version of what the ultimate, or universal, social psychology might be. My own version (Berry, 1978, 1979c) is based on the existence of biological, social, and cultural universals in adaptation to ecological contexts; these are taken as common dimensions of human variation which may provide a foundation for a universal social psychology (cf. Wertsch, this volume). For example, in attempting to comprehend the nature and distribution of independence and conformity across cultural groups, I have based my research on such cultural universals as socialization for the acceptance of group norms (Aberle, Cohen, Davis, Levy, & Sutton, 1950) and the dimension of cultural integration referred to as "tightness–looseness" by Pelto (1968). The former suggests that all individuals respond to normative pressure from their groups while the latter suggests that cultures vary in the degree of social pressure which is typically exerted by them on individuals. With such universals as a basis, comparison is legitimate, and cross-cultural generalizations, based on comparative integration, are valid. In principle, this approach can build up social psychological universals on the basis of both cultural universals and local cultural analyses.

In contrast, the approach of Triandis (1978) presents a logical and theoretical framework which is itself a set of social psychological universals. He has noted that "a general theory of social behaviour, applicable to all situations (across time and place), requires the identification of those fundamental constructs which are likely to maintian the same meaning across time and place" (p. 5). Triandis argued that there are known stimulus universals, process universals, and response universals which can form the basis of such a universal social psychological theory. However, in the view of Jahoda (1979, p. 146) "the price to be paid for this (global synthesis) is perhaps an excessively high level of abstraction."

Despite these variations in approach (one from "below" and another from "above"), it should be clear that our goal must be the development of a social psychology that is universal in its applicability: it should not be culture bound (neither inappropriately imported, nor single societal), and it cannot remain culture blind, if we are to comprehend all behavioral variation.

A Framework for the Future

An exhortation, to be meaningful, need only stand the test of analysis; to be useful, it need also stand the test of operationalization. How, then, can we actually pursue this universal goal for social psychology?

First of all, we need to have a period of "restraint and resistance" (Berry, 1979d, p. 90) in our international activity; the dominant social science communities might draw back for a while (see also Kumar, 1979), and the local communities might resist all those great temptations (research funding, co-publication with the patrons in *the* journals, etc.). This would allow more room for the development of local work and points of view.

Second, numerous societal social psychologies must be developed, with good material on the what and the how of social behavior, both firmly rooted in the local sociocultural reality. These will form the raw material for the eventual comparative integration.

Third, theoretical frameworks must be developed that have a basis in biological or cultural universals (cf. my own approach) or that are global to begin with (cf. the Triandis approach).

Fourth, the matching should begin. Can the societal materials be brought together, either on the basis of one of these theoretical frameworks or on some new basis discovered in the various societal social psychologies and common to all of them? If so, then the first step can be taken toward a universal social psychology; if not (over repeated attempts), then such a goal may be impossible to attain. However, given the existence of numerous universals in other disciplines, my own view is that it will be possible to develop a panhuman social sicence of human behavior.

A framework for this future effort is indicated in Figure 2. Basically it expands on the preliminary outline presented earlier (Figure 1) by adding a new dimension, that of societal variation along selected dimensions which are themselves cultural universals; this dimension is indicated along the top of the diagram. The two earlier dimensions (the what and the how) are indicated on the left of the diagram; here they are collapsed into one dimension on the assumption that the appropraite societal matches between content and theory which we have been advocating will have been achieved.

What must be done in order to fill in the framework is to identify all cultural universals that are relevant to social psychology, and then to identify all topics (with their appropriate theory and method) that may be related to each cultural universal.

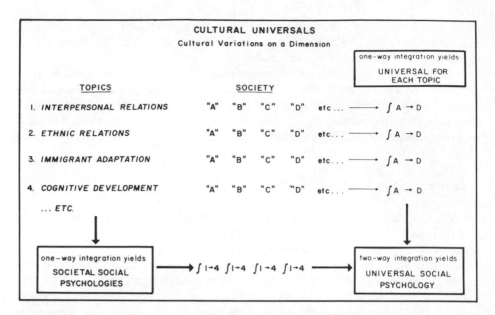

Figure 2. Framework for the future development of a universal social psychology.

For example, a cultural dimension (across the top of Figure 2) would be the universal dimension of cultural homogeneity–heterogeneity in a society (culturally monistic through to pluralistic). We then consider which kinds of social behaviour might be studied in relation to this dimension; for example, the nature of interpersonal and ethnic relations, of immigrant adaptation, or of cognitive development are all conceivably dependent on variation in this cultural context.

Studies may then be carried out on each topic within one or more societies representing each major position on the cultural dimension. The integration of social psychological knowledge across topics within a society (down the diagram) yields a societal social psychology; the comparative integration of social psychological knowledge across societies within a topic (across the diagram) yields a universal for that topic; and the comparative integration across all topics and societies produces our overall objective—a veritable universal social psychology. Within this framework, such a final product is demonstrably and visibly different from either a single societal social psychology or a cross-cultural sutdy of a single topic. And within such a framework, the variations in content, theory, method, and results, if related at all to cultural variation, will vindicate the thesis of this chapter—that at the present time social psychology is culturally relative, that it is culture bound and largely culture blind, and that as long as it remains so, it is hopelessly ethnocentric.

Sociogenesis and Social Psychology

The point of the argument in this chapter has been to demonstrate the cultural relativity of a single social science discipline. The position has been taken that the sociocultural context, be it the cultural characteristics within a single society or universals across cultures, has had and should have a clear and identifiable influence on social science. Only one element, that of cultural relativity, has been examined; others, such as social relativity (Danziger, 1980), historical relativity (Gergen, 1973), or political relativity (Apfelbaum & Lubek, 1976), could have been employed, but these arguments have already been made. Together, these statements provide substantial evidence for the sociogenesis, not only of human conduct, but of the *study* of human conduct. Together, they emphasize the necessity for each human community singly and collectively to reflect on its nature from a viewpoint based on both its cultural, social, and historical uniqueness and on its humanity. Without a sense of this uniqueness, intellectual domination from outside has created inappropriate local analyses and premature universals; but without a sense of our shared social character, as noted early on by Aberle *et al.* (1950), our futures would be grim indeed.

Acknowledgments

This chapter was begun while the author was on leave at the Institut d'Etudes et de Recherches Interethnique et Interculturelles (IDERIC), Université de Nice, France, and while holidng a leave Fellowship, from the Social Sciences and Humanities Research Council of Canada (SSHRC), Ottawa. I gratefully acknowledge their support, and the helpful interactions with my colleague, R. Kalin.

References

Aberle, D. F., Cohen, A. K., Davis, A. K., Levy, M. J., & Sutton, F. X. The functional prerequisites of a society. *Ethics,* 1950, *60,* 100–111.

Alcock, J. *Social psychology and the importation of values.* Paper presented to the Canadian Psychological Association, Ottawa, June 1978.

Apfelbaum, E., & Lubek, I. Resolution versus revolution: The theory of conflicts in question. In L. Strickland, F. Aboud, & K. Gergen (Eds.), *Social psychology in transition.* New York: Plenum Press, 1976.

Berry, J. W. On cross-cultural comparability. *International Journal of Psychology,* 1969, *4,* 119–128.

Berry, J. W. Canadian psychology: Some social and applied emphases. *Canadian Psychologist,* 1974, *15,* 132–139.

Berry, J. W. Critique of Triandis "Social Psychology and Cultural Analysis." In L. Strickland, F. Aboud, & K. Gergen (Eds.), *Social psychology in transition.* New York: Plenum Press, 1976.

Berry, J. W. Social psychology: Comparative, societal and universal. *Canadian Psychological Review,* 1978, *19,* 93–104.

Berry, J. W. Introduction to methodology. In H. C. Triandis & J. W. Berry (Eds.), *Handbook of cross-cultural psychology* (Vol. 2: Methodology). Boston: Allyn and Bacon, 1979. (a)

Berry, J. W. Social and cultural change. In H. C. Triandis & R. Brislin (Eds.), *Handbook of cross-cultural psychology* (Vol. 5: Social Psychology). Boston: Allyn and Bacon, 1979. (b)

Berry, J. W. A cultural ecology of social behavior. In L. Berkowitz (Ed.), *Advances in experimental social psychology* (Vol. 12). New York: Academic Press, 1979. (c)

Berry, J. W. Comparative social psychology: Societal roots and universal goals. In L. Strickland (Ed.), *Soviet and Western perspectives in social psychology.* Oxford: Pergamon Press, 1979. (d)

Berry, J. W., & Kalin, R. Reciprocity of inter-ethnic attitudes in a multicultural society. *International Journal of Intercultural Relations,* 1979, *3,* 99–112.

Berry, J. W., & Wilde, G. J. S. (Eds.). *Social psychology: The Canadian context.* Toronto: McClelland and Stewart, 1972.

Berry, J. W., Kalin, R., & Taylor, D. M. *Multiculturalism and ethnic attitudes in Canada.* Ottawa: Minister of Supply and Services, 1977.

Buss, A. The emerging field of the sociology of psychological knowledge. *American Psychologist,* 1975, *30,* 988–1002.

Buss, A. (Ed.). *Psychology in social context.* New York: Irvington-Halsted, 1980.

Cairns, A. C. Political science in Canada and the Americanization issue. *Canadian Journal of Political Science,* 1975, *8,* 191–234.

Crutchfield, R. S., & Krech, D. Some guides to the understanding of the history of psychology. In L. Postman (Ed.), *Pshchology in the making.* New York: Knopf, 1962.

Danziger, K. The social origins of modern psychology. In A. Buss (Ed.), *Psychology in social context.* New York: Irvington-Halsted, 1980.

Enriquez, V. G. Toward cross-cultural knowledge through cross-indigenous methods and persepctives. *Philippine Journal of Psychology* 1979, *12,* 9–16.

Faucheux, C. Cross-cultural research in experimental social psychology. *European Journal of Social Psychology,* 1976, *6,* 269–322.

Gergen, K. Social psychology as history. *Journal of Personality and Social Psychology,* 1973, *26,* 309–320.

Hofstede, G. *Culture's consequences: International differences in work-related values.* Beverly Hills, Calif.: Sage, 1980.

Jahoda, G. A cross-cultural perspective on experimental social psychology. *Personality and Social Psychology Bulletin,* 1979, *5,* 142–148.

Kalin, R. & Gardner, R. The cultural context of social psychology. In R. Gardner & R. Kalin (Eds.), *A Canadian social psychology of ethnic relations.* Toronto: Methuen, 1981.

Kumar, K. Some reflections on transnational social science transactions. *International Journal of Comparative Sociology,* 1979, *19,* 219–234.

Lamy, P. The globalization of American sociology: Excellence or imperialism? *American Sociologist,* 1976, *11,* 104–114.

McLeod, R. B. *Psychology in Canadian universities and colleges: A report to the Canadian social science research council.* Ottawa: Canadian Social Science Research Council, 1955.

Moscovici, S. Society and theory in social psychology. In J. Israel & H. Tajfel (Eds.), *The context of social psychology.* London: Academic Press, 1972.

Murphy, H. B. M. *Psychiatric concomitants of fusion in plural societies.* Paper presented to the conference on "Social Change and Mental Health", Honolulu, November 1969.

Pelto, P. The difference between "tight" and "loose" societies. *Transaction,* April 1968, pp. 37–40.

Pepitone, A. Toward a normative and comparative biocultural social psychology. *Journal of Personality and Social Psychology,* 1976, *34,* 641–653.

Sadava, S. Teaching social psychology: A Canadian dilemma. *Canadian Psychological Review,* 1978, *19,* 145–151.

Sampson, E. E., Psychology and the American ideal. *Journal of Personality and Social Psychology,* 1977, *35,* 767–782.

Sherif, M. & Sherif, C. *Social psychology.* New York: Harper & Row, 1969.

Social Science Federation of Canada. *Canadianization of the social sciences.* Ottawa: Author, 1978.

Symons, T. H. B. *To know ourselves* (Vols. 1 & 2). Ottawa: Association of Universities and Colleges of Canada, 1975.

Triandis, H. C. Cross-cultural social and personality psychology. *Personality and Social Psychology Bulletin,* 1977, *3,* 143–158.

Triandis, H. C. Some universals of social behavior. *Personality and Social Psychology Bulletin,* 1978, *4,* 3–16.

Wrightsman, L. *Social psychology in the 70's.* Monterey, Calif.: Brooks/Cole, 1977.

IV

The Paideia of Language: Historical, Educational, and Ethnic Praxis

26

Vernacular Values and Education

Ivan Illich

Introduction

This chapter was originally prepared for a lecture in New York at Teachers College, Columbia University, in the spring of 1979. It is a fragment from a larger study on which I am working. There, I distinguish between two domains of social activity that tend to be confused in current economics under the heading of "informal sector." Within this informal sector I discriminate between the area of shadow economics and the vernacular domain. I analyze the narrow and different constraints within which the concepts derived from formal economics can be applied to the one and then to the other of these areas. This distinction of two opposite domains within the informal sector is applicable to disciplines other than economics.

In the present draft, I begin to demonstrate the applicability of such an analysis to the field of education. I distinguish taught mother tongue and the process by which it is learned from vernacular language and the development of competence in its use. The former results from both formal and informal *educational* activities, while the concepts of pedagogics developed since the sixteenth century are only metaphorically applicable to the latter, the vernacular domain. By describing in general terms the limited appropriateness of pedagogical concepts to learning in primitive cultures, learning in preindustrial societies and, particularly, learning of certain competences in modern, commodity-intensive economics, I use insights gained through contemporary economic history and anthropology and apply them to the field of education. The inapplicability of pedagogical concepts to the learning of vernacular language can then be extended to other areas of learning, and the implicit limits to all education can then be understood. I hope with this chapter to encourage research *on* as distinct from research *in* education, that is, research that examines the myths, the practices, the structures, and the assumptions that are now common to all societies

Ivan Illich ● CIDOC, Cuernavaca, Morelos, Mexico.

where education has been "disembedded" as a distinct realm of activity, as a formal context or sphere.[1]

A Medieval Idea

The medieval mind firmly accepted the existence of heavenly spheres; the contemporary mind as certainly adheres to the existence of social spheres. My argument focuses especially on the educational sphere, but it can be generalized to the other modern spheres. On each of these spheres, two types of research can be done: that which does not go beyond the model of Copernicus, and that which tends to resemble the work of Kepler. The former is concerned with exploring the possible restructuring of the educational (or other) sphere by redefining its centerpiece, recalculating its amplitude, integrating more epicycles into its curriculum, or reassigning to it a new place or order within the hierarchy of social spheres. The latter research searches for the origins of the paradigm itself and, therefore, implicitly recognizes that, like heavenly spheres, modern social spheres might one day disappear.

Astronomers deal with a before and an after. They know that at some date human beings were able to reckon with a Copernican and then with a relativistic sky. They remember the change when planets were first perceived as physical objects that spin around the sun. They work within a paradigm that has an acknowledged beginning and, therefore, can plausibly end. Educators still lack such a historical perspective on their own work. The sphere of their competence appears to them as beginningless. They now need to recall that Ptolemy no less than Copernicus, Aristotle no less than Thomas Aquinas, were all convinced that planets were embedded in crystal spheres—transparent, hollow, perfect globes moving in uniform fashion (Litt, 1963). Today, these men's common, firm, and critical conviction (Braun, 1940)[2] about the existence of such heavenly spheres is almost beyond belief. Yet, Keynesians and Marxists, Curriculum Planners and Free Schoolers, Chinese and Americans, are all convinced that *homo* is *educandus,* that his well-being—nay, existence—depends on services from an educational sphere. Here, I shall describe how this sphere was first sighted in 1492, and then suggest that we begin to prepare to celebrate in 1992 the 500th birthday of the educational sphere—a worldwide festival to commemorate the generosity, fantasy, ingenuity, and occasional humor of the men and women whose lives were shaped by a belief that will be seen then as belonging to the past.

---

[1]This fragment, considerably enlarged, annotated, documented, and supplied with a "Guide to Research on Education," will be published in early 1984 as part of a volume in the series *Ideas in Progress,* Marion Boyars Publishers, 18 Brewer Street, London W1R 4AS.

[2]According to Thomas Aquinas, science was free to investigate (1) if heavenly spheres were driven by a soul, (2) precisely how many spheres there were, and (3) to what degree these spheres and their epicycles were eccentric. However, their existence, their substantive, three-dimensional nature, and their uniform circular motion could not be questioned without upsetting sound philosophical truth— and the latter was needed for the explanation of Christian dogma.

Columbus Finds the Nightingale

Early on August 3, 1492, Christopher Columbus sailed from Palos. The neighboring and much more important Cádiz was congested that year—it was the one port from which Jews were allowed to leave. Granada had been reconquered, and Jewish service no longer needed for a struggle with Islam. Columbus headed for Cipangu, the name for Cathay (China) during the short reign of the long dead Tamerlane. He had calculated the earth's degree as equivalent to 45 miles. This would place Eastern Asia 2,400 miles west of the Canaries, somewhere close to the Antilles in the Zaragoza Sea. He had reduced the ocean to the range of the ships he could master. Columbus had on board an Arabic interpreter to enable him to speak to the great Khan. He set out to discover a route, not new land, not a new hemisphere.

His project, however, was quite unreasonable. No learned man of the early Renaissance doubted that the earth was a globe—some believing that it rested at the center of the universe, and some that it whirled in its sphere. But not since Eratosthenes had anyone underestimated its size as badly as Columbus. In 255, Eratosthenes of Cyrene measured the distance from the great library that he directed in Alexandria to Syene (now the site of the Aswan dam) as 500 miles. He measured the distance using the camel caravan's remarkably steady gait from sunrise to sunset as his "rod." He had observed that on the day of the summer solstice, the rays of the sun fell vertically at Syene and seven degrees off the vertical at Alexandria. From this he calculated the earth's circumference to about 5 % of its real dimension.

When Columbus sought Isabella's support for his venture, she asked Talavera, the sage, to evaluate its feasibility. An expert commission reported that the West-to-the-Orient project lacked a firm foundation. Educated authorities believed its goal to be uncertain or impossible. The proposed voyage would require three years; it was doubtful that even the newest kind of ship, the caravel—designed for distant explorations—could ever return. The oceans were neither as small nor as navigable as Columbus supposed. And it was hardly likely that God would have allowed any uninhabited lands of real value to be concealed from his people for so many centuries. Initially, then, the queen rejected Columbus; reason and bureaucratic expertise supported her. Later, swayed by zealous Franciscan frairs, she contradicted her earlier decision and signed her stipulations with Columbus. She was moved by the same mystical mood that influenced her other decisions in that month of March, the mood called the "Grace of Granada," the mood that impelled her to sign the expulsion of the Jews and, as we shall see, to become the first sovereign to accept an educator's advice.

For five weeks Columbus sailed well-known waters. He put in at the Canary Islands to repair the rudder of the Pinta, to replace the lateen sail of the Niña, and to pursue a mysterious affair with Doña Beatriz de Peraza. Only on September 10, two days out of the Canaries, did he pick up the Easterlies, tradewinds on which he chanced and which carried him rapidly across the ocean. In October, he came upon land that neither he nor the queen's counselors had expected. In his diary entry for October 13, 1942, he beautifully described the song of the nightingale that welcomed him on Santo Domingo, though such birds never lived there. Columbus was and remained *gran marinero y mediocre cosmógrafo* (J. de Girava, cited in Menendez Pidal, 1957). To the end of his life he remained convinced of having found what he had sought—a Spanish nightingale on the shores of China.

Nebrija Engineers the Artifact: August 18, 1492

Let me now move from the reasonably well known to the unreasonably over-looked—from Columbus, immediately associated with 1492, to Elio Antonio de Nebrija, outside of Spain almost forgotten. During the time Columbus cruised south-west through recognizable Portuguese waters and harbors, in Spain the fundamental engineering of today's educational enterprise was developed and defended. Before Columbus chanced on the Western Hemisphere, Nebrija created the mental con-struct I call the educational sphere. If a single event in education can be compared to the burning of Giordano Bruno or to the appearance of Johannes Kepler's *The Harmony of the Worlds* (where the heavenly spheres dissolve), it is Nebrija's for-mulation of this proposal. His *Gramática Castellana* was published and presented to Queen Isabella.

I was deeply moved when I felt it in my hands—a quarto volume of five sig-natures set in Gothic letters. The epigraphy is printed in red, and a blank page pre-cedes the introduction:

> A la muy alta e assi esclarecida princesa dona Isabela la tercera deste nombre Reina i señora natural de españa e las islas de nuestro mar. Comienza la gra-mática que nuevamente hizo el maestro Antonio de Nebrixa sobre la lengua castellana, e pone primero el prólogo. Léelo en buena hora.

The Conqueror of Granada received a petition, similar to many others. But unlike the request of Columbus, who wanted resources to establish a new route to the China of Marco Polo, that of Nebrija urged the queen to invade a new domain at home. He offered Isabella a tool to colonize the language spoken by her own sub-jects; he wanted her to replace the vernacular speech of her people with a taught, standardized tongue.

I shall now translate and comment on sections of the six-page introduction to Nebrija's grammar. Remember, then, that the colophon of the *Gramática Castellana* notes that it came off the press in Salamanca on the 18th of August, just 15 days after Columbus had sailed.

> My Illustrious Queen. Whenever I ponder over the tokens of the past that have been preserved in writing, I am forced to the very same conclusion. Language has always been the consort of empire, and forever shall remain its mate. Together they come into being, together they grow and flower, and together they decline.

To understand what *la lengua,* "language," meant for Nebrija, it is necessary to know who he was (Bahner, 1956). Antonio Martinez de la Cala, descendant of Jewish converts, had decided at age 19 that Latin, at least on the Iberian peninsula, had become so corrupted that one could say it had died of neglect. Thus Spain was left without a language *(una lengua)* worthy of the name. The languages of Scripture—Greek, Latin, Hebrew—clearly were something other than the speech of the people. Nebrija then went to Italy where, in his opinion, Latin was least corrupted. When he returned to Spain, his contemporary Hernán Nuñez wrote that it was like Orpheus bringing Euridice back from Hades. During the next 20 years, Nebrija dedicated himself to the renewal of classical grammar and rhetoric. The first full book printed in Salamanca was his Latin grammar (1482).

When he reached his forties and began to age—as he put it—he discovered that he could make a language out of the speech forms he daily encountered in Spain. For this reason, he claimed, he wrote his Spanish grammar, the first in any modern European tongue. In the *converso,* Nebrija used his classical formation to extend the juridic category of *consuetudo hispaniae* to the realm of language (Maravall, 1964, p. 492). Throughout the Iberian peninsula, crowds speaking various languages gathered for pogroms against the Jewish outsider at the very moment when Nebrija, by way of the cosmopolitan *converso,* offered his services to the Crown—the creation of one language suitable for use wherever the sword could carry it (Castro, 1962, pp. xxii–xxiii). (When I speak to Brahmans in India, they are always surprised to learn that Europe, by the end of the fifteenth century, had produced only its shadows of Panini for Latin and Greek, but never a Prakrit grammarian. For Indians, grammars are descriptions; for Europeans, as we shall see, they are engineering manuals.)

While he worked on his grammar, Negrija also wrote a dictionary that, to this day, remains the single best source on Old Spanish. The two attempts made in our lifetime to supersede him both failed. Gili Gaya's *Tesauro Lexicográfico,* begun in 1947, foundered on the letter *E,* and R. S. Boggs *(Tentative Dictionary of Medieval Spanish)* remains, since 1946, an often copied draft. Nebrija's dictionary appeared the year after his grammar, and already contained evidence of the New World: the first Americanism, *canoa* (canoe), appeared.

Now note what Nebrija thought about Castilian.

> Castilian went through its infancy at the time of the judges . . . it waxed in strength under Alfonso the Learned. It was he who collected law and history books in Greek and Latin and had them translated.

Indeed, Alfonso (1221–1284) was the first European monarch to use the vulgar or vernacular tongue of the scribes as his chancery language. His intent was to demonstrate that he was not one of the Latin kings. Like a caliph, he ordered his courtiers to undertake pilgrimages through Muslim and Christian books, and transform them into treasures that, because of their very language, would be a valuable inheritance to leave his kingdom. Incidentally, most of his translators were Jews from Toledo. And these Jews—whose own language was Old Castilian—preferred to translate the oriental languages into the vernacular rather than into Latin, the sacred language of the Church.

Nebrija points out to the queen that Alfonso had left solid tokens of Old Spanish; in addition, he had worked toward the transformation of vernacular speech into language proper by using it to make laws, to record history, and to translate from the classics. He continues:

> This our language followed our soldiers whom we went abroad to rule. It spread to Aragon, to Navarra, even to Italy . . . the scattered bits and pieces of Spain were thus gathered and joined into one single kingdom.

Nebrija here reminds the queen of the new pact possible between sword and book. He proposes a convenant between two spheres, both within the secular realm of the Crown, a covenant distinct from the medieval pact between Emperor and Pope, which had been a covenant bridging the secular and the sacred. He knew well whom he addressed: the wife of Ferdinand of Aragon, a woman he once praised as the most enlightened of all men (*sic*). He was aware that she read Cicero, Seneca, and Livy in the original for her own pleasure, and that she possessed a sensibility that united the physical and spiritual into what she herself called "good taste." Indeed, historians claim that she was the first to use this expression (Menendez Pidal, 1957, p. 130). Together with Ferdinand, she was trying to give shape to the chaotic Castile they had inherited; together they were creating Renaissance institutions of government, institutions apt for making of a modern state, and yet, something better than a nation of lawyers (Mariejol, 1961, p. 307). Nebrija calls to their minds a concept that to this day is powerful in Spanish—*armas y letras*. He speaks about the marriage of empire and language, addressing the soverign who had just recently— and for a painfully short time—seized from the Church the Inquisition, in order to use it as a secular instrument of royal power. The monarchy used it to gain economic control of the grandees and to replace noblemen by the *letrados* of Nebrija on the governing councils of the kingdom. This was the monarchy that transformed the older advisory bodies into bureaucratic organizations of civil servants, institutions fit only for the execution of royal policies. These secretaries or ministries of "experts," under the court ceremonial of the Hapsburgs, were later assigned a ritual role in the processions and receptions incomparable to any other secular bureaucracy since the times of Byzantium.

Very astutely, Nebrija's argument reminds the queen that a new union of *armas y letras,* complementary to that of church and state, was essential to gather and join the scattered pieces of Spain into a single absolute kingdom.

> This unified and sovereign body will be of such shape and inner cohesion that centuries will be unable to undo it. Now that the Church has been purified, and we are thus reconciled to God [does he think of the work of his contemporary, Torquemada?], now that the enemies of the Faith have been subdued by our arms [he refers to the apogee of the *Reconquista*], now that just laws are being enforced, enabling all of us to live as equals [perhaps having in mind the *Hermandades*], what else remains but the flowering of the peaceful arts. And among the arts, foremost are those of language, which sets us apart from wild animals; language, which is the unique distinction of man, the means for the kind of understanding which can be surpassed only by contemplation.

Here, we distinctly hear the appeal of the humanist to the prince, requesting him to defend the realm of civilized Christians against the domain of the wild. "The wild man's inability to speak is part of the Wild Man Myth whenever we meet him during the middle ages . . . in a morally ordered world, to be wild is to be incoherent or mute . . . sinful and accursed" (White, 1972, p. 17). Formerly, the heathen was to be brought into the fold through baptism; henceforth, through education. Nebrija then points out:

> So far, this our language has been left loose and unruly and, therefore, in just a few centuries this language has changed beyond recognition. If we were to

compare what we speak today with the language spoken five hundred years ago, we would notice a difference and a diversity that could not be any greater if these were two alien tongues.

Nebrija describes the evolution and extension of vernacular tongues, of the *lengua vulgar,* through time. He refers to the untutored speech of Castile—different from that of Aragon and Navarra, regions where soldiers had recently introduced Castilian—but a speech also different from the older Castilian into which Alfonso's monks and Jews had translated the Greek classics from their Arabic versions. In the fifteenth century people felt and lived their languages otherwise than we do today. The study of Columbus's language made by Menendez Pidal helps us to understand this. Columbus, originally a cloth merchant from Genoa, had as his first language Genovese, a dialect still not standardized today. He learned to write business letters in Latin, albeit a barbarous variety. After being shipwrecked in Portugal, he married a Portuguese and probably forgot most of his Italian. He spoke but never wrote a word of Portuguese. During his nine years in Lisbon, he took up writing in Spanish. But he never used his brilliant mind to learn Spanish well and always wrote it in a hybrid, Portuguese-mannered style. His Spanish is not Castilian but is rich in simple words picked up all over the peninsula. In spite of some syntactical monstrosities, he handled this language in a lively, expressive, and precise fashion. Columbus, then, wrote in two languages he did not speak, and spoke several. None of this seems to have been problematic for his contemporaries. However, it is also true that none of these languages of Columbus would have satisfied Nebrija.

Continuing to develop his petition, he introduces the crucial element of his argument: *La lengua suelta y fuera de regla,* the unbound and ungoverned speech in which people actually live and manage their lives, has become a challenge to the Crown. He now interprets an unproblematic historical fact as a problem for the architects of a new kind of polity—the modern state.

> Your Majesty, it has been my constant desire to see our nation become great, and to provide the men of my tongue with books worthy of their leisure. Presently, they waste their time on novels and fancy stories full of lies.

Nebrija proposes to regularize language to stop people from wasting time on frivolous reading, "quando la emprenta aun no informaba la lengua de los libros" (Menendez Pidal, 1957, p. 132). And Nebrija was not the only late fifteenth-century person concerned with the "waste" of leisure time made possible through the inventions of paper and movable type. Ignatius of Loyla, 29 years later, while convalescing in Pamplona with a leg shattered by a cannonball, came to believe that he had disastrously wasted his youth. At thirty, he looked back on his life as one filled with "the vanities of the world," whose leisure had included the reading of vernacular trash.

Nebrija argues for standardizing a living language for the benefit of its printed form. This argument is also made in our generation, but the end now is different (cf. Williams, this volume). Our contemporaries believe that standardized language is a necessary condition to teach people to read, indispensable for the distribution of printed books. The argument in 1492 is the opposite: Nebrija was upset because people who spoke in dozens of distinct vernacular tongues had become the victims of a reading epidemic. They wasted their leisure, throwing away their time on books that circulated outside of any possible bureaucratic control. A manuscript was so precious and rare that authorities could often suppress the work of an author by literally seizing *all* the copies. Manuscripts, for example, could sometimes be extirpated. Not so books. Even with the small editions of two hundred to a thousand copies—typical for the first generation of print—it was never possible to confiscate an entire run. Printed books called for the exercise of censorship through an *Index of Forbidden Books*. Books could only be proscribed, not destroyed. But Nebrija's proposal appeared more than 50 years before the *Index* was published in 1559. And he wished to achieve control over the printed word on a much deeper level than what the Church attempted. He wanted to replace the people's vernacular with the grammarian's language. The humanist proposes the standardization of colloquial language to remove the new technology of printing from the vernacular domain—to prevent people from printing and reading in the various languages that, up to that time, they had only spoken. By this monopoly over an official and taught language, he proposes to suppress wild, untaught vernacular reading.

To grasp the full significance of Nebrija's argument—the argument that compulsory education in a standardized national tongue is necessary to stop people from wanton reading that gives them an easy pleasure—one must remember the status of print at that time. Nebrija was born before the appearance of movable type. He was 13 when the first movable stock came into use. His conscious adult life coincides with the Incunabula. When printing was in its 25th year, he published his Latin grammar; when it was in its 35th year, his Spanish grammar. Nebrija could recall the time before print, as I can the time before television. Nebrija's text, on which I am commenting, was by coincidence published the year Thomas Caxton died. And Caxton's work itself furthers our understanding of the *vernacular* book.

Thomas Caxton was an English cloth merchant living in the Netherlands. He took up translating, and then apprenticed himself to a printer. After publishing a few books in English, he took his press to England in 1476. By the time he died (1491), he had published 40 translations into English and nearly everything available in English vernacular literature, with the notable exception of William Langland's *Piers Plowman*. I have often wondered whether he left this important work off his list because of the challenge it might present to one of his best sellers—*The Art and Crafte to Knowe Well to Dye*. This volume of his Westminster Press belongs to the first series of self-help books. Whatever would train for a society well informed and well mannered, whatever would lead to behavior gentle and devout, was gathered in small folios and quartos of neat Gothic print—instructions on everything from manipulating a knife to conducting a conversation, from the art of weeping to the art of playing chess to that of dying. Before 1500, no less than 100 editions of this last book appeared. It is a self-instruction manual, showing one how to prepare to die with dignity and without the intervention of physican or clergy (O'Connor, 1966).

Four categories of books first appeared in the peoples' languages: vernacular, native literature; translations from French and Latin; devotional books; and, already, the how-to-do-it manuals that made teachers unnecessary. Printed books in Latin were of a different sort, comprising textbooks, rituals, and lawbooks—books at the service of professional clergymen and teachers. From the very beginning, printed books were of two kinds: those which readers independently chose for their pleasure and those professionally prescribed for the reader's own good.

It is estimated that before 1500, more than 1,700 presses in almost 300 European towns had produced one or more books. Almost 40,000 editions were published during the fifteenth century, comprising somewhere between 15 and 20 million copies (Wells, 1964). About one third of these were published in the various vernacular languages of Europe. This portion of printed books is the source of Nebrija's concern. To appreciate more fully his worry about the freedom to read, one must remember that reading in his time was not silent. Silent reading is a recent invention. Augustine was already a great author and the Bishop of Hippo when he found that it could be done. In his *Confessions,* he described the discovery (Marrou, 1958, pp. 209–314). During the night, charity forbade him to disturb his fellow monks with noises he made while reading. But curiosity impelled him to pick up a book. So he learned to read in silence, an art that he had observed in only one man, his teacher, Ambrose of Milan. Ambrose practiced the art of silent reading because otherwise people would have gathered around him and would have interrupted him with their queries on the text. Loud reading was the link between classical learning and popular culture (Albertini, 1923).

Habitual reading in a loud voice produces social effects. It is an extraordinarily effective way of teaching the art to those who look over the reader's shoulder; rather than being confined to a sublime or sublimated form of self-satisfaction, it promotes community intercourse; it actively leads to common digestion of and comment on the passages read. In most of the languages of India, the verb that translates into *reading* has a meaning close to *sounding.* The same verb makes the book and the vina sound. To read and to play a musical instrument are perceived as parallel activities. The current, simpleminded, internationally accepted definition of literacy obcures an alternate approach to book, print, and reading. If reading were conceived primarily as a social activity as, for example, competence in playing the guitar, fewer readers could mean a much broader access to books and literature.

Reading aloud—except for Latin—was common in Europe before Nebrija's time. Print multiplied and spread opportunities for this oral reading in an epidemic manner. Further, the line between literate and illiterate was different from what we recognize now. Literate was he who had been taught Latin. The great mass of people, thoroughly conversant with the vernacular literature of their region, either did not know how to read and write, had picked it up on their own, had been instructed as accountants, had left the clergy, or, even if they knew it, hardly used their Latin. This held true for the poor and for many nobles, especially women. And we sometimes forget that even today the rich, many professionals, and high-level bureaucrats have assistants report a verbal digest of documents and information and call on secretaries to write what they dictate.

To the queen, Nebrija's proposed enterprise must have seemed even more improbable than Columbus's project. But, ultimately, it turned out to be more fundamental than the New World for the rise of the Hapsburg Empire. Nebrija clearly showed the way to prevent the free and anarchic development of printing technology and exactly how to transform it into the evolving national state's instrument of bureaucratic control.

Today, we generally act on the assumption that books could not be printed and would not be read in any number if they were written in a vernacular language free from the constraints of an official grammar. Equally, we assume that people could not learn to read and write their own tongue unless they were taught in the same manner as students were traditionally taught in Latin. Let us listen again to Nebrija.

> By means of my grammar, they shall learn artificial Castilian, not difficult to do, since it is built up on the base of a language they know; and, then, Latin will come easily.

Nebrija already considers the vernacular as a raw material from which his Castilian art can be produced, a resource to be mined, not unlike the brazilwood and human chattel that, Columbus sadly concluded, were the only resources of value or importance in Cuba.

Nebrija does not seek to teach grammar that people learn to read. Rather, he implores Isabella to give him the power and authority to stem the anarchic spread of reading by the use of his grammar.

> Presently, they waste their leisure on novels and fancy stories full of lies. I have decided, therefore, that my most urgent task is to transform Castilian speech into an artifact, so that whatever henceforth shall be written in this language may be of one standard tenor.

Nebrija frankly states what he wants to do and even provides the outline of his incredible project. He deliberately turns the mate of empire into its slave. Here the first modern educational expert advises the Crown on the way to make, out of a people's speech and lives, tools that befit the state and its pursuits. Henceforth, people will have to rely on the language they receive from above, rather than to develop a tongue in common with one another. The switch from the vernacular to an officially taught mother tongue is perhaps the most significant—and, therefore, least researched—event in the coming of a commodity-intensive society. The radical change from vernacular to taught language foreshadows the switch from breast to bottle, from subsistence to welfare, from production for use to production for market, from expectations divided between state and church to a world where the Church is marginal, religion is privatized, and the state assumes the maternal functions heretofore claimed only by the Church. Formerly, there had been no salvation outside the Church; now, there would be no reading, no writing—if possible, no speaking—outside the educational sphere. People would have to be reborn out of the monarch's womb, and be nourished at her breast. Both the citizen of the modern state and his state-provided language come into being for the first time, both are without precedent anywhere in history.

But dependence on a formal, bureaucratic institution to obtain for every individual a service that is as necessary as breast milk for human subsistence, while radically new and without parallel outside of Europe, was not a break with Europe's past. Rather, this was a logical step forward—a process first legitimated in the Christian Church evolved into an accepted and expected temporal function of the secular state. Institutional maternity has a unique European history since the third century. In this sense, it is indeed true that Europe is the Church and the Church is Europe.

Nebrija and education in the modern state cannot be understood without a close knowledge of the Church, insofar as this institution is represented as a mother. Further, one must examine the secularization of this priest-ridden motherhood in the fifteenth and sixteenth centuries.

From the very earliest days, the Church was called "mother." Marcion the Gnostic used this designation in 144. At first, the community of the faithful was meant to be mother to the new members whom communion engenders. Soon, however, the Church became a mother outside of whose bosom it was hardly worthwhile to be called human or to be alive. But the origins of the Church's self-understanding as mother have been little researched. One can often find comments about the role of mother-goddesses in the various religions scattered throughout the Roman Empire at the time Christianity began to spread. But the fact that no previous community had ever been called mother has yet to be noticed and studied. We know that the image of the Church as mother comes from Syria, and that it flourished in the third century in North Africa. On a beautiful mosaic near Tripoli, where the claim is first expressed, both the invisible community and the visible building are represented as mother (Leclercq, 1903). And Rome is the last place where the metaphor is applied to the Church. The female personification of an institution did not fit the Roman style; the idea was first taken up only late in the fourth century in a poem by Pope Damasus.

This early Christian notion of the Church as mother is of a very peculiar type. No direct gnostic or pagan influence nor any direct relationship to the Roman mother cult has thus far been proven. The description of the Church's maternity is, however, quite explicit. The Church conceives, bears, and gives birth to her sons and daughters. She may have a miscarriage. She raises her children to her breast to nourish them with the milk of faith. She herself is born from the blood of Christ. In this early period, the institutional trait is clearly present, but the maternal authority exercised by the Church through her bishops and the ritual treatment of the Church building as a female entity are still balanced by the insistence on the motherly quality of God's love and of the mutual love of his children in baptism (Delhaye, 1964). The image of the Church as a prototype of the authoritarian and possessive mother became dominant in the Middle Ages (Plumpe, 1943). The popes then insisted on an understanding of the Church as *Mater, Magistra,* and *Domina* (Congar, 1964)—mother, authoritative teacher, sovereign. Thus Gregory VII (1073–1085) named her in the struggle with the emperor Henry IV.

Nebrija's introduction is addressed to a queen intent on building a modern state. And his argument implies that, institutionally, the state must now assume the universally maternal functions heretofore claimed only by the Church. Actually, when Nebrija proposes to transform Castilian into an artifact, as necessary for the queen's subjects as faith for the Christian, he appeals to the hermetic tradition. In the language of his time, the two words he uses—*reducir* and *artificio*—have both an ordinary and a technical meaning. In the latter case, they belong to a language of alchemy.

According to Nebrija's own dictionary, *reducir* in fifteenth-century Spanish means "to change," "to bring into obeissance," and "to civilize." In this last sense the Jesuits later understood the *Reducciones de Paraguay.* In addition, *reductio—*

throughout the fifteenth and sixteenth centuries—means one of the seven stages by which ordinary elements of nature are transmitted into the philosopher's stone, into the panacea that, by touch, turns everything into gold. Here, *reductio* designates the fourth of seven grades of sublimation. It designates the crucial test that must be passed by gray matter to be promoted from the primary to the secondary grades of enlightenment. In the first four grades, raw nature is successively liquefied, purified, and evaporated. In the fourth grade, that of *reductio,* it is nourished on philosopher's milk. If it takes to this substance, which will occur only if the first three processes have completely voided its unruly and raw nature, the chrysosperm, the sperm of gold hidden in its depth, can be brought forth. This is *educatio.* During the following three stages, the alchemist can coagulate his *alumnus*—the substance he has fed with his milk—into the philosopher's stone. The precise language used here is a bit posterior to Nebrija. It is taken almost literally from Paracelsus, another man born within a year of the publication of the *Grámatica Castellana.*

Now let us return to the text. Nebrija develops his argument:

> I have decided to transform Castilian into an artifact so that whatever shall be written henceforth in this language shall be of one standard tenor, one coinage that can outlast the times. Greek and Latin have been governed by art, and thus have kept their uniformity throughout the ages. Unless the like of this be done for our language, in vain Your Majesty's chroniclers . . . shall praise your deeds. Your labor will not last more than a few years, and we shall continue to feed on Castilian translations of foreign tales about our own kings. Either your feats will fade with the language or they will roam among aliens abroad, homeless, without a dwelling in which they can settle.

The Roman Empire could be governed through the Latin of its elite. But the traditional, separate elite language used in former empires for keeping records, maintaining international relations, and advancing learning—like Persian, Arabic, Latin, or Frankish—is insufficient to realize the aspirations of nationalistic monarchies. The modern European state cannot function in the world of the vernacular. The new national state needs an *artificio,* unlike the perennial Latin of diplomacy and the perishable Castilian of Alfonso the Learned. This kind of polity requires a standard language understood by all those subject to its laws and for whom the tales written at the monarch's behest (that is, propaganda) are destined. However, Nebrija does not suggest that Latin be abandoned. On the contrary, the neo-Latin renaissance in Spain owed its existence largely to his grammar, dictionary, and textbooks. But his important innovation was to lay the foundation for a linguistic ideal without precedent: the creation of a society in which the universal ruler's bureaucrats, soldiers, merchants, and peasants all pretend to speak one language, a language the poor are presumed to understand and to obey. Nebrija established the notion of a kind of ordinary language that itself is sufficient to place each man in his assigned place on the pyramid that education in a mother tongue necessarily constructs. In his argument, he insists that Isabella's claim to historical fame depends on forging a language of propaganda—universal and fixed like Latin, yet capable of penetrating every village and farm, to reduce subjects into modern citizens.

How times had changed since Dante! For Dante, a language that had to be learned, to be spoken according to a grammar, was inevitably a dead tongue. For him, such a language was fit only for schoolmen, whom he cynically called *inventores grammaticae facultatis*. What for Dante was dead and useless, Nebrija recommended as a tool. One was interested in vital exchange, the other in universal conquest, in a language that by rule would coin words as incorruptible as the stones of a palace:

> Your Majesty, I want to lay the foundations for the dwelling in which your fame can settle. I want to do for our language what Zeno has done for Greek, and Crates for Latin. I do not doubt that their betters have come to succeed them. But the fact that their pupils have improved on them does not detract from their or, I should say, from our glory—to be the inventors of a necessary craft just when the times for such invention was ripe. Trust me, Your Majesty, no craft has ever arrived more timely than grammar for the Castilian tongue at this time.

The expert is always in a hurry, but his belief in progress gives him the language of humility. The academic adventurer pushes his government to adopt his idea now, under threat of failure to achieve its imperial designs. This is the time!

> Our language has indeed just now reached a height from which we must fear more that we sink, than we can ever hope to rise.

Nebrija's last paragraph in the introduction exudes eloquence. Evidently the teacher of rhetoric knew what he taught. Nebrija has explained his project; given the queen logical reasons to accept it; frightened her with what would happen if she were not to heed him; now, finally, like Columbus, he appeals to her sense of a manifest destiny.

> Now, Your Majesty, let me come to the last advantage that you shall gain from my grammar. For the purpose, recall the time when I presented you with a draft of this book earlier this year in Salamanca. At this time, you asked me what end such a grammar could possibly serve. Upon this, the Bishop of Avila interrupted to answer in my stead. What he said was this: "Soon Your Majesty will have placed her yoke upon many barbarians who speak outlandish tongues. By this, your victory, these people shall stand in a new need; the need for the laws the victor owes to the vanquished, and the need for the language we shall bring with us." My grammar shall serve to impart to them the Castilian tongue, as we have used grammar to teach Latin to our young.

We can attempt a reconstruction of what happened at Salamanca when Nebrija handed the queen a draft of his forthcoming book. The queen praised the humanist for having provided the Castilian tongue with what had been reserved to the languages of Scripture—Hebrew, Greek, and Latin. (It is surprising and significant that the *converso,* in the year of Granada, does not mention the Arabic of the Koran!) But while Isabella was able to grasp the achievement of her *letrado*—the description of a living tongue as rules of grammar—she was unable to see any practical purpose in such an undertaking. For her, grammar was an instrument designed solely for use by teachers. She believed, however, that the vernacular simply could not be taught. In her royal view of linguistics, every subject of her many kingdoms was so made by nature that during his lifetime he would reach perfect dominion over his tongue *on his own*. In this version of "majestic linguistics," the vernacular is the *subject's* domain. By the very nature of things, the vernacular is beyond the reach of the ruler's authority. Isabella's initial rejection underscores the originality of Nebrija's proposal.

This discussion of Nebrija's draft about the need for instruction to speak one's mother tongue must have taken place in the months around March 1492, the same time Columbus argued his project with the queen. At first, Isabella refused Columbus on the advice of technical counsel—he had miscalculated the circumference of the globe. But Nebrija's proposal she rejected out of a different motive: from royal respect for the autonomy of her subject's tongues. This respect of the Crown for the juridic autonomy of each village, of the *fuero del pueblo,* the judgment by peers, was perceived by people and sovereign as the fundamental freedom of Christians engaged in the reconquest of Spain. Nebrija argued against this traditional and typically Iberic prejudice of Isabella—the notion that the Crown cannot encroach on the variety of customs in the kingdoms—and called up the image of a new, universal mission for a *modern* Crown.

Ultimately, Columbus won out because Franciscan friends presented him to the queen as a man driven by God to serve her mystical mission. Nebrija proceeded in the same fashion. First, he argued that the vernacular must be replaced by an *artificio* to give the monarch's power increased range and duration; then, to cultivate the arts by decision of the court; also, to guard the established order against the threat presented by wanton reading and printing. But he concluded his petition with an appeal to "the Grace of Granada"—the queen's destiny, not just to conquer, but to civilize the whole world.

Both Columbus and Nebrija offered their services to a new kind of empire builder. But Columbus proposed only to use the recently created caravels to the limit of their range for the expansion of royal power in what would become New Spain. Nebrija was more basic—he argued the use of his grammar for the expansion of the queen's power in a totally new sphere that he proposed to create through the act of conquest itself. He intended the creation of the sphere of a taught mother tongue— the first invented part of universal education.

The Conquest of the Vernacular

Historians have chosen Columbus's voyage from Palos as a date convenient for marking the transition from the Middle Ages to modern times, a point useful for changing editors of textbooks. But the world of Ptolemy did not become the world of Mercator in one year, nor did the world of the vernacular become the age of education overnight. Rather, traditional cosmography was gradually adjusted in the light of widening experience. Columbus was followed by Cortéz, Copernicus by Kepler, Nebrija by Comenius. Unlike personal insight, a change in world view takes time.

How often the hand of the clock advances depends on the language of the ciphers on the quadrant. The Chinese speak of five stages in sprouting, and dawn approaches in seven steps for the Arabs. If I were to describe the evolution of *homo economicus* from Mandeville to Marx or Galbraith (Dumont, 1977), I would come to a different view of epochs than if I had a mind to outline the stages in which the ideology of *homo educandus* developed from Nebrija through Radke to Comenius. And again, within this same paradigm, a different set of turning points would best describe the decay of untutored learning and the route toward the inescapable miseducation that educational institutions necessarily dispense.

It took a good decade to recognize that Columbus had found a new hemisphere, not just a new route. It took much longer to invent the concept *New World* for the continent whose existence he had denied. Later, it took exactly a hundred years from the posthumous publication of the *Heavenly Revolutions*—in which Copernicus reorganized and perfected the planetary spheres around the sun rather than the earth— to the posthumous publication of Kepler's *Dream*—in which, as we shall see, he advocated interplanetary travel unhampered by any crystal sphere. A full century and a half separated the claim of Nebrija—in the queen's service he *had* to teach all her subjects to speak—and the claim of John Amos Comenius—the possession of a method to teach everybody everything perfectly.

By the time of Comenius (1592–1670), the ruling groups of both the Old and the New Worlds were deeply convinced of the need for such a method. An incident in the history of Harvard College aptly illustrates the point. On the 150th birthday of Nebrija's grammar, John Winthrop, Jr. was on his way to Europe searching for a theologian and educator to accept the presidency of Harvard (Spinka, 1943). One of the first persons he approached was the Czech Comenius, leader and last bishop of the Moravian Church. Winthrop found him in London, where he was organizing the Royal Society and advising the government on public schools. In *Magna Didactica, vel Ars Omnibus Omnia Omnino Docendi,*[3] Comenius had succinctly defined the goals of his profession. Education begins in the womb, and does not end until death. Whatever is worth knowing is worth teaching by a special method appropriate to the subject. The preferred world is the one so organized that it functions as a school for all. Only if learning is the result of teaching can individuals be raised to the fullness of their humanity. People who learn without being taught are more like animals than men. And the school system must be so organized that all, old and young, rich and poor, noble and low, men and women, be taught effectively, not just symbolically and ostentatiously.

These are the thoughts written by the potential president of Harvard. But he never crossed the Atlantic. By the time Winthrop met him, he had already accepted the invitation of the Swedish government to organize a national system of schools for Queen Christina. Unlike Nebrija, he never had to argue the need for his services— they were always in great demand. The domain of the vernacular, considered untouchable by Isabella, had become the hunting ground for job-seeking Spanish *letrados,* Jesuits, and Massachusetts divines. A sphere of formal education had been disembedded.[4] Formerly taught mother tongue professionally handled according to abstract rules had begun to compete with and encroach upon the vernacular. This

---

[3]The *Magna Didactica* was first published in Czech (1627); the Latin translation was finished in 1638 and circulated thereafter in excerpts. It was first completely printed in Amsterdam (1657). Chapter 20, section 15, deals with the idea "that everything which ought to be known must be taught."

[4]This term was coined by Karl Polanyi in 1948. I use it on purpose to underline the fact that my analysis tries to broaden several trends of research that have been initiated by Polanyi.

gradual replacement and degradation of the vernacular by its costly counterfeit heralds the coming of the market-intensive society in which we now live.

Vernacular comes from an Indo-Germanic root that implies "rootedness" and "abode." *Vernaculum* as a Latin word was used for whatever was homebred, homespun, homegrown, homemade, as opposed to what was obtained in formal exchange. The child of one's slave and of one's wife, the donkey born of one's own beast, were vernacular beings, as was the staple that came from the garden or the commons. If Karl Polanyi had adverted to this fact, he might have used the term in the meaning accepted by the ancient Romans: sustenance derived from reciprocity patterns imbedded in every aspect of life, as distinguished from sustenance that comes from exchange or from vertical distribution.

Vernacular was used in this general sense from preclassical times down to the technical formulations found in the Codex of Theodosius.[5] It was Varro who picked the term to introduce the same distinction in language. For him, *vernacular speech* is made up of the words and patterns grown on the speaker's own ground, as opposed to what is grown elsewhere and then transported. And since Varro's authority was widely recognized, his definition stuck. He was the librarian of both Caesar and Augustus and the first Roman to attempt a thorough and critical study of the Latin language. His *Lingua Latina* was a basic reference book for centuries. Quintillian admired him as the most learned of all Romans. And Quintillian, the Spanish-born drill master for the future senators of Rome, is always proposed to normal students as one of the founders of their profession. But neither can be compared to Nebrija. Both Varra and Quintillian were concerned with shaping the speech of senators and scribes, the speech of the forum; Nebrija with the language of the common man who could read and listen to readings. Simply, Nebrija proposed to substitute a mother tongue for the vernacular.

Vernacular came into English in the one restricted sense to which Varro had confined its meaning. Just now, I would like to resuscitate some of its old breath. We need a simple, straightforward word to designate the activities of people when they are not motivated by thoughts of exchange, a word that denotes autonomous, non-market-related actions through which people satisfy everyday needs—the actions that by their very nature escape bureaucratic control, satisfying needs to which, in the very process, they give specific shape. Vernacular seems a good old word for this purpose, and should be acceptable to many contemporaries. There are technical words that designate the satisfaction of needs that economists do not or cannot measure—social production as opposed to economic production, the generation of use-values as opposed to the production of commodities, household economics as opposed to market economics. But these terms are specialized, tainted with some ideological prejudice, and each, in a different way, badly limps. Each contrasting pair of terms, in its own way, also fosters the confusion that assigns vernacular undertakings to unpaid, standardized, formalized activities. It is this kind of confusion that I wish to

---

[5] *Vernaculum, quidquid domi nascitur, domestici fructus, res quae alicui nata est, et quam non emit. Ita hanc vocem interpretatur Anianus in leg. 3 Cod. Th. de lustrati collatione, ube Jacob. Gothofredus.* Thus C. D. Du Cange (1883–1887).

clarify. We need a simple adjective to name those acts of competence, lust, or concern that we want to defend from measurement or manipulation by Chicago Boys and Socialist Commissars. The term must be broad enough to fit the preparation of food and the shaping of language, childbirth, and recreation, without implying either a privatized activity akin to the housework of modern women, a hobby, or an irrational and primitive procedure. Such an adjective is not at hand. But vernacular might serve. By speaking about vernacular language and the possibility of its recuperation, I am trying to bring into awareness and discussion the existence of a vernacular mode of being, doing, and making that in a desirable future society might again expand in all aspects of life.

Mother tongue, since the term was first used, has never meant the vernacular, but rather its contrary. The term was first used by Catholic monks to designate a particular language they used, instead of Latin, when speaking from the pulpit. No Indo-Germanic culture before had used the term. The word was introduced into Sanskrit in the eighteenth century as a translation from the English. The term has no roots in the other major language families now spoken on which I could check. The only classical people who viewed their homeland as a kind of mother were the Cretans. Bachofen suggests that memories of an old matriarchal order still lingered in their culture. But even in Crete, there was no equivalent to "mother" tongue. To trace the association which led to the term *mother tongue,* I shall first have to look at what happened at the court of Charlemagne, and then at what happened later in the Abbey of Gorz.

The idea that humans are born in such fashion that they need institutional service from professional agents in order to reach that humanity for which by birth all people are destined can be traced to Carolingian times. It was then that, for the first time in history, it was discovered that there are certain basic needs, needs that are universal to mankind and that cry out for satisfaction in a standard fashion that cannot be met in a vernacular way. The discovery is perhaps best associated with the Church reform that took place in the eighth century. The Scottish monk Alcuin, the former chancellor of York University who became the court philosopher of Charles the Great, played a prominent role in this reform (Heyer, 1959). Up to that time the Church had considered its ministers primarily as priests, that is, as men selected and invested with special powers to meet communitary, liturgical, public needs. They were engaged in preaching at ritual occasions and had to preside at functions. They acted as public officials, analogous to those others through whom the state provided for the administration of justice, or, in Roman times, for public work. To think of these kinds of magistrates as if they were "service professionals" would be an anachronistic projection of our contemporary categories.

But then, from the eighth century on, the classical priest rooted in Roman and Hellenistic models begun to be transmogrified into the precursor of the service professional: the teacher, social worker, or educator. Church ministers began to cater to the personal needs of parishioners, and to equip themselves with a sacramental and pastoral theology that defined and established these needs for their regular service. The institutionally defined care of the individual, the family, the village community, acquired unprecedented prominence. The term *holy mother of the Church* ceased almost totally to mean the actual assembly of the faithful whose love, under the impulse of the Holy Spirit, engenders new life in the very act of meeting. The term *mother* henceforth refered to an invisible, mystical reality from which alone those services absolutely necessary for salvation can be obtained. Henceforth, access to the good graces of this mother on whom universally necessary salvation depends was entirely controlled by a hierarchy of ordained males. This gender-specific mythology of male hierarchies mediating access to the institutional source of life was without precedent. From the ninth to the eleventh century, the idea took shape that there are some needs common to all human beings that can be satisfied only through service from professional agents. Thus the definition of needs in terms of profession- ally defined commodites in the service sector preceded by a millennium the industrial production of universally needed basic goods.

Thirty-five years ago, Lewis Mumford tried to make this point. When I first read his statement that the monastic reform of the ninth century created some of the basic assumptions on which the industrial system is founded, I could not be convinced by something I considered more of an intuition than a proof. In the meantime, though, I have found a host of converging arguments—most of which Mumford did not seem to suspect—for rooting the ideologies of the industrial age in the earlier Carolingian Renaissance. The idea that there is no salvation without *personal ser- vices* provided by professionals in the name of an institutional Mother Church is one of these formerly unnoticed developments without which, again, our own age would be unthinkable. True, it took 500 years of medieval theology to elaborate on this concept. Only by the end of the Middle Ages would the *pastoral* self-image of the Church be fully rounded. And only in the Council of Trent (1545) would the self- image of the Church as a mother milked by clerical hierarchies become formally defined. Then, in the *Constitution* of the Second Vatican Council (1964), the Cath- olic Church, which had served in the past as the prime model for the evolution of secular service organizations, aligned itself explicitly in the image of its secular imitations.

The important point here is the notion that the clergy can define its services as needs of human nature, and make this service commodity the kind of necessity that cannot be forgone without jeopardy to eternal life. It is in this ability of a nonhere- ditary elite that we ought to locate the foundation without which the contemporary service or welfare state would not be conceivable. Surprisingly little research has been done on the religious concepts that fundamentally distinguish the industrial age from all other epochs. The decline of the vernacular conception of Christian life in favor of one organized around pastoral care is a complex and drawn-out process constituting the background for a set of consistent shifts in the language and insti- tutional development of the West (cf. Parker, this volume).

When Europe first began to take shape as an idea and as a political reality, between Merovingian times and the High Middle Ages, what people spoke was unproblematic. It was called "romance" or "theodisc"—peoplish. Only somewhat later, *linguia vulgaris* became the common denominator distinguishing popular speech from the Latin of administration and doctrine. Since Roman times, a person's first language was the *patrius sermo,* the language of the male head of the household. Each such *sermo* or speech was perceived as a separate language. Neither in ancient

Greece nor in the Middle Ages did people make the modern distinction between mutually understandable dialects and different languages. The same holds true today, for example, at the grass roots in India. What we know today as monolingual communities were and, in fact, are exceptions. From the Balkans to Indochina's western frontiers, it is still rare to find a village in which one cannot get along in more than two or three tongues. While it is assumed that each person has his *patrius sermo,* it is equally taken for granted that most persons speak several "vulgar" tongues, each in a vernacular, untaught way. Thus the vernacular, in opposition to specialized, learned language—Latin for the Church, Frankish for the Court—was as obvious in its variety as the taste of local wines and food, as the shapes of house and hoe, down to the eleventh century. It was at this moment, quite suddenly, that the term *mother tongue* appeared. It shows up in the sermons of some monks from the abbey of Gorz. The process by which this phenomenon turned vernacular speech into a moral issue can only be touched upon here.

Gorz was a mother abbey in Lorrain, not far from Verdun. Benedictine monks had founded the monastery in the eighth century, around bones believed to belong to Saint Gorgonius. During the ninth century, a time of widespread decay in ecclesiastical discipline, Gorz, too, suffered a notorious decline. But only three generations after such scandalous dissolution Gorz became the center of monastic reform in the Germanic areas of the Empire. Its reinvigoration of Cistercian life paralleled the work of the reform abbey of Cluny. Within a century, 160 daughter abbeys throughout the northeastern parts of central Europe were established from Gorz.

It seems quite probable that Gorz was then at the center of the diffusion of a new technology that was crucial for the later imperial expansion of the European powers: the transformation of the horse into the tractor of choice. Four Asiatic inventions—the horseshoe, the fixed saddle and stirrup, the bit, and the cummett (the collar resting on the shoulder)—permitted important and extensive changes. One horse could replace six oxen. While supplying the same traction, and more speed, a horse could be fed on the acreage needed for one yoke of oxen. Because of its speed, the horse permitted a more extensive cultivation of the wet, northern soils, in spite of the short summers. Also, greater rotation of crops was possible. But even more importantly, the peasant could now tend fields twice as far away from his dwelling. A new pattern of life became possible. Formerly, people had lived in clusters of homesteads; now they could form villages large enough to support a parish and, later, a school. Through dozens of abbeys, monastic learning and discipline, together with the reorganization of settlement patterns, spread throughout this part of Europe. Thus we see concentrations accompanying one another. "Motorized" power grows; and control over colloquial language, as I shall show, goes with it.

Gorz lies close to the line that divided Frankish from Romance types of vernacular, and some monks from Cluny began to cross this line. In these circumstances, the monks of Gorz made language, vernacular language, into an issue to defend their territorial claims (Heising, 1958). The monks began to preach in Frankish, and spoke specifically about the value of the Frankish tongue. They began to use the pulpit as a forum to stress the importance of language itself, perhaps even to teach it. From the little we know, they used at least two approaches. First, Frankish was the lan-

guage spoken by the women, even in those areas where the men were already beginning to use a Romance vernacular. Second, it was the language now used by Mother
Church.

How charged with sacred meanings motherhood was in the religiosity of the
twelfth century, one can grasp through contemplating the contemporary statues of
the Virgin Mary, or from reading the liturgical Sequences, the poetry of the time.
The term mother tongue, from its very first use, instrumentalizes everyday language
in the service of an institutional cause (Daube, 1940).[6] The word was translated from
Frankish into Latin. Then, as a rare Latin term, it incubated for several centuries.
In the decades before Luther, quite suddenly and dramatically, mother tongue
acquired a strong meaning. It became the language taught in school.

Modernity: The Predominance of Uniquack

I have now dealt with two stages in the "reduction" of vernacular into industrial
uniquack—a term that James Reston first used when Univack was the only commerical computer. One step I have analyzed is the appearance of the term mother
tongue among the monkish tutors of vernacular medieval speech. Another is the
transformation of mother tongue into national language under the auspices of the
imperialist Crown's grammarians. But since then, since Nebrija, language has
become enormously expensive. This capitalization of language in the industrial
nation-state is the third stage of reduction on which I would like to dwell. In this
article, I cannot describe and dissect the stages through which the idea of Comenius—to teach everything—approached complete implementation. I have space only
for a phenomenology of mother tongue 50 years after the loudspeaker began to
approximate the human voice and was installed in motion pictures, the kitchen, and
the concentration camp.

As language teaching has become a job, it has cost a lot of money. Words are
now one of the two largest categories of marketed values that make up the gross
national product (GNP). Money decides what shall be said, who shall say it, when
and what kind of people shall be targeted for the messages. The higher the cost of
each uttered word, the more determined the echo demanded. In schools people learn
to speak as they should. Money is spent to make the poor speak more like the
wealthy, the sick more like the healthy, and the minority more like the majority. We
pay to improve, correct, enrich, update the language of children and of their teachers.
We spend more on the professional jargons that are taught in college, and more yet
in high schools to give teenagers a smattering of these jargons; but just enough to
make them feel dependent on the psychologist, druggist, or librarian who is fluent in
some special kind of English. We go even further: We first allow standard language
to degrade ethnic, black, or hillbilly language, and then spend money to teach their
counterfeits as academic subjects. Administrators and entertainers, admen and
newsmen, ethnic politicians and "radical" professionals form powerful interest
groups, each fighting for a larger slice of the language pie.

---

[6]A mediocre doctoral thesis, but a repertory of quotations.

I do not really know how much is spent in the United States to make words. But soon someone will provide us with the necessary statistical tables. Ten years ago, energy accounting was almost unthinkable. Now it has become an established practice. Today you can easily look up how many "energy units" have gone into growing, harvesting, packaging, transporting, and merchandising one edible calorie of bread. The difference between the bread produced and eaten in a village in Greece and that found in an American supermarket is enormous—about 40 times more units are contained in each edible calorie of the latter. Bicycle traffic in cities permits one to move four times as fast as on foot for one fourth of the energy expended—while cars, for the same progress, need 150 times as many calories per passenger mile. Information of this kind was available ten years ago, but no one thought about it. Today, it is recorded and will soon lead to a change in people's outlook on the need for fuels. It would now be interesting to know what language accounting looks like, since the linguistic analysis of contemporary language is certainly not complete, unless for each group of speakers we know the amount of money spent on shaping the speech of the average person. Just as social energy accounts are only approximate and at best allow us to identify the orders of magnitude within which the relative values are found, so language accounting would provide us with data on the relative prevalence of standardized, taught language in a population—sufficient, however, for the argument I want to make.

But mere per capita expenditure employed to mold the language of a group of speakers does not tell us enough. No doubt we would learn that each paid word addressed to the rich costs, per capita, much more than words addressed to the poor. Watts are actually more democratic than words. But taught language comes in a vast range of qualities. The poor, for instance, are much more blared at than the rich, who can buy tutoring and, what is more precious, hedge on their own vernacular by purchasing silence. The educator now comes with a loudspeaker to Oaxaca, to Travancore, to the Chinese commune, and the poor immediately forfeit the claim to that indispensable luxury, the silence out of which vernacular language arises.

Yet even without putting a price tag on silence, even without the more detailed language economics on which I would like to draw, I can still estimate that the dollars spent to power any nation's motors pale before those that are now expended on prostituting speech in the mouth of paid speakers. In rich nations, language has become incredibly spongy, absorbing huge investments. High expenditures to cultivate the language of the mandarin, the author, the actor, or the charmer have always been a mark of high civilization. But these were efforts to teach elites special codes. Even the cost of making some people learn secret languages in traditional societies is incomparably lower than the capitalization of language in industrial societies.

In poor countries today, people still speak to each other without the experience of capitalized language, although such countries always contain a tiny elite who manage very well to allocate a larger proportion of the national income for their prestige language. Let me ask: What is different in the everyday speech of groups whose language has received—or shall I say absorbed? resisted? survived? suffered? enjoyed?—huge investments, and the speech of people whose language has remained outside the market? Comparing these two worlds of language, I want to focus my curiosity on just one issue that arises in this context. Does the structure and function of the language itself change with the rate of investment? Are these alterations such that all languages that absorb funds show changes in the same direction? In this introductory exploration of the subject, I cannot demonstrate that this is the case. But I do believe my arguments make both propositions highly probable, and show that structurally oriented language economics are worth exploring.

Taught everyday language is without precedent in preindustrial cultures. The current dependence on paid teachers and models of ordinary speech is just as much a unique characteristic of industrial economies as is dependence on fossil fuels. The need for taught mother tongue was discovered four centuries earlier, but only in our generation have both language and energy been effectively treated as worldwide needs to be satisfied for all people by planned, programmed production and distribution. Because, unlike the vernacular of capitalized language we can reasonably say that it results from *production.*

Traditional cultures subsisted on sunshine, which was captured mostly through agriculture. The hoe, the ditch, the yoke, were basic means to harness the sun. Large sails or waterwheels were known, but rare. These cultures that lived mostly on the sun subsisted basically on vernacular values. In such societies, tools were essentially the prolongation of arms, fingers, and legs. There was no need for the production of power in centralized plants and its distant distribution to clients. Equally, in these essentially sun-powered cultures, there was no need for language production. Language was drawn by each one from the cultural environment, learned from the encounter with people whom the learner could smell and touch, love or hate. The vernacular spread just as most things and services were shared, namely, by multiple forms of mutual reciprocity, rather than clientage to the appointed teacher or professional. Just as fuel was not delivered, so the vernacular was never taught. Taught tongues did exist, but they were rare, as rare as sails and mills. In most cultures, we know that speech resulted from conversation embedded in everyday life, from listening to fights and lullabies, gossip, stories, and dreams. Even today, the majority of people in poor countries learn all their language skills without any paid tutorship, without any attempt whatsoever to teach them how to speak. And they learn to speak in a way that nowhere compares with the self-conscious, self-important, colorless mumbling that, after a long stay in villages in South America and Southeast Asia, always shocks me when I visit an American college. I feel sorrow for those students whom education has made tone deaf; they have lost the faculty for hearing the difference between the dessicated utterance of standard television English and the living speech of the unschooled. What else can I expect, though, from people who are not brought up at a mother's breast, but on formula? —or tinned milk, if they are from poor families, and on a brew prepared under the nose of Ralph Nader if they are born among the enlightened? For people trained to choose between packaged formulas, mother's breast appears as just one more option. And in the same way, for people who were intentionally *taught* to listen and to speak, untutored vernacular seems just like another, albeit less developed, model among many.

But this is simply false. Language exempt from rational tutorship is a different kind of social phenomenon from language that is purposefully taught. Where untutored language is the predominant marker of a shared world, a sense of power within the group exists, and this sense cannot be duplicated by language that is delivered.

One way this difference shows is the sense of power over language itself, over its acquisition. Even today, the poor in nonindustrial countries all over the world are polyglot. My friend the goldsmith in Timbuktu speaks Songhay at home, listens to Bambara on the radio, devotedly and with some understanding says his prayers five times a day in Arabic, gets along in two trade languages on the Souk, converses in passable French that he picked up in the army—and none of these languages was formally taught him. He did not set out to learn these tongues; each is one style in which he remembers a peculiar set of experiences that fits into the frame of that language. Communities in which monolingual people prevail are rare except in three kinds of settings: tribal communities that have not really experienced the late neolithic, communities that for a long time lived through exceptional forms of discrimination, and among the citizens of nation-states that, for several generations, have enjoyed the benefits of compulsory schooling. To take it for granted that most people are monolingual is typical of the members of the middle class (Tanla-Kishani, 1967).[7] Admiration for the vernacular polyglot unfailingly exposes the social climber (cf. Roberts & Williams; Appel; DeTerra, this volume).

Throughout history, untutored language was prevalent, but hardly ever the only kind of language known. Just as in traditional cultures some energy was captured through windmills and canals, and those who had large boats or those who cornered the right spot on the brook could use their tool for a net transfer of power to their own advantage, so some people have always used a taught language to corner some privilege. But such additional codes remained either rare and special, or served very narrow purposes. The ordinary language, until Nebrija, was prevalently vernacular. And this vernacular, be it the ordinary colloquial, a trade idiom, the language of prayer, the craft jargon, the language of basic accounts, the language of venery or of age (for example, baby talk) was learned on the side, as part of meaningful everyday life. Of course, Latin and Sanskrit were formally taught to the priest, court languages such as Frankish or Persian or Turkish were taught to the future scribe. Neophytes were formally initiated into the language of astronomy, alchemy, or late masonry. And, clearly, the knowledge of such formally taught languages raised a man above others, somewhat like the saddle lifts the free man above the serf in the infantry, or the bridge lifts the captain above the crew. But even when access to some elite language was unlocked by a formal initiation, it did not necessarily mean that language was being taught. Quite frequently, the process of formal initiation did not transfer to the initiate a new language skill, but simply exempted him henceforth from a tabu that forbade others to use certain words, or to speak out on certain occasions. Male initiation in the language of the hunt or of sex is probably the most widespread example of such a ritually selective language detabuization.

But, in traditional societies, no matter how much or how little language was taught, the taught language rarely rubbed off on vernacular speech. Neither the existence of some language teaching at all times nor the spread of some language through professional preachers or comedians weakens my main point: Outside of

[7]"The ordinary man on the streets of Africa can at times be led to think that one is only bilingual when one can manipulate two European languages, since African languages are graded as dialects, vernacular, patois" (Tanla-Kishani, 1967, p. 127).

those societies that we now call Modern European, no attempt was made to impose on entire populations an everyday language that would be subject to the control of paid teachers or announcers. Everyday language, until recently, was nowhere the product of design; it was nowhere paid for and delivered like a commodity. And while every historian who deals with the origins of nation-states pays attention to the imposition of a national tongue, economists generally overlook the fact that this taught mother tongue is the earliest of specifically modern commodities, the model of all "basic needs" to come.

Before I can go on to contrast taught colloquial speech and vernacular speech, costly language and that which comes at no cost, I must clarify one more distinction. Between taught mother tongue and the vernacular, I draw the line of demarcation somewhere else than linguists when they distinguish the high language of an elite from the dialect spoken in lower classes, somewhere other than the frontier that separates regional and superregional languages, somewhere else than restricted and corrected code, and somewhere else than at the line between the language of the literate and the illiterate. No matter how restricted within geographic boundaries, no matter how distinctive for a social level, no matter how specialized for one sex role or one caste, language can be either vernacular (in the sense in which I here use the term) or of the taught variety. Elite language, trade language, second language, local idiom, are nothing new. But each of these can be formally taught and the taught counterfeit of the vernacular comes as a commodity and is something entirely new.

The contrast between these two complementary forms is most marked and important in taught everyday language, that is, taught colloquial, taught standardized everyday speech. But here again we must avoid confusion. Not all standard language is either grammar-ridden or taught. In all of history, one mutually understandable dialect has tended toward predominance in a given region. This kind of principal dialect was often accepted as the standard form. It was indeed written more frequently than other dialects, but not, for that reason, was it taught. Rather, diffusion occurred through a much more complex and subtle process. Midland English, for example, slowly emerged as that second, common style in which people born into any English dialect could also speak their own tongue. Quite suddenly, the language of Mogul hordes (Urdu) came into being in northern India. Within two generations, it became the standard in Hindustan, the trade language in a vast area, and the medium for exquisite poetry written in the Sanskrit and Arabic alphabets. Not only was this language not taught for several generations, but poets who wanted to perfect their competence explicitly avoided the study of Hindu-Urdu; they explored the Persian, Arabic, or Sanskrit sources that had originally contributed to its being. In Indonesia, in half a generation of resistance to Japanese and Dutch, the militant fraternal and combative slogans, posters, and secret radios of the freedom struggle spread Malay competence into every village, and did so much more effectively than the later efforts of the Ministry of Language Control that was established after independence.

It is true that the dominant position of elite or standard language was always bolstered by the technique of writing. Printing enormously enhanced the colonizing power of elite language. But to say that because printing was invented elite language is destined to supplant vernacular variety results from a debilitated imagination— like saying that after the atom bomb only superpowers shall be sovereign. The historical monopoly of educational bureaucracies over the printing press is no argument that printing techniques cannot be used to give new vitality to written expression and new literary opportunity to thousands of vernacular forms. The fact that printing was used since the early sixteenth century (but not during the first 40 years of its existence) primarily for the imposition of standard colloquials does not mean that written language must always be a taught form. The commerical status of taught mother tongue, call it national language, literary standard, or television language, rests largely on unexamined axioms, some of which I have already mentioned: that printing implies standardized composition; that books written in the standard language could not be easily read by people who have not been schooled in that tongue; that reading is by its very nature a silent activity that usually should be conducted in private; that enforcing a universal ability to read a few sentences and then copy them in writing increases the access of a population to the content of libraries. These and other such illusions are used to enhance the standing of language teachers, the security of their jobs and an increase in the GNP.

Vernacular spreads by practical use; it is learned from people who mean what they say and who say what they mean to the person they address in the context of everyday life. This is not so in taught language. With taught language, the one from whom I learn is not a person whom I care for or dislike, but a professional speaker. The model for taught colloquial is somebody who does not say what he means, but who recites what others have contrived. In this sense, a street vendor announcing his wares in ritual language is not a professional speaker, while the king's herald or the clown on television are the prototypes. Taught colloquial is the language of the announcer who follows the script that an editor was told by a publicist that a board of directors had decided should be said. Taught colloquial is the dead, impersonal rhetoric of people paid to declaim with phony conviction texts composed by others, who themselves are usually paid only for *designing* the text. People who speak taught language imitate the announcer of news, the comedian of gag writers, the instructor following the teacher's manual to explain the textbook, the songsters of engineered rhymes, or the ghost-written president. This is language that implicitly lies when I use it to say something to your face; it is meant for the spectator who watches the scene. It is the language of farce, not of theater, the language of the hack, not of the performer. The language of media always seeks the appropriate audience profile that the sponsor tries to hit and to hit hard. While the vernacular is engendered in me by the intercourse between complete persons locked in conversation with each other, taught language is syntonic with loud speakers whose assigned job is gab.

The vernacular and taught mother tongue are like the two extremes on the spectrum of the colloquial. Language would be totally inhuman if it were totally taught. That is what Humboldt meant when he said that real language is speech that can only be fostered, never taught like mathematics. Speech is much more than communication, and only machines can communicate without reference to vernacular roots. Their chatter with one another in New York now takes up about three quarters of the lines that the telephone company operates under a franchise that guarantees access by people. This is an obvious perversion of a legal privilege that results from political aggrandizement and the degradation of vernacular domains to second-class commodities. But even more embarrassing and depressing than this abuse of a forum of free speech by robots is the incidence of robot-like stock phrases that blight the remaining lines on which people presumably "speak" to each other. A growing percentage of personal vocalization has become mere formula in content and style. In this way, the colloquial moves on the spectrum of language increasingly from vernacular to capital-intensive "communication," as if it were nothing more than the human variety of the exchange that also goes on between bees, whales, and computers. True, some vernacular elements or aspects always survive—but that is true even for most computer programs. I do not claim that the vernacular dies; only that it withers. The American, French, or German colloquials have become composites made up of two kinds of language: commodity-like taught uniquack and a limping, ragged, jerky vernacular struggling to survive. Analogously, French and German have also been bastardized. They have absorbed English uniquack to the degree where certain standard exchanges in European stores and offices have all the formal characteristics of pidgin.

The Eclipse of Vernacular Value

A resistance, sometimes as strong as a sacred tabu, prevents the recognition of the difference with which we are dealing—the difference between capitalized language and the vernacular, which comes at no economically measurable cost. It is the same kind of inhibition that makes it difficult for those who are brought up within the industrial system to sense the fundamental distinction between nurture from the breast and feeding by bottle, between literature and textbook, between a mile moved on my own and a passenger mile, between housing as activity and housing as commodity—areas where I have discussed this issue over the past years.

Most people would probably be willing to admit that there is huge difference in taste, meaning, and satisfaction between a home-cooked meal and a TV dinner. But the examination and understanding of this difference can be easily blocked, especially among those committed to equal rights, equity, and service to the poor. They know how many mothers have no milk in their breasts, how many children in the South Bronx suffer protein deficiencies, how many Mexicans—surrounded by fruit trees—are crippled by vitamin deficits. As soon as I raise the distinction between vernacular values and the values susceptible to economic measurement and, therefore, to being administered, some self-appointed tutor of the so-called proletariat will tell me that I am avoiding the critical issue by giving importance to noneconomic niceties. Should we not seek first the just distribution of commodities that correlate to basic needs? Poetry and fishing shall then be added without more thought or effort. So goes the reading of Marx and the Gospel of St. Matthew as interpreted by the theology of liberation.

A laudable intention here attempts an argument that should have been recognized as illogical in the nineteenth century, and that countless experiences have shown false in the twentieth. So far, every single attempt to substitute a universal commodity for a vernacular value has led, not to equality, but to a hierarchical modernization of poverty. In the new dispensation, the poor are no longer those who survive by their vernacular activities because they have only marginal or no access to the market. No, the modernized poor are those whose vernacular domain, in speech and in action, is most restricted—those who get least satisfaction out of the few vernacular activities in which they can still engage.

To clarify this point, I distinguish between transit and transportation, home-made food and packaged nutrition, autonomous learning and tutored socialization. Now, are not the distance covered on foot and by wheel, the terms used in vernacular and in taught language, the calories ingested in the two kinds of foods the same? Yes, but the similarity makes each of the two activities involved comparable in a narrow, nonsocial sense alone. The symbols engendered by the two sets are not only different in color and texture and taste but, above all, in fundamental meaning. The value to the person of the vernacular word, movement, food, or dwelling is to a large measure determined by the subjective enjoyment of the person or community that engenders it; the need for the commodity is determined and shaped for the consumer by the producer who defines its value. What makes the world modern is a replacement of vernacular values by commodities; the reorganization of the environment into a place for the production, storage, and exchange of these commodities; the definition of the human being as an *animal economicum;* and the destruction of those characteristics in the environment that permit the existence of vernacular domains (cf Parker, this volume).

Among people who feel "modern," needs that correlate to commodities tend to dampen or even extinguish the desire to engage in vernacular activities. For them, human progress consists in the application of scientific or technological discoveries to commodity production rather than to the enlargement of vernacular competence. The use of writing and printing at the service of standard colloquial in preference to its use for the expansion of the vernacular reflects this ingrained prejudice. One sees that speech and work, leisure, and even suffering have become modern in the increased intensity with which human activity is managed and planned. Modernization is also seen in the decreased significance of those activities in which people do or make things that are destined for themselves and their primary groups rather than for evaluation by measurement and exchange on the market. The press, as such, can be used in the vernacular and in the economic domain; the best the *rotary* press can do is the mass production of books that probably encroach on the expansion of vernacular printing and writing.

Our analysis of taught mother tongue and its encroachment on the vernacular has led us to recognize the imminent limits of the educational enterprise. These are somewhat analogous to those which now emerge as the boundaries beyond which mass-produced goods no longer provide satisfaction. But to get at these limits, we need a survey of the literature that results in a total reclassification. In order to carry out such a survey, William Leiss (1976) could serve as a guide. In *The Limits to Satisfaction* (1976), Leiss argued that the radical transformation of individual wants in the process of industrialization is the hidden complement of the Western attempt to dominate nature. Since the seventeenth century, this attempt has progressively shaped every aspect of public pursuit, thereby characterizing Western societies. Nature is increasingly interpreted as the source from which a social production process is fed, an enterprise undertaken *for* people rather than *by* them.

Indirectly, then, the attempt to dominate nature has shaped a vision of man. Human needs are defined as a series of rights to the outputs of this process. They are not seen as the fundamental claim for the freedoms to survive in an environment fit for providing direct subsistence to individuals equipped with tools under *their* control. As the environment (traditionally referred to as "nature") became ruthlessly exploited as a resource and a trash can for the commodities being produced for the satisfaction of ever newly defined needs, human nature (today called the "psyche") began to avenge itself. People became radically needy, when formally many might have thought of themselves only as being poor. In a commodity-dominated environment, human wants can no longer be satisfied without being translated into the need for access to stores, to markets, to the action of shopping. Individual feelings about one's own needs are now associated primarily with the sensation of impotence. For those whose sensibilities are not completely dulled, the rare occasions when satisfaction is obtained without dependence on a mass product are experienced as delightful surprises. The general picture, however, is rather bleak. Every experience of a commodity-determined fulfillment of a need necessarily entails its component of frustrated, unrealized self-reliance. This specifically modern, inevitable, albeit often subliminal element of frustration, which accompanies the use or consumption of commodities, can now be understood as the individual correlate to the hidden curriculum that I have tried to get into sharp focus above (see also, Illich, 1971).

Leiss also calls our attention to the fact that each act of consumption implies a renewal of the experience of isolation—a further dismantling of the reciprocity context that in less commodity-intensive societies demands and patterns reliance on the persons who are around. In a commodity-intensive environment, the person whom I touch and cherish is no longer able to provide me with the elements of immediate sustenance, cannot teach me how to obtain them for and by myself, is too embarrassed to encourage me to do without them. Every filling of a commodity-shaped need thus further undermines the experience of self-reliance and of trust in one another, the two basic threads forming the warp and woof of all societies except the historically unique one which I name the late industrial age.

Leiss then goes further. He examines the situation when the number and variety of goods and services grow, when these increased numbers of commodities are interpreted as correlative to needs and, therefore, each symbolically constituting a utility. In such a society, the individual is constantly forced to relearn how to need. His wants crumble into progressively smaller components; they lose their subjective coherence. The individual loses the ability to fit his need fragments into a whole that would be meaningful to him. Human needs are thus transformed from culture-determined longings that orient creative action that satisfies—or, at least, assures sustenance—into disorienting, learned lacks that demand professional service. The service is needed not only to provide and deliver the commodity, but also to prescribe the appropriate one and to coordinate this one with others that must be administered simultaneously.

In such a high "convenience" setting, the response to any commodity-determined need ceases to possess the qualities traditionally associated with the term *satisfaction*. Utility, then, can be pursued increasingly without the achievement of meaningful satisfaction. Thus, conclusions drawn from the observation of economic behavior must be attributed to an ever more illusory *homo economicus,* in which the specific individual recognizes nothing resembling his or her real self. *Homo econ-*

omicus is forever in need. And as needs become limitless, one feels increasingly needy. Thus paradoxically, the more time and resources are expended on acquiring commodities, commodities supposedly necessary for the satisfaction of needs, the more shallow each individual want becomes and the more one feels indifference to the specific form in which it will be met. Beyond a very low threshold, the substitution of vernacular forms of subsistence by commodity-shaped needs and the goods or services that fit them causes the person to become increasingly needy, teachable, and frustrated. These observations suggest a possible theoretical formulation to understand both the paradoxical counterproductivity of modern institutions—and, specifically, the educational institution—and the degradation of the cultural ecology necessary for satisfactory activity outside commodity-monopolized spheres.

This encroaching monopolization is seen dramatically in the transformation of most colloquial language into taught uniquack, and the institutional expansion of the educational system to fill, finally, the prescription of Comenius—events that have happened in our lifetime. As recently as the period between World Wars I and II, most people, rich and poor alike, learned most of their first language from persons who spoke either directly to them or from others whose conversations they overheard. Only a small fraction of language learning resulted from being in the audience of actors, teachers, or preachers—except for the children and cousins of parsons and performers. It can probably be argued that, at the beginning of this century, the child born into the lower classes in California or Toronto was not subject to more public utterances by schoolmasters and parsons than the typical child in Java who, through centuries, has attended several hundred hours of shadow plays a year. Today this is changed. Language is fed to young and old through channels to which they are hooked. What they learn is no longer a vernacular that, by definition, we draw into us from roots that we send out into the social context in which we are anchored. Our roots have become weak, and the soil itself has become dry or cemented over by schoolyards. For those adults who get hooked on adult education, trust in the ability to figure things out on their own has rotted away. People increasingly resemble plants grown in hydroponics. The young and their linguists cannot even distinguish between the vernacular and the high-class, groomed, and taught slang that they take to be gutsy. Language competence now, to a large degree, depends on costly access to the right teachers.

This decay of sovereignty over the tongue and its vernacular domains appears clearly in the way people speak about teaching. Were I lecturing, I would be speaking *to* you, and I could, if we were together, speak *with* you. But neither then, nor now, do I have any intention of teaching. I think I am arguing a point, presenting an opinion, I tell you how I believe things to have been; perhaps some readers think that I am entertaining—and that would please me. But I refuse to be pressed into your service as a teacher. Much less am I educating you. I do not want to have anything to do with the kind of task for which nature did not give me the appropriate organs. *Educatio prolis* is a term that in Latin grammar calls for a female subject. It designates the feeding and nurturing in which mothers engage, be they bitch, sow, or woman. Among humans only women educate. And they educate only infants, which etymologically means those who are yet without speech. To educate has etymologically nothing to do with "drawing out" as pedagogical folklore would have it. Pestalozzi should have heeded Cicero: *educit obstetrix—educat nutrix:* the midwife draws—the nurse nurtures. Men do neither in Latin. They engage in *docentia* (teaching) and *instructio* (instruction). The first men who attributed to themselves educational functions were early bishops who led their flocks to the *alma ubera* (milk-brimming breasts) of Mother Church from which they were never to be weaned. This is why they, like their secular successors, call the faithful *alumni*— which means sucklings or suckers and nothing else. It is this transfer of woman's functions to specialized institutional spheres governed by clergies that Nebrija helped to bring about. In the process the state acquired the function of a many-uddered provider of distinct forms of sustenance, each corresponding to a separate basic need, and each guarded and managed by a clergy, always male in the higher reaches of the hierarchy. What this means for the perception of sex roles in industrial societies, making them different from those in any other society whatsoever, must be left to another essay (cf. Phillips, this volume). Suffice it here to say that this is the reason why I will not permit my conversation with you to be called education. I hope that my chapter has convinced you that it is more than a terminological nicety when I insist that teaching is a very peculiar and always hierarchical form that conversation or even the performing arts can sometimes take, even when conducted in the vernacular. But for the act and the art of teaching, the hypothesis of an educational sphere is unnecessary, as unnecessary as spheres for the movement of planets and, *if* you insist, even for astrological effects of the stars on humankind. Unfortunately, many of our contemporaries cannot grasp this anymore. Language has become for them so much a commodity that education's primary task is the provision of institutions or factories in which language producers can equip citizens with ever-increasing shares in the language stock (cf. Bain, Introduction, this volume).

Aristotle once said that a thing's nature can often be known only when that thing has reached maturity and can be contemplated together with the fruits it has brought forth. Perhaps the time has come to consider the educational sphere fully grown, and to look at its fruits. This is what I did a short time ago, while back in New York City in an area that a few decades earlier I had known quite well, the South Bronx. I went there at the request of a young college teacher, married to a colleague. This man wanted my signature on a petition for compensatory prekindergarten language training for the inhabitants of a partially burnt-out, high-rise slum. Twice already, quite decidedly and yet with deep embarrassment, I had refused. To overcome my resistance against this expansion of educational services, he took me on visits to brown, white, black, mostly single-parent so-called households. I saw dozens of children dashing through uninhabitable cement corridors, exposed all day to blaring television and radio in English, Spanish, and even Yiddish. They seemed equally lost in language and landscape. As my friend pressed for my signature, I tried to argue for the protection of these children against further castration and inclusion in the educational sphere. We talked at cross-purposes, unable to meet. And then, in the evening, at dinner in my friend's home, I suddenly understood why. This man, whom I viewed with awe because he had chosen to live in this hell, had ceased to be a parent and had become a total teacher. In front of their own children this couple stood *in loco magistri*. Their children had to grow up without parents, because these two adults, in every word they addressed to their two sons and one daughter, were "educating" them—they were at dinner constantly conscious that they were modeling the speech of their children, and asked me to do the same.

Copernicus

Three decisive steps toward the integration of ideology, self-perception, and institutional structure led to what is called, uncritically, education: the idea of a mother tongue from Gorz, the imposition of standardization by Nebrija, the teaching of all things through the method of Comenius. These developments resulted in the peculiar belief that growing up should occur within an educational sphere. It is precisely this well-knit assumption that becomes the subject of the research on education I would recommend, but only as part of a wider research on the process by which economics, politics, wage labor, and domestic serfdom came into being. And this is the moment for such research, because the orthodox members of the cloister have lost the innocence of their convictions, while the heterodox have not yet found their new paradigm outside. The character of the approaching paradigm change is not yet clear, for the educational community is at a stage similar to that of astronomy at the Renaissance.

One of the principal figures in the development of astronomy at that time was Copernicus (1473–1543). And he is one of the most popular examples cited when people write on paradigm changes in world views. In the literature, one finds an enormous appreciation of the importance of his *De Revolutionibus Coelorum.* All testify to his undoubted worth as a mathematical astronomer. But de Solla Price challenged this view (1969). He actually believed it to be a dangerous myth. Since similar myths now envelope some antischool prophets, I shall comment on Copernicus and his influence.

Importantly, he reopened the question of the earth's mobility. And he showed that no mathematical damage was incurred by assuming that it rotated around its axis. In a sense, he did go back to the Pythagorean position that the sun is at the center of the planetary orbs. Mathematically, he was the first to create a planetary system. All his predecessors had dealt with each planet separately; he integrated them. But he did not differ in method or in basic assumptions from Ptolemy. His demonstrations are derived from the so-called *Almagest,* and he accepted the existence of heavenly spheres. In terms of received knowledge, he admitted even more. He prided himself for having philosophically restored a strictly uniform circular motion to the heavenly bodies. However, this necessitated the positing of more circles than Ptolemy in order to avoid the use of eccentrics.

It can be argued that Copernicus did replace the potential crystal spheres that Dante—or, before him, Mohammed of the Ladder-Book—could visit by making planets move along prosaic spherical sections. But these neither he nor the young Kepler would think of renouncing. These men could not bring themselves to believe that there is not a natural difference between the movement of the heavens, which is perfect, and that of the sublunar, that is, sinful sphere. Perhaps for this reason the Inquisition did not bother them at all. But in 1600, Giordano Bruno was burned at the stake. Bruno, like the young Kepler, was influenced by Copernicus. But unlike him, he was not an observer of nature, nor did he know any mathematics. Probably wrongly, he imputed to Copernicus the power to prove that the universe is immense, peopled by innumerable stars, and uniform throughout in its nature. With this opinion, he was suggesting that one could think about the universe without spheres—and that led him to the stake.

But Bruno's relationship to astronomy is somewhat akin to that of the outsider in the educational debate today. Therefore, he is of no direct interest in speaking about research on education. Before Kepler, and with the one exception of Bruno, the sky of common sense was also that of philosophical cosmology and mathematical astronomy. The common subject, however, was not the stars themselves, but rather, the spheres that carried the planets and the empyrean. The common interest lay in the perfectly circular movements of transparent concentric material realities of a special kind. Each such sphere carried a planet, was generated by it, and was named after the star. The star in turn indicated the influence that the sphere exercised in the world. Copernicus was a heavenly reformer, a rearranger of these spheres. He cannot serve as an example for educators.

The Options in a Crisis: Brahe and Kepler

In his day, Tycho Brahe (1546–1601) was the foremost observer of the heavens. Coming from a powerful Danish family, he was born when Copernicus died and, two years before his own death in 1601, accepted the young Kepler as an apprentice. During his lifetime, Brahe substantially corrected the accepted value of nearly every astronomical quantity. He was the first to allow for the refraction of the atmosphere, to introduce methods for correcting instrumental error, to suggest correctly the nature of a nova, to map the location of more than 7,000 fixed stars. As a practical astronomer, he surpassed all before him and, like them, he still looked at the sky with the naked eye alone.

Kepler approached him to learn because he felt that only Brahe could teach him the observational skills necessary to prove Copernicus correct. But from the beginning of the apprenticeship, Brahe strongly dissuaded Kepler from undertaking such a foolish project. Again, Brahe was the first to point out that the mathematical changes introduced by Copernicus were on the whole such that they increased enormously both the complexity of calculation and the heavenly mechanism without increasing the accuracy of prediction for the location of stars. Dissatisfied with both Ptolemy and Copernicus, Brahe designed a third system, constructed on a middle ground between Ptolemaic and Copernican assumptions. He retained the immobility of the earth, but the other planets were made to revolve around the sun. The latter, with these planets, annually circuited the earth. In addition, all planets performed a diurnal rotation with the sphere of fixed stars. His correct claim, that this system was more elegant and simple mathematically than that of Copernicus, indicates the monstrous complexity of the Copernican system. Experimentally, none of the three systems could be verified. Due to their constant improvement, the Ptolemaic predictions possessed an edge. Pascal was correct in believing that only because of a cosmological prejudice could one possibly choose among the three. Instruments to observe the parallax of fixed stars became available only three centuries later.

When Brahe died, Kepler edited his monumental catalog of the stars. Then he began to see the point on which all three of his great predecessors—Ptolemy, Copernicus, and Brahe—were wrong: None of them could conceive of heavenly movements detached from heavenly spheres. Kepler did not attempt to replace the spheres with something else; he simply eliminated them.

Johannes Kepler (1571–1630) had a poetic and critical mind. Already as a student, in 1593 (a hundred years after the first return of Columbus), he had written out a series of speculations derived from Maestlin's attempts to estimate the elevations on the lunar surface by measuring, in Tübingen, the shadows on the moon, a technique the ancient Greeks had already tried to use. During the summer of 1609, he wrote out a plan for landing on the moon, earth's closest neighbor in the sky. Kepler mentioned this project, never before conceived in scientific literature, in a letter to Galileo Galilei (April 19, 1610). He confided to his Italian friend:

> Last summer, the manuscript begun in 1593 has been expanded into a complete geography of the moon. . . . who would have believed that a huge ocean could be crossed more peacefully and safely than the narrow expanse of the Adriatic, the Baltic Sea or the English Channel . . . ? Provide ship or sail adapted to the heavenly breezes, and there will be some who will not fear even that void. . . . so for those who will come shortly to attempt this journey, let us establish the astronomy: Galileo, you, that of Jupiter, and I that of the moon.

As Bruno had done by reasoning on general principles, so Kepler, concerned with ordering his observations, replaced a mechanism of spheres by heavenly bodies following their orbits. Voyaging from earth to other planets of the sun thus became a reasonable subject for intellectual speculation in 1609[8] (Lear, 1965). *Mundus* became a new *Cosmos* interpreted by a new set of myths (Kranz, 1958).

I am under the impression that the educational debate, no matter how radical, is still only concerned with a rearrangement of social spheres on the model of pre-Kepler stargazers. Correct observations on shared imagery and shared competence are still used, like those of Brahe, to fit an outlived paradigm. Discussion rages, and research moves about the convenience or the necessity to redefine, to relate, to develop, or to appropriately add new epicycles within this one sphere. And when such educational policy alternatives pretend to be fundamental, then the relationship of the educational to the other spheres takes prominence as an issue. Should production or politics be at the center of the social system? Or should the two be related in a more complex way, perhaps on the model of Tycho Brahe? Should we prefer an all-encompassing system of spheres on the Copernican model? Or is it better to muddle through without an overall system, but relying on the proven approximations that Al

---

[8]Kepler confided his transgression of the "spheric tabu" to a private dairy written in the form of a dream. Through an indiscretion, some pages of this manuscript became known, and led to the arrest of Kepler's mother and her confrontation with the instruments of torture, an experience from which she soon died. The "Somnium" was published two years after Kepler's death and was first translated into English in Lear (1965).

Shatir's eccentrics and epicycles permitted one to calculate, even though such a theory deals with only one Ptolemaic planet at a time? Shall the school system remain at the center? Or shall school be but one adjunct to the education that goes on, for example, in a Chinese commune? How shall we rank the different tools of education? Or how shall we relate the spheres of education, health, welfare, research, finance, economics, politics? I think that research on the model of Copernicus is not what we need in education.

Following Kepler's example, we now need to recognize that the educational sphere is a construct analogous to the sphere of Mercury, and that the need of humans to be educated can be compared with the need of humans to live at the static center of the universe. This educational construct is mapped by an ideology that brought into being our convictions about *homo educandus*. The construct is socially articulated by a specific set of institutions, for which *Alma Mater Ecclesia* is the prototype. It is implanted into the world view of each individual by a double experience: first, by the latent curriculum of all educational programs, through which vernacular learning is inevitably debased, and, second, through life in the opaque, passive, and paralyzing life-style that professional control over the definition and satisfaction of needs inevitably fosters. Finally, the construct of the educational sphere is zealously guarded by the various bodies of educators who identify educational needs in terms of problems for which they alone possess the social mission to find institutional solutions in and out of schools.

This construct of an educational sphere is thoroughly consistent with other similar constructs, especially the spheres of economics and politics. The process through which each of these spheres has been disembedded to the point of achieving a radical monopoly that paralyzes its corresponding vernacular homologue can be studied separately for each one. But research on the educational sphere can claim a certain priority. Studying the process through which this sphere, in its ideological construction between Nebrija and Comenius, and in the degradation and replacement of vernacular languages by taught mother tongue after the invention of the loudspeaker, permits unique insights into the analogous elements that went into the constitution of other social spheres. Education as a subject matter and as a discipline has been defined by the construct and constrained by its basic assumptions up to now. This cannot be otherwise for research *in* education. But research on the relations of the educational domain to the global ideology of a society, together with the history of these relations, constitutes the kind of study which ought to be called research *on* education.

References

Albertini, E. *La composition dans les ouvrages philosophiques de Séneque.* Paris: D. Boccard, 1923.
Bahner, W. *Beitraege zum Sprachbewusstsein in der spanischen Literatur des 16 & 17 Jh.* Berlin: Ruttner Verlag, 1956.
Braun, H. Der Heilige Thomas und der gestirnte himmel, oder die Stellung des Hlg. Thomas zu den astro physikalischen Doktrinen seiner Zeit. *Angelikum,* January 1940, pp. 32–76.
Castro, A. *La realidad historica de Espana* (Revised ed.). Mexico: Porrua, 1962.

Congar, M. J. Introduction. In K. Delhaye. *Ecclesia Mater chez les pères des trois premiers siècles.* Paris: Editions Du Cerf, 1964.

Daube, A. *Der Aufstieg der Muttersprache im deutschen Denken des 15 & 16 Jh.* Deutsche Forschungen, Band 34, Verlag Diesterweg, 1940.

Delhaye, K. *Ecclesia Mater chez les pères des trois premiers siècles.* Paris: Editions Du Cerf., 1964.

Du Cange, C. D. *Glossarium mediae et infimae latinitatis.* Niorte, Spain: L. Sovre, 1883–1887.

Dumont, L. *From Mandeville to Marx.* Chicago: University of Chicago Press, 1977.

Heising, K. Muttersprache: Ein romanistischer Beitrag zur Genesis eines deutschen Wortes und zur Entstehung der deutsch-franzoesischen Sprachgrenze. *Mundartforschung,* 1958, *23* (3), 144–174.

Heyer, B. Alcuin zwischen autike und mittelater. *Zeitschrift fur Katholische Theologie,* 1959, *81,* 306–350, 405–453.

Illich, I. *Deschooling society.* New York: Harper & Row, 1971.

Kranz, W. Kosmos. *Archiv. fuer bergriffsgeschichte.* Bonn: Bouvier, 1958.

Lear, J. *Kepler's Dream.* Los Angeles: University of California Press, 1965.

Leclercq, dom H. Englise: I. Le mot. II. Le symbole. *Dictionnaire d'archeologie chrètienne et de liturgie, s.v.,* columns 2220–2237. Paris: Societé Nouvelle des Editions Letouzey et Ane, 1903.

Leiss, W. *The limits to satisfaction.* Toronto: University of Toronto Press, 1976.

Litt, T. OCSO, *les corps celestes dans l'univers de Saint Thomas d'Aquin.* Louvain: Centre de Wulf-Mansion, Philosophes Medievaus, 1963.

Maravall, J. A. *El concepto de España en la edad media* (2nd ed). Madrid: Instituto de Estudios Politicos, 1964.

Mariejol, J. H. *The Spain of Ferdinand and Isabella.* New Brunswick, N.J.: Rutgers University Press, 1961.

Marrou, H.-I. *Saint Augustin et la fin de la culture angique.* Paris: Editions Boccard, 1958.

Menéndez Pidal, R. *España y su historia.* Madrid: Minotauro, 1957.

O'Connor M. C., Sister. *The art of dying well: The development of the ars moriendi.* New York: AMS, 1966.

Plumpe, J. C., *Mater Ecclesia: An inquiry into the concept of the church as mother in early Christianity.* Ph.D. dissertation, Catholic University of America, 1943.

de Solla Price, D. J. Contra-Copernicus: A critical re-estimation of the mathematical planetary theory of Ptolemy, Copernicus and Kepler. In M. Clagett (Ed.), *Critical problems in the history of science.* Madison: University of Wisconsin Press, 1969.

Spinka, M. *John Amos Comenius, that incomparable moravian.* Chicago: University of Chicago Press, 1943.

Tanla-Kishani, B. African cultural identity through Western philosophies and languages. *Presence Africaine,* 1967, *98* (2nd trimester), 127.

Wells, J. M. History of printing. In *Encyclopaedia Britannica* (Vol. 18). 1964.

White, H. The forms of wildness. In E. Dudley & M. Novak (Eds.), *The wild man within: An image in Western thought from the Renaissance to romanticism.* Pittsburgh: University of Pittsburgh Press, 1972.

27

Language, Education, and Reproduction in Wales

Glyn Williams and Catrin Roberts

Theoretical Orientation[1]

Traditionally, the study of bilingualism has always taken the minority language as its "problem." Once defined, the problem was conventionally couched in terms of the individual, in the sense that it was seen to confront individuals rather than to form an inherent part of the social structure. The tendency to view bilingual education within a framework of individual liberalism was derived from this orientation. Recently, however, one of the striking developments in the sociology of education has been a sharp shift of focus from viewing education as an agency for social mobility and the differential conferment of rewards to a reappraisal of the ideological potency of education as an agency of social and cultural control. Although, to our knowledge, bilingualism has not been discussed within this framework, there is no reason why it cannot be, and indeed it can be claimed that viewing bilingualism in terms of a liberal philosophy is itself an element of social control on the part of the dominant language group.

Concentrating on the power and control implications of majority–minority relationships raises critical issues regarding viewing language or culture—or both—as the handicaps which impair individual mobility. The tautology of "explaining" the concept of minority, within the context of its subordination, by the failure of individual members of the minority to achieve *because* of the "disadvantage" of their knowledge of the minority language and/or culture, or because of their lack of familiarity with the dominant language and/or culture, is then brought into focus. Inequality is

---

[1]Our theoretical position is presented in greater detail in Williams and Roberts (1982).

Glyn Williams ● Department of Social Theory and Institution, University of North Wales, Bangor LL572DG, Great Britain. ***Catrin Roberts*** ● Department of Education, University of Manchester, Manchester, England.

explained solely in culturalist terms of language rather than viewed as related to social structure. If inequality is culturally derived, then it is hardly surprising that the egalitarian thrust of liberalism should seek to alleviate this inequality via programs of cultural compensation such as minority compensatory education. It is through the agency of such programs that minority groups are "educated" to a standard sufficient to enable their members to interact with dominant group members and thus reap the "benefits" of being a majority language speaker. The evaluative assumption of the inferiority of minority languages, and thus of minority language speakers, is evident.

The fallacy of this argument is demonstrable on three grounds. We should recognize, first, that social mobility within capitalism is in itself ideological, focusing as it does on the individual without changing the social structure; second, that education is part of the process whereby the social structure is reproduced; and third, that minorities are defined by reference to their lack of power, which is a corollary of their generalized low position within a cultural division of labor. Consequently, bilingual education will inevitably be seen as a means whereby the minority is functionally integrated into the system of production without presenting any threat to the state and its system of domination (cf. Maseman, this volume). Individual mobility is simply a meaningless by-product, albeit one which has tremendous ideological potential.

The conventional view of minority problems reflects the ideological position of the power holders in society—a position characterized by the minority language, which thus implicitly entails a denigration of the minority language in order to legitimize the institutionalization of the majority–minority power relationship. This position also results in the problem being viewed as the prerogative of a uniform minority, and its solution the responsibility of the individual. However, it does not preclude the minority being allocated "rights" within a liberal democracy, since these may serve to guarantee the power of the majority insofar as the concessions granted to the minority do not threaten this power (cf. Appel, this volume). Such rights are granted by the power holders, whose power is thereby confirmed. An associated concept is that of *discrimination* which conveys the impression of an unfair condition of inequality and implies the existence of some abstract form of rights within a democratic framework. It also suggests the existence of a preconceived plan constructed by some unspecified force. If we accept that discrimination in this sense is a manifestation of the power relationship between dominant and subservient language groups, then any rights associated with it are themselves ideological—being part of the process of language planning conducted by power holders on behalf of the minority. The problem is expropriated from those to whom it is claimed to pertain. It is within this context that a discussion of bilingual education should be located.

Within a Marxian perspective, the important point is to understand the dynamic relationship involving infrastructure, superstructure, ideology, and social formation. The driving force must inevitably be infrastructural, and the changes in the social formation must be those which infrastructural changes generate. The superstructure serves to legitimize the relations of production; the most sophisticated discussion of this legitimization process is found in the concept of ideological hegemony. It is seen to be far stronger than ideology, operating at the level of the unconscious rather than mere opinion or manipulation. Thus, hegemony defines common sense for those under its influence. Evidently, if there are changes in the infrastructure and the social formation, then there must be a corresponding response at the superstructural level—a response which may well involve a shift in what comes to constitute common sense. However, within what is known as liberal democracy, this procedure is by no means straightforward, in that conflicting parts of the social formation may present different interpretations of what constitutes common sense, and, if democracy is to be seen to be in operation, the dominant interests must respond to an interpretation that may well oppose their interests. However, this response occurs only if it does not supercede the prevailing interests, but can be accommodated. Thus, common sense is subject to interpretation, negotiation, and reinterpretation (cf. Harris, this volume).

In this chapter, our objective is to consider this totality in terms of its dynamics by reference to the manner in which conflict over bilingual education has developed in Wales. Before proceeding to a consideration of the specifics of the conflict in terms of language institutionalization, the control of education, and the ideological positions of the relevant groups involved in the conflict, it is necessary to consider briefly the infrastructural changes so that the groups can be located in terms of the contradictions which emerge at the level of social formation.

Infrastructural Changes[2]

The most common feature of the economy in Wales since 1930 has been the increasing role of state intervention, a policy which has been encompassed in various forms of "regional development programmes," through which capitalism has been spatially reorganized. Associated with this process of economic restructuring is an involved polarization, since the benefits of the economic changes are not uniformly distributed. Thus, in very broad terms, we envisage a distinction between an enclave development and an associated marginalized sector. The monopolistic economy thrives in the enclave and serves to marginalize the preexisting structure. It generally depends neither on local resources nor on local markets and grants the host area a minimum of control over its activities. Within the marginalized sector, there exists a pool of labor which permits some capital accumulation within the residual capitalism of this sector. It does not appear to be relevant to accumulation at the highest level and thereby becomes marginalized.

It is in the marginalized sector that the petite bourgeoisie is unable to compete with businesses of scale in the enclave. The falloff in trade frequently results in the closure of small businesses, thereby not only proletarianizing the petite bourgeoisie but also complicating further the lives of the old and the unemployed. The labor force within this marginalized sector displays a distinctive structure. While the bourgeoisie may well show extremely high returns for its investments, the earning of the proletariat tends to be well below its counterpart in the enclave. There is a tendency to

[2]For a more detailed analysis of economic marginalization with specific reference to Wales, see Williams and Roberts (1981).

work extremely long hours for limited returns, and it is evident that, because of the absence of secondary employment opportunities, self-employment and occupational pluralism are often the only means of survival. Furthermore, there is a high degree of mobility between "skilled worker" (proletariat) and "self-employed" (petite bourgeoisie) categories in both directions. The financial distinction between the skilled worker and the self-employed is minimal, and the influence of enclave development is largely responsible for the proletarianization of the self-employed.

Most of the enterprises in the enclave sector that derive advantage from state intervention have their source outside the periphery. A cultural distinction exists between core and periphery of the state, with repercussions for both the social and cultural order. Most of the core and international establishments that enter the periphery resort to the local population for their labor force at the lower level. At the managerial and key worker level, the picture is entirely different. These occupational categories consist mainly of *spiralists,* that is, those who combine social and geographical mobility. Their period of expected residence in the periphery, together with the nature of their occupation, manifests against local integration. Thus, while there is an erosion of the local bourgeoisie and petite bourgeoisie, there is a parallel development of a new, externally derived bourgeoisie whose orientations lie outside the periphery and whose consequent political ideology is strongly centralist. Of course, there are some of the local bourgeoisie who stand to gain from the new developments and will align themselves with the new bourgeoisie as a comprador class. Thus, a fragmentation of the local bourgeoisie develops, as well as a fragmentation of the proletariat, which is broadly divisible into those involved in enclave developments and those who find themselves marginalized by the same developments. The most evident feature is the emergence of a cultural division of labor (cf. Williams, this volume).

The heterogeneity of the low-income groups in the marginalized sector, together with the false sense of economic opportunity associated with self-employment opportunities, serves to generate a cohesion which cuts across and manifests against the development of a proletarian consciousness. It also serves to cloud the issue of what, or who, is responsible for their marginal status and relative impoverishment. The relationship between the dominant classes and the marginalized groups is increasingly precarious, unstable, and fragmentary. For the marginals, the state, despite the limitations of its services, remains the major source of survival, but the majority of them remain outside the state's compensatory mechanism; it is also evident to many that it is the state in its collusion with capitalist enterprises that is responsible for their marginal position. The disarticulation of the economic positions and of the social relations attached to them makes class action difficult. The types of economic arrangements characteristic of marginalized economies tend to individualize the problems of making a living. This individualization obscures the exploitation of the proletariat while emphasizing the limited opportunity for the enterprising individual. It leads to a fragmentation of classes that oppose one another because of their different relationships to the system of domination. It is in such situations that there is a tendency to align along ethnic lines in opposition to both the master and the "foreigner," who are usually one and the same; the emphasis is on the community defined by exploitation or by an exclusion that demands collective action.

A quest for national liberation develops. As a process, it is particularly conspicuous when the dominant indigenous stratum is threatened by the externally based dominant bourgeoisie of the enclave. Local identity will tend to be employed to create a local solidarity against the outside. Those of the local petite bourgeoisie who find themselves not only excluded from the new developments but also increasingly marginalized as a result of such developments rely on the idea of local community integration and solidarity as the basis for the retention of their power. The dominant bourgeoisie of spiralists drawn from the core aligns with those members of the entrenched local bourgeoisie who stand to gain from the new developments, in opposition to local interests, and rejects local integration, expecting instead to be accepted in terms of supralocal integration. It is inevitable that, if the locality is partly identified in terms of the minority language, one of the issues of contention will be that of language, which consequently becomes increasingly politicized. A conflict of ideology develops in what amounts to a peripheral nationalism of the state which the capitalist class, in collusion with the state, employs to mask and legitimize the maintenance of disparities in the geographic division of labor. It is based on an awareness that ethnic groups are stratified within the general division of labor.

Ideological Response and the Course of Language Conflict

Institutionalization of the Welsh Language

Having established the nature of the infrastructural changes and identified the respective groups within the resultant social formation, we can now proceed to a consideration of the manner in which the interests of these groups are constituted in language conflict and the associated ideological constructs. It should be clear from the preceding discussion that, although infrastructural interests determine superstructural responses, the relationship between them is dynamic in nature. Thus, there must exist some agency which provides the dynamic for the process, which ensures the reproduction of the process and makes it legitimate inasmuch as its acceptance is guaranteed by the groups involved. Thus, although in one sense ideology is not constituted before the act but is constructed through the act itself, the common sense that underlies ideological production is subject to negotiation, assessment, and reassessment. By focusing attention on specific issues of conflict inherent in the economic contradictions of social group interests, the dynamics of ideological mediation between infrastructure and superstructure can be recognized and clarified.

With reference to the Welsh language as an issue of conflict, it is perhaps apt to proceed with a discussion of the Welsh Language Act of 1967, which served to impose a degree of legitimacy on the Welsh language within a legal and administrative framework. Our claim is that it is only when this form and degree of recognition is afforded a minority language that further claims for the institutionalization of that language in public sector activities can be realistically and methodically pursued. Furthermore, if these claims can be realized and legitimized, they will in turn generate an awareness of further possibilities of minority language domain extension. Given such expansion of the minority language, there will be infrastructural spin-offs for the role of the minority language in the relations of production, and that language will begin to have relevance in terms of social mobility. Of course, there will be limitations to such extensions of the institutionalization and legitimization of the minority language in new public sector domains, since such action will be conceptualized as opposing the interests of those who hold power and control within those domains. Nonetheless, it is precisely such a process which serves to highlight the ideological arguments and presuppositions that manifestly relate to the issue of language, but that latently reflect group tension within a dynamic social formation (cf. de Terra, this volume).

It seems inevitable in a liberal democracy that minority language rights pertain to the majority and thus implicitly contravene the interests of the minority language and its preservation. Thus, although some aspects of recognition must be seen to be allocated to the minority language, they invariably constitute little more than action serving to keep the minority language lobby quiet. Conflict among various rights is negotiated in such a political setting by ideology, which is influenced by presenting the aims and objectives of the dominant group as advantageous to the minority. In so doing, the legitimization of policies that manifest the inequality among the different language groups can be perpetuated.

As recently as 1962 the High Court rejected the claim that the Welsh language was one of the "national" languages of the United Kingdom, and it was not until 1965 that the government saw fit to consider its legal and administrative status. This reviewing process reflected the need for the government of a liberal democratic system to respond to a minority demand, while simultaneously ensuring that its own power is not prejudiced. Following the conventional British format, the state nominates a committee whose brief it is to investigate the question at hand before reporting to the government. It is then the prerogative of the government in power and the House of Lords to consider the evidence and recommendations and subsequently to decide whether or not to proceed toward passing a bill. Clearly, there is an implicit bias in this process in that the selection of the committee is undertaken by the state, although it would appear that this committee is allocated the power to act within what is assumed to be a democratic process. In this case, the committee consisted of Welsh speakers who had reached positions of prominence either in public office or in a professional capacity. Their prominence had been achieved within the formal state structure and without recourse to the Welsh language. Thus, although their interests lay in the existing power structure, they had attributes that conveyed an impression of representing the Welsh minority. It is axiomatic that the consideration of any position that represents a contradiction between the Welsh minority and the power of the state was thus precluded.

The committee, in turn, was responsible for selecting witnesses and, thereby, the evidence which was presented. It seems that these witnesses were selected primarily from among representatives of public bodies and institutions within Wales; thus, an image of democratic representation was maintained while in reality the status quo was upheld. It is clear that the witnesses, as a consequence of the means of selection and their function as representatives, constituted a conservative rather than a radical element. Although rights are held to be the prerogative of the individual, the bulk of the evidence offered claimed to represent the views of institutions. Indeed, the entire process involved the explication of what are referred to as language rights within a

liberal democracy without recognizing that rights are conferred by—or at least negotiated with—power holders and thereby are better conceived of as concessions. Thus,
the explicit aspect of language planning can be seen as the response required of
power holders by the demands of minorities, while the retention of power by the
dominant group becomes its implicit aspect. It is perhaps relevant to recognize that
language planning, like other forms of planning, constitutes control on the part of
agencies of the state rather than serving the interests of the people that its ideological
referent claims.

On the basis of the evidence, the committee *subjectively constructed* and considered three positions with regard to the Welsh language:

1. The principle of necessity, advocating no change, with Welsh to be used only
   when any individual disadvantage could be shown by its refusal
2. The principle of equal validity, by which Welsh would have the same status
   as English within the law in Wales, which meant that the legal status of
   English in Wales would remain unimpaired
3. The principle of bilingualism, advocating that all legal and administrative
   business should be carried out in both languages side by side

Two points emerge: First, a fourth position, the converse of Position 1, was ignored.
We do not wish to impute any conspiratorial content to such action; we maintain
merely that such a consideration would lie outside the common sense of the established hegemony. Second, the three positions considered represent a continuum. By
labeling Position 3 extremist—and the view of a minority rather than the majority,
who presumably constitute the norm of the status quo—it became inevitable that the
committee would choose to advocate Position 2. Thus, by claiming Position 2 as reasonable, the fourth position—even if considered—becomes untenable. The selection
of evidence determines the outcome, and an impression of democracy is conveyed by
numerism.

The government of the day readily seized upon the recommendations of the
committee, which clearly contained proclamations compatible with its interests, and
passed the Welsh Language Act. Minimal concession was made to improving the
status of the Welsh language in Wales; simultaneously the hegemony of the English
language in Wales was retained, and any extension of Welsh language rights into
parts of the United Kingdom outside Wales was denied. Thus, the minority status
of the Welsh language was consolidated and legitimized.

In practice, the fact that the Welsh Language Act viewed bilingualism as
impractical meant that many of those who wished to conduct their lives through the
medium of Welsh in their own country found themselves in the position of continuously having to pressure for the right to use Welsh in public affairs. More often than
not, this right was denied them on the grounds of the principle of minimizing cost—
even though it appeared to be legally safeguarded. Furthermore, the terms of reference of the Welsh Language Act were restricted to the activities of the public
sector of the economy.

In terms of the manner in which the above procedure of representation was
undertaken, an interesting contrast may be found in the case of the Welsh Language
Council (Cyngor yr Iaith Gymraeg). This body was established by the government

in 1976 with the brief of providing a report which could serve as the basis of a comprehensive policy for the Welsh language in Wales. Although the members of the
committee held prestigious positions in institutions that by and large represented the
status quo, they nonetheless and in contrast to the committee of 1965 were men (the
committee included only one woman) who lived and worked in Wales and were in a
position to put a finger on the pulse of Welsh society. Rather than simply regarding
interviewing the officials of institutions as constituting a form of democratic process,
the council, in addition, chose to call a number of public meetings throughout Wales
and invited the public to attend and to air their views. Regardless of prior knowledge
about the propensity of the public to attend such meetings, it would appear from the
number of scheduled meetings and the seating capacity of the venues that the council
was not expecting anything more than minority (in numerical terms) participation.
Furthermore, it seems that the manner in which evidence was solicited implicitly
accepted the probability that such meetings would be attended by language activists.
Yet it was popular to refer to these proceedings as "an excellent exercise in participatory democracy."

Although in many respects conservative in its recommendations, the report of
the council went significantly further than any previous report. Indeed, it may be
that the recommendations went so far as to present an explicit threat to the status
quo and the interests that lie behind it. Given that the objective of the council was
to make proposals which would arrest the erosion of the Welsh language, even an
elementary understanding of the process of language erosion would lead to proposals
which would inevitably undermine the power basis of the status quo, since it is precisely that basis that is responsible for the erosion. The following were the council's
recommendations:

1. The government should announce a positive policy of effective bilingualism
   in Wales.
2. A permanent body should be set up to promote the Welsh language.
3. Substantial financial support should be forthcoming.
4. A propaganda campaign should be mounted to gain public support.
5. Bilingual education should become the norm throughout Wales.
6. A television channel for Welsh language broadcasting should be established.
7. Money should be set aside for preparing Welsh language reading material.
8. The Welsh language should receive special consideration in all planning matters within Wales.
9. Provision should be made for adults to learn Welsh.

The nature of the above recommendations suggests either that they represent an
ideological position quite distinct from and in some respects opposed to the recommendations of the Committee of 1965, or that there has been a shift in common sense
with reference to the Welsh language during a period of 10 years. We would suggest
that both are true and that the publication of the Council's report will represent and
contribute to a further modification of that common sense. Little wonder that the
Council's report has been ignored by successive governments since its publication.
This lack of response suggests that the ideological position of the government relative
to the Welsh language does not extend far enough to encompass the position repre-

sented by the council. It reflects Gramsci's (1971) point that a counterideology is created by intellectuals before being filtered to the public. As the counterideology gathers momentum, it obliges the power forces within a liberal democratic framework to respond by modifying the existing hegemonic position. In the above case, although the response of the government did not extend to accepting the recommendations of the council in their entirety, it was obliged to grant some concessions to the Welsh language lobby and thereby to modify its ideological stance.

In the last analysis, perhaps the notion that the position of a minority language is created by the unequal distribution of power in society is best revealed by the fact that the Welsh language must still continually justify itself. Thus, the mere fact that the language is forced into a position of self-defense precludes the idea that it exists as a natural phenomenon within Wales.

Language and the Control of Education

A clearer picture of the role of social groups as actors in the development of a counterideology can be obtained by considering the issue of language in education in Wales. Central to the discussion must be a concern with the question of who controls education.

The demand for extending bilingual education in Wales has been held to derive from a concern about the ability of the conventional agencies to reproduce the Welsh language on the one hand (Roberts, 1980) and from an awareness among some actors of a relationship between language and individual social mobility on the other (Williams, Roberts, & Isaac, 1978). The first issue relates to the manner in which ever increasing state intervention in all areas of society institutionalizes a new form of relationship between the masses and the state. Within this perspective, Gramsci's (1971) "integral state" comes to be identified with the monopoly capitalist state which is not restricted to political society but permeates civil society. The state permeates all forms of organization and mass consciousness, provoking a diffusion of hegemony and simultaneously organizing the whole of social reproduction. The second issue derives from the success of the language community in reoccupying part of the space lost by this process and involves an increasing politicization of social conflicts. It involves the insertion of the Welsh language in the domains of direct social reproduction with a resultant reinterpretation of the relevance of the minority language for social reproduction.

Within the pluralism of the British educational system, subject to the conditions of the 1944 Education Act, the local authority is responsible for the education process. However, head teachers are given wide discretionary powers with regard to curriculum and school organization. In hiring, for example, although the various teachers' associations jealously guard the relative autonomy of educators with reference to curriculum matters, the advice of the head teacher is vital. Yet even in cases of appointment, the role of specialists such as the Local Education Authority (LEA) language advisors can be crucial. The creation of the Welsh Office in 1964 and the transfer of responsibility for all education other than higher education from the Department of Educational Service (DES) to the Secretary of State for Wales in 1970 created an intermediary between the LEAs and Whitehall. While it is the Whitehall departments that take the initiative in the development of new policies, the Welsh Office is consulted by Whitehall at all stages in the formulation of policy as well as in resolving any conflicts arising from implementation. According to the 1944 Act, the Secretary of State is required

> to promote the education of the people of Wales and the progressive develop-ment of institutions devoted to that purpose, and to secure the effective execu-tion by local authorities, under his control and direction, of the national [*sic*] policy for providing a varied and comprehensive educational service in every area. (Rawkins, 1979, p. 21)

S/He is able to impose central government policy on the LEAs by utilizing "admin-istrative actions alone," and s/he can intervene only when and where it might be determined that the local education authority is acting "unreasonably." Yet the Welsh Secretary can decide in which areas s/he will act independently in dealing with problems specifically Welsh in character. However, because of the delicacy of the language issue, mediation is usually via informal networks of influence rather than the imposition of central authority. Crucial as mediators in this process are the school inspectorate and the Welsh Joint Education Committee (WJEC), a forum for the exchange of ideas, for sponsoring and conducting research, for establishing com-mon standards through public examinations, and for linking education with the needs of industry and society. Among its areas of concern are questions about "the curric-ulum of schools maintained by the appointing councils, with special reference to the teaching of the Welsh language and culture" (WJEC, 1970, p. 6). Although the WJEC can not make policy or impose its recommendations on local authorities, it provides an important forum for generating the acceptance of new ideas and approaches to education. It is significant in this respect in its overall control over the curriculum. Whereas the 1944 Act upheld the autonomy of head teachers in word, the common sense notion of what constitutes a good school includes the performance of that school in the external examinations organized by examining bodies such as the WJEC. Thus, the necessity of achieving successful examination results is ulti-mately what decides a school curriculum, and thus we may regard the autonomy of educators over the content of the curriculum as largely illusory.

What emerges from a scrutiny of who controls education with reference to the sensitive issue of bilingual education in Wales has been noted elsewhere in a different context (Williams, 1980b, p. 173): the presentation of the state as a benign agency of control. The channeling of power and resources through local or devolved govern-ment has the diversionary effect of making these resources appear to be used in local interests and in solving local problems, while distancing the state from any respon-sibility for policy repercussions. As Rawkins has demonstrated, "by effectively leav-ing the initiative in the hands of the LEA's, the government is abdicating its respon-sibility to Welsh speakers" (1979, p. 101). By the absence of any coordination plan or overall policy for the language, the state not only wastes resources but also stim-ulates, with minor modification, a perpetuation of the status quo. With reference to the Welsh language, this involves a perpetuation of its limited status and prestige on the one hand and a continuation of its erosion on the other. Yet in assigning respon-sibility, the state is able to absolve itself of any blame. It accepts the legitimacy of bilingualism in education but fails to give leadership and resources for its effective implementation. Thus, despite the appearance and ideology of local control, it is the state which is the single most important factor in determining the direction and terms of educational development. On the one hand, there is the claim that the state provides the maximum possible assistance for the language, with planning involving the control of resources; on the other, by leaving the LEAs to deal with issues of conflict within a guideline which involves obliging them to respond to parental demand and strictly educational criteria, it leaves a legacy that is at best highly complicated. Yet we should not be surprised by such a situation since it is one of the extremely efficient legacies of liberal policies of capitalist states. In this respect, it is not conspiratorial but simply part of a process wherein the negotiation of disaffection involves a preference for piecemeal measures in response to short-term political pressures rather than longrange policy coordination. Although this strategy may, in the long run, generate conflict which might lead to a shift in ideological consensus, the locus of authority and control is never in doubt. The informal legitimacy of bilingualism may have been established, but a framework for its implementation will inevitably be denied, since it would contradict the administrative structure of professed "responsibility" which is itself an integral part of policy.

Language Conflict and Ideological Stance

The most evident feature of the recent developments in bilingual education and the associated conflicts in Wales is the lack of uniformity within the nation's territory. In a sense, this variation should not be surprising given the uneven development of capitalism on the one hand and the existence of various LEAs who exercise their power as discrete entities on the other. It can be comprehended—as can the involvement of different social groups in the controversies—by considering cases of conflict in two locations: Gwynedd and the Cardiff area.

It is evident that because of the autonomy and apparent power of the LEAs, the issue of conflict is highly localized, in the sense that the actors embroiled in the conflict are invariably relatively few in number and focus on certain localities and individual schools. It is only when the issue is abstracted from its local significance and transmitted via the media that it becomes a national issue which carries a much wider significance. Thus, what language activists see as a national phenomenon is treated by the LEAs as a local issue. Nonetheless, the conflict itself and much of the process of negotiation are still conducted at a local level. It is only the resolution that is mediated through Her Majesty's Inspectors (HMIs), councillors, and Members of Parliament to the Welsh Office and ultimately to London, a process which involves a wider connotation. Even the publicity that makes it an issue of the entire community of Wales rarely boils over into the media outside Wales. In a sense, it is this ignoring of Welsh issues by the English media that makes the hegemonic order relatively weak in its ideological impact and that allows the counterideology to gain so much ground in the reassessment of common sense vis-à-vis the Welsh language.

Another feature of the tendency for language conflict in education to be acted out on a local level is that it commonly focuses on the enclave. One reason is that the relations of production, as well as other productive forces in the enclave, are invariably those which undermine the salience of the Welsh language. Furthermore, it is in the enclave that the new bourgeoisie emerges and finds itself in conflict with the entrenched bourgeoisie—with the result that the issue of language in education becomes the focus of a struggle between the diverse factions of the bourgeoisie. The proletariat and petite bourgeoisie may still be drawn into the conflict, but it appears that the conflict is fomented where the fragmentation of a sizable bourgeoisie is most evident. It should not be surprising, therefore, that much of the conflict has focused on the university towns of Bangor and Aberystwyth and the nearby administrative towns, since these comprise a sizable Welsh bourgeoisie and an intellectual bourgeoisie of English origin. Although the English academics hold significant power in that they constitute a majority within what they see as an important institution—the university—they view themselves as a minority, albeit a high-status minority, within a local community. The situation is reversed among Welsh academics, who refer to the University of Wales as the University of England in Wales. Thus, the struggle for control of single institutions manifests itself in local politics outside that institution. Whereas the English academics may be adept at manipulating the English media, the fact that the issue is ignored by those media enhances the importance of the manipulation of the media in Wales.

In Gwynedd, a county where the majority of the population speaks Welsh, one of the contentious issues has involved the role of Welsh as a compulsory component of the curriculum up to the age of 16. While this requirement is seen by many as an extreme extension of the teaching of Welsh, in no way can it be regarded as bilingual education, for although the county authorities purport to have a policy of bilingual education, few parents can have their children educated through the medium of Welsh, whereas all parents can have their children educated through the medium of English. Furthermore, even when provision is made for the teaching of Welsh or for Welsh-medium teaching, the response of individual head teachers or teachers often manifests against it in practice. Nonetheless, some opposition to the role of Welsh in education has arisen in the form of a pressure group which labels itself POW—Parents for Optional Welsh. Our objective should be to identify the social categories locked in this struggle over the Welsh language.

Given that the ownership and management of much of the private sector derives from outside Wales and given that the management invariably involves spiralist career patterns (i.e., the combination of social and geographic mobility), it is inevitable that Welsh-medium education will at best be of little relevance to this fraction of the bourgeoisie. On the other hand, those members of the nonlocal bourgeoisie whose residence is more permanent find it difficult to integrate with constituency networks because of linguistic and other integrational characteristics. Among them are the university personnel referred to above, who often constitute what might be categorized as frustrated spiralists, seeing their careers as involving more prestigious universities in England but for one reason or another not possessing the necessary qualities for mobility. There is a frequent tendency to blame the local environment and work situation for this failure. There are also those who are long-term residents by choice and who may not adopt an integrational stance. When they do not, they form part of active pressure groups such as POW which serves as a useful basis for political mobilization. Frequently, the nature of the employment of the members of this fraction does not demand any local integration. As is the case with most of the enclave enterprises, if the employing institution has a British or international orientation, their own orientation will tend to be extralocal, especially with reference to education, which is seen as the constituency of employment opportunity rather than community integration. Much of the leadership and membership of POW is drawn from this fraction. It is in this sense that we may conceive of their adoption of an *offensive* position relative to the Welsh language.

In contrast, the support for the role of Welsh in education derives mainly from the local population employed in the public sector and the residual establishments of the premonopolistic economy. The leadership is constituted by the fraction of the bourgeoisie that is associated with these categories and that often contains those who have employed their local and ethnic affiliations to attract a constituency that elects them to public office. In a sense, their position is one of *defense* of the Welsh language, consisting of attempts to safeguard it against continual threat.[3] In this respect, they are often supported by the HMIs and educational advisors who, despite the limitations on formal political alignment associated with the professional ethic of their positions, are nonetheless in positions to promote the recommendations of the LEA. We should also note that because the issue of community is politicized around the issue of language, there is a tendency for the proletariat within the marginalized sector to support Welsh language policies.

In the Cardiff area, different conditions exist. The most evident feature of recent economic development in this area is the expansion of the service sector as a result of decentralization. Associated with the devolution of public sector functions, including the media, education, and state administration, has been the extension of a bourgeoisie in this area. In a sense, there has developed something of a national bourgeoisie associated in part with the demands for the extension of the domains of Welsh language use following the passing of the Welsh Language Act. Thus, a significant proportion of this fraction of the bourgeoisie are Welsh speakers within an area with a low proportion of Welsh speakers. As such, they are visible, highly organized, and extremely articulate. Initially, demands for an extension of bilingual education derive from this fraction, and as such these demands represent an *offensive* stance. It is only after some ground has been gained that support emanates from a local proletariat drawn, more often than not, from the marginalized sector, which sees the language as a potential basis for intergenerational social mobility within what amounts to a highly restricted labor market (Williams, Roberts, & Isaac, 1978).

The opposition in this case derives from an entrenched local, non-Welsh-speaking leadership which feels threatened by such developments. It is not unusual for language issues to integrate both of the main British political parties in opposition in an area where the enmity between them is in other respects considerable. The leaders are often those whose grandparents were Welsh speakers who, in line with the nineteenth century ideology concerning the role of language, sacrificed the Welsh language in favor of educational and occupational opportunity. Their local integration is considerable, and their expression of interest derives from this integration. As lead-

---

[3]Clearly the categories *defensive* and *offensive* do not simply refer to the language but also to the postures of class fractions relative to one another, as fractions struggling for ascendancy.

ers of an opposition, they often ally with the immigrant bourgeoisie of English origin, whereas in other contexts, polarization would be more evident.

On initial scrutiny, we might expect a simple bifurcation of ideological position relative to the Welsh language into pro and anti categories. However, the situation is complicated by the differentiation into defensive and offensive demarcations and also by the localized nature of the disputes. Thus, in Figure 1, a fourfold typology is suggested. The preceding discussion sought to clarify the infrastructural location of the actors involved in these four categories; their ideological location may now be considered briefly.[4] Clearly, the most important categories are the offensive ones, and because of limitations of space, the emphasis will be on the interpretation of Positions 1 and 2.

Position 1. The fundamental principle here is that Welsh is the ancestral language of Wales and the basis of its cultural heritage. Within this historical outlook, there is a tendency to view features associated with the English language as external to Wales and emanating from its domination. Thus, the subversion of one language by the other is central. The community thus is defined as a language community consisting of all Welsh speakers, which potentially encompasses everyone living in Wales. However, the existing nature of language relations are such that there is a realistic threat to the existence of the Welsh language, and it is held that since the state is thought to have the power to arrest this process, a failure to do so implies, at best, complacency. Thus, there is an implicit vision of representing the Welsh community in direct opposition to an ambivalent state bureaucracy. Having adopted a conflict position, the resultant strategy tends to be aggressive. A major premise of this strategy is that the state should lead rather than follow public opinion with reference to language policy. Regarding Welsh as the national language of Wales in contrast to English, which is seen as a world language, it becomes essential that all inhabitants of Wales be able to speak Welsh. In a sense, the concept of nationhood is defined by this ability, to the extent that the disappearance of the language involves the disappearance of the condition of nationhood. However, since current institutions are seen to be inadequate in reproducing the language, and since so much new ground must be gained to realize the objective, education is seen as a crucial agency for language production and reproduction. Consequently, a universal policy of bilingual education is advocated and the teaching of Welsh as a second language is abandoned. Bilingualism is seen as a situation in which each individual achieves sufficient facility in both languages to be able to choose which language to use on all occasions and for all purposes in Wales. Clearly, language use is placed within the context of individual liberalism; the choice is made by the individual and is sufficient to guar-

	Offensive	Defensive
Pro-Welsh	1	3
Anti-Welsh	2	4

Figure 1. Typology of ideological positions.

[4]The following discussion derives from discourse analysis of relevant texts undertaken in conjunction with Pierre Achard of the Maison des Sciences de l'Homme, Paris. We are grateful to the British Academy for funding this particular piece of research.

antee the survival of the language. Consequently, language rights are couched in terms of providing the necessary ingredients for opportunity, and in this respect the discussion closely resembles liberal discussions about the provision of educational opportunity in relation to a search for the eradication of social inequality. The neglect of structural causes of language erosion, with the associated inequality vis-à-vis rights, consolidates the liberal position and make it an issue of policy in terms of public administration rather than in infrastructural terms. The role of Welsh in education is justified by arguments pointing to the extent to which early bilingualism facilitates the learning of a third language and by the claim that the study of Welsh is as intellectually satisfying as the study of any other language.[5] The academic success of the existing bilingual schools that are seen as nonselective (i.e., enrollment is on the basis of parental choice) reinforces this view.

Position 2. In some respects this position resembles the base point of the ideological consensus that existed in the nineteenth century, when the Welsh language was denigrated and relegated to the position of a noninstrumental patois. Again, a liberal stance is evident in that the right of the Welsh (they are presumably the only ones who would wish to use the language) to speak their language is acknowledged. However, the introduction of bilingual education is seen to involve forcing others to speak it. It would imply treating English residents as immigrant foreigners in their own country, Britain. Thus, a distinctive boundary closure defines a field of operation as one which encompasses Wales. The nationalism encompassed in making a nation (England) synonymous with a state (Britain) is ignored, as is the implicit polarization of "Welsh" and "English" people. The issue is couched in terms of Welsh nationalist "fanatics" who constitute a minority challenging the "citizens" who constitute a democratic majority. Thus, the language is politicized, and bilingual education is treated in overtly political terms. The policy of bilingual education may be acceptable, but it can not be implemented practically, because it interferes with the freedom of the individual and introduces community division. On initial scrutiny these two principles appear to be contradictory, but the definition of the community as one where the norm involves the English-speaking majority means that individualism must be similarly defined. Yet there is a clear focus on an argument that is couched strictly in educational terms. This focus involves viewing the Welsh language pejoratively as one that has no instrumental value. In this respect, it contrasts with the English language, which is the language of government (democracy), law (citizenship), and engineering (progress)—in brief, the language of reason. Thus, the allocation of both time and financial resources to teaching through the medium of Welsh is held (1) to restrict the choice of a more rational alternative, and (2) to contribute to the lowering of educational standards. In sum, there appears to be a limited liberal commitment to supporting the rights of minorities, but only insofar as these do not interfere with the interests of the majority.

---

[5]That the acquisition of the language is felt to require such justification merely serves to underline the fact that this position reflects but a limited degree of offensiveness: it is an offensive stance merely in terms of reference to conditions as they exist. An example of a more extreme offensive position is discernible in the stance of the pressure group Adfer, which clearly views the use of English in communities where Welsh-speaking ability predominates as untenable, undesirable, and unnecessary.

Positions 3 and 4. What is interesting about these two positions is not so much their liberal stance with reference to concepts such as *individual, democracy, minority,* and *rights,* but the focus on community as a point of reference. This should not be surprising, given that the positions purport to uphold local interests. What is different, of course, is the relationship of the community to language. In both cases, the idea of community that is upheld is that of an undifferentiated, geographically bounded population. Since the majority of the population in Gwynedd is Welsh speaking, the term *community* in Position 3 refers to an indigenous language community whose interests are held to be represented in action aimed at preserving the link between language and community. Thus, the language is viewed as crucial not only for entry into social institutions but also for comprehension of a culture that is reproduced within these institutions. In a sense, there is a tendency to counterpose the idea of an integrative community with a sense of alienation not unlike that found in the community dualisms of liberal social science. It follows that the loss of language results in the loss of all that is held to be good in this view of community. Thus, bilingual education is presented as a benevolent means of integrating the non-speaker into all that is of benefit in the concept of community. While Position 4 shares the tendency to present the community as undifferentiated and thereby to obscure any explicit interest inherent in internal differentation and community conservation, it deviates from position 3 in the relationship of language to community. The inability of the majority to speak Welsh means that the community language is held to be English. Education is seen as comprising "community" schools whose function is, in part, to socialize pupils through interaction into membership in the community. Thus, the introduction of Welsh will result in a social closure that inhibits such integration and thereby generates social divisiveness. Evidently, both positions draw upon the idea of democracy as constituting the will of the numerical majority, while the autonomy of the LEA serves to define the boundary by which *majority* and *minority* are defined.

A comparison of Positions 1 and 2 highlights two issues. The first is a contrast between Wales and Britain as nations in the sense of points of identity allegiance. It is a contrast of two *nationalisms.* However, because it is taken for granted, British nationalism does not exist within Britain (even though there is a tendency to refer to Britain as "the nation" and for most English people to see *Britain* and *England* as coterminous in that sense); the result is that Welsh nationalism assumes an explicit posture. The second issue involves a contrast in the evaluation of the Welsh language within Wales. Since in both positions the English language is taken for granted, either as a world language or as the language of the British "people," it is a matter of evaluating the degree of minority status allocated to the Welsh language. In Position 2, Welsh tends to be viewed as an atavistic attachment to an outmoded and irrational past. In a sense, this view is almost akin to placing the language—and by implication its speakers—in "nature," or certainly outside of total integration into civilization with its associated rational superiority.[6] Position 1, on the other hand,

---

[6]This theme also emerges in the various studies of communities in Wales undertaken by English anthropologists.

sees the language and its speakers as being in an underprivileged position within the pseudopolitical domain of the Welsh nation. The ensuing unfairness emanates from being a minority within a democratic context which under no condition allows the Welsh to assume a majority position and thereby to benefit from democratic principles. The problem is held to derive from the majority's failure to act as trustees of the minority and its interests.

These four positions can be conceptualized as a continuum ranging from Position 2, which represents the most vehement opposition to formal bilingual education, to Position 1, which constitutes an equally strong stance in favor of a concerted policy of bilingual education throughout Wales. Focusing conflict on local arenas means that alliances that would integrate positions into two polarized camps do not occur even if the resultant ideological positions would be congruent with the interests of the relevant class fractions. What seems apparent is that, as was suggested in the comparison of the two reports earlier, since 1960 there has been a significant shift in what constitutes acceptable common sense toward the Position 1 end of the continuum. This shift represents the success of the counterideology. However, it does not mean that the entire range of ideological positions ceases to exist, nor that a concerted backlash could not reverse these developments. What is likely to occur is that as the Welsh language continues to erode, probably to the point where it becomes a minority language within all LEAs, the ideological composition of each position will change. A defensive stance in Position 3 will not be tenable, and the nature of the boundary by which *majority* is defined in Position 2 will also change with an associated modification in the resultant rationalization.

Two developments appear to have precipitated this shift. First of all, the Welsh language was legitimized in the form of the Welsh Language Act, which justified the use of Welsh in law and administration—both important parts of the public sector of the economy. Second, the decentralization of services associated with the restructuring of the economy in Wales after the Second World War, especially during the 1960s, not only created a new bourgeoisie within the public sector in the Cardiff area but also tied many of the relevant occupations to the Welsh language. This increased *prestige,*[7] or relevance for social mobility, of the Welsh language through its extension into new domains is of utmost importance in the reassessment of the status of the language. Although it may lead to a reaction among those threatened by such developments, Welsh will no longer be trivialized and treated in a pejorative manner.

Conclusion

In this chapter, we have sought to identify the manner in which ideological production with reference to the issue of bilingualism in Wales is negotiated, assessed, and reassessed. Rather than treat this issue in the abstract, we have chosen to try to

---

[7]This concept is discussed in detail in Williams, 1980a.

identify the implicit interests of the respective class fractions involved in the struggle over language before considering the nature of their ideological output. In order to accomodate this line of argument, the issues of control and negotiation—inherent features of ideology in themselves—had to be considered. Thus, an attempt was made to overcome the major weakness of most approaches to both education and language: namely, the abstraction of ideology or infrastructure from discussions of the institutional administration of power and the implicit link between base and superstructure (cf. Parker; Illich, this volume).

Our conclusions from the preceding analysis are the following: We recognize that none of the protagonists in the struggle constitutes a threat to the existing capitalist hegemony nor to the associated class structure, but that the struggle is the manifestation of class fragmentation deriving from uneven capitalist development and the associated competition for control. In this setting, a delicate situation is developing whereby the indigenous fraction appears to be gaining ground in the sense that an ideological shift has occurred in its favor. Simultaneously, however, the issue (i.e., the Welsh language) that forms the focus of its demands is losing ground because of state disinvolvement and the process of language erosion, which derives from the absence of the minority language in the direct forces of social reproduction.

The process whereby this ideological shift has occurred involves the initial legitimation of the minority language, followed by the resultant implementation of the terms of legitimation on the part of new indigenous bourgeoisie. This process, together with the results of concerted pressure on the part of interested class fractions leads to a limited shift of the language into domains that constitute direct forces of social reproduction. Although this shift has profound repercussions—too complex to discuss here—for the relationship between linguistic features of the language and the social structure, it also brings the issue of the relationship between minority cultural reproduction and social reproduction into focus.

If culture is the basis for social control through the reproduction of the class structure and if education is a primary institutional agency for such processes, then the introduction of bilingual education presents a challenge to the state and its associated class interests. For if the minority culture, transmitted through the medium of the minority language, is seen to generate a counterideology which in some sense constitutes a threat to existing power relationships, then action must be taken. Even if—as is probable—the threat is a limited one, in the sense that the counterideology merely substantiates social reproduction, the context in which this substantiation occurs may constitute a threat. The two alternatives for action would appear to be to eliminate the minority language or to expropriate it. In a sense, the establishment of bilingual schools by the state constitutes expropriation in that it removes from the institutions of civil society the onus for minority language and cultural reproduction and places it within the domain of the state. It is here that we witness the firm control that the state exerts on ideological transmission, regardless of which language is employed for that transmission in education. As we have suggested, the liberal democratic administrative structure merely clouds the issue of control. Thus, although the minority language may predominate in education, it will be employed to transmit the hegemonic ideology. As a consequence, the minority language may well be reproduced, but the minority culture will not. The autonomy of the individual school and the individual teacher may allow for some scope in reproducing the minority culture, but the firm control of the state in terms of curriculum and the like manifests against such developments. Thus, while there may well be an ideological shift in progress concerning the reproduction of the minority language through the extension of bilingual education, any threat that this shift might constitute is firmly controlled by the process of expropriation.

References

Gramsci, A. *Selections from prison notebooks.* London: Lawrence and Wishart, 1971.

Rawkins, P. M. *The implementation of language policy in the schools of Wales* (Studies in Public Policy No. 40). Glasgow: University of Strathclyde, 1979.

Roberts, C. *Cultural reproduction and the bilingual school.* Paper delivered at the annual conference of the British Educational Research Association, Cardiff, October 1980.

Welsh Joint Education Committee (WJEC). *The Joint Committee comes of age, 1948–1969.* Cardiff: Her Majesty's Stationery Office, 1970.

Williams, G. Language group allegiance and ethnic interaction. In H. Giles & B. Saint-Jaques (Eds.), *Language and ethnic relations.* Oxford: Pergamon Press, 1980. (a)

Williams, G. Industrialization, inequality and deprivation in rural Wales. In G. Rees & T. L. Rees (Eds.), *Poverty and social inequality in Wales.* London: Croom Helm, 1980. (b)

Williams, G., & Roberts C. Language and social structure in Welsh education. In E. Hoyle & J. Megarry (Eds.), *World year book of education 1981: Education of minorities.* London: Kogan Page, 1981.

Williams, G., & Roberts, C. Institutional centralization and linguistic discrimination. In G. Braga & M. Civelli (Eds.), *Linguistic problems and European unity.* Milan: Franco Angeli Editore, 1982.

Williams, G., Roberts, E., & Isaac, R. Language and aspirations for upward social mobility. In G. Williams (Ed.), *Social and cultural change in contemporary Wales.* London: Routledge and Kegan Paul, 1978.

28

Minority Languages in the Netherlands: Relations between Sociopolitical Conflicts and Bilingual Education

René Appel

Introduction

Children from linguistic minority groups often have serious educational problems which are in good measure caused by the language discrepancy between home and school. The minority language is typically not used at school, and school subjects are taught in a language in which the children are often insufficiently competent. Instruction in the mother tongue of minority children in bilingual education programs is thought to be an answer to the educational problems of these children (Skutnabb-Kangas & Toukomaa, 1976). The maintenance of the children's first language is also considered an important effect of mother tongue teaching. According to Hernandez-Chavez (1978, p. 528), the goals of bilingual education in the United States are commonly seen "to be the attainment of scholastic skills in English and the use of the native language to advance conceptual development and academic achievement as well as for the enrichment of children's personal lives."

The reality of bilingual education in the United States shows, however, that the position of minority languages is mostly marginal (Spolsky, 1977; cf. Masemann, this volume). Bilingual education programs exist mainly to help children whose English is inadequate improve their proficiency. Hernandez-Chavez (1978) has pointed out that they are assimilationist in character and that they do not promote minority language maintenance, with the result that language shift from the minority to the majority language continues, although perhaps at a slower rate.

René Appel ● Institute for General Linguistics, University of Amsterdam, Amsterdam, Holland.

The assimilationist character of bilingual education programs can best be understood if proposals for bilingual and/or bicultural education are analyzed not as answers to linguistic and educational problems of minority children, but as reactions to sociopolitical conflicts between minority groups and majority society (cf. de Terra, this volume). An important, but perhaps hidden, aim of bilingual education is to reduce these conflicts by helping minority children assimilate in mainstream society. Mother tongue teaching can only play an important part in bilingual education if the minority group considered is already integrated in mainstream society: for example, indigenous minority groups with the same ethnic background as the speakers of the majority language.

I will illustrate this conception of the objectives and possible outcomes of bilingual education with a description of the social, linguistic, and educational situation of five minority groups in the Netherlands: the Frisians, the Indo-Europeans, the Moluccans, the Surinamese, and the so-called foreign workers. Like other European countries, Dutch society is becoming more and more multiethnic and multilingual. The need for bilingual education for children from linguistic minority groups is widely discussed, and the first steps in the direction of bilingual programs are being taken.

The Linguistic Situation in the Netherlands

The Netherlands has about 14,000,000 inhabitants (in 1981). Dutch is the national language, and, for more than 90% of the population, it is the mother tongue. However, many people have a social or regional variety of Dutch as their first language. For example, in the eastern and southeastern parts of Holland, regional varieties of Dutch are spoken which differ strikingly from standard Dutch. It is known that children who speak such regional varieties will encounter educational difficulties, because standard Dutch is the primary language of the classroom (although current practices are changing in favor of using nonstandard varieties).

The linguistic situation of Holland has been stable for some time, but is now rapidly changing due to the settlement of migrant workers (the so-called foreign workers) and people from the former colony of Surinam. In Rotterdam, after Amsterdam the second largest city in Holland, it is expected that by 1985, half of the newborn infants will have a non-Dutch ethnic background, and most of these children will grow up with a native language other than Dutch.

Minority Groups and Minority Languages

Frisians

The Frisians are the traditional linguistic minority in Holland. According to an estimate by Wijnstra (1976), about ⅔ of the 550,000 inhabitants of the province of Friesland (in the northwestern part of Holland) use Frisian as their vernacular. About 15% use Dutch at home, and another 15% a regional language or dialect.

Is there really a language problem in Friesland, except for the survival of Frisian? It is difficult to say something about this with any degree of certainty. Regarding educational difficulties, it is assumed that children will have problems if the language in the school is not the same as at home. However, hardly any concrete empirical data on the situation in Friesland are to be found.

Although only a few people want to fight for the promotion of the Frisian language, in general the inhabitants of Friesland place a high value on Frisian, and they want more status and prestige for it (Pietersen, 1969). In their opinion, Frisian and Dutch should be considered equivalent languages, and people should be encouraged to use Frisian in as many contexts as possible. To accomplish this end, it is necessary for all inhabitants of Friesland to be competent in Dutch as well as in Frisian. Education is a means of attaining this goal.

As early as 1907, courses in Frisian had been organized outside school hours with financial support from the province of Friesland. In 1973, Dutch law was changed, making it possible to include a regional language within the scope of Dutch language courses. Since 1980, Frisian is an obligatory subject in primary schools in Friesland (see also Boelens, 1977). Before the Second World War, some people were arguing for the use of Frisian as the medium of instruction in primary schools. In 1950, within the permission of the Ministry of Education, an experiment started with schools in which Frisian was used in the first two grades as the medium of instruction. In 1955, the law on primary education was changed to make possible a bilingual school with Frisian as the language of instruction in the first three grades. In 1974, the law was further changed so that Frisian could be used as the medium of instruction throughout elementary school.

Indo-Europeans

During and after the struggle for independence in the Dutch East Indies, which resulted in the official settlement of the Republic of Indonesia in 1948, thousands of people with Dutch nationality came to Holland. It is estimated that in 1969 there were about 250,000 of these so-called repatriateds in Holland (Surie, 1973). Most of them had a mixed Dutch-Indonesian ethnic background. In Holland, they were called *Indische Nederlanders;* I will use the expression *Indo-Europeans.*

The integration of the Indo-Europeans in Dutch society has taken place without major social conflicts, although individual people have experienced many social-psychological problems. In general, the Indo-Europeans, like the other repatriateds, held the opinion that they should assimilate as soon as possible.

Most of the adults were bilingual, with one of the varieties of Malay or Javanese as a first language, and Dutch as a second (or third) language. Most of the children were also bilingual, but many of them had Dutch as a first language. According to Surie (1973), Indo-Europeans had language problems in Holland. The level of proficiency in Dutch was especially low among the women. Children fared better, but school achievement showed that even after some years in Holland the problems had not been solved; their language deficiency had a negative effect on school subjects such as arithmetic.

There has never been an official effort to try to solve the language problems or other educational difficulties of these people. There were no compensatory language classes organized; the teaching of Malay to promote language maintenance for adults and children was not considered. The attitude seemed to be that the language problems of the Indo-Europeans could be neglected, because of their strong wish to assimilate in Dutch society. They did not cause social problems and conflicts; hence, their language problems went unnoticed.

Moluccans

Because of the pressure of the political situation in Indonesia and commitments made by the Dutch government, about 3,500 Moluccan soliders of the former Royal Dutch-Indian Army came to Holland with their families in April 1951. The Dutch government as well as the Moluccans did not consider this migration a real or attractive resolution to the problems, but regarded it as temporary.

There are no exact figures, but it is estimated that in 1978 approximately 32,000 Moluccans lived in Holland (Penninx, 1979). Today, about 4,000 Moluccan children are attending primary school, and 65% of these children are from families where (Moluccan) Malay is spoken in the home.

Most publications on the social position and problems of the Moluccans deal only indirectly with possible language problems. Because of the lack of empirical data, it is difficult to determine to what extent the social problems of the Moluccans are also caused by a possible language problem; the fact that the social problems are very large cannot be disputed. For example, the unemployment rate of the Moluccans is three times higher than that of the Dutch working population. Along with factors such as discrimination in the job market, the relatively bad school results of Moluccan children can be held responsible for this situation. According to Van Amersfoort (1971), the language problems of Moluccan children are one of the main obstacles to good school achievement.

It is astonishing how few measures were taken to solve the educational problems of Moluccan children. It was not until 1964 that there were tentative efforts to do something about their language problems with the help of supplementary language exercises in Dutch. The government seemed (or wanted) to realize that more facilities were needed to cope with these problems and educational difficulties when the political activities of the Moluccans, who are striving for an independent state in the Indonesian archipelago, escalated with the event in Bovensmilde in 1977, when schoolchildren and their teachers were taken as hostages. In 1978, the government presented a paper on the problems of the Moluccan community in Holland. The presentation of this paper must be interpreted more as a reaction to the problems that *Holland* had with the Moluccans than as an answer to the problems the Moluccans encountered themselves. The 1978 paper was nonetheless a first attempt to formulate an actual policy. Several measures were announced, including:

1. Development of language programs for the improvement of competence in Dutch
2. Supplementary education of teachers in schools with many Moluccan children
3. Consultations with representatives of the Moluccan community to discuss possibilities for organizing bilingual education

4. Further research into possibilities for improving the relations between vernacular language and culture of the Moluccan children and the Dutch educational system
5. Organization of instruction of Malay and Moluccan culture for Moluccans

The last three announced measures are especially interesting. It seems that in government circles it had finally been realized that the "soft," gradual assimilation, which was formerly, perhaps implicitly, the heart of the policy, in the end would provoke violent reactions. To put it another way: if the language and culture of the minority is ignored, that group will retaliate in some manner or other. That the opportunity for minority-group members to experience their language and culture can be guaranteed through administrative controls in schools, thereby productively channeling their cultural angst, seems to dawn on establishments ever so slowly! However, discussion of the Moluccan minority's own language and culture (and similarly of other minority groups) will surely continue for a long time. An important topic in this discussion is the influence of minority language education on the social, political, and cultural attitudes of the minority groups. If progress in this realm is not made, the groups could become more separatist, resulting in new social conflicts and political action.

Surinamese

In the late sixties and early seventies, people from Surinam started coming to Holland in ever-increasing numbers. The number of people with a Surinam ethnic background now living in Holland is estimated at 250,000. (Surinam, a former colony of Holland and independent since 1975, now has the same number of inhabitants!) Since about 1970, the Surinam minority group has been mainly enlarged "with people who experience the Dutch norms and values, and hence also the Dutch language and the Dutch cultural system as 'strange'" (Haakmat, 1979, p. 4). Most people from Surinam are bilingual. They have Sranan (the creole vernacular of Surinam) or Sarnami (the language of the Hindustan people in Surinam) as their first language and the Surinam variety of Dutch as their second language. Many of the children born in Holland either acquire two languages more or less simultaneously or have Dutch as their first language.

Research data on the language problems of Surinam children are scarce. Until 1979, the government paid little attention to the problems of Surinam children in Dutch schools: only a few ad hoc measures had been taken. It seemed that people thought, or hoped, that the problems would not last—a policy that is often employed toward minority groups. It has become quite clear, however, that the problems will continue, and since 1979 the arrangements for educational facilities for children of foreign workers also apply to Surinamese children. That makes it possible to give more attention to the teaching of Dutch. The draft policy paper of the Minister of Education (Concept Beleidsplan, 1980) on cultural minorities in the educational system states that classes on the children's own culture must be integrated into the regular program. Unfortunately, no provision was made for the teaching of the Surinamese languages.

Foreign Workers and Their Families

The first foreign workers from Mediterranean countries came to Holland in the early sixties. The law regulating the reunion of families made it possible in the seventies for many women to come and join their husbands and to bring their children. In 1979, there were about 200,000 people from countries with which Holland had made labor migration contracts. About 40% are of Turkish nationality, and 25% are Moroccan. Despite the fact that the hiring of new foreign workers has stopped, it is expected that the number of foreigners will increase. More families will probably reunite (in Holland), and the birthrate among foreigners is more than two times higher than that of the Dutch. Most of the foreign workers do unskilled or semiskilled labor. They form a kind of sub-proletariat with a social position more or less comparable to the position of migrant workers from Mexico in the United States.

The number of foreign children (i.e., children of foreign workers) has risen quickly: in 1972, there were 10,000 foreign children; in 1978, there were more than 32,000. According the Ministry of Education, this number grew to about 40,000 in 1979—an increase of 25% in one year. In the future, the number of foreign children will presumably grow at a similar or higher rate.

It is quite evident that this heterogeneous group of foreign workers and their families is faced with serious language problems. Most of the adults have a low level of proficiency in Dutch. The situation of the children is better, yet nearly all of them can still be considered to have serious majority language deficits. Although there are no research data on this issue, it seems that foreign children born and raised in Holland have fewer Dutch-language problems. However, parents sometimes complain that their children cannot speak their mother tongue well enough (see also Bain, 1980).

The educational policy regarding foreign children which was formulated around 1975 was not supported by clear ideas concerning the position and future of foreigners in Holland. The main part of the policy was the so-called facilities arrangement. On the basis of this arrangement, schools or groups of schools with a relatively large number of foreign children could engage special teachers for the introduction and teaching of Dutch, as well as a foreign teacher in charge of classes in the children's native language and culture (for about four hours a week). These classes were originally organized because it was expected that many of the foreign workers and their families would return to their respective countries of origin after a few years. Little attention was paid to the content and form of the education of foreign children. The result was that schools everywhere improvised—in their own manner—the reception and the teaching of foreign children.

In 1980, new measures were announced for improving the educational situation of foreign children. The measures are based on the conclusion that most of these children will stay in Holland. A form of bicultural education is planned, in which teaching of the minority groups' own languages and cultures is possible; the principal aim, however, is adaptation to the Dutch school system with much attention to the compensatory teaching of Dutch. According to the policy paper of 1980, the teaching of the children's own language and culture "should not hinder the unfolding in Dutch society, for example by the promotion of a certain kind of segregation" (Concept Beleidsplan, 1980, p. 36).

Five Minority Groups Compared: Sociopolitical Conflicts and Bilingual Education

I will now try to compare the educational situation of the five minority groups from a general sociopolitical perspective. The position of the Frisians is rather special, because they form the only indigenous linguistic minority. Of all the groups, this one has experienced the fewest language problems and educational difficulties; the education system has been working on the introduction of Frisian into the elementary schools and on the evaluation and planning of bilingual schools for a considerable period of time. Plans to make Frisian an obligatory subject in the school have been supported by nearly everyone in Parliament. At the same time, there is still much sharp political discussion about vernacular language and culture education for other minority groups. "The Frisians are our own linguistic minority and do not constitute a political or social danger for the rest of society" constitutes much of the political wisdom. However, if Frisian nationalists decide to promote their demands for a truly bilingual education by occupying the Afsluitdijk (an important road connecting Friesland and the western part of Holland) or by taking the prime minister hostage on one of the northern isles, Frisian bilingual education will also become a subject for more representative discussion.

Perhaps the policy toward Frisian in the schools is to be more cultural or linguistic than educational. An indication of this trend is the fact that in 1970, money was reserved for the maintenance and promotion of Frisian language and culture in the budget of the Ministry of Culture, Recreation, and Social Work. Of course, it should not be forgotten that the Frisian linguistic minority is a traditional one. Moreover, Frisians, as well as others with positive attitudes toward Friesland and the Frisian language, are represented in political parties, councils, and so on. As far as I know however, none of the members of the Dutch Parliament has a non-Dutch ethnic background.

The orientation of Dutch society is strongly monoethnic. The Frisians are indeed a linguistic minority, but they apparently wish to be part of Dutch society. The situation of the Moluccans, the Surinamese, and the foreign workers (and their families) is quite different. They are obviously marginal groups, to be left alone or ignored as long as the majority are not confronted with too many problems. I have already pointed out that immediately after some serious political action, attention was given to the education of Moluccan children. Educational measures were not taken because educational problems were growing; rather, they were taken in response to increasing political and social problems caused by the Moluccans. The same applies, to a large extent, to the Surinamese and the foreigners. People are afraid of problems with the second generation; the number of young foreigners who have tasted Dutch prosperity but who cannot really profit from it is growing. As with the Moluccans, people are talking about the young foreigners in the in-between position: they belong neither to their own culture nor to the Dutch culture. Maladjusted and antisocial behavior is feared. In discussions about education for minority children, issues such as the use of hard drugs, juvenile delinquency, and prostitution are often raised. In an interview on the position of minorities with *Elseviers Magazine,* the Minister of the Interior, who is responsible for the coordination of the policy on minorities, said ominously: "If we don't change our policy drastically, I am afraid we shall have to face violent explosions between Dutch people and foreigners" ("Minister Wiegel," 1980).

The position of the Indo-Europeans is well known by social scientists in Holland and in other countries. Their individual problems, among them language problems, have been ignored because they do not cause social or political conflicts. They have an apparent assimilative attitude. Likewise, the language problems of generations of Chinese people in Holland are not addressed. The reason is obvious: they maintain a low profile politically and socially.

It seems inevitable to compare this situation with the language compensation movement in the United States in the sixties. The efforts to reduce the educational problems of black children in large northern cities were partly motivated by social problems and political stirrings in black neighborhoods. The integration of the black population in American society was an important but hidden aim; for the legitimization of these efforts, one referred to the notion of equal educational opportunities. However, for everyone who analyzed the educational problems in their socioeconomic and political context, it was obvious that the idea of equal opportunities was an illusion (see Bowles & Gintis, 1976). I do not want to argue that people who devise educational policy for minority children have only secret, perfidious intentions. Their ostensible aim is to improve the situation of the minority groups concerned. In addition to this objective, or behind it, however, is often the desire to safeguard society against problems which minorities "cause." The basic question is whether these two objectives would not lead to contradictory and clashing practices.

Earlier, I referred to the draft policy paper on cultural minorities in the educational system by the Dutch Minister of Education (Concept Beleidsplan, 1980). Remarkably enough, in this paper there is not one word said about the century-old cultural minority in Friesland. It can be concluded from the paper that the position of schooling in the vernacular language and culture is still unclear. The more general parts of the paper lead to the conclusion that the ethnic minorities' own cultures should be brought into the schools, because that is important for a reciprocal cultural adjustment of Dutch children and minority children, of Dutch society and minority community. In contrast with this conclusion, there are many signs in the paper that point to the view that the main objective of schooling in the vernacular language and culture is a faster and more complete adjustment to the Dutch educational system. "To relieve the 'culture shock' is an important argument for reception in vernacular language and culture and a smooth *transition* to the *regular* Dutch school situation" (p. 34, emphasis added).

In the policy paper, the Minister does not seem to realize that arguments derived from language policy or language planning should be used in discussions of bilingual education. Proposals are made for teaching in the vernacular language and culture, but they are only motivated by the idea that "development of personality and identity" will occur (p. 60), or that the "self-concept" of the child will be positively influenced (p. 36). Kjolseth (1972) stated in a classic article that bilingual education can have two different objectives: (1) a pluralistic model: one strives for a stable form of multilingualism and multiculturalism; (2) an assimilative model in which multilingualism and multiculturalism are considered transitional stages to monolingualism and monoculturalism.

In the policy paper, the pluralistic society is taken as a starting point; however, it is obvious that the public authorities have no stable, long-term language policy. The question as to whether it is desirable, useful, necessary, or possible for Holland to have, for example, a permanent Turkish-speaking minority in the future is not dealt with. The comments in the paper on the value of teaching in the vernacular language lead to the conclusion that the proposed school model is assimilative in nature. Therefore, there is perhaps only an implicit language policy: to allow Turkish, Moroccan Arabic, and other nonindigenous minority languages to disappear from the Dutch speech community.

Concluding Remarks

In the Netherlands, there is a strong relationship between the sociopolitical situation of minority groups and the way their language problems are dealt with, a condition which, in my opinion, is not dissimilar to that which exists in other West European countries (cf. Roberts & Williams, this volume). A remarkable difference can be noticed between indigenous and nonindigenous minority groups. For the indigenous linguistic minority, that is, the Frisians, bilingual education is commonly accepted because they do not cause sociopolitical problems; language maintenance efforts are not disputed and are officially supported. In contrast, bilingual education for nonindigenous linguistic minorities is promoted only when sociopolitical conflicts arise or are expected to arise. Language problems of nonindigenous minority groups are more readily recognized and officially acknowledged if the groups concerned are considered to be the cause of (potential) social or political conflicts. New educational measures are often not a direct reaction to the problems the minority groups experience themselves, but to the problems majority society encounters when minority groups do not fit into the system in an assimilative way. These problems, or sociopolitical conflicts, are often interpreted as being caused by language problems alone; in this way, the socioeconomic and political aspects of the conflicts are unjustly ignored. The focus of bilingual education for nonindigenous minority children invariably turns out to be compensatory majority-language teaching. The official attitude toward minority languages is defensive: mother tongue teaching is stimulated only in a limited way, because it is feared that too much of this education will serve to strengthen minority-group political and cultural identity, thereby fostering additional sociopolitical conflicts.

References

Bain, B. *English as a second language needs assessment*. Edmonton, Alberta: Edmonton Public Schools, 1980.

Boelens, Kr. Bilingualism in primary schools of Friesland. In W. F. Mackey & T. Andersson (Eds.), *Bilingualism in early childhood*. Rowley, Mass.: Newbury House, 1977, pp. 209–213.

Bowles, S., & Gintis, H. *Schooling in capitalist America: Educational reform and the contradictions of economic life*. London: Routledge and Kegan Paul, 1976.

Concept Beleidsplan *Culturele minderheden in het Onderwijs*. 's Gravenhage: Staatsuitgeverij, 1980.

Haakmat, A. R. Het onderwijs aan Surinaamse kinderen in Nederland: Probleemvelden en perspectieven. *Span'noe*, 1979, *VI*(6/7), 4–9.

Hernandez-Chavez, E. Language maintenance, bilingual education and philosophies of bilingualism. In J. Alatis (Ed.), *Georgetown University Round Table on Languages and Linguistics*. Washington, D.C.: Georgetown University Press, 1978, pp. 527–550.

Kjolseth, R. Bilingual education programs in the United States: For assimilation or pluralism? In B. Spolsky (Ed.), *The language education of minority children*. Rowley, Mass.: Newbury House, 1972, pp. 94–121.

Minister Wiegel over minderheidsproblemen. *Elseviers Magazine*, May 24, 1980, pp. 48–49.

Penninx, R. Naar een algemeen etnisch minderhedenbeleid? In Wetenschappelijke Raad voor het Regeringsbeleid, *Etnische minderheden*, 's-Gravenhage: Staatsuitgeverij, 1979, pp. 1–174.

Pietersen, L. *De Friezen en hun taal*. Drachten: Uitgeverij Breuker, 1969.

Skutnabb-Kangas, T., & Toukomaa, P. *Teaching migrant children's mother tongue and learning the language of the host country in the context of the socio-cultural situation of the migrant family* (Tutkimuksia Research Reports). Finland: The University of Tampere, 1976.

Spolsky, B. The establishment of language education policy in multilingual societies. In B. Spolsky & R. Cooper (Eds.), *Frontiers of bilingual education*. Rowley Mass.: Newbury House, 1977, pp. 1–21.

Surie, H. G. De gerepatrieerden. In H. Verwey-Jonker (Ed.), *Allochtonen in Nederland*. 's-Gravenhage: Staatsuitgeverij, 1973, pp. 45–108.

Van Amersfoort, J. M. M. *De sociale positie van de Molukkers in Nederland*. 's-Gravenhage: Staatsuitgeverij, 1971.

Wijnstra, J. M. *Het onderwijs aan van huis uit friestalige kinderen*. 's-Gravenhage: Staatsuitgeverij, 1976.

29

The Linguagenesis of Society: The Implementation of the National Language Plan in West Malaysia

Diane de Terra

The sociogenesis of language and human conduct implies a general attitude or orientation toward the nature of the relationship between the individual, language, and society. So, too, does *linguagenesis*. However, there is a fundamental difference. The sociogenesis view is that the origins of language and human conduct are to be found within the matrix of social relations among people, while what I call the linguagenesis view is that the origins of social relations among people and of a united, modern nation are to be found in a common language. This single language will create a national soul, integration, and solidarity and will ensure the advent of modernity, technology, and economic development. Attempts to create united, modern societies by linguagenesis are the purview of language planning. Language is not the only aspect of national unity and development plans, but my focus is language in the context of national language-plan implementation in West Malaysia.

With the view to assessing the impact of national language planning on a target population, I lived in a non-Malay, working-class community in West Malaysia from 1975 to 1978. Evaluation of the speakers' responses is a neglected but vital part of the language planning process. My aim was to find out how a non-Malay speaking community reacts to planned language, to investigate the socioeconomic impact of planned language change, and to observe the process of linguagenesis and the social relations it creates.

Malaysia has a well-documented history of language planning both prior to independence, when English was the official language, and after independence (1957), when Malay became the national and official language. National language planning and engineering continue in Malaysia today. Language policy was a subject

Diane de Terra ● School of Oriental and African Studies, University of London, and Consultant, Development Anthropology, Washington, D.C. 20008.

of debate well before Article 152 of the Constitution (1957) established that "the National Language shall be the Malay language." To facilitate the implementation of this ruling, the Language and Literature Agency (Dewan Bahasa dan Pustaka), a corporate body, was set up in 1959 to develop the Malay language as well as literature in Malay and to produce books and textbooks. The national language for this multiracial country—approximately 46% Malay, 34% Chinese, 9% Indian, 4% Dayaks, 2% Kadazans, 3% other natives, and 2% other—was called either *Bahasa Melayu* or *Bahasa Kebangsaan* (National Language). In 1969, the Government adopted a new name, *Bahasa Malaysia,* to stress that this was the language of the entire nation and not just one section. The Constitution (Amendment) Act (1971) removed sensitive issues from the realm of public discussion and gave power to Parliament to pass laws prohibiting the question of, among others, Article 152, National Language. Such prohibition, however, does not apply to questioning in relation to the implementation of the provisions as specified by law.

In the non-Malay community, hereafter called the *Kampong* (Malay for village), in which I lived, I found little evidence of implementation, adaptation, or language shift. Kampong dwellers who did not speak Bahasa Malaysia were not learning it, although many wished to do so. Those who knew some Malay had little or no opportunity to speak it, and children who were learning it at school never uttered a word. Many people were aware of the importance of speaking the national language but found access to it impossible.

It is my conviction that attachment to language as a marker of ethnic identity is insufficient explanation for the absence of shift to Bahasa Malaysia. Rather, understanding the politics and economics of language planners and the socioeconomic activities of people living in the Kampong is essential to adequate explanation. I shall explore possible explanations for planners' failure to implement and speakers' responses. Failure to learn Bahasa Malaysia may have more to do with language planners than with language speakers/learners. Deficiency cannot be attributed to speakers alone. By not teaching Bahasa Malaysia while advocating a policy of a single language for national unity, a policy of divide and rule can be pursued at the same time. What language is for Bahasa Malaysia language planners is not what it is for working-class, non-Malay speakers. There are two distinct ideologies. At the outset, language-policy makers set themselves the task of solving societal problems by means of planned language change. Theirs is not Bernstein's view, that changes in the social structure are major factors in shaping or changing a given culture through their effect on the consequences of speaking, but Wittgenstein's idea, that language generates social modes. However, they fail to remember that for Wittgenstein the generation of social modes is only part of a cumulative dialectic: language generates social modes, and different social modes further divide languages. Language did generate social modes, but not the planned modes. Instead of unity, languages and their speakers were further divided. Communication became more difficult and less frequent.

Those studies that examine the relationship of language and political economy usually examine the influence of economic pressures on language shift. The role of economic factors in language shift is depicted in terms of direct or indirect pressure. Direct economic pressure compels people to adopt elite or standard languages in preference to minority languages, whereas indirect pressures prompt prestige usage—the adoption of an elite language by lower-class speakers wishing to emulate a socially dominant group. Direct economic pressure usually means that proficiency in a standard language is a job requirement. For economic survival, language shift is essential. Indirect pressure results from industrialization and rural–urban migration and influences a shift from minority languages to standard languages. Shift arises out of economic need, regardless of speakers' attitudes toward language.

Both the direct and indirect models suggest that the inhabitants of the Kampong are ripe for shift to Bahasa Malaysia. There is increasing economic need; there is increasing awareness of Malay elitism. However, there is little evidence of shift.

That no attempt is now being made to implement the national language plan—that is to teach Bahasa Malaysia in the Kampong—suggests that there may be aims other than those stated. For instance, by not implementing the plan, racial or ethnic divisions are maintained among the working class. The onus for learning falls on non-Malay speakers. They are responsible for failure to learn, and they must endure the consequences of their incompetence and their inability to break the language monopoly. The language campaigns of the 1960s are long gone. There never was one in the Kampong. There are no literacy programs at the village level; there is no pedagogy for these oppressed. There is no dialogue "between those who deny other men the right to speak their word and those whose right to speak has been denied them," nor any understanding that "neither language nor thought can exist without a structure to which they refer" (Freire 1968, p. 76; cf. Schubert, this volume).

Language for Unity and Modernity

There is nothing new about language planning other than its name and the attempt by some practitioners—language planners, architects of twentieth century Towers of Babel—to carve out a niche for it in the taxonomy of disciplines. It is not only the stuff that myth is made of—

> And the whole earth was of one language, and of one speech. . . . "Behold, the people is one, and they have all one language; and this they begin to do: and now nothing will be restrained from them, which they have imagined to do. Go to, let us go down, and there confound their language, that they may not understand one another's speech." (Gen. II: 01–08)

—but a problem that was pondered in ancient China, Greece, and other societies past as it is pondered today in nations both new and old.

There have been countless attempts to create universal languages, to restore primordial linguistic unity to the world. But though all have been in vain, the pursuit remains a tantalizing challenge. On a smaller scale, however, linguistic unity is no longer considered an unattainable goal or a myth immemorial. It is national and regional policy in many parts of the world.

For planners in Malaysia, the product of language planning and engineering will be this single national language without which unity and modernity will be impossible. But between modernizing Malaysia and ancient Babel there are differences, not the least of which is reality and myth. In the Federation of Malaysia, the goals of language planning are several, and assurance that these goals will be attained derives from the planners', not the speakers', ideas about what language can do, what can be done to language, and what can be done in the name of language. Some goals, such as graphization and standardization, are being met. According to Alisjahbana,

> the problem of paramount importance was how to change the more or less pidgin-like lingua franca into a stable, sophisticated, mature and official modern language which could be the vehicle of modern Indonesian and Malaysian thought and culture. (1972, p. 12)

Aside from this linguistic aim, the stated aims of language planning are national unity and modernity.

Unity

Bahasa Malaysia, the national and official language, is vital to national unity, identity, and integration. In the words of former Prime Minister Tengku Abdul Rahman:

> It is only right as a developing nation we should want to have a language of our own. If the national language is not introduced, our country will be devoid of unified character and personality—a nation without a soul and life. (Kee & Hong, 1971, p. 78)

Deputy Prime Minister and former Minister of Education Dr. Mahathir Mohamad believes that if people are educated in one language the result is a united nation in which people do not have unfounded prejudices against one another. This idea seems to be a variation on Fox's theory of lexical penetration from an alien language, whereby the way is paved for wider adoption of the contrasting culture represented by that language. Language provides a "softening up process."

"The primary divisive factor was language. This has always been the factor which placed the major racial components of the Malaysian population into separate compartments" (Omar, 1979, p. 19). Omar explains national language as a "symbol of national identity, just like the national flag and the national anthem, a symbol that called for reverence and devotion to one's country (p. 14). Such sentiments echo Herder, for whom language, mother tongue, was not just part of soul but was soul expressed. It was Herder's view that

> the mother tongue expressed a nationality's soul or spirit, that since it was a collective achievement par excellence, language was also the surest way for individuals to safeguard (or recover) the authenticity they had inherited from their ancestors as well as to hand it on to generations yet unborn. (Cited in Fishman 1972, p. 46)

But where current Malaysian language policy differs from Herder is in the notion that "worldwide diversity in language and in culture was a good and beautiful thing in and of itself, whereas imitation led to corruption and stagnation" (Fishman, 1972,

p. 46). Diversity in language in Malaysia is neither good nor beautiful; it thwarts national integration and development. Fishman (1972) noted that

> only language implied an ideal genotypic unity that could counteract the phenotypic horrors of the day. From the very first a distinction of the langue-parole type permitted Herder and other language nationalists both to have their cake and to eat it too; to champion an ideal norm and to create it at the same time. (p. 46)

In Malaysia, Bahasa Malaysia advocates seem to have taken to heart Herder's judgment that "without its own language, a Volk is an absurdity, a contradiction of terms (Fishman, 1972, pp. 48–49); they seem to interpret *Volk* to mean a Malay-speaking state. Ultimately, "language equals nationality and nationality equals language" (p. 48).

Modernity

Bahasa Malaysia is vital not only to the quest for unity, but to the quest for modernity as well. National language is also official language. An amendment to Article 152 defines *official purpose* as any purpose of the Government, whether Federal or State, and includes any purpose of a public authority. Official language has several functions: language of government, tool of communication, medium of instruction.

Omar (1979, p. 14) explained that

> beyond [national language] was something else, official language, something which sensitivized the human values other than the emotional need for a symbol, and these were the economic and academic values which in the last analysis identified themselves with ethnicism and chauvinism. This was so because the economic or/and academic achievements or the reverse could be clearly identified with specific ethnic groups. It has been the objective of the Malaysian government since Independence to erase this identification of ethnic group with achievement, and one of the ways of attaining this objective was to have the national language play the two functions previously mentioned, that is the functions of official language and medium of instruction.

The language chosen to erase the identification of one ethnic group with economic and/or academic achievement is the language of another ethnic group. Within that other ethnic group, it is the language of one class that makes use of ethnicity to further its own class interests (Lim, 1979).

Planners advocate bureaucratic rationality in the functional organization of linguistic resources in a country (Habermas, 1970). A single national language is a specialized tool pressed into service in the name of national development. The multiplicity of languages is considered irrational and a barrier to progress. Alternatively, language may be considered a resource which can be planned for situations of scarcity and abundance, linguistic haves and have-nots. Industrialization, modernization, and technological progress are the goals. For technical resources alone, a single official language is justified, but, as Marcuse suggests, the concept of technical reason may be ideological.

Language is a convenient tool to be used for the functions of modernization. But it is also a tool that can translate political advantage into economic and class-related advantage. Instrumentalism in language planning leads to the reification of one aspect of language, not necessarily the most important one. The implicit assumption is that a single national and official language enhances progress. The American assimilationist model prevails, not the Swiss language integrity model. When the aim is technological change, rational maximization—new uses for available means—is involved. But the term *rational* is subjective. Malaysian language planners are not finding new uses for the available means of Chinese and Tamil.

In the Third Malaysia Plan, Bahasa Malaysia is one of many factors considered in relation to the economic goals of the nation. For industrialization and socioeconomic development, a common language for literacy, bureaucracy, wider communication, science, and technology is needed. This same language is also the national language. But just as national language alone does not create national unity and identity, bureaucratic, technical language alone does not engender socioeconomic development. It emerges from Gonzalez's (1979) analysis of language and social development in the Pacific area that

> socioeconomic development has low correlation with national language development. One can have countries with high socioeconomic development not having solved the national language problem and one can have developing countries which have solved the national language problem but which have not achieved adequate socioeconomic development. (p. 3)

Language and Political Economy

Vološinov maintained that "language acquires life and historically evolves . . . in concrete verbal communication, and not in the abstract linguistic system of language forms, nor in the individual psyche of speakers" (1973, p. 75). Whiteley (1971) stressed the importance of the informal and ideological aspects of language policy as opposed to the technological aspects by which it is implemented.

If the advocates of unity and modernity by means of Bahasa Malaysia were classified according to the trends of thought which Vološinov identified in the philosophy of language, the national unity and identity contingent would be classified "individualistic subjectivists," while the modernity, efficiency, and development advocates would be classified "abstract objectivists." The former consider "the basis of language to be the individual creative act of speech"; the latter dramatically opposed, consider the basis to be "a linguistic system, a system of the phonetic, grammatical and lexical forms of language" (Vološinov, 1973, pp. 48–52). Of the latter, Vološinov noted that "the divorce of language from its ideological impletion is one of abstract objectivism's most serious errors" (pp. 70–71; cf. Parker, this volume).

Formal linguists and abstract objectivists all tell us that universals in linguistic structure are currently best identified through transformational-generative grammars. For them, language is an abstract, isolated system divorced from the social, cultural, and historical determinants of speech which I consider to be basic components. Lévi-Strauss reminded us that each language retains only certain of the elements at its disposal, "at least some of which remain the same throughout the most varied cultures and are combined into structures which are always diversified" (1963, p. 38).

The domain of language is interindividual territory of individuals organized socially, and the word is the ideological phenomenon *par excellence,* as well as the most sensitive index of social change. For Vološinov (1973, p. 70), "the economic conditions that inaugurate a new element of reality into the social purview . . . are exactly the same conditions that create the forms of ideological communication and semiotic expression." Although the various classes within a community use the same language, different accents intersect in every word. "Language (sign) becomes an arena of the class struggle" (p. 24).

Bahasa Malaysia is advocated for both affective (national identity) and instrumental (modernity) reasons. Conflict arises between the "spheres of symbolic interaction and the sphere of technologically or bureaucratically motivated instrumental communication, the latter increasingly invading the former" (Habermas, 1970). On the one hand, instrumental, goal-oriented, highly formalized interactions are sought in business, the marketplace, and with officialdom. On the other hand, a soul is to be created.

Not only is language reduced to an implement, but implement is then confused with affect. Language planners reduce language to abstract objectivism and confuse abstract objectivism with individualistic subjectivism. Abstract objectivism errs in divorcing language from its ideological impletion, individualistic subjectivism in adopting as basis the individual creative act of speech. "Language, in the process of its practical implementation is inseparable from its ideological or behavioral impletion" (Vološinov, 1973, p. 70). When language planning aims at deliberate language change, it is also aiming at ideological and behavioral change.

Colonialism and Language in Malaya

To a great extent colonial history is the history of all the languages of Malaya, not just of English. Omar classified English as the only colonial language, but all languages were bound up in the system of colonialism. The Malay spoken by sultans, paddy farmers, and fisherman; the Chinese languages spoken by gambier farmers, tin miners, and merchants; the Indian languages spoken by rubber tappers, railway workers, and policemen; and the English spoken by British governors, bureaucrats, and schoolboys—all were colonial languages in the sense of social function during the colonial period. Colonialism—capitalism in its imperial phase—is primarily an economic and political phenomenon. But it is not only economic and political; it is also cultural and linguistic. Indeed, English may be called *the* colonial language because it was the dominating, exclusive language of the class in power (cf. Roberts & Williams, this volume). But Malay, Chinese, and Tamil were also colonial languages, albeit dominated vernacular.

In his excellent analysis of languages and colonialism, Calvet (1974) defined linguistic superstructure not as language (language is not superstructure), but as the social organization of language. In the colonial context of dominating language and dominated languages, language become superstructure. There is a social and geo-graphical organization of multilingualism which has certain statistical and functional characteristics. Calvet recalls Marx and Engels's phrase in the Communist Mani-festo, "the history of all society to date has been the history of class struggle." The history of language as superstructure is a chapter in the history of class struggle. Language is not only a means of communication; it is also a means of oppression. In a colony, only a small percentage of the population speaks the dominant and official language, whereas the majority of the people speaks a dominated language or lan-guages. Only speakers of the dominant language may hold responsible jobs. It is clear that this language serves the interests of a class. Just as language serves colonialism, it also serves neocolonialism.

When Calvet referred to linguistic superstructure it was to that language status which characterizes certain power relationships: bilingualism (or multilingualism) with opposition between dominated and dominating language and the crushing of one or more languages by this exclusive language. If anything is primordial, it is the economic and political base. Calvet noted that linguistic superstructure is founded on the same model as are economic and social organization. Further, the relationship of languages reinforces social relationships. Colonial language and colonial economy are isomorphic. So too are neocolonial language and neocolonial economy (Calvet, 1974, pp. 75–78).

Vološinov's philosophy of language is substantive and relates to Marx, Engels, and Lenin on language, rather than to Stalin. Stalin's is a purely functional view: "Language does not differ from implements of production, from machines, let us say, which are as indifferent to classes as language" (Stalin 1951, p. 4). His notion of linguistic homogeneity is sheer illusion, an illusion that many national language-pol-icy makers might like to perpetuate. "History shows that national languages are not class, but common languages, common to the members of each nation and consti-tuting the single language of that nation (p. 6). Indeed, any language that serves one social group to the detriment of another is doomed to disappear.

Stalin's main concern was to refute the idea of the class character of language which is basic to Lenin, Marx, and Engels. He concluded:

(a) Language as a means of intercourse, always was and remains the single language of a society, common to all its members.
(b) The existence of dialects and jargons does not negate but confirms the exis-tence of a language common to the whole of the given people, of which they are offshoots and to which they are subordinate.
(c) The 'class character' of language formula is erroneous and non-Marxist.
(p. 11).

Stalin's bête noire was Marr (1864–1934), who insisted on language as super-structure, whence the origin of class language. The war of languages is a question of nationalities—autonomy, assimilation, colonialization. Marr echoed Vološinov: lan-guage, like work, is a collective activity and should be studied at the level of produc-tion. The new japhetic theory of language is by definition a theory of ideology. Its origins are the work of Marx, Lenin, and Engels. Marr realized that both practical and theoretical problems abound, "parce que le langage, inpensable sans la pensée qui lui est indissolublement liée, est la superstructure de tous les aspects et de tous les moments de la production et des rapports de production"[1] (Marr, 1979, p. 140). But at the same time, this new language doctrine constitutes "en tant qu'outil marxiste-leniniste, . . . l'outil de lutte du prolétariat dans la terrible lutte de classes que nous vivons, outil irremplacable et peu utilisé sur le front scientifico-cultural"[2] (p. 141).

The process of the production of language has the same origins as does the process of the production of capital. While Lenin stressed the importance of language to modernity, he never lost sight of its thought content ("car le langage n'est pas simplement sonorité, mais pensée"[3]) and the class character of language, which leads to class thinking or ideology:

> Chez les différentes classes sont presentes différentes langues différenciées, et chaque classe possède avec sa propre langue une pensée de classe également différente[4] (Cited in Marr 1979, pp. 113–114).

The following quotation could be attributed to a language planner in Malaysia, but, in fact, it is Lenin in *The Right of Nations to Self-determination:*

> Throughout the world, the period of the victory of capitalism over feudalism has been linked up with national movements. For the complete victory of commodity production, the bourgeoisie must capture the home market and there must be politically united territories whose population speak a single language, with all obstacles to the development of that language and to its consolidation in literature eliminated. Therein is the economic foundation of national movements. Language is the most important means of human intercourse. Unity and unimpeded development of language are the most important conditions for genuinely free and extensive commerce on a scale commensurate with modern capitalism, for a free and broad grouping of the population in all its various classes, and, lastly, for the establishment of a close connection between the market and each and every proprietor, big or little, and between seller and buyer. (1977, p. 8)

Stalin claimed that Lenin understood national language as a necessity. He did—a necessity for modern capitalism.

In *The German Ideology* (1845–1846/1972), Marx and Engels described language as a social product which arises from the necessity of intercourse with others. For them, and later for Lenin, the need for speech arises in collective and productive enterprises.

A national language is shaped by history: language contact with other nations and between dialects within the nation. Marx stressed the class character of language exemplified by "bourgeois language." It is this language, a product of the bourgeoi-

---

[1] " . . . because language, unthinkable without thought, which is indissolubly linked to it, is the superstructure of all the aspects and all the moments of production and the relations of production."

[2] " . . . a Marxist-Leninist tool, . . . the proletariat's tool of struggle in the terrible class struggle in which we are living, an irreplaceable tool little used on the scientifico-cultural front."

[3] "language [speech] is not just sonority, but thought."

[4] "In different classes there are different, distinct tongues, and each class possesses with its own tongue class thought which is also different."

sie, which becomes national language as a result of economic and political concentration. Engels illustrated class language in *The Condition of the Working Class in England* (1971):

> The English working class has gradually become a race wholly apart from the English bourgeoisie.... the workers speak other dialects, have other thoughts and ideals, other customs and moral principles, a different religion and other politics than those of the bourgeoisie. (p. 71)

This is a class, not an ethnic group.

Marx, Engels, Vološinov, and Lenin demonstrated the class character of language. Given their concept of language, the class character of ideology is implicit in the class character of language.

In Malaysia today, I contend, Bahasa Malaysia meets some of the needs suggested by Lenin—but not entirely. The dilemma occurs, however, at the level of the working class, which remains divided by ethnicity (race). Such divisions prevent class formation, which could well be more disruptive than ethnic tensions. Despite claims to the contrary, Bahasa Malaysia is not accessible to all. There is no literacy campaign for the working class similar to campaigns in China or Guinea-Bissau.

It appears that the target population is the civil servant, the teacher—the middle class. The main vehicle for spreading the national language is the school. Education has become as much a political as an academic issue. The process of planned language change is managed by the elite.

> Like language status planning (which deliberately effects social changes in a country) language corpus planning (which causes changes of language codes) is elite-conditioned. In the former type of planning it is the politicians and those in power who allocate the various statuses and uses of the languages of a country, while in the latter it is the linguists and those involved with the use and dissemination of language materials. (Omar, 1979, p. 79)

Bahasa Malaysia creates social stratification by its elitist nature but neither education nor language alone can unite or divide a nation.

We can ask ourselves two questions: (1) who accepts and disseminates these doctrines? and (2) what are the stated aims as opposed to the unstated ones? A third question is; what suggests that the stated aims may not be the real aims? Chomsky's answer to the first question is the modern, technocratic, scientific intelligentsia whose social role has been manipulation and social control. It is this modern intelligentsia in capitalist societies that has access to prestige and power by serving the state. It serves formation of a middle class. The structure of Malaysian society remains much the same as it did prior to independence; the cast has changed. The neocolonial elite, both Malay and foreign, still speaks English, but Bahasa Malaysia, relegated to vernacular status in colonial times, has become the national and official language and is making inroads (cf. Illich, this volume). Chinese and Indian languages remain vernaculars, while English is an important second language for science and technology. There may be unity for the bourgeoisie, but the working class remains divided and ruled. Lim (1979) concluded that

> it is too simplistic to view the divide and rule policy of the colonial state as one which seeks actively to pit one ethnic community against the other.... How-

ever, the precondition for the operation of capital is stability and order, not unrest. Thus, what is required is not actual conflict between different ethnic groups but their inability to unite along class lines. Such a policy requires compartmentalization and separation rather than interaction. (p. 10)

Linguistic isolation of working-class speech communities is useful in implementing such a policy.

Planned Language in the Kampong

People who lived in the Kampong did so because of poverty; with no money, they had no other place to go. The Kampong was described as poor but peaceful, a place where you could build your own home. Some said that because they had so many children, they could not afford to live elsewhere. At each new year, people forecast more hardship, more difficulties than in the preceding year. At weddings and funerals, gods' birthday parties and celebrations, the entire community participated. Although village organization was informal, people identified the same leaders.

> The village folks and common labourers are in general able to converse in Malaysian. Their deficiency with the Malaysian language was their inability to read and write it; but with a majority of these people reading or writing any language at all was lacking. The implementation of the language policy had bestowed upon them two blessings simultaneously: one is a knowledge of polished Malaysian, and the other literacy. (Omar, 1979, p. 39)

In the Kampong (population 945), 929 considered languages other than Malay their mother tongue. Many people were monolingual in a language other than Malay: a full 40%, in fact. For every illiterate male, there were two illiterate females.

Despite the fact that many people said they wanted to learn Bahasa Malaysia, they also said they did not know how to go about it. They thought they could not learn or that even if they did learn, it would never be good enough. The nearest Bahasa Malaysia classes were held at night in a school in town where Mandarin and English classes were also held. People who had never been to school or had not been there in years found it a daunting prospect to register or enroll. They also found it expensive and inconvenient.

No one had studied Bahasa Malaysia in adult education classes, and no one had attended a National Unity class, despite the assertion that

> adult education became a very important programme of the Alliance government in the 1950's and 1960's with the two-pronged goal mentioned above. Later on, in 1970, when illiteracy had been wiped off, the teaching of the language to people who still required it was conducted under the auspices of the Office of National Unity. These language classes were known as National Unity Classes. People registering for such classes were those already literate but whose language proficiency had not reached the level required to enable them to participate in communication other than the one conducted at the market places. (Omar, 1979, p. 39)

Given a chance to learn a new language, the majority (60%) replied that they could never learn a language because they never had, were too old, or too busy. The ages of those who said they were too old ranged from 18 to "90 and over." Even if they had had the ability to learn, which they knew they didn't, where would they ever find the time? Either they had to work hard or look hard for work. Half had no formal education: 20% had 1 to 3 years; 19%, 4 to 6 years; 9%, 7 to 9 years, and 3%, 10 or more years. It is of such people that Tunku Abdul Rahman remarked that those who wanted to make the country their home should "make the grade." They had to learn Malay. If they were serious about it, they could learn it within three months.

When women left the Kampong, they usually went to the market nearby. Many preferred not to go out at all and waited for hawkers and vendors to appear. A trip to town was an event, not a routine trip. Bus fare was also an issue, especially for unemployed men. One man who lost his job as a waiter did attend night classes, despite the fact that his friends jeered at him. After two night classes, sitting cramped at a desk designed for an 8-year-old, he dropped out. The only other people to attend night classes were female factory workers. They studied with little success, since they often missed classes when working the night shift. They studied in hopes of getting a better job one day. One young woman, an aspiring teacher, was trying to improve her Malay, but she despaired of ever learning, since no matter how much she studied her books, she never had a chance to speak. Though the advantages of learning Bahasa Malaysia were understood in the Kampong, she was the only adult whose efforts to learn were made in vain.

Ten years, say Bahasa Malaysia language planners, was a sufficiently long period for the people to prepare themselves for fluency in the national language. They argue that "fresh foreigners" take less time than that to learn and to become fluent in the language. No consideration is given to the fact that these "fresh foreigners" may be university lecturers rather than fresh fruit hawkers. They also argue that the acquisition of Malay should not have posed a difficulty since two important factors for language learning were already present at the time of establishing the language as national and then as official language. These factors were (1) the existence of a supporting speech community and (2) the already existing role of the language as medium of intergroup communication. Neither of these two important factors existed in the Kampong—or, more accurately, there was indeed a supporting speech community, but of non-Malay speakers.

A waiter at a large resort hotel no longer sets out before dawn to go to work on his motor scooter. He lost his motor scooter registration and driving license when he failed to renew it at City Hall. Although proficient in English and his mother tongue, he could no longer understand forms that were in Malay. By the time he had found someone to help him fill out the forms, the deadline had passed. He was afraid to go to the Bureau of Vehicle Registration, since he might have to admit to neither reading nor writing Malay. Without a license, he continued driving his unregistered scooter to work. This practice lasted until he was stopped for a routine check, which put an end to his predawn transport. Shortly thereafter, he lost his job when he was late for work. Now he spends his days in the Kampong helping to repair and build houses or doing some desultory fishing. His earnings as a waiter had supported a family of five.

An 18-year-old woman works shifts in one of the multinational electronics firms at the Bayan Lepas Free Trade Zone. During her 8- or 16-hour shifts, she peers through a microscope, assembling minute parts with the aid of tweezers held in her white-gloved hands. She has been doing that for a year, ever since she failed the teacher-training college entrance exam due to insufficient knowledge of Bahasa Malaysia. Several of her friends are at the factory for the same reason.

A middle-aged man had one of the most coveted jobs of all, that of driving instructor. It was one of the most prestigious and best-paid jobs held by a Kampong dweller. Although he had never taught a single Malay student driver, his company enacted a policy requiring all instructors to learn the national language. He found it impossible to learn and was sacked.

Such examples abound. A salesman no longer travels to Thailand; he had been unable to meet the language requirements for citizenship. A hawker no longer peddles her steamed chick-pea and peanut cart to town every day; she failed to fill in registration forms.

During my fieldwork, economic activity and household income declined in the Kampong, while unemployment and self-help and religious activity increased. Although many factors contributed to these trends, for the purposes of this chapter, I focus on inability to speak the official language and relate it to decline in economic activity. The Kampong became more isolated, more closed. This development coincided with a breakdown of traditional channels of communication and a loss of employment. Most people were either wage earners or own account (self-employed) workers. The main occupations of the self-employed or own-account workers were: trishaw peddling; boat repairs; hawking satay, fruit, fish, vegetables, and cooked food; and fishing for oysters, cockles, and prawns. Wage earners were divided into two main categories: service and industry. Most female factory workers were employed by the multinational electronics firms, and the remainder of the wage earners worked in fish, rubber, tin, oil, textile, and steel-processing plants. Service employees worked as amahs, cooks, caterers, waiters, doormen, hospital attendants, and so on. The man considered to be the best-educated person in the Kampong, who spoke Malay most fluently, was a school caretaker. More men claimed either laborer or odd job occupations. "I am jobless" and "No choice" were common phrases for men; rather than declare themselves unemployed many preferred to say "laborer," "odd jobs," or "fisherman."

In the Kampong, inability to speak Bahasa Malaysia had a definite impact on people's lives. Language planning has had and continues to have economic repercussions. There are changes due to planned language change, but not necessarily in the avowed directions of unity and modernization. For the Kampong, a single language for national solidarity and development has resulted in isolation and greater marginality. A few examples of Kampong dwellers with insufficient or no competence in Malay illustrate this claim.

A hawker's license here, a motor-scooter license there; factory worker instead of teacher or secretary; laborer or unemployed instead of waiter: each case represents a personal drama, the plight of a family. When considered together, they reflect the declining economy of a community of 1,000 people. Although other factors were at play, Kampong residents did recognize the inability to speak and write Malay as a serious handicap.

Malay-speaking Kampong residents also lost jobs, but not at the same rate. Their experience and attitudes differed from those of nonspeakers. Language competence had not been sufficient reason for retaining a job, and they attributed unemployment to other factors.

If language is considered inherently social and not an abstract, objectified process, then planned language change cannot be separated from social change. The issue is not simply what kind of *language* is being planned but what kind of *society*. To restructure society, Bahasa Malaysia was implemented in order to promote national integration and unity, development and modernization. But for some, inadequate implementation has restricted not only language choice but also social and economic choice. Communication has become more difficult or impossible for them. In such cases, rather than wider communication, unity, and integration, the result is isolation and division; rather than modernization and development, marginality and decline.

References

Alisjahbana, S. T. *The modernization of languages in Asia*. Kuala Lumpur: Malaysian Society of Asian Studies, 1972.

Calvet, L. J. *Linguistique et colonialisme*. Paris: Payot, 1974.

Engels, F. *The condition of the working class in England*. Oxford: Blackwell, 1971.

Fishman, J. A. *Language and nationalism*. Rowley, Mass.: Newbury House, 1972.

Freire, P. *Pedagogy of the oppressed*. New York: Seabury Press, 1968.

Gonzalez, A. *Language and social development in the Pacific area*. Khabarovsk, USSR: XIVth Pacific Congress, 1979.

Habermas, J. *Towards a rational society*. Boston: Beacon Press, 1970.

Kee, F. H., & Hong, E. T. *Education in Malaysia*. Singapore: Heineman Educational Books (Asia), 1971.

Lenin, V. I. *The right of nations to self-determination*. Moscow: Foreign Languages Publishing House, 1977.

Lévi-Strauss, C. *Structural anthropology*. New York: Basic Books, 1963.

Lim, M. H. *Ethnic and class relations in Malaysia*. Stockholm: JCA Tenth Anniversary Conference, 1979.

Marr, N. I. Le langage et la modernité. In F. Gadet, J. M. Gayman, Y. Mignot & E. Roudinesco *Les maîtres de la langue*. Paris: Librairie François Maspero, 1979.

Marx, K. & Engels, F. *The German ideology*. New York: International Publishers, 1972. (Originally published, 1845–1846.)

Omar, A. H. *Language planning for unity and efficiency*. Kuala Lumpur: Penerbit Universiti Malaya, 1979.

Stalin, J. *Marxism and linguistics*. New York: International Publishers, 1951.

Vološinov, V. N. *Marxism and the philosophy of language*. New York: Seminar Press, 1973.

Whiteley, W. H. Some factors influencing language policies in Eastern Africa. In J. Rubin & B. Jernudd, *Can language be planned?* Honolulu: University Press of Hawaii, 1971.

30

Cultural Reproduction in the Bilingual Classroom

Vandra Lea Masemann

Introduction

Research on bilingual education in the United States in the last decade has been more profuse in terms of publications, whether books, reports, dissertations, or journal articles, than in any other country, except perhaps, in relation to population, Canada. The vast bulk of the material has consisted of attempts to evaluate programs or to assess children's linguistic and academic competence and even psychological well-being (Dissertation Abstracts International, 1978, 1979, 1980). The underlying research models are derived from educational psychology or linguistics, with an ethnographic component where necessary. When anthropological insights have been used, they have generally been in the subfield of "ethnography of communicative competence" (Bauman & Sherzer, 1974). However, comparatively little research has been published using a theoretical perspective that does not fit in with prevailing evaluation models.[1] Indeed, in the climate of the 1970s, there was a particularly urgent need for the development of such models, in order for programs to be legitimated publicly and to be funded and expanded (Rosario & Love, 1979).

This chapter is based on a theoretical perspective which does not address the same kinds of concerns as do those evaluation models, although it was originally a study to explore interdisciplinary models for evaluation of the bilingual classroom (using methods from anthropology and educational psychology). In this analysis however, the bilingual classroom will be examined from a more critical approach, in terms of the prevailing cultural messages that are transmitted in the classroom through language, through the material culture of the classroom, and through classroom organization itself. The hypothesis to be examined is that the culture of the

---

[1]A noteworthy exception is Yu (1981).

Vandra Lea Masemann ● Inter Cultural Associates, Toronto, Ontario M4C 4V9, Canada.

dominant group is still purveyed in the bilingual (and monolingual) classroom in spite of explicit attempts by the program administrators and teachers to organize a pluralistic approach.

First, the study as it was conducted and its main findings will be described in brief. Then a theoretical formulation deriving from Bourdieu and Passeron's (1977) "theory of symbolic violence" will be presented. The ethnographic data on classroom language use, material culture, and the organization of teaching will then be examined with reference to such a formulation.

The Study: Some Theoretical Considerations

The study was undertaken with the purpose of exploring methodologies for the evaluation of bilingual education in the classroom setting. The substantive problem that this study addressed was bilingual education for Spanish-speaking (Mexican, Puerto Rican, and Cuban) children in three Milwaukee inner-city schools at the point when they were making the transition from reading in their first language (English or Spanish) to reading in both languages (second or third grade). Spanish speaking children in a fourth school in a monolingual program were also included as a comparison group.

The methodological problem that was originally the central concern of the study was the attempt to explore the relative contributions of methodologies derived from anthropology and from educational psychology in the study of a common substantive concern, specifically by the use of participant observation, classroom ethnography, and testing of reading. It was considered that a combination of the two methodologies could elucidate a complex situation more fully than either could alone and that an interdisciplinary approach to the evaluation of bilingual education could give a more satisfactory account of the linguistic, cognitive, and sociocultural processes operating in the bilingual classroom than could one methodology alone (cf. Okun, Fisk, & Brandt, this volume). Ethnographic observations were made over a period of one semester in the fall of 1976, and testing and interviews were carried out at the end of this period.

Earlier analyses of the results of the study have been reported by Masemann (1978) and Cooley (1979). However, both of these analyses rest on a functionalist theoretical perspective and discuss primarily linguistic or educational issues. The major ethnographic finding of the study was that the teacher's use of time and space in the classroom had a significant impact on the linguistic climate and the opportunities for language use in English or Spanish. In brief, the bilingual teacher who used designated times of day and places in the classroom for specific language use was far more successful in approaching the program ideal of a 50–50 ratio of Spanish use to English use. On the other hand, the teachers who were more informal and who used concurrent translation and techniques of individualized instruction were more likely to find English predominating as the spontaneous language of use among their students, except for the Spanish monolingual children. These findings resemble those of Legarreta (1977) in a study of five bilingual kindergartens in California, in which concurrent translation was associated with ever-increasing use of English by teachers and students. In the Legarreta study this occurred even in classrooms containing 65% native Spanish-speaking children (p. 11), whereas the proportion was generally lower in the Milwaukee study (27%, 54%, and 71% Spanish-surnamed students in the schools with a bilingual program, and 22% in the monolingual school).

An interesting phenomenon, which is alluded to in Legarreta's study, is that

> in the short span of about nine weeks of formal schooling, children who speak only Spanish in their homes, neighbourhoods and churches, are apparently already reflecting the vastly different language input in the schools by bilingual teachers/aides. . . . Despite a sincere and conscious commitment to bilingual teaching by the teachers/aides, they seem overwhelmed by the pull of the dominant language and the dominant culture, with the result that English again becomes the dominant language. (1977, pp. 14–15)

This "pull" was also noted by the observers in the Milwaukee classrooms and is the focus of this paper (see also Bain, 1981).

Two concepts that could help to illuminate this pull toward English are those of *cultural reproduction* and *hegemony*. One can postulate that the culture of the dominant society is being reproduced in the bilingual classroom through the very forms which are meant to be bilingual, such as bilingual instructional materials or the Pledge of Allegiance repeated in English and Spanish. Particularly if instructional materials are individualized, their being bilingual becomes an extension of the "illusion of choice" that a student can exercise in individualized instruction (Smollett, 1974).

To return to the original concept, however, *cultural reproduction* is a term used by Bourdieu and Passeron (1977) in their analysis of the distribution of cultural— that is, symbolic—capital (as distinct from material wealth) among the various classes (or in this case ethnic groups) in a society (cf. de Terra, this volume). They assert that all pedagogic actions (education)

> because they correspond to the material and symbolic interests of groups or classes differently situated within the power relations . . . always tend to reproduce the structure of the distribution of cultural capital among these groups or classes, thereby contributing to the reproduction of the social structure. (p. 11)

Moreover, they refer directly to bilingualism as a case in point:

> The problems posed by situations of early bilingualism or biculturalism give only a faint idea of the contradictions faced by a pedagogic action claiming to take as its practical didactic principle the theoretical arbitrariness of linguistic or cultural codes. (p. 12)

Thus, they see a linguistic code as the embodiment of the cultural capital of the group that possesses it; therefore, whereas linguistic relativism and equality are imaginable in the mind of a linguist, the speaker of a language exemplifies the power relations of that language with reference to other languages. This point is often totally neglected in studies of classroom bilingualism.

Bourdieu and Passeron also state that "all pedagogic action is, objectively, symbolic violence in that it is the imposition of a cultural arbitrary [i.e., language] by an arbitrary power" (p. 5), but that it is not seen as arbitrary, since it is carried out by an authority which is seen as legitimate. Thus, in turn, the "cultural arbitrary" itself is seen as legitimate culture (p. 22). Bourdieu and Passeron see all school culture as "necessarily standardized and ritualized, i.e., 'routinized' by and for the routine of the work of schooling" (p. 59).

Their "theory of symbolic violence" is similar to Antonio Gramsci's writings on cultural hegemony, and the function of schooling and all civil institutions of society in establishing and maintaining the cultural domination of groups in power (Apple, 1979; Gramsci, 1971). Gramsci saw hegemony as established through all cultural forms in civil life, as well as through overt forms of political, military, or economic domination. Moreover, he saw the possibility of developing a "counter-hegemony" as remote except in some concerted struggle by those who have been educated in a unitary school system that teaches the subordinate groups the dominant cultural forms well enough for them to counter the claims to hegemony of groups in power in an overt fashion. This analysis is slightly more optimistic than that of Bourdieu and Passeron, who see the imposition of the cultural arbitrary (i.e., hegemony) as producing "misrecognition of the objective truth of cultural arbitrariness" (1977, p. 22). Moreover, the more successful the dominant culture is in imposing itself on members of dominated groups the more "it tends at the same time to impose on them, by inculcation or exclusion, recognition of the illegitimacy of their own cultural arbitrary" (1977, p. 41). The comparison of Bourdieu and Passeron's theory of symbolic violence and Gramsci's concept of cultural hegemony, therefore, exposes the essential contradiction in the goals for bilingual education in any country, particularly the United States, whose cultural arbitrary spreads far beyond its borders in terms of the symbols of popular culture, the symbols of economic prosperity, and the use of English as a world language. It is possible, therefore, to see bilingual education as an attempt to offer both hegemonic (Anglo) and counterhegemonic (Hispanic) views of the world in the classroom, either by concurrent translation or by the use of alternating languages in specific time periods. The two views can thus to some extent be kept separate, their contradictions can be overlooked, or the dominant view can simply prevail. Alternatively, bilingual education can be thought of as the much more difficult task of teaching two cultural arbitraries of equal value at once in the same classroom. The basic contradiction in such a task is not acknowledged, and, if Bourdieu and Passeron are correct, it will remain covert (cf. Roberts & Williams, this volume). Analysis of observations in the four classrooms in this study will reveal that this contradiction can, in fact, be detected, but that it does, indeed, remain covert.

The Ethnicity of the Students

The students in the study were of predominantly Mexican and Puerto Rican background. The four schools observed were on the north and south sides of the industrial heart of Milwaukee. On the south side reside the descendants of Mexican factory laborers recruited after World War I, while on the north side live Puerto Rican immigrants who migrated in the 1950s to work in factories and foundries. In addition, there has been a continual migration and "settling out" of migrant Mexican farm workers, and migration from Mexico, Puerto Rico, and Cuba has continued

Table I. Milwaukee Public-School Enrollment by Ethnic Category (September 1976)

	American Indian		Black		Asian		Hispanic[a]		White/other		Total enrollment
	n	%	n	%	n	%	n	%	n	%	n
School 1	13	1.88	1	.14	7	1.01	494	71.49	176	25.47	691
School 2	41	8.07	0	0	1	.2	276	54.33	190	37.40	508
School 3	5	.88	232	41.20	0	0	155	27.53	171	30.37	563
School 4	15	3.17	136	28.75	12	2.53	104	21.98	206	43.55	473
Milwaukee elementary schools	760	1.30	23,633	40.44	333	.56	3,147	5.38	30,564	52.30	58,437
All Milwaukee schools	1,217	1.11	40,138	36.77	520	.47	4,937	4.52	62,334	56.71	109,146

[a]Spanish surname only.

until the present (Richards, 1976, p. 8). The ethnicity of students in the schools observed is compared with the general representation in Milwaukee public schools in Table I. The four classrooms were in schools that ranked among the highest six in the city in terms of Spanish-speaking population.

The students in these classrooms were, then, of predominantly working-class background, Spanish-speaking, and ranged from long-time American residents of Mexican or Puerto Rican background to completely new immigrants or cyclical migrants. The bilingual education provisions were similar for all Spanish-speaking students within their regular classrooms, although withdrawal instruction in English as a second language (ESL) was given to those who spoke little or no English.

With reference to language use in various domains, interviews were conducted with children in the four classrooms, asking them what language they used in various situations. These results can probably be generalized to students in all bilingual classes in these schools. Students claimed to speak predominantly Spanish with parents and grandparents and at church, but English more than Spanish with teachers, with classmates, with friends at recess, with children in other classes at the school, in the neighborhood, and when going to the store. Their preferences for language when talking to siblings occupied an intermediate position, in that nearly half (45%) claimed to speak only Spanish or more Spanish than English to siblings, a small minority (10%) spoke equally in both languages, and the other half (45%) claimed to speak more English than Spanish or English only to siblings. Yet these children were all in the bilingual program (except for four students in the monolingual classroom who were Spanish-speaking). When their exposure to the mass media was examined, it was evident that they were exposed to English for a large proportion of their day. Two-thirds of them watched television programs every day, primarily in English, and one-half listened to the radio every day, although there was a greater tendency to listen to Spanish programs on radio than on television. Half of them read comics, primarily in English, and most of them used the library, choosing predominantly English books.[2]

[2]Statistical analysis of all testing and quantitative data from the study are found in Cooley (1979).

It would indeed be impossible to discern what pressures caused these children to prefer speaking English to speaking Spanish. It is clear that in their time away from school they were exposed to the English media, and that it was primarily within the close family circle that they chose to speak Spanish. It is evident from the interviews that the bilingual program did not provide a language climate in which they chose to speak Spanish spontaneously, unless they were Spanish monolingual (cf. Appel, this volume).

The Bilingual Classroom

It should be emphasized at this point that the bilingual program in Milwaukee is considered "developmental" rather than transitional (Milwaukee Bilingual Education Project, 1977). It aims at increasing the level of Spanish proficiency in each grade, even through the high-school level. This goal is in marked contrast to transitional programs, which aim at an eventual switch to English by the end of three or four years. However, the legislation and regulations for bilingual education in the United States are aimed not so much at linguistic enrichment as at protection for individual civil rights as guaranteed by the American Constitution and the Civil Rights Act of 1964. The legislation enacted at the state level and carried out at the local level is worded in terms of a *needs model,* in which children's deficiencies (such as lack of English-speaking ability) are diagnosed, assessed, and remedied. Such needs are assessed on an individual level, as is response to a program of treatment. Thus, questions of ethnic loyalty and group membership are completely sidestepped in favor of equality of educational opportunity for each individual in the society (Masemann, 1979). The preservation of ethnic culture as a group phenomenon is thus not a goal of such programs.

An analysis of the organization and activities of a bilingual classroom can reveal still more of the pressures to speak English to which children are subject, pressures which teachers feel and try to resist. Two of the three bilingual classroom teachers mentioned spontaneously to the observer that they tried to speak Spanish as much as possible "so that the children won't forget it." In all three classrooms the teachers made conscious and consistent efforts to realize the 50–50 ratio of English use to Spanish use. In comparison with the monolingual classroom, their efforts were clearly successful. The Spanish-speaking children felt that they had a right to speak Spanish in a bilingual classroom and to learn to read and write in Spanish. In the monolingual classroom, they neither spoke, read, nor wrote Spanish. However, the pressures toward English still existed in the bilingual classroom, and the purpose of this chapter is to examine in some detail how these pressures were exemplified.

Important aspects to examine are the organization and material culture of the classroom. A close examination of the material culture in all of the four classrooms bore out Cohen's (1971) argument that the classroom material culture symbolically represents national, rather than local, sociocultural orientations and traditions. As in the classrooms analyzed by Johnson (1980), there were clocks, calendars, and an American flag in each room, but the ephemera varied from room to room. Each classroom had a relatively open plan, with tables in the center and learning areas around the periphery, for reading groups, a library area, or mathematics and science equipment. The only exception was the monolingual classroom, which had a similar floor plan, but in which students sat only on one side of the tables, since they all faced in one direction for the predominantly teacher-directed instruction. The displays on the walls emphasized over time the holidays of Halloween, Thanksgiving, and Christmas in all four classrooms, although there was some slight reference to Puerto Rican days of celebration in two of the bilingual classrooms.

The walls of the classrooms reflected each teacher's individual style, and it was there that symbols of bilingualism were more evident. In the classroom in the school with the largest Hispanic population, but with a bilingual Anglo teacher, there were the usual alphabet and number strips, as well as a clock with movable hands and a globe. Equally prominent signs on two bulletin boards said "He who speaks shall find" and "Quien busca, halla." Notices on the blackboard and bulletin boards were written in both languages. More of the printed matter, curriculum kits, teacher guides, mathematics texts, and readers were in English than Spanish, although the children had suitable basal readers and library books in Spanish. (The latter was by far the most evident point of contrast with the monolingual classroom.) In this bilingual classroom, the teacher made strenuous attempts to adhere to the 50–50 language ratio, and his attempt was reflected in the somewhat structured nature of the material culture of the classroom. It was also reflected in his organization of classroom time into Spanish-speaking time and English-speaking time and of classroom space into places where only one language or the other was used. However, the dominant cultural symbols and values (such as the flag), the emphasis on efficient and productive use of time, the emphasis on individual responsibility for learning, and the flexible use of space remained rooted in a progressive Anglo cultural matrix.

In the second classroom, in the school with the second largest Hispanic population (54%), there were very lavish bulletin board displays with theme titles prominent in both languages. The months, days, and numbers were also listed bilingually. Learning areas had labels pasted on them in both languages. The teacher's desk had on it small American and Mexican flags. In contrast to the first classroom, this one had a *concurrent translation* model in regard to decoration, in which a display in one language was duplicated in the other. The first classroom had what could be called an *alternate space* model. There were also some whimsical touches in the second classroom, such as a display of owls labeled "Wooo finishes work on time" and, on the door of the classroom, a series of masks surrounding a masked Charlie Brown saying "A Haunting We Will Go."

This classroom's arrangement of material culture was also a good reflection of the teaching method used, which strongly emphasized individualized instruction, concurrent translation, and the worth of the work and feelings of each child. There was ample evidence of the value placed on each child's work in the plethora of displays in the room.

In the third bilingual classroom, in the school with 27% Hispanic population, the classroom was also arrayed with bilingual notices on all the bulletin boards and furniture. However, perhaps as a matter of the teacher's individual style, there was much less material posted on any of the walls. This was the only classroom, however, to have a display of posters specifically showing Hispanic children engaged in various activities. In this classroom also a concurrent translation model was used, but there was much more evident division of labor by language between the teacher and the aide than in the other classrooms. However, again the bilingual motif was evident in the material culture of this classroom.

The monolingual classroom contrasted sharply with these three bilingual classrooms. The environment was in every way Anglo, although there was a multicultural, multiracial component to some of the illustrations in posters. There were the usual alphabet, season, month, and number lists, and there were also elaborate displays of the children's work hung in neat rows. There was a poster entitled "Our Civil Rights," which outlined the rights of a child in the classroom in terms of human relations. There was also a row of paper pockets underneath the blackboard holding a comb for each child. A very artistic arrangement of pumpkins and corn formed the theme display for October. There were signs under the windows of various polite forms of address, such as "Good morning" or "I'm sorry." Displays of the children's drawings of their family and their houses were arranged on the walls. Near the flag were hung lists of the reading groups by their level. All of the displays of library books and readers were entirely in English.

The material culture of this classroom also reflected accurately the teaching style of the teacher. She was very concerned with fostering language and mathematics achievement in the children; hence many of the displays concerned vowel and consonant sounds. She was also very interested in imparting habits of politeness, good citizenship, and self-respect in her students and used many opportunities to have students practice politeness and graciousness. She considered English proficiency and good citizenship to be the cardinal attainments in a pluralist democratic society and thus felt that emphasis on national symbols of patriotism was very important. As in Johnson's (1980) analysis of classroom material culture, her emphasis was decidedly national. When she discussed local issues, they were more likely to refer to Milwaukee as a city than to the Hispanic or Puerto Rican community. The most notable aspect of Hispanic culture produced during the semester-long observation period was a piñata which the children broke for Halloween.

In summary, the material culture and organization of all four of these classrooms exhibited the fundamental hegemonic pressures of the interests of the nation-state. The flag, clock, and calendar were standard components, as were lists of alphabets, numbers, months, days, and seasons. The teachers' record books, school supplies, curriculum kits, reference books, and instructional materials were all standardized and purchased in accordance with local school board and state policy. Even in the bilingual classrooms, such materials were predominantly in English, although the children had access to ample supplies of Spanish material. Each school was basically administered in English, and the emergency signals notice in each classroom was printed only in English.

Opportunities for self-expression of students and teachers occurred primarily on the bulletin boards, which were, in a sense, framed by all the standardized material around them. Johnson noted that the profusion of artwork occurs primarily in the lower grades, as noted here, while in the upper grades "informal contextual learning is over-shadowed by a formal text and subject-oriented standardized curriculum established by federal and state agencies" (1980, p. 183). Thus, since bilingual classrooms in a transitional kindergarten–third-grade program are the norm in America (Masemann, 1979), the emphasis on child-centered contextual learning can be allowed freer rein than if bilingual classrooms were concentrated in the higher grades.

The second framework, other than material, in which these classrooms exist is an organizational one. The standard forms of modern educational practice are evident in these bilingual classrooms with reference to organization of both time and space. Aspects of an "invisible pedagogy" (Bernstein 1977; cf. Kvale, this volume) are evident in the flexible arrangement of tables and learning areas or activity centers. Children are given certain key instructions and are then deployed to various tasks for which they accept some degree of responsibility. Because the bilingual classrooms contain both a teacher and an aide, more opportunity is available for individualizing instruction. There is a strong emphasis on the wise and productive use of time; this concern may increase in the bilingual classroom if teachers feel they have twice as much language teaching to perform.

In all the classrooms there was an acknowledgement of the child as an individual with feelings, wants, and needs. Of course, one of the main rationales for a bilingual program is that Hispanic children have different needs (Milwaukee Bilingual Education Project, 1977). The individual characteristics of each child are seen in the assessment of their language dominance, their test scores in language and mathematics, and their reading levels. The provision of a bilingual program is thus a way of responding to these needs and guaranteeing students equality of educational opportunity (Masemann, 1979). The strong emphasis on the individual rights of the child is a specifically American emphasis which overrides group definitions of participation in a particular cultural subgroup. A somewhat analogous situation is that of the Amish, whose individual rights as American citizens to education in state schools which are separate from religious influence conflict with their own wishes as a group to have their children raised in a religious atmosphere (Keim, 1975). In the case of Hispanic children in Milwaukee, their rights to a bilingual education do not include rights to practice their culture in the schools, as for instance in religious observances or in somewhat less aggressively competitive classroom demeanor (cf. Smith, 1979).

The emphasis on individualism is also expressed in the human-relations emphasis in some classrooms, with the interest in having children express their feelings, develop a stronger self-concept, or take pleasure in dramatic projections of their personality. In all of these activities, it is not an expression of Mexican or Puerto Rican culture that is expected, but indication of a greater ability to deal with individuals in a specifically American setting (cf. Ruskin & Varenne, this volume).

Language Use: Conclusions

This discussion concludes on the question of language use. In the context of an English-framed and American-organized classroom, it is evident that the pressures toward increased English usage and cultural assimilation are strong. The teachers who aim most consistently for a 50–50 language ratio may be those who achieve bilingualism (spoken, written, and read) in their students (cf. Legarreta, 1979). However, it appears that the framework of dominant cultural forms is still basically unquestioned in the bilingual classroom, although the interstices contain two languages. A review of any recent publisher's catalogue of Spanish instructional materials will show them to be solidly in the mainstream of evolving educational packaging. The fragmentation of curricular knowledge and its rearrangement into "information management systems" are as prevalent in bilingual education as in monolingual programs. There is little inculcation of cultural forms that could undermine the routine practices of a classroom teacher or the stratagems of a curriculum developer. This discussion of four classrooms has demonstrated that the dominant language prevails in nearly every aspect of classroom life.

Acknowledgments

Support for this study was given by the Spencer Foundation and the School of Education, the University of Wisconsin—Madison, for which I thank them. I also acknowledge with thanks the work of the two research assistants on the project, Julia Becker Richards and H. William Cooley. In addition my thanks to all the school personnel and children who assisted in the study. All errors are the responsibility of the author.

References

Apple, M. W. *Ideology and curriculum*. London: Routledge and Kegan Paul, 1979.
Bain, B. C. *Edmonton Public Schools: English as a second language needs assessment*. Edmonton: EPS, 1981.
Bauman, R, & Sherzer, J. *Explorations in the ethnography of speaking*. London: Cambridge University Press, 1974.
Bernstein, B. *Class, codes, and control* (Vol. 3). London and Boston: Routledge and Kegan Paul, 1977.
Bourdieu, P., & Passeron J. C. *Reproduction in education, society and culture*. London: Sage, 1977.
Cohen, Y. The shaping of men's minds: Adaptations to imperatives of culture. In M. L. Wax, S. Diamond, & F. O. Gearing (Eds.), *Anthropological perspectives on education*. New York: Basic Books, 1971.
Cooley, H. W. *Multiple measures of second language acquisition among Hispanic children in a bilingual program*. Ph.D. Dissertation, Department of Educational Psychology, University of Wisconsin—Madison, 1979.
Dissertation Abstracts International. *Section A: Humanities and social sciences*. Ann Arbor, Mich.: University Microfilms, 1978, 1979, 1980.
Gramsci, A. *Selections from the prison notebooks*. London: Lawrence and Wishart, 1971.
Johnson, N. The material culture of public school classrooms: The symbolic integration of local schools and national culture. *Anthropology and Education Quarterly*, 1980, *11*, 173–190.
Keim, A. N. *Compulsory education and the Amish*. Boston: Beacon Press, 1975.
Legarreta, D. Language choice in bilingual classrooms. *TESOL Quarterly*, 1977, *11*, 9–16.
Legarreta, D. The effects of program models on language acquisition by Spanish-speaking children. *TESOL Quarterly*, 1979, *13*, 521–534.
Masemann, V. Ethnography of the bilingual classroom. *International Review of Education*, 1978, *24*, 295–307.
Masemann, V. Bilingual education in the United States. *Compare*, 1979, *9*, 171–178.
Milwaukee Bilingual Education Project. *Application for continuation, ESEA Title VII funding, fiscal year 1977–78*. Milwaukee: Milwaukee Public Schools, 1977.

Richards, J. *Two approaches to education of Hispanic children in Milwaukee, Wisconsin.* Madison, Wisc.: Department of Educational Policy Studies, University of Wisconsin, 1976. (Mimeo)

Rosario, J., & Love J. M. On the reproductive function of evaluative research: A case study in the use of evaluations for shaping public policy. In R. V. Padilla (Ed.), *Bilingual education and public policy in the United States.* Ypsilanti, Mich.: Bilingual Bicultural Education Programs, Eastern Michigan University, 1979.

Smith, J. The education of Mexican Americans: Bilingual, bicognitive, or biased? *Teacher Education and Special Education,* 1979, *2,* 37–48.

Smollett, E. Schools and the illusion of choice: The middle class and the "open" classroom. In G. Martell (Ed.), *The politics of the Canadian public school.* Toronto: James, Lewis, and Samuel, 1974.

Yu, A. Y. *The implications of language, culture, social class and cognitive style in higher cognitive processes: A cross-cultural, developmental study.* Ph.D. dissertation, the University of Alberta, 1981.

31

The Production of Ethnic Discourse:
American and Puerto Rican Patterns

Francine Ruskin and Hervé Varenne

> Even if any given terminology is a *reflection* of reality, by its very nature as a terminology it must be a *selection* of reality; and to this extent it must function also as a *deflection* of reality. (Burke, 1966, p. 45)

Ethnicity: Social Reality or Discourse?

The persistence of ethnicity as a topic of discourse and other symbolic performances—food identification, fairs, special days, parades—in the United States is generally considered obvious evidence for statements to the effect that the melting pot has not worked as it was supposed to have worked. The melting pot was to erase cultural differences between immigrant groups, mold them into a new form, dissolve perceptions of differences, and make moot any talk of such differences. It is now evident that this characterization of the probable history of the United States is fundamentally inaccurate. Immigration is continuing, and pockets of altogether foreign forms are being continually replenished. Even more significant is the fact that many children and grandchildren of immigrants can talk fluently about ethnic difference and in a way that reveals that the making of distinctions between people on the basis of expected life-style differences is still for them a live experience, a constituent part of their social environment. These people can use, for purposes of identification, labels in which the "American" is qualified by an adjective referring to a foreign group—even when their ancestry is in fact extremely mixed. What has rarely been considered, however, is the possibility that, in important cases, this experience of

Francine Ruskin • New York, New York 10024. *Hervé Varenne* • Department of Family and Community Education, Teachers College, Columbia University, New York, New York 10027.

ethnicity, particularly as it is mediated by the structured discourse people must use to express it, is in fact a fully "melted," *American* experience. This is the possibility which we will explore here through a comparison of various statements about a common story that reveal the presence of two ways of expressing ethnicity that can be found in the United States, one "Puerto Rican," and the other "American."

This possibility is a matter of interest both to sociologists and to educators. Both have repeatedly called for a deeper awareness and understanding of the phenomena grouped under the label "ethnicity in the United States." But the ensuing debates have often been more passionate than clarifying. In the heat of these debates, questions of value have come up with much more insistence than any others. For example, Novak wrote: "I disliked the general American desire to believe that ethnic groups do not exist, or if they do, should not" (1971, p. 63). He did not deal systematically with the interesting fact that even those who fear the persistence of ethnic identification in the United States can still talk about ethnic differences. Like many, he called for shifts in attitudes. Though not universal, a shift has occurred. Many in sociology, education, and the helping professions are now "aware." And yet it is possible to say that understanding has not progressed with awareness. Could it be that the matter is more complex, particularly if it is confirmed that, as anthropologists have been arguing since Sapir and Whorf at least, the form of knowledge as it expresses itself in discourse is more powerful than one's abstract, inner awareness?

In this paper we take the position that, to the extent that one can hear people talk about ethnicity in all parts of the United States, it is reasonable to postulate the existence of a form of discourse—discourse about life-style differences that are the product of the origin of one's direct ancestry; in short, *ethnic discourse*—that is systematically different from other possible forms that this discourse can also take. This form is a subsample, though probably politically dominant, of the forms that can be observed to occur in the United States. It can be labeled an *American* discourse in that its structure is homologous to the structure of the talk that Americans can produce on other matters (e.g., family life, religion, education). This American ethnic discourse will display the features of individualization, psychologization, the tendency to assume the need for even superficial unanimity and conformity that have widely been recognized as characteristic of the American way. The possibility that such homologies in structure would be found between content domains has most recently been stressed by Schneider (1969) and the work of one of us confirms the fruitfulness of the line of inquiry (Varenne, 1977, 1978a, b).

If indeed it can be shown that there exists in the United States an American ethnic discourse that is available to the people who live there, if indeed this discourse is so culturally shaped as to convince those who initiate it of its verisimilitude even as it prevents them from seeing the truly "others" in their own terms, and if it is prevalent and powerful enough to oblige all these others to take it seriously as they respond to it, then it will also be shown (1) to educators, that the problem created for them by the multicultural nature of United States society is far more complex than was first thought; and (2) to sociologists, that the melting pot may have worked, and may still be working, even though it has not been working quite in the expected manner. It now seems probable that ethnic identifications will survive in the United States for the foreseeable future. But these identifications will be made *in American terms,* thus confirming the victory of American culture over the people who came to the shores of the United States.[1]

The chapter begins with general considerations about discourse processes. These provide the theoretical background for recasting the traditional studies on the place of ethnicity (as a cultural phenomenon) in the United States. This discussion will be followed by a presentation of a research methodology which we consider particularly well suited for the demonstration of similarities and differences in the structuring of discourse about a certain topic. We will then move to a brief summary of the salient features that differentiate American from Puerto Rican kinds of ethnic discourse. We will close this chapter with a discussion of a text that reveals a person in transition, and we will draw conclusions.

The Production of Culturally Specific Kinds of Discourse about Ethnicity

As mentioned, few sociologists have taken seriously the possibility that the very presence of a discourse about something, a named group of people for example, is *not* proof enough that something is happening at any level other than the level of discourse itself.[2] As Glazer and Moynihan, rather typically, wrote:

> We are suggesting that a new word reflects a new reality and a new usage reflects a change in that reality. The new word is "ethnicity"; and the new usage is the steady expansion of the term "ethnic group" from minority and marginal subgroups at the edges of society . . . to major elements of a society. (1975, p. 5)

With little respect for the kind of intuitions that have driven the work of many semioticists, linguists, and cultural anthropologists, they assume that discourse forms are transparent windows on social structures and that the further reality "behind" can be directly reached. They move on to sketch this new reality, and they suggest that it is of universal validity. They never consider that any discourse has a structure as well as a topic, and that this structure directly participates in shaping both the experience that the people have of what they are talking about and the subsequent actions that they take in terms of their understanding of this experience. As many have said within the frameworks of various disciplines and from various points of view, no discourse is, in any simple way, "about" a social experience that imposes its own structure on it. A discourse is a creative act, something that somebody shapes for a purpose and addresses to an audience. The main requirement for a successful discourse is not that it be "true" to what it is about. It is, rather, that it be *intelligible* (semiot-

---

[1] It should be evident that this chapter is not concerned with the creation or maintenance of ethnic identifications through boundary maintenance, of either the type described by Suttles (1968) or that described by Erikson (1975). If the chapter says something about this issue, it is the suggestion that, in some cases, boundary displays can be performed even in the absence of "differences" between the groups. Indeed, it is probable that certain boundary-maintaining sequences are directly produced by a cultural patterning shared by the people on both sides of the boundary.

[2] See Varenne (1982) for a more extended discussion of the same kind of myopia as exemplified in sociological writing about cliques in American high schools (cf. Dittmar, this volume).

ically—see Lévi-Strauss, 1962/1963) and *persuasive* (rhetorically—see Burke, 1950/1969), particularly if its goal is to lie or to mystify (something that discourse can do very practically and efficaciously—see Eco, 1976). Thus, it is important that we understand the formal conditions that make a discourse intelligible and persuasive even when, and perhaps particularly *if,* we want eventually to reach social conditions that transcend discourse apprehension. These are general principles of discourse production and analysis. They apply directly to all kinds of ethnic discourse.

A discourse about ethnicity, like any other discourse, is uttered for a practical purpose by a person who is reacting to a practical situation which is in part constituted by the previous talk of the participants in the situation. Both the discourse situation and the pursued goal establish a framework for the actor/speaker who must answer, in some ways, in the terms suggested by this framework. But, as Bourdieu has emphasized in a series of publications in which he reanalyzed Mauss's work on gift transactions (1972/1977, 1980), the framework provided by the ensemble [preceding situation/practical goal] does not mechanically determine the action of the person (cf. Stein, this volume). In any situation, all involved persons have a range of possible things that they can do and/or say (to help us keep track of this historical process, we will refer to this response to an initial situation as R1). These things are not all equivalent, and they have differential powers as acts that create new frameworks for subsequent possible responses by another actor (R2). Even a totally new response is possible, one that has never been offered before. The response (R3) to this response (R2), however, may or may not deal with the novelty as something to be taken seriously. It may not take into account the novelty and may be constructed as if the response (R2) had been stereotypical. It (R3) can also recognize the preceding response (R2) as unusual and take the form of a xenophobic statement of rejection or a metastatement of education into the proper response. There are many other possibilities. Given the relative powers of interlocutors, the kind of interaction into which they must enter, and other historical factors, it is probable, as Bourdieu well saw, that a stock range of possibilities for the development of interactions in time becomes established and that this stock range can then be considered characteristic of a social group. Bourdieu labeled this stock range of responses a *habitus.* We will refer to it as a *culture* in deference to the more usual American vocabulary.

An ethnic discourse, as a discourse about the interaction one has with foreigners—real or imagined—is necessarily a quasi-universal discourse, since most human societies are in more or less constant contact with others. However, given the historical dimension of these interactions, there is no reason to expect that the practices that establish themselves around them would have many universal characteristics. We cannot even expect that the two sides in such an interaction will produce similar kinds of discourse—even though they may have "understood" each other during the actual interaction.[3] When each side goes back to its own people and reports on the

---

[3]The possible presence of such "understandings" in at least apparently cross-ethnic interaction has been demonstrated in the work of McDermott and Gospodinoff (1979). This important point has often been obscured in the earlier enthusiasm for explanations of differential treatment in interaction based on the idea of culturally produced misunderstandings. It remains that the presence of understandings-in-situation does not imply, *per se,* that the same coherence principles that organize this situation will be found in a homologous fashion in other situations produced by the protagonists separately.

interaction it has had with the strangers, it constructs something that is now a response to be made within the framework of a traditional sequence ("Let's talk about them among ourselves"). In the United States, we can postulate the presence of many different kinds of discourse about ethnicity. Indeed, we can postulate that there are as many as there are cultures.

Ways of Discovering

The theoretical framework just sketched dictated our research procedures. First, we had to ensure that informants would talk about the topic and produce a linguistic artifact, an instance of discourse, or *text,* which we could then analyze. This text had to be produced in comparable circumstances to hold elements of content as stable as possible. Second, we had to choose informants who were likely to handle the content in various ways. Finally, we had to ensure that the informants would have a rather direct experience of the topic that they were to discuss.

To fulfill the first requirement, we settled on a methodology in part inspired by Laura Bohannan's (1968) account of her attempts to tell the story of Hamlet to the Tiv. She recounted that her audience of Tiv elders continually "corrected" her account and, in the process, transformed the story, the personae, their motivations, the dramatic progression, and the denouement so that the ensemble would correspond structurally to one of their own stories. They have used Hamlet as a pretext; a pre-text from which they could move to construct their own text according to their own rules for the construction of such texts. Although Bohannan contributed the original impulse from the outside, the resultant interaction that produced the new text was very much an insider event. Indeed, the situation in which people are obliged to confront a new event generated from outside their own environment and must reinterpret it to make it fit this environment is a common and altogether natural one.

To fulfill the second and third requirements, we decided to focus on experiences of and about a recent immigrant group, namely, people coming from Puerto Rico to New York City. We chose people who had spent at least some time in the United States. Some of them had come from Puerto Rico during their adult years, still spoke Spanish at home, and lived in the Puerto Rican neighborhoods of New York City. Others were those who had had direct experiences with Puerto Ricans through their professional activity but whose families did not come from Puerto Rico itself. Some were white or black Protestants, and others were Italian Catholics and Jews. They had all been born and raised in the United States—most of them in New York City. They were all social workers who had worked extensively with Puerto Rican clients.

Because of the added complexities of asking informants to react to a text like *Hamlet,* which is already strongly typified thematically and structurally, we decided to write a story in such a style that it would provoke our informants into ethnic talk without suggesting too strongly how this talk should be organized. The basis for the story was an actual case drawn from Ruskin's professional experience. The case displayed events common in Puerto Rican biographies—including events that are often used to stereotype Puerto Ricans. The story was written in such a way as to offer little more than an empty set of biographical details with no judgmental or explanatory phrases and no grammatical connectives suggestive of logical linkages. Here are excerpts from this story:

> Mrs. Dominguez, 39, came to New York from Puerto Rico at the age of 18. After a while she married. Her parents were separated.... She reported that the reason for the separation was that somebody in her father's family had cast a bad spell on them. Since then Mrs. Dominguez's mother has worked as a domestic.... Mrs. Dominguez's daughter has symptoms of selective mutism: She does not talk to her father and she does not talk in school. She does talk to her mother and to the grandmother who lives with them and shares a bed with a younger child....
>
> Mr. Dominguez does not want his mother-in-law to live with them. Mrs. Dominguez says she cannot tell her mother to leave, ... it would be disrespectful. Mr. Dominguez works as a janitor.... Mrs. Dominguez would like to work but her husband does not allow her to. She does not speak English.

The story was introduced to the informants as a real case of which Ruskin knew.[4] They either read it themselves or it was read to them, and they reacted to it immediately after this reading. Stylistically, the story is told from the point of view of an implicit narrator who is not specifically named or otherwise identified, leaving open the possibility that Ruskin was in fact this narrator. Besides the actors presented in the story, the interview situation provided the informants with at least two more protagonists: themselves and Ruskin, who conducted all the interviews. The absence of explicit connectives in the story and the relatively artificial requirement of having to make something with so little made all the informants uncomfortable. All of them eventually constructed their task as one in which they were to supply the missing connectives and to relate patterns of behavior to various types of social and psychological causes. As ethnomethodologists might say, all informants tried to teach Ruskin how to select facts, how to write a coherent story. In the process, the "flat" text became the occasion for a "thick" attempt at presenting one's understanding of the human condition in difficult circumstances. Our own task can be understood as involving the discovery of the principles that our informants used for making stories coherent.

The analysis focused on the whole interview (including the reaction of the informants to the interviewer as an interactant in the task). The corpus was the transcription of the audio recording of the interview. The analysis consisted in a modified version of the type of structural analysis adapted by Lévi-Strauss (1964–1971) from Saussurian principles for his analysis of Amerindian myths. The process consists of an initial identification of a text's episodic and topical content, followed by an examination of the manner in which the various parts of the text are sequenced and con-

---

[4]The research procedure involved the following steps: (1) Informants from four different groups were contacted in various ways (the groups were: New York Puerto Rican clients of several counseling centers, New York Puerto Rican mental health professionals, New York Puerto Rican spiritists, and North American mental health professionals). (2) Each informant was interviewed separately by Ruskin in English or Spanish. The interviews were tape recorded and fully transcribed. The purpose of the study was explained to the informants, and a short biography was obtained from them stressing in particular their relationship to Puerto Rico (when they left the island, how often they go back, etc.). (3) the story was then either given to them for them to read or was read to them, depending on the wishes of the informants. They were then asked to tell it back to the interviewer.

textualized. The content and the organization of each text are then compared to the content and the organization of the other texts in relation to variations in the situation of production.

This is not the place to defend a method that has been abundantly criticized in recent years. We will simply emphasize two things about the approach. First, it obliges one to be fully inductive since it requires that one start with carefully contextualized and situated texts and only then proceed toward making statements about their internal ordering. Each text is then compared to other texts. It is only later, if the internal evidence warrants it, that a set of texts can be separated from the whole corpus as being structurally homologous at a particular level. Second, the approach leads one to treat structural ordering not as a psychological event but as a historically produced intercommunicational one. This has the advantage of moving us away from the kind of methodological questions that have paralyzed the earlier work on cultural specificity (whether from the point of view of culture and personality or that of value-orientation theory). In this earlier work, culture was localized within the individual and had to become a statistical norm: "what *most* people do, say, think, believe, value, etc."—whatever the verb may have been. To the extent that one conceives of a cultural structure as a structure of communication and in communication, it cannot be treated as a statistical event. A culture either is or is not present in a particular interaction. It is not present "to a degree." Most important, a culture (from our point of view) cannot be "varied." Within a large enough group made of many subgroups who rarely communicate with each other, several different cultures may be used, but each culture is a discrete event.

American versus Puerto Rican: The Relating of Individual to Group

The structuring of the story and of the interview situation led the informants to spend most of their time establishing the missing connectives between the action of the people depicted in the story and their environment. All informants established such relationships both explicitly, in lexical terms, and implicitly, in their use of deictic forms. Consequently, the results of our analysis are summarized in terms of the way the informants integrated two sets of actors in their contexts. First, we examine how the informant set himself/herself in relation to the story and the interview situation. Second, we examine how the informant related the various members of the Dominguez family to each other. In addition, we talk of the informants' understanding of the relevance of the immigration experience for Puerto Ricans.

As we conducted the analysis, it soon become apparent that—as we had expected—the corpus of texts could be divided into two major groups, each of which exhibited similar discourse patterning. We labeled one pattern *Puerto Rican* and the other *American*. We did this for various reasons. One is that, while some of our Spanish-speaking informants used a pattern similar to the one used by our English-speaking ones, the contrary did not occur. Second, the pattern used by the English-speaking informants is homologous to patterns that have traditionally been associated with America in social science writing. Since all our informants were citizens of the United States, it should be clear by now that we do not equate America with the United States: The former is a cultural-ideological structure, the latter is a geopolitical location.[5]

The Informant/Speaker in Context

The research task was deliberately set up as an I–you situation in which researcher and informant were separated and in which the researcher asked the informant to focus on the manner in which the informant himself/herself would relate to the story. How the informants related the story is the primary datum of the study. As we mentioned, the story and interview offered various actors and locales that could be considered as pieces with which the informant could construct a social field in relation to himself. First, the informant had to place himself in relation to the interviewer. Her immediate presence (which, we assume, would preclude her being dealt with as a third person) gave the informant the option of treating her either in an inclusive or exclusive manner, as a "you" or as a "we." Being of Latin American and Jewish backgrounds, Ruskin had characteristics that could be used by most of the informants to place themselves at such a time and place either with her ("We are both Spanish-speaking foreigners in this land," or "We are both [Jewish] professionals") or not. In Puerto Rican discourse, Ruskin was included in the speaker's "we"; in American discourse, this pronoun was not used, and Ruskin was "you."

The informant also had to place himself in relation to the two places mentioned in the story, Puerto Rico and New York. He could place himself *in* or *out* either place, neither, or both. In Puerto Rican discourse, the speaker was systematically placed *in* in relation to Puerto Rico through the extensive and redundant use of first person plural forms ("nosotros puertorriqueños ... somos"). S/He systematically was placed *out* in relation to New York. The two environments were strongly differentiated. The informants talked of two different *culturas* and of the fact that "they" did not understand "us." Each culture was an overwhelming social event from which no individual could, or should, fully escape. In American discourse the speaker was placed *out* of both environments. It is not simply that the speaker was not identified with Puerto Ricans as "we," but that he was not identified either with New York, The United States, or America. America was never "we" to the speakers. America was not talked about as a specific environment with particularistic traits. If it was mentioned—generally implicitly—it was simply as "here," a generalized, characterless space to which one may or may not adapt but from which one can be presented as being independent.

Contextualizing the Members of the Dominguez Family

The members of the Dominguez family were a more complex set for the informants to organize, since there were six of them, they were of different sexes and

---

[5]In the following pages, in order to facilitate readability, we will write of *Puerto Ricans* and *Americans*. For these words one should read "those informants who use the particular pattern." We are not suggesting anything about the sociological reasons for their use of the pattern. The search for such reasons belongs to research other than ours. Nor do we imply that they have psychologically "internalized" the pattern.

ages, and they could not afford immediate feedback as to where they should be placed (in contrast to the feedback Ruskin necessarily gave). The Dominguezes were set as a context to each other in the story, and all the informants acknowledged this fact. They all agreed that, as one of them put it, "while the child is the primary patient, her functioning is related to her family difficulties." All informants also placed the Dominguezes in relation to Puerto Rico and New York. From then on things differentiated themselves.

The matter is delicate. A family, in English as in Spanish, can be approached either as a single unit or as the addition of a plurality of smaller single units. All informants talked about the family in general and about the members of the family in particular. Thus, differentiating between patterns is not as easy as in the case of the relation of speaker to culture, which could be treated as an either–or proposition, the evidence for the interpretation being the presence or absence of a type of identification. In the case of the relating of members of a family to one another, the situation is more complex and the evidence subtler. Let us look briefly at two texts about the relationship between parents and children:

> Si Ud. quiere que un hijo sea bueno. Sea comprehensivo con los problemas del hogar, entre los padres y los hijos. Ud. tiene que sentarse con ellos. Como yo hice con los mìos. Cuando queremos hablar como padre e hijo, hablamos como padre e hijo. Cuando queremos hablar como amigos, les digo: "Sí, hoy vamos hablar como amigas y amigos." Me contestan lo malo que yo hago y yo les contesto lo malo que Uds. hacen. Y asi podemos resolver nuestros problemas.[6]

> A lot of cultural aspects in the family: the father's dominance, and certainly not allowing certain things to happen, the mother living in a very confined, isolated kind of existence, where she is dependent upon all the other family members to help her get around and to manage. Sometimes there is the wish to be something other than what you are but not enough incentive to make the change on your own for fear of whatever retaliation would come, say, from a husband like hers. I think we often see the youngsters in families like this becoming rebellious. . . . She can see she is different from other youngsters at her age. . . . you start worrying . . . how she will break away from the family.

The first statement was made by Mendez, a man strongly involved in spiritism. The second was made by Tripp, a woman social worker. Both were trying to deal with a common dilemma: the source of, consequences of, and proper reactions to tensions between parents and children. Both are focusing on the father and on something that both consider cultural: the father's objections to his wife's going out in public and to his daughter's dating. For Mendez, the solution is a matter of all the people *understanding* how a household operates and of clearly marking what is happening when. Another informant expressed the same idea when she said about the same topic that the solution to the family's problems was for everybody to get his or her traditionally appointed place "dentro de su roll, el padre como padre, la abuela

---

[6]"If you want a child to become good, be understanding with the problems at home between parents and children. As I have done with mine, when we want to talk as father and son, we talk as father and son. When we want to talk as friends, I say: 'Yes, today we will talk as friends [feminine and masculine].' They tell me the wrong things that I do and I tell them the wrong things that you do. And so we solve our problems."

como abuela y la madre como madre."[7] For Tripp, the Dominguezes problems have to do with dominance, dependence, and wrongly channeled rebellion. She went on, in her interview, to give examples of positive processes she had observed among her own Puerto Rican clients. She talked of wives slowly disengaging themselves from their husbands through her intervention, of children establishing their independence from their parents. Tripp did not want to make her clients understand how the well-organized family works or to help them play competently their traditionally pre-scribed role. She wanted to liberate the individual members, renegotiate their posi-tioning so that the separateness of each can be preserved. Separation was not an issue for Mendez. He never even mentioned it to say that it is not an issue (just as no American ever talked about the need for each person to perform appropriately pre-defined roles[8]).

These differences are expressed by variation in the choice of subtopic within the larger topic of parent–child relationships. They are expressed in the variation in the vocabulary used to refer to the event. In the case of the Puerto Rican informants, there was a constant use of a vocabulary of social and customary order. The Puerto Ricans talked of respect, *machismo,* the roles of the various members of the family, *our* way of doing things, and so on. The Americans talked of individual psychological states: dependence, dominance, rebellion, assertion, immaturity, mental illness, and well-being. Indeed, we might say that the Puerto Ricans never really talked about the individual members of the Dominguez family. Even when they started with com-ments about the case, it was only as a jumping board toward a statement of the well-regulated (according to Puerto Rican rules) family system. When the Americans talked about culture and the family as a system (which they did explicitly and repeatedly), it was always as an introduction to the detailed discussion of individuals. Indeed, for the Americans, "culture" has become an aspect of the personality of the client. It is something that is to be taken into account in the overall diagnosis. It is a symptom. Troubles occur when independence is subverted either through forced compliance or through an unreflective ("primitive") internalization. In such a case, the task of the therapist involves the "real-ization" of the separation, cognitively and behaviorally: the patients must realize that they are separate; they must then act out this realization. Such a realization may properly involve a return to the family fold, but on a new footing, as an independent act.[9]

From Puerto Rico to New York

For all informants, the matter of immigration was of permanent importance for an understanding of the Dominguezes. Puerto Rico and New York are different social settings that put different constraints on the Dominguezes. This factor too was interpreted differently in the American and Puerto Rican patterns. In American dis-course, the problem is one of psychological adaptation. It concerns the need to accept

---

[7]"In their role, the father as father, the grandmother as grandmother and the mother as mother."

[8]Garrison, in her study of Puerto Rican spiritists as mental health professionals (1977) reported that this is indeed the most common prescription these spiritists make in cases of family difficulties.

[9]The same pattern for American Jewish social work intervention was noticed in Leichter and Mitchell's (1967/1978) work on a Jewish family agency.

and internalize new cultural objects which are external to oneself but which might be difficult to recognize as external given a long habituation sometimes joined with other personality flaws (e.g., immaturity or weakness). In Puerto Rican discourse, the problem is one of actualizing a pattern in a subsphere (the family in particular) when the larger social sphere is not supportive. The solution is to screen out the outside. As Mendez said: "Vivo en un circulo que [los americanos] llaman, ellos, 'los gettos,' no me molesta."[10] A Puerto Rican social worker quoted approvingly one of her clients who had told her: "Yo no permito que ninguno de afuera se meta con [mi familia].[11] For the Puerto Rican informants, what was wrong with the Dominguezes was that they were not successful in achieving the necessary social reconstruction. It was not wrong for them to try. No amount of cultural awareness among Americans led any of them to consider such an attempt as legitimate. None of them perceived the role of the therapist as helping the family isolate itself with a Puerto Rican circle ruled by Puerto Rican customs.

Transitions

Not all Spanish-speaking informants organized their response to the interviewer in a Puerto Rican fashion consistently. This phenomenon is well worth pursuing. The construction of a discourse, we have mentioned repeatedly, is a joint process during which both interlocutors participate in shaping the direction that will eventually be taken. It was therefore necessary for Ruskin to be relatively impassive during the interview. In many other situations found in real life, interlocutors are much more directly active in suggesting the appropriate direction that statements about the world should take. We can postulate that in general use there are two kinds of environments for ethnic discourse: one in which carriers of different cultures meet and challenge each other for the right to establish the major orientation of the discourse, and one in which carriers of the same culture reinforce each other as they talk in terms of their habitual discourse. All the informants we interviewed have probably found themselves in both kinds of situation—particularly the Puerto Rican social workers, some of whom were graduates of American schools. It is possible that had the interview been constructed differently, some informants might have been led to produce texts that would have appeared very American. Given Ruskin's impassivity, most chose to construct her as "one of us." Some, however, hesitated and produced texts in which the alternate pattern to the one that might have been expected to prevail appeared. Given the general power relationship between the societies, it is not surprising that we had cases only of Spanish-speakers using an American pattern and none of the reverse process.

Let us look briefly at the case of Mrs. Fernandez, a client. She was a student in bilingual education at City University. She was strongly aware of the substantive aspects of the Puerto Rican experience in New York. She talked about the misunderstanding of Puerto Rican culture by Americans, of respect, *machismo,* spiritism.

[10]"I live in a circle that [the Americans] call the ghetto, I don't mind."
[11]"I do not allow anyone from outside to interfere with [my family]."

From this point of view, she was very different from the English-speaking informants whose knowledge of the details of Puerto Rican life was always very limited. Fernandez knew what could be expected from such a father as Mr. Dominguez. She recognized that there is so much training of female children toward not going out in public that it is often a very difficult experience for them to do it, even when they have decided that there is nothing wrong with it, as she herself had done. She considered herself as moving out literally and symbolically, even in the face of opposition from her husband. She made her son vacuum the carpet, and she encouraged him to cry so that he would learn about his "feelings" (she used the English word in the midst of her Spanish). But what makes what she produced American in our view is not the overall balance of the traits exhibited. It is, rather, her manner of organizing her response. When discussing the story, she, too, placed most of the blame on the father. But she did not move on to statements about the appropriate roles fathers should play. She focused, rather, on his personal qualities. Perhaps because her training in psychology had been less intense and because she does not feel the professional commitment of social workers toward nonjudgmental attitudes, she used a vocabulary of moral characteristics that the social workers did not use. Mr. Dominguez, according to her, is "cold," "dry," "nonloving." Mrs. Dominguez is weak of character for accepting the orders of her husband. For Fernandez both of them are more extreme in these characteristics than Puerto Rican customs require. Let us show how she explains it:

> Se encogió de hombros y dijo: "le tengo que obedecer." I can't believe it, she's been in New York y 39 años, es vieja tiene 39 años pero es una señora vieja, you know, no lo puedo creer. Estoy segura que aparenta vieja también, porque es así. . . . cuando se casan ya uno deja de existir como mujer, ya no es uno de su persona, no se pertenece. . . . Ahora se pertenece al marido . . . como lo que és el y si el dice esta bién, that's all . . . o aunque que "si le tengo que obedecer pero lo tengo que hacer, no lo encuentro bién," no veo nada de eso . . . porque vió a sus padres divorciados y a lo mejor piensa, "yo no quiero ser divorciada como mi mamá y sufrir lo que ella sufrió."[12]

The Puerto Rican rules for the husband–wife relationship are stated but are prefaced (or sometimes followed) by statements that distance her ("I can't believe it") and lead to a statement about the potential impact of the rules on an individual and the possible internal motivation of this individual for her actions.

This pattern (distancing/statement of rule about customary behavior/potential impact and motivation) repeated itself several times in the course of the interview. Depending on the topic and the moment in the interview, Fernandez emphasized certain parts of the patterns over others. At times, the statement of the rule became

---

[12]"She shrugged her shoulders and said: 'I have to obey him,' *I can't believe it, she's been in New York* 39 years, she is old, she is 39 but she is an old lady, *you know,* I cannot believe it. I am sure she also looks old, because she is like this. . . . When they get married, one ceases to exist as a woman and one does not own oneself, does not belong to oneself. . . . now one belongs to one's husband . . . because what he is and what he says is right, *that's all.* . . . [Mrs. Dominguez is saying] 'if I have to obey him because I have to do it, I do not find it right,' I don't see nothing of that, because she saw her parents divorce, and maybe she believes, 'I do not want to be divorced like my mother was, and suffer what she suffered.'"

so extensive, complete, and forceful that it became all but indistinguishable from a statement about the same topic made by another Puerto Rican. This similarity was particularly strong when Fernandez talked about the treatment of aged relatives. At other times, it was her personal attempts at getting out from Puerto Rican constraints which were emphasized. But the very presence of such statements, as well as the intermittent use of stylistic constructions and vocabulary that focus the text on one person in its separateness, makes the whole interview stand out.

At least two of our informants exhibited this kind of ambivalence, where an intimate knowledge of Puerto Rican customs and an appreciation for some of them is joined to a conscious rebellion against those that apply most directly to the speaker. Whether this ambivalence can be interpreted as evidence that the boundary between Puerto Rico and America has been crossed may not be an issue that can easily be settled. One could imagine that the pressure of her interlocutors could lead a speaker like Fernandez to express herself differently with different persons depending on their own habitual way of constructing a discourse. Her wavering during the interview may have been partially the product of lapses in Ruskin's neutrality. Fernandez's most explicitly Puerto Rican statement, for example, came after Ruskin, halfway through the interview, specified that her research was concerned with misunderstandings of Puerto Rican culture. Fernandez's statements about her own rebellion came up as the conversation focused on her. But, of course, the process was reciprocal. It is probably not a matter of chance that Ruskin spent relatively more time during this interview talking to Fernandez about herself than she did with any other informant. In some ways, Fernandez must have prompted Ruskin in that direction.

The American Ethnic Experience

As we conclude, we focus again on the question of the constitution of an *American* ethnic discourse with which we started. Our interest in the Puerto Rican pattern was essentially instrumental: it helped us see more concretely how an American pattern could arise in interaction even at times when one might expect that the perception of the other would be the strongest. The processual perspective that we have used to abstract the patterns can also help us see how this pattern can contribute to the difficulties foreigners have in the United States. Most research on cross-cultural misunderstandings have focused on settings where members of the two cultures meet. But in a complex, bureaucratic society, the real danger to the less powerful group lies in the fact that the situations that may most effect its destiny in the United States (e.g., the making of laws, the designing of a curricula and helping treatments) are situations in which the group does not participate. At such times, the members of the dominant group, politicians, educators, and mental health specialists will use a pattern that can lead them to mistake their ability to talk about cultural difference (a matter of topic) with an ability to understand a foreign pattern in its own terms (a matter of structure). It is certain, for example, that as Puerto Ricans have settled in large numbers in places like New York City, the many who have come in contact with them have gained a certain amount of topical knowledge. The American social workers we interviewed knew something about Puerto Ricans, and what they knew was not completely false. It was always partial, often caricatural, and never adequate. But it was obviously grounded in certain interactions. The same things could be said of the Puerto Ricans' knowledge of American ways. Most social workers knew about spiritism, most Puerto Ricans mentioned the "freedom" Americans gave their children. The knowledge that certain informants had was in fact quite extensive, and a few could resist the urge to caricature. Most importantly, both Americans and Puerto Ricans were aware that the other group knew about them. They all were aware of New York City as a multiethnic society that is hostile to cultural difference. They all were aware that this hostility made life difficult for the weaker group. They all said that this was deplorable and that certain things should change so that life could become easier.

In other words, Puerto Rico and America, immigration, difficulties in adaptation, difference—all were easy topics of discourse for these people, whatever their backgrounds. As such, the ease with which they all entered into the discourse is proof of the immediate, existential relevance of ethnicity to an understanding of United States society. But it is not proof of how this experience is handled for communication. As we have shown, this experience can be handled through very different kinds of discourse that cannot be equated simply because they are built around the same topic. Indeed, the fact that some informants can talk about ethnicity and even identify with a particular group does not mean that they are not essentially "melted" Americans, even if this melting has not quite taken place according to the expectations of the original melting pot theory. Cultural structuring, precisely because it is a structur*ing,* cannot be approached from the point of view of the content of statements and behaviors. The test of Americanness is not the presence or absence of certain topics of conversation but the presence or absence of a certain mode of organizing conversation, whatever the topic. While we cannot demonstrate in detail at this point how the American ethnic discourse sketched earlier is indeed a direct structural transformation of other talks about different topics of the American experience, we would like to conclude this paper by briefly suggesting how such a demonstration could proceed.

The central characteristic of the pattern that revealed itself in the talk of some of the social workers is that it systematically separates a single subject (whether the speaker or a third person that serves as the point of reference for a while) from an environment of external pressures (including other subjects and various types of habits, cultural and otherwise); this environment is made up of objective events in relation to which the subject orients himself in a deliberate fashion, "freely" to the extent that the external world has not been unconsciously or uncritically "internalized." Culture or ethnicity is one aspect of this environment. It is assumed that cultural patterns can be described independently and that the behavior of the subject can then be measured in relation to it. This pattern is very familiar to anybody aware of the writing about America. It is the pattern that those of us who have tackled the complex and controversial task of mapping American specificity within the context of the modern theories of culture in anthropology have identified as that used to organize many different areas of social life, be it family life (Kelly, 1979; Schneider, 1968; Varenne, 1977), religious and political life (Dumont, 1961/1970; Varenne,

1977, 1978a), or the life of the school (Varenne, 1978b, 1982; cf. Masemann, this volume).

It is certain that we are far from the point when we have an adequate formalization both of the features of American discourse production and of the transformations in surface form that can occur under the many conditions of everyday interaction. And yet, we cannot ignore the possibility that America is indeed an overarching structure that organizes the most powerful events in the United States, be they political or educational. To ignore the possibility is to condemn oneself to blindness and a particularly insidious form of righteous false consciousness that insists on the need for certain kinds of awareness (e.g., "awareness of cultural differences") without giving itself the means of framing this awareness—on the grounds, for example, that there is no such thing as an American culture. The melting pot has worked. There is an American culture. It is necessary to learn the means of recognizing its presence, particularly in those settings where it hides itself. And then, when necessary, one must examine one's own productions so as to escape its overwhelming power.

Acknowledgments

The research on which this paper is based was originally conducted by F. Ruskin as part of her doctoral dissertation under the sponsorship of H. Varenne. The full report can be found in Ruskin (1979). We want to acknowledge our debt to the informants, to the Puerto Rican Family Institute, and to the Spiritist Center, without whom this research would not have been possible. Too many other persons have helped us for us to mention them all. We are very aware of their contribution and deeply thankful for it. We want to mention specifically the diffuse and enduring support of our spouses, Asa Ruskin and Susan Varenne.

References

Bohannan, L. Shakespeare in the bush. In A. Dundes (Ed.), *Everyman his way.* Englewood Cliffs, N.J.: Prentice-Hall, 1968, pp. 477–486.

Bourdieu, P. *Outline of a theory of practice* (R. Nice, trans.). Cambridge: Cambridge University Press, 1977. (Originally published, 1972.)

Bourdieu, P. *Le sens pratique.* Paris: Editions de Minuit, 1980.

Burke, K. *Language as symbolic action.* Berkeley, Calif.: University of California Press, 1966.

Burke, K. *A rhetoric of motives.* Berkeley, Calif.: University of California Press, 1969. (Originally published, 1950.)

Dumont, L. Caste, racism and 'stratification.' In L. Dumont, *Homo Hierarchicus* (M. Sainsbury, trans.). Chicago: University of Chicago Press, 1970, pp. 239–260. (Originally published, 1961.)

Eco, U. *A theory of semiotics.* Bloomington, Ind.: Indiana University Press, 1976.

Erikson, F. Gatekeeping and the melting pot: Interaction in counseling encounters. *Harvard Educational Review,* 1975, *45,* 44–70.

Garrison, V. The 'Puerto Rican syndrome' in psychiatry and *espiritismo.* In V. Crapanzano & V. Garrison (Eds.), *Case studies in spirit possession.* New York: John Wiley and Sons, 1977, 383–449.

Glazer, N., & Moynihan, P. (Eds.). *Ethnicity: Theory and experience.* Cambridge, Mass.: Harvard University Press, 1975.

Kelly, M. *Science, common sense, and love: A cultural account of symbol, myth and ritual in American child rearing manuals.* Doctoral dissertation, Teachers College, Columbia University, 1979.

Leichter, H., & Mitchell, W. *Kinship and casework.* New York: Teachers College Press, 1978. (Originally published, 1967.)

Lévi-Strauss, C. *Totemism* (R. Needham, trans.). Boston: Beacon Press, 1963. (Originally published, 1962.)

Lévi-Strauss, C. *Mythologiques* (4 vols.). Paris: Plon, 1964–1971.

McDermott, R., & Gospodinoff, K. Social contexts for ethnic borders and school failure. In A. Wolfgang (Ed.), *Nonverbal behavior.* New York: Academic Press, 1979, pp. 175–195.

Novak, M. *The rise of the unmeltable ethnics.* New York: Macmillan, 1971.

Ruskin, F. *A structural analysis of statements by Puerto Ricans and Americans about family relationships.* Doctoral dissertation, Teachers College, Columbia University, 1979.

Schneider, D. *American kinship: A cultural account.* Englewood Cliffs, N.J.: Prentice-Hall, 1968.

Schneider, D. Kinship, nationality and religion in American culture: Toward a definition of kinship. In V. Turner (Ed.), *Forms of symbolic action. Proceedings of the American Ethnological Association,* 1969, 116–125.

Suttles, G. *The social order of the slum: Ethnicity and territory in the inner city.* Chicago: University of Chicago Press, 1968.

Varenne, H. *Americans together.* New York: Teachers College Press, 1977.

Varenne, H. Is Dedham American? The diagnosis of things American. *Anthropological Quarterly,* 1978, *51,* 231–245. 231–245. (a)

Varenne, H. Culture as rhetoric: Patterning in the verbal interpretation of interaction between teachers and administrators in an American high school. *American Ethnologist,* 1978, *5,* 635–650. (b)

Varenne, H. Jocks and freaks: The symbolic structure of the expression of social interaction among American senior high school students. In G. Spindler (Ed.), *Doing the ethnography of schooling.* New York: Holt, Rinehart & Winston, 1982.

Epilogue

Guilem Rodrigues da Silva
Translated by Catharina Jonsson

My Language

To Sten Soler

When I say earth in Portuguese
TERRA
this double "rr" crunches between my teeth
like particles of earth
FLOR
blossoms on my lips
Moon may be more beautiful than LUA
but never sea more beautiful than MAR
with endless shores
where every sunbeam
transforms the grains of sand to diamonds
My language is the guarantee for my life
is a constant reminder
of sorrow
of happiness
of rage
Here I have received the most
I say thanks as a matter of course
I say "How are you" and it is difficult not to mean it
Non-alcoholic
non-smoking
the silence

Guilem Rodrigues da Silva ● Lund, Sweden.   *Catharina Jonsson* ● Lund, Sweden.

the quiet sighs
O, I know that I have the prerequisites
to be happy here
in spite of the prepositions
which still complain of violation
But my language
which is a vital necessity to me
like most of the things from my underdeveloped country
is suffocated by the unknown and by the well-known
It is a daily fight
with monologues in front of the mirror
with reading aloud
to keep my language alive
Every time I look up a word in a dictionary
for the spelling
I withdraw from my roots
Soon I shall be standing there without words and naked
in the cold northern wind.

About the Necessity of Having a Language

To Tove Skuttnab-Kangas

I love the birdlike gestures of people
when they do not look at me
I look at them
like the birds
outside my window
If I waved to them
they would fly away
forever and be scared
by my black hair
and my brown dreaming eyes

There are days when I cannot speak any language
without an accent
not even my own language
Then I would like to be
like Picolino the clown of Rio Grande
to step forward and say words of love
without being accused of

disorderly conduct
It would be like owning the world
without having a name
without having a face

"The Night Cometh When No Man Can Work"
(St. John 9:4)

To Ronald B. Antoine

Every word I forget
is a hidden threat
each forgotten word
is a palisade that falls
is water that grows
and beats against the dam
and defeats its resistance
For each word I forget
I fear the night
It will be hard to find the way
when the night comes
Who
What will save me
from the eventual submersion
when I have forgotten my language?
Who will give me a lantern
while there is still day
for searching for the lost words?
Soon soon
"the night cometh when no man can work"

Measures

To Agnes Yu

I predict a general subscription
where the goodness of the minority walks the streets

crying unheard like the baptist in the desert
I predict that in every town
bazaars fun-fairs and other activities will be arranged
to buy back for the poet the lost words
to return to the immigrant poets
the words they have lost
in the labyrinth of adaptation
on the sea of assimilation
Who can stop us from becoming shadows without bodies
Who can stop us from writing with gall
instead of ink
Who will be able to stop our songs
from stirring up a rebellion
The people without a language
those sentenced to wordlessness
gather in their hearts gunpowder instead of words
Who will be able to stop our songs
from lighting the fuse

to you

No man No woman
No nation has the right
to sentence hundreds of thousands of people
to wordlessness
to sentence hundreds of thousands of people
to a hybridization creating monsters
Let us together breed the day
the hour
the moment
which will let us return to our languages

Index